EMERGENCY POWERS IN ASIA

What is the relevance of contemporary debates over emergency powers for countries situated in Asia? What role does, and should, the constitution play in constraining these powers? The essays in this collection address these issues, drawing on emergency situations in over twenty countries in Asia as a ready-made laboratory for exploring the relationship between emergency powers and constitutionalism. This volume therefore rests squarely at the intersection of two debates – a debate over the ability of law to constrain the invocation and use of emergency powers by the executive in times of crisis, and a debate over the nature and viability of constitutionalism in Asia. At this intersection are fundamental questions about constitutionalism and the nature of the modern state, questions that invite legal, political, sociological and historical analysis.

VICTOR V. RAMRAJ is an Associate Professor in the Faculty of Law at the National University of Singapore, where he is also Vice-Dean for Academic Affairs.

ARUN K. THIRUVENGADAM is an Assistant Professor in the Faculty of Law at the National University of Singapore.

EMERGENCY POWERS IN ASIA

Exploring the Limits of Legality

Edited by
VICTOR V. RAMRAJ
ARUN K. THIRUVENGADAM

CAMBRIDGE
UNIVERSITY PRESS

CAMBRIDGE
UNIVERSITY PRESS

University Printing House, Cambridge CB2 8BS, United Kingdom

One Liberty Plaza, 20th Floor, New York, NY 10006, USA

477 Williamstown Road, Port Melbourne, VIC 3207, Australia

314-321, 3rd Floor, Plot 3, Splendor Forum, Jasola District Centre, New Delhi - 110025, India

103 Penang Road, #05-06/07, Visioncrest Commercial, Singapore 238467

Cambridge University Press is part of the University of Cambridge.

It furthers the University's mission by disseminating knowledge in the pursuit of education, learning and research at the highest international levels of excellence.

www.cambridge.org
Information on this title: www.cambridge.org/9780521768900

First published 2010

A catalogue record for this publication is available from the British Library

Library of Congress Cataloging in Publication data
Emergency powers in Asia : exploring the limits of legality / edited by Victor V. Ramraj, Arun K. Thiruvengadam.
p. cm.
ISBN 978-0-521-76890-0 (hardback)
1. War and emergency powers – Asia. I. Ramraj, Victor Vridar, 1968 –
II. Thiruvengadam, Arun K.
KNC956.E44 2009
342.5′0412 – dc22 2009043744

ISBN 978-0-521-76890-0 Hardback

For my parents, Ruby and Victor J.,
sine qua non
— V.V.R.

For Chandraleka and Ramaswamy Thiruvengadam
— A.K.T.

CONTENTS

CONTRIBUTORS

MAITRII AUNG-THWIN Assistant Professor, Department of History, National University of Singapore

ALBERT H. Y. CHEN Professor, Faculty of Law, University of Hong Kong

SIMON CHESTERMAN Associate Professor, Faculty of Law, National University of Singapore and Global Professor, New York University School of Law

JACQUES DELISLE Stephen A. Cozen Professor of Law, University of Pennsylvania Law School

R. MICHAEL FEENER Associate Professor, Department of History, National University of Singapore

MARK FENWICK Associate Professor, Faculty of Law, Kyushu University

ANDREW HARDING Professor of Asia-Pacific Law, Faculty of Law, University of Victoria

NADIRSYAH HOSEN Lecturer, Faculty of Law, University of Wollongong

ANIL KALHAN Associate Professor of Law, Drexel University Earle Mack School of Law

H. P. LEE Sir John Latham Professor of Law, Faculty of Law, Monash University

CLARK B. LOMBARDI Associate Professor, University of Washington School of Law

MICHELLE ANN MILLER Research Fellow, Deakin University

VASUKI NESIAH Director of International Affairs, Brown University

RAUL C. PANGALANGAN Professor, College of Law, University of the Philippines

VICTOR V. RAMRAJ Associate Professor, Faculty of Law, National University of Singapore

KEVIN Y. L. TAN Adjunct Professor, Faculty of Law, National University of Singapore and Adjunct Professor, S Rajaratnam School of International Studies, Nanyang Technological University

ARUN K. THIRUVENGADAM Assistant Professor, Faculty of Law, National University of Singapore

PREFACE

This book is the final instalment in an accidental trilogy. The 'trilogy' began with the publication by Cambridge University Press of a symposium volume, *Global Anti-Terrorism Law and Policy* (edited by Victor V. Ramraj, Michael Hor and Kent Roach), in 2005. The debate between David Dyzenhaus and Oren Gross over emergency powers in that book was the inspiration for another symposium (in which Arun was involved as a session chair) and another collection, *Emergencies and the Limits of Legality* (edited by Victor V. Ramraj), published in 2008. That collection in turn prompted the central question posed at the May 2008 symposium at the National University of Singapore Law School that shaped this volume: what relevance do the debates on emergency powers in liberal constitutional democracies have for the actual experience of and scholarly reflections on emergency powers in Asia?

Questions of this sort are important not only because of the reflections they stimulate. They are also important because they challenge an all-too-human tendency to look to the familiar first. We have both been struck in our research by the extent to which comparative constitutional studies in English are often limited to North American and European jurisdictions, Australia and increasingly, these days, South Africa. Rare is the study that engages Asian jurisdictions. Within Asia as well, we find a tendency to look within or to gaze outward to the West, rather than to reflect on the experiences in neighbouring countries. This is unfortunate when it comes to a study of emergency powers, since the experience of these powers in Asia, though often tragic, is rich, complex and varied. We are privileged to be part of a law school that encourages and supports broad-based comparative and theoretical inquiry and seeks to facilitate cross-cultural and cross-jurisdictional dialogue and supports projects of this sort.

This project would not have been possible without a research grant from the Singapore Ministry of Education's Academic Research Fund (MOE AcRF #R-241-000-058-112) and the confidence in our project on the part of: the Faculty Research Committee at the NUS Law School; our dean, Tan Cheng Han; and the Board of Directors of ASLI (the Asian Law Institute). The symposium was enriched by the heroic administrative efforts of Elizabeth Chua and Wendy Wee; the provocative contributions of Gary Bell, Gregory Clancey, Jörg Monar, M. Sornarajah, Alan Khee Jin Tan and Tey Tsun Hang; and the dedication of a superb team of research assistants: David Borgia, Shaun Lee, Lyndy Davies, Sang-Bonn Soth and Phang Liying. During the preparation of the manuscript, Kevin Leong and Kennedy Chen were of great assistance. We are especially grateful to Karin Loevy for her keen eye for detail, tireless work and substantive comments during the final stages of manuscript preparation. We are also indebted to Finola O'Sullivan and her colleagues at Cambridge University Press for their professionalism and support.

Victor would like to record his deep gratitude: to Sandy, who patiently endured a third edited volume, nourished his spirit and intellect and held the fort whenever it needed holding; to Eli and Satchel, who made him laugh, guided him through a wondrous world of play and sparked his imagination; and to Ruby and Victor J. who, long ago, taught him to write, indulged his curiosity and opened his eyes to new horizons.

Arun would like to thank: Victor, for his invitation to join this fascinating journey and for being a generous collaborator and mentor; his parents (to whom the book is dedicated), for the enduring gift of a love for the written word; and finally, Mayura, Ghazal and Sanjana, for their life-affirming love, which allows him to remain hopeful even while addressing the bleaker aspects of the human condition canvassed in this volume.

1

Introduction: emergency powers and constitutionalism in Asia

VICTOR V. RAMRAJ AND ARUN K. THIRUVENGADAM

I. Introduction

The invocation of emergency powers by the state in response to a perceived crisis is the subject of considerable controversy in liberal democracies because these powers appear on their face to pose a direct challenge to the liberal ideal of constitutional government.[1] Although emergency powers were the subject of constitutional theory long before the 11 September 2001 terrorist attacks in the United States,[2] the 9/11 attacks and their aftermath have reignited debates about how established liberal democracies should respond to terrorist attacks and other sorts of emergency, leading to the development of sophisticated theories of emergency powers.[3] Some of these theories defend a prominent, but qualified, role for the courts in checking the use of these powers. Others, mindful of the apparent deference to the executive shown by the courts in times of crisis, prefer to use constitutional or statutory emergency powers provisions to delimit the powers of the executive, often by subjecting them to stringent legislative procedures and oversight. Yet other theories stress the importance of extra-legal checks and the underlying social and political culture in preventing the abuse of executive power in an emergency. But what is the relevance of these debates and theories to the invocation of emergency powers in constitutional orders beyond the liberal democracies of 'the West'?

[1] See, for instance, Carl Schmitt's challenge to liberalism in *Political Theology: Four Chapters on the Concept of Sovereignty*, trans. G. Schwab (Chicago: University of Chicago Press, 2005).

[2] For an overview, see A. H. Y. Chen, 'Emergency Powers, Constitutionalism and Legal Transplants: The East Asian Experience' (Chapter 3), this volume, pp. 57–65.

[3] These theories are summarised and referenced in V. V. Ramraj, 'The Emergency Powers Paradox' (Chapter 2), this volume, pp. 23–8. For survey and analysis, see V. V. Ramraj (ed.), *Emergencies and the Limits of Legality* (Cambridge: Cambridge University Press, 2008).

The essays in this collection address this question, directly or implicitly, by drawing on the diverse emergency situations in Asia as a ready-made laboratory for exploring the relationship between emergency powers and constitutionalism. The volume therefore rests squarely at the intersection of two debates – a debate over the ability of law to constrain the invocation and use of emergency powers by the executive in times of crisis, and a debate over the nature and viability of constitutionalism in Asia. At this intersection are fundamental questions about constitutionalism and the nature of the modern state. In this introduction, we seek to show why this is so, framing the issues in a way that, we hope, facilitates our understanding of the two broad debates. First, however, two points of clarification are in order: What do we mean by emergency powers? And why do we focus on Asia?

At the symposium that inspired this collection, we deliberately refrained from defining 'emergency powers'. Had we defined emergency powers from the outset, we might have precluded, unnecessarily, an examination of powers that fall outside the stipulated definition, but function in the same way as 'formal' emergency powers, such as internal security legislation[4] or undeclared or informal '*de facto*' emergency regimes.[5] Refraining from providing a definition signalled that we invited disagreement about whether a particular law or action ought to have been included in or excluded from the scope of this study. Having said all this, the essays in this volume typically interpret 'emergency powers' to refer to coercive powers, claimed or invoked by or on behalf of the state, the purpose of which is to address a serious threat (usually to persons, property or social order) which, in the view of those who invoke it, cannot be addressed by 'ordinary' law. Whether this working definition covers all instances of emergency powers remains an open question. The central concern, though, is whether state powers exercised under this banner can be meaningfully constrained through law.

The second question concerns the category 'Asia'. Why define the scope of the inquiry in this way? In choosing this category, are we assuming that there is something different or unique about Asia? Are we engaged in an

4 Internal security legislation has in some jurisdictions become a standing power to deal with subversion: see, for instance, the Internal Security Act in Singapore and Malaysia, discussed in M. Hor, 'Law and Terror: Singapore Stories and Malaysian Dilemmas', in V. V. Ramraj, M. Hor and K. Roach (eds.), *Global Anti-Terrorism Law and Policy* (Cambridge: Cambridge University Press, 2005), pp. 278–9.

5 On the distinction between *de jure* and *de facto* emergencies, see J. Fitzpatrick, *Human Rights in Crisis: The International System for Protecting Rights During States of Emergency* (Philadelphia: University of Pennsylvania Press, 1994), pp. 3–21.

orientalist, and therefore suspect, exercise? We do not mean to imply that there is anything special or unique about the Asian societies considered in this volume (though neither do we repudiate this possibility). However, there are several reasons why a study of emergency powers in Asia is important. For one, as a vast continent, Asia contains a plurality of legal forms and systems of government, as well as a diversity of experiences with European and Asian colonialism (and in the case of Thailand, an absence of colonial rule altogether). It consists of states in the midst of or emerging from conflict, single-party communist states, economically successful semi-authoritarian or formally democratic states, and both nascent and aspiring democracies. A second reason is the depressingly large number of emergencies in Asia canvassed in this volume. Indeed, the range of emergencies is so broad that we can hardly do justice to them in these pages. We do not, for instance, examine recent states of emergency in Russia, Turkey, Iraq, Bangladesh, Nepal, the Middle East or Central Asia.[6] But our objective in this volume is not to provide a comprehensive survey of the actual experiences of emergency powers in Asia; rather, it is to use the particular instances of emergency powers recounted here as a vehicle for exploring the relationship between emergency powers and aspirations of constitutional government more generally. With this goal in mind, we have brought together a collection of essays which take as their starting points the experiences of emergency powers in Aceh, Afghanistan, Brunei, Burma/Myanmar, Cambodia, China, East Timor/Timor-Leste, Hong Kong, India, Indonesia, Japan, Laos, Malaysia, Pakistan, Philippines, Singapore, South Korea, Sri Lanka, Taiwan, Thailand and Vietnam. Finally, although this volume is grounded in Asia, our firm conviction is that this study holds lessons for *any* constitutional order that is struggling to come to terms with emergency powers, whether in Asia or elsewhere.

In this introduction, we identify four overarching themes that emerge from the chapters in this volume and correspond to the four parts of this book. There is, of course, some risk and artificiality in doing so. Most of the chapters in this volume examine a range of cross-cutting themes, and to classify them according to one main theme does not do them justice. Yet

[6] Websites maintained by the UN Security Council's Counter-Terrorism Committee (www.un.org/sc/ctc/) and the International Commission of Jurists (www.icj.org/) provide useful resources and databases for tracking the use of emergency powers in Asia and elsewhere. Though no longer updated, the Queen's University Belfast's States of Emergency Database is a useful historical resource: www.qub.ac.uk/schools/SchoolofLaw/Research/HumanRightsCentre/ Resources/StatesofEmergencyDatabase/.

there is some analytic clarity to be gained from this exercise, and so, with some apprehension, we group the chapters according to four main themes: perspectives from legal and political theory; postcolonial and post-conflict transitions; emergencies, executive power and constitutional order; and the role of the courts.

II. Perspectives from legal and political theory

As Albert Chen astutely observes in his contribution to this volume, the 'concept and theory of emergency powers are... inseparable from the concept and theory of constitutionalism'.[7] What then, is the impact of the transplantation of emergency powers in a constitution? For Victor V. Ramraj (looking at East Timor,[8] Thailand and Malaysia),[9] and Chen (referring to Hong Kong, Taiwan, South Korea and the People's Republic of China), this question makes sense only if we first distinguish between established liberal democracies and developing or aspiring constitutional orders. According to Ramraj, there is a crucial distinction in theory and practice between situations in which emergency powers are used to preserve or restore constitutionalism in established states, and situations in which they are used 'to bring about the basic conditions of stability upon which a constitutional order can take hold'.[10] Similarly, in many countries in Asia and elsewhere, argues Chen, the 'discourse of emergency may be no more than a substitute or surrogate for the idea that the prevailing circumstances make it impossible or impracticable to practise the liberal constitutional democratic system prescribed... for "normal" circumstances'.[11]

Ramraj and Chen are conscious of the potential for emergency powers to be abused. Ramraj argues that in developing constitutional orders, especially post-conflict ones, an 'emergency powers paradox' is apparent; emergency powers are 'seen as necessary to establish the conditions of relative stability needed for legal, political and economic reforms to take hold, and yet a propensity to invoke these powers... casts doubt on a government's commitment to constitutionalism in the first place'.[12] In his view, emergency powers are sometimes justified to establish stability,

[7] Chen, Chapter 3, p. 58.

[8] Officially, East Timor is known in Portuguese as República Democrática de Timor-Leste. However, since we have rendered the names of other countries in this volume by their names in English, we refer to Timor-Leste, for short, as 'East Timor'.

[9] Ramraj, Chapter 2. [10] *Ibid.*, p. 43.

[11] Chen, Chapter 3, p. 64. [12] Ramraj, Chapter 2, p. 29.

provided that (as in East Timor), the government remains committed to legality and constitutionalism. At the same time, however, he acknowledges the danger of abuse of such powers (as in Malaysia and Thailand), but argues that the struggle for constitutional constraints on emergency powers is more political than legal, at least until a constitutional culture is entrenched. Chen too is conscious that the use and discourse of emergency powers can become 'instruments for subverting constitutionalism', but argues that emergency powers laws can sometimes play an important role in constraining their use (as in Hong Kong and China[13]) and, in some circumstances, can serve to galvanise public support against authoritarian rule when those powers are abused or have outlived the events that justified their invocation in the first place (as in Taiwan and South Korea[14]).

In contrast with Chen and Ramraj, Anil Kalhan[15] and Vasuki Nesiah[16] are more overtly concerned about the potential for abuse in light of the experience of those powers in India, Pakistan and Sri Lanka. For example, Kalhan shows how Pakistani President and General Pervez Musharraf (in 2007) and Indian Prime Minister Indira Gandhi (in 1975) both invoked emergency powers, albeit in constitutionally distinct and contentious ways, to consolidate political power. In Pakistan, Musharraf proclaimed an emergency in part to neutralise what he considered an activist judiciary working 'at cross-purposes with the executive and the legislature'.[17] Musharraf used the emergency to purge the judiciary of potentially 'disloyal' judges and to detain political opponents, including 'opposition lawyers, judges and politicians'.[18] What was particularly remarkable about this emergency was the lack of a clear legal basis for it in the Constitution and the 'extraconstitutional' order it ushered in. In contrast, although Gandhi's emergency in 1975 was formally in accordance with the Constitution, it was motivated by similar concerns about the judiciary and had similar political consequences, rendering 'the distinction between constitution and extraconstitution largely formal'[19] and demonstrating 'that non-legal or political factors can loom large under both constitutional and extraconstitutional emergency powers regimes'.[20] So for Kalhan, rather than paving the way for the accountability of modern

[13] Chen, Chapter 3, pp. 65–8, 79–82. [14] *Ibid.*, pp. 68–72, 72–9.

[15] A. Kalhan, 'Constitution and "Extraconstitution": Colonial Emergency Regimes in Postcolonial India and Pakistan' (Chapter 4), this volume.

[16] V. Nesiah, 'The Princely Imposter: Stories of Law and Pathology in the Exercise of Emergency Powers' (Chapter 5), this volume.

[17] Kalhan, Chapter 4, p. 96. [18] *Ibid.*, p. 99. [19] *Ibid.*, p. 111. [20] *Ibid.*, p. 115.

constitutional government, 'emergency and emergency-like powers [are] in part designed precisely to avoid such accountability'.[21]

Nesiah is similarly sceptical. Drawing on the experience of Sri Lanka, she warns of the dangers that arise when emergency powers are normalised. For Nesiah, the usual remedies of liberal constitutionalism – 'better laws, institutions and norms'[22] – are problematic because of the way in which they conceive the problem. For liberal constitutional law theorists, the danger of emergency powers arises from the lack of adequate constraints, so they seek to refine emergency powers and fix doctrinal gaps, improve the political-legal institutional architecture and reform the 'political culture of constitutionalism'.[23] But the Sri Lankan example points to a deeper problem – a problem that arises when emergency powers become part of normalised, 'crisis constitutionalism'[24] that Nesiah claims (drawing on Giorgio Agamben[25]) is characteristic not only of the '"Sri Lankas" of the world'[26] but of constitutionalism more generally.

On one point, Ramraj, Chen, Kalhan and Nesiah seem to agree: the law of emergency powers is deeply political; law cannot play the same kind of constraining role in developing constitutional orders that it seeks to play in developed, liberal constitutional orders. Where they differ is on the potential for law to do so. In this respect, Ramraj and Chen are more optimistic concerning law's prospects; while conscious of the potential for abuse, they both see emergency powers as capable of securing a foundation on which a liberal constitutional order might eventually be built. In contrast, Kalhan sees emergency powers, whether constitutional or extraconstitutional, as undermining efforts to establish accountable government; Nesiah sees them as essentially uncontainable. Contexts of extreme power, she argues, show that 'more law can itself enable, exacerbate and authorise such abuse' and that 'exceptions are not outside of law but are themselves its products'.[27]

The deep tension between emergency powers and the constitutional order reverberates through this volume in different contexts. Two contexts have already been identified. The first is the link between emergency powers and colonialism, which emerges indirectly in Ramraj's account of Malaysia and Chen's discussion of Hong Kong. It is also confronted squarely in Kalhan's recognition of the 'shared origins' of

21 *Ibid.*, p. 120. 22 Nesiah, Chapter 5, p. 121.
23 *Ibid.*, pp. 121, 129 and (in quotes) 131. 24 *Ibid.*, p. 124.
25 G. Agamben, *State of Exception* (Chicago: University of Chicago Press, 2005).
26 Nesiah, Chapter 5, p. 139. 27 *Ibid.*, p. 144.

emergency powers in India and Pakistan 'in the British colonial state'[28] and Nesiah's claim that the normalisation of emergency powers 'stretches back into the country's colonial history as a central component of colonial governance'.[29] The second is the important and contentious role of emergency powers in transitional, post-conflict states, such as East Timor. In the next part of this chapter, we consider the role that emergency powers play in mediating legal transitions in postcolonial and post-conflict contexts.

III. Postcolonial and post-conflict transitions

The invocation of emergency powers often straddles formal changes in the legal and political order. Here we consider two such changes: the first occurs when former colonial powers withdraw; the second takes place in the transition from conflict to peace. Kevin Tan's chapter provides an overview of the use of emergency powers during transitions of the first kind – through the process of decolonisation and its immediate aftermath in Southeast Asia.[30] Maitrii Aung-Thwin examines the use of emergency powers by British colonial authorities in Burma between 1930 and 1932 and explores its implications for contemporary Myanmar and postcolonial societies in Asia.[31] The contributions by Simon Chesterman[32] and by Michelle Miller and Michael Feener[33] examine the role of emergency powers as societies embark on a transition from conflict to peace, but show strong connections to the problems of colonialism highlighted by Tan and Aung-Thwin.

In his chapter, Tan describes the transfer of power between colonial authorities and indigenous leaders across Southeast Asia, focusing on the use of emergency powers by the four colonial regimes: the American regime (in the Philippines); the British (in Burma, Malaya, Singapore, Borneo and Brunei); the French (in Vietnam, Laos and Cambodia); and

[28] Kalhan, Chapter 4, p. 116.

[29] Nesiah, Chapter 5, p. 123. See also M. Aung-Thwin, 'Discourses of Emergency in Colonial and Postcolonial Burma' (Chapter 7), this volume. Colonialism figures prominently in the history of emergency powers in Southeast Asia and Hong Kong as well: see K. Y. L. Tan, 'From Myanmar to Manila: A Brief Study of Emergency Powers in Southeast Asia' (Chapter 6), this volume; Chen, Chapter 3.

[30] Tan, Chapter 6. [31] Aung-Thwin, Chapter 7.

[32] S. Chesterman, 'UNaccountable? The United Nations, Emergency Powers, and the Rule of Law in Asia' (Chapter 9), this volume.

[33] M. A. Miller and R. M. Feener, 'Emergency and Islamic Law in Aceh' (Chapter 8), this volume.

the Dutch (in Indonesia). The nationalist leaders who came to power often denounced the use of emergency powers by colonial rulers, Tan shows, but were quick to accept and adopt those same powers to maintain a stronghold over their new nations. Most political leaders argued that this was necessary to preserve their new constitutional orders, even if this meant sacrificing elements of constitutionalism, thereby reinforcing the paradox on which Ramraj focuses. Tan appears sympathetic to this development. He argues that basic law-and-order issues were not settled by the formal adoption of constitutions, and the nations in Southeast Asia constantly have had to face challenges to their survival; attempts at insurrection and subterfuge were regular features of the history of these postcolonial nations. Faced with such challenges, explains Tan, most nations used one of two constitutional options: to constitutionally eradicate opposition to power (an option exercised by Vietnam, Laos and Burma, and by Indonesia until the Suharto era), or to retain and use emergency powers when necessary (the option chosen by the Philippines, Malaysia and Singapore). Thailand, Cambodia and Brunei did not fit into these two models, and were exceptional on account of specific circumstances within each nation.

Like Tan, Maitrii Aung-Thwin is equally concerned about the understudied impact of colonialism on current legal regimes in Asia. His chapter focuses on a single instance of the use of emergency powers in Burma between 1930 and 1932, in what came to be known as the 'Burma Rebellion'. This one event at the height of colonial rule in Burma shows how the colonial authorities employed emergency powers in dubious ways, often with full knowledge that there was no justifiable basis for their use, in order to maintain control over colonial subjects. Aung-Thwin traces the worldview that influenced the colonial authorities' use of emergency powers; in his view, this mindset went on to affect the thinking of leaders in post-independence Burma. Aung-Thwin is less accepting of the legitimacy of the use of emergency powers in postcolonial Asia. He suggests that at least in postcolonial Burma, the political elite's perception of Burma as being continuously under siege and the Burmese people as not being 'ready to embrace alternative forms of government'[34] had strong parallels with the perspectives of the colonial authorities who imposed the emergency to quell the Burma Rebellion.

Simon Chesterman takes us from the colonial context to what some have called our neo-imperial era[35] – specifically, recent exercises of emergency

[34] Aung-Thwin, Chapter 7, p. 211.
[35] J. Stromseth, D. Wippman and R. Brooks, *Can Might Make Rights? Building the Rule of Law after Military Interventions* (New York: Cambridge University Press, 2006), esp. pp. 1–17.

powers by the United Nations in Asia under international law.[36] How does the rule of law, an important dimension of constitutionalism, apply to the state-building activities of the United Nations? More specifically, how does the UN Security Council use the rule of law as a tool, and to what extent are its own actions constrained by the rule of law in its operations in East Timor and Afghanistan? Chesterman begins and ends his chapter with references to colonialism in Asia, and his overall analysis is persuasive in making the connection between UN operations and some of the mistakes of colonialism: the uncritical use of foreign legal models without making efforts to adapt those models to local conditions, and the extensive use of preventive detention to bring peace, often in violation of widely accepted international norms. Reflecting the colonial legacy highlighted by Tan and Aung-Thwin, Chesterman concludes that 'the contradictions between what international administrators say and . . . do have complicated [the task of governing these societies] and left an uncertain legacy for those who inherit it'.[37]

In their chapter, Miller and Feener examine the interplay between the use of emergency powers and the introduction of religious law (specifically, Shari'a law) in the Indonesian province of Aceh, where an armed separatist movement was active for decades.[38] Like East Timor, Aceh is a post-conflict society, but the devastation of the 2004 tsunami added a further layer of complexity to the governance of postcolonial Aceh, leading to intervention by international aid authorities. Miller and Feener describe attempts by successive governments in Jakarta to contain the separatist movement in Aceh by imposing emergency rule and simultaneously offering Shari'a law to the Acehnese – moves that have both strengthened and constrained Indonesian authority within Aceh in different ways. Drawing parallels to Northern Ireland, Miller and Feener argue that while the formal imposition of harsh emergency laws led to greater Indonesian control over the territory of Aceh, it also alienated and radicalised the Acehnese, providing popular support for the separatist movement. The introduction of Shari'a law, they argue, though unsuccessful when first introduced alongside military measures, later proved useful for embedding stable political authority in post-conflict Aceh, instilling hope for many Acehnese that there will be 'an alternative legal order for post-conflict Aceh as a special autonomous region within Indonesia'.[39] This analysis draws attention to a common problem in postcolonial societies: tensions between the centre and the periphery that are articulated as disputes over

[36] Chesterman, Chapter 9. [37] *Ibid.*, p. 262.
[38] Miller and Feener, Chapter 8. [39] *Ibid.*, p. 236.

federalism. What makes these cases so intractable is that many are a direct result of the messy arrangements left when colonial powers withdrew and borders were redrawn based on considerations other than national identity. Taken together, these chapters reinforce the need to study more closely the impact of colonialism on the contemporary use of emergency powers in Asia.

IV. Emergencies, executive power and constitutional order

Emergency powers evidently play a controversial role in transitions from colonial rule to independence and from conflict to relative tranquillity. They also raise critical questions about constitutionalism in states with a history of strong executive government, but where colonial rule is distant or non-existent. The chapters by Nadirsyah Hosen (Indonesia),[40] Andrew Harding (Thailand),[41] Mark Fenwick (Japan),[42] and Jacques deLisle (China),[43] though dealing with societies vastly different in terms of their political and legal structures and their social and economic conditions, provide a useful lens to examine the complex relationship between emergency powers and strong executive government.

In his contribution, Hosen traces the development of emergency powers in post-independence Indonesia through Presidents Sukarno and Suharto into the modern era, alongside the evolution of a substantive conception of *negara hukum* – a concept akin to the rule of law. In particular, he shows how the shift away from authoritarian government toward a more substantive conception of the rule of law in Indonesia has taken place in response to internal political changes and external pressure from international financial institutions. Hosen also demonstrates how this shift toward the rule of law stands in sharp contrast with the post-9/11 pressure, again both internal and external, to strengthen and invoke emergency powers in response to terrorist bombings in Bali and Jakarta. Hosen observes, however, that these powers have also been used, controversially, to issue permits to mining companies in protected forests, renewing concerns about the

[40] N. Hosen, 'Emergency Powers and the Rule of Law in Indonesia' (Chapter 10), this volume.
[41] A. Harding, 'Emergency Powers with a Moustache: Special Powers, Military Rule and Evolving Constitutionalism in Thailand' (Chapter 11), this volume.
[42] M. Fenwick, 'Emergency Powers and the Limits of Constitutionalism in Japan' (Chapter 12), this volume.
[43] J. deLisle, 'States of Exception in an Exceptional State: Emergency Powers Law in China' (Chapter 13), this volume.

strength of the rule of law as a substantive constraint on government in contemporary Indonesia.

The strength of constitutionalism as a check on strong executive power is equally evident in Thailand, which has seen regular military intervention, often with the support of the King, in times of political crisis. Thailand has also seen the invocation of emergency powers, both in response to a bloody insurgency in its southern provinces and, at least formally, in response to mass political protests in Bangkok in 2008. Harding examines recent developments in Thailand as part of a long project 'of building constitutionalism and the rule of law'[44] that began in earnest in 1991, and tracks the legal development of emergency and emergency-like powers in Thailand following the September 2006 military coup and the promulgation of the 2007 Constitution. He makes two central observations. The first concerns Thailand's attempt to deal with political instability through the law, as it has attempted to do through emergency and emergency-like legislation. Harding shows how the emergency provisions in the Thai Constitution, including provisions relating to martial law and the newly enacted Internal Security Act 2007 introduced by the interim government following the 2006 military coup, pose serious threats to human rights and to the prospect of constitutional government. For Harding, the Internal Security Act is particularly problematic, moving Thailand – 'a country that has been making much progress in other areas of constitutional experimentation – further down the path of making the rule of law an exception'.[45] His second observation concerns how the military coup has been normalised as a mechanism for handling political crises with impunity, a development that Harding recognises has important parallels with Pakistan, as described by Kalhan.[46] These two observations lead Harding to conclude that in contemporary Thailand the law 'imposes virtually no restraint on executive powers in emergency and security contexts and only public and international opinion act as anything near to a check'.[47]

Unlike Indonesia's and Thailand's Constitutions, both currently in the midst of significant transformation, Japan's Constitution appears to be relatively stable. In his chapter, Fenwick describes the significant informal power wielded by the Japanese executive and examines the recent enactment of emergency power provisions authorising 'a systematic derogation from constitutional norms'.[48] These emergency powers, in his view, are

[44] Harding, Chapter 11, p. 295. [45] *Ibid.*, p. 311.
[46] *Ibid.*, p. 296, referring to Kalhan, Chapter 4.
[47] *Ibid.*, pp. 312–13. [48] Fenwick, Chapter 12.

not readily amenable to liberal constitutional analysis, for two reasons. First, constraints on executive power in post-war Japan 'have not been legal . . . at least not to any significant degree'.[49] The pervasive use of informal 'guidance' by the executive and the significant role of factionalism and consensus politics in constraining executive power serve to demonstrate that extra-legal constraints have been normalised even in ordinary cases. Second, the absence of a strong constitutional culture can be traced in part to the 'illegitimate' foundation of the post-war Constitution. This shows why, in Japan, the introduction of emergency powers should be seen not as part of a quest 'for rule of law legitimation', but rather 'as a symptom of the failure of constitutionalism' and as 'a challenge to the authority of the Constitution' by those critical of the illegitimacy of its foundation.[50]

If emergency powers in Indonesia, Thailand and Japan reveal the inability of constitutional law to constrain executive power, the formalisation of these powers presents both a challenge and an opportunity in China. The very idea of emergency powers in China is puzzling given that a 'regime of China's type (at least in pure form) operates in a permanent, but almost never-declared, state of emergency'.[51] How, then, can we make sense of emergency powers law in China? In response to this question, deLisle identifies four broad factors that help to explain the appeal of emergency powers to China's leadership: the consistency of these powers with China's 'legal development' project; their resonance with a 'power-creating' concept of law; their instrumental value in helping to realise the leadership's priorities; and the way in which they allow the regime to draw on law's legitimacy in its use of extraordinary power.[52] However, while conscious of the dangers of formalizing emergency powers, deLisle argues that a formal emergency powers regime in China 'has the potential to constrain the state' by forging 'restraints on derogations [from legal rights] where few otherwise would exist'.[53] Formalised emergency powers can limit the scope of legitimate state conduct and reduce the likelihood that exceptional powers will be used to deal with 'lesser threats'[54] and shift debates about the use of such powers onto the terrain of law. Here, the contrast with liberal constitutional theories of emergency powers is apparent. While theorists of emergency powers warn of a 'seepage' of emergency norms into the ordinary legal system,[55] in China, according

[49] *Ibid.*, p. 317. [50] *Ibid.* [51] deLisle, Chapter 13, p. 342.
[52] *Ibid.* (see Parts II to V). [53] *Ibid.*, pp. 375, 376. [54] *Ibid.*, p. 381.
[55] O. Gross, 'Chaos and Rules: Should Responses to Violent Crises Always be Constitutional?', (2003) 112 *Yale Law Journal* 1011 at 1097.

to deLisle, we find the potential for the principle of legality that inspires emergency powers to seep into the ordinary legal system: 'Once laws and power-holders articulate the conditions for emergencies and the processes for arrogating exceptional power, disregard of ordinary legal limits likely becomes more illegitimate in other contexts'.[56]

These diverse studies of the interplay between constitutionalism and strong executive government show some of the difficulties in generalising about legal constraints on emergency powers within Asia, let alone across developing and developed legal systems. A range of factors, including many 'local' factors, may be relevant.[57] But there is one crucial factor that directly invokes the agency of legal actors and that remains to be considered in this chapter. It is hard to imagine a modern state committed to constitutionalism in which the judiciary does not play a key role in safeguarding constitutional norms. What role does and should the judiciary play in constraining the exercise of emergency powers? Is it possible for the judiciary, at least in some circumstances, to serve as a check?

V. The role of the courts

In sharp contrast with deLisle's account of emergency powers in China, H. P. Lee argues that the true villain in the tragic abuse of emergency powers in Asia is the formal inclusion of these powers in the constitution.[58] Lee begins by noting that this feature is conspicuously absent in the Anglo-American tradition, and asserts that such provisions – the main culprits that account for the dismal record of misuse of emergency powers in Malaysia and India – should be similarly banished from Asia. Lee therefore argues that a better solution would be to embody emergency powers in ordinary statutes, where courts would be more free and able to regulate them through judicial doctrines such as 'proportionality'. The main problem with constitutionalised emergency provisions, he explains, is that judges feel far more constrained when dealing with constitutionally entrenched emergency powers. Lee's difficulty with constitutionalised emergency powers thus stems from his concern about the ability of judges and courts to act as checks on their abuse. His solution is designed to

[56] deLisle, Chapter 13, pp. 387–8.

[57] Tan, Chapter 6. Echoing this view, Chesterman observes that East Timor is very much bound, due to its ongoing ties with Portugal, Australia and the UN, to a 'global (and perhaps Western) discourse' (Chapter 9, p. 262).

[58] H. P. Lee, 'Constitutionalised Emergency Powers: A Plague on Asian Constitutionalism?', (Chapter 14), this volume.

empower courts to exercise a stronger role in the context of emergency powers.

Raul Pangalangan is also sceptical of the existing capacity of courts and judges to make a tangible difference in preventing misuse of emergency powers.[59] He focuses on the manner in which Philippine Presidents Ferdinand Marcos and Gloria Macapagal-Arroyo abused or otherwise sidestepped formal constitutional constraints on emergency powers. Pangalangan's principal argument is that the 'formal' and 'legalistic' notions of law that are prevalent among legal actors in the Philippines (including the courts) are incapable of restraining the dictatorial tendencies of presidents. Echoing Lee's concern that courts are reluctant to review the use of constitutionalised emergency powers, Pangalangan notes that the Supreme Court endorsed Marcos's use of such powers, avoiding a decision on merits by taking refuge in the 'political questions' doctrine. Under President Arroyo, however, the judiciary has become more activist; perhaps in response, Arroyo has frustrated constitutional review by invoking emergency-like powers that fall short of formal emergency provisions, thus 'remaining below the radar of the courts'.[60] Pangalangan acknowledges that the courts have tried to rein in some of Arroyo's measures, but he believes that these efforts have had little effect; formal constraints and judicial review offer little hope that ordinary Filipinos will be shielded from abuses of emergency powers.

In contrast with Lee and Pangalangan, Clark Lombardi[61] and Arun Thiruvengadam[62] are more optimistic about courts. Lombardi focuses on the thought of one of the most famous judges in Pakistan's early post-independence era, Justice A. R. Cornelius. Cornelius wrote powerful dissents in cases arising out of Pakistan's first state of emergency (1954) and first martial law (1958), in which he decried his colleagues' reluctance to challenge executive assertions of power, while defending the importance of fundamental rights in times of emergency. Lombardi's analysis suggests that judicial reactions to emergency powers in the 1950s and 1960s in Pakistan approximate those detailed by Lee and Pangalangan; Cornelius was alone in his dissents, and the majority of the judges in Pakistan meekly surrendered to the wishes of the ruling executive in such cases. As

59 R. Pangalangan, 'Political Emergencies in the Philippines: Changing Labels and the Unchanging Need for Legitimacy,' (Chapter 15), this volume.
60 *Ibid.*, p. 432.
61 C. B. Lombardi, 'Islamism as a Response to Emergency Rule in Pakistan: The Surprising Proposal of Justice A. R. Cornelius' (Chapter 16), this volume.
62 A. K. Thiruvengadam, 'Asian Judiciaries and Emergency Powers: Reasons for Optimism?', (Chapter 17), this volume.

Lombardi explains, Cornelius concluded that there was a need to create a 'culture of constitutionalism' in Pakistan, which would only take root when ordinary people felt invested in their legal system. For Cornelius, this meant connecting the legal system to the liberal ideas of Islam, the predominant religion in Pakistan, which he believed would 'resanctify' the judges' constitutional role 'as checks on executive power'.[63] It would facilitate the emergence of a liberal constitutional order by imparting to it a legitimacy which the transplanted colonial legal order lacked. Cornelius's concern for a more expansive role for judges in the context of emergency power thus led him to an unusual solution.

Thiruvengadam's chapter considers whether the 'conventional view' that the judiciary is an ineffective check on emergency powers fairly reflects the potential for judicial review in Asia. He starts by showing why the historical record bears out the fears of judicial-sceptics, but argues that times are changing in much of Asia. He draws empirical support from the fact that in recent decades, courts in India, South Korea and Taiwan have begun to exercise strong forms of review over constitutional claims, at least in areas other than national security and emergency powers. This shift, argues Thiruvengadam, can be traced to a number of socio-political changes in these countries, which have emboldened judges and heralded the emergence of a constitutional culture in which citizens and political leaders alike accept the legitimacy of judicial review as a fact of democratic governance. Thiruvengadam argues that the political and sociological conditions that provide support for judiciaries to extend their review jurisdiction to sensitive cases involving emergency powers appear to be emerging in a number of Asian nations. He also sets out the normative arguments for judicial review of emergency powers, arguing that judges in Asia (such as Cornelius in Pakistan and H. R. Khanna in India, both in dissent) have long been familiar with them. For Thiruvengadam, the institutional legitimacy of the courts (at least in some countries in Asia) has improved significantly, such that prospects for judicial intervention in emergency powers cases are much brighter than they were in Cornelius's time.

VI. Emergency powers in Asia: intellectual crossroads

How should emergency powers in Asia be understood? The essays in this volume suggest two broad reasons to think that the abstract theories of emergency powers originating in established liberal democracies might

[63] Lombardi, Chapter 16, p. 464.

not be immediately relevant in Asia. First, a range of factors from the colonial history to the interplay of law and religion to the simmering ethnic and political conflicts in the region suggest that a contextual account of emergency powers is apposite. Destabilising internal struggles, often dating to colonial times, from Sri Lanka to East Timor, suggest a need for a nuanced understanding of emergency powers distinct from those in established liberal democracies post-9/11. Second, in many (but not all) of the jurisdictions canvassed in this volume, legal and political institutions, including the courts, are not sufficiently stable – nor are the norms of those institutions sufficiently entrenched – to allow legal and constitutional norms governing emergency powers to take firm hold. Moreover, as Harding's and Kalhan's chapters demonstrate (and others imply), the military often plays a much greater role domestically in parts of Asia than it has historically in many liberal constitutional democracies.

At the same time, however, there is some convergence (both within Asia and between Asia and elsewhere) in terms of the issues and challenges that arise from the invocation of emergency powers by the state. First, the potential for emergency and emergency-like powers to be abused by the state and to become normalised are ever-present in developing and developed legal orders. So there is reason to believe that the *problem* of emergency powers is similar even if the potential solutions are distinct. The liberal constitutional remedy of 'better laws, institutions and norms',[64] identified and critiqued by Nesiah, may not be easily transferred to developing constitutional orders in Asia. However, if we bear in mind three things – the danger of allowing 'the exception' into the constitutional order; the contextual and historical particularities of the particular society (highlighted by Tan, Aung-Thwin, Kalhan and Miller and Feener); and the special challenges involved in establishing a constitutional order (noted by Chen and Ramraj) – alongside 'better laws, institutions and norms', we might yet find a useful starting point for analysing emergency powers in Asia.

A second area of convergence of issues, if not solutions, concerns the question of whether the constitutionalisation of emergency powers – with or without the active supervision of the courts – is able to provide an effective check on emergency powers, or if instead it invites their abuse. In their contributions to this volume, Lee, Nesiah, Kalhan and Pangalangan are deeply sceptical of emergency powers and of the ability of the law to contain them. Fenwick shows how emergency powers can develop opportunistically, rather than in response to a concrete threat; Hosen

[64] Nesiah, Chapter 5, p. 121.

and Chesterman, in different ways, demonstrate that external pressures to invoke emergency or emergency-like powers might at times influence the domestic agenda in ways that stand in tension with other legal priorities and aspirations. Others, however, are more optimistic. Ramraj, Chen and deLisle all see a qualified role for emergency powers as part of a move toward a constitutional order, although they are, to varying degrees, sceptical about the ability of law to contain these powers in the same manner that it does in established liberal democracies; Justice Cornelius (in Lombardi's account) and Thiruvengadam see the emergence of a constitutional culture as a precondition of effective judicial review.

A third area of convergence can be seen in the way that Asian constitutionalists, lawmakers, judges and activists have historically resisted the executive's abuse of emergency powers, using arguments that resonate with those of contemporary liberal constitutionalists. The essays in this volume provide several examples: the framers of the Indian Constitution who opposed incorporating constitutional sanction for preventive detention laws in the text of the Constitution in 1949;[65] the members of the Burma Legislative Council who managed to vote against and strike down the preventive detention law proposed by the British colonial authority in Burma in 1931;[66] the strict limitations imposed by the East Timorese National Parliament on the invocation of a state of emergency in 2008;[67] the courageous dissents of Justice Cornelius in the 1950s, invoking ideas of the rule of the law in opposing martial law and emergency powers in post-independence Pakistan;[68] and the Korean activists who, with tragic consequences, took to the streets in 1980 to protest martial law.[69] These historical episodes show that although contextual differences remain important, scholars of emergency powers in and outside Asia have much to share and discuss.

VII. Conclusion: out of the shadows

A study of emergency powers might seem at first to be an arcane area of constitutional law. The essays in this collection show that it is not. On the contrary, a study of emergency powers quickly leads us to the bedrock of constitutionalism and conceptual foundations of constitutional theory. It forces us to consider the relationship between law, politics, history and the modern state and to ask whether and in what circumstances liberal constitutionalism is the best way forward. This collection invites readers to

[65] Thiruvengadam, Chapter 17. [66] Aung-Thwin, Chapter 7.
[67] Ramraj, Chapter 2. [68] Lombardi, Chapter 16. [69] Chen, Chapter 3.

consider their assumptions and views in a new light. For those interested in contemporary debates over emergency powers in legal and political theory, the collection invites us to reconsider the way we frame the issues in light of the special challenges for legality canvassed here. For those whose primary interests are in constitutionalism in Asia, it poses questions rarely asked about the socio-political conditions in which constitutionalism can be sustained and the prospects for its evolution and survival alongside emergency situations, real, exaggerated or invented. For those interested in problems of political authority, political sociology and the development of the modern state, these essays offer a fresh perspective on the displacement of traditional structures of political authority and their replacement with alien ones, often through force or hegemonic influence.

What emerges from this collection is that we cannot fully comprehend the legal and constitutional complexities of emergency powers from a narrow disciplinary perspective. The essays in the volume engage collectively with emergency powers from historical, sociological, comparative and theoretical perspectives. Some chapters draw on historical narratives in particular societies, reminding us that the exercise of emergency powers is deeply rooted in the colonial era. Others stress the importance of political and sociological forces in enabling law to regulate the exercise of extraordinary coercive powers in times of crisis. The importance of comparative analysis is equally evident. Studying emergency powers in a constitutional laboratory shows how these powers can be used cautiously, in a manner narrowly delimited by law, and can also reveal the tendency of governments to use these powers as a tool for consolidating political control, often with tragic consequences. It also provides us the opportunity to test our normative arguments and develop and refine our legal and political model for responding to crises, and facilitates theoretical engagement. A careful use of theory enriches discussions about emergency powers and constitutionalism, forcing us to abstract from concrete experiences, while mindful of their nuances and particularities. We hope that this collection does justice to these larger interdisciplinary aims – but most of all, we hope it will bring the study of emergency powers in Asia out of the intellectual shadows, prompting others to take a closer look.

PART I

Perspectives from legal and political theory

2

The emergency powers paradox

VICTOR V. RAMRAJ

I. Introduction

The basic principles enshrined in the constitutions of many Southeast Asian states bear at least a superficial resemblance to those in their Western, liberal-democratic counterparts. Ostensibly, these principles guarantee fundamental freedoms and place general limits on the use of coercive powers by the state. And as in liberal democracies, emergencies – especially those involving political violence – occasionally pose a serious threat to the constitutional order. Liberal-democratic theories of emergency powers, it seems, should have some relevance for anyone seeking to understand the use of formal or informal emergency powers in Southeast Asia. Yet it is precisely in the context of an emergency that the profound differences between Southeast Asian states and established liberal democracies in the practice of constitutionalism – and, more generally, the aspiration of legality – are exposed.

Theories of emergency powers in the liberal-democratic tradition tend to focus on the capacity of law and formal legal institutions, including the courts, to constrain state power and preserve the normative legal order. This is true not only of the classical theories of legality in times of crisis,[1] but also of contemporary theories of emergency powers.[2] These theories are important and illuminating, but they are limited in one important

I am grateful to Chairat Charoensin-O-Larn, Michael Feener, Karin Loevy, M. Sornarajah, Arun K. Thiruvengadam, and especially to A. P. Simester, for constructive criticism, and to students in my Emergencies and Legal Theory seminar at the National University of Singapore in 2008, who, through their rigorous discussion and debate, helped me refine my arguments.

[1] See, for example, John Locke's theory of the prerogative in *Two Treatises of Government*, ed. P. Laslett (Cambridge: Cambridge University Press, 1988), pp. 374–81, and A. V. Dicey's conception of the rule of law in *Introduction to the Study of the Law of the Constitution*, 8th edn (London: Macmillan, 1920), pp. 179–201.

[2] See, for example, V. V. Ramraj (ed.), *Emergencies and the Limits of Legality* (Cambridge: Cambridge University Press, 2008).

respect. They typically assume the presence of liberal-democratic institutions, a fully developed legal infrastructure and an entrenched culture of accountability. Yet in Southeast Asia, where many states have invoked emergency powers, often in response to political violence, many – and in some cases, all – of these conditions are lacking. We find, for example, the invocation of emergency powers in situations where, following a conflict, the basic institutions of the state are not fully developed and basic technical capacity is lacking; where the military periodically intervenes, ostensibly to stabilise the political order and adjust the constitutional order; and where, at least in the sphere of public power, there is little formal legal accountability for those who wield the coercive power of the state. There are, of course, several states outside Southeast Asia where similar conditions exist. I do not mean to preclude the possibility that my analysis could be extended, cautiously, to other situations. But with all its diversity, Southeast Asia provides a useful laboratory in which ideas about constitutionalism might first be tested.

At the heart of this chapter stand two propositions. The first is that the difference between liberal-democratic and Southeast Asian experiences of emergency powers can best be understood by distinguishing between two constitutional contexts in which emergency powers are invoked: where states seek to *establish* legality and where they seek to *preserve* it.[3] The implications of this distinction are crucial because emergency powers operate differently in an established rule-of-law state than in a state in which the basic constitutional infrastructure and culture of accountability are weak or lacking. The second proposition is that the key to understanding the unique problem that emergencies pose in states seeking to establish legality is what I call the *emergency powers paradox*: in states that are struggling to establish legality in the face of a violent political crisis, emergency powers may be seen by the government as necessary to establish the conditions of relative stability in which a legal infrastructure and culture of accountability can take hold; yet the invocation of these powers throws into question the government's commitment to legality and constitutional government in the first place. Drawing on these propositions, I argue in this chapter, first, that emergency powers may at times be necessary to establish the political conditions upon which a liberal-democratic

[3] This chapter focuses on emergency powers invoked to address political violence, though I am mindful of the complexities of that term and the possibility that emergency powers invoked to address natural disasters and other crises might be used for malign purposes, such as political oppression. These other uses (and abuses) of emergency powers also warrant careful analysis.

constitutional order can be built, provided that those powers are exercised proportionately and in a manner consistent with the establishment of such an order; and, second, that a political struggle is needed to prevent abuse and to secure the transformation of the political order into a fully constitutional one.

Part II of this chapter begins with a survey of contemporary theories of emergency powers. In this part, I show that these theories typically assume the presence of liberal-democratic institutions, a developed constitutional infrastructure and an entrenched culture of accountability; and while the theories differ, sometimes dramatically, in their prescriptions for emergency powers, they are united in their understanding of the challenge of emergencies as one of *preserving* legality. Part III considers the experience of emergency powers in three states in Southeast Asia – East Timor, Thailand and Malaysia – that invoked emergency powers in response to political violence in distinct political and constitutional contexts. What emerges from this survey is that despite their differences, in each of these examples a key background objective is not to preserve legality, but to *establish* it in the first place. In Part IV, I reframe the emergency powers problem as a paradox confronting states seeking to establish legality, and I explore the practical and normative implications of this approach. My aim in this part is to understand better how emergencies operate in the context of a developing constitutional order, and to shed light on the challenge that emergencies pose for legality more generally, whether in liberal democracies or in the developing legal systems of Southeast Asia and elsewhere.

II. Contemporary theories of emergency powers

The foil for my analysis of emergency powers in Southeast Asia in this chapter is the contemporary literature in the liberal-democratic West on emergency powers, a literature that has grown in breadth and sophistication post-9/11. I begin the discussion in this part by distinguishing two levels at which the contemporary debate over emergency powers takes place: at the level of specific emergency powers, such as preventive detention and torture, where the controversy is framed as one of balance, in which the effectiveness of these powers in preventing terrorist acts is measured in some fashion against the threat these powers pose to constitutional or human rights; and at the level of fundamental notions of legality, where the debate is framed in response to Carl Schmitt's challenge to the legal order itself,[4] the central issue being whether and, if so, how the state can preserve legality in times of emergency. I then focus on the second of these issues. The solutions to the Schmittian challenge are varied, but, as I shall argue, they all assume the presence of liberal-democratic institutions, a developed legal infrastructure, and an entrenched culture of accountability; and while they differ, sometimes dramatically, in their prescriptions for emergency powers, they are united in their understanding of the challenge of emergencies as one of *preserving* legality. This is significant because the aim of preserving legality that dominates the liberal-democratic literature is conceptually and, as I shall argue, normatively distinct from the goal of *establishing* it.

On the first level, the concern is the use by governments in times of crisis of controversial emergency powers such as preventive detention and torture or 'rendition' to torture. The concern is often expressed in terms of the threat these specific powers pose to the constitutional rights, civil liberties or human rights of those persons against whom these powers are used. It might be cast as a tension between competing values: 'No matter how long they last, emergency powers pose a host of difficult tradeoffs, between values of liberty, privacy, autonomy, and equality on the one hand, and those of efficacy, efficiency, and security on the other.'[5] This is the essence of the hard cases on emergency powers that, post-9/11, have made their way to the highest courts in the United States, the United Kingdom and Canada.[6] In response to the challenges posed at this level, proposed solutions might involve, for example: a constitutional emergency powers framework that specifies, in advance of an emergency, the powers that can be exercised in an emergency, sometimes described as the neo-Roman model[7]; an 'ordinary legislation' model, which advocates a non-constitutional, statutory framework for dealing with emergency powers,

[4] C. Schmitt, *Political Theology: Four Chapters on the Concept of Sovereignty*, trans. G. Schwab (Chicago: University of Chicago Press, 2005).

[5] D. Cole, 'The Priority of Morality: The Emergency Constitution's Blind Spot' (2004) 113 *Yale Law Journal* 1753 at 1769.

[6] See, for example, some of the early post-9/11 decisions by these courts, respectively: *Hamdi* v. *Rumsfeld*, 124 S Ct 2633 (2004); *A.* v. *Secretary of State for the Home Department* [2004] UKHL 56; *Charkaoui* v. *Canada Citizenship and Immigration* [2007] 1 SCR 350, 2007 SCC 9.

[7] Variations on this model have been defended in the post-9/11 literature by J. Ferejohn and P. Pasquino, 'The Law of the Exception: A Typology of Emergency Powers' (2004) 2 *International Journal of Constitutional Law* 210; B. Ackerman, 'The Emergency Constitution' (2004) 113 *Yale Law Journal* 1029; and W. E. Scheuerman, 'Presidentialism and Emergency Government', in Ramraj (ed.), *Emergencies*, pp. 258–86.

often premised on the need for democratic legitimacy[8]; a judicial review model according to which either the courts[9] or specialised administrative tribunals under their supervision[10] play a key role in scrutinising the use of emergency powers; an extra-legal measures model according to which public officials confronted with grave dangers might disobey the law and then openly admit their illegal conduct, seeking public ratification but otherwise accepting legal condemnation after the fact.[11] An important issue in the debate over these solutions is whether *ex ante* or *ex post* checks on powers are preferable, given the importance of the rights or liberties in question and the demands of national security.

On the second level, however, the debate leaves to one side the specific rights and liberties that are called into question by emergency powers and confronts a more fundamental question about emergency powers. Can the state, faced with a violent emergency, take steps necessary to suppress the emergency while remaining faithful to the demands of legality? Carl Schmitt argued, notoriously, that it cannot. In times of crisis, he insisted, 'the state remains, whereas law recedes'.[12] Schmitt's challenge directly or indirectly has preoccupied contemporary legal and constitutional theorists. Their proposed solutions to the problems posed by emergency powers – whether constitutional, legislative or judicial and whether *ex ante* or *ex post* – can also be understood as a response to the question of whether and, if so, how the state can preserve legality in times of crisis. Most post-9/11 theorists reject Schmitt's thesis, arguing or implying that the state can preserve legality, at least in the long term, while confronting an emergency.

Notably, even Oren Gross – who takes seriously the challenge posed by Schmitt but accepts that public officials might, in extreme situations, have to act outside the law – believes that the prospect of *ex post* democratic-political and legal checks on extra-legal measures will deter public officials

[8] See, for example, T. Campbell, 'Emergency Strategies for Prescriptive Legal Positivists: Anti-Terrorist Law and Legal Theory' and K. Roach, 'The Ordinary Law of Emergencies and Democratic Derogation from Rights', in Ramraj (ed.), *Emergencies*, pp. 201–28 and 229–57 respectively.

[9] Cole, 'The Priority of Morality'.

[10] D. Dyzenhaus, 'The State of Emergency in Legal Theory' in V. V. Ramraj, M. Hor and K. Roach (eds.), *Global Anti-Terrorism Law and Policy* (Cambridge: Cambridge University Press, 2005), pp. 65–89. See also D. Dyzenhaus, *The Constitution of Law: Legality in a Time of Emergency* (Cambridge: Cambridge University Press, 2006), pp. 121–73.

[11] O. Gross, 'Chaos and Rules: Should Responses to Violent Crises Always be Constitutional?' (2003) 112 *Yale Law Journal* 1011; 'Stability and Flexibility: A Dicey Business', in Ramraj, Hor and Roach (eds.), *Global Anti-Terrorism Law and Policy*, pp. 90–106.

[12] Schmitt, *Political Theology*, p. 12.

from using them. Also, by taking pressure off the courts to endorse illegal but practically necessary actions, Gross insists that his extra-legal measures model will, over the longer term, better preserve legality, leaving intact the core values of the legal order.[13] For David Dyzenhaus, the courts continue to play a key role in preserving legality in an emergency, although modifications to the formal separation of powers may be required to address legitimate national security concerns in times of crisis.[14] These modifications can, however, be made in a manner consistent with legality; modern administrative law shows us how specialised administrative tribunals – as participants in a broader rule-of-law project in which all branches of government participate[15] – can address concerns about, for example, the confidentiality of intelligence sources, while preserving legality. Other theorists are less sanguine about the role of the courts, urging that emergency powers be entrenched in the constitution.[16] The provision *ex ante* of the tools that can be used by the state in an emergency accepts that a different set of norms is appropriate, but then, as in the neo-Roman model, places strict limits on the scope and duration of the emergency regime.[17]

There are many important normative differences and tensions even among these three models of emergency powers. Yet they have two features in common: first, they all assume the presence of liberal-democratic institutions; second, they all see the challenge of emergencies as that of *preserving* legality. Consider the first assumption, about liberal-democratic institutions. While many of the theories we have been looking at purport to have broad relevance beyond the liberal democracies of the North Atlantic,[18] a closer look at their theories shows the crucial role that liberal-democratic institutions and practices play in making theories plausible. For instance, Ackerman's 'supermajoritarian escalator', which requires increasingly large majorities to sustain emergency executive powers, depends on the existence of an independent legislature that,

[13] O. Gross, 'Extralegality and the Ethic of Political Responsibility', in Ramraj (ed.), *Emergencies*, pp. 60–94 at p. 62.

[14] Dyzenhaus, 'The State of Emergency'.

[15] *Dyzenhaus, The Constitution of Law*, p. 17.

[16] Above, note 7.

[17] A related approach is to provide an *ex ante* statutory, rather than constitutional, framework of emergency powers: see Campbell, 'Emergency Strategies' and Roach, 'The Ordinary Law'.

[18] For example, Gross insists that his is 'not an "American" study, nor is it a post-September 11th one' and should be 'treated as generally applicable to constitutional democratic regimes faced with the need to respond to extreme violent crises' ('Chaos and Rules', at 1027); Dyzenhaus criticises Gross's theory as too narrow, having little to say about 'well-ordered' societies that are 'neither liberal nor democratic' ('The State of Emergency', p. 72); Ackerman focuses self-consciously on liberal democracies generally and, at times, on the 'distinctive character of the US Constitution' ('The Emergency Constitution', at 1030).

in practice, plays a significant role in checking the power of the executive – an assumption that is dubious in some Southeast Asian countries. Dyzenhaus's theory of legality depends not only on a robust, independent judiciary, but also on a sophisticated understanding of the administrative state and the relationship between the courts, the legislature and specialised administrative tribunals, with each consciously aware of its role in the 'rule of law project'.[19] And Gross's extra-legal measures model, which turns on the prospect of *ex post* public repudiation or ratification of official disobedience, envisions that the extra-legal measures taken by the government be 'openly, candidly, and fully disclosed to the public',[20] which then decides 'either directly or through its elected representatives, to ratify, *ex post*, those actions that have been taken on its behalf and in its name, or to denounce them'.[21] Crucially, his model 'calls for public deliberation and, eventually, for the taking of responsibility by each and every member of the community'.[22] Yet transparency on the part of public officials in his theory, which is idealistic even in liberal democracies, rings hollow outside this context, as does his faith in the possibility of a robust public debate through which the public and the society as a whole assume responsibility for and pass judgement on the tragic choices of public officials in an emergency. These theories therefore take for granted the presence of liberal-democratic institutions and practices, whose presence cannot be assumed in other contexts – thus throwing into question each theory's claim to broad or universal relevance.

The second common feature is that these models of emergency powers tend to regard the main goal of the emergency powers regime as that of preserving the legal order, including its core substantive norms and principles. Ferejohn and Pasquino associate this goal with the neo-Roman or constitutional model, in contrast with the legislative model, which seeks to tackle emergencies using ordinary legislation; for them, one key feature of this model is its conservative aim – 'to restore the constitutional status quo and not to impose any permanent change on the legal ordering'.[23] While they recognise as an aim of the legislative model that the President would 'deal with an emergency without fundamentally altering the constitutional system'[24] through the use of temporary powers authorised by Congress, they acknowledge a 'special danger' posed by this model – the danger that 'the authority by which the president takes action is an

[19] Dyzenhaus, *The Constitution of Law*, p. 3 and *passim*.
[20] Gross, 'Chaos and Rules', at 1111.
[21] *Ibid.*, at 1111–12. [22] *Ibid.*, at 1126.
[23] Ferejohn and Pasquino, 'The Law of the Exception', at 235. [24] *Ibid.*, at 236.

ordinary statute, and statutes have, intrinsically, the potential to change the legal system in a permanent way'.[25]

I shall not pursue this debate on the permanence of ordinary emergency powers here, except to reject the assumption that the conservative aims that Ferejohn and Pasquino attribute to the neo-Roman model are exclusive to that model. The common goal of emergency powers in the liberal-democratic tradition is precisely to ensure the continuity of the normative constitutional order; where theorists in this tradition differ is in how to do this. The neo-Roman model relies on constitutional mechanisms that empower the executive for a specified, time-limited term to exercise extraordinary powers with the goal of restoring constitutional order. Dyzenhaus's legality model seeks to preserve constitutional norms through the use of innovative institutional arrangements that acknowledge the needs of national security operations while respecting the demands of legality. For his part, Gross seeks through his extra-legal measures model to preserve legality in the longer term, by providing for *ex post* democratic-political, rather than exclusively legal, checks on official disobedience.

It is precisely this aspect of emergency powers in liberal democracies – the goal of preserving the fundamental values of the constitutional order – that distinguishes liberal democracies from aspiring constitutional orders. For, in the latter, legality may not be fully established or embraced, nor is the legal infrastructure and culture necessary to sustain it fully entrenched. And so the threat posed by emergency powers to the legal order differs significantly; emergency powers pose a threat not to an established legal order with a deep tradition of constitutionalism, but to a nascent and fragile legal order struggling to establish its rule-of-law credentials. This difference in the nature of the threat posed by emergency powers in these contexts has important normative and practical implications for our understanding of emergency powers in Southeast Asia – or so I will argue in the next two parts of this chapter.

III. Emergency powers and constitutionalism in Southeast Asia

Through colonialism and the rise of the international legal and economic order in the postcolonial period, a modern state structure has been superimposed on the political structures of Southeast Asia.[26] This state structure

[25] *Ibid.*

[26] J. Tully, 'The Imperialism of Modern Constitutional Democracy', in M. Loughlin and N. Walker (eds.), *The Paradox of Constitutionalism: Constituent Power and Constitutional Form* (Oxford: Oxford University Press, 2007), pp. 315–38.

now typically includes a written constitution whose content differs considerably from one country to another within the region[27] and whose words point to the general goal of legality – the subordination of political authority to law. But the words of a constitution tell us little about its practical impact, and less still about the underlying political and institutional culture needed to give effect to many of the constitution's values and aspirations, including the aspiration of legality. So the challenge is typically one of closing the gap between aspiration and reality, between constitutionalism in theory and practice. Political violence poses a special problem for those aspiring to constitutional order because of the temptation it presents to governments to invoke emergency powers. And this in turn leads to a paradox – emergency powers are seen as necessary to establish the conditions of relative stability needed for legal, political and economic reforms to take hold, and yet a propensity to invoke these powers (and the ever-present possibility of their abuse) casts doubt on a government's commitment to constitutionalism in the first place. To confront this paradox, we need to better understand the unique challenges posed by emergency powers in legal orders in nascent democracies where legal institutions and practices are not fully established. In this part of the chapter, I attempt to describe these challenges in a general way, drawing on examples from Southeast Asia, specifically East Timor, Thailand and Malaysia; in the next part, I consider their normative and practical implications.

A. *East Timor: emergency powers and post-conflict constitutionalism*

On 31 August 1999, after nearly four centuries of Portuguese rule and twenty-four years of Indonesian occupation, the East Timorese voted overwhelmingly (78.5 per cent) against a proposal for special autonomy within Indonesia, in favour of independence,[28] unleashing a wave of political violence in which thousands were killed, many at the hands of pro-integration (with Indonesia) militias supported by the Tentara Nasional Indonesia (TNI), the Indonesian military.[29] The widespread

[27] See K. Y. L. Tan, 'The Making and Remaking of Constitutions in Southeast Asia: An Overview' (2002) 6 *Singapore Journal of International and Comparative Law* 1.

[28] For details, see the UNAMET website: www.un.org/peace/etimor99/.

[29] See generally, D. Kingsbury, 'East Timor: The Difficult Birth of a New State', in *Southeast Asia: A Political Profile*, 2nd edn (Melbourne: Oxford University Press, 2005), pp. 393–413; see also H. Charlesworth, 'The Constitution of East Timor, May 20, 2002' (2003) 1 *International Journal of Constitutional Law* 325; N. Hosen, 'Emergency Powers and the Rule of Law in Indonesia' (Chapter 10), this volume.

unrest prompted the United Nations to back a peace-enforcement mission, the Australian-led International Forces to East Timor (INTERFET), which stabilised the volatile political situation and paved the way for the UN Transitional Authority in East Timor (UNTAET). UNTAET's mandate was, in short, to maintain security and order in East Timor, to ensure the delivery of essential services and to assist in capacity-building toward self-government. On 20 May 2002, the Democratic Republic of East Timor became Southeast Asia's newest independent state. It is still very much in the process of rebuilding and has twice, in 2006 and 2008, assumed emergency powers. In his contribution to this volume, Simon Chesterman focuses on the UN's record in facilitating East Timor's transition.[30] In this section, I consider the relationship between East Timor's invocation of emergency powers and its constitutional aspirations.[31]

Several major obstacles stood in the way of East Timor's transition into a stable, self-governing state, including widespread poverty and unemployment,[32] violence and displacement of persons. Building legal and political institutions is a complex and difficult task at the best of times, but it is especially challenging when it takes place in a volatile political situation with limited infrastructure and weak public institutions. Such was the case in East Timor, where, as a result of the TNI's scorched earth policy in retreat, 'Infrastructure, including communications and water-supply, was almost non-existent, most major buildings were destroyed or damaged and industry was non-existent'.[33] The transition from conflict to relative peace also left many former guerrillas unemployed. While many were retrained and redeployed to join the new military or civilian police forces, others remained unemployed, and tensions between civilian police and military forces continue to create instability.

As Chesterman observes, legal capacity building has been difficult, given the dearth of East Timorese with professional qualifications and relevant

[30] See S. Chesterman, 'UNaccountable? The United Nations, Emergency Powers and the Rule of Law in Asia' (Chapter 9), this volume.

[31] I gratefully acknowledge the assistance of Marcelino Magno, Fernando La Sama de Araojo, Marcelina Tilman, Rita Sutil Roque, Vasco Soares, João Azevedo, Bruno Teixeira, Silverio Pinto Baptista, Amândio de Sá Benevides, Vital dos Santos, Campbell Watson, Preston Pentony, Gordon Peake, Marcus Boorman and Edward Rees, who met me in Dili in November 2008. Although my discussions with them were of great assistance in helping me to understand recent events in East Timor, my interpretation of those events and my conclusions in this section may be contentious and does not necessarily reflect the views of any one of them. I am also indebted to Simon Chesterman, Jim Della-Giacoma, Daniel Fitzpatrick and Adérito de Jesus Soares for their pre-trip assistance.

[32] Kingsbury, 'East Timor', p. 393. [33] *Ibid.*, p. 408.

practical experience.[34] And as for public confidence in the legal system, under Indonesian administration, many 'viewed the Indonesian legal system with deep distrust' and so 'had no experience or understanding of the rule of law and would rarely access the formal legal system'.[35] Against this background, the challenge of establishing an effective constitution that is not dismissed simply as another foreign imposition,[36] but is, or can be, integrated into the society in a way that respects local traditions, remains daunting.[37] As the former UN Secretary-General observed of transitional justice mechanisms generally, 'due regard must be given to indigenous and informal traditions for administering justice or settling disputes, to help them to continue their often vital role and to do so in conformity with both international standards and local traditions'.[38] Yet even these laudable goals seem secondary to the need to diffuse the most pressing political disputes before they escalate into violence, and to channel them into public institutions that command some degree of public confidence.

In these circumstances, it is unsurprising that both UNTAET and the post-independence state considered it necessary to invoke emergency or emergency-like powers in the face of political volatility and violence. Chesterman explains in his chapter how, in the immediate violent aftermath of the independence poll, INTERFET assumed emergency-like powers to detain many persons as 'security risks', who were later handed over to UNTAET. Since then, the East Timor government has twice assumed emergency powers. The first instance occurred in May 2006, as initially peaceful protests by disgruntled soldiers who complained of discrimination rapidly escalated, resulting in widespread violence, looting and the burning of houses, and culminating in the deaths of thirty-seven police officers and civilians and the displacement of some 150,000 others.[39] At the request of the East Timor government, an Australian-led peacekeeping force arrived in Dili and started patrolling the streets on 26 May 2006. Four days later, President Kay Rala Xanana Gusmão issued a declaration

[34] Chesterman, Chapter 9, p. 249.

[35] L. Grenfell, 'Legal Pluralism and the Rule of Law in East Timor' (2006) 19 *Leiden Journal of International Law* 305 at 314–15.

[36] See N. Feldman, 'Imposed Constitutionalism' (2005) 37 *Connecticut Law Review* 857.

[37] Grenfell, 'Legal Pluralism'.

[38] 'The Rule of Law and Transitional Justice in Conflict and Post-Conflict Societies' (23 August 2004), S/2004/616, at para. 36.

[39] B. V. E. Wilson, 'Joint Command for PNTL and F-FDTL Undermines Rule of Law and Security Sector Reform in Timor-Leste' [2008] *East Timor Law Journal* 2, available at: www.eastimorlawjournal.org/ARTICLES/2008/Joint-Command-PNTL-F-FDTL-Undermines-Rule-of-Law-Wilson.html.

by which – in accordance with his role as 'the guarantor of the unity of the State, of the national independence and of the regular functioning of the democratic institutions' and ostensibly in consultation with the Prime Minister and the president of the National Parliament – he formally assumed control of the police and armed forces under a joint command.[40] These actions helped to quell the violence, although tensions remained heightened for many months as a political crisis continued to unfold, leading to the eventual resignation of Prime Minister Mari Alkatiri on 25 June 2006 and the revocation of the 'crisis' measures in late August 2006.

Following presidential elections and legislative elections in May and June 2007, a second emergency occurred on 11 February 2008 when an assassination attempt was made on President José Ramos-Horta and now-Prime Minister Gusmão. This time, a national state of emergency was formally declared, initially for forty-eight hours, and restrictions were placed on assemblies and demonstrations, and on movement, the latter by way of a curfew.[41] During the assassination attempt, President Horta's assailant was killed in a shoot-out, but Gusmão's assailant remained at large. On 13 February 2008 and again on 22 February 2008, the emergency was renewed as a nationwide 'state of siege'[42] under Article 25 of the Constitution.[43] The state of siege was renewed again in March, but only in seven districts,[44] and again in April, but only in the District of Ermera.[45]

Both Article 25 and the framework law on states of siege and emergency place significant limitations on emergency powers. The state of siege or state of emergency is limited to thirty days (though subject to renewal) and, according to Article 25(5), the following rights cannot be suspended:

[40] President Kay Rala Xanana Gusmão, 'Emergency Measures to Overcome the Crisis' (30 May 2006). See also Articles 74 and 85(b) of the Constitution, setting out the President's powers. The Presidential Declaration of 30 May 2006 was supported unanimously by the National Parliament on 5 June 2006.

[41] Presidential Decree No. 43/2008 (11 February 2008), signed by Acting President Viente da Silva Guterres.

[42] Presidential Decrees Nos. 44/2008 and 45/2008 respectively, signed by Acting President Fernando La Sama de Araújo. The second renewal was made pursuant to new framework emergency legislation enacted the same day, 22 February 2008: Law No. 3/2008, on the Regulation of the State of Siege and Emergency.

[43] Article 25 provides that in the event of 'effective or impending aggression by a foreign force, of a serious disturbance or threat of serious disturbance to the democratic constitutional order, or of a public disaster', the President may, with the approval of the legislature and upon consulting key government bodies, declare a state of siege or a state of emergency.

[44] Presidential Decree No. 48/2008 (20 March 2008), renewing the state of siege only in the districts of Aileu, Ermera, Bobonaro, Covalima, Ainaro, Liquica and Manufahi.

[45] Presidential Decree No. 49/2008 (22 April 2008).

'the right to life, physical integrity, citizenship, non-retroactivity of the criminal law, defence in a criminal case and freedom of conscience and religion, the right not to be subjected to torture, slavery or servitude, the right not to be subjected to cruel, inhuman or degrading treatment or punishment, and the guarantee of non-discrimination'. The framework law on states of siege and emergency specifies that the character, territorial scope, duration, affected rights, powers of the military and civilian forces and the jurisdiction of the military courts all be set out expressly.[46] It places further limitations on the suspension of rights, requiring, for example, that arrests are reported within seventy-two hours, that searches are conducted in the presence of witnesses, that restrictions on movement make allowances for the maintenance of those affected; and that compensation is made to those illegally deprived of their liberty.[47] And it requires that the courts and the office of the Ombudsman for Human Rights and Justice will remain open.[48] Article 25(6) of the Constitution directs that the authorities 'restore constitutional normality as soon as possible'.

The invocation of these powers in East Timor has prompted concerns that the measures taken would 'further undermine the fragile rule of law' by subordinating the police force to military control, leading to further abuses of power, including arbitrary arrests.[49] The lesson elsewhere in Southeast Asia is that it is tempting for weak governments to invoke emergency powers ostensibly to secure the state, and then use those powers opportunistically to consolidate power and oppress political opponents.[50] However well-crafted emergency powers might be, there may yet be a gap – as there was in East Timor in 2006 – between the law in theory and its implementation. Even so, the experience of East Timor demonstrates that emergency powers can be used by nascent democracies to restore political stability in a manner consistent with constitutional aspirations. The 2006 declaration of an emergency might not have conformed strictly to the wording of the Constitution, but in an extremely fragile situation, the stability was quickly established and the emergency powers were soon revoked. In 2008, the state of emergency complied more closely with the Constitution: the powers invoked were relatively narrow (limited to restrictions on assembly and movement, and the temporary joining of

46 Law No. 3/2008, Article 15. 47 *Ibid.*, Article 3.

48 *Ibid.*, Article 7. 49 Wilson, 'Joint Command'.

50 See, respectively, H. P. Lee, 'Constitutionalised Emergency Powers: A Plague on Asian Constitutionalism?' (Chapter 14) and R. Pangalangan, 'Political Emergencies in the Philippines: Changing Labels and the Unchanging Need for Legitimacy' (Chapter 15), both in this volume.

the police and military under a joint command)[51] and were progressively rolled back; reports of abuse during the curfew were relatively minor (limited mostly to manhandling by the security forces).[52] Throughout this period, the language and symbolism of the Constitution formed an important part of the political discourse – not surprising, perhaps, in a nation whose leaders, despite their differences, struggled for decades to have their own constitution.

The experience of emergency powers in East Timor must be understood against a backdrop of escalating and destabilising violence in a fragile state with limited institutional capacity. Faced with residual episodes of political violence, the political legitimacy of a post-conflict state depends not only on its ability to maintain the peace, but to do so in a manner consistent with its commitment to govern through law rather than by unrestrained force – in short, its commitment to legality and constitutionalism. East Timor found itself in a precarious position in 2006 and 2008 and was forced to manage, as adeptly as possible, the emergency powers paradox – invoking emergency powers to maintain a fragile peace, while striving to do so within its nascent constitutional framework.

B. *Thailand: emergency powers and constitutional instability*

Thailand's constitutional order poses complex questions concerning the nature of constitutionalism in times of crisis, although for reasons very different from those in East Timor. For one, Thailand's constitutional history is much older, with its modern inception in 1932.[53] Since then, Thailand has seen eighteen different constitutions,[54] a detailed study of which reveals a struggle among 'rightists, leftists, royalists, liberals, progressives, civilians and the military'[55] elements of the political elite to define Thailand's constitutional order and to consolidate political power. Critical to this political struggle has been the role of the King within the constitutional monarchy. Although initial attempts were made after 1932

51 See Wilson, 'Joint Command', for a more sceptical view.

52 My interviews at the office of the Ombudsman for Human Rights and Justice in November 2008 indicated that only some forty cases of abuse were reported during the 2008 emergency, mostly minor cases involving manhandling by police officers.

53 See, for an overview, K. Suwannathat-Pian, *Kings, Country and Constitutions: Thailand's Political Development 1932–2000* (London: RoutledgeCurzon, 2004), pp. 3–67.

54 C. Traimas and J. Hoerth, 'Thailand: Another New Constitution as a Way Out of the Vicious Cycle?' in C. Hill and J. Menzel (eds.), *Constitutionalism in Southeast Asia* (Singapore: Konrad Adenauer Stiftung, 2008), vol. II, pp. 287–310.

55 Suwannathan-Pian, *Kings, Country and Constitutions*, p. 8.

to limit the King to a largely ceremonial role, the monarchy has emerged as the most stable and influential institution of the modern Thai state, in large part because of the compelling personal attributes of King Bhumibol, Thailand's king since 1946, who commands widespread respect and admiration. He is popularly regarded as a benevolent monarch who intervenes and plays a power-broking role in Thai politics only as necessary in the interests of his subjects.[56] Yet, because the public support for the King is due to the personal respect he has earned, it has been argued that Thai constitutionalism, as it is currently practised, 'cannot be institutionalized' since it 'is personal, non-transferable, and thus unpredictable'.[57]

These unique features of Thailand's constitutional landscape forewarn us that the relationship between constitutionalism and emergency powers in Thailand is bound to be complex. For almost ten years prior to 2006, Thailand appeared to be moving into a period of relative constitutional stability. However, the bloodless military coup in September 2006, which was followed by another round of constitutional redrafting and the promulgation of a new constitution in 2007[58] is yet another reminder of the ongoing constitutional instability in Thailand and the thorny political and constitutional context against which emergency powers may be invoked.[59] Before the 2006 coup, in response to the insurgency in the predominantly Malay-Muslim southern provinces, the Thai government in July 2005 had issued an Emergency Decree on Government Administration in States of Emergency, conferring on the authorities special powers to deal with the insurgency, including special powers of investigation, arrest, detention and confiscation of weapons.[60] The coup appears to have been triggered by a general dissatisfaction with Prime Minister Thaksin Shinawatra's government among several political constituencies, especially in Bangkok, rather than as a direct response to the exercise of emergency powers in the southern provinces; yet the government's abuse of powers in the southern provinces would have to be considered in any credible account of the political context and contributing causes of the 2006 coup.[61]

56 *Ibid.*, pp. 62–7. 57 *Ibid.*, p. 67.

58 Constitution of the Kingdom of Thailand, BE 2550 (24 August 2007).

59 See A. J. Harding, 'Emergency Powers with a Moustache: Special Powers, Military Rule and Evolving Constitutionalism in Thailand' (Chapter 11), this volume.

60 BE 2548 (16 July 2005). The Thai government reported these measures to the UN Security Council's Counter-Terrorism Committee in June 2006: see S/2006/399. This and other country reports are available through the Committee's website: www.un.org/sc/ctc/countryreports.shtml.

61 D. McCargo (ed.), *Rethinking Thailand's Southern Violence* (Singapore: NUS Press, 2007). In his postscript, McCargo observes that Thaksin's 'deeply divisive leadership had eroded

As Andrew Harding observes in his contribution to this volume, concerns about the Thaksin government's abuses of power include its 'war on drugs' in which an estimated '2,500 people, alleged drug-traffickers, died . . . effectively executed without any resort to judicial procedure'[62] and the Tak Bai incident in the south of Thailand in 2003, in which eighty-seven people died from suffocation when they were stacked on top of one another during an operation against insurgents (some of whom have also committed unspeakable atrocities).[63] The challenge in Thailand has been to create effective mechanisms for holding the government to account, and at the same time provide the tools needed to address security concerns in the restive south. It is not surprising, then, that the 2007 Constitution follows its predecessor in attempting to entrench constitutional norms and institutions to check the executive powers, while at the same time retaining the emergency powers under which the 2005 Emergency Decree was issued – powers that stand in tension with fundamental rights.[64] These powers allow the King to issue an emergency decree, subject to the confirmation of the Council of Ministers that it is a case of 'emergency and necessary urgency which is unavoidable' and subject further to ratification of the decree by the National Assembly without delay.[65]

Thailand's constitutional order is not easily classified. Its current Constitution is newer than East Timor's, but its constitutional principles and institutions are not. Its Constitutional Court has, in its modern incarnations, experimented with judicial review.[66] Even so, Thailand's constitutional order is, as we shall see, considerably less stable than Malaysia's, which marked the fiftieth anniversary of its post-independence constitution in 2007. As far as the relationship between emergency powers and constitutionalism is concerned, two points are worthy of note. First, Thailand's 2005 state of emergency has survived intact through three formal

democratic politics and triggered the return of the military. While Thaksin's downfall boded ill for the future of Thai politics, it was greeted with great enthusiasm by many Malay Muslims in the southern border provinces . . . For better or worse, the end of the Thaksin regime signaled a new opportunity to address the worsening violent conflict' (p. 173).

62 Harding Chapter 11, p. 298.

63 The atrocities committed by both sides are recounted in a Human Rights Watch report, 'No One is Safe: Insurgent Attacks on Civilians in Thailand's Southern Border Provinces' (27 August 2007), vol. 19, no. 13(C): www.hrw.org/en/reports/2007/08/27/no-one-safe.

64 *Ibid.* 65 Section 184 of the Emergency Decree.

66 See generally, A. J. Harding, 'Buddhism, Human Rights, and Constitutional Reform in Thailand' (2007) 2 *Asian Journal of Comparative Law* 1.

constitutions: the 1997 Constitution, the 2006 Interim Constitution and the post-coup 2007 Constitution. In Western terms, the exception in Thailand has eclipsed the norm.[67] Second, although constitutional law and the courts have done little to prevent abuses of power,[68] other informal social, political and institutional checks on power are nevertheless present. In contrast with the bloody events of May 1992, in which protesters were killed at the hands of the military, recent Thai history suggests that the most serious abuses of state power have been held in check not by the courts, but by the military itself, often with the support of broad segments of Thai society and at least the tacit support of the King.[69] But while the 2006 coup might have put a temporary end to some of the abuses of an errant government, the current constitutional arrangements are deeply personal to King Bhumibol, such that the monarchy, as an institution, cannot be relied on as a constraint on the abuse of emergency powers beyond the inevitable end of the King's reign.[70] Neither the courts nor the legislature currently has the social or political standing to assume the role of checking abuses of power, particularly when emergency powers are invoked in Thailand;[71] the only other institution that has this standing is the very institution entrusted with enforcing those powers in the first place – the military. As the continued volatility in Thailand suggests, the precise shape of its constitutional order remains very much in flux.

[67] Note, however, that two recent attempts to declare a state of emergency in Bangkok, in September and December 2008, following anti-government protests, encountered difficulties when the military refused to act against the protesters: see also K. Y. L. Tan, 'From Myanmar to Manila: A Brief Study of Emergency Powers in Southeast Asia' (Chapter 6), this volume, p. 180.

[68] Thailand's Constitutional Court is increasingly immersed in Thai politics. Recent decisions have sided with opponents of former Prime Minister Thaksin's party (previously Thai Rak Thai, later revived as the People's Power Party), twice barring the party and several party members from competing in elections, most recently (in December 2008) following mass anti-government protests at Bangkok's Suvarnabhumi airport, and once forcing the resignation of the Prime Minister on the ground that he had 'unlawfully accepted payments to appear on television cooking shows': see S. Mydans and and T. Fuller, 'Thai Protesters Ending Airport Blockade', *New York Times*, 1 December 2008, www.nytimes.com/2008/12/03/world/asia/03thai.html?partner=permalink & exprod =permalink.

[69] C. Charoensin-O-Larn, 'Military Coup and Democracy in Thailand', in J. Funston (ed.), *Thailand's Continuing Crises: The Coup, and Violence in the South* (Canberra: National Thai Studies Centre, Australian National University, 2007), pp. 48–78.

[70] See Suwannathat-Pian, *Kings, Country and Constitutions*, pp. 28–9.

[71] For example, during the 1997 financial crisis, the courts adopted a deferential posture toward emergency financial measures: Harding, Chapter 11, p. 302.

C. *Malaysia: constitutionalism and emergency powers at the crossroads*

East Timor and Thailand illustrate the challenges of invoking emergency powers while attempting to establish the basic conditions of constitutional government. Yet even in those countries in Southeast Asia with a stronger rule-of-law culture – particularly in the resolution of private disputes – such as Malaysia, questions remain as to whether a commitment to legality extends fully to the domain of public law. Just as a key litmus test for the health of a democracy could be the government's reaction to opposition successes, an important litmus test for the acceptance of legality as a constitutional ideal may well be the government's response to legal constraints imposed by the courts in a state of emergency. In Malaysia, the test is a critical one because Malaysia was conceived in a state of emergency[72] and has remained under a state of emergency for most of its modern existence.[73] The historical record shows that the Malaysian government has been loath to accept judicial constraints on emergency powers, and has held on to those powers long after the conditions that triggered them have abated.

Consider, for instance, the 1969 Emergency and its aftermath.[74] In May 1969, following a strong showing by the opposition in the general elections, which in turn provoked communal riots in which many were killed,[75] the Yang di-Pertuan Agong (the Malaysian king) formally proclaimed a state of emergency throughout the Federation,[76] which paved the way for 'emergency regulations' to be issued by a Director of Operations assisted by a National Operations Council. At the time that the emergency was proclaimed, the newly elected parliament had not yet sat. And while the Constitution required Parliament to be summoned 'as soon as may be practicable' after an emergency is proclaimed, Parliament did not sit again for some twenty-one months. In the interim, the Director of Operations had 'virtually dictatorial powers . . . restrained only by the

[72] On 31 August 1957, the Federation was already under a state of emergency proclaimed on 7 July 1948 by Emergency Regulations Ordinance 1948 (No. 10), which continued beyond Merdeka and formally ended on 31 July 1960 (see LN 185/1960). See Wu Min Aun, *The Malaysian Legal System*, 2nd edn (Petaling Jaya: Pearson, 1999), pp. 251–2.

[73] For an overview of constitutional developments, see A. J. Harding and H. P. Lee (eds.), *Constitutional Landmarks in Malaysia: The First 50 Years 1957–2007* (Singapore: LexisNexis, 2007).

[74] This and the three following paragraphs draw on V. V. Ramraj, 'The *Teh Cheng Poh* Case', in Harding and Lee (eds.), *Constitutional Landmarks*, pp. 145–55.

[75] C. Das, 'The May 13th Riots and Emergency Rule', in Harding and Lee (eds.), *Constitutional Landmarks*, pp. 103–13.

[76] PU (A) 145.

Prime Minister's advice and the moderating counsel of the NOC' and used emergency regulations to deal with 'many routine government matters . . . including fiscal, pensions, civil service and even land matters'.[77] The use of emergency regulations continued well after Parliament had sat. Among the regulations that were promulgated after Parliament had sat were the Essential (Security Cases) (Amendment) Regulations 1975, which set out a special procedure for security cases, departing from the normal procedures in the Criminal Procedure Code.

The constitutional validity of the regulations was challenged in *Teh Cheng Poh* v. *Public Prosecutor*,[78] a death penalty case in which the defendant was charged with the unlawful possession of a firearm and ammunition under the Internal Security Act. The case was ultimately decided by the Privy Council, in one of its last appeals from Malaysia. Although a range of arguments were presented to it, the Privy Council refused to consider whether the facts which gave rise to the declaration of a state of emergency remained present; instead it held that eight years' worth of emergency regulations, including the security case regulations, were invalid from 20 February 1971, the date following the declaration of the state of emergency, on which Parliament first sat. On the one hand, this was a bold decision. It put the government in the awkward position of having to pass legislation to validate retrospectively every emergency regulation made after 20 February 1971, which it did swiftly in 1979.[79] On the other hand, the Privy Council's decision was largely formalistic – it refused to articulate any significant constitutional constraints on the use of emergency powers.[80] We could, of course, fault the Privy Council for not taking a bolder stand on the use of emergency powers. But to have done so may well have been in vain. In the aftermath of *Teh Cheng*

77 A. J. Harding, *Law, Government and the Constitution in Malaysia* (Kuala Lumpur: *Malayan Law Journal*, 1996), p. 43 and n. 98.

78 [1980] AC 458.

79 It did so through the Emergency (Essential Powers) Act 1979, which placed the emergency legislation on a proper constitutional footing and purported to validate retroactively every piece of 'subsidiary legislation whatsoever made or purporting to have been made' and every prosecution instituted, trial conducted, decision or order given . . . or any other proceeding whatsoever' purporting to have been made under Ordinance No. 1 on or after 20 February 1971, respectively, ss. 9(1) and 9(3) of the Act.

80 The closest the Privy Council came to a substantive constitutional principle was its discussion of *mala fides*, in which it warns of latent judicial power, in an appropriate case, to grant *mandamus* where the government, through the Yang di-Pertuan Agong, abuses its discretion by failing 'to exercise his power of revocation, and to maintain the proclamation for some different purpose' (at 473). Since *mala fides* is difficult to prove, this hardly amounts to a significant limitation.

Poh, the Malaysian government, in 1981, amended the Constitution to make the proclamation of an emergency, its continued operation, any emergency ordinances and continuation in force of those ordinances, all non-justiciable.[81]

The 1969 proclamation was never rescinded, so Malaysia remains today formally under a state of emergency. But this legal status hardly reflects the contemporary reality. As H. P. Lee observes, when 'one walks the streets of Kuala Lumpur or any major city in Malaysia today, one does not sense a serious threat to the security or economic life of the Federation'. This leads him to ask: 'How is it possible to maintain the validity of the Proclamation of Emergency when the very factual substratum nourishing it no longer exists?'[82]

The problem in contemporary Malaysia is not, as it is in East Timor, the need to ensure the stability and legitimacy of the government in the aftermath of a protracted conflict and to create a legal infrastructure effectively from the ground up. Nor is the problem, as it is in Thailand, that the constitutional order remains in flux. Rather, the problem in Malaysia seems to be an inability or unwillingness on the part of key elements in the 'legal complex' – including not only lawyers and judges, but 'all legally-trained personnel in a society who undertake legal work, including prosecutors and civil servants involved in the administration of justice'[83] – to build on the existing legal infrastructure and legal culture with the intention of bringing about a complete transition to a rule-of-law state.[84] Malaysia is much closer to establishing a 'culture of justification', which, argues

81 See Constitution (Amendment) Act 1981 (Act A 544), s. 15, amending Article 150(8) of the Constitution to provide, by sub-paragraph (b), that 'no court shall have jurisdiction to entertain or determine any application, question or proceeding, in whatever form, on any ground, regarding the validity' of the proclamation or continued operation of an emergency or of any emergency ordinances made under it. The amendments also enhanced the Yang di-Pertuan Agong's power to promulgate durable emergency ordinances, giving the executive 'unbridled power . . . to declare an emergency at will, and to perpetuate emergency rule'. See H. P. Lee, *Constitutional Conflicts in Contemporary Malaysia* (Kuala Lumpur: Oxford University Press, 1995), p. 104. For a parallel episode in Singapore, see *Chng Suan Tze* v. *Minister of Home Affairs*, [1988] SLR 132, and its aftermath, recounted in M. Hor, 'Law and Terror: Singapore Stories and Malaysian Dilemmas', in Ramraj, Hor and Roach (eds.), *Global Anti-Terrorism Law and Policy*, pp. 273–94.

82 Lee, Chapter 14, p. 397.

83 T. C. Halliday, L. Karpik and M. M. Feeley, 'The Legal Complex in Struggles for Political Liberalism', in Halliday, Karpik, and Feeley (eds.) *Fighting for Political Freedom: Comparative Studies of the Legal Complex and Political Liberalism* (Oxford: Hart, 2007), p. 7.

84 For theoretical account of Malaysia's incomplete transition to a rule-of-law state, see R. R. Balasubramaniam, 'Indefinite Detention: Rule by Law or Rule of Law', in Ramraj (ed.), *Emergencies*, pp. 118–41.

Dyzenhaus, comes about when 'a political order accepts that all official acts, all exercises of state power, are legal only on condition that they are justified by law, where law is understood in an expansive sense, that is, as including fundamental commitments such as those entailed by the principle of legality and respect for human rights'.[85] Malaysia has shown, in the context of emergency powers and national security cases, a respect for legality only in a very formal sense;[86] it has responded to judicial challenges with formal amendments to the law, making the executive legally unaccountable for the use of these powers – and thereby casting doubt on the extent to which legality in the public sphere is firmly entrenched. Yet at this point in its constitutional development, the fate of its emergency regime is no longer dependent on volatile political conditions, but on the will of judges and others within the wider 'legal complex' to nurture and sustain a rather different kind of legal culture.

D. *Emergency powers and constitutionalism in Southeast Asia*

East Timor, Thailand and Malaysia provide remarkably different social, political and constitutional contexts for invoking emergency powers. Emerging from a long period of occupation and internal conflict, East Timor faces the perilous challenges of nation-building, attempting to stabilise the political order by channelling violent political conflicts into nascent public institutions designed to resolve disputes. Yet when faced with lingering political violence, including assassination attempts on its political leaders, the government has invoked constitutional emergency powers in an effort to re-establish political stability and secure its legitimacy through legal means. Thailand's invocation of emergency powers in response to the insurgency in the south takes place against the backdrop of a different kind of constitutional instability, in which public institutions are regularly dismantled and recalibrated in response to political conflict. The instability of the constitutional order throws into question any attempt to subject coercive state power to legal and constitutional control and undermines the credibility of any ostensible commitment to constitutionalism. Finally, Malaysia's experience with emergency powers shows how difficult it is, even with a developed legal infrastructure and a relatively stable political order, to make a transition away from

[85] See D. Dyzenhaus, 'Deference, Security, and Human Rights', in B. Goold and L. Lazarus (eds.), *Security and Human Rights* (Oxford: Hart, 2006), pp. 125–56 at p. 137.

[86] Balasubramaniam, 'Indefinite Detention', pp. 119–29.

emergency rule and toward the rule of law.[87] It demonstrates also how the invocation of emergency powers, in which the exercise of the most coercive powers of the state is perpetually shielded from judicial review, can, over time, undermine efforts to establish a constitutional culture. These experiences support the claim that the interplay between emergency powers and legality in these developing constitutional orders is distinct from the corresponding interaction in liberal democracies. But is this difference normatively relevant and, if so, what implications does this difference have for our understanding of constitutionalism in developing legal orders? It is time to turn our attention to these critical questions.

IV. Emergency powers, politics and the struggle for legality

In response to Schmitt's challenge, theorists in contemporary liberal democracies seek to show how the state can confront an emergency through law while *preserving* or, after a brief interval, *restoring* fundamental constitutional norms. It is easier to adapt the existing framework and to address the emergency through legal means because a stable legal order and constitutional culture are already firmly in place. As Mark Tushnet observes, bureaucrats and professionals have internalised a 'degree of commitment to the rule of law', which mitigates even the most egregious departures from ordinary constitutional principles, such as the post-9/11 detention of 'enemy combatants' at the US naval base at Guantánamo Bay.[88] Part III of this chapter suggests that the experience of emergency powers in East Timor, Thailand and Malaysia supports two claims. The first is that there is a prima facie empirical and conceptual distinction between preserving and establishing legality, the latter better reflecting the experience of emergency powers in East Timor, Thailand and Malaysia. The second is that the emergency powers paradox is experienced differently depending on the context. While emergency powers might seem justified to enable a nascent government to stabilise a politically volatile situation, as in East Timor, they seem less warranted in a relatively stable and prosperous country, such as contemporary Malaysia. Does the latter claim (that the range of developing constitutional orders seeking to establish legality differs significantly) undercut the former claim (that there is a significant normative difference between preserving and establishing

[87] See generally, T. Ginsburg and T. Mustafa, 'Introduction', in *Rule by Law: The Politics of Courts in Authoritarian Regimes* (New York: Cambridge University Press, 2008), pp. 1–22.

[88] M. Tushnet, 'The Political Constitution of Emergency Powers: Some Conceptual Issues', in Ramraj (ed.), *Emergencies*, p. 155.

legality)? Is it not better to see the difference as a matter of degree, rather than allow governments in developing constitutional orders to claim that they should be judged by a different standard?

In this part, I answer these questions by exploring the normative implications of the distinction between preserving and establishing legality and the differences within developing constitutional orders, and then by considering and responding to possible objections. My primary argument is this. First, in developing contexts, emergencies that would not pose a serious threat to the viability of an established constitutional order may well pose an existential threat to a nascent or developing constitutional order. Emergency powers might therefore be needed to bring about the basic conditions of stability upon which a constitutional order can take hold. Second, in periods of constitutional transition and development, the goal of legality will be aspirational and will require what is primarily a *political* struggle. Third, until a point is reached when a constitutional culture is fully entrenched, the normative questions raised by the invocation of emergency powers will have to be approached in a distinct way; however, the principle of proportionality can provide a unifying normative standard to regulate the invocation of emergency powers politically and legally, in both established and developing constitutional orders.

A. *Existential threats and emergency powers*

In recent work, Ackerman argues that although liberal democracies such as the United States are unlikely to face an existential threat from terrorist attacks, it remains necessary for the government to take steps to reassure its citizens in the wake of an attack.[89] His proposal for how to do this is controversial and has attracted considerably scholarly attention, but what is of particular interest for present purposes is the less contentious claim that terrorist attacks, including the detonation of a 'suitcase A-bomb' in a major US city, would not pose an existential threat and the 'American government would survive the day'.[90] This confident assertion would be distinctly out of place in most nascent, post-conflict constitutional orders. What has at times been threatened in post-independence East Timor is the survival of organised government.

In posthumously published work, Bernard Williams has described what he calls the 'first political question'.[91] By this he means 'the securing of

[89] Ackerman, 'The Emergency Constitution'. [90] *Ibid.*, at 1036.

[91] B. Williams, 'Realism and Moralism in Political Theory', in G. Hawthorn (ed.), *In the Beginning was the Deed* (Princeton: Princeton University Press, 2005), pp. 1–17 at p. 3.

order, protection, safety, trust, and the conditions of cooperation'.[92] Until these basic conditions of organised government are secured, nuanced (or even basic) debates about political morality and constitutionalism seem distinctly out of place. The first challenge, as the Australian-led International Forces appreciated in 1999 in East Timor, was to stabilise the situation on the ground so that the long process of state-building could begin.[93] Emergency-like powers of preventive detention (for example) were used by INTERFET in what was effectively a constitutional vacuum, to resolve Williams's 'question' so that the basic constitutional questions could be asked. A similar approach is reflected in the post-conflict, state-building literature, in which several scholars have defended a core understanding of the rule of law.[94] In their view, the rule of law helps to 'establish non-violent mechanisms for resolving political disputes',[95] while requiring 'a normative commitment to the project of law itself, a commitment to the orderly and nonviolent resolution of disputes and a willingness to be bound by the outcome of legal rules and processes'.[96] What this core of legality tells us is that apart from whatever economic motives governments might have or pressures they might face in embracing the 'rule of law' as articulated by the World Bank and other international financial institutions,[97] a government committed to the rule of law is committing itself to a measure of self-restraint.

Aspiring to even this core of legality, however, and to the 'orderly and non-violent resolution of disputes' requires something of a leap of faith: it requires that political disenchantment be expressed through nascent institutions that are yet untested and perhaps not even fully functional. Laying the foundation for these institutions to work might in some circumstances require a degree of state coercion. Political stability, as the UN's involvement in East Timor suggests, will often require interim coercive measures to ensure that new institutions have a chance to develop and adapt to local circumstances.[98] The emergency powers paradox arises precisely because of the challenge of realising even the core conception of legality and the need to invoke powers ostensibly at odds with the aspiration of legality in

92 *Ibid.* 93 Chesterman, Chapter 9.

94 On the competing definitions of the rule of law, see below, notes 111 to 119 and accompanying text.

95 S. Chesterman, 'An International Rule of Law?' (2008) 56 *American Journal of Comparative Law* 331 at 341.

96 J. Stromseth, D. Wippman and R. Brooks, *Can Might Make Rights? Building the Rule of Law after Military Interventions* (New York: Cambridge University Press, 2006), p. 75.

97 On this approach to the rule of law, see Hosen, Chapter 10, pp. 278–80.

98 Chesterman, Chapter 9.

the name of legality. *Absit*, perhaps, an existential emergency (of the sort Ackerman thinks is unlikely), the paradox does not arise in the same way in liberal democracies because, contrary to Schmitt, we can easily conceive in *that* context how we might respond to emergency powers within the broad 'normative universe' of law, even if we might disagree on how precisely to do so.[99] The vulnerability of nascent and, in particular, post-conflict constitutional orders to violent political emergencies shows why the distinction between establishing and preserving legality is normatively relevant: emergency powers can more readily be justified in an unstable environment to help create a constitutional order, than they can in an established constitutional order which has a sophisticated range of legal tools and constraints at its disposal.

B. *Transitional constitutionalism and the struggle for legality*

As we have seen in this chapter, nascent, post-conflict states represent only one kind of constitutional order that falls outside the liberal-democratic mould. Not every state is as vulnerable to emergencies as East Timor has been. Thailand has survived the insurgency in its southern provinces even in the midst of its constitutional instability. And although in its pre-independence and early postcolonial days, Malaysia might have been similarly vulnerable to political instability and violence in a manner that possibly justified the invocation of emergency powers, the 'very factual substratum nourishing' the emergency (as Lee reminds us) 'no longer exists'.[100] How then are we to understand the relationship between emergency powers and legality in these less extreme situations, and to what extent, if any, is the distinction between establishing and preserving legality normatively significant? In my view, the distinction retains a normative significance, although in a different way than in East Timor; for in these situations, it tracks a categorical difference between political and legal paradigms for responding to an emergency, a difference that has important normative implications. The normative significance of the distinction between establishing and preserving legality lies in two important dimensions of legality in developing constitutional orders such as Thailand

[99] See generally, Ramraj (ed.), *Emergencies*. The reference to the 'normative universe' of law echoes Mark Tushnet's imagery in his chapter in the same volume. See also Scheuerman's survey article, 'Emergency Powers and the Rule of Law after 9/11' (2006) 14 *The Journal of Political Philosophy* 61, contesting Schmitt's claim that liberal democracy is unable to respond consistently to an emergency.

[100] Lee, Chapter 14, p. 397.

and Malaysia: both are transitional constitutional orders[101] and both are engaged in a political struggle for legality.[102]

Consider first the transitional role that constitutions often play in a post-authoritarian or post-conflict context. In these situations, a constitution typically marks a break from the past and an aspiration to a different kind of political order. Ruti Teitel argues that transitional constitutionalism plays a distinct role in 'mediating periods of political change.'[103] Because transitional constitutions confront the past while aspiring to a better constitutional order, 'what is considered constitutionally just is contextual and contingent, relating to the attempt to transform legacies of past injustice'.[104] In a post-authoritarian context, transitional constitutions 'broker the political shifts from authoritarian rule' by constructing 'interim periods of substantial liberalizing political change, albeit not equivalent to a fully democratic order'.[105]

Recognition of the political role of law in periods of transition is not new; it is apparent, for instance, in the Hart–Fuller debate over legality in post-war Germany. Redressing the wrongs committed by 'grudge informers' who collaborated with the Nazi regime meant convicting them for conduct that was ostensibly legal under Nazi laws. H. L. A. Hart's recommendation was to pass a frankly retrospective law to make conduct illegal that at the time (assumed Hart) was legal, though morally objectionable.[106] In response, Lon Fuller (who sympathised with Gustav Radbruch's view that 'extreme injustice is no law'[107]) stressed the transitional nature of the problem confronting post-war Germany and the need to re-establish respect for the legal system:

> While I do not subscribe to all of Radbruch's postwar views . . . he saw, much more clearly than does Professor Hart, the true nature of the dilemma confronted by Germany in seeking to rebuild her shattered legal institutions. Germany had to restore both respect for law and respect for justice.

[101] R. Teitel, 'Constitutional Justice', in *Transitional Justice* (Oxford: Oxford University Press, 2000), pp. 191–211.

[102] Others have invoked the imagery of a struggle for legality, notably, in the emergency powers context, D. Dyzenhaus, 'The Compulsion of Legality', p. 39, and K. Jayasuriya, 'Struggle over Legality in the Midnight Hour: Governing the International State of Emergency', pp. 360–84, both in Ramraj (ed.), *Emergencies*.

[103] Teitel, 'Constitutional Justice', p. 197.

[104] *Ibid.*, p. 196. [105] *Ibid.*, p. 197.

[106] H. L. A. Hart, 'Positivism and the Separation of Law and Morals' (1958) 71 *Harvard Law Review* 593 at 619.

[107] This is R. Alexy's formulation: see 'A Defence of Radbruch's Formula', in D. Dyzenhaus (ed.), *Recrafting the Rule of Law* (Oxford: Hart, 1999), pp. 15–39 at p. 17.

> Though neither could be restored without the other, painful antinomies were encountered in attempting to restore both at once, as Radbruch saw all too clearly.[108]

Fuller wanted to resolve the dilemma in a manner that respected the post-war aspiration of legality. His solution, like Hart's, was to enact a retroactive statute, though his reasons were different. For Fuller, a retroactive law was 'a way of symbolizing a sharp break from the past, as a means of isolating a kind of clean-up operation from the normal functioning of the judicial process'.[109] Despite their differences, Hart and Fuller agreed that the attempt to establish legality following the Nazi atrocities was not easily amenable to ordinary legal norms.[110] To put the point more generally, in times of constitutional transition a *political* struggle is needed to facilitate the creation of a new legal order.

To see more concretely why this struggle is political, we need to consider first what kind of constitutional order a particular state might aspire to. In East Timor, a commitment to a core sense of legality can be seen in the government's attempts to resolve political disputes (including violent episodes) through legally constituted institutions and mechanisms. But to what extent are governments in Southeast Asia committed to a more robust conception of the rule of law? According to Randall Peerenboom, many Asian governments are ostensibly committed to some form of the rule of law, even if the content of that ideal is contested.[111] Formal or 'thin' conceptions – which view law as consisting of 'a body of clear, stable, and prospective rules, capable of obedience, and faithfully applied by judges and other public officials'[112] – command broader support in many parts of Asia largely because they do not assume a shared conception of political

108 L. Fuller, 'Positivism and Fidelity to Law – A Reply to Professor Hart' (1958) 71 *Harvard Law Review* 630 at 656–7.

109 *Ibid.*, at 661.

110 For a critique of this debate for its failure to focus 'on the distinct problem of law in the transitional context', see Teitel, *Transitional Justice*, p. 13.

111 Contemporary legal theorists distinguish between two conceptions of the rule of law – formal and substantive: see P. Craig, 'Formal and Procedural Conceptions of the Rule of Law: An Analytic Framework' [1997] *Public Law* 467. For a parallel distinction between 'thin' and 'thick' conceptions of the rule of law, see R. Peerenboom, 'Varieties of the Rule of Law: An Introduction and Provisional Conclusion', in R. Peerenboom (ed.), *Asian Discourses of the Rule of Law* (London: Routledge, 2004), pp. 1–55, at pp. 2, 4.

112 T. R. S. Allen, *Constitutional Justice: A Liberal Theory of the Rule of Law* (Oxford: Oxford University Press, 2001), p. 61, referring to L. L. Fuller, *The Morality of Law* (New Haven: Yale University Press, 1969).

morality, as do substantive conceptions.[113] Emergency and emergency-like powers might therefore be invoked and extended in formal compliance with the constitution, or authorised by constitutional amendment, even when those powers effectively undermine any real constraint on executive power – thus amounting to no more than rule *by* law.[114]

For some, a substantive conception of the rule of law flows conceptually or normatively from a commitment to governing through law.[115] These arguments are contentious. Rule *by* law is *conceptually* coherent, in that it is compatible with different approaches to political morality, including those of one-party states.[116] Contrary to Balasubramaniam's view, a commitment to rule by law need not be premised on a respect for the legal subject;[117] it might instead be premised on rather more pragmatic considerations. The normative consequences of committing to the rule of law are contentious precisely because we can distinguish formal and substantive conceptions and can conceive of a commitment to rule by law in a non-liberal democratic state.[118] But since there is genuine doubt as to whether a commitment to rule of law leads conceptually or normatively to a substantive commitment to the rule of law, it would be more fruitful to consider under what conditions a substantive conception of the rule of law might emerge in a state committed only to rule by law.[119] And this line of inquiry leads to the view that the rule of law requires a *political* struggle – by a network of lawyers, judges and civil society[120] – to establish the 'laws, norms and institutions'[121] needed to sustain a *substantive* conception of legality that commits the government in more than a purely formal way.

[113] Substantive conceptions, while embracing the minimum requirements of the formal account, also include requirements of justice, whether in relation to the economic or political structure of the state or in relation to human rights: Craig, 'Formal and Procedural Conceptions'; Peerenboom, 'Varieties of the Rule of Law'.

[114] See Balasubramaniam, 'Indefinite Detention'. A formal conception of the rule of law is consistent with 'great iniquity' – a point famously made by H. L. A. Hart in his debate with Lon Fuller: see H. L. A. Hart, *The Concept of Law*, 2nd edn (Oxford: Oxford University Press, 1994), p. 207.

[115] Respectively, Balasubramaniam, 'indefinite Detention'; T. Nardin, 'Emergency Logic: Prudence, Morality and the Rule of Law', in Ramraj (ed.), *Emergencies*, pp. 97–117.

[116] In China, ruling the country 'according to law' is seen officially as compatible with 'a socialist rule of law state': Peerenboom, 'Varieties of the Rule of Law', p. 17.

[117] Balasubramaniam, 'Indefinite Detention'. [118] *Ibid.*

[119] Ginsburg and Mustafa, 'Introduction'.

[120] Halliday, Karpik and Feeley, 'The Legal Complex'. See also Ginsburg and Mustafa, on the importance of 'judicial support networks' that 'facilitate the expansion of judicial power by actively initiating litigation and/or supporting the independence of judicial institutions if they come under attack' (*ibid.* p. 13).

[121] V. Nesiah, 'The Princely Impostor: Stories of Law and Pathology in the Exercise of Emergency Powers' (Chapter 5), this volume, p. 121.

To see legality in this way, as a goal to be achieved, in part through political struggle, is not to deny law's normative force or the agency of courts or judges in this struggle;[122] rather it is to recognise a political struggle is needed to secure the normative force of law, particularly in aspiring constitutional orders that are tempted to invoke emergency powers.[123] Such a political struggle for legality is evident in Malaysia and – as other contributors to the volume imply – in Pakistan as well. Despite its developed legal infrastructure, the Malaysian courts are reluctant to hold the executive in check in its exercise of emergency powers; its attempts to do so have resulted in legislative and constitutional reversal of decisions against the government. So the courts have acted strategically, adopting a strategy of 'running away to live and fight again another day'.[124] Clark Lombardi's account of Justice Cornelius's principled stand on emergency powers in Pakistan is illuminating precisely because Cornelius, finding himself squeezed into a dissenting role in the court, took his struggle for legality outside the courtroom, making his case directly – and extra-judicially – to the military in his 1962 speech at Rawalpindi.[125] In these circumstances, it is not sufficient for judges to declare solemnly to the public, as judicial 'weathermen', that constitutional storm clouds are coming, as Dyzenhaus suggests;[126] they must, at times, enter the political arena in struggling for legal change.[127] Recent political developments in Malaysia suggest that the day for legal change may be at hand, as the government has been pressured to launch an inquiry into interference with judicial independence in the late 1980s; and newly emboldened opposition parties, with the support of civil society groups, have vowed to abolish the Internal Security Act if elected.[128] The courts have also recently started to show renewed courage

[122] See A. K. Thiruvengadam, 'Asian judiciaries and emergency powers: reasons for optimism?' (Chapter 17), this volume.

[123] See, for instance, A. H. Y. Chen, 'Emergency Powers, Constitutionalism and Legal Transplants: The East Asian Experience' (Chapter 3), this volume, in particular pp. 72–9, on the political struggle for legality in South Korea.

[124] Hor, 'Law and Terror', p. 286.

[125] C. Lombardi, 'Islamism as a Response to Emergency Rule in Pakistan: The Surprising Proposal of Justice A. R. Cornelius' (Chapter 16), this volume, p. 455.

[126] Dyzenhaus, 'The Compulsion of Legality', p. 51; see also Thiruvengadam, Chapter 17, p. 491.

[127] As Anil Kalhan suggests in his contribution to this volume, little has changed in Pakistan since Cornelius's time, with the courts still struggling with the executive legally and extra-legally to secure their place in the legal order: see A. Kalhan, 'Constitution and "Extraconstitution": Emergency Powers in Postcolonial India and Pakistan' (Chapter 4), this volume.

[128] 'Malaysian Opposition Leader Seeks Peaceful Transformation', *New York Times*, 17 September 2008, www.nytimes.com/2008/09/17/world/asia/17malay.html.

in supervising the use of preventive detention in national security cases.[129] These are the sorts of political developments that might eventually pave the way for a substantive conception of legality to take hold.

To be fair, some theorists of emergency powers in liberal democracies also acknowledge the crucial role that the political and social culture plays in supporting the constitutional order. Dyzenhaus, for instance, acknowledges that the 'liberal aspiration to have the rule of law rather than the rule of men requires not only a political struggle to subordinate politics to the rule of law, but also a political struggle within practice about how that is best done'.[130] Others, such as Mark Tushnet, are more direct; formal legal constraints on state power, he argues, 'cannot succeed at all without sociology and politics at their back'.[131] The key difference between the role of politics in established liberal democracies and aspiring ones is that, in the latter, a constitutional culture is not yet entrenched. In these societies, it may be that we reach a constitutional tipping-point where 'the wheels of justice may simply have too much momentum to stop'.[132] But until that point is reached, constraints on state power, including constraints on the use of emergency powers, will depend at least as much (and probably *more*) on politics than on law.

C. *The proportionality principle*

Does this mean, then, that governments in developing constitutional orders are unconstrained in their invocation of emergency powers? Do they effectively have a 'free pass' to invoke emergency powers as an interim measure in the name of political stability?[133] If, as the previous section suggests, legal principles minimally constrain governments in developing constitutional orders that are determined to use emergency powers, the answer seems to be 'yes'. Practically, there remains a gulf between the practice of constitutionalism in established and developing constitutional orders, and this in turn has significant implications for the transition from

[129] See *Raja Petra bin Raja Kamarudin* v. *Menteri Hal Ehwal Dalam Negeri* (7 November 2008), file no. MTJ1: 44-217-2008 (Malaysia H. C.), *per* Datuk Syed Ahmad Helmy bin Syed Ahmad J. (ordering the release of a detainee held under the Internal Security Act on the ground that his blogs 'were critical of and insulted Muslims, the purity of Islam, and the personality of the Prophet Mohammad S. A. W.', because such grounds for detention did not fall within the jurisdiction of the Internal Security Act).

[130] Dyzenhaus, 'The Compulsion of Legality', pp. 38–9.

[131] Tushnet, 'The Political Constitution', p. 155.

[132] Ginsburg and Mustafa, 'Introduction', p. 21.

[133] I am grateful to Arun Thiruvengadam for extensive discussion on this point.

an authoritarian political order to a constitutional one. There is, however, an important normative principle that can unify the legal and the political when it comes to emergency powers – the principle of proportionality. This principle, if understood as both a political and a legal one, may well be able to bridge the normative gap between the political struggle and the commitment to legality.

In its legal form, the principle of proportionality, as a principle of international law, is set out in Article 4(1) of the International Covenant on Civil and Political Rights, which provides for limited derogation from fundamental rights in times of emergency:

> In time of public emergency which threatens the life of the nation and the existence of which is officially proclaimed, the States Parties to the present Covenant may take measures derogating from their obligations under the present Covenant *to the extent strictly required by the exigencies of the situation*, provided that such measures are not inconsistent with their other obligations under international law and do not involve discrimination solely on the ground of race, colour, sex, language, religion or social origin (emphasis added).

Faced with a public emergency threatening 'the life of the nation', the government may, excepting the non-derogable rights set out in Article 4(2),[134] derogate from its legal obligations 'to the extent strictly required by the exigencies of the situation'. This requirement of strict necessity is significant because it suggests a way of addressing the emergency powers paradox; states may use such measures as are strictly necessary to deal with the emergency.

Political arguments to respect proportionality in times of crisis amount, in effect, to an appeal to constitutionalism itself – to the principle that the state cannot derogate from fundamental rights, except where such derogation is consistent with constitutionalism itself. This basic principle is found in the jurisprudence of the European Court of Human Rights and the Supreme Court of Canada, and in the text of the South African Constitution.[135] In all three contexts, the principle plays a pivotal role in

[134] Article 4(2) prohibits derogation from the right to life, the prohibition of torture and of cruel, inhuman or degrading treatment or punishment, the prohibitions of slavery and servitude, the prohibition on imprisonment for breach of contract, the prohibition of retroactive criminal laws, the right to legal personality, and freedom of thought, conscience and religion.

[135] On the fundamental importance of proportionality (and rationality) in Canada (as well as Europe and elsewhere), see D. Beatty, *Constitutional Law in Theory and Practice* (Toronto: University of Toronto Press, 1995), pp. 15–17. The principle of proportionality is entrenched in s. 36 of the Constitution of the Republic of South Africa, 1996.

justifying when the state may properly interfere with fundamental rights. In the context of developing constitutional orders that have invoked or seek to invoke emergency powers, the invocation of this principle may be more rudimentary and more political than legal. It is a visceral appeal to a principle of political morality that holds, as it would in response to abuses of state power in the southern Thailand provinces, that emergency powers should not be used beyond what is 'strictly required' to suppress political violence, and as in Malaysia, that they should no longer be used when the 'life of the nation' is no longer threatened.

A substantive conception of legality might eventually become embedded as a legal principle infused with greater constitutional value and importance. It could well develop in a nuanced way to preclude practices, such as torture, that are 'unlegalisable' even in times of crisis.[136] But until those aspirations are realised, the principle of proportionality will have more political than legal purchase; precisely how it functions as a political principle in aspiring constitutional orders deserves further analysis.

D. *Final clarifications*

We are now in a position to respond to three questions about emergency powers that might arise from the approach to emergencies in this chapter and from the broader themes of this book. The first question raised in this part of the chapter is whether the distinction between preserving and establishing legality signifies a difference of degree or kind. The second, which arises most directly from the Malaysian experience, is whether emergency powers should be constitutionally entrenched. A third question arises from a concern about the extent to which constitutionalism itself is a postcolonial or imperial imposition by liberal democracies on weaker, developing states. I have but a few brief words about these questions before I conclude.

Consider first whether the distinction between preserving and establishing legality is a difference of degree or kind. My analysis concludes that it is both. The proportionality standard implies that it is a matter of degree what sorts of measures would be justified, subject perhaps to limits on the kinds of measure (such as torture) that might be 'unlegalisable' under any circumstances. Moreover, even within the transitional constitutional context, the implications of a strict necessity test would vary according to the circumstances: the more politically volatile

[136] Dyzenhaus, 'The Compulsion of Legality', pp. 52–6.

the situation and the greater the potential for widespread violence, the stronger the force of the emergency powers paradox, and the greater the need (in some cases) for emergency powers; the less politically volatile the situation and the more entrenched a culture of legality, the harder it would be to justify emergency powers and the more compelling the case for responding to political conflict without recourse to extraordinary legal powers. In the politically vibrant but stable context of present-day Malaysia, for instance, the case for the continued reliance on emergency powers is increasingly suspect; and its internal security legislation is more convincingly seen as a tool too readily invoked to 'suppress political dissent'.[137]

But a proportionality or strict necessity standard is also consistent with a categorical distinction between preserving and establishing legality. As noted in my discussion of Ackerman, even the most extreme emergencies confronting stable liberal democracies are unlikely to pose an existential threat. This implies that these democracies will better be able to respond through ordinary legal means. Crucially, however, it suggests that law and legal principles will be able to play a greater role in checking the use of emergency powers. In stressing, by way of contrast, the important role that politics plays in aspiring constitutional orders, I do not mean to say that the courts could not have a role in constraining emergency powers – although it would be a rare bench that is confident to take on the executive constitutionally in these circumstances. The principle of proportionality recognises that states may, at times, require extraordinary powers to address emergency situations but insists that they do so in a manner maximally consistent with basic legal norms.[138] Where the courts are able to intervene to enforce this principle, they should.

Second, several contributors to this volume argue that entrenching emergency powers constitutionally opens the door to abuse. Specifically, Lee argues in his chapter that emergency powers should not be entrenched.[139] My answer is twofold. First, Lee's argument assumes that the problem lies in the constitutional framework; the analysis in this chapter suggests, however, that the problem might equally arise from the

137 T. Lee, 'Malaysia and the Internal Security Act: The Insecurity of Human Rights after September 11' (2002) *Singapore Journal of Legal Studies* 56 at 60, 71.

138 This is not only normatively recommended; it is also strategically sound. Abuses of state power in an emergency have been shown to mobilise violent opposition: C. Campbell, 'Law, Terror, and Social Movements: The Repression–Mobilisation Nexus', in Ramraj (ed.), *Emergencies*, pp. 172–98.

139 Lee, Chapter 14.

absence of a constitutional culture,[140] which takes seriously the role of the constitution and the courts in constraining executive power. Second, the role of politics is essential in constraining state power. In this volume, Raul Pangalangan and Jacques deLisle show the extraordinary steps governments will take to avoid invoking emergency powers even when they are readily available and unlikely to meet judicial resistance,[141] suggesting that there may be a *political* cost to invoking them without good cause.

My third point concerns the limits of legality as a response to politically violent emergencies. This chapter takes for granted that the states we are considering are committed to being governed through law and that law ought therefore to play a key role in constraining the exercise of emergency powers. But formal legal structures and processes need not be the only elements charged with this responsibility. Modern legal transplants have long been displacing informal and traditional means of controlling state power.[142] Conceptions of honourable rulers, deeply entrenched in cultural norms and practices, have been disrupted, only to be replaced with alien political institutions and practices. On this account, transitional constitutionalism signifies a profound transformation in which norms of liberal legality are gradually absorbed into the local political and social culture. These changes might be welcomed as modern or condemned as the consequences of neo-imperialism.[143] But whatever our position might be on the imperialism of liberal democracy, we should be conscious of the importance of informal means of controlling excesses of state power, and of the role that politics and sociology play in sustaining a normative constitutional order.

V. Conclusion

Understanding why liberal-democratic theories of emergency powers fail to resonate in Southeast Asia is enlightening in several respects. First, and most obviously, it gives us a basis for a moderately sceptical stance toward

[140] Lee himself seems to acknowledge as much in his conclusion: 'the judicial role in countries without an entrenched "culture of accountability" is severely constrained', *ibid.*, p. 410.

[141] Respectively, Pangalangan, Chapter 15, and J. delisle, 'States of Exception in an Exceptional State: Emergency Powers Law in China' (Chapter 13), this volume.

[142] See Chen, Chapter 3.

[143] Tully, 'The Imperialism of Modern Constitutional Democracy'. For a closer look at the concept of 'power' in Southeast Asia, including its colonial and anthropological dimensions, see the papers presented at the conference, *Continuity and Change: (Re)conceptualising Power in Southeast Asia*, Centre for Research in the Arts, Social Sciences and Humanities, University of Cambridge, 26–28 March 2009.

the wholesale transplantation of liberal-democratic theories and practices, while directing our attention to the more fundamental question of a government's commitment to legality. If the goal is to move toward legality and to bring about a stronger culture of accountability in government, it is important to ensure that the invocation of emergency powers does not become counter-productive; being conscious of the emergency powers paradox sheds light on the dangers of emergency powers for countries with developing legal systems that aspire to a stronger culture of legality. Second, reflecting on emergency powers in Southeast Asia helps us to understand better the assumptions – sometimes unarticulated – behind theories of emergency powers in liberal democracies. In particular, it allows us to appreciate how these theories depend on the assumed presence of the basic conditions of legality and on a constitutional culture that is independent of formal legal structures and documents.

But crucially, a deeper appreciation of the distinction between establishing and preserving legality allows us to see how the same problem might be viewed differently depending on the context. Emergency powers will likely play out in a very different way when a commitment to legality is strong, but the conditions of legality have not been fully realised, or when those conditions are realised but key actors in the 'legal complex' have yet to embrace constitutionalism; they would play out yet differently when, as in a modern liberal democracy, the conditions for legality are fully realised and entrenched. Does this mean that a comprehensive theory of emergency powers is untenable? Not necessarily. But it does mean that a theory of emergency powers that resonates beyond established liberal democracies must account for the distinct roles that law and politics play, and the special challenges emergency powers pose, in aspiring constitutional orders.

3

Emergency powers, constitutionalism and legal transplants: the East Asian experience

ALBERT H. Y. CHEN

I. Introduction

The concepts of emergency powers and the state of siege are the products of the modern age of constitutionalism, although the idea of 'constitutional dictatorship' can be traced back to republican Rome.[1] With the spread of constitutionalism from Europe and North America to all continents of the world, the theory, discourse, constitutional and legal texts and practice of emergency powers were also transplanted all over the world. In the post-9/11 world, theoretical debates on the relationship between emergency powers and liberal constitutional democracy or the rule of law have reached a new climax. Thus in *Law in Times of Crisis*, Gross and Ní Aoláin wrote about 'a tension of "tragic dimensions" between democratic values and responses to violent emergencies'.[2]

Yet in the world today, most countries are not long-established or well-established liberal constitutional democratic states. There are fragile post-colonial states, weak democracies, authoritarian states, one-party states, military dictatorships, communist states, facade democracies, quasi-democracies, and so on. All of them have written constitutions, and most of them have constitutional or statutory provisions on states of emergency or emergency powers. Provisions on states of emergency are frequently invoked in the non-Western world or Third World, much more so than in Western liberal constitutional democracies. Actually, in these non-Western

The author is grateful for helpful comments on the draft of this chapter from the editors of this volume, Andrew Harding (fellow contributor to this volume), Fu Hualing, P. J. Yap (both the author's colleagues at the University of Hong Kong) and P. Y. Lo, barrister in Hong Kong.

1 C. J. Friedrich, *Constitutional Government and Democracy*, rev. edn (Boston: Ginn and Co., 1950), chap. XXVI ('Constitutional Dictatorship and Military Government').

2 O. Gross and F. Ní Aoláin, *Law in Times of Crisis: Emergency Powers in Theory and Practice* (Cambridge: Cambridge University Press, 2006), p. 7.

states, the 'tragedy' lies not so much in the possible conflict between the exigencies of emergency and liberal constitutional democratic or rule-of-law values, but rather in the difficulties of and obstacles to the building of a liberal constitutional democratic state based on the rule of law, and in the circumstances of 'emergency' that contribute to such difficulties or constitute such obstacles. The experience of the use of emergency powers in such developing countries may therefore be quite different from that in well-established liberal constitutional states.[3]

It is the purpose of this chapter to undertake a preliminary exploration of the former experience. The title of the chapter covers 'emergency powers, constitutionalism and legal transplants', because both constitutionalism and the concept of emergency powers were transplanted to non-Western states from the European soil on which they originally grew. Part II of the chapter explores the European origins of emergency powers and related concepts, and reflects on the possible problems of their transplant to political environments in the non-Western world. The chapter (in Parts III, IV, V and VI respectively) then provides four case studies from East Asia – Hong Kong, Taiwan, South Korea and mainland China. It concludes with some comparative reflections on both the case studies and the general theory.[4]

II. Emergency powers: origins and transplant

In the *ancien régime* of the age of absolutism, the powers of monarchs and states were not subject to express constitutional limitations. There was no formal separation of powers, system of checks and balances or constitutional guarantees of civil liberties or human rights. There was therefore no room and no need for the concept of emergency powers. The concept itself is premised on a distinction between normalcy and exception, between normal times and extraordinary times of emergency or special danger to the state. In normal times constitutional government should be practised.

[3] For the latter experience, see generally, C. Rossiter, *Constitutional Dictatorship: Crisis Government in the Modern Democracies* (New Brunswick, N.J.: Transaction, 2002) (on, *inter alia*, France, Britain and the USA); M. Freeman, *Freedom or Security: The Consequences for Democracies Using Emergency Powers to Fight Terror* (Westport, Conn.: Praeger, 2003) (on, *inter alia*, Northern Ireland and Canada); Shao-chuan Leng (ed.), *Coping With Crises: How Governments Deal With Emergencies*, vol. II (Lanham, Md: University Press of America, 1990) (on, *inter alia*, Israel, Italy and Northern Ireland).

[4] Due to space limitations, this chapter will focus on emergency powers, martial law and state of siege, and will not extend to national security law and terrorism law that does not employ these concepts even though they may perform functions similar to such concepts.

This is the theory of constitutionalism. Constitutionalism requires the rule of law, the separation of powers, checks and balances, judicial review of administrative action, the protection of civil liberties and human rights and the non-intervention of the military in civil affairs.[5] But the concept or theory of emergency powers suggests that there are exceptional times when departures from these requirements of constitutionalism would be justified. In these exceptional circumstances, which include war, rebellion, riots or other large-scale violence or crises that threaten the very survival of the social order, government – particularly the executive branch of government – or even the military, needs to be given greater powers, the rights and liberties of individuals need to be subject to greater restrictions and the separation of powers – horizontal or vertical – needs to be superseded by greater concentration of powers, in order that the government or the military be able to defend the nation against extreme perils.[6]

The concept and theory of emergency powers are therefore inseparable from the concept and theory of constitutionalism. In order to be complete or comprehensive, any theory of constitutionalism must address the question of what is to be done when those exceptional or emergency circumstances arise that necessitate a departure from the norms of constitutional government. Thus Abraham Lincoln asked at the time of the American Civil War in 1861 whether a republic must 'of necessity, be too strong for the liberties of its own people, or too weak to maintain its own existence?'[7] Carl Schmitt, a leading theorist on commissarial and sovereign dictatorships in times of emergency,[8] wrote:

> Every general norm demands a normal, everyday frame of life to which it can be factually applied and which is subjected to its regulations . . . This effective normal situation is not a mere 'superficial presupposition' that a jurist can ignore; that situation belongs precisely to [the norm's] immanent

[5] As Nino points out, the word 'constitutionalism' 'has a range of meanings that vary in their conceptual thickness', and he identifies eight possible meanings: see C. S. Nino, *The Constitution of Deliberative Democracy* (New Haven: Yale University Press, 1996), pp. 3–7.

[6] See generally, P. B. Heymann, 'Models of Emergency Powers' (2003) 33 *Israel Yearbook on Human Rights* 1.

[7] J. Richardson (ed.), *Messages and Papers of the Presidents*, vol. VI (1898), p. 20, as quoted in J. Lobel, 'Emergency Powers and the Decline of Liberalism' (1989) 98 *Yale Law Journal* 1385 at 1386.

[8] See generally, J. P. McCormick, 'The Dilemmas of Dictatorship: Carl Schmitt and Constitutional Emergency Powers', in D. Dyzenhaus (ed.), *Law as Politics: Carl Schmitt's Critique of Liberalism* (Durham, N.C.: Duke University Press, 1998).

> validity. There exists no norm that is applicable to chaos. For a legal order to make sense, a normal situation must exist, and he is sovereign who definitely decides whether this normal situation actually exists.[9]

In the modern constitutional and legal history of the West, the first major attempt to seek accommodation between constitutionalism and state powers to cope with emergency occurred in the aftermath of the French Revolution: 'it is important not to forget that the modern state of exception is a creation of the democratic-revolutionary tradition and not the absolutist one'.[10] In 1791, the French Constituent Assembly enacted a law regarding the classification of military areas; the law introduced the distinction between state of peace, state of war and state of siege (*état de siège*).[11] Rossiter in his classic work on *Constitutional Dictatorship* described the state of siege as 'the foremost emergency institution of modern times';[12] '[i]t is in this typically French solution to the ancient problem of constitutional dictatorship that modern emergency government reaches its peak of institutional and legal perfection'.[13] The concept of the state of siege in the 1791 law applied only to fortified cities and military posts under attack by enemy troops; in such circumstances the authority of civilian officials would be transferred to the military commanders. In 1797, another law extended the scope of application of the concept from circumstances of foreign invasion to those of domestic rebellion, and from military posts to cities and towns generally. The legal consequences of the state of siege included not only the subjection of civilians to military jurisdiction, but also the possible suspension of certain constitutional rights.[14]

In the course of the nineteenth century the French law on the state of siege continued to evolve. The most significant developments were the relevant laws of 1849 and 1878.[15] Under these laws, the state of siege could only be declared by a law enacted by Parliament. In the state of siege, the powers of the police and civil authorities passed to the military, which was expressly given powers of search, deportation and prohibition of publications and meetings. It was, however, also provided that '[d]espite

9 C. Schmitt, *Political Theology: Four Chapters on the Theory of Sovereignty*, trans. G. Schwab (Cambridge, Mass.: MIT Press, 1985), p. 13.

10 G. Agamben, *State of Exception*, trans. K. Attell (Chicago: University of Chicago Press, 2005), p. 5.

11 B. Loveman, *The Constitution of Tyranny: Regimes of Exception in Spanish America* (Pittsburgh: University of Pittsburgh Press, 1993), p. 21.

12 Rossiter, *Constitutional Dictatorship*, p. 77. 13 *Ibid.*, p. 79.

14 Loveman, *The Constitution of Tyranny*, pp. 21–2; Agamben, *State of Exception*, p. 5.

15 The 1878 law supplemented and did not supersede the 1849 law: Rossiter, *Constitutional Dictatorship*, pp. 82–3.

the state of siege, citizens continue to exercise the rights guaranteed by the Constitution whose enjoyment is not suspended by the preceding articles'.[16]

Another significant development in the nineteenth century was the enactment of a Prussian law on the state of siege (*Preussisches Gesetz ueber den Belagerungszustand*) in 1851.[17] This law made provisions for the transfer of power from civilian to military authority, military courts' jurisdiction over civilians, and the suspension of citizens' rights. In 1871, the Bismarckian Constitution in its Article 68 provided that 'the Kaiser can, if the public safety in the federal territory is threatened, declare the state of war [*Kriegszustand*]', and incorporated by reference the terms of the 1851 law.[18] When the Weimar Republic was established after the end of the First World War, Article 48 of its Constitution governed emergency powers. This article is probably the most famous – and some would say notorious, as it was ultimately exploited by Hitler – provision in the modern legal history of emergency powers. Rossiter describes it as 'the most forthright provision for emergency dictatorship in modern constitutional history'.[19] It provided, *inter alia*:

> If the public safety and order in the German Reich are seriously disturbed or endangered, the President . . . may take the measures necessary to the restoration of public safety and order, and may if necessary, intervene with the assistance of the armed forces. To this end, he may temporarily suspend in whole or in part, the fundamental rights established in Articles 114, 115, 117, 118, 123, 124, and 153.
>
> The President . . . must immediately inform the Reichstag of all measures taken in conformity with sections one or two of this Article. The measures are to be revoked upon the demand of the Reichstag.[20]

The state of siege and Article 48 of the Weimar Constitution were products of the continental European legal tradition. In the Anglo-American tradition, the functional equivalents were martial law and emergency legislation. Martial law refers to 'the common law right of the Crown and its servants to repel force by force in the case of invasion, insurrection, riot, or generally of any violent resistance to the law' 'at whatever cost of blood or property may be necessary'.[21] Martial law has not been used in

[16] *Ibid.*, p. 83. [17] Loveman, *The Constitution of Tyranny*, p. 24.
[18] Agamben, *State of Exception*, p. 14. [19] Rossiter, *Constitutional Dictatorship*, p. xix.
[20] This translated text is taken from J. E. Finn, *Constitutions in Crisis: Political Violence and the Rule of Law* (New York: Oxford University Press, 1991), p. 147.
[21] A. V. Dicey, *An Introduction to the Study of the Law of the Constitution*, 10th edn, ELBS edn (London: Macmillan, 1968; first pub. 1885), pp. 288, 290.

Britain itself since 1800,[22] but was 'frequently resorted to throughout the nineteenth century'[23] in British colonies. During the twentieth century, in both Britain itself[24] and throughout the British Empire,[25] emergency powers were conferred on government by legislative enactments, such as the Defence of the Realm Act 1914,[26] the Emergency Powers Act 1920 (both applicable to Britain itself), the Emergency Powers Orders in Council 1939 and 1956 (for colonies), and local emergency regulations ordinances enacted by colonial legislatures.[27] In the USA, the Constitution does not contain elaborate provisions on emergencies,[28] but it was estimated in 1974 that there existed more than 470 federal statutes conferring powers on the executive to deal with various kinds of emergency.[29] In the Anglo-American tradition, the courts play a pivotal role in adjudicating the legality or constitutionality of governmental or legislative acts during alleged emergencies and in determining their legal consequences.[30]

Growing from its European origins, constitutional and statutory devices to empower governments in what are considered emergency or extraordinary circumstances have found their way into almost all legal systems in the contemporary world.[31] In his comparative study of constitutional provisions on emergencies around the world, Gross found that '[m]ost modern

22 Gross and Ní Aoláin, *Law in Times of Crisis*, p. 182.

23 N. Hussain, *The Jurisprudence of Emergency: Colonialism and the Rule of Law* (Ann Arbor: University of Michigan Press, 2003), p. 108.

24 Rossiter, *Constitutional Dictatorship*, part III.

25 D. C. Holland, 'Emergency Legislation in the Commonwealth', in G. W. Keeton and G. Schwarzenberger (eds.), *Current Legal Problems*, vol. XIII (London: Steven & Sons, 1960); A. W. B. Simpson, 'Emergency Powers and Their Abuse: Lessons From the End of the British Empire' (2003) 33 *Israel Yearbook on Human Rights* 219.

26 Gross and Ní Aoláin, *Law in Times of Crisis*, pp. 182–3.

27 Holland, 'Emergency Legislation'. The author points out that the Emergency Powers Orders in Council 'are much more drastic in their effect in the colonies than is the Emergency Powers Act, 1920, in the United Kingdom – in particular, in imposing none of the restrictions on the executive imposed by the latter law'. (p. 151)

28 The US Constitution (Article 1, Section 9(2)) does provide for the possible suspension of the writ of habeas corpus 'when in the cases of rebellion or invasion the public safety may require it'. This may be regarded as a constitutional provision on emergency power.

29 W. E. Scheuerman, 'Emergency Powers and the Rule of Law After 9/11' (2006) 14 *Journal of Political Philosophy* 61 at 64; M. Neocleous, 'The Problem with Normality: Taking Exception to "Permanent Emergency"' (2006) 31 *Alternatives* 191 at 198.

30 Friedrich, *Constitutional Government and Democracy*, p. 579; Hussain, *The Jurisprudence of Emergency*, pp. 115–17; L. H. Tribe and P. O. Gudridge, 'The Anti-Emergency Constitution' (2004) 113 *Yale Law Journal* 1801.

31 For the significance of the colonisation and decolonisation processes for emergency powers in Southeast Asia, see K.Y. L. Tan, 'From Myanmar to Manila: A Brief Study of Emergency Powers in Southeast Asia', (Chapter 6), this volume.

constitutions contain explicit, frequently detailed, emergency provisions. The European . . . concept of the "state of siege" as an emergency mechanism underlies the great bulk of modern constitutional systems.'[32] Some constitutional emergency provisions are quite elaborate, and provide for multiple states of exception which may be understood with reference to a sliding scale of higher and lower levels of emergency or crisis.[33] What is even more interesting is another finding, by Ferejohn and Pasquino, that whereas constitutional emergency provisions have almost never been used in the 'advanced democracies'[34] after the Second World War, their use 'remains common in newer and more fragile democracies: Latin America, Africa, and southern Asia have seen repeated uses of such constitutional powers'; 'emergency powers remain alive and well in less stable democracies'.[35] A set of data compiled by Neocleous demonstrates the following:[36] in the decade preceding 1963, more than 100 states of emergency had been declared in African states; in 1978, 30 of the 150 countries in the world were in a state of emergency; in 1986, approximately 70 states were undergoing some type of emergency; in the period 1985–97, approximately 100 states or territories were under a state of emergency at some point.

Even in well-established liberal constitutional democracies, the challenges to constitutionalism and the rule of law posed by emergency situations such as war and terrorism have been well recognised. In some circumstances, 'constitutional dictatorship' may be justified, but the purpose must be to restore the constitutional order of the status quo ante, and sufficient institutional safeguards must be put in place. As Ramraj points out in this volume,[37] 'the common goal of emergency powers in the liberal-democratic tradition is precisely to ensure the continuity of the normative constitutional order'. One risk of the use of emergency powers is that they become gradually absorbed into the general law and continue after the original 'emergency' has passed; thus the exception

[32] O. Gross, 'Providing for the Unexpected: Constitutional Emergency Provisions' (2003) 33 *Israel Yearbook on Human Rights* 13 at 18 (footnotes omitted from quotation).

[33] *Ibid.*

[34] J. Ferejohn and P. Pasquino, 'The Law of the Exception: A Typology of Emergency Powers' (2004) 2 *International Journal of Constitutional Law* 210 at 215; an exception (in which such provisions were resorted to) was the use of constitutional emergency powers by France in 1961 with regard to the Algerian situation. Ferejohn and Pasquino also point out that in advanced democracies in the past few decades, the 'legislative model' has been used in dealing with emergencies instead of constitutional provisions: ordinary legislation is enacted to confer emergency powers on the executive.

[35] *Ibid.*, at 217, n. 19.

[36] Neocleous, 'The Problem with Normality', at 197.

[37] See V. V. Ramraj, 'The Emergency Powers Paradox' (Chapter 2), this volume.

becomes the norm.[38] The gravest danger of constitutional dictatorship is that it may become permanent and absolute. The lesson of Article 48 of the Weimar Constitution contributing to the rise of Nazi Germany is a painful one.[39] But history also demonstrates that constitutionalism may be able to survive emergencies. Thus Rossiter concludes his study of constitutional dictatorship as follows: '[i]f the crisis history of the modern democracies teaches us anything, it teaches us that power can be responsible, that strong government can be democratic government, that dictatorship can be constitutional'.[40] Freeman points out in his study of the use of emergency powers by democratic governments to fight terrorism that there has been successful experience of abuses being prevented or minimised where the emergency powers concerned are limited in duration and scope, and where constitutional safeguards such as freedom of speech and press, the right to vote and the separation of powers remain intact during the emergency.[41]

Unfortunately, the same can hardly be said for dictatorship for allegedly emergency circumstances in the world outside the well-established constitutional democracies. As mentioned above, the Western concepts, theory and discourse of constitutionalism and emergency powers give rise to the dichotomy between normalcy and exception: whereas constitutional government is the norm, departure from the norm may be justified in states of exception. But as Carl Schmitt wrote in his famous opening sentence of *Political Theology*: 'Sovereign is he who decides on the exception.'[42] In practice, rulers of states rather than the people decide on the exception, and therefore abuses are bound to occur. In many countries in Latin America,[43] Africa[44] and Asia,[45] political, social and economic crises often occur that may be perceived as emergency circumstances justifying the

[38] K. Jayasuriya, 'The Exception Becomes the Norm: Law and Regimes of Exception in East Asia' (2001) 2 *Asian-Pacific Law and Policy Journal* 108.

[39] Rossiter, *Constitutional Dictatorship*, part I; Finn, *Constitutions in Crisis*, chap. 4.

[40] Rossiter, *Constitutional Dictatorship*, p. 314.

[41] Freeman, *Freedom or Security*, chaps. 1, 7. For example, with free speech, abuses will be publicised and pressure put on the government; with separation of powers, an independent legislature may investigate abuses, and courts may review the exercise of emergency powers.

[42] Schmitt, *Political Theology*, p. 5.

[43] G. L. Negretto and J. A. Aguilar Rivera, 'Liberalism and Emergency Powers in Latin America: Reflections on Carl Schmitt and the Theory of Constitutional Dictatorship' (2000) 21 *Cardozo Law Review* 1797.

[44] B. O. Nwabueze, *Constitutionalism in the Emergent States* (London: C. Hurst & Co., 1973); see especially chap. VII ('Constitutionalism and the Frequent Incidence of Emergencies in New Nations').

[45] See, for example, A. Kalhan, 'Constitution and "Extraconstitution": Colonial Emergency Regimes in Postcolonial India and Pakistan' (Chapter 4), and R. Pangalangan, 'Political

invocation of constitutional or statutory emergency powers. Sometimes it is really justified; sometimes it is not, but the rulers who hold power at the time nevertheless declare a state of emergency and the action is often not subject to any meaningful political, legislative or judicial checks and review.[46] Thus often rulers use the discourse and law of emergencies and emergency powers to legitimise their holding on to power and suppressing their political opponents.[47] Sometimes the military use such discourse and law to seize power in a *coup d'état*.[48] In these ways, the discourse and law of emergency powers become instruments for subverting constitutionalism rather than for defending it, which is the original purpose of constitutional emergency powers and constitutional dictatorship.

But it should also be pointed out that in many countries in Latin America, Africa and Asia, the social, cultural and economic conditions may be such that it is difficult to operate a liberal constitutional democratic system of government. If the conditions are such that an authoritarian system of government is more suitable for a particular nation at a particular stage of its development, then the discourse of emergency may be no more than a substitute or surrogate for the idea that the prevailing circumstances make it impossible or impracticable to practice the liberal constitutional democratic system prescribed in the constitution for 'normal' circumstances.[49] In this case, then, emergency provisions in the constitution or the law should probably not take all the blame for giving legitimacy to authoritarian rulers. At least it cannot be easily assumed that if such provisions had not existed, then the political system of the country concerned would have been less authoritarian. To argue in this way would be to overestimate the importance and power of constitutional and legal provisions.

Emergencies in the Philippines: Changing Labels and the Unchanging Need for Legitimacy' (Chapter 15), both in this volume; I. Omar, *Rights, Emergencies and Judicial Review* (The Hague: Kluwer Law International, 1996) (on the cases of Malaysia, Sri Lanka and Bangladesh); V. Iyer, *States of Emergency: The Indian Experience* (New Delhi: Butterworths India, 2000); R. Coomaraswamy and C. de los Reyes, 'Rule by Emergency: Sri Lanka's Postcolonial Constitutional Experience' (2004) 2 *International Journal of Constitutional Law* 272.

46 However, the growing significance of judicial review as such a check in some Asian countries should not be underestimated: see A. K. Thiruvengadam, 'Asian Judiciaries and Emergency Powers: Reasons for Optimism?' (Chapter 17), this volume.

47 See, for example, H. P. Lee, 'Constitutionalised Emergency Powers: A Plague on Asian Constitutionalism?' (Chapter 14), this volume.

48 See, for example, A. Harding, 'Emergency Powers with a Moustache: Special Powers Military Rule and Evolving Constitutionalism in Thailand' (Chapter 11), this volume.

49 As Ramraj points out (Chapter 2), in many developing countries 'emergency powers are seen as necessary to establish the conditions of relative stability needed for legal, political, and economic reforms to take hold' (p. 29).

We now turn from general observations and reflections to the case studies of this chapter. It is hoped that after conducting the case studies, we will be in a better position to understand the operation and significance of emergency laws in their transplanted environments in East Asia.

III. The case of Hong Kong

Hong Kong was a British colony from 1842 until its reunification with China in 1997. The constitutional arrangements in colonial Hong Kong were similar to those applicable to conquered colonies in other parts of the Empire. The British tradition of the rule of law was transplanted to the colony,[50] but not the full civil liberties or the democracy in Britain itself.[51] The establishment of the rule of law, both as a set of institutions and procedures and as a doctrine or ideology, was nevertheless significant. As Hussain points out in his study of British colonialism and the jurisprudence of emergency:

> Government by rules became the basis for the conceptualisation of the 'moral legitimacy' of British colonial rule. The applicability of rules to all was understood as the distinguishing feature of British rule, and counterpoint to the 'personal discretion' found in a theory of precolonial sovereignty known as Oriental Despotism.[52]

Hussain also considers that 'colonialism is the best historical example for any theoretical study of norm and exception, rule of law and emergency'.[53]

In colonial Hong Kong, two main sources of law granted to the executive extensive powers in times of emergency. The Orders in Council 1939–73 issued by the British Crown authorised the Governor of Hong Kong, if satisfied that a public emergency existed, to make regulations which may override other laws.[54] The Emergency Regulations Ordinance, enacted in 1922, the year of a large-scale strike by seamen and other workers in Hong Kong, provided that '[o]n any occasion which the Governor in Council may consider to be an occasion of emergency or public danger he may make any regulations whatsoever which he may consider desirable in the public interest'.[55] The regulations may provide for, *inter alia*, censorship,

[50] P. Wesley-Smith, *An Introduction to the Hong Kong Legal System* (Hong Kong: Oxford University Press, 1987).

[51] R. Wacks (ed.), *Civil Liberties in Hong Kong* (Hong Kong: Oxford University Press, 1988).

[52] Hussain, *The Jurisprudence of Emergency*, p. 4.

[53] *Ibid.*, p. 31.

[54] P. Wesley-Smith, *Constitutional and Administrative Law in Hong Kong* (Hong Kong: China and Hong Kong Law Studies, 1988), vol. II, p. 445.

[55] Section 2(1) of the Ordinance.

arrest, detention, deportation, search of premises, taking possession of property, etc.; they may also create criminal offences and provide for punishment thereof. The regulations would prevail over any other law inconsistent with them. The main set of regulations made under the Ordinance was the Emergency (Principal) Regulations made in 1949 – the year of the establishment of the People's Republic of China after the communist takeover – which consisted of a total of 137 regulations. Such regulations were, however, to remain dormant, and would only come into force when expressly activated by the colonial government.

Unlike the case of most colonies in the British Empire, the British did not apply the decolonisation policy to Hong Kong after the Second World War. Also, unlike most other British colonies in Asia and Africa, there was in Hong Kong no political and social movement for independence. Neither was there a movement for reincorporation of Hong Kong into (communist) China. Compared to many parts of the non-Western world, post-war Hong Kong enjoyed relative social and political stability,[56] and rose economically to become one of the Four Little Dragons of Asia. The greatest challenge to its political and social order and the most serious emergency situation it faced in the second half of the twentieth century occurred in 1967. In the middle of that year, communist elements in Hong Kong, inspired by the radical Maoist ideology of the 'Cultural Revolution' which was sweeping mainland China at the time, launched a movement against British colonial rule in Hong Kong. For several months in the second half of 1967, Hong Kong witnessed the severest civil disturbances in its colonial history. The protesters marched, demonstrated and threw stones at the police; workers went on strike; there were clashes between demonstrators and police with casualties on both sides. Vehicles were set alight; bombs were planted in streets and public places; an anti-communist radio programme presenter was murdered. The riots resulted in 51 people (including policemen, rioters and civilians) being killed and more than 1,100 injured.[57]

The colonial government resorted to the Emergency Regulations Ordinance in dealing with the crisis. In the period May–October 1967, nine new sets of regulations were enacted by the Governor in Council (Executive Council) under the Ordinance; the existing Emergency (Principal) Regulations were amended four times; six orders were made activating

[56] Lau Siu-kai, *Society and Politics in Hong Kong* (Hong Kong: Chinese University Press, 1982).

[57] S. Tsang, *A Modern History of Hong Kong* (Hong Kong: Hong Kong University Press, 2004), chap. 13.

various provisions of the Emergency (Principal) Regulations; in addition, one other order and two other sets of rules were introduced under the Emergency Regulations Ordinance.[58] The government also saw the need to codify and tighten up the existing law on assemblies, processions and demonstrations: the Public Order Ordinance on this subject was enacted by the colonial Legislative Council in late 1967.

One of the powers exercised by the police under the Emergency Regulations Ordinance during the period of civil disturbances was that of detention without trial. The subject attracted some attention in the House of Commons of the British Parliament: in its 1967–8 session, twenty-six questions were asked in the House on the detainees' conditions and related matters.[59] By contrast, there was very little discussion of the riots, and no scrutiny of the government's handling of them, in the Legislative Council of Hong Kong itself,[60] which consisted at that time entirely of government officials and unofficial members (members of the community) appointed by the Governor.

Even though colonial Hong Kong was not a liberal-democratic polity with constitutional guarantees of civil liberties or human rights, the distinction between normalcy and emergency that its emergency laws presupposed is still of some significance. It has been pointed out that 'the difference between the ordinary law and the emergency laws of [British] dependent territories is one of degree rather than of kind'.[61] This is true, because the absence of a constitutional bill of rights and the concentration of powers in the person of the Governor under colonial constitutional law even in 'normal' times[62] imply that from the constitutional perspective no special arrangements need to be introduced in times of emergency. But British colonial rule had indeed brought to Hong Kong the British tradition of the rule of law, as well as some degree of civil liberties though not as plentiful as in Britain itself. Emergency circumstances such as those in 1967 necessitated a departure from the pre-existing standards of the rule of law and civil liberties. Fortunately, the departure was no more than temporary, and as the confrontation between the communists and the colonial government came to an end, the emergency regulations activated

58 See the *Hong Kong Government Gazette* 1967.

59 N. Miners, *The Government and Politics of Hong Kong*, 4th edn (Hong Kong: Oxford University Press, 1986), p. 70, n. 8.

60 See *Hong Kong Hansard* (*Proceedings of the Legislative Council of Hong Kong*) 1967.

61 Holland, 'Emergency Legislation', p. 170.

62 Thus the government system of colonial Hong Kong has been described as 'gubernatorial government': P. Wesley-Smith, *Constitutional and Administrative Law* (Hong Kong: Longman Asia, 1995), p. 122.

in 1967 were discontinued in 1968, and legal 'normalcy' was restored. In the 1970s Hong Kong entered a golden age in terms of economic development and social reform, so that by the time the Sino-British negotiation on the future of the colony began in 1982, there was consensus in Hong Kong that the existing economic, social and legal systems should be preserved as far as possible. That, indeed, was the objective of the policy of 'one country, two systems' that was enshrined in the Sino-British Joint Declaration of 1984 and the Basic Law of the Hong Kong Special Administrative Region enacted by the Chinese legislature in 1990 and coming into force in Hong Kong in 1997.[63]

IV. The case of Taiwan

Taiwan was ceded by the Qing empire in China to Japan after its defeat in the Sino-Japanese War of 1894–5. Japanese colonial rule in Taiwan came to an end in 1945 with Japan's defeat in the Second World War, and Chinese rule was restored. The Chinese government at the time was the government of the Republic of China (ROC) established in 1911 when the Qing dynasty fell. The government was led by Chiang Kai-shek, leader of the Nationalist Party (Kuomintang, or KMT). In the late 1940s, civil war engulfed mainland China, ending in the victory of the Chinese Communist Party led by Mao Zedong. In 1949, the People's Republic of China (PRC) was established in mainland China, while the Nationalist government retreated to Taiwan. The constitutional and legal regime of the ROC has survived in Taiwan to this day.

The constitutional foundation of the regime in Taiwan has been the Constitution of the ROC enacted by the National Assembly in Nanjing, then capital of the ROC, in December 1946.[64] The Constitution attempts to establish a Western-style liberal constitutional democratic state, while incorporating features of the political theory of Dr Sun Yat-sen, the revered founding father of the ROC, such as the doctrine of the five-branch government (i. e. in addition to the Legislative, Executive and Judicial Yuans (*yuan* means organ), there should also be an Examination Yuan and a Control (or supervision) Yuan, with the National Assembly being the

[63] P. Wesley-Smith and A. Chen (eds.), *The Basic Law and Hong Kong's Future* (Hong Kong: Butterworths, 1988).

[64] See generally, A. H. Y. Chen, 'A Tale of Two Islands: Comparative Reflections on Constitutionalism in Hong Kong and Taiwan' (2007) 37 *Hong Kong Law Journal* 647 at 651–3.

supreme body which is responsible for electing the President and amending the Constitution).[65] As far as emergency powers are concerned, the Constitution contains two provisions which have continental European and Japanese roots.[66] Article 39 governs *jieyan* (which is often translated in the literature on Taiwan as 'martial law', although 'state of siege' would be a better translation given the continental European and Japanese origins of this Chinese term), while Article 43 deals with emergency orders. The subject of *jieyan* is further regulated by a pre-existing Jieyan Law enacted in 1934 (and amended in 1948 and 1949).

The 1946 Constitution never had the chance of being fully implemented. The emergency circumstances of the civil war soon precipitated the suppression, or at least the suspension, of constitutionalism or aspirations toward it. In July 1947, the Nationalist government declared that China had entered a Period of National Mobilisation to Suppress the Communist Rebellion.[67] In December 1947, the Constitution that had been enacted one year previously came into force. In March–April 1948, the National Assembly elected from all over China in areas under the control of the Nationalist government in 1947–8 in accordance with the Constitution met and adopted a constitutional amendment in the form of the Temporary Provisions for the Period of National Mobilisation to Suppress the Communist Rebellion ('the Temporary Provisions'). The main theme of the Temporary Provisions was to expand the emergency powers of the President:

> During the Period of Mobilisation for Suppression of Communist Rebellion[,] to prevent the nation or the people from suffering imminent dangers or to deal with serious unforeseen economic or financial crisis, the President may, by the resolution of the council of the Executive Yuan, take emergency measures without being restricted by Articles 39 or 43 of the Constitution . . .[68]

On the basis of the provision on emergency measures in the Temporary Provisions, *jieyan* was declared by the ROC government with regard

65 Chi-tung Lin and Herbert H. P. Ma, 'The Republic of China (Taiwan)', in L. W. Beer (ed.), *Constitutional Systems in Late Twentieth Century Asia* (Seattle: University of Washington Press, 1992), p. 88.

66 Chen Xinmin, *Constitutional Law of the Republic of China* (*Zhonghua minguo xianfa shilun*), 4th edn (Taipei: Sanmin, 2001), p. 449.

67 Chen Xinmin, *Constitutional Law of the Republic of China* (*Zhonghua minguo xianfa shilun*), 5th edn (Taipei: Sanmin, 2005), p. 925.

68 This English translation of the original Chinese text is taken from Lin and Ma, 'The Republic of China (Taiwan)', p. 95.

to the Chinese mainland in December 1948.[69] In May 1949, the Taiwan Provincial Garrison Headquarters promulgated a *jieyan* decree with regard to the Taiwan province.[70] This *jieyan* decree was adopted by the Executive Yuan in November 1949 and ratified by the Legislative Yuan in March 1950.[71] Article 4 of the *jieyan* decree provided for the use of capital punishment in respect of ten types of behaviour that were disruptive of public order (including, for example, 'spreading rumours', 'assembling for riots', 'disrupting finance', robbery, going on strike, 'inciting student protest activities', etc.).[72] For the purpose of implementing *jieyan* in Taiwan, various executive measures or decrees were promulgated. Examples included: Measures Governing Implementation of the Provisions for Preventing Illegal Assembly, Association, Demonstration, Petition, or Strike; Measures Governing the Control of Publications; Measures for Dividing What Kinds of Cases Are To Be Tried by Military Organs and What Kinds Are To Be Turned Over to the Civil Court for Trial;[73] Measures Governing the Control of Entry into and Exit from the Taiwan Region, etc.[74] Thus civil liberties were restricted not by laws enacted by the legislature but by executive *jieyan* measures. Other restrictions on civil liberties were imposed by emergency measures under the National General Mobilisation Law enacted in 1942 during the Sino-Japanese War,[75] and laws such as the Regulations on Punishment for Rebellion.[76]

The circumstances of the civil war and of the ROC government retreating to Taiwan not only triggered the state of *jieyan* which led to the suspension of some crucial civil liberties (until the *jieyan* decree was finally lifted in July 1987), but were also used as the pretext for the suspension of the democratic rights of the people in Taiwan. In 1954, the Council of Grand Justices – the constitutional court established under the 1946

[69] The *jieyan* decree was not applicable to the four border regions nor to Taiwan. This decree was lifted in January 1949, but was reinstated in July 1949 with regard to the Chinese mainland. See Chen, *Constitutional Law*, 5th edn, p. 464.

[70] The major event in Taiwan before this was the massacre and repression of the '28 February incident' of 1947 initiated by protests by Taiwanese against Nationalist rule in Taiwan.

[71] Chen, *Constitutional Law*, 5th edn p. 464.

[72] *Ibid.*, pp. 457–8; Chen Xinmin, *The Basic Theory of Fundamental Constitutional Rights* (*Xianfa jiben quanli zhi jiben lilun*), 5th edn, vol. II (Taipei: Yuanzhao, 1999), p. 323.

[73] See Hungdah Chiu, 'Constitutional Development in the Republic of China in Taiwan', in S. Tsang (ed.), *In the Shadow of China: Political Developments in Taiwan since 1949* (Hong Kong University Press, 1993), p. 17 at pp. 26–8.

[74] Tao-tai Hsia and W. Zeldin, 'Laws on Emergency Powers in Taiwan', in Leng (ed.), *Coping With Crises*, p. 173 at p. 183.

[75] *Ibid.*, pp. 178, 183.

[76] Chen Xinmin, *The Rule of Law* (*Fazhi guojia lun*) (Taipei: Xuelin wenhua, 2001), p. 236.

Constitution – issued its Interpretation No. 31, ruling that because of 'major changes in the nation' and the 'impossibility' of holding nationwide elections (in the whole of China), the incumbent members of the Legislative Yuan and Control Yuan (elected from the whole of China before the ROC government retreated to Taiwan) could continue to hold office indefinitely although their term of office as stipulated in the Constitution had expired.[77] The same practice was followed in the case of the National Assembly. Thus members of these representative institutions continued to serve until 1991 (except of course those who died or retired voluntarily before then), when they were finally forced to retire by the constitutional court's Interpretation No. 261 issued in June 1990, which ruled that Interpretation No. 31 was no longer applicable because of changed circumstances.[78] Since 1969, the people of Taiwan had been given the right to elect some members into the parliamentary institutions in accordance with amendments to the Temporary Provisions introduced in 1966 and 1972 (although under the *jieyan* decrees there was no right to form political parties to compete in the elections), but this only concerned a small portion of the total number of seats.[79]

Apart from the promulgation of *jieyan* for the whole nation in 1948, the provision on emergency measures in the Temporary Provisions was invoked on ten other occasions[80] during the Period of National Mobilisation to Suppress the Communist Rebellion, which only ended in 1991, when the Temporary Provisions were finally repealed and new constitutional amendments were introduced in the form of the Additional Articles. Among these ten occasions, the first six were in 1948–9, and five of these six concerned economic and financial matters. The other four occasions were in 1959 (emergency measure on reconstruction after flooding), 1978 (emergency measure, at the time of the establishment of diplomatic relations between the USA and the PRC and the US de-recognition of the ROC, to put the armed forces on full alert and to postpone elections in Taiwan), 1979 (supplementing the preceding measure by extending the term of office of incumbent parliamentary members elected from Taiwan for two years),[81] and 1988 (emergency measure, at the time of the death of President Chiang Ching-kuo, on the restriction of assembly and

77 Chen, 'A Tale of Two Islands', 653–4. 78 *Ibid.*, 667.

79 As of 1990, three-quarters of the seats in the National Assembly (766 out of 979) were still occupied by those elected in China in the late 1940s: Chen, 'A Tale of Two Islands', 667.

80 Chen, *Constitutional Law*, 4th edn, p. 477.

81 Chen, *Constitutional Law*, 5th edn, p. 933.

association).[82] After the end of the Period of National Mobilisation to Suppress the Communist Rebellion, the president's power to issue emergency orders, now governed by the Additional Articles,[83] was used in the aftermath of the great earthquake of 21 September 1999.[84]

The ROC in Taiwan was under one-party (KMT) rule and the leadership of the political 'strongmen' Chiang Kai-shek and Chiang Ching-kuo, who succeeded his father upon the former's death in 1975. The emergency measure of *jieyan* and the Temporary Provisions that were grafted onto the Constitution, which continued in effect for thirty-eight years and forty-three years respectively, provided the legal basis for authoritarian rule in Taiwan for four decades. Shortly before his death (in January 1988), President Chiang Ching-kuo lifted the *jieyan* decree in July 1987, and Taiwan entered its age of liberalisation. Democratisation was realised in the 1990s under Lee Teng-hui's presidency, with elections to all seats in the National Assembly and the Legislative Yuan by the Taiwanese people being introduced in 1991 and 1992 respectively, and direct election of the president by the Taiwanese people in 1996. At the same time, the Council of Grand Justices grew into an activist guardian of the Constitution as it issued numerous interpretations overturning the laws, regulations, decrees and measures of the authoritarian era.[85] The promises of the 1946 Constitution in terms of liberal constitutional democracy, held in abeyance for nearly four decades, were finally fulfilled. The Taiwan story of constitutionalism and emergency powers is thus a moving and telling one. It demonstrates that in the long run, constitutionalism can triumph over emergency. Whether it took too long in Taiwan's case, and whether the 'developmental state' of the KMT should have pursued democratic reform earlier than it did, is for history and posterity to judge.

V. The case of South Korea

Korea was under Japanese colonial rule from 1910 to 1945. At the end of the Second World War, Korea became divided into two parts under the influence of the USSR and the USA respectively. In 1948, the Democratic People's Republic of Korea was established in North Korea, and the Republic of Korea in South Korea. Although South Korea's legal system has been

[82] Chen, *Constitutional Law*, 4th edn, p. 477; Hsia and Zeldin, 'Laws on Emergency Powers', 178.

[83] Chen, *Constitutional Law*, 5th edn, p. 493. [84] *Ibid.*, p. 497.

[85] T. Ginsburg, *Judicial Review in New Democracies* (Cambridge: Cambridge University Press, 2003), chap. 5.

largely shaped by its Japanese heritage and follows the continental Civil Law tradition, American constitutionalism has been a significant influence on South Korean constitutional law.[86] The first Constitution of the Republic of Korea was adopted in 1948. Sources of influence on it included not only the US Constitution, but also the Constitution of the Weimar Republic of pre-war Germany and the Constitution of the Republic of China mentioned above.[87] The Constitution provided for a Western-style liberal constitutional democracy. Article 64 of the Constitution provided for the President's power to proclaim martial law.[88] Article 57 dealt with emergency measures in the forms of orders and financial dispositions.[89]

After the Constitution had been promulgated, the National Assembly, which was elected at the first general election in South Korea, elected Dr Syngman Rhee as President of the Republic of Korea. The first instance of the use of emergency power in South Korea was not to cope with the general situation of the Korean War 1950–3, but to achieve President Rhee's personal goal in domestic politics, which was to change the mode of election of the President to direct election by the populace, a change which the National Assembly did not originally support. On 25 May 1952, martial law was imposed on Pusan, the temporary wartime capital, using the pretext of the murder of four American soldiers and the need to fight communist guerillas. The President made use of his expanded powers under martial law to intimidate the National Assembly, with the result that the constitutional amendment he proposed regarding presidential election by direct popular vote was approved on 4 July 1952.[90] Shortly thereafter, Rhee was elected for a second term. In 1954, Rhee secured by dubious means a second constitutional amendment,[91] which created an

[86] Kyong Whan Ahn, 'The Influence of American Constitutionalism on South Korea' (1997–8) 22 *Southern Illinois University Law Journal* 71; Tscholsu Kim and Sang Don Lee, 'The Influence of US Constitutional Law Doctrines in Korea', in L. W. Beer (ed.), *Constitutional Systems in Late Twentieth Century Asia* (Seattle: University of Washington Press, 1992), p. 303.

[87] G. H. Flanz (ed.), *Constitutions of the Countries of the World* (Dobbs Ferry, N.Y.: Oceana, looseleaf), 'Korea'.

[88] Young C. Kim, 'Politics of Emergency Powers: The Case of Korea', in Leng (ed.), *Coping with Crises*, p. 129 at pp. 138–9.

[89] *Ibid.*

[90] J. Kleiner, *Korea: A Century of Change* (Singapore: World Scientific, 2001), pp. 110–11; B. Cumings, *Korea's Place in the Sun: A Modern History* (New York: W. W. Norton, 1997), p. 342; Dae-kyu Yoon, *Law and Political Authority in South Korea* (Boulder, Colo.: Westview, 1990), p. 98.

[91] Yoon, *Law and Political Authority*, p. 99; Kleiner, *Korea*, p. 111; Cumings, *Korea's Place*, pp. 342–3.

exception to the two-term limit on the presidency by allowing the first President of the Republic to run for office for an unlimited number of terms. In 1955, Rhee was re-elected for a third term. In March 1960 he was again re-elected.

This time the election result was not accepted by significant numbers of citizens, who believed that the election had been rigged. Student-led demonstrations led to the police opening fire into the crowd in Seoul on 19 April 1960, killing more than a hundred and injuring approximately 1,000 people.[92] On the same day the President declared martial law and called in the troops. But demonstrations and riots continued every day after 19 April. Rhee was forced to resign on 26 April. The event became known as the 'Righteous Student Uprising of 19 April'.[93] Martial law was terminated on 16 July 1960.[94]

After Rhee's resignation, an interim government was formed, and the existing National Assembly introduced amendments to the Constitution in June 1960 which substituted a parliamentary system for the presidential system.[95] The National Assembly of the Second Republic was elected in July 1960, and Chang Myon became Prime Minister. The liberal democracy of the Second Republic was however short-lived. The new government proved to be ineffective. Economic conditions worsened; there were almost daily demonstrations; and pro-communist and radical elements seemed to be gaining influence. The political instability, social chaos and economic crises of the Second Republic in 1960–1 thus constituted the background of the military coup in 1961.

The *coup d'état* was launched by General Park Chung-hee on 16 May 1961. Seoul was put under military occupation, and a self-appointed Military Revolutionary Committee proclaimed martial law throughout the nation on that day. On 18 May, President Yun Po-san, president of the Second Republic (a ceremonial head of state), acting on the advice of Prime Minister Chang Myon, also proclaimed martial law under Article 64 of the 1960 Constitution,[96] in effect acknowledging the validity of the earlier action of the Military Revolutionary Committee. Prime Minister Chang then resigned, and the military established the Supreme Council of

92 Cumings, *Korea's Place*, p. 344; Kleiner, *Korea*, p. 126; A. C. Nahm, *Korea: Tradition and Transformation*, 2nd edn (Elizabeth, N.J.: Hollym, 1996), p. 406.

93 Nahm, *Korea*, p. 406. 94 Kim, 'Politics of Emergency Powers', p. 147.

95 A major source of influence on the 1960 Constitution was the Constitution (Basic Law) of the Federal Republic of Germany (West Germany) enacted in 1949: see Flanz (ed.), *Constitutions*, 'Korea'.

96 Kim, 'Politics of Emergency Powers', p. 148.

National Reconstruction to take over the powers of government and the National Assembly (which was dissolved). In June, the Council enacted the Emergency Measures Law on National Reconstruction which overrode the Constitution. Martial law was only terminated on 6 December 1962. On 17 December, an amended Constitution which reintroduced the presidential system[97] was approved in a national referendum. In October 1963, a presidential election was held under the 1962 Constitution, and Park was elected President of the Third Republic.

The next time martial law was invoked was in 1964. In spring that year, political and social unrest began as a result of popular opposition to the government's talks with Japan on the normalisation of relations between the countries. There were again large-scale demonstrations, involving violent confrontations between student demonstrators and the police. Martial law was proclaimed in Seoul on 3 June 1964. Martial Decree No. 1 prohibited all assemblies and demonstrations and imposed press censorship and curfew. Public trials by court martial of student activists and other protesters were held. Martial law was terminated on 28 July 1964. The treaty on normalisation of relations was subsequently concluded and ratified by both South Korea and Japan in 1965.

In 1967 Park was re-elected President for a second term. In 1969, he secured a constitutional amendment, approved by both the National Assembly (despite opposition by the opposition party) and a referendum, which allowed an incumbent president to run for a third term.[98] In 1971 Park was re-elected for a third term, narrowly defeating the opposition candidate Kim Dae-jung.

The year 1971–2 saw another turning point in South Korea's political and constitutional history. In order to quell student unrest, the Garrison Law was invoked in October 1971; troops moved into university campuses in Seoul. On 4 December 1971, President Park proclaimed a state of national emergency, alleging national security concerns and possible invasion by North Korea.[99] Shortly thereafter, on 27 December, the Law on Special Measures for National Protection and Defence was enacted by the National Assembly, empowering the President to proclaim an emergency when this was necessary to counter a grave threat to national security

[97] Articles 73–5 of this Constitution dealt with emergency powers. For example, Article 75(5) provided that the President shall lift the proclaimed state of siege if so requested by the National Assembly: see Flanz (ed.), *Constitutions*, 'Korea', pp. 7–8.

[98] Yoon, *Law and Political Authority*, pp. 102–3; Kim and Lee, 'The Influence of US Constitutional Law Doctrines', pp. 312–13.

[99] Kim, 'Politics of Emergency Powers', p. 155.

or to maintain social peace and order.[100] The law authorised restrictions on human rights and press freedom,[101] emergency economic measures and requisition of property.[102] The law was given retroactive effect, thus purporting to validate the declaration of a state of emergency on 4 December.[103] Insofar as this law attempted to expand the emergency powers of the President beyond the limits stipulated in the Constitution, its constitutionality was in doubt.[104]

President Park took an even more drastic step toward authoritarianism in 1972. On 17 October, nationwide martial law was suddenly proclaimed. Assemblies and demonstrations were banned; press censorship was imposed; the National Assembly was dissolved 'by an extra-constitutional power';[105] political parties' activities were banned; and an Emergency State Council was formed to take over power. Park claimed that the measures were necessary in order to establish a new system that would facilitate dialogue between South and North Korea and eventual unification.[106] As pointed out by Kleiner, Park 'did not try to find legal justification for his measures. This would have been impossible because the measures of 17 October 1972 were an attack against the constitution. Park Chung-hee had plotted against his own constitution.'[107]

The Emergency State Council was given the task of drafting a new constitution, which it completed by 27 October. On 21 November 1972, with the nation still under martial law, the Constitution was approved in a referendum. It was known as the Yushin (meaning 'revitalising reforms')[108] Constitution, and purported to introduce a 'Korean-style democracy'.[109]

100 Kleiner, *Korea*, p. 153. 101 Nahm, *Korea*, pp. 425–6.

102 Flanz (ed.), *Constitutions*, 'Korea'.

103 This may be taken as implicit admission that the declaration on 4 December was not authorised by the provisions on emergency power in the existing Constitution.

104 The opposition argued that the law was unconstitutional: see Kim, 'Politics of Emergency Powers', pp. 155–6; Flanz (ed.), *Constitutions*, 'Korea'; Kleiner, *Korea*, p. 153. 'The alleged critical situation of national security could not . . . justify the declaration of an emergency. According to Art. 75 of the Constitution of the Third Republic, the proclamation of an emergency was only possible when there was a military necessity or when it was necessary to maintain public safety and order by the mobilisation of the armed forces': Kleiner, *Korea*, pp. 152–3.

105 Yoon, *Law and Political Authority*, p. 103.

106 Kim, 'Politics of Emergency Powers', pp. 156–7; Flanz (ed.), *Constitutions*, 'Korea'.

107 Kleiner, *Korea*, p. 154. Kim also referred to the actions on 17 October 1972 as 'extra-constitutional emergency measures': Kim, 'Politics of Emergency Powers', p. 139.

108 Yushin is the Korean equivalent of the Japanese term issin which was the slogan of the Meiji reform of 1868: Cumings, *Korea's Place*, p. 358; Kim and Lee, 'The Influence of US Constitutional Law Doctrines', p. 317.

109 Kim, 'Politics of Emergency Powers', p. 157; Yoon, *Law and Political Authority*, p. 104; Cumings, *Korea's Place*, p. 359; Kleiner, *Korea*, p. 156.

On 13 December martial law was lifted. On 23 December, Park was elected President of the Fourth Republic by the National Conference for Unification (NCU) established under the new 1972 Constitution – 'a constitution which legalised authoritarian rule'.[110] South Korea entered a 'dark age' of constitutionalism.[111]

The 1972 Constitution expanded the emergency powers of the President, and expressly authorised the suspension of constitutional rights by emergency measures.[112] In the Fourth Republic of 1972–9, these powers were used extensively to introduce draconian measures to suppress movements for amendment of the Constitution, liberalisation and democratisation. A total of nine emergency decrees were promulgated by Park, including three decrees for the purpose of lifting previously issued decrees.[113] Among them, Emergency Decree No. 9 lasted for the longest time. Issued on 13 May 1975 to suppress opposition to the Yushin Constitution and Park's government, it was only lifted in December 1979 after Park's death. In the meantime, the Yushin system was reaffirmed by a national referendum in February 1975, and Park was re-elected President by the NCU in 1976.

The political situation further deteriorated in 1979. After the expulsion from the National Assembly of Kim Young-sam, a leading opposition politician, a large-scale student demonstration took place on 16 October 1979 in Pusan. Martial law was imposed on Pusan on 17 October. As the demonstrations spread to Masan and Changwon, garrison decrees were issued in these cities.[114] As 'the most serious student uprising since 1960'[115] developed, Park was assassinated on 26 October 1979 by the Director of the Korean Central Intelligence Agency (KCIA). Martial law was immediately proclaimed on 27 October throughout South Korea, except for the Cheju Islands.[116] Prime Minister Choi Kyu-hah became Acting President in accordance with Article 48 of the Constitution. On

110 Kleiner, *Korea*, p. 156.

111 Kim and Lee, 'The Influence of US Constitutional Law Doctrines', p. 318.

112 Article 53 of the Constitution deals with emergency measures; Article 54 deals with martial law: see Flanz (ed.), *Constitutions*, 'Korea'.

113 Emergency Decrees (ED) nos. 1 and 2 were issued on 8 January 1974 to prohibit opposition to the Yushin Constitution and to provide for 'emergency courts-martial' for offenders. ED no. 3 on 14 January 1974 introduced measures for economic stabilisation, and was lifted by ED No. 6 on 31 December 1974. ED no. 4 on 3 April 1974 was aimed at suppressing students' political activities. ED no. 5 on 23 August 1974 lifted ED nos. 1 and 4. ED no. 7 on 8 April 1975 closed down twenty-one universities and restricted press freedom, and was lifted by ED no. 8 on 13 May 1975, the same day as the promulgation of ED no. 9.

114 Nahm, *Korea*, pp. 430–1; Kleiner, *Korea*, pp. 165–6.

115 Nahm, *Korea*, p. 431.

116 Kim, 'Politics of Emergency Powers', p. 162.

6 December 1979, Choi was elected president by the NCU. On 7 December, he terminated Emergency Decree No. 9, which had been promulgated by Park in 1975.

In the meantime, the proclamation of martial law resulted in a shift of power to the military. On 12 December 1979, General Chun Doo-hwan seized power within the military. In April 1980, Chun, then Commander of the Defence Security Command, became Acting Director of the KCIA as well. In May, demonstrations erupted all over the country demanding the termination of martial law and democratisation. The government opted for repression. On 17 May 1980, the level of martial law was elevated from 'emergency martial law' to 'extraordinary martial law', and its scope was extended to the entire country.[117] At the same time, Emergency Decree No. 10 was promulgated. Leading politicians were arrested; universities were closed; censorship was imposed; political activities were prohibited. The National Assembly was indefinitely suspended.[118]

To protest the government's repression, what became known as the 'Kwangju Uprising' occurred in the period 18–27 May 1980. The military's brutal suppression of the initial demonstrations in Kwangju provoked citizens' resistance and demonstrations on an even larger scale. 'In the early hours of 27 May 1980, Kwangju was conquered by troops in an assault like in times of war.'[119] The event was 'Korea's Tiananmen nightmare in which students and young people were slaughtered on a scale the same as or greater than that in "People's" China in June 1989'.[120]

Following Choi's resignation from the presidency on 16 August 1980, the NCU elected Chun as President on 30 August. A new constitution was prepared and was approved by a referendum on 22 October,[121] when South Korea was still under martial law. Martial law was lifted on 25 January 1981, and on 25 February 1981, Chun was elected President of the new Fifth Republic by an electoral college in accordance with the new Constitution. The democracy movement in South Korea continued during Chun's rule to strive for direct election of the President by citizens themselves. The movement escalated into large-scale demonstrations in 1987. On 29 June that year, Roh Tae-woo, Chun's designated successor, opted for conciliation rather than repression, and by consensus between the government and the opposition a new constitution (providing for direct election of the

[117] *Ibid.*, p. 164. [118] Nahm, *Korea*, p. 434; Kleiner, *Korea*, p. 176.

[119] Cumings, *Korea's Place*, p. 177. [120] *Ibid.*, p. 338.

[121] The new Constitution, unlike the Yushin Constitution, was a liberal-democratic one. The emergency powers granted to the President by the Yushin Constitution were curtailed by the 1981 Constitution. See Nahm, *Korea*, p. 437.

President) was produced and approved by the National Assembly on 12 October and in a referendum on 25 October 1987.[122] This Constitution is still in force today. As one historian of modern Korea writes: 'democracy is not a gift or a political regime that one is born with but something that must be fought for every inch of the way, in every society. In this sense, the Korean struggle has been so enduring that there may be no country more deserving of democracy in our time than the Republic of Korea'.[123] And, as we have just seen, side by side with the story of the Korean struggle for democracy stands the story of the use of martial law and emergency powers by holders of political power. We shall return to this point in the conclusion of this chapter.

VI. The case of mainland China

The first Constitution of the People's Republic of China (PRC), which was adopted in 1954, was largely based on the constitutional model of the Soviet Union.[124] It established the National People's Congress (NPC) as the supreme organ of state power, a system which is still in force today. Article 31(18) provided that the Standing Committee of the NPC had the power to decide on *jieyan* (the same Chinese term as that used in the ROC Constitution mentioned above, which may be translated as 'martial law' or 'state of siege') for the whole nation or part of it. During the chaos of the Cultural Revolution that began in 1966 and lasted for several years, military rule was imposed in some areas and institutions in order to restore order, but the concept of *jieyan* was not employed.[125] In the 1975 Constitution, which reflected the extreme leftist ideology of the Cultural Revolution era, the provision on *jieyan* in the 1954 Constitution was deleted, but *jieyan* was nevertheless practised to suppress the anti-government demonstration at Tiananmen Square on 5 April 1976 to mourn the death of Premier Zhou Enlai.[126] The 1978 Constitution, which restored many features of the

[122] Kim and Lee, 'The Influence of US Constitutional Law Doctrines', p. 324. The new Constitution further curtails the President's power to issue emergency decrees. See Nahm, *Korea*, p. 443.

[123] Cumings, *Korea's Place*, p. 339.

[124] A. H. Y. Chen, *An Introduction to the Legal System of the People's Republic of China*, 3rd edn (Hong Kong: LexisNexis, 2004), p. 42.

[125] Mo Jihong, 'Wanshan jinjizhuangtai lifa baozhang gongmin de xianfa he falu quanli' ('Developing the Law on the State of Emergency, Protecting Citizens' Constitutional and Legal Rights'), www.chinalawinfo.com (accessed 1 July 2008).

[126] *Ibid.*

1954 Constitution, did not provide for *jieyan*.[127] The 1982 Constitution, a product of Deng Xiaoping's policy of 'reform and opening', provided that the NPC Standing Committee may decide on *jieyan* for the whole nation or an individual province, autonomous region or municipality directly under the central government (MUC),[128] while the State Council may decide on *jieyan* for part of a province, of an autonomous region or of a MUC.[129] However, unlike the case of the ROC, there was no law governing further details of *jieyan* until the enactment of the Jieyan Law in 1995.

In 1989, the constitutional power of *jieyan* was activated twice,[130] first on 8 March to suppress riots in Lhasa, and then on 20 May in Beijing to suppress the students' democracy movement which had grown out of activities since mid-April to mourn the death of Hu Yaobang, the former General Secretary of the Chinese Communist Party who had been deposed in 1987. The interaction of law and politics in the making of the latter *jieyan* decree is particularly noteworthy. Under the Constitution, as mentioned above, *jieyan* in Beijing (which is a MUC) would require action by the NPC Standing Committee. However, the authorities did not convene any meeting of this committee to discuss how to deal with the student movement. The decision to impose *jieyan* was instead made by the State Council. Under the Constitution, the State Council has power to impose *jieyan* only on part of a MUC, not the whole of it, and this was what it chose to do. Acting under the *jieyan* decree, the municipal government of Beijing imposed *jieyan* on all of urban Beijing but not all of its suburban and rural areas.[131] Thus there was compliance 'with the letter of the Constitution but not its spirit'.[132] Before and after the day of the *jieyan* proclamation, there were calls from members of the public and from NPC members for an extraordinary meeting of the NPC

[127] However, both the 1954 and the 1978 Constitutions provided for the state of war: see Article 31(16) of the former and Article 25(12) of the latter.

[128] Article 67(20). Article 80 provides, *inter alia*, that after the NPC Standing Committee has decided on *jieyan*, the President of the PRC shall promulgate the relevant *jieyan* decree. Articles 67(18) and (19) provide respectively for the state of war and for military mobilisation.

[129] Article 89(16).

[130] Mo, 'Developing the Law'. Both *jieyan* decrees were lifted in 1990. The *jieyan* power was not used in dealing with the riots in Lhasa in March 2008.

[131] [1989] *Zhonghuarenmingongheguo guowuyuan gongbao* (*Gazette of the State Council of the PRC*), p. 392.

[132] J. A. Cohen, 'Tiananmen and the Rule of Law', in G. Hicks (ed.), *The Broken Mirror: China After Tiananmen* (Harlow: Longman, 1990), p. 323 at p. 325.

or the NPC Standing Committee to deal with the situation,[133] but these were deliberately ignored by the top party leadership, which, under the control of Deng Xiaoping, ousted Zhao Ziyang, General Secretary of the Chinese Communist Party who sympathised with the protesting students and opposed *jieyan*. After *jieyan* was imposed, there was large-scale civil disobedience and continued protests. On the night of 3 June and in the early hours of 4 June, martial law troops, who had surrounded Beijing after the imposition of *jieyan* on 20 May, finally forced their way into the city, opened fire on the crowds and conquered Tiananmen Square, which the student demonstrators had occupied for weeks. The NPC Standing Committee was convened only at the end of June 1989, by which time all that was left for it to do was to endorse the report from Chen Xitong, mayor of Beijing, on the suppression of the 'counter-revolutionary rebellion' that had taken place.[134]

The first decree promulgated by the Beijing municipal government to implement *jieyan* prohibited, *inter alia*, demonstrations and processions. The large-scale demonstrations of the Beijing student movement exposed a gap in Chinese law which the NPC Standing Committee recognised and filled in October 1989 when it enacted the Law on Assemblies, Processions and Demonstrations. On the other hand, the lack of a law regulating *jieyan* was only remedied in 1995, when the NPC Standing Committee enacted the Jieyan Law (also translated as 'Martial Law'). The law governs *jieyan* in situations of riot and civil disturbance. While it was pointed out in the explanatory speech on the bill for this law that the Chinese concept of *jieyan* was similar to that of the state of emergency abroad, it was also explained that circumstances involving natural disasters and epidemics would not necessitate the measures provided for in the Jieyan Law.[135]

When the PRC Constitution was amended in 2004, one set of amendments related to *jieyan*: all the references to *jieyan* in the existing constitutional text were replaced by 'state of emergency'.[136] After the national

133 A. H. Y. Chen, 'Human Rights in China: A Brief Historical Review', in R. Wacks (ed.), *Human Rights in Hong Kong* (Hong Kong: Oxford University Press, 1992), p. 176 at p. 200. See also A. Kent, *Between Freedom and Subsistence: China and Human Rights* (Hong Kong: Oxford University Press, 1993), pp. 177–86.

134 [1989] *Zhonghuarenmingongheguo quanguorenmindaibiaodahui changwuweiyuanhui gongbao (Gazette of the Standing Committee of the National People's Congress of the PRC)*, pp. 244–6.

135 [1996] *Zhonghuarenmingongheguo quanguorenmindaibiaodahui changwuweiyuanhui gongbao (Gazette of the Standing Committee of the National People's Congress of the PRC)*, pp. 9–12 (explanatory speech on the bill), esp. p. 10.

136 The amendments relate to Articles 67, 80 and 89 of the Constitution.

crisis caused by the SARS (severe acute respiratory syndrome) epidemic in spring 2003, it was recognised that legal provisions on emergency situations like this ought to be introduced. The constitutional amendment relating to *jieyan* was premised on the idea that the state of emergency is a broader and more modern concept than *jieyan*, and is more widely used in the contemporary constitutional law of other nations and in international human rights law.[137] After the constitutional amendment was introduced, the drafting of a law on the state of emergency was put onto the legislative agenda of the NPC Standing Committee.[138]

During the drafting and legislative process, it was eventually decided that the new law would mainly cover emergency situations such as natural disasters, accidents and epidemics rather than riots and civil disturbances. The title of the law that was enacted in 2007 is the Law on Responses to Emergency Events (also translated as Emergency Response Law). One of the controversies that arose during the drafting of the law concerned the extent to which the media could freely report on emergency events without official permission. The draft provided for restrictions, which were relaxed in the final version of the law in response to criticisms.[139] The effectiveness of this law was put to the test during the snowstorms that swept China in early 2008 and the great earthquake in Sichuan on 12 May 2008.[140]

VII. Concluding reflections

Scholars of comparative political systems distinguish between different types of modern state. For example, Finer identifies three main forms of modern government – the liberal-democratic state, the totalitarian state, and the Third World state (which include various kinds of autocracy and oligarchy, including the facade-democracy, the quasi-democracy and the military regime).[141] Blondel identifies five main types of modern political system – liberal-democratic, egalitarian-authoritarian, traditional inegalitarian, populist and authoritarian-inegalitarian.[142] Brooker's study of

137 *Shijie quanguo renda erci huiyi wenjian fudao duben* (*Reader on the Second Session of the Tenth National People's Congress*) (Beijing: Renmin Press, 2004), pp. 235–8; Mo, 'Developing the Law'.

138 Mo, 'Developing the Law'.

139 See Articles 54 and 65 of the law as enacted.

140 For a more detailed discussion and analysis of the law of emergency powers in China, see J. deLisle, 'States of Exception in an Exceptional State: Emergency Powers Law in China' (Chapter 13), this volume.

141 S. E. Finer, *Comparative Government* (Harmondsworth: Penguin, 1970).

142 J. Blondel, *Comparative Government* (New York: Prentice Hall/Harvester Wheatsheaf, 1995).

non-democratic regimes theorises about two types of regime (the military regime and the party regime) and four forms of government (totalitarian, authoritarian, communist and fascist).[143]

The case studies in this chapter suggest that the study of emergency powers should take into account the context of the political systems in which such powers are established and exercised. Thus the practice of emergency powers in authoritarian states, or states in which democracy is weak, unstable and functioning feebly, may be affected by factors other than those applicable to the practice of emergency powers in a well-established liberal constitutional democracy.[144]

As pointed out in Part II of this chapter, the concept of emergency powers is inseparable from that of constitutionalism itself. Where the state exercises arbitrary and absolute power, no special principles or rules are necessary to cope with emergencies. Conversely, special principles or rules which constitute the theory and law of emergency powers are essential to the liberal constitutional democratic state. Such theory and law, as mentioned in Part II, are premised on the dichotomy between normalcy and states of exception.

The question therefore arises as to what happens to emergency powers when they are transplanted from the Western liberal democracies in which they originated to countries which are not liberal democracies or which are newly born and fragile liberal democracies. In Part II of this chapter, the possibility of the abuse of emergency powers when so transplanted to Latin America, Africa and Asia has been highlighted. In the light of the four case studies on East Asian jurisdictions in this chapter, we are now in a better position to gain further insight into the matter.

The four cases are all different from one another in terms of the nature of the political system that has existed and in which emergency powers have been exercised. Hong Kong was (until 1997) under colonial rule. The political system was authoritarian but the British tradition of the rule of law and a certain degree of civil liberties (not as extensive as in Britain itself) had been transplanted to the colony. Mainland China, or the PRC, was a totalitarian state in which the principle of the leadership of the Chinese Communist Party had been enshrined in the Constitution. It was a lawless nation in the Cultural Revolution era, but since the 'reform and opening' of the late 1970s it has reconstructed its legal system and rehabilitated the concept of the rule of law. In Taiwan, the ROC Constitution that has been

[143] P. Brooker, *Non-Democratic Regimes: Theory, Government and Politics* (Basingstoke: Macmillan, 2000).

[144] For the latter practice, see notes 3 and 41 above.

in force is a liberal-democratic one. But from the late 1940s to the late 1970s, Taiwan was in practice a one-party authoritarian state. Like the ROC Constitution, the Constitutions that were in force in South Korea from 1948 to 1971 were liberal-democratic ones. But South Korea was at best a quasi-democracy or semi-democracy in the 1950s and 1960s under the authoritarian personalities of Rhee and Park, and in the 1970s moved further toward authoritarianism and military dictatorship.

We now first consider the cases of colonial Hong Kong and the PRC, both of which, unlike South Korea and Taiwan, did not have on paper a Western-style liberal-democratic constitution. Hong Kong's Emergency Regulations Ordinance, activated in 1967 when the colonial government faced the only major challenge to its rule in the whole of the second half of the twentieth century, demonstrates that the distinction between normalcy and exception is not meaningless even in the absence of a liberal-democratic constitution instituting the separation of powers and guaranteeing human rights. The emergency circumstances of the riots in 1967 justified a temporary departure (e.g. executive law-making, severe restrictions on civil liberties) from the normal standards of the rule of law and civil liberties that the British authorities practised in the colony. The law on emergency powers had a positive role to play in confining such departures to the emergency circumstances. Thus when the emergency was over, there was no further excuse for using the Emergency Regulations Ordinance. On the other hand, a few provisions introduced during the emergency did pass into the general law with the enactment of the Public Order Ordinance in late 1967, which is consistent with the 'familiar pattern'[145] elsewhere of temporary provisions introduced for an emergency sometimes becoming permanent, with the consequent 'normalisation of the exception'.[146] However, post-war Hong Kong did not have the internal security acts like those in Malaysia and Singapore which authorised preventive detention.

Similarly, the existence of the provision on *jieyan* in the PRC Constitution of 1982 may be perceived as a positive phenomenon from the perspective of the rule of law, even though the PRC does not practise Western-style liberal constitutional democracy. The restoration of the provision on *jieyan* in the 1982 Constitution after its disappearance in the two preceding constitutions itself testifies to the Chinese project of rebuilding 'socialist legality' after the lawlessness of the Cultural Revolution era. The events of 1989 show that the constitutional provisions on

[145] Gross and Ní Aoláin, *Law in Times of Crisis*, p. 178. [146] *Ibid.*, p. 228.

jieyan were not merely semantic but had an authentic normative effect in shaping the behaviour of power-holders. This is evidenced by the fact that the *jieyan* decree was promulgated by the State Council with regard to only parts of Beijing, which as discussed above was probably a deliberate attempt to avoid the issue going before the NPC Standing Committee in which dissenting views would most probably have been aired. The lesson of this is that the precise content of constitutional texts on emergency powers and their procedural constraints do matter, even in a communist state like the PRC. If the Constitution had provided that only the NPC Standing Committee could authorise *jieyan* in any part of the capital city, history might have had to be rewritten. Since the events of 1989, China has enacted its Jieyan Law and Emergency Response Law and substituted the 'state of emergency' for *jieyan* in relevant provisions in the Constitution. These developments reflect the increasing commitment of the Chinese state to the rule of law. Indeed, it is now recognised in the PRC that the level of development of its law on emergency and emergency powers is a sign of the maturity of its legal system.[147] On the other hand, it should also be noted that the Chinese state has broad powers at its disposal under ordinary law and there is no effective constitutional review of executive and legislative actions; hence the practical need to rely on the concept, discourse and law of emergency is minimal.

We turn finally to Taiwan and South Korea. In Taiwan, the effect of the *jieyan* decree that lasted for thirty-eight years and the 'temporary' provisions in the Constitution dealing with the exigencies of 'national mobilisation to suppress the communist rebellion' that lasted for forty-three years was to freeze the liberal-democratic promises of the ROC Constitution during these decades. The case of Taiwan is therefore an extreme case of constitutional emergency powers being used to suspend key provisions of the Constitution for an extraordinarily long period of time. Although there existed a constitutional court, and although the Legislative Yuan technically had the power to terminate an emergency measure,[148] the political reality of one-party rule had meant that these institutions were powerless to constrain the executive exercise of emergency powers.

[147] See generally, deLisle, Chapter 13. As deLisle points out, Chinese emergency powers law is 'potentially a double-edged sword'; while it 'allows the regime to draw upon law's emergent legitimacy in China to support extraordinary authority', it can also 'help limit state power and implement promises that laws – and policies – make to Chinese citizens' (p. 345).

[148] Lin and Ma, 'The Republic of China (Taiwan)', p. 95.

Critics of constitutional emergency powers[149] can argue that this case vividly demonstrates the evils of the abuse of such powers. On the other hand, optimists can point out that compared to having an authoritarian or totalitarian constitution, having a liberal-democratic constitution that contains emergency provisions is still the lesser of two evils for a nation which is young and struggling to become democratic. In the case of Taiwan, those who struggled for democracy could reason and argue that the emergency circumstances that originally justified *jieyan* and the enactment of the Temporary Provisions in the late 1940s no longer existed, and therefore these measures should be lifted and the original text of the Constitution practised. And this was what happened in Taiwan eventually.

Thus constitutional emergency provisions, when transplanted to countries that aspire toward liberal constitutional democracy and express such aspirations in the text of their constitutions, can be a two-edged sword. On the one hand, they may be easily abused by power-holders for the purpose of legitimising their authoritarian rule. On the other hand, insofar as they presuppose the distinction between normalcy and states of exception, those who struggle for democracy can use the discourse of normalcy and emergency to challenge the justifications for emergency and demand the return of normalcy. The case of South Korea illustrates this vividly. As this chapter has shown, among the four cases studied in this chapter, South Korea is the case in which emergency powers and martial law have been abused to the greatest extent. But South Korea is also the case where the people's struggle for democracy has been fiercest and most persistent. Time and again, the declaration of martial law or state of emergency by the government only served to provoke the people to protest even more, and to demand the lifting of martial law or the state of emergency and the return to the normalcy of civil liberties and political freedoms promised by the Constitution. Thus over the years the power-holders came to appreciate the heavy cost of martial law and repression, and finally accomplished the 'constitutional miracle'[150] of 1987 when the momentous decision was made to choose the path of constitutionalism rather than that of martial law and emergency powers.

The case of South Korea is also instructive in three other ways. First, even without formally and expressly resorting to emergency powers, the state already had at its disposal the draconian provisions of the National Security

[149] See, for example, Lee, Chapter 14.

[150] Kim and Lee, 'The Influence of US Constitutional Law Doctrines', p. 322.

Law (enacted in 1948 and further tightened in 1958)[151] and the Anti-Communist Law (1961)[152] which could be easily used against political forces and voices opposed to it. In a sense these laws were also emergency laws. Thus the line between emergency laws and ordinary laws was not so clear. Second, the National Assembly has had the constitutional power to request the termination of the state of emergency or martial law,[153] a power which it did use successfully in 1964 (regarding the martial law decree)[154] and 1979 (regarding Emergency Decree No. 9).[155] This shows that the constitutional constraint on emergency powers in South Korea when it was a quasi-democracy was more effective than that in Taiwan when it was an authoritarian one-party state. On the other hand, the courts in South Korea were not able to exercise such constraint.[156] Third, having learnt the lessons of previous abuse of emergency powers, the relevant constitutional provisions have now been improved in terms of procedural controls and human rights protection.[157] The same has taken place in Taiwan.[158]

The cases of Hong Kong and the PRC show that in jurisdictions that are not liberal-democratic but nevertheless practise or aspire toward the rule of law and certain minimum levels of human rights and civil liberties, the development of the law on emergency powers and the dichotomy between normalcy and exception can make a positive contribution to the project of legality.[159] The cases of Taiwan and South Korea demonstrate that where a new nation adopts a liberal-democratic constitution that provides

[151] Cumings, *Korea's Place*, p. 343; Kleiner, *Korea*, p. 115; Nahm, *Korea*, p. 405.

[152] Nahm, *Korea*, p. 416; Kleiner, *Korea*, p. 182.

[153] Kim, 'Politics of Emergency Powers', pp. 131, 137–8; Flanz (ed.), *Constitutions*, 'Korea'.

[154] Kim, 'Politics of Emergency Powers', p. 153. In 1960, the National Assembly also introduced a resolution calling for the termination of martial law, and the government responded by changing the state of extraordinary martial law to that of security martial law on 25 April 1960: *ibid.*, p. 146.

[155] Nahm, *Korea*, p. 431.

[156] Under the Constitution of the Third Republic (1962–72), the courts enjoyed the power of constitutional review: Kim and Lee, 'The Influence of US Constitutional Law Doctrines', pp. 313–15; Flanz (ed.), *Constitutions*, 'Korea'. The Constitution of the Fourth Republic (1972–9) expressly excluded the President's emergency powers from judicial review: Kim, 'Politics of Emergency Powers', p. 133.

[157] See Articles 76 and 77 of the 1987 Constitution; Articles 51 and 52 of the 1980 Constitution.

[158] See Article 2 of the Additional Articles of the Constitution of the ROC.

[159] For a less optimistic view suggesting that the distinction between normalcy and exception is being effaced by contemporary developments in the use of internal security law and terrorism law, see e.g. Jayasuriya, 'The Exception Becomes the Norm'; Neocleous, 'The Problem with Normality'.

for emergency powers of the state,[160] there is indeed the possibility of abuse of emergency powers; but insofar as the concept of and justification for emergency powers presuppose the distinction between normalcy and exception and affirm the requirements of liberal constitutional democracy as the norm, the struggle for democracy can be sustained and propelled forward by the idea that it is the struggle for return to normalcy. We do not want to live in the state of exception any more. We want to return to normal life. And normal life is where constitutionalism and human rights flourish.

If this concluding observation sounds too optimistic, particularly in light of some of the other chapters in this volume, readers may bear in mind that it is made only on the basis of the experience to date of the four jurisdictions studied in this chapter, and is not intended to be generalised into a universally applicable theory of emergency powers and constitutionalism. This chapter reveals no more than one possible and contingent pathway of the operation of emergency powers and their relationship to constitutionalism, but has not discovered any logic of necessity that is of universal application. Indeed, if this chapter were written twenty-five years ago – before Taiwan and South Korea emerged from their eras of the abuse of emergency powers by authoritarian rulers and before China made significant progress in building its legal system – the concluding observation would have been a very different – and pessimistic – one: perhaps one which, as H. P. Lee in this volume does, emphasises the negative function of the legitimation of abuse performed by constitutional emergency powers;[161] or one which, as Vasuki Nesiah in this volume does, suggests that emergency states are 'the norm not the exception'.[162] The experience of Malaysia, Sri Lanka, India and Pakistan, on which these authors' views are based, must therefore be taken seriously, and compared with that of the jurisdictions studied in this chapter. In this way, perhaps, we can work toward the development of a general theory of emergency powers and constitutionalism in the Asian context.

160 For a different evaluation of the constitutionalisation of emergency powers, see Lee, Chapter 14.

161 *Ibid.*

162 V. Nesiah, 'The Princely Impostor: Stories of Law and Pathology in the Exercise of Emergency Powers' (Chapter 5), this volume, p. 140.

4

Constitution and 'extraconstitution': colonial emergency regimes in postcolonial India and Pakistan

ANIL KALHAN

I. Introduction

On 3 November 2007, Pakistan's President and Chief of Army Staff, General Pervez Musharraf, issued a 'proclamation of emergency', nominally predicated upon the rise of extremism and terrorist violence which, he asserted, 'pos[ed] a grave threat to the life and property' of Pakistan's citizens.[1] In a televised address, Musharraf went further, defending the emergency as necessary to 'save Pakistan' and to prevent nothing less than the country's 'suicide'.[2] Despite these existential overtones, the emergency was widely criticised as a pretextual attempt for Musharraf to maintain power, not a means to combat terrorism. In the weeks that followed, Musharraf assumed sweeping executive powers and cracked down heavily on regime opponents.

Notably, Musharraf's opponents resisted not only the crackdown itself, but also his characterisation of those measures as involving 'emergency' at all. Like other constitutions, Pakistan's explicitly authorises the executive to invoke emergency powers to address crises posing a severe threat to the

I am grateful to Victor Ramraj and Arun Thiruvengadam for inviting me to participate in the Symposium on Emergency Powers in Asia and for their helpful feedback. Many thanks to the symposium participants and to Manan Ahmed, Ali Ahsan, Elizabeth Angell, Michael Dorf, Stephen Ellmann, Sadiq Reza, Sahar Shafqat, Mitra Sharafi and Ayesha Siddiqa, and to presentation attendees at New York Law School, the Open Society Institute and the University of Wisconsin's Annual Conference on South Asia for comments on earlier drafts and valuable exchanges on the issues addressed in this chapter.

1 Proclamation of Emergency (3 November 2007) (Musharraf), www.pakistani.org/pakistan/constitution/post_03nov07/proclamation_emergency_20071103.html.

2 G. Witte, 'Musharraf Declares Emergency Rule in Pakistan', *Washington Post*, 4 November 2007, www.washingtonpost.com/wp-dyn/content/article/2007/11/03/AR2007110300214.html.

nation.[3] However, Musharraf's decree was self-consciously extraconstitutional, aimed at objectives not typically associated with the constitutional idea of 'emergency'. Following a script established during earlier moments in Pakistan's history, Musharraf sought to preserve the political status quo, but by transforming Pakistan's institutional and legal order, purging independent judges from their posts and promulgating constitutional amendments and other laws by decree, rather than through normal law-making processes.

Implicit in the critics' resistance to Musharraf's characterisation of his actions as involving 'emergency' is a suggestion that the exercise of *constitutional* emergency powers would have been more benign, restrained or legitimate than these *extraconstitutional* actions. To what extent, however, is this suggestion warranted? This chapter explores the experiences with emergency and emergency-like powers in postcolonial Pakistan and India to illustrate the ways in which constitutional and extraconstitutional states of exception can converge in their application.

On the one hand, the experiences in Pakistan demonstrate, perhaps unsurprisingly, that extraconstitutional assertions of emergency authority can provide a ready means for authoritarian rulers to usurp power, violate fundamental rights and transform the constitutional landscape in the guise of addressing a crisis. The authoritarianism in such moments is not entirely 'lawless'. To the contrary, in exercising these extraordinary powers, Musharraf and his predecessors have imposed upon Pakistan a parallel higher law regime – call it an 'extraconstitution' – which effectively functions as the existing constitution's legal *doppelgänger*. Even as the constitution has been explicitly suspended, the extraconstitution seeks to create an appearance that legality has been maintained and a foundation for its own legal supremacy. Nevertheless, the extraconstitution undermines legality by seeking to displace the existing constitutional order – even after the period of supposed crisis has ended and the constitution purportedly has been 'revived'. While executive power under the extraconstitution ostensibly remains subject to limits, the deference afforded to the executive during the crisis period, in most practical respects, leaves that power unfettered.

On the other hand, the experiences of both Pakistan and India suggest that constitutionally authorised emergency powers can be as difficult to constrain as extraconstitutional regimes of the sort seen in Pakistan, and can lead to excesses and lasting transformations that are at least as severe. Most notably, the constitutional emergency imposed by Indira Gandhi in

[3] Pakistan Constitution, Articles 232–7.

1975 in India, which bears a striking, although perhaps superficial, resemblance to Musharraf's extraconstitutional emergency in 2007, illustrates the ways in which the exercise of constitutional and extraconstitutional emergency powers can functionally resemble one another. Gandhi invoked India's constitutional emergency powers ostensibly to combat internal disturbances presenting a grave threat to the Indian state, but like Musharraf, in reality to prolong her tenure of office. Like Musharraf, Gandhi suspended fundamental rights, sidelined political opponents and the upper judiciary, and effectively ruled by decree. She also used this crackdown to impose a number of constitutional, statutory and institutional changes that were intended to be permanent. Though formally constitutional, Gandhi's emergency similarly ushered in a parallel legal regime that – by design – threatened to displace the existing Constitution in order to preserve the political status quo.

Together, these experiences may be understood as distinct instantiations of a shared emergency powers discourse inherited from the British colonial state.[4] While India and Pakistan both have been governed by constitutions incorporating commitments to democracy and fundamental rights, both countries' legal frameworks build upon colonial-era laws, institutions and norms that were designed not to facilitate democratic governance and accountability, but rather to establish and maintain centralised control by the executive.[5] Emergency and emergency-like powers were vitally important to this end, and their use in independent India and Pakistan – whether constitutionally or extraconstitutionally – has often continued to function as a means of displacing democratic processes, rather than primarily as a 'provisional and exceptional measure' to deal with existential crises of the order of war or rebellion.[6] This anti-democratic quality can be seen not only in extreme circumstances, such as the emergencies

[4] Cf. A. Jalal, *Democracy and Authoritarianism in South Asia: A Comparative and Historical Perspective* (Cambridge: Cambridge University Press, 1995), pp. 249–50 (challenging a 'simple dichotomy between democracy in India and military authoritarianism in Pakistan and Bangladesh', and arguing instead that India, Pakistan and Bangladesh 'appear to exhibit alternate forms of authoritarianism').

[5] See V. Iyer, *States of Emergency: The Indian Experience* (New Delhi: Butterworths, 2000), pp. 67–75; I. Omar, *Emergency Powers and the Courts in India and Pakistan* (New York: Kluwer Law International, 2002), pp. 13–14; A. Kalhan, 'Colonial Continuities: Human Rights, Terrorism, and Security Laws in India' (2006) 20 *Columbia Journal of Asian Law* 93 at 111, 125–9.

[6] G. Agamben, *State of Exception*, trans. K. Attell (Chicago: University of Chicago Press, 2005), p. 3; see also N. Hussain, *The Jurisprudence of Emergency: Colonialism and the Rule of Law* (Ann Arbor: University of Michigan Press, 2003), pp. 136–40; Omar, *Emergency Powers and the Courts*, p. 129 (arguing that 'every Proclamation of Emergency under the Constitutions of India and Pakistan has been used for extraneous purposes').

ordered by Gandhi and Musharraf, but also in the more routinised use of constitutional, emergency-like executive authority in both countries – for example, to dismiss elected governments at both the national and subnational level, to legislate by ordinance or to engage in preventive detention.

In arguing that the experiences of India and Pakistan with emergency and emergency-like powers have in these respects converged, I do not mean to suggest that constitutionality is necessarily irrelevant in constraining potential excesses or legitimising the use of emergency powers regardless of context.[7] In postcolonial South Asia, however, the significance of constitutionality has had limits, illustrating Giorgio Agamben's observation that the development of emergency powers may be independent of whether such powers are constitutionally formalised.[8] Owing in part to the colonial legacy's persistence, anti-democratic tendencies have continued to manifest themselves in the laws and institutions of India and Pakistan, albeit in different ways in each country. Whether those tendencies have operated through constitutional or extraconstitutional means, the basic results have in some respects been strikingly similar.

II. Emergency as 'extraconstitution'

Modern constitutions frequently incorporate provisions explicitly authorising resort to extraordinary powers during designated periods of emergency.[9] While such provisions vary in their details, a shared assumption underlying such provisions – and arguably, underlying liberal-democratic conceptions of emergency powers more generally – is

[7] Nor do I necessarily mean to equate the broader circumstances that led Musharraf to invoke emergency powers with those that led Gandhi to do so. For early commentary comparing and contrasting those circumstances, see, for example, V. Venkatesan, 'Pakistan 2008, India 1977', *Law and Other Things*, 19 February 2008, http://lawandotherthings.blogspot.com/2008/02/pakistan-2008-india-1977.html; H. Haqqani, 'Will Musharraf Learn From Indira?' *Gulf News*, 13 February 2008, www.gulfnews.com/opinion/columns/world/10189242.html; A. Jaitley, 'A Tale of Three Emergencies: Real Reason Always Different', *Indian Express*, 5 November 2007, www.indianexpress.com/story/235992.html; S. Dam, 'Pakistani SC and Constitutional Space', *Daily Times*, 19 October 2007, www.dailytimes.com.pk/default.asp?page=2007\10\19\story_19-10-2007_pg3_4; A. Kalhan, 'The Looming Clouds of Emergency?' *AsiaMedia*, 18 May 2007, www.asiamedia.ucla.edu/article.asp?parentid=70208.

[8] Agamben, *State of Exception*, p. 10.

[9] O. Gross and F. Ní Aoláin, *Law in Times of Crisis: Emergency Powers in Theory and Practice*, pp. 35–66 (Cambridge: Cambridge University Press, 2006) (discussing 'constitutional accommodation' models of emergency powers).

that emergency powers exist to advance 'fundamentally conservative' purposes.[10] When faced with a sufficiently grave threat, the government may respond by assuming sweeping powers and taking severe, even troubling actions – disregarding, for example, fundamental rights and other constitutional constraints that otherwise would apply. However, it is assumed not only that the emergency period itself will be temporary, but that legal and institutional changes implemented to respond to the emergency will not outlast that temporary period. Once the crisis has been resolved and the emergency declared over, laws and institutions are to be restored to their pre-emergency condition. As John Ferejohn and Pasquale Pasquino argue, if constitutional emergency powers are instead used to implement permanent changes to the legal or constitutional order, then their invocation 'no longer properly [involves] an exercise of an emergency power at all', but instead amounts to an 'exercise of constituent power'.[11]

Pakistan's *extraconstitutional* experiences with extraordinary powers appear to illustrate this dichotomy. When Pakistan's civilian executive and army leaders have invoked extraconstitutional powers, they typically have used those powers to transform, rather than preserve, the underlying legal and constitutional order – invoking, in other words, 'constituent' power rather than 'emergency' power. At the same time, the distinction is not quite as sharp as Ferejohn and Pasquino suggest. While Pakistan's extraconstitutional assertions of emergency power have permitted transformations of the legal and constitutional order, they simultaneously have been justified in the name of other purposes that may fairly be characterised as 'conservative' – namely, preservation of the political status quo and, through the courts' invocation of the doctrine of 'state necessity', of the state itself. This extraconstitutional pattern has recurred on several occasions in Pakistan's history, most recently in the emergency imposed by Musharraf in 2007.

A. *Pakistan's 2007 judicial crisis*

Musharraf's emergency was the culmination of an eight-month period in which he clashed with Pakistani lawyers and judges over judicial

[10] J. Ferejohn and P. Pasquino, 'The Law of the Exception: A Typology of Emergency Powers' (2004) 2 *International Journal of Constitutional Law* 210 at 210–11; see V. V. Ramraj, 'The Emergency Powers Paradox' (Chapter 2), this volume, p. 27 (arguing that the 'main goal' of liberal-democratic emergency powers regimes is 'to ensure the continuity of the [pre-emergency] normative constitutional order').

[11] Ferejohn and Pasquino, 'The Law of the Exception', at 223.

independence and his own political future.[12] In March 2007, Musharraf 'summoned' the Chief Justice of Pakistan, Iftikhar Muhammad Chaudhry, to meet with him and other uniformed generals. Musharraf confronted Chaudhry with a raft of allegations of misuse of power and tried to prevail upon Chaudhry to resign, assuring him that he would be 'accommodated'. When Chaudhry refused, Musharraf formally referred Chaudhry to a judicial disciplinary body, the Supreme Judicial Council.[13] Acting without clear legal authority, Musharraf also ordered Chaudhry's suspension and swore an acting chief justice into office. Chaudhry was subsequently detained for several days and when he appeared before the Supreme Judicial Council the following week, he and his wife were manhandled by the police.[14]

As Pakistani citizens watched these events unfold on television, lawyers and bar associations responded with outrage, launching a mass movement in support of the Chief Justice and the rule of law. The 'lawyers' movement' catalysed a broader anti-Musharraf movement in Pakistan's civil society, filling a vacuum caused by Musharraf's success in sidelining Pakistan's leading political parties.[15] As the movement gained momentum – with Chaudhry as its leading symbol, attracting massive crowds of non-lawyers as he travelled across Pakistan to speak to bar associations – the government began to crack down on both protesters and the media, whose coverage of the movement fuelled the growing anti-Musharraf sentiment.[16] Rumours began circulating as early as May 2007

[12] See Pakistan Institute of Legislative Development and Transparency (PILDAT), 'The Judicial Crisis, March–July 2007' (December 2007), www.pildat.org/publications/publication/judicialcrisis/The%20Judical%20Crisis.pdf; Human Rights Watch (HRW), 'Destroying Legality: Pakistan's Crackdown on Lawyers and Judges' (December 2007), www.hrw.org/en/reports/2007/12/18/destroying-legality-0; S. A. Ghias, 'Miscarriage of Chief Justice: Lawyers, Media, and the Struggle for Judicial Power in Pakistan, 2005–07', http://papers.ssrn.com/sol3/papers.cfm?abstract_id=1163642; S. Shafqat, 'The Movement to Restore the Judiciary' (presentation at 37th Annual Conference on South Asia, University of Wisconsin, 17 October 2008).

[13] Reference by the president of the Islamic Republic of Pakistan, under Article 209 of the Constitution (9 March 2007), available at www.dawn.com/2007/03/21/nat2.htm; text of Chief Justice's affidavit filed in the Supreme Court (30 May 2007), available at www.thenews.com.pk/top_story_detail.asp?Id=8188.

[14] See PILDAT, 'The Judicial Crisis'.

[15] The leaders of those leading parties, Benazir Bhutto and Nawaz Sharif, were in exile outside of Pakistan throughout the entire period in which the lawyers' movement sought the Chief Justice's reinstatement. Shafqat, 'The Movement to Restore'.

[16] See Pakistan Electronic Media Regulatory Authority (Amendment) Ordinance, 2007; see 'Sweeping Curbs on Media', *Dawn*, 5 June 2007, www.dawn.com/2007/06/05/top1.htm; S. Sengupta, 'A Lawyer Who Turned a Judge Into a National Cause', *New York Times*, 28 July 2007, www.nytimes.com/2007/07/28/world/asia/28islamabad.html.

that Musharraf might declare a constitutional emergency to curb the escalating movement, especially after Chaudhry's visit to Karachi was met with organised, pro-Musharraf violence.[17]

Observers have speculated extensively about what initially prompted Musharraf's decision to seek Chaudhry's ouster, a decision that ultimately cost Musharraf tremendous support. While Musharraf has stood by his allegations against Chaudhry, most observers believe that Musharraf and his allies were motivated primarily by concern over the independence exhibited by the Supreme Court during Chaudhry's tenure.[18] Under Chaudhry, the court had demonstrated an unprecedented willingness to challenge government action – for example, expanding use of its *suo motu* powers in human rights and public interest cases,[19] invalidating the regime's effort to privatise certain state-owned enterprises[20] and initiating an investigation into disappearances since 2001 arising from the US-led counterterrorism campaign.[21] With Musharraf's opponents questioning his eligibility to be re-elected as president in the elections due to be held by late 2007, Musharraf may have hoped that by sidelining the Chief Justice he could pre-empt the court holding him ineligible.[22]

In July 2007, the Supreme Court dismissed Musharraf's reference and reinstated Chaudhry as Chief Justice by a 10–3 margin.[23] After Chaudhry's reinstatement, the court resumed its nascent assertiveness, proceeding with the investigation into disappearances and its review of the legality of the regime's privatisation initiatives, and dramatically affirming the

[17] See Kalhan, 'The Looming Clouds of Emergency?'; Human Rights Commission of Pakistan, 'Carnage in Karachi' (September 2007), http://hrcp-web.org/carnage%20in%20karachi.pdf.

[18] See, for example, J. Khan, 'An Extraordinary Encounter With Musharraf', *Independent* (UK), 17 February 2008, www.independent.co.uk/news/world/asia/an-extraordinary-encounter-with-musharraf-783388.html; PILDAT, 'The Judicial Crisis', at 9; A. Kalhan, 'Five Questions for Aitzaz Ahsan, Leader of the Lawyers' Movement', *SAJAforum*, 1 July 2008, www.sajaforum.org/2008/07/pakistan-five-q.html.

[19] Pakistan Constitution, Article 184(3); see Ghias, 'Miscarriage of Chief Justice', at 24–6; Dam, 'Pakistani SC and Constitutional Space'; S. B. Khan, 'I Am Innocent, Want Open Trial: Justice Iftikhar', *Dawn*, 23 March 2007, www.dawn.com/2007/03/23/top1.htm.

[20] See *Watan Party* v. *Pakistan*, 2006 PLD S Ct 697.

[21] See Ghias, 'Miscarriage of Chief Justice', at 32–4; D. Walsh, 'Without a Trace', *Guardian* (UK), 16 March 2007, www.guardian.co.uk/world/2007/mar/16/alqaida.pakistan.

[22] See, for example, Human Rights Watch, 'Pakistan: Release Chief Justice of Supreme Court' (12 March 2007), www.hrw.org/en/news/2007/03/12/pakistan-release-chief-justice-supreme-court.

[23] *Iftikhar Muhammad Chaudhry* v. *President of Pakistan*, 2007 PLD S Ct 578, www.supremecourt.gov.pk//sub_links/judgements/ConstitutionPetitionNo.21Of2007.zip; see S. Sengupta, 'Chief Justice Is Reinstated in Pakistan', *New York Times*, 20 July 2007, www.nytimes.com/2007/07/20/world/asia/20cnd-pakistan.html.

right of exiled Musharraf opponent Nawaz Sharif to return to Pakistan in advance of parliamentary elections. When the government blocked Sharif's return, by detaining him upon his arrival in Islamabad and summarily rendering him to Saudi Arabia, the court initiated contempt proceedings against the senior officials responsible for Sharif's expulsion. The court also initiated an inquiry into the controversial military operation against militants lodged in Islamabad's Lal Masjid.[24]

Perhaps most explosively, as the time for elections drew closer, the court entertained petitions challenging Musharraf's eligibility to be re-elected president. While Chaudhry recused himself from cases involving Musharraf, and the court dismissed an initial challenge to Musharraf's eligibility on procedural grounds, the court considered a second challenge on the merits, permitting the election to take place but ordering the results not to be certified until the court had issued its final decision. Following arguments, it was widely expected that the court ultimately would rule against Musharraf.[25]

B. *Musharraf's 'emergency'*

On 3 November 2007, before the Supreme Court could issue a final decision concerning his eligibility, Musharraf declared his emergency, confirming fears held by many since the earliest days of the judicial crisis. While Musharraf justified the emergency as necessary to make special powers available to fight extremist violence, few observers took that justification seriously, especially given the prolonged conflict over the judiciary. The proclamation singled out the judiciary as a source of the supposed crisis, stating that 'some [judges]' had 'work[ed] at cross purposes with the executive and legislature' across a range of policy areas and even had 'humiliat[ed]' government officials 'on a routine basis during court proceedings'.[26] Moreover, the government already had been exercising extraordinary powers to combat extremist violence and had little apparent need for additional authority.[27] As with emergencies in other

[24] *Pakistan Muslim League (N)* v. *Pakistan*, 2007 PLD S Ct 642; N. Iqbal 'Destruction of Evidence Annoys Apex Court: Lal Masjid–Jamia Hafsa Case', *Dawn*, 18 August 2007, www.dawn.com/2007/08/18/top3.htm.

[25] HRW, 'Destroying Legality', at 17–18.

[26] Proclamation of Emergency (2007).

[27] In fact, reports indicated that even as the government cracked down on civil society, it was simultaneously accommodating the very insurgent groups ostensibly being targeted. P. Wiseman and Z. M. Sheikh, 'Musharraf's Motivations Scrutinized', *USA Today*, 5 November 2007, www.usatoday.com/news/world/2007-11-05-pakistan-musharraf_N.htm.

circumstances, Musharraf's emergency – far from helping to resolve a genuine threat – instead exacerbated the crisis that had been mounting since March 2007.[28]

Under Pakistan's Constitution, the president may exercise emergency powers if satisfied that Pakistan's security is threatened by a present or imminent danger of war, external aggression or internal disturbance.[29] The powers available during a constitutional emergency are considerable. While the emergency is in effect, the government may legislate or act in contravention of several enumerated fundamental rights and may suspend the ability to obtain judicial enforcement of fundamental rights.[30] Parliament may legislate on matters otherwise within the competence of provincial governments, and the federal executive may direct the manner in which provincial executive authority may be exercised.[31] The term of Parliament itself may be extended for up to one year.[32] Finally, the Constitution curtails judicial review of the validity of the emergency proclamation or any order issued pursuant to it.[33]

These powers are not completely unlimited. The Constitution provides that the emergency proclamation and orders suspending fundamental rights automatically expire if not approved by Parliament within two months.[34] In addition, any emergency laws and orders that would otherwise be invalid automatically lapse when the emergency period has ended.[35] While the Constitution purports to eliminate judicial review of emergency proclamations and orders, the Supreme Court has asserted its ability, albeit under a limited scope of review, to review both the emergency's initial validity and, subsequently, its continuing validity.[36]

[28] See V. Nesiah, 'The Princely Impostor: Stories of Law and Pathology in the Exercise of Emergency Powers' (Chapter 5), this volume, p. 123 (arguing that use of emergency powers in Sri Lanka 'ha[s] helped provoke and entrench a prolonged political crisis'); Kalhan, 'Colonial Continuities', at 128–9 (discussing the crisis provoked by the extension of emergency-like powers in colonial India following World War I).

[29] Pakistan Constitution, Article 232(1); *Farooq Leghari* v. *Pakistan*, 1999 PLD S Ct 57.

[30] Pakistan Constitution, Article 233(1)–(2).

[31] *Ibid.*, Article 232(2). [32] *Ibid.*, Article 232(6). [33] *Ibid.*, Article 236(2).

[34] *Ibid.*, Articles 232(7), 233(3). If the National Assembly has been dissolved at the time when the emergency proclamation is issued, then the proclamation shall expire after four months unless approved by a resolution of the Senate: *ibid.*, Article 232(8).

[35] Laws that Parliament would otherwise not have competence to enact outside the period of emergency automatically expire six months after the emergency is no longer in effect (*Ibid.*, Article 232(5)). Laws or orders contravening fundamental rights, as permitted under Article 233, cease to have effect immediately upon revocation or cessation of the emergency (*Ibid.*, Article 233(1)).

[36] *Leghari*, 1999 PLD S Ct 57; see Omar, *Emergency Powers and the Courts*, pp. 42–4.

Most fundamentally, the Constitution itself remains in effect during an emergency. The emergency provisions do not confer authority to fashion structural changes to the underlying constitutional order or contemplate special procedures for constitutional amendments.

At least on their face, therefore, these provisions comport with the conventional notion of emergency powers as 'conservative', in the sense discussed above. Musharraf's emergency, however, was not rooted in this conventional understanding. The proclamation – which was issued by Musharraf in his capacity as Chief of Army Staff, rather than President – declared that the government 'cannot be carried on [in a]ccordance with the constitution', and that the 'constitution provides no solution for [the country's] situation'. On that basis, the proclamation ordered the Constitution to be held 'in abeyance'. Pursuant to the proclamation, Musharraf simultaneously issued a 'provisional constitutional order' (PCO), which explicitly suspended the Constitution's fundamental rights provisions and conferred on the president ultimate lawmaking authority, including authority unilaterally to promulgate constitutional amendments and other laws. The PCO also prohibited any court from questioning the validity of the emergency or other actions taken by the president or prime minister.[37]

During the six weeks in which the emergency remained in effect, Musharraf exercised these powers extensively.[38] First and foremost, Musharraf sought to guarantee his ability to remain president, issuing constitutional amendments designed to insulate his eligibility from further legal challenge. He also instituted structural changes taking direct aim at the independence of Pakistan's judiciary and legal profession. Like his predecessors, Musharraf purged judges unwilling to confirm their loyalty by requiring Supreme Court and High Court judges to take new oaths of office under the PCO or cease to be judges altogether.[39] Musharraf also amended the Constitution to establish a new Islamabad High Court, a move that observers viewed as designed to make it easier for the government to engage in forum-shopping, and amended other laws to make it

[37] Provisional Constitutional Order No. 1 of 2007 (3 November) (Musharraf).

[38] See A. Kalhan, '"Emergency" as Institution Laundering', *Dorf on Law*, 7 November 2007, http://michaeldorf.org/2007/11/emergency-as-institution-laundering.html.

[39] Oath of Office (Judges) Order 2007 (3 November); see HRW, 'Destroying Legality', at 19.

easier to interfere with bar associations' operations and to punish lawyers critical of the government.[40]

Musharraf also imposed widespread curbs on civil and political rights. Soon after the emergency was proclaimed, the government began detaining opposition lawyers, judges and politicians, charging them in some instances under anti-terrorism and other criminal laws and in many others under preventive detention laws. Ultimately, thousands of individuals were detained.[41] Changes to the Army Act authorised the trial of civilians in military tribunals for a wide range of ordinary offences – and with retrospective effect from January 2003. Trials conducted by these tribunals would not be subject to ordinary procedural and evidentiary rules and could be held in secret.[42] Cable operators were immediately pressured to take independent television networks off the air, and existing restrictions on both print and electronic media were expanded, including a controversial government-imposed 'code of conduct'.[43]

C. *Constitution versus 'extraconstitution'*

Musharraf's opponents vigorously resisted his characterisation of the crackdown as involving 'emergency' at all, highlighting – notwithstanding the constitutional terminology – the extraconstitutional nature of his actions. Former prime minister Benazir Bhutto and others immediately charged that Musharraf's actions involved nothing less than 'martial law', a 'coup within a coup' given that Musharraf had originally come to power through extraconstitutional means.[44] Indeed, under the Pakistan

[40] Constitution (Amendment) Order, President's Order No. 5 of 2007 (3 November) (Pakistan Constitution, purporting to amend Article 175); Islamabad High Court (Establishment) Order, President's Order No. 7 of 2007 (14 December); Legal Practitioners and Bar Councils (Amendment) Ordinance 2007 (24 November); see HRW, 'Destroying Legality', at 25–8; I. A. Rehman, 'Undo Emergency First', *Dawn*, 29 February 2008, www.dawn.com/2008/02/29/top11.htm.

[41] HRW, 'Destroying Legality', at 21.

[42] A. Assails, 'Changes in Army Act', *Dawn*, 12 November 2007, www.dawn.com/2007/11/12/top6.htm.

[43] Press, Newspapers, News Agencies and Books Registration (Amendment) Ordinance 2007 (3 November); Pakistan Electronic Media Regulatory Authority (Third Amendment) Ordinance 2007 (3 November); see International Federation of Journalists, 'Emergency in Pakistan' (January 2008), http://asiapacific.ifj.org/assets/docs/111/067/a893f6f-1aaf343.pdf; M. Abbas, 'Media in Chains', *Daily Times*, 3 November 2008, www.dailytimes.com.pk/default.asp?page=2008\11\03\story_3-11-2008_pg3_6.

[44] See, for example, Shamim-ur-Rahman, 'Benazir Calls It Martial Law on Dash Back Home', *Dawn*, 4 November 2007, www.dawn.com/2007/11/04/top6.htm; T. Ali, *The Duel: Pakistan*

Constitution, Musharraf's actions constituted not a legitimate exercise of emergency authority, but an act of treason, punishable by the death penalty.[45]

However, Musharraf and his allies never claimed that the emergency was constitutional. To the contrary, his prime minister matter-of-factly acknowledged its extraconstitutional nature almost as soon as it was imposed.[46] In following this extraconstitutional path, Musharraf replicated a pattern established and refined during previous moments in Pakistan's history, beginning with the country's earliest constitutional crises in the 1950s and proceeding through Musharraf's own 1999 coup.[47] The pattern has typically proceeded in three stages. First, the executive declares a state of emergency or martial law, ostensibly based on an existential or near-existential threat.[48] These exigent circumstances are used to justify displacement of the existing constitution in favour of a parallel, newly fashioned legal framework founded on the emergency declaration

on the Flight Path of American Power (New York: Scribner, 2008), p. 163 (characterising crackdown as a 'coup within a coup'); see also International Crisis Group, 'Winding Back Martial Law in Pakistan' (2007), 2; Amnesty International, 'Pakistan: Fatal Erosion of Human Rights Safeguards Under Emergency' (2007), 3; National Lawyers Guild and Lahore University of Management Sciences, Rule of Law Project, 'Defending Dictatorship: US Foreign Policy and Pakistan's Struggle for Democracy' (2008), 3–4.

45 See Pakistan Constitution, Article 6 (providing that any effort to abrogate or subvert the Constitution 'by use of force or other unconstitutional means' constitutes treason).

46 See Kalhan, '"Emergency" as Institution Laundering'. Government ministers readily acknowledged that the crackdown entailed more than an ordinary constitutional 'emergency', referring to the crackdown from the outset as 'emergency plus'. M. Ahmed, 'Pakistan: The Emergency Plus Edition', *Informed Comment*, 3 November 2007, http://icga.blogspot.com/2007/11/pakistan-emergency-plus-edition.html; A. Hassan, 'Govt Undecided Over Constitutional, Extra-Constitutional Steps', *Dawn*, 3 November 2007, www.dawn.com/2007/11/03/top1.htm.

47 See H. Khan, *Constitutional and Political History of Pakistan* (Karachi: Oxford University Press, 2001); A. Ahsan, 'Why Pakistan Is Not a Democracy', in D. Page (ed.), *Divided By Democracy* (New Delhi: Lotus, 2005), pp. 75–144; Z. K. Maluka, 'Reconstructing the Constitution for a COAS President: Pakistan, 1999 to 2002', in Craig Baxter (ed.), *Pakistan on the Brink: Politics, Economics, and Society* (Karachi: Oxford University Press, 2002), pp. 53–100; P. R. Newberg, *Judging the State: Courts and Constitutional Politics in Pakistan* (Cambridge: Cambridge University Press, 1995); T. Mahmud, 'Praetorianism and Common Law in Post-Colonial Settings: Judicial Responses to Constitutional Breakdowns in Pakistan' (1993) *Utah Law Review* 1225.

48 See, for example, Proclamation of Emergency (2007); see also Proclamation of Emergency (14 October 1999) (Musharraf); Proclamation of Martial Law (5 July 1977) (Zia-ul-Haq); Address by Gen. Yahya Khan (26 March 1969), http://therepublicofrumi.com/archives/69yahya26.htm (announcing imposition of martial law); Proclamation of Martial Law (7 October 1958) (Mirza); Proclamation of Emergency (24 October 1954) (Mohammed).

itself – a regime I refer to as an 'extraconstitution', given its aspirations to function, paradoxically, as the Constitution's legal *doppelgänger*. Fundamentally and self-consciously, the extraconstitution places itself beyond the Constitution's authority, establishing the foundation for a new legal regime that disregards and displaces the Constitution altogether. The justification for the emergency is external to the existing Constitution, and as such, the new regime does not purport to be constrained by the Constitution's limits.

At the same time – and just as self-consciously – the extraconstitution aspires to create the simulacrum[49] of adherence to legality, constitutional norms and existing institutions, as a means of establishing its own authority and, ultimately, acquiescence to its supremacy, if not full legitimacy.[50] As Imtiaz Omar notes, Pakistan's extraconstitutional forms of emergency and martial law resemble 'albeit in a deviant form', constitutional states of emergency, in that such states of exception are 'inaugurated by a proclamation to this effect, and [are] terminated formally'.[51] In more recent iterations of the pattern, the very use of the term 'emergency', rather than 'martial law', also contributes to the appearance of legality.[52] Thus, Musharraf's 2007 emergency proclamation and PCO did not 'abrogate' the Constitution altogether but merely held it 'in abeyance', implying that it later might be restored. Even as the Constitution was suspended, the PCO provided for the Constitution to continue to govern, and therefore

[49] I adapt the use of this term by Bruce Ackerman. B. Ackerman, *We the People: Transformations* (Cambridge, Mass.: Belknap Press, 1998), pp. 269–70; cf. Sujit Choudhry, 'Ackerman's Higher Lawmaking in Comparative Constitutional Perspective: Constitutional Moments as Constitutional Failures?' (2008) 6 *International Journal of Constitutional Law* 193.

[50] See also T. Moustafa and T. Ginsburg, 'Introduction: The Functions of Courts in Authoritarian Politics', in T. Moustafa and T. Ginsburg (eds.), *Rule By Law: The Politics of Courts in Authoritarian Regimes* (Cambridge: Cambridge University Press, 2008), pp. 1–22 at pp. 5–7 (discussing use of courts by authoritarian regimes to 'make up for their questionable legitimacy by preserving judicial institutions that give the image, if not the full effect, of constraints on arbitrary rule'); J. deLisle, 'States of Exception in an Exceptional State: Emergency Powers Law in China' (Chapter 13), this volume, p. 370 (explaining China's use of law to 'authorise and define emergency powers' in part as a means of tapping the 'legitimacy that law holds in society').

[51] Omar, *Emergency Powers and the Courts*, p. 53.

[52] E.g., Maluka, 'Reconstructing the Constitution', p. 55 (arguing that Musharraf characterised the 1999 coup as constituting an 'emergency', rather than martial law, 'to make the military intervention acceptable . . . and to give it a benign political appearance to the outside world'); see M. Neocleous, 'From Martial Law to the War on Terror' (2007) 10 *New Criminal Law Review* 489 at 506 (arguing that authoritarian regimes have increasingly preferred the language of 'emergency powers', which 'better connotes neutrality and necessity', to that of 'martial law').

to guide and constrain government action, 'as nearly as may be' – albeit subject to the enveloping caveats that fundamental rights would be suspended and the executive would claim plenary authority to amend both the PCO and the Constitution as 'deemed expedient'.[53]

Second, the executive seeks judicial validation of the takeover under the 'doctrine of state necessity', which recognises extraconstitutional authority for the executive to take extraordinary action as necessary against existential threats to the state. This doctrine was first articulated by Pakistan's Federal Court in the 1950s, amidst a conflict between the Constituent Assembly, which was poised to ratify Pakistan's first postcolonial constitution, and the Governor-General, who was apparently 'stung by the Assembly's action in curtailing his powers' under that constitution.[54] Declaring that the 'constitutional machinery' of Pakistan's provisional government 'had broken down', the Governor-General proclaimed an emergency and effectively dissolved the Assembly before it could ratify the new Constitution.[55] Subsequent executive and judicial responses deepened the crisis by effectively creating a legal and constitutional vacuum.[56] The Federal Court then sought to resolve the crisis, validating the Governor-General's assertion of emergency powers as justified not by Pakistan's existing legal and constitutional framework, but rather by 'state necessity'.[57]

Since then, through several subsequent extraconstitutional interventions, Pakistan's courts have developed a significant body of jurisprudence elaborating the doctrine of necessity.[58] Given the doctrine's derivation

[53] Proclamation of Emergency (2007); Provisional Constitutional Order (2007); see also Provisional Constitutional Order No. 1 of 1999 (15 October) (Musharraf); Proclamation of Emergency (1999); Provisional Constitutional Order, Chief Martial Law Administrator's Order No. 1 of 1981 (24 March) (Zia-ul-Haq); Laws (Continuance in Force) Order, Chief Martial Law Administrator's Order No. 1 of 1977 (5 July) (Zia-ul-Haq); Provisional Constitutional Order 1969 (4 April) (Yahya Khan); Laws (Continuance in Force) Order 1958 (10 October) (Ayub Khan); see *Governor-General's Reference*, 1955 PLD Fed Ct 435 (advisory opinion endorsing validity of Governor-General's proclamation assuming emergency powers to 'maintain the government . . . in its existing condition' (proclamation quoted in Mahmud, 'Praetorianism and Common Law', at 1236 n. 40)).

[54] Khan, *Constitutional and Political History*, pp. 130–1; see Newberg, *Judging the State*, pp. 39–42. Pakistan had been governed since independence by the colonial-era constitutional framework, with the Constituent Assembly serving both as the body charged with drafting a new constitution and as a provisional legislature and the Federal Court continuing to function as the country's apex court: *ibid.*, pp. 36–8.

[55] Proclamation of Emergency (1954).

[56] *Tamizuddin Khan* v. *Pakistan*, 1955 PLD Fed Ct 240; *Usif Patel* v. *The Crown*, 1955 PLD Fed Ct 387.

[57] *Governor-General's Reference*, 1955 PLD Fed Ct 435.

[58] See, e.g., *Zafar Ali Shah* v. *General Pervez Musharraf*, 2000 PLD S Ct 869; *Begum Nusrat Bhutto* v. *Chief of Army Staff*, 1977 PLD S Ct 657; *Asma Jilani* v. *Punjab*, 1972 PLD

from British common law and colonial law principles concerning the invocation of martial law and emergency, the judiciary's application of this doctrine grafts principles developed in a different context onto a legal regime in which popular sovereignty and written constitutionalism were intended to reign supreme.[59] Thus transplanted, the doctrine has been used to validate extraconstitutional action, giving a judicial stamp of approval to these efforts to wrest control from democratic, legislative institutions.

This second step typically has taken place only after the executive has safely assured the judiciary's loyalty. With courts staffed with judges whose allegiance to the extraconstitution has been assured, there could be little doubt concerning the outcome of any case concerning the extraconstitution's very validity. At times, such loyalty has been assured informally.[60] More recently, loyalty has been assured by formally requiring judges to take fresh oaths of office under the extraconstitution.[61] Notably, however, mimicking existing constitutional forms remains vitally important. Not only does the executive rely upon the Supreme Court as an institution to validate the existing constitution's suspension, but the court itself purports to adjudicate that validity within its existing body of jurisprudence, without sharply distinguishing between constitutional and extraconstitutional norms. As with the extraconstitution's promulgation, creating the simulacrum of constitutionalism, legality and continuity remains centrally important at this second stage of seeking the extraconstitution's validation.

Third, after the emergency period has been terminated, the Constitution is 'revived', ostensibly returning the legal order to some semblance of normalcy. However, contrary to the conventional assumptions underlying emergency powers, this 'normalcy' does not restore the Constitution as

S Ct 139; *State* v. *Dosso*, 1958 PLD S Ct 533; see Newberg, *Judging the State*; Mahmud, 'Praetorianism and Common Law'.

[59] See *Governor-General's Reference*, 1955 PLD Fed Ct, at 478 (describing the doctrine of necessity as constituting 'part of the common law of all civilized States and which every written Constitution of a civilized people takes for granted'); Gross and Ní Aoláin, *Law in Times of Crisis*, pp. 30–5 (discussing principles of necessity governing the imposition of martial law in British common law); Hussain, *Jurisprudence of Emergency*, pp. 106–9 (discussing role of necessity in colonial martial law).

[60] See, for example, A. Jalal, *The State of Martial Rule* (Cambridge: Cambridge University Press, 1990), pp. 192, 202–3 (discussing consultations between the Governor-General and the Chief Justice).

[61] See, for example, Oath of Office (Judges) Order 2007; Oath of Office (Judges) Order 2000; Provisional Constitutional Order 1981; see also Maluka, 'Reconstructing the Constitution', pp. 59–60; S. Nawaz, *Crossed Swords: Pakistan, Its Army, and the Wars Within* (Karachi: Oxford University Press, 2008), p. 363.

it existed before the emergency. Rather, the 'revival' seeks to usher in a 'new normal',[62] completing the transformation from one legal regime to another by assimilating the extraconstitution into that normalised legal order. Thus, when Musharraf purported to 'revive' the Constitution after terminating the emergency in December 2007, he intended the legal and constitutional changes imposed during the emergency period to remain in place permanently.[63]

At this point, two parallel legal regimes directly contend with each other for supremacy: the existing Constitution, now supposedly 'revived', and the extraconstitution, whose very existence, constitutionally speaking, is an act of treason. Accordingly, the emergency's termination does not herald the end of the crisis, but merely marks the passing of that crisis to a new stage. To be sure, the emergency's termination may well restore some measure of normalcy. After Musharraf 'lifted' his emergency in December 2007, for instance, fundamental rights were restored, detainees were released, and parliamentary elections were soon held. However, the incoming parliament that came to power after those elections was immediately handed the challenge of wrangling with Musharraf and other actors over whether the 'revived' Constitution, the extraconstitution or some hybrid would reign legally supreme.[64]

With Pakistan's earlier 'extraconstitutional moments',[65] the parliament convening upon the Constitution's 'revival' has adopted formal constitutional amendments explicitly acquiescing to the changes implemented during the emergency or martial law period and assimilating them into the existing constitutional order.[66] Because of the lingering possibility of treason, these amendments also have typically indemnified the extraconstitutional actions taken during that period.[67] One might characterise such provisions as akin to the kind of indemnity contemplated by

[62] Compare, in the US context, Lawyers Committee for Human Rights, 'Assessing the New Normal: Liberty and Security for the Post-September 11 United States' (2003), www.humanrightsfirst.org/pubs/descriptions/Assessing/AssessingtheNewNormal.pdf, p. i.

[63] See, for example, Rehman, 'Undo Emergency'; Kalhan, '"Emergency" as Institution Laundering'; see also Legal Framework Order, Chief Executive's Order No. 24 of 2002 (Musharraf); Revival of the Constitution 1973 Order, President's Order No. 14 of 1985 (Zia-ul-Haq).

[64] See A. Kalhan, 'The Math of Rollback', *Dorf on Law* (23 February 2008), http://michaeldorf.org/2008/02/math-of-rollback.html.

[65] The term is again adapted from Ackerman; for example, Ackerman, *We the People: Transformations*; cf. Choudhry, 'Ackerman's Higher Lawmaking'.

[66] See Constitution (Seventeenth Amendment) Act 2003; Constitution (Eighth Amendment) Act 1985.

[67] See Pakistan Constitution, Articles 270A, 270AA; cf. A. Harding, 'Emergency Powers with a Moustache: Special Powers, Military Rule and Evolving Constitutionalism in Thailand'

A. V. Dicey, transforming an illegal act into something legally justified, and advocated by Oren Gross as a means of tolerating the 'little wrong' of illegality in the short term to achieve the 'great[er] right' of 'preserv[ing] not only . . . the constitutional order, but also . . . its most fundamental principles and tenets' in the long term.[68] For Gross, this *ex post* indemnification depends upon effective institutions of accountability when the emergency has ended. In Pakistan, by contrast, Parliament's *ex post* acquiescence has typically been attained through more dubious means.[69]

III. Constraining extraconstitutionality

As it has developed, Pakistan's extraconstitution carries ambiguous legal status. From the internal perspective of the existing Constitution, the extraconstitution rather plainly is *ultra vires*, resembling what David Dyzenhaus, following Johan Steyn, calls a 'legal black hole': a 'zone in which officials can act unconstrained by [the Constitution] and [which] in advance declares what they do to be legal', and which 'declares . . . that official decisions are by definition both necessitous and made in good faith'.[70] To the extent that the extraconstitution displaces the existing legal order, it involves an exercise of 'constituent' power. At the same time, from the internal perspective of the extraconstitution itself, the extraconstitution purports to be governed by a set of quasi-legal norms, deriving from the Supreme Court's jurisprudence on the doctrine of necessity and Parliament's traditional practice of adopting amendments that assimilate the extraconstitution into the Constitution and indemnify officials from liability for their extraconstitutional actions.[71] The aspiration to maintain some *semblance* of legality remains, and the extraconstitution's justification even may be understood as resting on assumptions akin to

(Chapter 11), this volume, p. 297 (noting routine grants of immunity for military coup leaders in Thailand).

68 O. Gross, 'Chaos and Rules: Should Responses to Violent Crises Always Be Constitutional?' (2003) 112 *Yale Law Journal* 1011 at 1024; Gross and Ní Aoláin, *Law in Times of Crisis*, pp. 130–2.

69 See, for example, Khan, *Constitutional and Political History*, pp. 674–7 (discussing adoption of the Eighth Amendment); H. Khan, *Constitutional and Political History of Pakistan*, rev. abridged edn (Karachi: Oxford University Press, 2005), pp. 501–4 (discussing adoption of the Seventeenth Amendment); A. R. Wilder, 'Elections 2002: Legitimizing the Status Quo', in Baxter (ed.), *Pakistan on the Brink*, pp. 101–30.

70 D. Dyzenhaus, 'Schmitt v. Dicey: Are States of Emergency Inside or Outside the Legal Order?' (2007) 27 *Cardozo Law Review* 2005 at 2032; see J. Steyn, 'Guantanamo Bay: The Legal Black Hole' (2004) 53 *International and Comparative Law Quarterly* 1.

71 See Agamben, *State of Exception*, pp. 28–9.

the 'conservative' premises underlying conventional understandings of 'emergency' power.

Of course, within both Parliament and the Supreme Court, those extra-constitutional customs and quasi-legal norms have developed under the gravitational pull of the extraconstitution's 'legal black hole'. From the perspective of constitutionalism, therefore, Pakistan's early experiences with the extraconstitution have not helped to 'establish legality' or 'preserve legality', in the manner discussed by Victor Ramraj, but have instead established a template and body of jurisprudence, akin to US Supreme Court Justice Robert Jackson's famous 'loaded weapon', which have repeatedly enabled actions *undermining* legality.[72] Indeed, Pakistan's doctrine of necessity has proven remarkably durable. Since courts and lawyers have not sharply distinguished between decisions rendered under the Constitution and those under the extraconstitution, it has been difficult to marginalise and discredit this extraconstitutional jurisprudence as illegitimate.[73] As a result, the jurisprudence under Pakistan's extraconstitution has been normalised and assimilated into the mainstream of Pakistani law to a considerable extent – just as the institutional role of the Pakistani Army in civilian affairs itself has become normalised.[74] Ironically, while concern over precisely this kind of 'normalization of the extraordinary' leads Gross to favour an emergency powers regime founded on extralegal measures – to keep 'the ordinary legal system clean and distinct from the dirty and messy reality of emergency' – Pakistan's experience demonstrates that extralegality itself can be normalised in much the same fashion.[75] As one Supreme Court justice noted during arguments in the litigation over Musharraf's

[72] Ramraj, Chapter 2; *Korematsu* v. *United States*, 323 US 214, 243–4 (1944) (Jackson J, dissenting) ('[O]nce a judicial opinion . . . rationalizes the Constitution to show that the Constitution sanctions such an [emergency] order, the Court for all time has validated the principle. . . . The principle then lies about like a loaded weapon ready for the hand of any authority that can bring forward a plausible claim of an urgent need.').

[73] As a superficial example, Supreme Court cases arising under the extraconstitution have been published in the same case reporters as the Court's constitutional case law, helping to assimilate that extraconstitutional case law into the broader stream of Supreme Court jurisprudence more generally.

[74] See Newberg, *Judging the State*, pp. 172–9 (discussing the High Court's enforcement and implementation of the Supreme Court decision in the *Nusrat Bhutto* case); M. Aziz, *Military Control in Pakistan* (London: Routledge, 2008), p. 2 (arguing that the military's 'relatively "small . . ."' involvement in civil administration after independence eventually became 'institutionalized . . . [and] very difficult to reverse').

[75] Gross, 'Chaos and Rules', at 1089, 1132; see D. Cole, 'Judging the Next Emergency: Judicial Review and Individual Rights in Times of Crisis' (2003) 101 *Michigan Law Review* 2565 at 2585–94 (arguing that Gross's model, 'while lacking the attributes of the formal legal process, would nonetheless generate a more informal common law of extralegal emergency

eligibility to be re-elected president, 'We keep on burying the . . . doctrine of necessity but it keeps haunting us.'[76] In this context, the extent to which Musharraf closely drew upon Pakistan's long-standing pattern is striking, but not particularly surprising, especially given the potential for path dependence in precedent-based, common law systems.[77] Indeed, Pakistan's jurisprudence on necessity has shaped the prospects for constitutionalism and legality well beyond Pakistan's borders, as courts have looked to Pakistan's case law for persuasive guidance in countries such as Uganda, Rhodesia, Seychelles, Grenada and Lesotho.[78]

At the same time, Musharraf's 2007 emergency illustrates the possibility of at least some constraints upon assertions of extraconstitutional power. What distinguishes Musharraf's 2007 emergency from Pakistan's earlier experiences is not a greater commitment by the regime to heed legality-enforcing and abuse-constraining modalities, but rather the degree of resistance in defence of constitutionalism at each stage of that process. While such constraints may find their justification in principles of legality, the manner in which they operate appears largely non-legal in nature.[79]

First, in Pakistan's earlier extraconstitutional experiences, the executive's principal targets have been the legislature and its elected politicians, leading to greater success in getting the judiciary to accept and validate the extraconstitution by invoking the doctrine of necessity. In 2007, however, the judiciary itself was the principal target of Musharraf's emergency and offered unprecedented resistance from the outset. Indeed, before Musharraf even was able to implement and enforce his emergency proclamation and PCO, a seven-judge bench of the Supreme Court, acting under the authority of the existing Constitution, enjoined Musharraf's emergency and ordered all civilian and military officials not to act under the PCO or

authorities'). For a different critique of Gross in light of the experiences of postcolonial India and Pakistan, see A. Z. Huq, 'Uncertain Law in Uncertain Times: Emergency Powers and Lessons from South Asia' (2006) 13 *Constellations* 89 at 99–102.

76 N. Iqbal, 'SC Urged to Bury Doctrine of Necessity', *Dawn* (23 October 2007), www.dawn.com/2007/10/23/top3.htm.

77 See O. A. Hathaway, 'Path Dependence in the Law: The Course and Pattern of Legal Change in a Common Law System' (2001) 86 *Iowa Law Review* 101; cf. Gross, 'Chaos and Rules', at 1089.

78 T. Mahmud, 'Jurisprudence of Successful Treason: Coup d'Etat and Common Law' (1994) 27 *Cornell International Law Journal* 49 at 57–65, 82–93.

79 See, for example, M. Tushnet, 'The Political Constitution of Emergency Powers', in V. V. Ramraj (ed.), *Emergencies and the Limits of Legality* (Cambridge: Cambridge University Press, 2008), pp. 145–55.

administer new oaths of office to any judges.[80] Ultimately, over sixty High Court and Supreme Court justices, including the Chief Justice of Pakistan, refused or were not asked to take new oaths of office under the PCO, a number unprecedented in Pakistan's history.[81]

Second, past extraconstitutional takeovers have been effective, at least in the short term, at coercing opposition and garnering some measure of acquiescence from the public.[82] Musharraf's emergency, by contrast, was ineffectual in suppressing opposition. The institutions that support and reinforce constitutional ideals in Pakistan – though still precarious – had grown stronger than in the past, and certainly appear to have been stronger than in other Asian countries facing comparable situations. By the time Musharraf declared the emergency, Pakistan's civil society already had nurtured significant anti-Musharraf resistance, which only grew stronger in the face of his crackdown. The lawyers' movement and the broader anti-emergency movement it triggered were facilitated by the emergence of a vibrant, transnational electronic media, including private television channels, the Internet and mobile telephone communications, which the regime hindered but could not stop altogether.[83] These domestic developments were reinforced and supported by international pressure from both governments and civil society institutions, such as bar associations.[84] In this context, the regime's ability and willingness to crack down on opponents may have been more limited than in the past.

Finally, the elections held following termination of the emergency proved to be more 'free and fair' than expected, delivering a resounding

[80] The Court's order is reprinted at 'SC Bench Verdict over Emergency', *The News*, 3 November 2007, http://thenews.com.pk/updates.asp?id=31604. The post-purge 'supreme court' assembled by Musharraf under the extraconstitution later deemed this order a nullity, invoking the doctrine of necessity to validate Musharraf's emergency: *Wajihuddin Ahmed* v. *Chief Election Comm'r, Islamabad*, 2007 PLD S Ct 25, declared void *ab initio*, *Sindh High Court Bar Ass'n* v. *Pakistan*, 2009 PLD SCt, www.supremecourt.gov.pk/web/page.asp?id=655.

[81] HRW, 'Destroying Legality', at 19.

[82] See, for example, A. Siddiqa, *Military Inc.: Inside Pakistan's Military Economy* (London: Pluto, 2007), pp. 84–8 (discussing measures taken by the Zia regime to consolidate power); *ibid.* p. 98 (discussing the Musharraf regime's 'subtle' tactics to 'penetrate the political system and the society').

[83] See Shafqat, 'The Movement to Restore' (discussing the lawyers' movement); Abbas, 'Media in Chains' (discussing the journalists' resistance to emergency); above, notes 12–17 and accompanying text.

[84] See, for example, 'NYC Bar Association Denounces Suspension of Pakistan's Constitution' (7 November 2007), www.nycbar.org/PressRoom/PressRelease/2007_1107.htm; P. Webster and D. Byers, 'Pakistan Suspended From Commonwealth Over Musharraf Emergency Rule', *The Times* (UK), 23 November 2007, www.timesonline.co.uk/tol/news/world/asia/article2925847.ece.

rebuke to Musharraf and bringing to power a government disinclined to affirmatively validate the extraconstitution or to affirmatively indemnify Musharraf.[85] Perhaps anticipating parliamentary hostility, Musharraf promulgated, before lifting the emergency, constitutional amendments that purported to indemnify himself, denying any need for parliamentary action at all.[86] This widely ridiculed attempt at self-indemnification departed even from Pakistan's traditional pattern, which has typically contemplated some *ex post* role for Parliament, however timid or irregular, before full assimilation of the extraconstitution into the normal constitutional order.

One should not be overly eager to celebrate the potential effectiveness of these non-legal constraints upon extraconstitutionality.[87] Indeed, despite its unprecedented popular mandate to roll back Musharraf's extraconstitution – especially to reinstate the judges ousted by Musharraf – even the government that came to power following Pakistan's 2008 elections found itself stymied by the challenge of exercising meaningful constraints upon the extraconstitution by rolling back the changes wrought during the emergency. While Musharraf himself was eventually forced to resign in the wake of the elections, the new government proved to be deeply reluctant to summarily reverse Musharraf's extraconstitution as illegitimate, perhaps hoping to avoid a confrontation with the Army or seeing some merit or convenience in keeping some of Musharraf's legal and institutional changes.[88] At the same time, the new government also failed

[85] See J. Perlez and C. Gall, 'In Pakistan, Musharraf's Party Accepts Defeat', *New York Times*, 20 February 2008, www.nytimes.com/2008/02/20/world/asia/20pakistan.htm.

[86] Constitution (Amendment) Order, s. 6 (purporting to add Article 270AAA to the Constitution).

[87] Cf. Cole, 'Judging the Next Emergency', at 2585–94 (criticising recognition of extraconstitutional emergency powers in part for their lack of meaningful constraints).

[88] C. Rondeaux, 'Musharraf Exits, But Uncertainty Remains', *Washington Post*, 19 August 2008, www.washingtonpost.com/wp-dyn/content/article/2008/08/18/AR2008081800418.html; M. A. Noorani, 'Nov 3 Actions Cannot Be Undone: Naek', *The News*, 28 August 2008, http://thenews.jang.com.pk/top_story_detail.asp?Id=16877 (discussing the opinion of the PPP-led government's law minister that Parliament 'could not reverse' Musharraf's extraconstitutional actions because they had been 'validated' by the Supreme Court constituted under Musharraf's PCO); see also Abbas, 'Media in Chains' (noting the failure of the PPP-led government to reverse Musharraf's 'code of conduct' for electronic media). Soon after Musharraf's resignation, the new government began to return many of the ousted judges to the bench. However, those judges were not fully reinstated, but in effect were newly 'reappointed', after being asked to take new oaths of office. Other judges, including Chief Justice Chaudhry, were not immediately reappointed in this manner, although following renewed pressure from the lawyers' movement and opposition politicians, Chaudhry ultimately was restored to his position in March 2009. By the same token, the government declined to remove or discipline judges who illegally cooperated

to take any affirmative steps explicitly endorsing Musharraf's transformation in whole or in part, leaving the state of Pakistan's constitutional order exceedingly muddled. Even under arguably the most favourable circumstances for constitutionalism that Pakistan has seen in its history, for well over a year the government risked affording *de facto* validity to Musharraf's extraconstitution (and necessarily, *de facto* indemnity for his actions) without the considered, *ex post* decision concerning accountability and validity that Dicey or Gross would require – acting only much later when its hand was forced by a landmark Supreme Court judgment invalidating Musharraf's emergency.[89]

IV. Constitution as extraconstitution

Pakistan's experiences raise questions concerning the difference that constitutionality makes in this context. Had Musharraf instead imposed a *constitutional* emergency, would that have been more benign or less troubling than his extraconstitutional crackdown? The answer implicit in some critiques of Musharraf's actions is yes – a perspective consistent with the views of scholars who favour 'constitutional accommodation', in the form of explicit articulation of emergency powers and constraints upon those powers in a written constitution's text.[90]

At one level, the critics' implication is unremarkable, for it hardly strains reason to argue that from the perspective of constitutionalism and legality, forcible displacement of the Constitution in favour of a parallel legal regime might be troubling, especially given the foundation such a move can create for future extraconstitutional actions and the extent to which non-legal constraints have tended to fail.[91] The resort to extraconstitutional means also might undermine more than the Constitution, for the tolerance of large projects undermining legality might create a space in which a range of other, smaller acts flouting the rule of law are also tolerated.[92] Moreover, as discussed above, the exercise of constitutional emergency powers at least formally is subject to some defined

with or were appointed under Musharraf's extraconstitution until spurred to take action by the Supreme Court: see *Sindh High Court Bar Ass'n*.

89 *Sindh High Court Bar Ass'n*; Syed Shoaib Hasan, 'Pakistan Emergency Judges Removed', *BBC News*, 3 August 2009, http://news.bbc.co.uk/2/hi/south-asia/8182314.stm.

90 Gross and Ní Aoláin, *Law in Times of Crisis*, pp. 35–66; see also A. H. Y. Chen, 'Emergency Powers, Constitutionalism and Legal Transplants: The East Asian Experience' (Chapter 3), this volume.

91 See, for example, Choudhry, 'Ackerman's Higher Lawmaking', at 200 ('[D]ispensing with the rules governing constitutional amendment can subvert the goals of constitutionalism itself.').

92 Gross and Ní Aoláin, *Law in Times of Crisis*, pp. 143–5.

limits. While the extraconstitution also purports to have limits, emerging from both case law and customary practice, these constraints might not appear as explicit or robust as the constraints found in the text of a written constitution[93] – especially given the apparently self-justifying character of the extraconstitution's means of validation.

At the same time, the comfort given by constitutional text can prove illusory. By pushing the constitutional order to the outermost frontiers of legality, the exercise of constitutional emergency powers can itself approximate and create the simulacrum of extraconstitutionality, what David Dyzenhaus has termed a legal 'grey hole'.[94] India's experience during the 1970s under Indira Gandhi illustrates how the use of constitutional emergency powers can render the distinction between constitution and extraconstitution largely formal.[95] While Gandhi initially came to power with tremendous popular support, she eventually faced mounting opposition and unrest, along with an escalating conflict with the Supreme Court over judicial independence. Like Musharraf, Gandhi also faced the prospect of an unfavourable judicial decision threatening her eligibility to remain in office. In response, on 26 June 1975, Gandhi declared a state of emergency under constitutional provisions that at the time, like the similar provisions of the Pakistan Constitution, authorised the executive to exercise emergency powers if a present or imminent threat of war, external aggression or internal disturbance endangered the country's security.[96] Gandhi went through the motions of justifying the emergency in these constitutional terms, asserting that 'agitations have... [led] to violent incidents' and that '[c]ertain persons have... incit[ed] our armed forces to mutiny and

[93] For example, Chen, Chapter 3, pp. 61–2.

[94] Dyzenhaus, 'Schmitt v. Dicey', at 2018 (defining a legal 'grey hole' as 'a legal space in which there are some legal constraints on executive action . . . but the constraints are so insubstantial that they pretty well permit government to do as it pleases').

[95] On Gandhi's emergency, see G. Austin, *Working a Democratic Constitution* (New Delhi: Oxford University Press, 1999), pp. 293–390; Iyer, *States of Emergency*, pp. 152–205; Omar, *Emergency Powers and the Courts*, pp. 97–111; Kalhan, 'Colonial Continuities', at 137–41; L. I. Rudolph and S. H. Rudolph, *In Pursuit of Lakshmi: The Political Economy of the Indian State* (Chicago: University of Chicago Press, 1987), pp. 103–24; R. Jethmalani, 'Commentary: The Indian Crisis' (1976) 23 *Wayne Law Review* 247; R. L. Kidder, 'Law and Political Crisis: An Assessment of the Indian Legal System's Potential Role' (1976) 16 *Asian Survey* 879.

[96] Indian Constitution, Articles 352–60; G. Subramanium, 'Emergency Provisions Under the Indian Constitution', in B. N. Kirpal *et al.* (eds.) *Supreme But Not Infallible: Essays in Honour of the Supreme Court of India* (New Delhi: Oxford University Press, 2000), pp. 134, 136. A state of emergency had already been in effect in India since 1971, arising from the war over Bangladesh's secession from Pakistan – even though that conflict had ended soon after the emergency had been declared: Iyer, *States of Emergency*, pp. 131–41.

our police to rebel'.[97] However, Gandhi's real motivation was to maintain the political status quo and advance her substantive agenda. The declaration came soon after a High Court decision invalidating her election to Parliament, on account of allegedly corrupt practices, and temporarily barring her from public office.[98] Gandhi herself later acknowledged that the emergency was designed to prevent 'subver[sion of] the government's progressive programmes'.[99]

Gandhi's exceptionally severe crackdown, which continued until early 1977, far overshadowed the extraconstitutional but comparatively mild measures imposed by Musharraf in 2007. As provided by the Indian Constitution, the emergency automatically suspended several fundamental rights and authorised the central executive to suspend judicial enforcement of others. Ultimately, over 111,000 individuals were arrested and detained, and publications were subjected to sweeping censorship and prepublication review. Gandhi also invoked emergency authority to impose direct central government rule in the two states with opposition-led governments, bringing all state governments within her control.[100]

Gandhi's use of these measures to sideline would-be challengers – within civil society and opposition parties, but also within her own Congress party – created an environment that facilitated, by formally constitutional means, the same kind of legal and institutional transformation that her counterparts in Pakistan have pursued extraconstitutionally.[101] Soon after the emergency was declared, Parliament adopted a series of constitutional amendments designed to insulate both the emergency and Gandhi's contested election from legal challenge.[102] A divided Supreme Court infamously acquiesced. While the court invalidated a provision purporting to eliminate judicial review of election decisions involving the Prime Minister, it upheld the validity of her election, and refused to scrutinise Gandhi's emergency declaration or suspension of habeas corpus.[103] In providing

97 Iyer, *States of Emergency*, p. 159 (quoting 26 June 1975 address).
98 See *ibid.*, pp. 153–4.
99 Austin, *Working a Democratic Constitution*, pp. 314–19 (discussing the Indira Gandhi election case); *ibid.*, pp. 307–8 (discussing Gandhi's justifications for the emergency).
100 Kalhan, 'Colonial Continuities', at 137.
101 See J. A. Lukas, 'India Is As Indira Does', *New York Times Magazine*, 4 April 1976, at SM5.
102 Austin, *Working a Democratic Constitution*, pp. 319–25 (discussing the Thirty-Eighth, Thirty-Ninth, Fortieth and Forty-First Amendments).
103 *A.D.M. Jabalpur* v. *Shukla*, AIR 1976 SC 1207; *Indira Gandhi* v. *Raj Narain*, AIR 1975 SC 2299; see A. Thiruvengadam, 'Asian Judiciaries and Emergency Powers: Reasons for Optimism?' (Chapter 17), this volume, p. 492; J. K. Krishnan, 'Scholarly Discourse, Public Perceptions, and the Cementing of Norms: The Case of the Indian Supreme Court and a

legal cover for Gandhi's emergency, the court played a functionally comparable role to that played time and again by Pakistan's Supreme Court in applying the doctrine of necessity, validating extraordinary measures whose legitimacy was deeply contested.

With opponents detained, publications censored and the courts quiescent, Gandhi proceeded to consolidate her political position by seeking more far-reaching changes to the legal and institutional landscape – the functional equivalent, in constitutional form, of a Pakistan-style extra-constitution. Gandhi's transformative intentions, like Musharraf's, were strikingly open. Gandhi insisted that 'India can never go back to what it was',[104] and by late 1975, she and her associates had commenced an active effort to effect a fundamental and permanent transformation to the constitutional order.[105] One theatre in that campaign was the Supreme Court itself, where the government unsuccessfully sought reversal of the 'basic structure' doctrine that the court had expounded, over Gandhi's strenuous resistance, since the early 1970s.[106] Gandhi found greater success in Parliament, which in November 1976 adopted the Forty-Second Amendment, a comprehensive package of changes – so sweeping, argue Lloyd Rudolph and Susanne Rudolph, as to be '[t]antamount to a new constitution'[107] – that, among other things, gave the Constitution's directive principles precedence over its fundamental rights provisions and altered the basic structural balance of powers between the branches of government.[108]

Plea for Research' (2007) 29 *Journal of Appellate Practice and Process* 255 at 272; Austin, *Working a Democratic Constitution*, pp. 323–4.

104 W. Borders, 'Mrs. Gandhi Is Cleared, but Questions Cloud the Future', *New York Times*, 10 November 1975, at 2; see also D. Binder, 'Permanent Shift for India Is Seen', *New York Times*, 10 August 1975, at 5 (noting US officials' view that 'Mrs. Gandhi will [not] permit a return to the pre-June 25 conditions'); Omar, *Emergency Powers and the Courts*, p. 129 (characterising Gandhi's emergency as 'attempted "revolution"').

105 For example, W. Borders, 'Mrs. Gandhi Gives New Hints of Plans to Alter Constitution', *New York Times*, 28 December 1975, at 3; Lukas, 'India Is As Indira Does'; Austin, *Working a Democratic Constitution*, pp. 348–69. Like Musharraf and his predecessors, Gandhi also sought to manipulate the personnel within the upper judiciary, formulating plans to transfer as many as seventy judges to different High Courts. Ultimately, sixteen High Court judges were transferred without their consent: Austin, *Working a Democratic Constitution*, pp. 344–7; Kidder, 'Law and Political Crisis', at 891–2.

106 Krishnan, 'Scholarly Discourse', at 273; Austin, *Working a Democratic Constitution*, pp. 328–33; see R. Ramachandran, 'The Supreme Court and the Basic Structure Doctrine', in Kirpal *et al.* (eds.) *Supreme But Not Infallible*, pp. 107–33.

107 Rudolph and Rudolph, *In Pursuit of Lakshmi*, p. 115.

108 See Iyer, *States of Emergency*, pp. 160–77; Austin, *Working a Democratic Constitution*, pp. 370–90; W. Borders, 'India's New Order Has Look of Permanence', *New York Times*, 8 November 1976, at 1.

Effective resistance to Gandhi's emergency came only after it formally was over – and not from constitutional safeguards, but from the people of India. Gandhi lifted her emergency in early 1977, and as with Musharraf, the subsequent elections brought a decisive repudiation, as opposition parties harnessed pent-up anti-Gandhi sentiment to win over two-thirds of all parliamentary seats.[109] But with Gandhi having implemented major legal and institutional changes during the emergency, the incoming government, led by the Janata party, faced similar questions to those confronted by post-emergency governments in Pakistan over whether, how and to what extent those changes should be rolled back. The Janata government's 'first great substantive issue', notes Granville Austin, 'was whether the Forty-second Amendment should be repealed entirely with one stroke of the pen, or its provisions repealed selectively'.[110] While leading advocates favoured a 'one-line repeal' – on the ground that the emergency's changes, in the words of Supreme Court lawyer Soli Sorabjee, 'had been conceived in sin' – the government instead conducted a more elaborate, year-long amendment exercise, concluding that some provisions in the Forty-second Amendment and other laws should be repealed but others 'were worth keeping'.[111]

The challenge faced by the Janata government closely resembles that faced by Pakistan's post-emergency government over whether Musharraf's extraconstitutional changes should be deemed illegitimate and summarily reversed, or instead be afforded some modicum of legal respect and addressed affirmatively, through an Act of Parliament or a constitutional amendment 'package'. Like Pakistan's post-emergency government, the strife-ridden Janata government struggled in its effort to roll back Gandhi's emergency. While the Janata government eventually adopted constitutional amendments affirmatively rolling back much of the emergency's legacy – and even incorporating additional safeguards to constrain future use of emergency powers – significant parts of the emergency's constitutional legacy survived.[112] The new government also moved fitfully to reverse other features of the emergency, such as the use of preventive

[109] See Venkatesan, 'Pakistan 2008, India 1977'; Kalhan, 'Colonial Continuities'.

[110] Austin, *Working a Democratic Constitution*, p. 410.

[111] *Ibid.*, p. 418 (quoting Soli Sorabjee and noting views of Law Minister Shanti Bhushan); *ibid.*, pp. 432–3 (discussing preventive detention statutes).

[112] See, for example, J. N. Kasibhatla, 'Constituting the Exception: Law, Literature, and the State of Emergency in Postcolonial India', unpublished PhD dissertation, Duke University (2005), pp. 126–8 (describing the Janata government's attempt to roll back the emergency as 'hopelessly incomplete').

detention, encroachments upon judicial independence and expansion of central government power.[113]

The experiences of Pakistan and India demonstrate that non-legal factors can loom large under both constitutional and extraconstitutional emergency powers regimes. When political opposition, legislatures, the judiciary or civil society institutions are sufficiently strong and independent, as to some extent was the case in Pakistan during Musharraf's emergency, there may be real limits on the executive's exercise of extraconstitutional emergency powers. By the same token, the absence of strong political and institutional counterweights can render ineffectual the formal limits on emergency powers drawn up in a written constitution.[114] If Musharraf had greater political strength – and had the judiciary and civil society offered less resistance – he might have been able to accomplish many of his objectives by exercising constitutional emergency powers, as Gandhi had done before him in India. In either case, post-emergency governments may find themselves confronting similar challenges in deciding whether or how to roll back or reconcile themselves to the legacy of emergency, whether constitutional or extraconstitutional.

V. The colonial period and its legacy

What factors explain these continuities in the experiences of India and Pakistan with emergency powers? It may be tempting to understand these experiences simply as illustrations of the abuse of authority, failure in constitutional design or the lack of an established culture of accountability, and nothing more. To be sure, these and other explanations might well be important.[115] However, to understand the use of emergency powers

[113] Austin, *Working a Democratic Constitution*, pp. 431–49; Kalhan, 'Colonial Continuities', at 140–1.

[114] Cf. Ramraj, Chapter 2, p. 54 (acknowledging this importance of 'informal means of controlling excesses of state power').

[115] For example, in the aftermath of Gandhi's emergency, the Janata government amended the Constitution to narrow and constrain the exercise of emergency powers: Kalhan, 'Colonial Continuities', at 139. No subsequent government has resorted to the constitution's nation-wide emergency provisions; in the wake of Gandhi's emergency, the political costs of doing so would probably be considerable: Thiruvengadam, Chapter 17, p. 475. One therefore might fairly argue that through its own constitutional evolution, India has managed to place a meaningful combination of legal and non-legal constraints on emergency powers. See L. H. Tribe and P. O. Gudridge, 'The Anti-Emergency Constitution' (2004) 113 *Yale Law Journal* 1801 at 1846–50. As Thiruvengadam notes, however, such an argument does not account for the myriad ways in which emergency-like powers, such as preventive detention and anti-terrorism laws, continue to play an important role largely free from

in postcolonial India and Pakistan – both constitutional and extraconstitutional – their shared origins in the British colonial state must also be considered. Ayesha Jalal has discussed how the 'bureaucratic authoritarianism' of the colonial state 'remained largely intact' in both India and Pakistan at independence, rendering it 'difficult at the very onset [of independence] to establish the principle of legislative supremacy over the executive'.[116] While it is not possible to develop a complete account here, no less than the famed 'steel frame' of the colonial bureaucracy, the inherited legal framework of colonial constitutionalism – with its prominent place for emergency and emergency-like powers – has contributed to creating the challenge of fully establishing legality and legislative primacy.

Far from treating emergency powers simply as a 'conservative' institution to be used in response to a temporary but severe crisis – in the sense conventionally associated with emergency powers – the British incorporated a broad range of exceptional laws and institutions into the very heart of the colonial state, ensuring their availability in a variety of forms both within and outside formal 'emergencies'.[117] Beginning in 1861, the colonial state's framework statutes granted the executive authority to legislate outside normal lawmaking processes by unilaterally issuing emergency 'ordinances' to ensure the 'peace and good government' of India.[118] The colonial state also invoked emergency powers during periods of heightened crisis, such as the two world wars, and at times imposed martial law to address perceived threats to law and order, most notably in Punjab following the Amritsar Massacre of 1919.[119]

As the colonial state increasingly faced Indian demands for democratic self-government, the British understood themselves to be facing a dilemma: how to 'liberalize their power while still retaining control'.[120] To resolve that distinctively colonial quandary, the British sought to implement a form of 'constitutional autocracy', a governing framework that would allow for consultation with Indian representatives, to inform the colonial state's policies, but only in an advisory capacity that would leave

these emerging constraints (Thiruvengadam, Chapter 17, pp. 475–6); Kalhan, 'Colonial Continuities'.

116 Jalal, *Democracy and Authoritarianism*, p. 18.

117 Iyer, *States of Emergency*, pp. 67–75; Kalhan, 'Colonial Continuities', at 126–31.

118 Kalhan, 'Colonial Continuities', at 126.

119 *Ibid.*; see T. R. Metcalf, *Ideologies of the Raj*, pp. 229–30 (Cambridge: Cambridge University Press, 1994) (discussing 1919 martial law); Hussain, *Jurisprudence of Emergency*, pp. 99–131 (discussing evolution of martial law principles in Britain and its colonies).

120 V. P. Menon, *The Transfer of Power in India* (Princeton: Princeton University Press, 1957), p. 7.

the executive with sweeping powers. Thus, as early as 1911, a colonial official advised London that in addressing Indian demands for democratic self-government, 'the question will be how this devolution of power can be conceded without impairing the supreme authority of the Governor-General in Council'.[121]

Emergency powers became central to this discourse of quasi-democratic governance. As Omar explains, framework statutes governing the colonies 'regularly linked the establishment of representative institutions with the reservation of special "emergency" powers to the Representative of the Crown', in an effort to reconcile 'the doctrinal inconsistency between the notions of local representative government patterned on the British model, and the needs of centralised, imperial control'.[122] Indeed, this enhanced role for exceptional laws and institutions only became more aggressive as the British gradually involved Indians more directly in 'responsible government'.[123] The colonial state backed away from the frontal use of martial law and the army, which were understood to have 'widened the distance between India and England', but increasingly relied upon emergency powers and civilian forces such as the armed police, establishing a regime that D. A. Low has termed 'civil martial law'.[124]

Thus, a central purpose of colonial-era emergency powers was neither exclusively to 'establish legality' nor to 'preserve legality', though in some circumstances such powers might indeed have been used to advance those purposes. Rather, the availability of emergency powers was also crucial to ensuring colonial executive supremacy over even the limited space established during the decades preceding independence for democratic participation. For the colonial state, democratic self-governance *itself* was understood as a potential threat as dangerous as war, rebellion or internal disturbance. The nature of the emergency powers conferred upon the colonial state reflected that understanding. For example, in addition to authorising the Governor-General to declare a state of emergency

[121] Quoted in *ibid.*, pp. 12–13. [122] Omar, *Emergency Powers and the Courts*, p. 13.

[123] See Kalhan, 'Colonial Continuities', at 111, 130. Such an approach also characterised the emergency and reserve powers frameworks established in other British colonies. K. Y. L. Tan, 'From Myanmar to Manila: A Brief Study of Emergency Powers in Southeast Asia' (Chapter 6), this volume, pp. 151, 153–63.

[124] Metcalf, *Ideologies*, p. 229; Kalhan, 'Colonial Continuities', at 130 (quoting Low). This shift from martial law to emergency powers may be understood as part of a broader trend, in which governments have sought to 'liberalize' martial law so that its 'key practices . . . [could] be carried out under a conceptual form more easily defended on liberal terms': Neocleous, 'From Martial Law to the War on Terror', at 490.

in the event of war or internal disturbance,[125] and authorising both the Governor-General and provincial governors to assume the executive functions of government to address threats to 'peace and tranquillity', the Government of India Act of 1935 also authorised the Governor-General and provincial governors to supersede the central and provincial legislatures and govern by ordinance upon a declaration that the government 'could not be carried on in accordance with the [Act's] provisions'.[126] The 1935 Act also maintained the Governor-General's authority to legislate by ordinance even during non-emergency periods.[127]

The postcolonial constitutions and legal systems in both India and Pakistan inherited these understandings. The legislation conferring independence provided that the 1935 Act would continue to serve as the provisional constitution in both India and Pakistan until their respective Constituent Assemblies had approved new constitutions, and in both countries, the new constitutions that ultimately were adopted drew extensively from the colonial constitutional framework.[128] The influence of the colonial framework was particularly important in shaping the emergency powers provisions in the two countries' constitutions.[129] Both countries have preserved versions of the colonial executive's authority to legislate by ordinance and supersede legislative authority, and in both countries such authority has been extensively used to supersede elected state and provincial legislatures. In Pakistan, this executive authority has been extended even further than originally contemplated, with the amendment of the Constitution to confer the President with near-plenary authority under Article 58(2)(b) to dissolve Parliament, and as noted above, the legal principles underlying Pakistan's extraconstitutional 'doctrine of state necessity' also derived from British colonial and common law.[130]

Certainly, the adoption of emergency and emergency-like powers in both India and Pakistan can be justified on grounds consistent with modern constitutional premises – after all, many modern constitutions

[125] Government of India Act 1935, 25 and 26 Geo. 5, s. 102; see Iyer, *States of Emergency*, pp. 71–3.

[126] Government of India Act, 1935, ss. 45, 93.

[127] *Ibid.*, ss. 42–4.

[128] Indian Independence Act 1947, s. 8(1)–(2); M. C. Setalvad, *The Common Law in India*, 2nd edn (Bombay: N. M. Tripathi, 1970), pp. 177–82 (India); Khan, *Constitutional and Political History* (2001 edition), pp. 166–7, 486–87 (Pakistan).

[129] See Iyer, *States of Emergency*, at 80–102; Khan, *Constitutional and Political History* (2001 edition), pp. 188–92, 502–3; above, notes 54–9 and accompanying text.

[130] See Kalhan, 'Colonial Continuities', at 133–4; O. Siddique, 'The Jurisprudence of Dissolutions: Presidential Power to Dissolve Assemblies under the Pakistani Constitution and Its Discontents' (2006) 23 *Arizona Journal of International and Comparative Law* 615.

include emergency powers provisions.[131] At the same time, given the close relationship between these postcolonial frameworks and their colonial antecedents, it should not be altogether surprising to see the anti-democratic premises of the colonial state periodically resurface. 'When a crisis occurs', argues Nasser Hussain, 'the postcolonial state declares emergency much like its colonial predecessor and through similar institutional mechanisms.'[132]

VI. Conclusion

In distinguishing between situations in which emergency powers may be justified to 'preserve legality' from those in which they are invoked to 'establish legality', Ramraj also distinguishes between different constitutional baselines. In the liberal democracies traditionally contemplated by theories of emergency powers, he argues, the baseline is one of 'a fully developed legal infrastructure and an entrenched culture of accountability', while in states such as East Timor, the baseline is messier, with the state 'attempting to stabilise the political order by channelling violent political conflicts into nascent public institutions designed to resolve disputes'.[133]

Postcolonial India and Pakistan offer baselines falling somewhere on the continuum between these two extremes. While both countries faced major challenges in establishing themselves as stable, pluralistic nation-states, both countries also inherited reasonably well-developed laws and institutions, including constitutions that drew heavily from the colonial constitutional framework.[134] Narrowly understood, therefore, the need to 'establish legality' may have been less acute than in other, more transitional contexts. At the same time, the conception of legality established by the colonial state was more 'formal' than 'substantive'. The use of emergency and emergency-like powers by the colonial state may well have functioned to preserve *this* narrower, formal conception of legality, along with the colonial state's existing political and social hierarchy. But the colonial state never sought to establish the richer conception of legality that Ramraj associates with contemporary understandings of the 'rule of

[131] See, for example, Subramanium, 'Emergency Provisions under the Indian Constitution'.

[132] Hussain, *Jurisprudence of Emergency*, p. 140.

[133] Ramraj, Chapter 2, pp. 22, 41.

[134] Formally, both India and Pakistan inherited the same legal framework at the moment of independence. However, government institutions in India were certainly better developed than in Pakistan at independence, owing to the differential impact of partition on each country. Jalal, *Democracy and Authoritarianism*, p. 5.

law', including commitments to 'accountability' and 'self-restraint'.[135] To the contrary, not only did the colonial state seek to prevent the development of meaningful forms of internal democratic accountability, but its emergency and emergency-like powers were in part designed precisely to avoid such accountability.

The experiences of postcolonial India and Pakistan suggest that their exercise of emergency and emergency-like powers poses a challenge even deeper than 'throw[ing] into question the government's commitment to legality', as Ramraj argues.[136] Rather, they also expose a fundamental tension embedded within the postcolonial legal framework itself: while India and Pakistan have committed themselves to democracy, constitutionalism, fundamental rights and the broader conception of legality that Ramraj describes, their inherited emergency and emergency-like powers – both constitutional and extraconstitutional – rest on fundamentally different premises. To the extent that such powers continue to serve the now-anachronistic function of constraining democratic self-governance, their use will invariably risk preserving 'illegality' as much as they might help establish legality, with potential to reinforce this vestigial colonial discourse at the expense of postcolonial commitments more consistent with broader, contemporary conceptions of legality and constitutionalism.

[135] Ramraj, Chapter 2, pp. 22, 44. [136] *Ibid.*, p. 22.

5

The princely impostor: stories of law and pathology in the exercise of emergency powers

VASUKI NESIAH

I. Introduction

The dominant approach to 'emergency powers' in liberal constitutional law is characterised by a preoccupation with how to produce legitimacy in exceptional moments. Reflecting a liberal concern with the abuse of power, the jurisprudential focus is on how to allow exceptions to constitutional order without undermining constitutionalism. In effect, we can understand this as an effort directed at delineating the character of 'a legitimate prince' so that sovereign identity is recognisable even in conditions of crisis and, concomitantly, so that we are better positioned to expose, deter and exclude impostors from the throne.[1] The dominant solutions are threefold – better laws, institutions and norms. The field of constitutional law has been devoted in many ways to developing constitutional solutions that better delineate the conditions of its suspension. Thus there are many treatises on how to define and restrict what constitutes the 'exceptional' circumstances that can trigger the invocation of emergency powers, raise the threshold on the procedural checks that need to be satisfied for such powers to be passed and then limit the extent of the abrogation of 'normal' constitutionalism. Alongside this, there are those who look specifically to the societal internalisation of the norms of rights and democracy that sustain constitutionalism – what some have described as the 'norm cascade'[2] that normalises rights expectations by citizens and

[1] My reference here is to Partha Chatterjee's essay on the *Princely Impostor* where he describes how a community grappled with the indeterminacy of princely identity in trying to identify the legitimate Kumar of Bengal. I return to the metaphor of the Princely Impostor in the concluding section of this chapter. See P. Chatterjee, *A Princely Impostor? The Strange and Universal History of the Kumar of Bhawal* (Princeton: Princeton University Press, 2002).

[2] Finnemore and Sikkink describe a national–international dynamic of norm diffusion: M. Finnemore and K. Sikkink, 'International Norm Dynamics and Political Change' (Autumn 1998) *International Organization*, 887.

rights-conforming behavior by states even in exceptional times. Different theorists may place differential emphasis on law and norms, and draw the dots differently between checks and balances, regulatory limits and normative habitus. However, they are united in subscribing to political legitimacy as produced through a common project to ensure emergency powers are constrained and limited by a self-referential legality that limits power rather than authorises it.

Working through the postcolonial constitutional history of Sri Lanka I urge a counter-interpretation – namely, that in its preoccupation with the challenges of legal legitimacy, liberal constitutionalism in fact engaged in the conferring of political legitimacy on specific zones of abuse. Dominant traditions of constitutionalism mobilise legitimacy by generating a distinction between contexts of order and disorder, of legal norms and their absence, of the normal and the pathological. The Sri Lankan story of emergency powers offers a symptomatic window on how this is not about the parameters of lawlessness but about the parameters of political legitimacy, about how power is authorised through the very delineation of constitutional limits. It is a call to be attentive to the continuities between times and approaches that are categorised as 'ordinary' and those classified as 'extraordinary', those that are perceived as 'normal' politics and those that are categorised as 'pathological', the nature of the prince and that of the princely impostor.

II. Producing a state of emergency

A. *What edible-salt laws have to do with the fight against terror*

On 12 August 1953 a hartal (peaceful demonstration) protesting the lifting of rice subsidies in the budget of then Finance Minister J. R. Jayewardene was met with the UNP government of the day decrying what it termed the rise of 'hooliganism'; it moved to declare an emergency that extended from 12 August to 11 September of that year.[3] Less than five years later, the Public Security Ordinance of 1947 was invoked and an emergency was declared once again, but this time by the SLFP government of S. W. R. D. Bandaranaike. On 27 May 1958 a state of emergency was called after five days of anti-Tamil riots that were part of the protracted majoritarian response to the 1957 Bandaranaike–Chelvanayakam pact. Since that time, emergency rule has been a dominant dimension of governance in

[3] In the wake of these protests, the Prime Minister, Dudley Senanayake, resigned and John Kotalawela took over the premiership.

Sri Lanka by both major political parties. Extraordinarily for a country that has been routinely characterised as a constitutional democracy,[4] some measure of emergency regulation has been in place for most of its post-independence history.[5] Emergency regulations have been invoked for matters that range from extended detention without trial to the regulation of the quality of edible salt.[6] Which category of regulation has constituted the greater violation of a democratic ethos in Sri Lanka is debatable: draconian regulations that have crushed democratic space and entrenched regimes of authoritarianism or trivial ones that have routinely subverted the legislative process and facilitated the abuse of power in the everyday lives of its citizens.[7] In either case, it *is* clear that at this point in Sri Lanka's history, the invocation of a state of emergency is not merely a reaction to a crisis, but indeed that emergency regulations themselves have helped provoke and entrench a prolonged political crisis. The state of emergency has, in effect, willed itself into being as the state of things as such – not an aberration but the norm.

This normalising dimension of emergency regulations in Sri Lanka stretches back into the country's history as a central component of colonial governance. In negotiating the perennial tensions between 'local representation' and 'imperial control',[8] between the dual imperatives of 'promoting self-rule' in the periphery and asserting metropolitan authority, colonial

[4] In fact, Sri Lanka's constitutional tradition is lauded with reference to how it has never succumbed to military rule; suggesting that the rule it has enjoyed must therefore be democratic, constitutional and legitimate.

[5] In the 1989 to 1992 period, 449 emergency regulations were passed under the Public Security Ordinance (see States of Emergency Database, School of Law, Queen's University Belfast, www.law.qub.ac.uk/Research/HumanRightsCentre/Resources/html/Filetoupload,53200,en.htm). The Queen's University of Belfast database lists those regulations as well as the following seventeen periods of emergency rule in the period leading up to 1989: '(1) 12 August 1953 – 11 September 1953; (2) 27 May 1958 – 26 March 1959; (3) 25 September 1959 – 3 December 1959; (4) 17 April 1961 – 4 April 1963; (5) 5 March 1964 – 4 April 1964; (6) 8 January 1966 – 7 December 1966; (7) 19 December 1966 – 18 January 1969; (8) 26 October 1970 – 25 November 1970; (9) 16 March 1971 – 15 February 1977; (10) 29 November 1978 – 28 May 1979; (11) 3 July 1979 – 27 December 1979; (12) 16 July 1980 – 15 August 1980; (13) 3 June 1981 – 9 June 1981; (14) 17 August 1981 – 16 January 1982; (15) 20 October 1982 – 20 January 1983; (16) 18 May 1983 – 11 January 1989; (17) 20 June 1989 to the present'.

[6] Emergency (Edible Salt) Regulation No. 635/7 (7 November 1990).

[7] For discussion of how the normal legislative process has been subverted through reliance on emergency powers for regulations that include 'adoption, the quality of edible salt issue and driving licenses', see R. Coomaraswamy and C. de los Reyes, 'Emergency Powers and Constitutionalism' (2004) 2 *International Journal of Constitutional Law* 272 at 277.

[8] See I. Omar, *Rights, Emergencies and Judicial Review* (The Hague: Kluwer Law International, 1996), p. 73.

rule increasingly embedded normality into crisis governance. Thus in many ways colonial government was the first phase of crisis constitutionalism; a state where counter-hegemonic dissent provoked a sense of emergency codified in the 1947 Public Security Ordinance and like measures.

What then is the emergency regime that the 1947 Ordinance launched? The Public Security Ordinance enables the executive to enact emergency regulations on declaration that an emergency exists through a two-part legal mechanism: 'Part I empowers the President to declare a state of emergency, thereby making Part II of the ordinance, which governs the nature of emergency regulations, effective.'[9] While subsequent legislative endorsement is needed for extension, 'Rule 1(2A)(b) gives supreme authority to the President to issue any emergency regulation under Part II.'[10] These powers have been reinforced and extended by the Prevention of Terrorism Act of 1979 (suspended with the 2002 ceasefire and then reinstated in December 2006). Such regulations have to be extended periodically by the legislature; but rather than use those opportunities to provide a check on executive excess, the legislature has deferred to the executive with little dissent. In theory the Public Security Ordinance and the Prevention of Terrorism Act are intended to curtail and limit the abuse of power but they have functioned as a legal regime to enable and legitimise such violations. Rights advocates have pointed out that emergency regulations have enabled a range of different powers in Sri Lanka that have conflicted with both the fundamental rights guarantees of the Sri Lankan Constitution and the laws and norms entrenched in the international human rights framework.[11] Amongst the most significant and commonly utilised set of powers relate to arrest and detention. In fact, each phase of emergency regulations has allowed for more discretion

[9] A. Zanzi, 'Sri Lanka's Emergency Laws' (seminar paper presented April 2002), available at www.india-seminar.com/2002/512/512%20abizer%20zanzi.htm.

[10] *Ibid.*

[11] For instance the annual reports of the Law and Society Trust (www.lawandsocietytrust.org) and the periodic reports of the Asian Center for Human Rights (www.achrweb.org) and Human Rights Watch (www.hrw.org) document how Sri Lanka's emergency laws contravene its international human rights obligations. For instance, see analysis of the emergency regulations passed in 2000 by Suriya Wickramasinghe in 'Emergency Rule', in *Sri Lanka – State of Human Rights 2001* (Colombo: Law and Society Trust, 2001) and then a 2008 analysis that also addresses emergency regulations passed in the preceding half-decade in 'Recurring Nightmare: State Responsibility for "Disappearances" and Abductions in Sri Lanka', Human Rights Watch (March 2008) at www.hrw.org/en/reports/2008/03/05/recurring-nightmare-0.

and arbitrariness and less accountability.[12] In addition there have been crippling restrictions on civil liberties. For instance, the Colombo-based Centre for Policy Alternatives criticises the 2006 regulations because they threaten to 'curtail legitimate democratic activity, dissent and the autonomy of civil society groups'.[13] At various points we have also seen recourse to emergency powers to ease the passage of laws related to a range of private, partisan interests. Be they individual corruptions, or abuses of the state, the far-reaching scope of emergency powers has given licence to wide impunity for the abusive actions of politicians and the security services.

Neil DeVotta is not wrong in highlighting the particularly perverse role of the 1978 Constitution and the 'near-dictatorial powers' that it bestowed to Jayewardene and his successor Ranasinghe Premadasa in entrenching a regime of 'illiberal governance'.[14] On the one hand, the 1978 Constitution introduced the notion of justiciable fundamental rights in Sri Lanka, but, on the other hand, the unprecedented power that it gave the executive branch chilled courts and contributed to the fact that it took another decade for the Supreme Court to invalidate emergency regulations; it did this for the first time in 1987.[15] However, when conversations about emergency powers circulated in the 1977–8 period, the situation looked decidedly grim. Citing Jayewardene's boast upon coming to power that he was going 'to demolish and completely destroy the opposition politically', DeVotta notes that Jayewardene advised the country to 'roll up the election map of Sri Lanka. You will not need it for another ten years.'[16] That rolling of the electoral map was accompanied by the unrolling of a series of oppressive measures that militarised the conflict, politicised the military and chilled political dissent.

The year 2008 marked the sixtieth anniversary of Sri Lankan independence. Looking back at those sixty years, 1978 emerges as a pivotal

[12] For instance, Amnesty International argues that the 2005 regulations allow 'detention orders to be made in an even more arbitrary and capricious manner': 'Sri Lanka – New Emergency Regulations: Erosion of Human Rights Protections', Amnesty International (1 July 2000) www.amnesty.org/en/library/asset/ASA37/019/2000/en/dom-ASA370192000en.html. The 2006 regulations were even more problematic in authorising a tribunal by presidential appointment to bypass the court system and allowing public officials wide immunity from prosecution.

[13] Centre for Policy Alternatives (CPA), 'Statement on the Introduction of Emergency' (2006); see http://eyesonsrilanka.blogspot.com/2006/12/cpa-statement-on-introduction-of.html.

[14] N. DeVotta, 'Illiberalism and Ethnic Conflict in Sri Lanka' (2002) 13 *Journal of Democracy* 84 at 91.

[15] *Joseph Perera* v. *Attorney-General* (1992)1 Sri LR 199.

[16] DeVotta, 'Illiberalism and Ethnic Conflict', at 91.

half-way point in the country's postcolonial history. By many measures, the three decades following 1978 have been extraordinarily inimical to the space for democracy and dissent; the frequency with which emergency rule has been invoked and the abuses it has licensed are a big part of that post-1978 story.[17] Today the Rajapakse government has escalated abuses of power against citizens in a regime that has been widely condemned not only for its intensification of the military offensive in the North and East, but also for the mobilisation of emergency regulations for the concerted persecution of minorities, political opponents and voices of dissent all over the country.

B. The compulsion to legality

Dyzenhaus describes the compulsion to legality as the effort to establish 'a legal framework, whether prospectively or retrospectively, in which public officials act . . . (such that) . . . the constitution of authority is not political, or at least not only political; it is also legal'.[18] With such a framework as the regulative ideal, liberal constitutional law scholars, judges and activists have studied the history of emergency laws in Sri Lanka to identify the factors that enabled the abuse of power, and develop proposals for addressing emergencies that will enable authority to be exercised in accordance with constitutionalist principles. One can identify three principal strands of analysis, and related proposals – namely, a law deficit, an institution deficit and a norm deficit, and, concomitantly, a remedy that focuses on doctrinal reform, a remedy that focuses on institutional reform and a remedy that addresses political culture. These strands of analysis are distinct but potentially interrelated and often proposed in tandem. Lamenting inadequacies in all these spheres, liberal constitutionalists in Sri Lanka make proposals that include laws that can provide better checks on arbitrary and

[17] This does not mean that there was a continuous downward slide; the history is more complicated – for instance the 1990s also opened up remarkable rich conversations on constitutionalism and democracy in the public sphere, including that catalysed in opposition to emergency laws. Given the accelerated frequency with which emergency regulations were invoked and also the stronger judicial support when they were contested, after 1978 debates on emergency regulations played a more significant role in the public sphere. One impact of this was that political debate became much more militarised and more fraught with the weight of regulations advanced in the name of public security.

[18] D. Dyzenhaus, 'State of Exception', in M. Troper (ed.), *Traité international de Droit constitutional* (Paris: Presse Universitaire de France, forthcoming). See also D. Dyzenhaus, 'The Compulsion of Legality', in V. V. Ramraj (ed.), *Emergencies and the Limits of Legality* (Cambridge: Cambridge University Press, 2008), pp. 33–59.

wide-ranging emergency powers, judicial review to provide institutional checks and balances, and the infusion of a culture of rights in the public sphere. In effect, thc compulsion to legality that guides these proposals is seeking to anticipate the exercise of extraordinary powers within the framework of ordinary constitutional order – or as Dyzenhaus puts it, to ensure that 'Legal authority – an idea which presupposes legal limits on what its delegates may do – is invoked to suspend the limits on the delegates.'[19]

1. Law deficits and doctrinal remedies

Many critics of the abuse of power through emergency rule in Sri Lanka locate the problems in emergency doctrine. The powers granted by the emergency regulations are seen as excessively broad because the doctrine lends itself to interpretive indeterminacy in regard to the powers that it authorises and/or the circumstances that warrant such powers. Moreover, its provisions are often too deferential to executive and military power, and, concomitantly, too neglectful of international human rights norms or even the need for grounding emergency regulations in the non-derogation of fundamental rights that are entrenched in the Sri Lankan Constitution. Summarising these various criticisms, Coomaraswamy and de los Reyes say that 'In short, the powers conferred on the national security forces and police enforcement officials were too often broadly framed, over extensive, or asymmetrical relative to the actual emergency situation.'[20]

In addressing these doctrinal deficits, there are two solutions that are proposed. First, there is the argument that the circumstances that warrant invocation of emergency powers should be more narrowly and clearly defined. The Supreme Court has advanced this argument in invalidating emergency regulations for being excessively broad such that it was unable to discern a 'reasonable nexus' between 'the areas the regulation covered' and any threat to national security.[21] The argument has been that more delineation and narrowing is needed of the specific circumstances that warrant emergencies to ensure that these powers are not abused. There is a need to avoid emergency regulations (such as the 'edible-salt' order, or

[19] Dyzenhaus, 'States of Emergency', in R. Goodin, P. Pettit and T. Pogge (eds.), *A Companion to Contemporary Political Philosophy* (Oxford: Blackwell, 2007), p. 804.

[20] Coomaraswamy and de los Reyes, 'Emergency Powers and Constitutionalism', at 282.

[21] See *Karunathilaka and Another* v. *Dayananda Dissanayake, Commissioner of Elections and Others*, Case No. 1 in (1999) 1 Sri LR 157, where the court strikes down the president's suspension of the poll date for Provincial Council elections; see the discussion in Coomaraswamy and de los Reyes, 'Emergency Powers and Constitutionalism', at 288.

in this case, an order cancelling the election date) that are not accountable to the 'fact' of emergency conditions in the area being regulated. Thus emergency regulations need to be narrowly crafted and grounded in the doctrinal and policy rationale enabling extraordinary powers, be it the Public Security Ordinance or the Prevention of Terrorism Act. In fact, the supreme Court has argued that the government must subject itself to the reasonableness test by showing that it relied on impartial information and good reasons for determining that emergency powers were needed.[22]

A related argument giving content to what constitutes a reasonable nexus is that emergency regulations need to be proportionate to the public security crisis. If the previous argument was that the area being regulated must be one where there is a genuine emergency, here there is the argument that even when emergency conditions do prevail, the regulations must be proportionate to the threat. The mere fact of emergency conditions does not provide an open-ended licence to impunity. For instance, the court has invalidated detention powers authorised by emergency regulations when they have not detailed the period of detention, i.e., even when emergency conditions prevail, indefinite detention is disproportionate.[23]

A second line of responses focusing on doctrinal gaps pays attention to how doctrine has been developed in relation to fundamental rights. For instance, in some cases courts have argued that emergency regulations need to be crafted in ways that do not violate fundamental rights such as equal protection[24] or sharply delineate powers to inhibit interference with basic rights of citizenship such as free speech.[25] Here the doctrinal solution requires the constitutional entrenchment of fundamental rights. A review of the case law suggests that the post-1978 court has an inconsistent, although not insignificant, record of invalidating emergency regulations on the basis of their threat to civil liberties such as rights to exercise the franchise, freedom of speech, personal liberty and equal treatment before the law. It gradually developed a fundamental-rights jurisprudence in

22 See Justice Amarasinghe's opinion in *Sirisena Cooray* (1997) 3 Sri LR 265 at 286–7, and the discussion in Coomaraswamy and de los Reyes, 'Emergency Powers and Constitutionalism', at 293.

23 *Gamini Perera, Attorney-at-Law* v. *W. B. Rajaguru, Inspector General of Police and Others* (1997) 3 Sri LR 141.

24 *Lilanthi de Silva* v. *Attorney-General and Others* (2000) 3 Sri LR 230, where the court recognises a substantive equality position in invalidating the differential distributive impact on the poor of an emergency law restricting electricity consumption through a uniform percentage consumption reduction requirement on all citizens.

25 See *Joseph Perera* on the preventive detention of Young Socialists of the Revolutionary Communist League for circulation of anti-UNP pamphlets.

relation to emergency regulations, and, ironically, did this in the context of one of Sri Lanka's bleakest periods, politically and militarily. Referring to the 1987 to 2001 period, Coomaraswamy and de los Reyes review the fundamental-rights jurisprudence of the court to argue that 'freedom of speech and expression experience the most fruitful development among the fundamental rights articulated in the Constitution during the most intense period of emergency rule'.[26]

2. Institution deficits and Institutional reform

Many liberal constitutionalists locate problems with emergencies in inadequacies in the politico-legal architecture of the system. This is about both the micro-technology of how emergencies are dealt with in practice (i.e. who are the relevant institutional actors? What role do they play in governance?), as well as a broader institutional orientation toward liberal constitutionalism (i.e. what is the normative anchor of these institutions? What is the ideology of governance?).

For many commentators the institutional culture of the judiciary provides a telling indicator of the factors that have contributed to the abuse of emergency powers in Sri Lanka and the discussion of the judiciary provides an illustrative window on the analysis of institutional deficits and institutional reform remedies. For instance, Imtiaz Omar clearly locates 'the self-denial of the Court of its status as constitutional court' and the 'permeative influence' of excessively statist ('conventional') notions of 'law and justice' as contributing to the corrosion of constitutional liberties in Sri Lanka in the face of emergency proclamations.[27] The history of judicial review reveals a marked deference to the executive branch in determining when an emergency proclamation is warranted and what the content of the emergency regulations will be. In a series of cases the court repeatedly affirmed that it would defer to the reasons provided by the President or Defence Secretary.[28] Moreover, by treating the government's good faith as the default assumption, courts place the onus of proving illegitimate reasons in declaring an emergency on the petitioner contesting it; and, relatedly, there was a very high bar in making that case.[29] The Thirteenth Amendment to the 1978 Constitution sought to codify this restriction

[26] Coomaraswamy and de los Reyes, 'Emergency Powers and Constitutionalism', at 290.

[27] Omar, *Rights, Emergencies and Judicial Review*, p. 238.

[28] *Yasapala* v. *Wickremasinghe* (1982) FRD (1)143 and *Hirdanaramani* v. *Ratnavale* (1975) NLR 67; see discussion in Coomaraswamy and de los Reyes, 'Emergency Powers and Constitutionalism', at 287 and 286.

[29] *Hirdanaramani* v. *Ratnavale* (1972).

on judicial review of emergency proclamation. Article 154(J) stipulates that an emergency proclamation 'shall be conclusive for all purposes and shall not be questioned in any Court and no Court or Tribunal shall inquire into, or pronounce on, or in any manner call into question, such Proclamation'.[30]

As Coomaraswamy and de los Reyes note, however (paradoxically in 1987, the very same year that this amendment was certified), the court also invalidated an emergency law for the first time in *Joseph Perera* v. *Attorney-General*.[31] The Supreme Court construed Article 154(J) in ways that restricted the reach of these provisions and gave itself space to engage with the reasonableness 'nexus between the national emergency and the corresponding regulation'. [32] From this point, the court has often asserted its authority more actively to review emergency regulations in terms of the reasonableness nexus, with particular attention to the threat that such regulations may pose for fundamental rights. Omar notes that in the pre-1978 period the court's approach was entirely formalist and conservative; the post-1978 period has seen greater willingness to question executive authority but in ways that have not been sufficiently robust in advancing 'the rights of citizens'.[33]

On this account, the Supreme Court's jurisprudence itself reflects a recognition of its own potential role in governance; a recognition that Sri Lanka needs stronger institutional mechanisms (such as judicial and legislative review of emergency regulations) that can provide the checks and balances that monitor and contest illegitimate emergencies, but also institutions that reinforce an approach to governance that asserts citizens' interest and protests the derogation of fundamental rights. Omar argues that contesting the abuse of emergency powers requires a transformation of the structural and ideological elements of judicial institutions so that courts are empowered to safeguard fundamental rights; performing this

[30] Passed in 1987, the thirteenth amendment to the 1978 Constitution was introduced on the promise that it was paving the way toward a politics of inclusion and decentralisation by recognising Tamil as an official language and making provision for provincial councils, including provincial courts; however, this did not impede the dynamic toward majoritarianism and centralisation that has characterised the two decades that have followed. Undoubtedly constitutional language such as that noted here strengthened this dynamic – thus the creation of provincial institutions and the clarification of their powers was also the very process of delimiting their reach, and indeed, entrenching them in a broader dynamic of centralisation. For the full text of the Constitution, see www.priu.gov.lk/Cons/1978Constitution/Introduction.htm.

[31] Coomaraswamy and de los Reyes, 'Emergency Powers and Constitutionalism', at 287.

[32] *Ibid.* [33] Omar, *Rights, Emergencies and Judicial Review*, p. 199.

function also requires that the judiciary cultivate a tradition of rights à la Dworkin that will normatively anchor this institutional mandate even in contexts of crisis.[34]

3. Norm deficits and political culture remedies

The preceding subsections focused on problems with law or institutions that were to be remedied by better doctrine and institutional reform, but we now turn to analyses that locate problems with the abuse of emergency powers in inadequacies with the political culture of constitutionalism. The political culture of constitutionalism refers to the integration of rule-of-law norms into political and legal practice but also in the public sphere at large. For instance, DeVotta asserts that political culture is the root of Sri Lanka's problems; he argues that while Sri Lanka may have the appearance of maintaining democratic institutions, 'the true essentials of constitutional liberalism . . . have been perverted, crippled or destroyed in an atmosphere of ethnic hatred'.[35] This broader diagnosis of the role of a majoritarian public culture in sanctioning emergency measures is underscored by Deepika Udagama who argues that when the Prevention of Terrorism Act (PTA) was first introduced in Sri Lanka the draconian emergency measures it authorised faced little opposition from the general public. 'Despite the protests of Amnesty International, CRM and other civil libertarians, many Sri Lankans did not question the law initially when it was enacted because they believed that it applied only to Tamil separatists.'[36]

Udagama in fact suggests that the emergency regime in Sri Lanka is designed to curb a public culture of democratic engagement with emergency laws. As already mentioned the 1978 Constitution sought to prohibit judicial review of emergency regulations. In addition, Article 80 of the 1978 Constitution disallows constitutional challenges to laws once enacted by Parliament and allows only a narrow one-week window to challenge draft laws once they are placed on the official agenda of Parliament. 'The public often had no knowledge of or access to draft laws to challenge them within that short period.'[37] Hundreds of emergency regulations (ERs) have been

[34] Omar makes the argument in relation not only to Sri Lanka but also to Malaysia and Bangladesh; see Omar, *Rights, Emergencies and Judicial Review*.

[35] DeVotta, 'Illiberalism and Ethnic Conflict', at 84.

[36] D. Udagama, 'Taming of the Beast: Judicial Responses to State Violence in Sri Lanka' (1998) 11 *Harvard Human Rights Journal* 269 at 277–8.

[37] *Ibid.*, at 275.

passed over the last two decades[38] but the system is designed to make it difficult for the public to track these. Udagama describes a Kafkaesque world where citizens have little knowledge of the laws that can be used against them: 'The public has limited information about the prohibitions contained in the ERs because they are not easily accessible. The government does not publish an index to the ERs nor a separate compilation of ERs. To find the individual ERs, one has to wade through innumerable Gazettes and sometimes the Gazettes themselves are not available.'[39] The combination of the proliferation of ERs authorising a wide range of powers and the public's lack of knowledge of the legal landscape of emergency produces conditions that 'instilled fear in Sri Lankan citizens and chilled the exercise of legitimate democratic rights'.[40]

The arena of political culture is closely intertwined with the legal and institutional reforms noted above. For instance, Coomaraswamy and de los Reyes assert that the entrenching of judicial review in the 1990s, together with the influence exercised by the international human rights community, has served to limit the abuse of emergency powers in Sri Lanka in this period.[41] This combination of the legal architecture for judicial review and the greater role of human rights norms in the public sphere has functioned as a key element in the political culture remedy that liberal constitutionalism advocates in addressing emergency powers. On this view these two elements need to be strengthened to ensure that the emergency regime that exists is one that has political legitimacy.

III. Crisis constitutionalism

A. *Producing legitimacy in exceptional moments*

As noted earlier, liberal constitutional law scholarship on 'emergency powers' is preoccupied with how to produce legitimacy in exceptional moments. Thus constitutional theorists have sought to devise approaches that allow exceptions to constitutional order while adhering to constitutionalism. As described in the preceding section, in the Sri Lankan context the dominant solutions that have been advocated are, simply put, threefold – better laws, institutions and norms. This is consistent with the broader discussion in the field internationally. David Dyzenhaus's

[38] As noted earlier (note 5), in the 1989 to 1992 period, 449 emergency regulations were passed under the Public Security Ordinance.

[39] Udagama, 'Taming of the Beast', at 278. [40] *Ibid.*, at 280.

[41] Coomaraswamy and de los Reyes, 'Emergency Powers and Constitutionalism', at 294.

analysis of how contemporary constitutional theory has dealt with the idea of a 'state of exception' surveys theorists who advance these approaches in different ways. For instance, Bruce Ackerman's proposal of a 'supermajoritarian escalator' is an ingenious doctrinal package that would impose tighter requirements on the passage of emergency legislation. It would place an ever increasing burden on government to prove that emergency powers are needed, because with the passage of time each 'renewal' of the emergency would require the support of an ever larger legislative majority.[42] The same impulse that called for public articulation of impartial evidence and good reasons in cases such as *Sirisena Cooray*, is channelled into doctrine regarding procedural requirements for the renewal of emergency powers in Ackerman's proposal.

Interestingly, while the 'supermajoritarian escalator' proposal is an argument for doctrinal reform, it is also a proposal for institutional reform; in particular, it is an institutional reform proposal that places greater weight on legislative review in the legal architecture of emergencies. While the dominant institutional reform proposal of those engaged with the Sri Lankan context was for judicial review, Ackerman's bets on the legislature as providing the more reliable institutional home for constitutional checks and balances. The specifics of the institutional reform proposal are undoubtedly a question of context – in the US case Ackerman may find that judges have been too ready to defer to the executive's assessment of the need for emergency regulations, while in the Sri Lankan case Udagama found that majorities have proved too ready to defer to anti-minority emergency regulations such as the PTA. David Dyzenhaus has argued that creative institutional architecture is in fact the key to balancing constitutionalism with responsible responses to emergencies. He has proposed that 'experiments in institutional design' that co-ordinate the roles for the judiciary, executive, the legislature and other public officials in order to complement and check the excesses of any one branch can preserve legality even in conditions of emergency. His discussion of judicial reasoning in the *Belmarsh* case suggests a potential role for judges there that is closely analogous to how the Sri Lankan Supreme Court created space in *Joseph Perera* for judicial review of emergency laws. In both cases judges neatly manoeuvered around bars on courts assessing

[42] For a short commentary summarising this proposal, see B. Ackerman, 'In Case of Emergency', *American Prospect* (18 August 2006), www.prospect.org/cs/articles?article=in_case_of_emergency. For a more extended deliberation, see B. Ackerman, *Before the Next Attack: Preserving Civil Liberties in an Age of Terrorism* (New Haven: Yale University Press, 2007).

whether 'a state of emergency exists', by asserting their role in assessing 'whether the government's response is correctly calibrated to the emergency', even while they demurred from directly assessing whether the emergency obtained.[43] Most importantly for us these are instances suggestive of the idea that the counter to the abuse of emergency powers lies in asserting institutional platforms that are empowered to scrutinise and monitor, check and repeal. Like Ackerman, Dyzenhaus is keen to point out that the 'institutional parochialism' of relying solely on judicial vigilance has been misplaced. Moreover, he notes that it is potentially counter-productive in enabling a 'sham legality' that preserves the form of the rule of law when the substance is defeated. Rather, his suggestion is that we need institutional experiments governed by the rule of law (this could include special functions for public officials, such as the role of the Special Advocate in the UK to engage with the European human rights system) to ensure that the system is oriented toward increasing the chances that emergency powers are deployed in ways that reinforce constitutional legitimacy.

While Dyzenhaus emphasised institutional experiments, Oren Gross and Mark Tushnet, in different ways, place their bets on public culture rather than legal or institutional reform. For instance, Gross argues famously for preserving the purity of law by disallowing legalised emergency powers in favour of a system for retroactive democratic legitimation of publicly disclosed extra-legal crisis responses by public officials.[44] In garnering such legitimation, Gross relies on the broader ethos of constitutional citizenship rather than explicit constitutional provision for emergencies: 'The model promotes, and is promoted by, ethical concepts of political and popular responsibility, morality, and candor.'[45] He wants the socio-political dynamics of democratic power to ensure that the extra-legal deployment of emergency powers by officials is subject to the test of democratic legitimacy. Although their philosophies and motivations may be different *vis-à-vis* the law as such, Gross and Tushnet both look beyond any specific doctrinal or institutional tweaking in the belief that the system of constitutional order is both more complex and more resilient.[46]

[43] Dyzenhaus, 'States of Emergency', p. 810.

[44] O. Gross, 'Chaos and Rules: Should Responses to Violent Crises Always be Constitutional?' (2003) 112 *Yale Law Journal* 1011.

[45] *Ibid.*, at 1011.

[46] *Ibid.*; M. Tushnet, 'The Political Constitution of Emergency Powers' (2008) 3 *International Journal of Law in Context* 275. See also Dyzenhaus, 'The Compulsion to Legality', pp. 40–1, referring to Gross.

Thus even if anti-liberal measures are adopted in the shorter term, in the broader picture and the longer term, constitutionalism will be secured.

The quest for constitutional solutions that better delineate the conditions of the constitution's suspension has informed efforts to provide both more precise and more demanding definitions of circumstances that are exceptional enough to trigger the invocation of emergency powers. It has also informed more demanding procedural checks for such powers to be authorised and renewed, and then limited the extent to which constitutional constraints can be clawed back. Concomitantly, there has been interest in engendering widespread diffusion of norms that sustain constitutionalism to heighten rights expectations by citizens and the pressure on rights-conforming behavior by states even in exceptional times. As noted in the preceding sections, liberal constitutional law theorists may differ in how they draw the dots between checks and balances, regulatory limits and normative habitus. However, they are united in the effort to locate political legitimacy in ensuring that emergency powers are defined by a self-referential legality; they are united in seeing this endeavour as directed at limiting power rather than authorising it. Accordingly, when emergencies are not adequately constrained, this is explained by deficiencies in the realm of 'legality' as we have discussed above in relation to Sri Lanka. Such emergencies are seen as departures from the normal operation of law and legal institutions.

B. *Continuities and ruptures: the pathology of the everyday*

As Coomaraswamy, Udagama, Omar and others note, emergency regulations have been operative for most of the sixty or 50 years of Sri Lanka's postcolonial history. In rendering the state of emergency a constant rather than an exception, the Sri Lankan history of emergency laws provides an important perspective on crisis constitutionalism. Thus, shifting away from the emphasis of the other observers of Sri Lankan constitutionalism, my own reading of this history focuses on what it reveals about the order maintained by constitutionalism, not just the disorder threatened by crisis. It illustrates how the dominant legal traditions of constitutionalism mobilise legitimacy by seeking to assert a distinction between situations in which legal norms are present and ones from which they are absent; yet in constitutional states of exception it is a distinction that presses against the very mantle of legitimacy that it is intended to engender.

In addition to, and in some ways more important than, the sheer ubiquity of constitutional rule by emergency power in Sri Lanka are the distinctive patterns of how and when emergency rule has been triggered (and when it has not). Closer scrutiny of when emergencies have been proclaimed and to what end is also indicative that emergencies are not deviations from public order but reinforce and advance particular structures, hierarchies and biases of public order. For instance, as noted above the first emergency came in the context of the 1953 hartal protesting the distributive impact of the UNP budget. Emergency powers have been invoked in crushing struggles for socio-economic justice many times in the decades since then – most significantly in the crippling of the unions in the context of the 1980 labour strikes and the persecution of the traditional and 'new' left in the context of the JVP insurgency in the late 1980s. The work done by constitutionalism in constituting the 'normal' within a zone of political legitimacy contributes to emergency regulations being redeemed by the rule of law rather than being condemned by it.

From 1953, emergencies were deployed in ways that reproduced and normalised a particular status quo and it is important to pry under the normalising discourse of the 1947 Public Security Ordinance to look at the political economies of meanings and resources that were at stake. What were unleashed were not only police batons but also a discourse of 'riot' and 'hooliganism' (as the actions of the 1953 hartal activists were termed) as threats to peace; seamlessly it is the non-violent hartal that becomes coded as violence.[47] The project of understanding the work of legal norms undergirding constitutional emergencies (such as 'the reasonableness nexus', ideas of 'public security' or the procedural checks and balances of the ER regime) is not then just about fine-tuning these elements but also about scrutinising how a discourse of reasonableness or public security scripts protest in relation to 'the law'; how the subjectivity of 'protest' becomes coded and prefigured as deviant through the discursive and performative violence of emergency regulations (the curfew, the police baton, the 'police as sovereign'[48] etc.). Emergency regulations have been an integral part of the technologies of colonial and postcolonial governance that have marginalised and delimited counter-hegemonic social forces; in fact, producing such forces as exceptional, deviant threats to the norms of democratic legitimacy that undermine liberal constitutionalism and so on. In sum, to understand the consequences of the use and abuse of these emergencies, we need to go beyond constitutional checks and balances

[47] This is particularly striking given the dominant equation of liberal democracy with 'non-violent reasoned argument'. See V. V. Ramraj, 'The Emergency Powers Paradox' (Chapter 2), this volume.

[48] See G. Agamben, *Homo Sacer: Sovereign Power and Bare Life* (Stanford: Standford University Press, 1998).

to look at both (1) the new maps of 'meaning' through which counter-hegemonic social forces emerge into the public sphere in emergency talk, and (2) the distributive consequences for those sectors of the population that have had most to lose in Sri Lanka's macro-economic policy trajectory. Rather than being aberrations of 'business-as-usual' constitutionalism,[49] these constitutional emergencies reinforced and strengthened business as usual.[50]

Perhaps even more starkly than in struggles over distributive justice, emergencies have also been used to reinforce and advance majoritarian power. The silences, the times when ERs are *not* deployed, tell the story. In contexts of anti-Tamil riots, the government has been conspicuously slow in proclaiming an emergency and addressing majoritarian violence – from 1958 to 1983 this was consistent. This record is highlighted when set alongside the use of emergency regulations against Tamils – in fact, one can define the nature of constitutional governance of minorities since 1983 as of being in a prolonged state of emergency, *de jure* and *de facto*. Thus in different ways, emergency powers are embedded in the normal not the pathological; they refract social dynamics of prejudice, hierarchy and exclusion into supportive legal technologies. Moreover, we find that rather than limiting emergencies, by delineating what circumstances trigger the exercise of emergency powers, the constitutional provisions for emergencies have in fact normalised a political order that has harnessed law to persecute and prosecute dissidents, minorities, labour movements and other voices for economic justice.

If the preceding paragraphs have described the structural tilt of public order that was normalised and reinforced by emergencies in Sri Lanka, it is equally useful to attend to the specific ways in which emergencies have done this work. At least two specific technologies of normalisation are worth highlighting here. First, emergency powers have served to produce Sri Lankan citizenship as always-already split or internally differentiated. This is evinced in different ways – for instance, substantive challenges to majoritarianism in the public sphere can themselves trigger the use of emergency powers;[51] in addition, however, there is a routinised performative element to the regulation of Sri Lankan identity in the application

49 I borrow the phrase 'business-as-usual' from Oren Gross but invoke that phrase here to convey a somewhat different orientation toward constitutional normalcy than intended by Gross, 'Chaos and Rules'.

50 Sri Lanka is hardly an exception here. See the discussion of emergencies in Indonesia in relation to mining contracts and the IMF's structural adjustment policies in N. Hosen, 'Emergency Powers and the Rule of Law in Indonesia' (Chapter 10), this volume.

51 See Coomaraswamy and de los Reyes, 'Emergency Powers and Constitutionalism', at 288, on *Visuvalingam* v. *Liyanage* and the successful use of emergency powers to close down

of emergency powers (triggers of dress code, accent, etc. that shape how one 'presents' ethnicity, class, etc.[52]) that also constitutes and reinforces differentiated citizenship at checkpoints, cordons and search operations, etc. Ethnic targeting has proved ineffective in identifying those who may pose a danger to public security but the labour accomplished in these checkpoints is not about security but identity – it is in the reproduction of differentiated citizenship, precisely through this hyperbolic accentuation of the power to stop, search, arrest, detain and thereby inscribe as 'minority.'[53]

A second and related use of emergency power is in the performative aspect of legally authorised 'surplus repression'. Surplus repression indicates a generative, revolutionary violence that heralds the new 'normal'. The invocation of the Public Security Ordinance in responding to hartals on economic policy marks the rightward shift of the 1950s, which was even more emphatic in the 1980s and beyond. This was a harbinger not just of the rightward shift of the government of the day but of a fundamental reordering of the longer-term socio-political compact. Similarly the enactment of the PTA in 1979 was a marker of a particularly virulent, violent majoritarianism as the basis for political order from the 1970s. The use of the PTA to target and persecute minorities in the public sphere became an enabling contributing factor for the 1983 riots and the war that followed; it signalled through law and legal authority that Tamils were a legitimate target. There is synergy here with the preceding point about emergencies enacting differentiated citizenship through ethnic targeting in contexts such as checkpoints. The public sphere aspect of this is particularly important in communicating what Lenta, following Foucault, calls spectacular torture because it provides public ownership of this majoritarian orientation – the message being not that all are complicit but that all are redeemed.[54] Interestingly, spectacular inaction also does this work; thus,

the *Saturday Review* for criticising 'police brutality' and evincing 'sympathy for the Tamil people'.

[52] Note parallels with Maitrii Aung-Thwin's discussion of how tattoos function in Myanmar; see M. Aung-Thwin, 'Discourses of Emergency in Colonial and Postcolonial Burma' (Chapter 7), this volume.

[53] Patrick Lenta describes how, when emergencies were declared in Algeria and South Africa, these were exercised for ends that do not bear rational resemblance to the efficient consolidation of state power. For instance, in South Africa emergency powers were not used to extract information but to humiliate. In Algeria, emergency regulations did not help the state obtain information but they served as an outlet for the occupying soldiers to vent frustration and release steam; see P. Lenta, 'Waiting for the Barbarians After September 11' (May 2006) 42:1 *Journal of Postcolonial Writing* 71 at 73.

[54] See *ibid.*, at 75–6, where he refers, following both Comaroff and Foucault, to 'a condensing of power to make it visible'.

to the extent that emergencies are about responding to exceptional crisis, regulating the pathological and steering the situation back to normalcy, the decision not to proclaim an emergency or delay such proclamations in the context of anti-Tamil riots also signals that this violence is normal, authorised and legitimate. Emergencies are symptomatic expressions of the perversities of the rule of law.

C. *From the 'compulsion of legality' to the 'force of law'*

The enduring politico-military crisis that has characterised Sri Lanka has made it a ready example of the enduring state of exception, of normalised emergencies.[55] Significantly, however, Sri Lanka post-9/11 is symptomatic of the world at large. As Nadirsyah Hosen notes in this volume, part of the rule-of-law package advanced by the IMF, the United States and Australia in contexts such as Indonesia includes emergency regimes as central components of the rule of law.[56] In China, Jacques deLisle underscores the paradoxical situation where legal legitimacy is seen to be advanced by licensing its suspension.[57] Unlike in Indonesia this is not a result of pressure from other countries as much as an understanding that modernisation of legal systems requires the enacting of regulations for the suspension of legal constraints. Today all states are states of emergency in a permanent war against terror. From Guantanamo to rendition, there are new states of exception from national constitutions and Geneva Conventions; ongoing, indefinite states of legal limbo. In this light, I would argue that the Sri Lankan case, by throwing into relief that the central problem is not about 'constitutionalism in crisis' but 'crisis constitutionalism', provides an illustrative window on a constitutional problem of more general relevance. The constitutive myth of constitutionalism is that emergencies figure as a problem for liberal constitutionalism only in those exceptional contexts of crisis, only in the 'Sri Lankas' of the world. On this view there is a normative settled field that is safely within the realm of law; it is under the jurisdiction of the constitution, in most contexts, most of the time, while the legitimacy crisis emerges only when exceptional circumstance require that we break out of that settled field and change the rules

[55] Aung-Thwin's disussion suggests that like Sri Lanka, Burma may play a parallel symptomatic role – there too the state has advanced a notion of permanent war and defined governance as the management of that enduring crisis through emergency measures; see Chapter 7.

[56] See Hosen, Chapter 10.

[57] See J. deLisle, 'States of Exception in an Exceptional State: Emergency Powers Law in China' (Chapter 13), this volume.

of the game. Today, however, 'crisis constitutionalism' shifts the starting point of the constitutional theory question; it challenges the notion that an authoritative centre is settled, and that it is the pathological periphery that is the issue. Thus we find ourselves in a context such as Japan where, as Mark Fenwick notes, emergency regulations are put in place even when there is no obvious domestic catalyst – rather, enacting such regulations and providing for a suspension of law emerges as a definitive dimension of a country's effort to advance the rule of law and establish good governance.[58] Sri Lanka's rule by emergency may be symptomatic of post-9/11 governance as such.

The Italian political philosopher Giorgio Agamben reaches for contexts even bleaker than Sri Lanka to urge that 'the concentration camp – the spatial form of the state of exception – is not exceptional but rather, the paradigmatic political space of modernity itself'.[59] While I do not subscribe to his larger metaphysics, Agamben's masterful probing of the genealogy of emergencies illuminates the counter-reading of Sri Lankan constitutional emergencies that I want to advance here – emergency states as the norm not the exception, redeemed by law rather than condemned by it.[60] Agamben traces the notion of emergency from the Roman Empire through the historic 'state of siege' in French legal doctrine and the Weimar Constitution right up to the authorising legal regime invoked for Guantanamo Bay.[61] He urges that when we are presented with distinctions such as those between 'law and lawlessness', 'law and anomie', 'public and private', rather than lamenting the 'diminution' of one side of these equations we need to interrogate their 'interweaving' because 'the system always operates in doubles, it works always by means of opposition'.[62] Illustrating this doubling, Agamben notes that the Roman figure of *homo sacer* is caught between a legal prohibition on killing and a legal prohibition on accountability *vis-à-vis* the killing of men designated *homo sacer*, sacred life. By prohibiting killing, the Roman concept of *homo sacer* defines their murder as something not sanctioned by law, but by prohibiting accountability for that murder, it also places their lives beyond the reach of the

[58] See M. Fenwick, 'Emergency Powers and the Limits of Constitutionalism in Japan' (Chapter 12), this volume.

[59] M. Kohn, 'Bare Life and the Limits of the Law' (2006) 9:2 *Theory and Event*, at para. 1. The term 'bare life' is problematic if it is taken to imply a contrast between a life protected by law and a life that is completely outside legal domains; the contrast is not between law and its absence but between alternative legal architectures.

[60] G. Agamben, *State of Exception* (Chicago: University of Chicago Press, 2005).

[61] Kohn, 'Bare Life and the Limits of the Law', at para. 2.

[62] U. Raulff, 'An Interview with Giorgio Agamben' (2004) 5 *German Law Journal* 1 at 4.

law.[63] When Alan Dershowitz advocates for courts disbursing torture warrants, law emerges again on both sides of the equation.[64] By prohibiting torture these warrants define such practice as something outside the law, but by authorising it under certain conditions, they also place torture within the ambit of the law, evidence of legality not lawlessness. Agamben argues that 'the state of exception establishes a fundamental relationship between law and the absence of law. It is a void, a blank and this empty space is constitutive of the legal system.'[65] Law's legislation of a space external to it emerges as a management technique rather than as a threat to legal authority.

The insight into law's own production of the space between law and that which it characterises as the absence of law is helpful to us in underscoring the way the legal system legitimates injustices as internal to legality. Thus notwithstanding the polarity of rule v. exception being defined as what is present when the other is absent, the machinery of 'exceptions to the rule' involves a range of doctrinal levers and pulleys that are, in effect, central to the machinery of 'rules'. Agamben's discussion extends beyond specific doctrines such as *homo sacer* to emergency proclamations and how states of exception function as something of a limit category for law – not a counter to law or a threat to law but a way of bringing into relief the figure of law through its own portrayal of its suspension. Agamben derives from the relationship between law and the absence of law the concept of 'force of law' to convey how 'law seeks to annex anomie itself'; it conveys the shadow of law even when law is suspended. In the suspension of the constitution to save constitutionalism (à la Ackerman, Dershowitz or any of the others) we see this shadow – 'The term' force of law conveys how 'acts that do not have the value of law can acquire the "force-of-law".[66]

[63] Already in his first book on sovereign power and bare life, Agamben draws attention to the interstices between law and lawlessness through the Roman figure of *homo sacer*, the sacred man or sacred life. Manslaughter was prohibited in Roman law, but there was also a regime of impunity for certain killings. In particular, the doctrine, of *homo sacer* prohibited killing of men designated as sacred but also prohibited performing sacrificial rituals in their death, and even more striking, prohibited holding someone who killed a sacred man culpable for murder. Agamben notes (quoting Bennet) that in opening this zone void of justice and holding his murder unaccountable and deritualised, the law (secular and religious) essentially authorises his killing but it does so in complex and contradictory ways; ironically, the men the Roman law refers to as sacred are precisely those whose lives emerge as the least sacrosanct. See Agamben, *Homo Sacer*, Part III, esp. pp. 65–8.

[64] A. Dershowitz, *Why Terrorism Works* (New Haven: Yale University Press, 2002).

[65] Raulff, 'An Interview', at 1.

[66] B. Neilson, 'A Review of *Stato di eccezione*' (*State of Exception*), Generation Online (2003). See: www.generation-online.org/p/fpagambenreviewed.htm. As Neilson notes, Agamben

The distinction between law and its exception is integral to politics, and has 'strategic' import for the force of law in the exercise of sovereign power. Thus to contest sovereign power we cannot start with the illusion that more law will constrain it; we need to 'break the discursive lock on dominant ways of not seeing sovereign power' if we are to 'disrupt its hegemonic effects'.[67]

Moreover, this notion, this marshalling of anomie within law as its exception, is present not just in the 'Sri Lankas' of the world but is, according to Agamben, paradigmatic of law in modernity. The difference between law and its exception emerges in different ways; it is a split that becomes the foundation for constitutional politics. In South Asia, we have the fundamental rights amendment cases of the Indian Supreme Court in the 1970s on using the notion of a 'basic structure' to identify what is core to constitutional identity and what is not – Jacobsohn describes how the Indian court has explicitly split constitutionalism into, in Justice Gajendragadkar's words, 'what is basic and what is circumstantial . . . fundamental rights are given by the Constitution and therefore can be abridged or taken away by the amending process of the constitution itself'.[68] Moreover, with security and terror intertwined, the 'state of exception' has given way to a more generalised and pervasive 'paradigm of security' everywhere which provides a different way of 'splitting' the law. Similarly, engaging with the rights–security dynamic in Bolivia, Daniel Goldstein shows how 'security provision becomes the singular activity of the state, its key discourse and preoccupation, and principal source of legitimation'.[69] Thus the state of exception becomes normalised because, as Goldstein notes, implicit in this expansion of 'security talk' and security-making activity is the notion that rights may have to be sacrificed for security[70]. In fact it becomes internal to the rights regime with the notion of 'citizen security as a human right'.[71] This internalising of exception within the rule is not just integral to the work of state legitimacy on a national plane; Jared Schott describes

stresses that 'The state of emergency is always distinguished from anarchy and chaos and, in the legal sense, there is still order in it, even though it is not a legal order.'

67 Kohn, 'Bare Life and the Limits of the Law', at para. 4.

68 G. Jacobsohn, 'An Unconstitutional Constitution? A Comparative Perspective' (2006) 4 *International Journal of Constitutional Law* 460 at 472 and 474, quoting Justice Gajendragadkar in *Kesavananda Bharati* v. *State of Kerala* 1973 SC 1461 at 1624 and 1691.

69 D. Goldstein, 'Human Rights as Culprit, Human Rights as Victim: Rights and Security in the States of Exception', in M. Goodale and S. E. Merry (eds.), *The Practice of Human Rights: Tracking Law Between the Global and the Local* (Cambridge: Cambridge University Press, 2007), p. 54.

70 *Ibid.* 71 *Ibid.*, p. 61.

the 'regulative ideal of emergency', of norm and exception, in the work of the Security Council and its interpretation of its Chapter VII mandate to maintain peace and security.[72] Studying UN operations in contexts as diverse as Timor-Leste and Afghanistan, Simon Chesterman argues, elsewhere in this volume, that the UN's deployment of emergency powers demonstrates a remarkable similarity to that of its member states in its willingness to 'compromise' the rule of law in order to promote it.[73] This 'exception-in-rule rule of law' emerges then as the globalised currency of legal authority as such. I cite these very different examples not as a comparative law exercise but as an anecdotal mapping of the state of exception *as* the state of law.

IV. Conclusion: The Princely Impostor

In his story of the Princely Impostor, Chatterjee investigates the contested claims of who was the Kumar of Bengal to urge that identity is indeterminate. Even as the modern state mobilises an apparatus of governance through identity cards and passports in seeking to 'fix' identity, we are confronted with the challenges of determining what is, in fact, the identity of the state – the rule of law or its suspension? In effect, the preceding analysis suggests that in the world of constitutionalism, emergencies function as the princely impostor who is interrogated for how he wields the sceptre; emergency rule is tried and prosecuted for abuse of power and violations of citizens. Like impostors, it is understood as a state of exception that 'interrupts' legitimate authority. However, in our current context we need to look at what it means to regard emergencies as impostors – as deviations from governance rather than a window on governance as such. I have argued that contexts characterised as conflict-ridden such as Sri Lanka, provide us precisely that opportunity. This is a context where conflict and crisis have become internal to the challenges, norms and laws of governance; thus, the rule of law is in effect the law of exception.

What then is displaced when we interrogate the princely impostor rather than the prince – emergencies rather than the rule of law? The analysis of the Sri Lankan case suggests that the distinction between constitutional power and the state of emergency can obscure more than it reveals. The focus on emergency as the area where we worry about untrammelled

[72] J. Schott, 'Chapter VII as Exception: Security Council Action and the Regulative Ideal of Emergency' (2007) 6 *Northwestern University Journal of International Human Rights* 24.

[73] S. Chesterman, 'UNaccountable? The United Nations, Emergency Powers, and the Rule of Law in Asia' (Chapter 9), this volume.

abuse of power displaces attention from the normal; in effect, to sanction and legitimate the rest of constitutional authority. It distracts from the everyday injustices under constitutional order. It also displaces scrutiny of how discourses of constitutionalism and emergency interact through legal principles such as 'reasonable nexus' or 'public security' in ways that reinforce and reproduce a pathological public order. Rather than seeing these principles as constraining states of exception, we see them precisely as embodying the law/exception split *internal* to constitutionalism, i.e. the evidence of Agamben's force of law, of how 'acts that do not have the value of law can acquire the "force-of-law"'.[74] Like Chatterjee we may be led to conclude that the identities of the prince and the princely impostor are in fact indeterminate. We inhabit a paradoxical context where the impostor is identified through the very parameters of princely governance.

As noted above, the response of constitutionalism has been the compulsion to legality – more princely governance. What consequences follow from more law, legal institutions and legalistic norms in the public sphere? We know from contexts where there have been constitutionally authorised abuses of power that more law can itself enable, exacerbate and authorise such abuse.[75] Sri Lanka was illustrative here in showing us how incorporation into legitimate legal authority may be a two-edged sword that heightens our difficulties in distinguishing between the prince and the impostor – it could be argued that the discussions in this volume of contexts like Burma and the Philippines only underscore this challenge. Thus the remedy is not about devising doctrinal and other strategies to extend the rule of law further into the zone of the exception; emergencies are already expressive of the rule-of-law's underbelly. As discussed above in our reading of constitutional theorists such as Dyzenhaus and Gross on the one hand, and Agamben on the other, the legitimacy of legal norms requires that there be an extra-legal sphere that projects the 'force-of-law', legitimating the abuses in the jurisdiction of that sphere as much as it legitimates the abuses of the rule of law. We may often find ourselves arguing for laws that check the abuse of power but not *just* by bringing in the rule of law to the state of emergency but *also* by scrutinising the rule of law, in particular the exceptions it demarcates even in defining its own purview. These exceptions are not outside of law but are themselves its products; the impulse is not to delineate better the pathological but to make more

[74] Neilson, 'A Review of *Stato di eccezione*'.

[75] Which Dyzenhaus himself recognises as running the risk of legitimating anti-democratic policies.

space to interrogate what is designated as normal.[76] We need to be equally vigilant about the normalised emergencies that do not trigger exceptional interventions – legalised regimes of anti-minority measures in Sri Lanka that do not catalyse the Public Security Ordinance, the Indonesian mining contracts that do not trigger emergency regulations, the Pakistani financial deals that do not propel the state to suspend the Constitution and so on – contexts where emergency laws gather dust in cupboards from lack of use. Challenging the abuses of the princely impostor is important and necessary, but let us not permit that effort to distract us from interrogating the prince.

[76] Such as Spivak's scrunity, following Derrida, of the authorising narrative of 'We the people' as expressing the everyday paradox of invoking the people to authorise a declaration of independence that is itself tasked with constituting them as a 'people' – Spivak invokes how Derrida points to this quotidian sleight of hand that inheres in the very constitution (the document and the political act) of the United States; G. C. Spivak, 'Constitutions and Culture Studies' (1990) 2 *Yale Journal of Law and the Humanities* 133.

PART II

Postcolonial and post-conflict transitions

6

From Myanmar to Manila: a brief study of emergency powers in Southeast Asia

KEVIN Y. L. TAN

I. Introduction

Constitutions are supposed to step in when men fail. But what happens when constitutions themselves fail, or, more ironically, if constitutional orders have in-built mechanisms for the total suspension of the rule of law? What happens when courts bow in the face of naked executive might? Does the law have a place in such situations, or is it all down to politics? Nowhere is this seen more graphically than in the case of emergency powers.

In most liberal-democratic societies, emergency legislation and the power of preventive detention are considered aberrations; a necessary but illegal intromission on the rule of law. British Prime Minister Winston Churchill called such a power 'in the highest degree odious'.[1] Scholars have thus often tried to deal with the emergency conundrum by reference to politics and executive prerogatives, and courts have dealt with it using the doctrine of necessity.[2] But in Southeast Asia, states of emergency have been so common in the decolonisation period and its immediate aftermath that clauses empowering the executive to proclaim states of emergency as well as to issue emergency laws or regulations have been routinely incorporated into the constitutions of these societies.

In this historical account, I consider how the legal systems of the region have dealt with these questions since the time of their creation. While situations within Southeast Asia are varied and complex, ranging from a total collapse of law and legality as in the case of Myanmar, with little pretence

[1] Quoted in A. W. B. Simpson, *In the Highest Degree Odious: Detention Without Trial in Wartime Britain* (Oxford: Clarendon Press, 1992), p. iv.

[2] See, for example, the Privy Council's landmark decision in *Madzimbamuto* v. *Lardner-Burke* [1968] 3 All ER 561; see also L. Wolf-Philips, *Constitutional Legitimacy: A Study of the Doctrine of Necessity* (London: Third World Foundation, undated).

of legality, to an American-style defence of the rule of law as in the case of the Philippines. Through this historical overview, I argue that emergency powers – that scourge of a liberal democracy – have long been a mainstay of Southeast Asian constitutions. This resulted mainly from the wars of independence and the desire by newly emergent Southeast Asian states to protect their hard-won independence. Nationalists, often hardened by bitter struggles to overthrow colonial regimes, have long centralised power in the executive branch of government, and the continuation and embedding of inherited emergency powers in the constitution is symptomatic of this tendency. I focus primarily on the postcolonial development of emergency powers, without denying the importance of the impact of colonial law. As Maitrii Aung-Thwin suggests later in this volume, we need to 'extend our gaze a bit further than the period of decolonisation'[3] but that would require a much longer chapter.

Rather than argue from a theoretical perspective, politicians in the region have approached the question of governance from a practical point of view. The need to operate within the confines of the rule of law have always been part of the constitutional culture, but governments of these states are not about to play by Queensberry Rules if the nation itself is at stake. Indeed, going back to the early days of the American republic, President Abraham Lincoln found himself in the same dilemma when faced with secession by the southern states. In a now-famous letter to Alfred Hodges, Lincoln wrote:

> I did understand however, that my oath to preserve the constitution to the best of my ability, imposed upon me the duty of preserving, by every indispensable means, that government – that nation – of which that constitution was the organic law. Was it possible to lose the nation, and yet preserve the constitution? By general law life and limb must be protected; yet often a limb must be amputated to save a life; but a life is never wisely given to save a limb. I felt that measures, otherwise unconstitutional, might become lawful, by becoming indispensable to the preservation of the constitution, through the preservation of the nation. Right or wrong, I assumed this ground, and now avow it.[4]

What is important to our understanding of Southeast Asian constitutions is the extent to which the governments of these states have been ready to resort to the use of emergency powers and in what circumstances

[3] M. Aung-Thwin, 'Discourses of Emergency in Colonial and Postcolonial Burma' (Chapter 7), this volume.

[4] Lincoln to Hodges, 4 April 1864, in A. Lincoln, *Speeches and Writings, 1832–1858: Speeches, Letters, and Miscellaneous* (New York: Library of America, 1989), p. 585.

these exercises of power took place. Part II of this chapter provides a historical overview of how the various Southeast Asian states gained their independence and the nature of the emergency powers found in their postcolonial constitutions. In Part III, I consider how these powers have been or have not been exercised in the postcolonial period. In the concluding Part IV, I attempt to draw out some themes and patterns to help locate these developments within the wider discourse on emergency powers and constitutionalism.

II. Reserve powers of the colonial masters

With the possible exception of the Philippines, states in Southeast Asia[5] do not have long or strong constitutional traditions.[6] Most of them emerged as independent entities only in the aftermath of the Second World War after the decolonisation of the great European powers. The Dutch occupied Indonesia as the Dutch East Indies right up till 1948; the British were lords over Burma, Malaysia, Singapore and Brunei, while the French controlled Cambodia, Vietnam and Laos as part of French Indochina. Only Thailand – then known as Siam – was never colonised. This short history of constitutionalism contributes significantly to the way reserve and emergency powers are embedded in the legal and social psyche of most Southeast Asian states. The decolonisation process, so crucial in the framing of legal institutions in new states, has resulted in a structural legacy that treats as normal the exceptional situation of emergencies.

Even though leaders of nationalist movements were often quick to denounce emergency legislation that gave colonial masters wide-reaching powers of detention and quite often the right to suspend the constitution, these same leaders were also quick to accept and adopt these reserve powers as part of their own constitutions even after the colonial powers have long gone.

[5] See generally, D. G. E. Hall, *A History of South-East Asia*, 4th edn (London: Macmillan, 1981); D. J. Steinberg (ed.), *In Search of Southeast Asia* (Honolulu : University of Hawaii Press, 1987); N. Tarling (ed.), *The Cambridge History of Southeast Asia*, 2 vols. (Cambridge: Cambridge University Press, 1992); J. M. Pluvier, *Southeast Asia from Colonialism to Independence* (Kuala Lumpur: Oxford University Press, 1974); C. D Neher, *Southeast Asia: Crossroads of the World* (DeKalb: Northern Illinois University Center for Southeast Asian Studies, 2000); M. Osborne, *Southeast Asia: An Introductory History*, 8th edn (Sydney: Allen & Unwin, 2000).

[6] On the development of constitutions in the region, see K. Y. L. Tan, 'The Making and Remaking of Constitutions in Southeast Asia: An Overview' (2002) 6 *Singapore Journal of International and Comparative Law* 1.

A. *The American influence and the Philippines*[7]

Spain ruled the Philippines for over 300 years before ceding it to the United States of America in 1898.[8] Being staunchly anti-imperialistic, America 'assumed colonial power with a bad conscience'.[9] In February 1899 the Senate passed a resolution not to annex the Philippines, and became the first colonial power to actively plan its own departure from the region.[10] In 1934, the Congress passed the Tydings–McDuffie Act (the Philippines Independence Act) to give the Philippines independence within ten years. Manuel Quezon's faction won the 1934 elections to select delegates for the Constitutional Convention and the transition period commenced in 1935 with a national plebiscite approving the new Constitution – which had earlier been approved by US President Franklin Roosevelt – and the country's first presidential election, which Quezon won.[11] The 1935 Constitution gave the executive a dominant position and provided for a unicameral legislature – the National Assembly.[12] Despite Japanese occupation of the Philippines during the Second World War, the 1935 Constitution remained in force until the Marcos Constitution of 1973.

As the Philippines was an unincorporated territory of the United States, its 1935 Constitution operated much along American lines[13] and, following from the American example, the Filipino Constitution provided for

[7] A more detailed description of developments in the Philippines is found in R. Pangalangan, 'Political Emergencies in the Philippines: Changing Labels and the Unchanging Need for Legitimacy' (Chapter 15), this volume.

[8] For a brief history of the Philippines, see J. S. Archilla, *An Introduction to Philippine History*, 4th edn (Quezon City: Ateneo de Manila University Press, 1998).

[9] See R. von Albertini, *Decolonization: The Administration and Future of the Colonies 1919–1960* (New York: Doubleday, 1971), p. 474.

[10] On the evolution of the Philippines Constitution, see E. M. Fernando, 'The American Constitutional Impact on the Philippine Legal System', in L. W. Beer (ed.), *Constitutionalism in Asia: Asian Views of the American Influence* (Berkeley: University of California Press, 1979), pp. 140–78; and E. M. Fernando and E. Quisiumbing-Fernando, 'The 1987 Constitution of the Philippines: The Impact of American Constitutionalism Revisited', in L. W. Beer (ed.), *Constitutional Systems in Late Twentieth Century Asia* (Seattle: University of Washington Press, 1992), pp. 571–627.

[11] *Ibid.*, p. 264.

[12] See generally, C. Benitez, 'The New Philippine Constitution' (1935) 8 *Pacific Affairs* 428.

[13] Fernando and Quisiumbing-Fernando observed that 'there was a great deal of truth to the charge that the working of the 1935 Constitution, especially the Bill of Rights, owed much to the first Ten Amendments of the American Constitution – its Bill of Rights – as well as the Thirteenth Amendment prohibiting slavery and the Fourteenth Amendment enshrining the principal guarantees of due process and equal protection': 'The 1987 Constitution of the Philippines' p. 573.

emergency or war powers for the executive in Section 10 of the document. The operative Section 10(2) provides:

> The President shall be commander-in-chief of all armed forces of the Philippines, and, whenever it becomes necessary, he may call out such armed forces to prevent or suppress lawless violence, invasion, insurrection, or rebellion. In case of invasion, insurrection, or rebellion or imminent danger thereof, when the public safety requires it, he may suspend the privilege of the writ of habeas corpus, or place the Philippines or any part thereof under Martial Law.

It is interesting to note that even the 1943 Constitution of the Republic of the Philippines, which operated during the Japanese occupation, maintained these emergency or war powers in its Section 9 which is word-for-word the same as Section 10(2) of the 1935 Constitution.

B. The British model

Prior to decolonisation, Britain held five territories in Southeast Asia: Burma, Malaya, Singapore, Borneo and Brunei.[14] In the twilight years of British colonial rule,[15] the Colonial Office began working out policies and procedures for granting independence to these colonies. Even though Britain was anxious to divest itself of its economic and military burdens, its exit had to be as dignified as possible. The British hoped that their former colonies would be self-governing and continue to owe allegiance to the Crown through the British Commonwealth. The transfer of power was to be 'carried out by gradual and orderly stages'.[16] The granting of independence was contingent on the fulfilment of four conditions:[17] first, the peaceful transfer of executive control from the colonial governor to local politicians democratically elected by the local population; second, the establishment of a stable local economy as the essential prerequisite of a fair standard of living; third, the local government should be able to

[14] See R. Allen, 'Britain's Colonial Aftermath in South East Asia' (1963) 3 *Asian Survey* 403.

[15] See generally, D. A. Low, *Eclipse of Empire* (Cambridge: Cambridge University Press, 1991); J. Mayall and A. Payne (eds.), *The Fallacies of Hope: The Post-Colonial Record of the Commonwealth Third World* (Manchester: Manchester University Press, 1991); J. Bastin and H. J. Benda, *A History of Southeast Asia: Colonialism, Nationalism and Decolonization* (Prentice Hall, 1968); B. O. Nwabueze, *Constitutionalism in the Emergent States* (London: Hurst, 1973).

[16] M. Perham, *Colonial Reckoning* (London: Collins, 1961), p. 79.

[17] See D. J. Morgan, *The Official History of Colonial Development Vol 5: Guidance Towards Self-Government in British Colonies, 1941–1971* (London: Macmillan, 1980), p. 21.

protect its territory from external attack; fourth, individuals and communities within its jurisdiction should be protected by the local government from arbitrary acts of oppression. The main method of drafting a post-colonial constitution of the Westminster export variety[18] was to hold a constitutional conference in which Britain actively participated, to protect its interests or act as a power-broker.[19]

Throughout the transition period, and often right up to the point of independence, the British ensured that their representative, the Governor, would retain reserve powers – including the power to suspend the constitution and to declare a state of emergency – if public security and order were threatened. The 'reserve powers' refer to unnamed powers the Crown reserved for itself or its representative under the residual royal prerogative. In his authoritative study of the reserve powers of the British monarch, Justice Herbert Vere Evatt argued that the concept of reserve powers had to be understood within the rubric of 'responsible government' of the colonies:

> The term 'Responsible Government' is frequently used to describe the method of government in which executive powers are required by custom to be exercised upon the advice of Ministers controlling a majority in the popularly elected House of Parliament. The term has been applied, in the main, to the British Dominions. But there are several aspects of the matter which should be distinguished. First of all, it may be that certain powers and prerogatives have not been committed to the Dominions at all, being reserved for Imperial control under certain conditions. Secondly, the problem may be that of determining in the Dominion how a power, admittedly within the competence of some local authority, ought to be exercised, e.g. whether the Governor General or Governor retains a sufficient reserve of discretionary authority either to act against, or to refrain from acting upon, the advice of Ministers in office.[20]

As we shall see below, these reserve powers found expression in the post-colonial constitutions in each of the former British territories.

[18] See generally, S. A. de Smith, 'Westminster's Export Models: The Legal Framework of Responsible Government' (1961–3) 1 *Journal of Commonwealth and Political Studies* 2; S. A. de Smith, *The New Commonwealth and Its Constitutions* (London: Stevens, 1964); and W. Dale, 'The Making and Remaking of Commonwealth Constitutions' (1993) 42 *International and Comparative Law Quarterly* 67.

[19] For a description of this process, see Y. P. Ghai, 'Constitution Making and Decolonisation', in Y. P. Ghai (ed.), *Law, Government and Politics in the Pacific Island States* (Suva: University of the South Pacific Institute of Pacific Studies, 1988), p. 9. See also D. Austin, 'The Transfer of Power: Why and How?', in W. H. Morris-Jones and G. Fischer (eds.), *Decolonisation and After: The British and French Experience* (London: Frank Cass, 1980), pp. 3ff.

[20] H. V. Evatt, *The King and His Dominion Governors: A Study of the Reserve Powers of the Crown in Great Britain and the Dominions* (London: Oxford University Press, 1935), p. 12.

1. Burma (Myanmar)

Of Britain's Southeast Asian colonies, Burma led the push for full self-government. Up till 1937, Burma was administered as part of British India.[21] In 1935, the Burma Act was passed to separate the two territories. The Act came into operation in 1937. Under the Act, a bicameral legislature was created. The British-appointed Governor retained discretionary powers under section 43 of the Act. On 23 February 1940, the Burmese House of Representatives passed a motion calling for the immediate recognition of Burma 'as an independent nation entitled to frame its own constitution'.[22] Winston Churchill, who became British Prime Minister in May 1940, was most reluctant to grant self-government to the colonies and pushed aside recommendations to allow Burma greater autonomy. In its place, it was proposed that Burma be granted dominion status, but only after the War. The Japanese invasion of Burma in 1942 provided the young Burmese anti-British intellectuals an opportunity to rush the timetable. Aung San and his comrades joined the Japanese and marched into Burma with a 'Burma Independence Army'.

Realising that a Japanese-backed independence would only mean replacing one colonial master with another, Aung San and his followers began negotiations with the British secret service to attack the Japanese to secure full independence for Burma. This gave the Burmese another opportunity to push Britain for an independence deadline. Churchill remained unmoved. Instead, Lord Louis Mountbatten, Supreme Commander for Southeast Asia, assumed the initiative as he wanted Burmese support to help reconquer Burma, and this entailed recognising Aung San's renamed Burma National Army as an Allied force under British high command. In June 1945, Aung San's Burma National Army marched into Rangoon as independent troops under a new Burmese flag.[23] Britain's decolonisation timetable had to be dramatically accelerated.

Aung San's Anti-Fascist People's Freedom League (AFPFL) rejected the conditions for independence stipulated in the May 1945 British White Paper on Burma.[24] The proposal provided for a British-appointed Governor to be in control for the first three years, to be followed by the bringing into force of the 1935 Burmese Constitution (Burma Act 1935). Thereafter, the Burmese could work out a new constitution for complete self-government within the British Commonwealth. Instead, Aung

[21] On the British administration of Burma, see C. Hobbs, 'Nationalism in British Colonial Burma' (1947) 6(2) *Far Eastern Quarterly* 113.

[22] See Von Albertini, *Decolonization*, p. 197. [23] *Ibid.*, p. 201.

[24] See A. Thorner, 'White Paper on Burma' (1945) 14 *Far Eastern Survey* 145.

San demanded the election of a national constitutional assembly.[25] The Labour government sped up negotiations and the new British Governor, Sir Hubert Rance, reorganised the Executive Council, making Aung San second-in-command with control over defence and foreign policy. In November 1946, the Burmese issued an ultimatum: elections for a constitutional assembly by 31 January 1947, and the granting of full independence to Burma within a year.[26] U Nu, who succeeded the recently assassinated Aung San, signed the independence treaty with Clement Attlee in October 1947.[27] On 4 January 1948, Burma became independent.

The new Constitution provided for a republican form of government with three autonomous states: Shan, Kachin and Karenni. The legislature was bicameral, with a Chamber of Deputies and a Chamber of Nationalities which would jointly elect the President, though in conformity with the Westminster model, the Prime Minister was accorded extensive powers. The Chief Justice and Supreme Court judges were appointed by the President, with Parliament's approval. Under the 1947 Constitution, the President may issue a Proclamation of Emergency if 'the security of the Union is threatened, whether by war or internal disturbance, or that a grave economic emergency affecting the Union has arisen in any part of the Union'.[28] Such a Proclamation may be revoked by a subsequent Proclamation and ceases to have effect after six months unless approved by Parliament.[29]

2. Malaysia and Singapore[30]

The territories that now constitute Singapore, Malaysia and Brunei were, like Burma, acquired in parts over time. With the British capitulation under Japanese attack in 1942, latent anti-colonial sentiment was fanned

[25] See Von Albertini, *Decolonization*, p. 203. [26] *Ibid.*, p. 204.

[27] The tough circumstances leading to the signing of this independence agreement are described in H. Tinker, 'Burma's Struggle for Independence: The Transfer of Power Thesis Re-examined' (1986) 20 *Modern Asian Studies* 461.

[28] Constitution of the Union of Burma 1947, Article 94(1). [29] *Ibid.*, Article 94(3).

[30] See generally, A. Lau, *The Malayan Union Controversy 1942–1948* (Kuala Lumpur: Oxford University Press, 1991); K. Y. L. Tan, 'A Short Legal and Constitutional History of Singapore', in K. Y. L. Tan (ed.), *The Singapore Legal System*, 2nd edn (Singapore: Singapore University Press, 1999), pp. 26–66; K. Y. L. Tan, 'The Development of Constitutional Government in Singapore 1945–1995', unpublished JSD thesis, Yale Law School (1995); Lim Hong Hai, 'The Eve of Independence Constitutional Debate on Fundamental Liberties and Judicial Review: A Window on Elite Views and Constitutional Government in Malaysia' (1989) 7 *Journal of Malaysian Studies* 1; and M. A. Yusoff, 'Post-War Political Changes, Constitutional Developments Towards Independence and Changing Conceptions of Judicial Review in Malaysia' (1982) 9 *Journal of Malaysian and Comparative Law* 19.

into flames. Plans for the post-war reoccupation involved the complete reorganisation of British possessions in the region, including the creation of a new state of Sabah (formerly North Borneo and Labuan) and colonial control over Sarawak.[31] The Straits Settlements of Penang, Malacca and Singapore was disbanded and Singapore became a separate crown colony on its own. Penang and Malacca were amalgamated with the Federated and Unfederated Malay States to form a new Malayan Union on 1 April 1946.[32]

Malay opposition led to the dismemberment of the Malayan Union. Less than two years later, the scheme was replaced by the Federation of Malaya Order-in-Council 1948,[33] establishing the new Federation of Malaya. Under this colonial-style constitution, the Head of State was the British High Commissioner.[34] On 12 June 1948, faced with the armed insurrection of the Communist Party of Malaya (CPM), the British proclaimed a state of emergency in Malaya under the British Military Administration (Essential Regulations) Proclamation 1948.[35] By this time, the Federation of Malaya Agreement 1948[36] was in force. The High Commissioner had reserve powers to 'act in opposition to the advice given to him by Members of the Federal Executive Council'[37] and to enact legislation which he considers 'expedient in the interests of public order, public faith, or good government of the Federation'.[38]

The British reserved powers in matters of public security and order from the outset, and this was a pattern that was to be repeated in Singapore as well. The 1948 Emergency Proclamation applied to the whole of Malaya

[31] This territory had previously been controlled by the Brooke family, the 'White Rajahs' of Sarawak. See, generally, C. Pybus, *White Rajah: A Dynastic Intrigue* (St Lucia: University of Queensland Press, 1996); and R. Payne, *The White Rajahs of Sarawak* (London: Hale, 1960).

[32] This was done through the Malayan Union Order-in-Council 1946, and in Royal Instructions dated 27 March 1946, collectively known as the Malayan Union Constitution. On the Malayan Union plan, see Lau, *The Malayan Union Controversy*; S. C. Smith, *British Relations with the Malay Rulers from Decentralization to Malayan Independence, 1930–1957* (Kuala Lumpur: Oxford University Press, 1995); and A. J. Stockwell, *British Policy and Malay Politics During the Malayan Union Experiment 1945–1948* (Singapore: Malaysian Branch of the Royal Asiatic Society, 1979).

[33] Federation of Malaya Order-in-Council 1948, GN no. 5 of 1948.

[34] See, Federation of Malaya Agreement, Part II.

[35] The British Military Administration governed Malaya under martial law from 1945 to 1948.

[36] Federation of Malaya Agreement 1948, GN no. 6 of 1948, reproduced in J. de V. Allen, A. J. Stockwell and L. R. Wright, *A Collection of Treaties and Other Documents Affecting the States of Malaysia 1761–1963* (London: Oceana Publications, 1981).

[37] Federation of Malaya Agreement 1948, s. 31.

[38] Ibid., s. 52.

on 18 June 1948, and to Singapore on 25 June 1948. Pursuant to the Emergency Proclamation, the colonial authorities enacted the Emergency Regulations Ordinance[39] on 21 July 1948 'to confer on the Governor power to make regulations on occasions of emergency or public danger'.[40] Section 3(1) of the Ordinance empowered the Governor in Council to proclaim a state of emergency

> whenever it appears to him that an occasion of emergency or public danger has arisen, or that any action has been taken or is immediately threatened by any persons or body of persons of such a nature and on so extensive a scale as to be calculated, by interfering with the supply and distribution of food, water, fuel or light, or with the maintenance of health or health services, or with the means of locomotion, to deprive the community, or any substantial portion of the community, of the essentials of life . . .

In addition, the Governor was empowered to make any regulations

> which appear to him to be necessary or expedient for securing the defence of the Colony, the public safety, the maintenance of public order and for maintaining supplies and services essential to the life of the community including the maintenance of health and health services and to prescribe penalties to be imposed for any offence against any such regulation, and to provide for the trial, by such Courts as may be specified in such regulations, of persons guilty of such offences.[41]

As a prelude to the grant of independence, a constitutional commission under the chairmanship of Lord Reid was appointed to recommend the form of constitution for a fully self-governing and independent Federation of Malaya. Extensive extracts of this commission's report are quoted below as they demonstrate the underlying thinking about the nature of emergency powers that Britain considered necessary for Malaya, and which impacted constitutional development in Singapore a few years later.

On whether emergency powers should be allowed to eclipse fundamental rights, the Reid Commission opined:

> Neither the existence of fundamental rights nor the division of powers between the Federation and the States ought to be permitted to imperil the safety of the State or the preservation of a democratic way of life. The Federation must have adequate power in the last resort to protect these essential national interests. But in our opinion infringement of fundamental rights or of State rights is only justified to such an extent as may be necessary to meet any particular danger which threatens the nation. We

[39] Emergency Regulations Ordinance, 1948, (no. 17 of 1948).
[40] *Ibid.*, Preamble [41] *Ibid.*, s. 4(1)

therefore recommend that the Constitution should authorise the use of emergency powers by the Federation but that the occasions on which, and so far as possible the extent to which, such powers can be used should be limited and defined.[42]

The Reid Commission took cognisance of the prevailing state of emergency (first declared in 1948) and recommended that when the new Constitution came into force, any existing emergency legislation should be continued only for a year, and if it was deemed necessary to retain such legislation, this should only be 'done by resolution of both Houses of Parliament'.[43] The Commission further recommended that Parliament be authorised to enact provisions to deal with 'any further attempt by any substantial body of persons to organise violence against persons or property'.[44] In addition, the Commission recommended that Parliament be authorised to enact such provisions notwithstanding that they might infringe fundamental or State rights.[45] In emergencies

such as war, or internal disturbance, which constitute an immediate threat to the security or economic life of the country . . . there should be a Proclamation of Emergency, and . . . the Federal Government should then have power to give directions to any State Government or State officer or authority. In such an emergency we recommend that Parliament should have power to enact any provision notwithstanding that it infringes fundamental rights or State rights. We do not think that it is possible or desirable to set general limits to this power, and we think that it is even necessary to authorise Parliament to extend its own duration for a year, or, if the emergency should last so long, from year to year.[46]

Finally, on the issue of preventive detention, the Commission recognised that such a drastic measure 'may be necessary' but recommended that

a citizen of the Federation should not be detained under any emergency provisions for more than three months unless an advisory board appointed by the Chief Justice has reported that there is in its opinion sufficient cause for such detention. In order that the person detained may have as full an opportunity as possible of submitting his case we recommend that he should be told the grounds and allegations of fact on which he has been detained, subject to the right of the detaining authority to refuse to disclose facts whose disclosure would in its opinion be against the national interest.[47]

[42] Lord Reid (Chairman), *Report of the Federation of Malaya Constitutional Commission* (Kuala Lumpur: HMSO, 1957), para. 172.

[43] *Ibid.*, para. 173. [44] *Ibid.*, para. 174. [45] *Ibid.*

[46] *Ibid.*, para. 175. [47] *Ibid.*, para. 176.

When Britain finally granted the Federation of Malaya independence on 31 August 1957, the reserve powers of the executive branch were retained under Part XI of the Constitution and all the recommendations of the Reid Commission were accepted and duly enacted.

Singapore's post-1945 constitutional development was slow, but it received a boost with the appointment in 1953 of the Rendel Constitutional Commission. The Commission recommended that the Legislative Council be transformed into a mainly elected assembly of thirty-two members, the majority of whom would be Unofficial Members; and the creation of a Council of Ministers. These recommendations were implemented by the Singapore Colony Order-in-Council of 1955. By this time, a new nationalism fuelled island-wide left-wing and communist-front activities. The 1955 election proved a watershed for Singapore politics and the Labour Front, led by the charismatic lawyer David Marshall, took every opportunity to push the envelope, forcing Britain to grant self-government to Singapore at the soonest possible date.

Under the 1955 Order-in-Council, more popularly called the Rendel Constitution, the head of state was the British Governor, who retained reserve powers to suspend the Constitution in an emergency. He also retained the legislative powers granted him under the Emergency Regulations Ordinance of 1948 which were discussed above. During the run-up to the election, Marshall's Labour Front vowed to repeal the Emergency Regulations, but it was forced to renege on its promise when the security situation worsened with communist-inspired strikes and sit-ins. Throughout this period, the British Governor retained the power to suspend the Constitution even though it was never used. Sir Robert Brown Black, the second-last Governor of Singapore stated that it was 'a piece of paper which was put in a bottom drawer and locked away and it was very much a last resort of desperation'.[48]

In 1958, following two constitutional conferences in London, a new Constitution was drafted and adopted, giving Singapore the right to self-government with its own head of state, the Yang di-Pertuan Negara. Britain retained responsibility for defence and foreign affairs. Internal security was managed by an Internal Security Council, comprising three British, three Singaporean and one Malayan representative. This was the prelude to full independence. In the meantime, the British government had turned its attentions to the self-government of North Borneo, Brunei and Sarawak. A joint British–Malayan commission – the Cobbold Commission – was

[48] Sir R. B. Black, Oral History Interview, July 1995 (Singapore: The National Archives).

established in April 1962 to determine if the people of Borneo wanted, with Singapore, to join Malaya to form the Federation of Malaysia. As a result of opposition from the Philippines and Indonesia, the UN Secretary-General was invited to send a mission to determine whether the people of these territories truly supported Malaysia. This mission announced on 15 September 1963 that the majority of people in North Borneo and Sarawak supported Malaysia, but this did not dispel Indonesian and Filipino opposition to Malaysia.

At a September 1961 meeting of the Commonwealth Parliamentary Association, the principle of merger with the Federation of Malaya was approved by representatives from Malaya, Singapore, North Borneo, Brunei and Sarawak. On 31 August 1963, Prime Minister Lee Kuan Yew declared Singapore's independence from Britain, and sixteen days later, Singapore became a part of the Federation of Malaya along with North Borneo (Sabah) and Sarawak. Brunei chose to remain a British colony.

When Singapore joined the Federation of Malaysia in 1963, Part IX of the Federal Constitution, which contained the emergency powers of the Head of State, applied to Singapore as well, as did the Internal Security Act which was enacted in 1960 to deal with the communist insurgency. When Singapore became independent on 9 August 1965, these same provisions were retained as part of Singapore's Constitution. Today, emergency powers are found under Part XII, 'Special Powers Against Subversion and Emergency Powers'.

3. Brunei[49]

Developments in the Federation of Malaya and Singapore were not paralleled in Brunei. Once a powerful kingdom covering the island of Borneo, its influence began to wane after Spanish settlement in the Philippines in the sixteenth century. In the nineteenth century, Brunei lost most of its territories to Sarawak under the 'White Rajahs' and North Borneo (Sabah) under the British. In 1906, the British created a 'Residency' in Brunei, establishing a system of indirect rule lasting until self-government was granted in 1959.[50]

[49] See A. Ibrahim and V. S. Winslow, 'Constitution and Monarchy in Brunei', in Beer (ed.), *Constitutional Systems*, pp. 365–73; and R. Kershaw, 'Brunei: Malay, Monarchical, Micro-state', in J. Funston (ed.), *Government and Politics in Southeast Asia* (Singapore: ISEAS, 2001), pp. 1–35.

[50] See A. V. M. Horton, 'British Administration in Brunei 1906–1959' (1986) 20 *Modern Asian Studies* 353.

Brunei's 1959 Constitution vested full executive authority in the Head of State, the Sultan, who was assisted and advised by five councils – the Religious Council, the Privy Council, the Council of Ministers (the Cabinet), the Legislative Council and the Council of Succession. The British High Commissioner was adviser to the government on all matters except those relating to the Muslim religion and Malay customs. Under this Constitution, elections for District Councils – which later sent members to an enlarged State Council[51] – were held in 1962 and the Partai Rakyat Brunei (Brunei People's Party, which had been formed in 1956) won fifty-four of the fifty-five seats on the platform of opposition to Britain's Federation of Malaysia plan. The British would not tolerate this and refused to convene the Legislative Council. This infuriated the PRB, which mounted an armed revolt on 8 December 1962. A state of emergency was proclaimed and the revolt was suppressed by British troops flown in from Singapore.

In 1971 constitutional changes reduced British power, making defence a joint responsibility and allowing Britain to retain control over foreign affairs. Brunei achieved full independence in 1984. Unlike Malaysia and Singapore, political power in Brunei is retained almost exclusively in the hands of the Sultan and the royal household. The Brunei Constitution has no bill of rights and its system of government revolves around the Sultan as the source of executive power. The power to proclaim a state of emergency and to promulgate legislation during an emergency resides, unsurprisingly, with the Sultan. Article 83 of the Brunei Constitution provides that:

> Whenever it appears to His Majesty the Sultan and Yang Di-Pertuan that an occasion of public danger exists whereby the security of economic life of Brunei Darussalam, or any part thereof, is threatened whether by war or external aggression or internal disturbance, actual or threatened, he may by Proclamation (hereinafter referred to as a Proclamation of Emergency) declare a state of emergency either in the whole of Brunei Darussalam or part of Brunei Darussalam as may be specified in the Proclamation.

A Proclamation is valid for a period of two years[52] and during such time, the Sultan 'may make any Orders whatsoever which he considers desirable in the public interest; and may prescribe penalties which may be imposed for any offence against any such Order, and may provide for the trial by any court of persons guilty of such offences'.[53] Since independence in 1984, the Sultan has ruled by decree and Royal Proclamation. It was only in 2004 that Sultan Hassanah Bolkiah issued amendments to the

[51] *Ibid.*, at 372. [52] Brunei Constitution, Article 83(2). [53] *Ibid.*, Article 83(3).

Constitution to reintroduce a thirty-one-seat appointed Legislative Council with minimal powers. Only five of the members are elected, indirectly by village leaders.

C. *The 'communisation' of French Indochina*

The French had three colonies in Southeast Asia: Vietnam, Cambodia and Laos, and they clung onto their post-war colonies far more tenaciously than the British did. This resulted in a completely different postcolonial experience. The failure of the French Union – the political entity created in 1946 under the Fourth Republic to replace the old colonial system – to contain nationalist anti-French sentiments can be attributed to several factors. First, metropolitan France was too concerned with its own permanent interests to accommodate the demands of colonial emancipation movements. Second, the newly formed United Nations adopted a strongly anti-colonialist stance. Third, France failed to make the institutions of the French Union acceptable to its overseas territories or involve them in policy-making. This was further exacerbated by a general French lack of interest in overseas affairs.[54] Consequently, preparation for the decolonisation of Indochina, and especially the drafting of constitutional documents and arrangements for transferring power were far less well managed than those of the British.[55] Unlike the British, the French were unable to stem the tide of communism. Indeed, all three French territories were to fall into communist hands by the time the French left Southeast Asia.

1. Vietnam

Vietnam was the most important of the French colonies and also proved the most problematic. Revolutionary leader Ho Chi Minh established the Indochinese Communist Party (ICP) in Hong Kong in 1930, and in 1941 formed the Vietminh (League for Vietnamese Independence) to work for Vietnamese independence. On 11 March 1945, while under Japanese administration, Vietnamese Emperor Bao Dai[56] proclaimed

[54] See Von Albertini, *Decolonization*, pp. 406–7. [55] *Ibid.*, p. 400.

[56] Born in 1913, Bao Dai was the last emperor of Vietnam. He succeeded his father in 1925 at the age of twelve but did not ascend the throne until 1932. During World War II, he collaborated with the Japanese but abdicated to collaborate with the Vietminh in 1945. He then went into exile, but was brought back by the French to rule as Head of State (1949–55) but was ousted by Ngo Dinh Diem. He died in exile in Paris in 1997. See M. E. Chamberlain, *The Longman Companion to European Decolonization in the Twentieth Century* (London: Longman, 1998), p. 211.

Vietnam independent of the French Empire. Five months later, he abdicated and Ho Chi Minh – who had recently been elected chairman of the National Liberation Committee – proclaimed his provisional government of the Democratic Republic of Vietnam (DRV) in Hanoi. When France returned to Indochina in 1946, Vietnam was pronounced a 'free state' within the French Union and was promised a referendum to determine if Tonkin (northern Vietnam, around Hanoi), Annam (central Vietnam) and Cochin China (southern Vietnam around Saigon and the Mekong Delta) should be reunited.

From May to September 1946, Ho Chi Minh negotiated with the French but only a limited agreement was reached. While Ho was in Paris negotiating with the French, Governor-General Admiral Thierry d'Argenlieu proclaimed the Republic of Cochin China on 1 June 1946. Three issues induced a stalemate in these negotiations: French insistence on the Union's integrity; the Vietminh's demand for the reunification of Vietnam; and the place of Vietnam in the Indochinese federation. On 23 November, d'Argenlieu ordered an attack on Haiphong. The Vietminh retaliated and, on 20 December, Ho Chi Minh declared a 'war of nationwide resistance' against the French, marking the First Vietnam War.[57]

The Vietminh controlled much of the north, but Cochin China in the south was more fractious. Attempts by the French to secure popular support by bringing Emperor Bao Dai back from exile led ultimately to full-scale war between the French, supported by the British and Americans, and Ho Chi Minh's DRV.[58] In 1954, the French suffered their biggest military defeat in Dien Bien Phu. Talks were immediately commenced to reach a ceasefire in Vietnam, Cambodia and Laos. In July 1954, an accord was reached in Geneva and Vietnam was partitioned into North and South, along the seventeenth parallel. By October that year, the French forces had left Hanoi.

Meanwhile, things were getting complicated in the south.[59] Ngo Dinh Diem was appointed Prime Minister in 1954. In October 1955, he defeated former Emperor Bao Dai in a heavily rigged referendum to become head of state. Three days later, he proclaimed the Republic of Vietnam with

[57] See A. J. Stockwell, 'Southeast Asia in War and Peace: The End of European Colonial Empires', in Tarling (ed.), *The Cambridge History of Southeast Asia*, vol. II, pp. 329–86 at p. 359.

[58] See R. F. Holland, *European Decolonisation 1918–1981: An Introductory Survey* (London: Macmillan, 1985), p. 98.

[59] See generally, G. S. Prugh, *Law at War: Vietnam 1964–1973* (Washington DC: Department of the Army, 1975), pp. 21–7.

himself as President and immediately began clamping down on Vietminh supporters in the South. After Diem took office, a long list of emergency decrees were promulgated to control the population and protect the state against insurgents. In all, seven different constitutions 'were promulgated, suspended, and replaced as a result of a series of coups and counter coups'.[60] The President was vested with broad emergency powers to rule by decree between the short sessions of the legislature, and, in time of war, internal disturbance, or financial or economic crisis, to exercise extraordinary power to institute any appropriate measures. There were hardly any effective checks against executive abuses of power.[61]

Diem's repressive regime ended when he was violently assassinated in a coup on 1 November 1963. A provisional charter replaced the 1956 Constitution and vested all legislative and executive power in the Revolutionary Military Council headed by Major-General Duong Van Minh. This was replaced by a second provisional charter on 2 July 1964, and a third on 16 August 1964. Both these charters emphasised the supremacy of the military leadership. This charter was later withdrawn when confronted with a barrage of criticism about its dictatorial tendencies. In October 1964, a fourth provisional constitution was enacted, providing for the transfer of authority to a civilian government. The civilian government was ineffective and eventually relinquished its authority to the military in June 1965. On 19 June 1965, Air-Marshal Nguyen Cao Ky was named Prime Minister and he promulgated a fifth constitution.[62]

In September 1966, a national ballot was conducted to elect a constituent assembly to draft another constitution providing for the return to civilian government. On 1 April 1967, the sixth constitution – after the American model – was promulgated which provided for a president, a bicameral legislature and an independent judiciary.[63] However, many of the emergency decrees promulgated earlier – which were of questionable validity – remained in effect. Furthermore, additional decrees were promulgated, further concentrating power in the executive. On 10 May 1972 President Nguyen Van Thieu declared martial law.[64]

In North Vietnam, the DRV promulgated another constitution in 1959 which was outwardly communist in character. With the reunification of North and South Vietnam in 1976 under communist rule, the 1959 Constitution was revised and a new Constitution was given unanimous approval by the National Assembly on 18 December 1980.[65]

[60] *Ibid.*, p. 21. [61] *Ibid.*, p. 22. [62] *Ibid.*, p 23. [63] *Ibid.* [64] *Ibid.*, p. 26.

[65] See W. Duiker, 'The Constitution of the Socialist Republic of Vietnam', in Beer (ed.), *Constitutional Systems*, pp. 333–4.

In 1986, the Vietnamese government adopted a policy of *doi moi* (renewal) at the Sixth National Party Congress and proceeded to amend its 1980 Constitution to reflect this. What started out as a constitution-amending exercise led to the adoption of a new Constitution in 1992. Emergency powers may be proclaimed by the Standing Committee of the National Assembly to ensure 'national defence and security' under Article 84(12), read with Article 91(9). In addition, the State President is empowered under Article 103(6) to declare a state of emergency 'in cases where the National Assembly Standing Committee cannot meet'.

2. Laos

Although part of the French Empire, political development in Laos and Cambodia lagged behind that in Vietnam, which was economically more important to France.[66] Laos was acquired by France in the latter part of the nineteenth century.[67] Like Vietnam, Laos experienced Japanese occupation during World War II and the royal family became involved in the struggle for nationhood. Under Japanese pressure, King Sisavangvong declared Laos's independence in April 1945 but retracted it four months later when Japan surrendered. Prince Phetsarath, the leader of the Lao Issara (Free Laos) nationalist movement reasserted Laos's independence a month later. The French returned in large numbers and Lao Issara leaders fled to Thailand. Phetsarath's half-brother, Prince Souphanouvong refused to accept French reoccupation and he and his supporters took to the jungles to fight for Laos's independence.[68] On 11 May 1947, King Sisavangvong promulgated a new constitution under which Laos was an independent associate state of the French Union in 1949, and in October 1953, Laos secured full sovereign status as a constitutional monarchy, the Royal Lao Government (RLG).[69]

Immediately after Laos became part of the French Union, anti-colonial forces under Prince Souphanouvong and his Pathet Lao forces, aided by the Vietminh, attacked central Laos. Under the 1954 Geneva Agreements and

[66] '[W]hen contrasted with the case of Vietnam, the paucity of pre-1941 Cambodian and Lao "nationalist" activity is striking. It is difficult to point to any organised parties, other than the Vietnamese-initiated ICP [Indochinese Communist Party], and only a handful of individuals emerge as identifiable "nationalists", compared to the scores of prominent figures in histories of the early Vietnamese anti-colonialist and nationalist movements.' See P. Kratoska and B. Batson, 'Nationalism and Modernist Reform', in Tarling (ed.), *The Cambridge History of Southeast Asia*, vol. II, pp. 249–323 at p. 282.

[67] See N. J. Freeman, 'Laos: Timid Transition', in Funston (ed.), *Government and Politics in Southeast Asia*, pp. 120–59 at p. 120.

[68] See Osborne, *Southeast Asia*, p. 177. [69] *Ibid.*, pp. 122–3.

the 1955 armistice, the two northern provinces were given to the Pathet Lao while the rest of the country went to the royal regime. In 1957, Prince Souvanna Phouma, the royal premier, and Prince Souphanouvong agreed to re-establish a unified government. However the agreement broke down in 1959 and further armed conflict ensued. The Laotian situation was further complicated when General Phoumi Nosavan, who controlled the royal army, established a pro-Western revolutionary government headed by Prince Boun Gum in the south. Prince Souvanna Phouma was driven into exile in Cambodia. In 1961, a cease-fire was arranged and the three princes agreed to form a coalition government headed by Prince Souvanna Phouma. In 1975, the Pathet Lao seized power completely and Prince Souphanouvong was installed as President and Kaysone Phomvihane as Prime Minister. On 2 December 1975, the monarchy was abolished and King Savang Vatthana abdicated. Drafting a new constitution assumed low priority with the new Lao government and the pace was excruciatingly slow and it was not until August 1991 that the Supreme People's Assembly (SPA) adopted a new constitution.[70] Under this Constitution, the President is empowered to proclaim a state of emergency under Article 53(10).

3. Cambodia

Cambodia gained its independence from France in 1953 without a war, thanks largely to the manoeuvring of King Norodom Sihanouk. Sihanouk ruled till 1955 when he abdicated in favour of his father to form a political party, the Sangkhum Reastr Niyum (People's Socialist Community), and became Cambodia's first prime minister. Sihanouk continued to dominate politics in Cambodia until he was overthrown by his armed forces chief, General Lon Nol in a 1970 military coup. The American-backed Lon Nol was himself overthrown by the communist Khmer Rouge in April 1975.

The Khmer Rouge, under the genocidal Pol Pot regime, began a programme of social reconstruction, plunging Cambodia into the Dark Ages. Throughout this period, the Cambodian Constitution was suspended and law and legal institutions hardly existed. In 1978, the Vietnamese army invaded Cambodia and overthrew Pol Pot. A new government was installed with the backing of Vietnam, and Hun Sen was Prime Minister from 1979 to 1989. Hun Sen's legitimacy was constantly challenged by the other key political actors: the royalist FUNCINPEC founded by

[70] See J. J. Zasloff, 'The Emergence of the Constitution in Laos', in 'Laos', in A. P. Blaustein and G. H. Flanz (eds.), *Constitutions of the Countries of the World* (New York: Oceana Publications, 1971), p. 41.

Sihanouk, the Khmer People's National Liberation Front (KPNLF) led by former Prime Minister Son Sann, and the surviving Khmer Rouge army and leadership.[71] In 1991, the warring factions signed a major peace accord and invited the UN to intervene in Cambodia. The United Nations Transitional Authority in Cambodia (UNTAC) was mandated to create a neutral political environment for free and fair elections. After two years, UNTAC held general elections in May 1993, and FUNCINPEC won 58 of the 120 seats. The Cambodian People's Party (CPP) won 51 seats, the KPNLF 10 seats and the independent Moulinaka one seat. The 120-member Constituent Assembly adopted a new constitution promulgated by the reinstated King Sihanouk as Head of State.

The 1993 Constitution was drafted by a twenty-six-member multi-party committee formed on 30 June 1993. Following a short period of parliamentary debate, the Constitution was adopted by the Constituent Assembly. It was amended in March 1999 after opposition parties argued that more checks and balances were needed. The main change in 1999 was the creation of a Senate.[72] The 1993 Constitution is replete with democratic aspirations and values,[73] rejecting political authoritarianism. In 1997, Hun Sen ousted Prince Ranariddh (Sihanouk's son) as his co-Prime Minister and emerged as Cambodia's strongman. Hun Sen's CPP won the 1998 elections handsomely. Despite the democratic aspirations of the 1993 Constitution, democracy has yet to gain a strong foothold in Cambodia. Under Article 22 of the Constitution: 'When the nation faces danger, the King shall make a proclamation to the people putting the country in a state of emergency after agreement with the Prime Minister and the President of the Assembly.'

D. Indonesia

The Dutch occupied what is modern-day Indonesia from 1602 when they first staked their claim on Batavia (modern-day Jakarta). Despite early attempts to secure self-government and independence, the Dutch held on tightly to their territory. Governor-General de Jonge declared: 'We have

[71] S. Peou, 'Cambodia: After the Killing Fields', in Funston (ed.), *Government and Politics in Southeast Asia*, pp. 36–73 at p. 38.

[72] *Ibid.*, p. 40.

[73] Article 51 of the Constitution actually states that 'Cambodia adopts a policy of liberal democracy and pluralism.' Article 153 forbids any revision or amendment that affects 'the system of liberal and pluralistic democracy and the regime of Constitutional Monarchy' (*ibid.*, pp. 41–2).

ruled here for three hundred years with the whip and the club, and we shall still be doing it in another three hundred years.'[74] However, World War II changed everything. On 6 December 1942, Queen Wilhelmina of the Netherlands declared that after the war, it would be 'possible to reconstruct the Kingdom on the solid foundation of complete partnership' and that a future conference would lead to 'a Commonwealth in which the Netherlands, Indonesia, Surinam and Curacao will participate, with complete self-reliance and freedom of conduct for each part regarding its internal affairs . . .'.[75] This declaration formed the bedrock of Dutch policy toward decolonisation after 1945.

However, the Japanese occupation of Indonesia in 1942 derailed this late initiative. Freedom-fighters Ahmad Sukarno and Mohamed Hatta collaborated with the Japanese and headed the government. On 17 August 1945, just two days after the Japanese surrendered, Sukarno proclaimed Indonesia a republic. A new constitution was promulgated the very next day. The Dutch tried to reassert control over Indonesia, eliciting immediate, fierce opposition from the Indonesians. In July 1946, the Dutch sought to re-establish order by launching a 'police action' which resulted in a two-year battle with nationalist forces. In December 1948, the Dutch captured both Sukarno and Hatta but could not overcome the resistance of the 65,000-strong Japanese-trained military. In December 1949, the Netherlands agreed to 'an unconditional and complete transfer of sovereignty of the entire territory of the former Dutch East Indies (except Western New Guinea) to the Republic of the United States of Indonesia by 30 December 1949 at the latest'.[76] On 27 December 1949, the transfer of sovereignty took place. A few days earlier, Sukarno had been proclaimed President of the United States of Indonesia.

III. Postcolonial developments

A. *The Philippines*[77]

Looking at Southeast Asia in 1945, no one could possibly have imagined that the Philippines would later be placed under martial law. Following the grant of the 1946 Constitution, the Philippines enjoyed some twenty years of free presidential elections even though Filipino politics was often

[74] See Von Albertini, *Decolonization*, p. 493. [75] *Ibid.*, pp. 494–5.
[76] *Ibid.* [77] Pangalangan, Chapter 15.

marred by sectoral and landed interests. In 1965, a war hero[78] who was former top student of the Filipino bar was elected President of the Philippines. Ferdinand Emmanuel Edralin Marcos (1917–1989) brought a breath of fresh air to Malacañang Palace and was expected to take the Philippines to first-world status with his plans for economic development and his vows to rid the country of corruption. His initial efforts at economic development enabled his re-election for a second term in 1969, but, by then, things were not going well for the Philippines.

Three factors contributed to this state of affairs. First, the economic situation worsened because of rising commodity and fuel prices and natural calamities resulting in damage to crops and livestock. Second, the restive student population became increasingly radicalised and this was manifested in massive rallies and demonstrations. On 30 January 1970, some 50,000 demonstrating students and labourers stormed Malacañang Palace, burnt part of the Medical Building and crashed a fire vehicle through its gates. Four people were killed and numerous others injured. This event was known as the First Quarter Storm. Further violent student protests broke out, leading to the 'occupation' of the office of the President of the University of the Philippines by student leaders. Third, the communist movement re-emerged as a major force and a challenge against the government.

Marcos suspended the writ of habeas corpus on 23 August 1971. On 21 September 1972, acting upon an ostensible attempt on the life of his Defence Secretary Juan Ponce Enrile, Marcos issued Proclamation 1081, declaring the Philippines to be under a state of martial law. The military arrested many opposition figures, journalists, student leaders and labour activists. In all, some 30,000 persons were arrested and detained. Weapons were also confiscated and 'private armies' associated with prominent politicians were disbanded. Newspapers were shut down and the mass media was reined in. Marcos also closed the Philippine Congress and in 1976, through the infamous Amendment No. 6, assumed legislative powers. The constitutionality of martial law was upheld by the Philippine Supreme Court in *Josue Javellana* v. *The Executive Secretary and others.*[79]

Prior to Marcos's declaration of martial law, a Constitutional Convention elected in November 1970 had reviewed the 1935 Constitution,

[78] Marcos was the leader of the Ang Maharlika guerilla force in north Luzon during the Second World War.

[79] [1973] Supreme Court Reports Annotated 50 [Philippines].

resulting in the adoption of the 1973 Constitution, which was very similar to the earlier one. Unique among the changes were the new provisions emphasising social and economic rights.[80] The 1973 Constitution was amended four times in the period until Marcos was overthrown in 1986. That year, Marcos called snap elections to stem the growing opposition to his corrupt regime, following Benigno Aquino's assassination in 1983. Aquino's widow, Corazon 'Cory' Aquino won a landslide victory, but Marcos declared himself duly re-elected. A spontaneous popular uprising called 'People Power' brought Marcos down, driving him from Malacañang Palace.

Cory Aquino was sworn in as President and immediately ordered a new constitution to be drafted. The revolutionary pedigree of this new constitution is evident as Aquino governed by decree and through one of these decrees created a Constitutional Commission composed of her appointees. In a statement appended to Proclamation No. 3, on the Provisional Constitution of the Revolutionary Government, Aquino declared:

> To hasten the restoration of full normal constitutional government, she shall appoint, within 60 days, men and women of probity and patriotism to a constitutional Commission which will draft a constitution that will be submitted to the people in a national plebiscite.[81]

The time frame for the drafting of the new constitution was one year. On 23 April 1986, Aquino issued Proclamation No. 8, the Law Governing the Constitutional Commission of 1986, providing that the Commission comprise 'not more than fifty (50) national, regional, and sectoral representatives who shall be appointed by the President'.[82] The draft of the 1987 Constitution was approved on 12 October 1986, signed on 15 October and ratified on 2 February 1987.

Commentators have noted that the 1987 Constitution took yet another step away from the American model which had influenced both the 1935 and 1973 Constitutions. The American influence is most evident in three areas: the separation of powers; the Bill of Rights; and judicial review. The emphasis on social and economic rights in the 1987 Constitution is

[80] Article 2(5) provides for state management of private property to ensure its equitable diffusion and enjoyment of its profits. Article 2(7) states: 'The State shall establish, maintain, and ensure adequate social services in the field of education, health, housing, employment, welfare, and social security to guarantee the enjoyment of the people of a decent standard of living.'

[81] See Fernando and Quisiumbing-Fernando, 'The 1987 Constitution of the Philippines', p. 579.

[82] *Ibid.*

unique among Southeast Asian democratic constitutions. The focus on social justice and protection for labour is taken to new heights. Article 2(9) provides for freedom from poverty 'through policies that provide adequate social services, promote full employment, a rising standard of living, and an improved quality of life for all.' Special provisions are also included to promote agrarian and natural resources reform; urban land reform and housing; science and technology; arts and culture; and sports. Women are given special protection under Article 13(4).[83]

The 1987 Filipino Constitution is the first revolutionary constitution in Southeast Asia with a strong democratic ethos. It is remarkable for including indigenous elements and third-generation rights (in this case, social and economic rights). Emergency powers under the 1987 Constitution are found in Article VII, section 18 which provides:

> The President shall be the Commander-in-Chief of all armed forces of the Philippines and whenever it becomes necessary, he may call out such armed forces to prevent or suppress lawless violence, invasion or rebellion. In case of invasion or rebellion, when the public safety requires it, he may, for a period not exceeding sixty days, suspend the privilege of the writ of *habeas corpus* or place the Philippines or any part thereof under martial law. Within forty-eight hours from the proclamation of martial law or the suspension of the privilege of the writ of *habeas corpus*, the President shall submit a report in person or in writing to the Congress. The Congress, voting jointly, by a vote of at least a majority of all its Members in regular or special session, may revoke such proclamation or suspension, which revocation shall not be set aside by the President. Upon the initiative of the President, the Congress may, in the same manner, extend such proclamation or suspension for a period to be determined by the Congress, if the invasion or rebellion shall persist and public safety requires it.

Aquino served the maximum single term as president, and was succeeded by her vice-president, Fidel Ramos. When Ramos's term ended, Joseph Estrada, a popular movie actor took office as president, but was driven from power by People Power 2 and was succeeded by his vice-president, Gloria Macapagal-Arroyo, in 2001. In 2004, Arroyo won the presidential election in her own right. However, her presidency was plagued by attempts to overthrow the government and charges of corruption and nepotism. Her popularity flagged dramatically over the years. On

[83] 'The State shall protect working women by providing safe and healthful working conditions, taking into account their maternal functions, and such facilities and opportunities that will enhance their welfare and enable them to realise their full potential in the service of the nation.'

24 February 2006, in the aftermath of an alleged attempted *coup d'état*, Arroyo, exercising her presidential powers under Article VII, section 18, issued Proclamation No. 1017 and declared the Philippines under a state of emergency. She lifted the state of emergency a week later on 3 March 2006 under Proclamation No. 1021.

B. *Indonesia*[84]

In 1955, Indonesia held its first general election since independence. However, the country was far from stable. In 1948, the Communists staged the Madiun Rebellion, and from 1950 to 1962, the Darul Islam movement fought for an Islamic state in the provinces of Aceh, West Java and South Sulawesi.[85] By 1956, Vice-President Mohd Hatta had fallen out with President Sukarno, and a number of local army commanders in Sumatra and Sulawesi proclaimed rival governments. By 1958 state institutions were beginning to crumble because of political infighting, and in 1959 Sukarno banned elections and announced that he would preside over a 'guided democracy'. He abrogated the 1950 Provisional Constitution, established the National Advisory Council and reverted to the 1945 Constitution that contained greater presidential powers. Relevant to us are Article 12 of the 1945 Constitution which provides:

> It is the President, with the agreement of the House of Representatives, who has the authority to declare a state of emergency. The conditions governing and the consequences of the state of emergency shall be laid down by law.

and Article 22(1) of the Constitution which further provides:

> In the event of a compelling emergency, the President has the right to issue government regulations in lieu of laws.

During this period, Sukarno also became increasingly radical. He grew close to the People's Republic of China and the Partai Kommunist Indonesia (PKI, the local communist party) and brooked no opposition.[86]

Sukarno's 'guided democracy' experiment did not bring prosperity or economic growth. The government was corrupt, and the country nearly

[84] For a more detailed study of developments in Indonesia, see N. Hosen, 'Emergency Powers and the Rule of Law in Indonesia' (Chapter 10), this volume; see also generally, P. Wahjono, 'Democracy in Indonesia: Pancasila Democracy', in Beer (ed.), *Constitutional Systems*, pp. 462–506; A. L. Smith, 'Indonesia: Transforming the Leviathan', in Funston (ed.), *Government and Politics in Southeast Asia*, pp. 74–119.

[85] See Smith, 'Indonesia: Transforming the Leviathan'. [86] *Ibid.*, p. 77.

collapsed. On 30 September 1965, a group of pro-communist military officers, calling themselves the September 30 Movement (*Gestapu*) tried to seize power. On 1 October, they captured the state radio station and announced the formation of a Revolutionary Council and cabinet to avert an attempted coup by corrupt generals allegedly in the pay of the United States Central Intelligence Agency.[87] Five generals were murdered and Defence Minister A. H. Nasution's daughter was wounded in an attempt on his life. Within hours of the coup attempt, General Suharto, a little-known commander of the Kostrad, the military's strategic reserve, assumed control. On 11 March 1966, acting on emergency powers given to him by Sukarno to restore order, Suharto 'arrested cabinet ministers and members of the Communist Party, and established an emergency body, the Provisional MPR, provided for in the 1945 Constitution, to strip Sukarno of his powers and transfer them to himself'.[88]

Suharto blamed the coup on the PKI and in the next two years allowed PKI supporters in central and east Java and Bali to be massacred by Muslims in a *jihad*. It is estimated that between 500,000 and a million people – many of whom were ethnic Chinese – were murdered. Sukarno was placed under house arrest and Suharto slowly assumed power. He was named Acting President in 1967. Suharto announced his New Order, emphasising 'authoritarian government, economic development and political stability'.[89] To ensure no change to the 1945 Constitution, Suharto convened the People's Consultative Assembly in 1983 and it passed a decree stipulating that before any amendments were made to the Constitution, a nationwide referendum was necessary. This requirement was made even more onerous in 1985 when a law was passed requiring such a referendum to have a 90 per cent turnout and for any changes to be approved by a 90 per cent vote.

Suharto for the most part brought economic prosperity and heightened living standards for Indonesians. However, corruption, nepotism and the regime's disrespect for human rights brought about his downfall.

[87] Subsequent declassified files and interviews have implicated the CIA. See, for example, P. D. Scott, 'The United States and the Overthrow of Sukarno, 1965–1967' (1985) 58 *Pacific Affairs* 239; Anon., 'The Latief Case: Suharto's Involvement Revealed' (1979) 9 *Journal of Contemporary Asia* 248; and W. F. Wertheim, 'Whose Plot? New Light on the 1965 Events' (1979) 9 *Journal of Contemporary Asia* 197; on the 1965 coup generally, see D. S. Lev, 'Indonesia 1965: The Year of the Coup' (1966) 6 *Asian Survey* 103–10; and J. M. van der Kroef, 'Origins of the 1965 Coup in Indonesia: Probabilities and Alternatives' (1972) 3 *Journal of Southeast Asian Studies* 282.

[88] See Hosen, Chapter 10. [89] See Neher, *Southeast Asia: Crossroads of the World*, p. 108.

In May 1998, after ten days of student-led anti-government demonstrations, Suharto resigned and his vice-president, B. J. Habibie, took over. Habibie had no choice but to embark upon political reform. He changed the law to allow new political parties to be formed, and an early general election was promised. Hundreds of political prisoners were also released. In June 1999, the first truly democratic elections were held in Indonesia since 1955.[90]

Even after Suharto's ouster, the 1945 Constitution remained in force. Under this Constitution, the Majelis Permusyawaratan Rakyat (MPR, or People's Consultative Assembly) is empowered to establish and amend the Constitution. In October 1999, the MPR decided to hold annual sessions to amend the Constitution. To that end, the First Amendment to the Constitution was passed in 1999 and the Second Amendment in August 2000. The Third Amendment was passed in 2001 and the Fourth in 2002.

C. *Burma (Myanmar)*[91]

Post-independence Burma faced several serious problems. The first was ethnic strife and secessionist movements from the minority ethnic groups, especially the Karens and Shans. These minority groups sought independence, opposing the government's insistence on a unified state. A civil war broke out between the minority groups and the central government. The second problem was a poorly trained civil service which often resulted in failed government initiatives. This led to problems within the central government itself. By 1958, the situation in Burma had become so chaotic that President U Nu voluntarily turned over state administration to a caretaker military government headed by General Ne Win. The military government restored law and order, and reorganised the bureaucracy. Two years later, elections were held and U Nu was returned to power.

The highly popular U Nu was committed to democracy and announced his plan to make Buddhism the state religion. This caused more uprisings among the non-Buddhist ethnic minorities. U Nu also announced a plan to turn Burma into a federation, giving hill tribes greater autonomy. This proposal upset the military who felt this would bring greater civil strife. On

90 Smith, 'Indonesia: Transforming the Leviathan', p. 79.

91 See generally, Neher, *Southeast Asia: Crossroads of the World*, at pp. 95–100; and Tin Muang Muang Than, 'Myanmar: Military in Charge', in Funston (ed.), *Government and Politics in Southeast Asia*, pp. 203–51.

2 March 1962, General Ne Win overthrew U Nu's government in a military coup. Ne Win disbanded Parliament, banned political parties, arrested U Nu for his political failures and restricted civil liberties. He then established the Burmese Revolutionary Council (BRC) comprising seventeen military leaders and announced a programme of radical economic and political reforms called the 'Burmese Way to Socialism'.[92]

These reforms were based on a mixture of Buddhist principles and Marxist economic thinking. In 1974, the BRC handed over power to an elected government in accordance with a new constitution establishing Burma as a one-party socialist unitary state. The state was led by the Burmese Socialist Programme Party (BSPP) which was formed by Ne Win and his BRC cadres. Under this Constitution, representation was based on a four-tier hierarchy elected once every four years. The legislature comprised the People's Councils (covering the ward/village, township and state/division levels) and the Pyithu Hluttaw (People's Assembly). As Burma was a one-party state, the 'election' of candidates was more akin to a Stalinist confirmation of party nominees. The BSPP ruled Burma thus from 1974 to 1988 when it was toppled by a popular rebellion, following the massive devaluation of the Burmese currency.[93] The 1988 demonstrations led to Ne Win's resignation as BSPP chairman. Ne Win's replacement, U Sein Lwin, was toppled within a few weeks and Maung Maung, a moderate leader, lasted a few months longer. By September 1988, the hardliners under General Saw Maung restored military rule, crushing all demonstrations. Saw Maung established the much-reviled State Law and Order Restoration Council (SLORC), composed of generals loyal to Ne Win.

In 1990, general elections were held and the newly established National League for Democracy (NLD), led by Aung San Suu Kyi (daughter of the revered Aung San), won a landslide victory with 80 per cent of the popular vote. However, the generals refused to hand over power to the civilians, voiding the elections, arresting NLD activists and placing its leader under house arrest. In 1997, Burma was admitted to ASEAN but remains a military dictatorship. Aung San Suu Kyi – who won the Nobel Peace Prize in 1991 – was released from house arrest in 2002, only to be rearrested the following year. The situation in Burma remains unresolved, with the military junta holding sway and remaining unmoved despite increasing isolation, even from its ASEAN neighbours.

92 Neher, *Southeast Asia: Crossroads of the World*, p. 98.
93 Tin Muang Muang Than, 'Myanmar: Military in Charge', p. 205.

D. *Thailand*[94]

Of all the countries surveyed, Thailand has rewritten its Constitution the most times. From the time the Chakri kings surrendered their absolute power in 1932, Thailand has promulgated and discarded seventeen constitutions. Thai constitutional development is characterised by periods of military dictatorship and repression of civil liberties, interspersed by periods of liberal democracy. Lt.-Col. Luang Pibilsongkram, who successfully quelled the 1933 attempted rebellion, became Prime Minister in 1938 and took Thailand in a nationalist, rightist direction, forging a military alliance with Japan. After World War II, a new constitution was promulgated and this remained in force only until 1949. A military coup in 1951 resulted in the abrogation of the 1949 Constitution and the country reverted to the 1932 Constitution. Late in 1958, this was abolished by Field Marshal Sarit Thanarak who promulgated a Provisional Constitution which lasted till 1968. A more 'permanent' constitution was drafted, but was quickly thrown out by Field Marshal Thanom Kittikachorn who abolished all political parties and dissolved Parliament in 1971. Thanom's regime lasted only till 1973 when student riots brought down his repressive government.

In late 1974, a new, liberal constitution was promulgated under the regime of Prime Minister Dr Sanya Dharmasakti. However, this democratic hiatus, marked by the prime ministerships of Seni Pramoj and Kukrit Pramoj, lasted only till 1976. In 1977, Thanin Kraivichien, a former Supreme Court Justice, was installed as Prime Minister. His repressive tenure was followed by that of General Kriangsak Chommanand, whose moderate government lasted till 1980.[95] During Kriangsak's regime, a relatively liberal Constitution was promulgated and it lasted till a bloodless coup led by General Sunthorn Kongsompong in 1991. Between 1978 and 1991, Thailand enjoyed relative political stability and the semi-liberal Constitution was respected. General Prem Tinsulanond, a former army general led a broad-based political coalition government. Several general elections were held, but the winning parties always asked Prem to continue as Prime Minister, as he enjoyed the support of the military, King

[94] For recent constitutional developments in Thailand, see A. Harding, 'Buddhism, Human Rights and Constitutional Reform in Thailand' (2007) 2 *Asian Journal of Comparative Law* 1; see generally, J. Funston, 'Thailand: Reform Politics', in Funston (ed.), *Government and Politics in Southeast Asia*, pp. 328–37; and P. A. F. Aakesson, M. Bunnag and R. Bunnag, 'The Development of Constitutionalism in Thailand: Some Historical Considerations', in Beer (ed.), *Constitutional Systems*, pp. 656–83.

[95] Aakesson *et al.*, 'The Development of Constitutionalism in Thailand', pp. 666–7.

Bhumibol and the people. Prem's final term of office ended in 1988 when elections were held and Chatichai Choonhavan, another former general, won the elections and formed a civilian government.

The Chatichai government lasted only three years before the military staged another coup. Realising that the military coup had little popular support, the generals installed Anand Panyarachun, a career diplomat as Prime Minister. Anand, who lacked political ambition, is generally acknowledged as Thailand's best prime minister in recent times. His tenure lasted just over a year before elections were again called. Suchinda Kraprayoon, a military strongman was made Prime Minister, but his tenure lasted only a few months. The people revolted and there was widespread rioting in Bangkok. In a rare instance of direct intervention, King Bhumibol lectured the feuding parties on national television and told them to work out a peaceful solution. Suchinda resigned and Anand Panyarachun was once again asked to take over as Prime Minister. Anand set about reorganising the government and left office after organising fresh elections. In the second election of 1992, a new coalition under Chuan Leekpai took power. As with most coalitions, it was difficult to hold the parties together, and Chuan Leekpai took turns with Banharn Siliparcha to helm the coalition. During this period, a Constitution Amendment Bill was passed in May 1996 to provide for the formation of a ninety-nine-member Constitution Drafting Assembly.[96] The Assembly was to conduct a survey of public opinion through hearings and was to finalise a draft for presentation to Parliament in 240 days. If it failed to secure a majority vote in Parliament, a public referendum would be held and a simple majority of eligible voters would suffice to approve it.

The draft Constitution recognised more rights and freedoms than any previous constitution and was designed to make elected politicians and public officials accountable. Civil liberties, although provided for in previous constitutions, were for the first time linked to the idea of 'human dignity'. To enhance political participation, access to the media was guaranteed through a number of measures. These included privatisation plans for state and private monopolies of radio, television and telecommunications and provisions allowing 50,000 electors to submit a piece of legislation to Parliament, or asking the Senate to remove high officials if they appeared 'unusually wealthy' or where they exercised their powers

[96] One member was drawn from each of the seventy-six provinces while the others were experts in public law, political science and public administration shortlisted by universities, to be chosen by Parliament.

unconstitutionally. Other social and economic rights included in the 1997 Constitution were the state's obligations to provide twelve years of free education, health care for the poor, pensions for the elderly without means of support and guarantees for accessible facilities for the handicapped.

Among other innovative provisions were measures intended to stop the buying of votes; the establishment of an independent Election Commission (working with non-government organisations); the implementation of the German-style party-list system of voting; anti-corruption measures prohibiting parliamentarians from receiving state concessions or monopolies; requirements for government ministers to transfer their assets into blind trusts; an asset and liability disclosure mechanism and the establishment of a National Counter-Corruption Commission; and the establishment of a Constitutional Court and a National Human Rights Commission.[97] Parliament passed the Constitution on 27 September 1997 at a joint sitting of the House of Representatives and the Senate with 518 votes for, 16 against and 17 abstentions. The King assented to the Constitution on 11 October 1997. In 2001, billionaire businessman Thaksin Shinawata became Prime Minister after his Thai Rak Thai Party won the elections under the new Constitution.

On 19 September 2006, following a year of political crises involving Thaksin and his political opponents, Thaksin and his government were overthrown by a military coup sanctioned by the King. This was the first unconstitutional change of government in fifteen years. The Constitution was suspended and martial law declared. The new military rulers, led by General Sonthi Boonyaratglin, established the Council for National Security and convened a new drafting committee to enact a new constitution. On 26 January 2007, martial law was lifted in forty-one of Thailand's seventy-six provinces. The elections, which were scheduled for October 2006, were cancelled, although the military promised elections within twelve months. In the meantime, the junta outlawed Thaksin's Thai Rak Thai Party and banned the party's executives from contesting elections for five years.

On 23 December 2007, general elections were held and members of the banned Thai Rak Thai Party, now contesting under the new banner of the People's Power Party (PPP), won 226 out of 400 seats in the House of Representatives. Samak Sundaravej, a close ally of Thaksin, became Prime Minister. Samak's premiership was fraught with controversy and, by July

[97] On the development of the Commission, see A. J. Harding. 'Thailand's Reforms: Human Rights and the National Commission' (2006) 1 *Journal of Comparative Law* 88.

2008, his government was under tremendous pressure from the right-wing People's Alliance for Democracy (PAD) – who sought to thwart a government attempt to amend the Constitution to reduce the proportion of elected representatives in Parliament – to resign. In late August, Government House and several ministries were seized by some 30,000 protesters and on 2 September 2008, Samak proclaimed a state of emergency. A week later, the Constitutional Court removed Samak as Prime Minister on account of his inappropriate involvement in commercial activities while holding the prime ministership. The state of emergency was lifted on 14 September 2008 by Acting Prime Minister Somchai Wongsawat. The PPP's Somchai – who secured 298 votes against Abhisit Najjajiva's 163 votes – was elected Prime Minister by the National Assembly on 17 September 2008. The election of Somchai – who is Thaksin's brother-in-law – as Acting Prime Minister did little to stem the tide of opposition against the ruling PPP. On 25 November 2008, tens of thousands of yellow-shirted PAD protesters marched into Bangkok's Suvarnabhumi Airport and took control of its control tower and key facilities. All flights were cancelled and over 3,000 passengers were left stranded in the airport. The protesters, led by Sondhi Limthongul, eventually left the airport after Somchai resigned as Prime Minister. However, the ongoing conflict between the two factions, which may be characterised as pro- and anti-monarchy, looks set to continue unabated until an acceptable succession plan is put in place by King Bhumibol.

E. Malaysia, Singapore[98] *and Brunei*

Singapore joined the North Borneo states of Sabah and Sarawak and the Federation of Malaya to form Malaysia on 16 September 1963. The effect of this union was the application of the Federation of Malaya Constitution of 1957 to all the new states. State Constitutions had to be drafted for

98 On the issue of separation, see *Singapore Breakaway* (Kuala Lumpur: Department of Information, 1965); *Separation* (Singapore: Ministry of Culture, 1965); N. Fletcher, *The Separation of Singapore from Malaysia* (Ithaca: Cornell University Press, 1969); Chan Heng Chee, *The Politics of Survival* (Singapore: Oxford University Press, 1971). On the legal aspects of merger and separation, see L. A. Sheridan, 'Constitutional Problems of Malaysia' (1964) 13 *International Comparative Law Quarterly* 1349; A. Ibrahim, 'The Position of Singapore in Malaysia' [1964] *Malayan Law Journal* cxi; and L. A. Sheridan, 'The Constitutional and Legal Implications and Problems in Separation of Singapore from Malaysia' (1966) 1 *Fiat Justicia* 47.

Singapore, Sabah and Sarawak,[99] and in the case of Singapore, the State Constitution of 1958[100] served as the base for the Constitution. Under the terms of the merger, Singapore was given special status, with its own Prime Minister (all other Malaysian states having only Chief Ministers or *menteri besars*). More importantly, Singapore had much greater autonomy than the other Malaysian states, retaining control over finance, labour, education and commerce. Singapore citizens would not, however, automatically qualify for Malaysian citizenship, and Singapore would enjoy a smaller representation in the Federal Government.

Almost as soon as the union was sealed, disagreements between Singapore and the Federal Government broke out. The internal politics of the Federation and the abortive attempt by Singapore's People's Action Party (PAP) proved fatal to the merger and, ultimately, Singapore was expelled from the Federation of Malaysia on 9 August 1965. Immediately after Singapore gained her independence, Prime Minister Lee Kuan Yew promised Singaporeans a new constitution. In the meantime, Singapore's parliament amended the State of Singapore Constitution 1963,[101] passed the Republic of Singapore Independence Act[102] and got on with the business of government.

The new constitution never came to pass. In 1979, Parliament passed an amendment to the Constitution to authorise the Attorney-General to consolidate and issue a reprint of the Constitution.[103] Under the 1980 Reprint, the President's power to declare an emergency is found in Part XII of the Constitution. In particular, Article 150(1) empowers the President to issue a Proclamation of Emergency if he 'is satisfied that a grave emergency exists whereby the security or economic life of Singapore is threatened'. If the Proclamation is made while Parliament is not sitting, the President is obliged to 'summon Parliament as soon as practicable' and in the meantime 'promulgate ordinances having the force of law' if he is

[99] This was done through the United Kingdom's Sabah, Sarawak and Singapore (State Constitutions) Order-in-Council 1963, 2 SI 1963, no. 2656.

[100] Singapore (Constitution) Order-in-Council 1958, 2 SI 1958, no. 1956.

[101] Act no. 9 of 1965. [102] Act no. 8 of 1965.

[103] The first Reprint of the Constitution of the Republic of Singapore was issued in 1980. All the provisions of the State Constitution of 1963, provisions of the Constitution of the Federation of Malaysia imported through the Republic of Singapore Independence Act, and all subsequent amendments were rearranged, rationalised and published in a single document for the first time. The old 1963 State Constitution of Singapore did not provide for a judiciary in Singapore, nor did it make any provisions to guarantee civil liberties to its people. These deficiencies were dealt with by 'importing' the relevant provisions from the Federation of Malaysia Constitution 1957.

'satisfied that immediate action is required.'[104] Such ordinances must be presented to Parliament and shall cease to have effect if Parliament annuls it or annuls the Proclamation.[105] During an Emergency, Parliament may make laws on any matter even if it goes against the fundamental liberties provisions. It may not, however, legislate to deprive the President of his constitutional powers.[106] All laws that have been promulgated during an Emergency automatically cease to be in force six months after the end of the Emergency.[107] None of these provisions has ever been invoked since Singapore attained its independence in 1965.

The situation in Malaysia was rather different. The Malayan Emergency, first proclaimed by the British in 1948, officially came to an end in 1960.[108] At that time, the emergency provisions of the Federal Constitution were amended to their present form[109] and the Internal Security Act was introduced as part of the government's anti-terrorism arsenal. As in the Singapore Constitution, the Malaysian emergency powers are found in Article 150 of the Federal Constitution.[110] These provisions were first invoked in September 1964[111] when a state of emergency was proclaimed following Indonesian President Sukarno's *Konfrontasi* or 'Confrontation' against the formation of the Federation of Malaysia.[112] The Confrontation, announced on 20 January 1963 by Indonesian Foreign Minister Subandrio, was a euphemism for a state of undeclared war in which Indonesian volunteers – ostensibly Indonesian Army personnel – infiltrated Sabah and Sarawak to engage in raids and sabotage. By 1964, these Indonesian troops began raiding areas in Peninsular Malaysia and in 1965, Singapore as well. This state of affairs lasted till Sukarno's ouster in 1966.

[104] Constitution of the Republic of Singapore, Article 150(2).

[105] *Ibid.*, Article 150(3). [106] *Ibid.*, Article 150(4). [107] *Ibid.*, Article 150(6).

[108] The Emergency came to an end on 31 July 1960; see Legal Notice 185 of 1960.

[109] For an introduction to the legal issues involved in emergency legislation, see S. Jayakumar, 'Emergency Powers in Malaysia: Development of the Law 1955–77' [1978] 1 *Malayan Law Journal* lx; S. Jayakumar, 'Legal Aspects of Emergency Powers in Malaysia' (1969) 2 *The Commentary* 17; H. P. Lee, 'Emergency Powers in Malaysia', in F. A. Trindade and H. P. Lee (eds.), *The Constitution of Malaysia: Further Perspectives and Developments. Essays in Honour of Tun Mohamed Suffian* (Singapore: Oxford University Press, 1986).

[110] See C. V. Das, *Governments and Crisis Powers: A Study of the Use of Emergency Powers Under the Malaysian Constitution and Parts of the Commonwealth* (Kuala Lumpur: The Malaysian Current Law Journal, 1986).

[111] See Legal Notice 271 of 1964 (3 September).

[112] On the Indonesian Confrontation, see, generally, H. James, *The Undeclared War: The Story of the Indonesian Confrontation, 1962–1966* (London: Leo Cooper, 1971); and G. Poulgrain, *The Genesis of Konfrontasi: Malaysia Brunei Indonesia 1945–65* (Bathhurst, NSW: Crawford House Publishing, 1998).

The Proclamation of Emergency, under which the Malaysian parliament enacted the Emergency Powers (Essential Powers) Act, was never formally expressly revoked.

Three further Proclamations of Emergency were made by the Yang di-Pertuan Agong (the Malaysian king) after the Confrontation. The first of these was on 14 September 1966 following the constitutional impasse resulting from the dismissal of Stephen Kalong Ningkan, Chief Minister of Sarawak.[113] The second came in the aftermath of widespread rioting and racial violence in the Malaysian capital, Kuala Lumpur, on 13 May 1969. The Yang di-Pertuan Agong issued a Proclamation of Emergency on 15 May applicable to the whole of Malaysia, and parts of the Constitution were suspended. Malaysia's management was placed under the charge of the Director of Operations, Deputy Prime Minister Tun Abdul Razak. Constitutional government was restored and Parliament was reconvened in February 1971. The final Proclamation, made on 8 November 1977 and applied to the state of Kelantan, vested state legislative authority in the Prime Minister of Malaysia. A constitutional crisis resulted when the Chief Minister Datuk Mohammed Nasir refused to step down following a motion of 'no confidence' in the State Assembly. This led to demonstrations in the state capital, Kota Baru, and troops had to be called in to restore order.

What is remarkable about the four Proclamations of Emergency in Malaysia is that they have hitherto not been revoked by the Malaysian parliament. This means that the various emergency laws that were enacted pursuant to these proclamations, including the Emergency (Essential Powers) Act 1964 (now known as the Emergency (Essential Powers) Act 1979); the Emergency (Public Order and Prevention of Crime) Ordinance 1969; and the Essential (Security Cases) Regulations 1975, remain on the statute book.

[113] See PU 339A (14 September 1966). The Sarawak crisis resulted in a slew of constitutional cases: *Stephen Kalong Ningkan* v. *Tun Abang Haji Openg and Tawi Sli* [1966] 2 MLJ 187; *Stephen Kalong Ningkan* v. *Tun Abang Haji Openg and Tawi Sli* (No 2) [1967] 1 MLJ 46; *Stephen Kalong Ningkan* v. *Government of Malaysia* [1968] 1 MLJ 119 (Federal Court); *Stephen Kalong Ningkan* v. *Government of Malaysia* [1968] 2 MLJ 238 (Privy Council). See also Y. Ghai, 'The Politics of the Constitution: Another Look at the Ningkan Litigation' (1986) 7 *Singapore Law Review* 147; see also Thio Su Mien, 'Dismissal of Chief Minister' (1966) 3 *Malaya Law Review* 283; V. Sinnadurai, 'Proclamation of Emergency – Reviewable? Stephen Kalong Ningkan v Government of Malaysia' (1968) 10 *Malaya Law Review* 130; and A. Ibrahim, 'Power to Dismiss the Prime Minister or Chief Minister in Malaysia' (1977) 58 *Parliamentarian* 34.

IV. Concluding observations

It is difficult to discern any overarching pattern of development with respect to emergency powers within the Southeast Asian states although some generalisations and observations may be made. Constitutional pedigree is no guarantee for liberal democracy. The Philippines, with the most liberally democratic of constitutions, modelled on the American system, succumbed just as easily to martial law. The key lies not in the inherited tradition or system, but in how the state and its governing elite view their own survival. The states of Southeast Asia have had a short but turbulent history. Independence from their former colonial masters did not spell the end of their quest for survival, as constant challenges to governments through insurrection or subterfuge were regular features of these post-colonial states. Basic law-and-order issues were not settled by the passing of a constitution, and the role of the military, so essential in the colonial struggle, continues to loom large. With so many challenges to legitimacy, governments in the region are faced with two possibilities. The first is to constitutionally eradicate opposition to power; the second, to retain and use emergency powers when necessary.

Countries like Vietnam, Laos and Burma chose the first option. They turned their societies into single-party states where opposition is illegal and where the rulers and military strongmen work hand in hand to suppress any form of dissent. In such cases, the integrity of the state is preserved, often at the expense of democratic values and human rights. The state ranks above the individuals who comprise it and this is reflected in the constitutional orders that have emerged. Though all these constitutions contain emergency provisions, these governments have had little need to invoke them since the executive needs no approval from any other branch to crush those who oppose it.

We might add Indonesia to this list of countries although its history is rather different. The close collaboration between the military and the civilian government in the first fifty years of its history ensured the survival of the Indonesian state but this also meant an increased role for the military under the doctrine of *dwifungsi*, or dual function.[114] However, Indonesia has chosen a different trajectory since the ouster of Suharto.

[114] See H. Crouch, 'Indonesia', in Z. H. Ahmad and H. Crouch (eds.), *Military–Civilian Relations in Southeast Asia* (Singapore: Oxford University Press, 1985), p. 50; H. Crouch, *The Army and Politics in Indonesia* (Ithaca: Cornell University Press, 1988); and T. Lee, 'The Nature and Future of Civil–Military Relations in Indonesia' (2000) 40 *Asian Survey* 692.

Since 1998, the concept of *dwifungsi* has been consciously abandoned. Military representation in the legislature was reduced from seventy-five to thirty-eight and eventually obliterated completely in 2004.

Countries which adopted the second option include the Philippines, Malaysia[115] and Singapore. The pattern of development is the same. These states inherited emergency powers from their colonial masters and they are prepared to use these powers when the situation warrants. Alas, the proclamation of emergencies is a singularly executive and political act. Most courts have refrained from adjudicating upon the correctness of such decisions. Whether there existed a state of affairs warranting the executive to act the way it did, or whether it was compelled to use these reserve powers, was often held unjusticiable.

The cases of Thailand, Cambodia and Brunei are exceptional. Looking back through time, Thailand deals with exceptional political situations through *coups d'état* rather than through the invoking of emergency powers.[116] The pattern is clearly discernible. When things get out of hand, the military step in, a bloodless coup is staged, a new government is sworn in and a new constitution follows. Cambodia could well have followed the same route of development as its Indochinese neighbours Vietnam and Laos had it not been for the personality and wiliness of King Sihanouk. The intervention of the United Nations and the staging of democratic elections in 1993, followed by the crushing of dissent by Hun Sen, indicate the country's tendency toward the Vietnamese model. The basic institutions of democracy have yet to take firm root in the country, and this makes the situation rather volatile.

Brunei is an unlikely state. It has a very small population of about 374,000 and relies almost entirely on its oil revenue for survival. It is perhaps the last surviving real monarchy in the region and, with such systems, constitutionally entrenched emergency powers are really quite unnecessary.

It is always tempting to conclude with a little crystal-ball gazing. With the strong entrenchment of emergency powers in the various Southeast

[115] The most thorough study of the Malaysian emergency powers is: Das, *Governments and Crisis Powers*. For an early comparison of the Malaysian and Filipino experiences, see E. M. Fernando, *Governmental Powers and Human Rights In Times of Emergency: A Brief Survey of the Malaysian and Philippine Constitutions* (Singapore: Malayan Law Journal, 1974); for a comparison between the Malaysian, Sri Lankan and Bangladeshi situations, see I. Omar, *Rights, Emergencies and Judicial Review* (The Hague: Kluwer Law International, 1996).

[116] See A. Harding, 'Emergency Powers with a Moustache: Special Powers, Military Rule and Evolving Constitutionalism in Thailand' (Chapter 11), this volume.

Asian constitutions, what are the prospects for the flowering of liberal-democratic regimes in the region? In his analysis of the development of Pakistani and Indian emergency powers, Anil Kalhan argues that the central purpose of emergency powers in the colonial state was not a simple case of establishing or preserving legality, but to ensure executive supremacy over the 'limited space' of democratic participation.[117] Taken to its logical conclusion, it would suggest that the continued presence and use of emergency powers in the constitutions of Southeast Asia will act as impediments to the development of democratic ideals and a constitutional culture that respects free choice and popular opinion. But then again, nothing is preordained. What are likely to emerge are societies with varying degrees of liberalism and democracy – right across the spectrum – tempered by their specific legal cultures and constitutional histories and traditions. They will be polities requiring new modes of analysis and classification, eschewing traditional categorisations that have, at one end, totalitarianism and authoritarianism, and at the other, liberal democracy.

[117] 'Constitution and "Extraconstitution": Colonial Emergency Regimes in Postcolonial India and Pakistan' (Chapter 4), this volume.

7

Discourses of emergency in colonial and postcolonial Burma

MAITRII AUNG-THWIN

I. Introduction

The notion of emergency has come to have a wide range of meanings and understandings that have stretched the range of possibilities for socio-legal research. Although emergency can refer to extraordinary medical, environmental, financial, and even perceived cultural crises, it is often discussed within the arena of politics and the law.[1] Conceptually, emergency might be situated anywhere between that which is considered 'normal' and that which is considered 'exceptional', suggesting a variety of temporal and qualitative conditions that might delineate its parameters. In many respects, the very idea of emergency as an exceptional set of circumstances depends on and enables an understanding of what constitutes 'non-emergency' situations. From the perspective of the state (and those officials managing its administrative structures), emergency might be considered a category designed to make threats to society 'legible' by incorporating those elements into a familiar vocabulary of governance.[2] For those seeking reform or advocating resistance to the state's definition of the status quo, the conditions associated with emergency can certainly come to mean very different things.[3] It is the socio-legal context underlying this ambiguity that makes the defining of emergency (and conversely the defining of normality) in different cultural-political settings a provocative area of comparative research.

[1] See G. Groemer, 'Fifteen Years of Folk Song Collection in Japan: Reports and Recordings of the "Emergency Folk Song Survey"' (1994) 53 *Asian Folklore Studies* 199.

[2] J. C. Scott, *Seeing Like a State: How Certain Schemes to Improve the Human Condition Have Failed* (New Haven: Yale University Press, 1998), pp. 53–83.

[3] S. E. Guggenheim and R. P. Weller, 'Introduction: Moral Economy, Capitalism, and State Power in Rural Protest', in S. E. Guggenheim and R. P. Weller (eds.), *Power and Protest in the Countryside: Studies of Rural Unrest in Asia, Europe, and Latin America* (Durham, N. C.: Duke University Press, 1982).

Determining how emergency fits within or without existing legal structures is one important area of scholarly attention. Some commentators have focused on emergency within the context of constitutional systems or as a function of authoritarian regimes, where security issues seem to characterise the discourse surrounding the application of such powers.[4] The ensuing paradox, as suggested by Victor V. Ramraj, is that in the effort to establish or retain legal and political stability through such special powers, the state's commitment to the rule of law immediately comes into question.[5] Much attention has been focused on how societies deliberate, rationalise, and prepare for these emergencies by incorporating special powers into their legal structures in order to protect the very principles that may be undermined by these provisions.[6] An interesting tension that emerges in the literature concerns questions of authority and the conceptual framework within which emergency functions: are emergency powers separate from the operating parameters of the law, do they continue to function within law's boundaries, or can emergency powers (and their influences) preside in contexts beyond constitutional law?[7] Much of what will be considered in this chapter is concerned with the role of emergency within colonial and postcolonial Burma (Myanmar), whose political history challenges our understanding of special powers and its relationship with constitutionalism.

In many respects, Asia has provided scholars with a legal 'laboratory'[8] within which to examine many of these questions, as fundamental differences (from the West) are often noticed that provide interesting points of inquiry and departure. Emergency situations have often provided the context for assessing, constructing and comparing political systems in the region with the wide range of liberal democracies in North America, Europe and Australia. More often than not, discourses of modernity, democracy and development inform these critiques as well,

[4] A. Lijphart, 'Emergency Powers and Emergency Regimes: A Commentary' (1978) 18 *Asian Survey* 401; C. Cotter, 'Constitutionalizing Emergency Powers: The British Experience' (1953) 5 *Stanford Law Review* 382; B. Ackerman, 'The Emergency Constitution' (2004) 113 *Yale Law Journal* 1029; L. H. Tribe and P. O. Gudridge, 'The Anti-Emergency Constitution' (2004) 113 *Yale Law Journal* 1801.

[5] V. V. Ramraj, 'The Emergency Powers Paradox' (Chapter 2), this volume, p. 22.

[6] N. Hussain, *The Jurisprudence of Emergency: Colonialism and the Rule of Law* (Ann Arbor: University of Michigan Press, 2003).

[7] O. Gross and F. Ní Aoláin (eds.), 'Introduction', in *Law in Times of Crisis: Emergency Powers Constitutionalism in Theory and Practice* (Cambridge: Cambridge University Press, 2006).

[8] V. V. Ramraj and A. K. Thiruvengadam, 'Introduction: Emergency Powers and Constitutionalism in Asia' (Chapter 1), this volume, p. 2.

producing contested and sometimes conflated images of the state and the societies under examination.[9] Such assessments require some caution as certain paradigms are automatically employed when in fact they may not be relevant or meaningful.[10] One must not assume, as pointed out by Anil Kalhan's contribution, that issues such as constitutionality or extra-constitutionality 'really matter' in the context of South Asia.[11] Efforts to categorise the political development of particular regional nations using criteria associated with more 'mature' liberal democracies may limit our ability to assess notions of emergency critically by overlooking how law, power and authority are translated and understood in a variety of Asian contexts. As Ramraj suggests in his contribution, the role of emergency powers can mean something quite different in an Asian context, where the challenge of such conditions lies in the threat not to an existing constitutional order, but to a fragile form of government trying to establish itself in the face of particular historical and political circumstances.[12] Reading emergency strictly through a lens of liberal democracy creates prescriptive oppositions that obfuscate the very differences that make comparative analyses useful in the first place.

Yet old paradigms die hard as Southeast Asian nations have appeared to resort to the use of constitutionally mandated special powers rather frequently, even at the risk of tainting the liberal-democratic principles upon which their constitutions supposedly rest.[13] One is led to consider why Southeast Asian legal systems are different when it comes to the use of emergency powers from (presumably) those that invoke them less frequently. Kevin Tan's contribution deals with this question directly and situates the place of emergency powers in Southeast Asia within the history of decolonisation and independence following the Second World War, arguing that conditions following the retreat of the Europeans provided the newly formed nations with a limited range of choices, considering the

[9] K. Heinz-Kramer, 'Nepal in 2002: Emergency and Resurrection of Royal Power' (2002) 43 *Asian Survey* 208; B. N. Shoenfeld, 'Emergency Rule in India' (1962) 36 *Pacific Affairs* 221; J. Das Gupta, 'A Season of Caesars: Emergency Regimes and Development Politics in Asia' (1978) 18 *Asian Survey* 315; Nicholas J. White, 'Capitalism and Counter-Insurgency? Business and Government in the Malayan Emergency 1948–1952' (1998) 32 *Modern Asian Studies* 149.

[10] E. Said, *Culture and Imperialism* (New York: Vintage, 1993).

[11] A. Kalhan, 'Constitution and "Extraconstitution": Colonial Emergency Regimes in Post-colonial India and Pakistan' (Chapter 4), this volume.

[12] Ramraj, Chapter 2.

[13] C. D. Neher and R. Marlay, *Democracy and Development in Southeast Asia: The Winds of Change* (Boulder, Colo.: Westview, 1995).

political, economic and social challenges that characterised this period. There is much truth in his observation that the manner in which these political transitions were managed influenced the extent to which emergency powers were employed.[14] At the same time, one must not overlook that emergency was also employed regularly by colonial powers to secure and entrench administrative control, suggesting that we might extend our gaze a bit further back than the period of decolonisation.[15] Similar to cases in British India, colonial administrations infused exceptional powers into the everyday governance of its subjects, rather than limiting these technologies of rule for temporary use. Contemporary (and perhaps regular) use of what might be considered 'extraordinary' powers by Southeast Asian governments may be connected, as Kalhan has noticed for Pakistan, to patterns of governance inherited from the colonial experience and its legal legacy.[16] Stretching our chronological gaze and exploring the connections between colonial understandings of emergency and contemporary settings may offer further insight into the relationships underlying power, authority and legitimacy as it is exercised in Southeast Asia today. In short, situating emergency exclusively within a liberal-democratic framework anchored in the post-war era may not only contribute to limited understandings of Southeast Asia governance systems, but also overlook the colonial legacy to which notions of emergency are directly tied. This chapter is concerned with these colonial moments in the history of emergency and the manner in which special powers were infused into the everyday governance of British Burma.

In doing so, the chapter will suggest that understanding the direct and indirect encounters with colonialism and its attendant forms can open new lines of inquiry in regard to the study of emergency in contemporary Asia. It will stretch the 'limits of law' methodologically by shifting attention away from emergency's relationship with constitutionalism toward a study of law's epistemological function as an active agent in the construction of historical knowledge.[17] From this perspective, emergency will be treated here as a particular lens through which cultures and communities are identified, categorised and ultimately criminalised to represent threats to the system. In order to demonstrate emergency's prescriptive nature,

[14] K. Y. L. Tan, 'From Myanmar to Manila: A Brief Study of Emergency Powers in Southeast Asia' (Chapter 6), this volume.

[15] *Ibid.*

[16] Kalhan, Chapter 4.

[17] A. Sarat and T. Kearns (eds.), *History, Memory, and the Law* (Ann Arbor: University of Michigan Press, 1999).

attention will be directed toward the way in which images of rebellion were preserved in the colonial archive through counter-insurgency legislation, tribunals and documentation projects that were employed to respond to such a crisis in British Burma between 1930 and 1932. This study will reconstruct how a notion of emergency was declared, how that crisis status relied on cultural profiles of Burmese and Bengalis and how special powers drawn from models of martial law were secured for a colonial administration that nonetheless negotiated to preserve its own rule from military intervention. To this end, the study concentrates primarily on how cultural discourses of emergency in Myanmar's colonial past produced particular images of Burmese political potential, representations that were ultimately adopted and reshaped by Myanmar's postcolonial government and by international critics as well.

II. Historical context

Imagining the place of law and the shape of the political future was decidedly mixed and often contentious for reformers in the 1920s and 1930s, partly on account of pre-existing rivalries, class divisions and generational differences that contributed to and were exacerbated by the colonial administrative policies. Particular systems of governance, designed to reflect economic and political priorities of the authorities affected the way in which power was interpreted and expressed by locals. Reform was often attempted through controlled channels within the colonial bureaucracy and many earlier reformers articulated their concerns through issues of religion and social welfare. Many indigenous communities within British Burma and sections of French Indochina experienced considerable change as a result of direct rule, requiring them to rethink the nature of law and authority, which no longer was sanctioned by religious or sacred ideals. Colonial rule, decidedly secular, bureaucratic and more intrusive than previous systems, was certainly more traumatic for people who would begin to call themselves 'Burmese', 'Indonesians' or 'Vietnamese' as the intensity of the changes they experienced were greater than those experienced by peoples living in Thailand, Malaysia, Singapore, Cambodia, Laos, Brunei and the Philippines.[18] As a result, differences in how 'legal normality' was

[18] N. G. Owen (ed.), *The Emergence of Southeast Asia* (Honolulu: University of Hawaii Press, 2005), pp. 201–68; N. Tarling (ed.) *The Cambridge History of Southeast Asia* (Cambridge University Press, 1999), vol. II, part 1, pp. 1–72 and pp. 245–320; N. Tarling (ed.), *Southeast Asia: A Modern History* (New York: Oxford University Press, 2001), pp. 44–96.

defined highlighted the range of experiences that were often connected to education, mobility, print media, Japanese/Chinese nationalist influence and anti-colonial ideologies.[19]

With these thoughts in mind, it is especially difficult to sustain a monolithic critique of Southeast Asian legal systems (and their understanding and employment of emergency powers) when one considers the wide range of pre-colonial indigenous notions of law, mediation, governance, authority and legitimacy – let alone the different applications of jurisprudence and constitutionalism that were associated with the colonial encounter. While Kevin Tan's contribution draws upon the challenges of the period after the Second World War and the often arduous transition to nationhood, many of the relevant debates and competitions amongst elite politicians, activists, students, communists, soldiers, monks and union leaders over the shape of the national community were actually a continuation of conversations that pre-dated the war, illustrating how deep and varied the divisions were by 1945. In fact, the vocabulary of liberal democracy was employed alongside many other concepts (such as Marxism, Fabianism and Japanese militarism) and systems that circulated amongst student dormitories, book clubs, study groups, volunteer associations, reform societies, monasteries and tea-shops. Differing educational policies were also a factor in that different domestic situations affected the intensity of colonial rule, which in turn governed the level of access students and future activists would have to external modes of governance, languages of reform and notions of law. Varying combinations of vernacular education and Western language schools produced similar types of civil servant ready to fulfil the needs within the respective administrations, but differing circumstances within each colonial setting created different needs, priorities and agendas. Some local elites would see themselves with colonial rulers, adopting the latter's world-view in shaping their notions of identity. Others would accept the essentialised discourses of difference between Europe and Asia, enabling them to denigrate certain characteristics of their past while simultaneously providing space to appropriate new (legal) models on their own terms. In short, assessing the role of emergency in a Southeast Asian context requires not only a closer understanding of the legal frameworks from which notions of constitutionalism were inherited, but also a recognition that the intensely complex ideological terrain from which many of the region's future leaders emerged also affected the ways in which legitimacy and authority were articulated.[20]

[19] Tarling (ed.), *Cambridge History*, pp. 245–320. [20] *Ibid.*

The notion of emergency in Burmese history may have many cultural understandings that include, but are not necessarily limited to, definitions emerging from the encounter with Western law. Following three wars that characterised the strained nature of Anglo-Burman relations in the nineteenth century, the British formally annexed the kingdom in 1886 and deported King Thibaw to India, essentially ending the long reign of kings that had stretched back to the eleventh century. In Burmese-Buddhist terms, the annexation and the fall of the throne has been regarded as the beginning of a socio-cultural emergency (*ayebaw*), as the monarchy was considered the custodian, benefactor and protector of the Buddhist religion – a role that would not be continued by the colonial administration but was crucial to the spiritual welfare of the Buddhist population. Moreover, such a crisis may have signalled for some that the end of the world was near, as the decline of Buddhism was also believed to correspond to the end of the world.[21] The dismantling of the monarchy, the subsequent decline in monastic standards, the disruption of social networks and the neglect of traditional rituals and religious festivals signalled a state of emergency (*ayebaw-achey-anay*) in terms that would intersect with the new vocabularies of colonial rule.

As a province of India, British Burma would eventually have its countryside 'pacified' and incorporated into the imperial legal system, administratively under the oversight of New Delhi but with its day-to-day business managed by its own civil service administration, governor-general, and eventually its own partially elected legislature under the 'dyarchy constitution'.[22] Following features of the Indian model, British Burma's judicial system featured a high court, several sessional courts and a network of local commissioners and magistrates that handled most of the more mundane affairs of the province by 1923. Indian civil servants were brought in to run the colony, though eventually Burmese were trained both locally and abroad in law to fill coveted positions in the administration. By the late 1920s a generation of Burmese barristers was active in the courts, while a growing number of political monks and students were beginning to articulate their views of political reform in the countryside, the universities, and the streets of Rangoon. With the onset of a worldwide drop in commodity prices toward the end of the decade, preexisting cultural, economic and social tensions among British Burma's

[21] M. Sarkisyanz, *Buddhist Backgrounds of the Burmese Revolution* (The Hague: Martinus Nijhoff, 1965). To be more precise, the decline of Buddhism signalled the end of this world cycle, which would eventually be renewed by a Buddha of the Future.

[22] R. H. Taylor, *The State of Burma* (Honolulu: University of Hawaii Press, 1987), pp. 66–79.

urban communities erupted in the form of riots, destruction of property and racially motivated violence. As a result of the rise in rent, the drop in rice-paddy prices, confiscation of land, unrelenting taxes and the erosion of secondary income options, conditions in the countryside took a turn for the worse in the heart of British Burma's rice-producing delta region.[23]

III. An epistemology of emergency

In late December 1930, British Burma experienced the first wave of what would become the largest peasant uprising since the annexation of the kingdom. It began with only a few hundred armed cultivators who had apparently attacked a small police force in the rural district of Tharrawaddy, killing a forestry official and a few subordinates. Though minor disturbances had occurred randomly since the annexation of the kingdom, the skirmishes that erupted in the paddy-fields of Lower Burma would eventually be treated more seriously by administrators based in the newly established capital of Rangoon, as one district after another succumbed to rebellion and civil disorder. Unlike the earlier pacification campaigns of the 1890s, officials reported that rural cultivators were now seemingly more organised, prepared and apparently united behind a mysterious leader who was said to be the new king of Burma. Rumours of his great powers and charisma allegedly attracted peasants to his campaign for tax-relief, a resurrection of the Burmese monarchy and the revitalisation of the Buddhist religion, which was perceived by many to have been in decline since the dismantling of the royal court and the exiling of the king to India. Calling himself Saya San, he reportedly claimed not only to be skilled in indigenous forms of healing and protection, but also to have experience in more contemporary forms of political mobilisation, having spent some time working for a radical wing of British Burma's largest nationalist organisation. Officials reported that Saya San had built a palace, held a coronation ceremony, made several royal proclamations and recruited followers, in order to appeal to long-standing beliefs held by rural communities that the monarchy had indeed returned. Saya San's allure was apparently so strong that the rebellion would take over two years to quell, resulting in 1,300 casualties, 9,000 arrests and many more displaced from their homes. Saya San was eventually captured in July 1931

[23] See M. Adas, *The Burma Delta: Economic Development and Social Change on an Asian Frontier 1852–1941* (Madison: University of Wisconsin Press, 1974); R. H. Taylor, *The State in Burma* (London: Hurst & Co., 1987); I. Brown, *A Colonial Economy in Crisis: Burma's Cultivators and the World Depression of the 1930s* (New York: Routledge/Curzon, 2005).

and, shortly after, brought before a tribunal which found him guilty of waging war under sections 121 and 121(A) of the Indian Penal Code. While colonial officials in London, New Delhi and Rangoon viewed what was termed the 'Burma Rebellion' as one among many throughout the Empire, scholars would eventually consider the 'Saya San Rebellion' as one of Southeast Asia's quintessential anti-colonial resistance movements.[24]

The above narrative is drawn from the official blue-book report that was published in 1934, two years after the violence was judged to have subsided into random acts of dacoity. Entitled *The Origins and Causes of the Burma Rebellion 1930–1932*, the report was commissioned by Parliament over matters of expenditure and mounting political pressure to explain the measures adopted by the local government.[25] Rangoon officials had constantly been under scrutiny for their counter-insurgency tactics; from opposition members of the local legislature, from sympathetic MPs in Parliament, and from colonial administrators in New Delhi, who were responsible for managing governance in what was technically a province under the British Raj in India. The report brought together four years of official documentation into a single document and argued that the rebellion was political in origin, caused by the gullibility of the peasantry on the one hand and the manipulative efforts of Saya San and his lieutenants on the other. It argued that superstitious beliefs in the protective powers of tattoos, a nostalgia for a returning monarch and an inherent restlessness on the part of the peasants typified the world-view of rural communities and demonstrated their inability to comprehend political reform in terms other than (what was identified as) the 'traditional'. Based on a security document written fifteen years earlier, the official explanation relied on a premise that colonial Burma was consistently under threat of pretender kings who would periodically emerge and rally discontented peasants against the authorities.[26] Emergencies were therefore something to be expected within Burmese culture; it was part of the 'hereditary disposition' of peasant communities to raise the standard of revolt in hope of resurrecting the monarchy. With few exceptions, the *Origins and*

24 A wide range of scholars have studied the Saya San Rebellion from a variety of perspectives. See a brief survey of this scholarship in M. Aung-Thwin, 'Genealogy of a Rebellion Narrative: Law, Ethnology, and Culture in Colonial Burma' (2003) 34 *Journal of Southeast Asian Studies* 393, and in 'Structuring Revolt: Communities of Interpretation in the Construction of the Saya San Rebellion' (2008) 39 *Journal of Southeast Asia Studies* 297.

25 Government of Burma (GOB), L/PJ/6/2020, Burma Rebellion General File (BRGF), *The Origins and Causes of the Burma Rebellion 1930–1932*, 1934.

26 GOB, L/PJ/6/2020, BRGF, B. S. Carey, 'Hints for the Guidance of Civil Officers in the Event of Outbreak of Disturbances in Burma', 1914.

Causes of the Burma Rebellion became the primary source that anchored nearly every subsequent study of the rebellion, providing the 'historical' evidence upon which the facts of the narrative and interpretations have been based. Although aware of the various administrative priorities that shaped the document, subsequent scholars accepted the report as containing what were perceived as the basic facts pertaining to the rebellion, relying on them and the document as the evidential foundation for a wide range of interpretations about the motivations, character and distinctiveness of peasant resistance in colonial Burma.[27]

With closer examination, one finds that the report relied primarily on the findings of special courts that oversaw the processing and conviction of detainees identified as rebels.[28] Whole sections of the report's text were lifted from the arguments that stemmed from government advocates and the decisions that were authorised by the tribunals. The report's content, narrative scaffolding and credibility were thus reliant upon and closely connected to the sources produced by the tribunals. Moreover, the arguments made in the report were directly drawn from the findings contained in earlier judgment summaries, revealing the manner in which the official blue-book report authorised and was authorised by these legal sources. Thus, the most important source for the history of the Saya San Rebellion was very much connected to the special tribunal system that was erected to process it.[29]

The relevant judgment summaries that emerged from nearly three years of this legal processing resulted in an impressive documentary record upon which this official report was based.[30] The trials of detainees under the special tribunals functioned as an important site of knowledge production, as the documents that emerged from them not only validated earlier assessments made by colonial authorities but became the textual basis for

[27] A wide range of literature is available. For a sample, see P. Ghosh, *Brave Men of the Hills: Rebellion and Resistance in Burma 1825–1932* (London: Hurst & Co., 2000); P. Herbert, *The Hsaya San Rebellion: Reappraised* (Melbourne: Monash University Centre for Southeast Asian Studies Working Papers, 1982); M. Adas, *Prophets of Rebellion: Millenarian Protest Movements Against the European Colonial Order* (Chapel Hill: University of North Carolina Press, 1979); J. C. Scott, *The Moral Economy of the Peasant: Rebellion and Subsistence in Southeast Asia* (New Haven: Yale University Press, 1977); Sarkisyanz, *Buddhist Backgrounds*; J. Cady, *A History of Modern Burma* (Ithaca: Cornell University Press, 1958).

[28] GOB, L/PJ/6/2022–3, BRGF.

[29] A fuller version of this argument can be found in Aung-Thwin, 'Genealogy of a Rebellion Narrative' and M. Aung-Thwin, 'British Counter-Insurgency Narratives and the Construction of a Twentieth Century Burmese Rebel', unpublished PhD dissertation, University of Michigan (2001).

[30] GOB, L/PJ/6/2022–3, BRGF.

the official report that would follow in 1934. However, these records were not detailed transcripts of the proceedings, but summaries that contained only the prosecution's arguments and the statements by the presiding judges. Specifically, only the arguments made by government advocates were recorded, along with various deliberations conducted by the tribunal when legal issues regarding procedure, admissibility of evidence and sentencing were raised. As a result, embedded within the official narrative were the prosecution's side of the story, the tribunal's deliberations and the administrative priorities directing the processing of detainees. The shape of *Origins and Causes of the Burma Rebellion 1930–1932* was thus determined by the contours of the prosecution's case, the reliability of the evidence presented to the tribunal, the manner in which the judges authenticated what it understood as 'rebellion' and, most significantly, the form in which these conclusions were rendered for documentation. A reassessment of the government's case against Saya San reveals that it rested on an untenable evidential foundation, drawing into question the entire historical narrative (and subsequent interpretations) that rely on it.[31] Yet the story of law's role in this rendering begins not with these trials, but in the declaration of an emergency situation and the legislation that was authorised to deal with it.

IV. Legislating emergency

In response to the outbreaks of unrest in late 1930, Rangoon officials quickly sent patrols to Tharrawaddy and other districts, to collect intelligence, assess the situation and engage the rebels if confronted. Upon finding that these advanced units were clearly outnumbered, troops were dispatched from local garrisons while reinforcements were requested from British India proper, as officials soon realised that the disturbances were not, as earlier suspected, merely limited in number and short-lived in nature. In addition to these measures, the Burma government quickly proposed key counter-insurgency legislation in order to provide civil authorities with extraordinary powers to deal with the rise in civil disorder. Two government-sponsored initiatives, the Burma Criminal Law Amendment Ordinance and the Burma Rebellion Trials Ordinance, provided special authority to respond to the crisis while providing the legal basis for what would eventually be called the Burma Emergency Powers Ordinance of 1931.

[31] Aung-Thwin, 'Genealogy of a Rebellion Narrative'.

The Burma Criminal Law Amendment Ordinance was promulgated in January 1931, providing specific powers to set up courts of special commissioners to try terrorist and revolutionary offences under the Indian Penal Code.[32] A key feature was the omission of committal proceedings and the ability of the courts to pass any sentence authorised by law. Another feature was the authority to make orders controlling the movements or detain without trial, persons suspected of offences under certain sections of the Indian Penal Code. Rangoon officials were obviously shaken by the spread of the rebellion as a bill was introduced into the Burma Legislative Council that would extend these temporary measures for five years. Although it faced fierce debate and rejection in the local legislature, it was ultimately certified by the Governor (who had the power to overrule the legislature) and supported by the Secretary of State for India. In essence, the Ordinance amplified existing power structures, hierarchies and 'biases of public order' that Vasuki Nesiah recognises in the Sri Lankan context.[33]

In March 1931, the Burma Rebellion Trials Ordinance was enacted in order to provide special tribunals that could oversee the hearings of arrested rebels and other detainees as well. In this format, judges from the existing civil courts would be used to preside over the cases. This piece of legislation also attempted to detain without trial those suspected of rebellion and waging war against the Crown or those who aided and abetted those who took part in the uprisings. Because of disagreement with the Government of India (which continued to oversee administrative affairs in Burma and managed communication with London), power to detain without trial was officially curbed. Rangoon officials, hoping to secure powers quickly, then moulded their proposals along the model of the Bengal Criminal Law Amendment Act of 1925, as this legislation would provide administrative precedence and seemingly quicker action. The Bengali Act was actually drafted using a template for legislating martial law, a copy of which was included in the correspondences between Rangoon and New Delhi. By creating tribunals with special procedural provisions that were designed to 'stop the activity of leaders of whose guilt they are convinced but of which they cannot produce sufficient evidence to secure conviction in the courts,' Rangoon officials 'seized on an Ordinance which

[32] GOB, L/PJ/6/2021, BRGF, 'Memorandum of Specific Powers Already Taken and How Asked for By the Government of Burma in Connection with Rebellion', June 1931.

[33] V. Nesiah, 'The Princely Impostor: Stories of Law and Pathology in the Exercise of Emergency Powers' (Chapter 5), this volume, p. 136.

would meet their immediate needs'.[34] In doing so, counter-insurgency officials bypassed the reach and authority of the existing courts, froze civil liberties and extended the ability of the state to search, seize and arrest – a sign that the conditions for the normal operation of the law had certainly changed.

The securing of these special powers depended on Burma officials convincing both their New Delhi and London superiors that such exceptional circumstances threatened the security and future of the state. But as legislative precedence was not available that could directly link what appeared to be a traditional rebellion with the type of special powers sought by the colonial authorities, other explanations that could refer to existing sources of legislation were thus deemed necessary to make their case. In this manner, constructing the appropriate ethno-historical context enabled a commensurate legal context to be established through which special powers could be secured. Such intersections between colonial law, politics and ethnology is, as Vasuki Nesiah observes in the case of Sri Lanka, about the parameters of legal legitimacy as it is an opportunity to problematise supposed periods of lawlessness.[35] Interestingly, gestures towards the maintenance of legal normality were offered through the participation of the Burmese Legislative Council in this process, while at the same time the powers invested in the suggested ordinances would significantly curb and isolate the powers of both the legislature and judicial sectors in rebellion matters. The appropriation of the Bengal Criminal Law Amendment Act to Burma needed justification along a different line, one that presented the situation in Burma as analogous to past experiences of terrorism in Bengal. Emergency in Burma would have to be defined through a different narrative of crisis.

V. The Burma Criminal Law Amendment Ordinance, monks and the Bengali connection

In an effort to secure the Burma Criminal Law Amendment Ordinance, Rangoon officials resurrected the Bengal Criminal Law Amendment Act which was originally enacted in 1925 to deal with the threat of revolutionary activities that had risen in Bengal toward the end of

[34] GOB, L/PJ/6/2021, BRGF, W. Johnston, Legal Advisor, Docket, Public and Judicial Department, 11 January 1931.

[35] Nesiah, Chapter 5.

1922.[36] Officials had in fact proposed its adoption in Burma as early as 15 December 1930 (a week before the Tharrawaddy outbreak), in order to deal with the 'terrorist movement' in Burma.[37] It is possible that the events in the paddy-fields finally provided Rangoon officials with the conditions needed to secure these special powers that had not existed earlier. Burma officials had sought permission from the Government of India to arrest and detain without trial revolutionaries suspected of committing terrorist acts. They feared that 'gullible' and 'excitable' university students might be attracted to the agenda of the Bengali terrorists and therefore special powers were required to dissuade Burmese youths from taking the mantle of revolution. Interestingly, authorities would eventually adopt these very same words to describe the limited political potential of Burmese rural communities.[38]

The outbreak in Tharrawaddy District, which occurred a few weeks later, was presented as a continuation of these Bengali operations, even as the 'royal' model (suggesting a returning king) was being communicated simultaneously through other official channels. While the ordinance was passed in order to curb the influence of foreign terrorists, the records surrounding the ordinance reveal how this emergency legislation used ethnology to define the profile of a Burmese Rebel. The Burma Criminal Law Amendment Ordinance expanded not only the ability to arrest, detain, search and seize, but also established what would be considered 'rebellious' acts against the Crown, revealing its ability to define emergency through behaviour, ritual, and symbols it identified as 'Burmese culture'. The criminalisation of Burmese beliefs, the movement of non-state authorities and the criminalisation of tattooing became important parts of Rangoon's counter-insurgency programme to make legible the character of Burmese resistance. Counter-insurgency legislation was the key phase that brought earlier ethnographic constructions of Burmese rebellion into the orbit of colonial legal culture.

At 11.45 a.m. on 8 January 1931, the Secretary of State for India received a telegram from India (on behalf of the Burma government), seeking special legislation to deal with terrorism in Burma that had occurred in

[36] GOB, L/PJ/6/2021, BRGF, 'A Brief Summary of the History of the Bengal Criminal Law Amendment Ordinance'.

[37] GOB, L/PJ/6/2021, BRGF, 'Proposal for Promulgation of an Ordinance', Confidential Minute Paper 9 January 1931.

[38] GOB, L/PJ/6/2021, BRGF, Government of Burma, Confidential Letter, 693W30, 15 December 1930.

Tharrawaddy District.[39] Although several situation reports had already identified Saya San as the prime suspect to British authorities, an entirely different story was being constructed for legislative purposes. At 12.00 noon, the Secretary of State for India began to receive detailed information that the outbreak was the work of Bengali terrorists, who were attempting to smuggle 'arms into Bengal from Singapore and the Far East' but were now assuming 'terrorist activities in Burma'.[40] These terrorists, functioning under the Bengal Revolutionary Party, were said to be 'mainly Bengali' and to number around 300.[41] Officials attributed recent reports of 'political dacoity' in Rangoon and the attempted derailment of a train in September and October 1930 respectively, to this terrorist organisation.[42] By 2.30 p.m., information from an informer provided government officials with new intelligence that indicated a slightly different story. According to this version, 'Burman monks were connected with the movement and involved in the importation of revolvers and ammunition from the Chinese border'.[43] Tattooing had occurred in several districts as the rebellion spread, indicating (according to officials) signs of 'excitement' and 'disaffection'.[44] This arrangement was apparently the 'definite plan' of the 'notorious revolutionary absconder' Rash Bihari Bose, the General Council of Burmese Associations (GCBA) (the most outspoken and well-organised opposition organisation in Burma) and U Oktama (political activist and monk) who had ties to the Bengal Revolutionary Party.[45] He was well known to British officials as a 'revolutionary firebrand' who had been imprisoned more than once for his

[39] GOB, L/PJ/6/2021, BRGF, Government of India, Home Department, to S/S for India, Secret Telegram, 8 January 1931 (11.45 a.m.).

[40] GOB, L/PJ/6/2021, BRGF, Government of India, Home Department, to S/S for India, Secret Telegram 8 January 1931 (12.00 noon).

[41] *Ibid.*

[42] *Ibid.* It is interesting to note that during this time, these same two events were being linked to the Tharrawaddy outbreak that occurred in late December 1930 and January 1931. When, however, the events in Tharrawaddy became associated with Saya San in the accepted narrative, these two events were removed from the story.

[43] GOB, L/PJ/6/2021, BRGF, Government of India, Home Department, to S/S for India, Secret Telegram, 8 January 1931 (2.30 p.m.).

[44] *Ibid.* Tattooing had already become a significant characteristic of *both* narratives and in this case, was being presented as 'evidence' for rebellion-related 'excitement'.

[45] GOB, L/PJ/6/2021, BRGF, Government of India, Home Department, to S/S for India, Secret Telegram, 8 January 1931 (3.15 p.m.). U Ottama (Oktama) was a monk who advocated that the monkhood be involved in secular affairs, particularly in the livelihood of peasants. His message was eventually taken up by the GCBA. See Taylor, *The State in Burma*, pp. 182–3.

activities.[46] A 1929 report described U Oktama as 'exceedingly excitable', 'intelligent', 'endowed with great energy and driving power . . . and is hand in glove with the most extreme Indian agitators'.[47] The spread of the rebellion to neighbouring districts was attributed to visits by U Oktama and his subordinates, making it 'impossible not to associate these risings with him' and the Bengal Revolutionary Party.[48] Due to the rapid expansion of the outbreak, the Burmese Government requested permission to search the headquarters of the Soe Thein General Council of Burmese Associations, in order to 'arrest leaders and declare the Association and its most important branches illegal'.[49] However, it was 'uncertain whether sufficient evidence will be obtained to convict leaders under ordinary law' and therefore a more favourable set of laws in the form of the Ordinance was desired.[50] In short, the securing of new counter-insurgency legislation was based on a completely separate narrative from the *minlaung*[51] explanation involving Saya San; British administrators had identified another monk (U Oktama), the GCBA and the Bengal Revolutionary Party as having planned and instigated the growing number of outbreaks in rural Lower Burma[52].

By 11 January, the Burma government recommended immediate promulgation of the Criminal Law Amendment Ordinance through the executive powers of the Governor-General. They reported that the rebellion was more widespread than originally believed, partly based on speculation that the GCBA and its affiliates had penetrated the local

[46] GOB, L/PJ/6/2021, BRGF, 'Proposed promulgation of an Ordinance to deal with the revolutionaries', Confidential Minute, 9 January 1931.

[47] *Ibid.*

[48] GOB, L/PJ/6/2021, BRGF, Government of India, Home Department, to S/S for India, Secret Telegram, Part II, 11 January 1931.

[49] *Ibid.* The 'Soe Thein General Council of Burma Associations' refers to a branch of the original GCBA which split off due to differing views on the Separation issue. It is quite possible that the rebellion and the nature of the government's response had to do with the Soe Thein stance of disagreeing with the government's position to separate from the administrative control of India. A brief synopsis of the GCBA and its branches can be found in Taylor, *The State in Burma*, pp. 174–88.

[50] GOB, L/PJ/6/2020, BRGF, Secret Telegram, 8 January 1931.

[51] *Minlaung* is a Burmese term that means 'embryo king', 'incipient king' or 'king-to-be'. In the context of the British pacification of the Kingdom (and in subsequent rebellions), the term was used to refer to anyone the administration deemed as a 'pretender king' or one who was illegitimately claiming to be a king.

[52] GOB, L/PJ/6/2021, BRGF, Government of India, Home Department, to S/S for India, Secret Telegram, 2 February 1931.

countryside and won the support of the monks.[53] U Oktama's involvement was further embellished, by describing his meetings with Rash Bihari Bose, his contact with other Bengali revolutionaries, and his membership of the executive committee of the General Council of Burmese Associations.[54] Curiously, the telegram closes with the statement:

> [i]nformation independently obtained received from Bengal Government to which reference was made in previous telegram, definitely states armed rising as object of *Burmese* Revolutionary Party acting in conjunction with Buddhist monks and other Burmans.[55]

Whereas the initial view posited that the Bengal Revolutionary Party, the GCBA and sympathetic monks were responsible for the outbreaks, three days later it was being reported that an entity known as the *Burmese* Revolutionary Party was now running the show, thereby shifting attention away from external influences on the rebellion to an internal one. Later documentation would eventually confirm that the legislation was meant not for some external terrorist group, but for Burmese accused of rebellion. For the moment, Rangoon officials were satisfied with the contrived Bengali connection because any delay in securing these extended powers would allow the Party to 'gravely embarrass Local government' even if it were found (as it was admitted) that the Party was 'not directly connected with the rebellion'.[56]

Internal documents on 11 January also indicate that the use of the Bengali narrative was crucial to guaranteeing the requested ordinances, even though officials quietly admitted that it 'was a little out of date'.[57] By creating the impression that the emergency in Burma was as serious as it was in Bengal, Rangoon would be able to seek special provisions

[53] GOB, L/PJ/6/2021, BRGF, Government of India, Home Department, to S/S India, Secret Telegram, 11 January 1931 (1.00 p.m.).

[54] *Ibid.*

[55] *Ibid.*, emphasis added. It is quite possible that this was merely a typo, but later statements seem to indicate that the legislation being sought was to be used against the Burmese.

[56] GOB, L/PJ/6/2021, BRGF, Government of India, Home Department, to S/S for India, Secret Telegram, 11 January 1931 (2.30 p.m.).

[57] GOB, L/PJ/6/2021, BRGF, Confidential Minute Paper, Public and Judicial Department, 5 January 1931. This comment by W. Johnston refers specifically to a report compiled by Lt.-Col. C. De Wellborne and Deputy Inspector-General of Police entitled 'Note On the Growth of the Bengal Revolutionary Movement in Burma from 1922 to 1930'. This report detailed the actions of Bengali terrorists in Burma thought to be responsible for numerous acts of violence. Although officials had begun implicating the GCBA in the rebellion, Rangoon still included Wellborne's 'Note' with the proposal for the new ordinance.

at least comparable to those imposed in Bengal.[58] In fact, advisors saw the situation in Burma as more precarious since it was thought that the terrorist party in Bengal was 'comparatively small in numbers' and that a revolutionary party in Burma that had the administrative apparatus of the GCBA posed a more serious threat.[59] Dealing with an organisation as politically experienced as the GCBA and one which had penetrated the countryside demanded quick and thorough action. As a result, extended powers, such as the authority to detain without trial, the denial of habeas corpus, the creation of special tribunals and provisions stated in the Bengal Criminal Law Amendment Act of 1925 were all deemed necessary by both the India and Burma governments. On 16 January, the government made it clear what it needed: one ordinance to deal with Bengal revolutionaries and one to give special powers for trials of rebels.

Thus, on 31 January, the Burma Criminal Law Amendment Ordinance was issued, along with a statement from the Governor-General explaining his actions.

> It has been known to Government for some years that there is a terrorist party in Burma which is closely associated with terrorist movement in Bengal. This party has of late engaged in commission of terrorist outrages and there is reason to believe that it was responsible for a political dacoity in Rangoon Town in September, 1930, and for derailment of a mail train in October, 1930, at Nyaungchidauk in Toungoo District, in which high officials of Government were traveling [*sic*]. A recent feature of its activities has been wide distribution among students and others of revolutionary pamphlets directly inciting violence. There is good ground for belief that it is privy to rebellion in Tharrawaddy District and that it was the intention of those responsible for that rebellion to organize [*sic*] risings in different parts of Burma with a view to overthrow of Government as established by law.[60]

In other words, the Burma Criminal Law Amendment Ordinance was deemed a response to the perceived connection between the rebellion and Bengali terrorists. The powers conferred by the Ordinance were to be used only against 'those in regard to whom there is reason to believe that they are members of terrorist party in Burma or are acting in furtherance of terrorist movement [*sic*]'.[61] As a result, the Tharrawaddy rebellion

[58] GOB, L/PJ/6/2021, BRGF, W. Johnston, Legal Advisor, Docket, Public and Judicial Department, 11 January 1931.

[59] *Ibid.*

[60] GOB, L/PJ/6/2021, BRGF, Government of India, Home Department, to S/S for India, Telegram, 2 February 1931

[61] *Ibid.*

was conceptualised as part of a Bengali narrative of resistance, thereby allowing action against it as prescribed by the Ordinance. Although the Governor-General of India issued the Ordinance as a supplement to 'ordinary Criminal Law' in Burma, its subsequent introduction as a bill in the Legislative Council would soon draw heavy criticism from its Burmese members, who also saw several problems in the Government's narrative.[62]

VI. Debating emergency

At the 14 February 1931 meeting of the Burma Legislative Council, Sir Joseph Maung Gyi, former Acting Governor-General, whose brief tenure saw the outbreak of rebellion in Tharrawaddy, introduced the Criminal Law Amendment Bill and urged for it to be formally considered.[63] Repeating the words from the current Governor-General's statement, Maung Gyi reiterated the need to extend the duration of the Ordinance as it was only a temporary measure with a limited period of operation. His argument attempted to convey much of the view that officials had sent on to London: namely, that the government had always been well aware of the presence of the terrorists in Burma but certain jurisdictional obstacles required a more substantive and concrete amendment. He states:

> The Government has been aware that [*sic*] since 1922 of the existence of a section of the Bengal Revolutionary Party in Burma, but hitherto they have contented themselves in keeping a careful watch on the activities of these men . . . Now when those members of the Association came to Rangoon the Police were aware of their arrival and they were not met at the wharf, but to all appearances and purposes these revolutionaries who were fugitives looked harmless people [*sic*], and as the Police had nothing to show against them, they could not take any steps to prevent these revolutionaries from carrying on their nefarious work. We have no law with which to deal with these revolutionaries. Until they acted overtly we could do nothing to them.[64]

Even more curious was Acting Governor-General Sir Joseph Maung Gyi's explanation of how geographical origins and the 'body' of the

[62] GOB, L/PJ/6/2021, BRGF, Statement by the Governor-General of India, Home Department, 31 January 1931.

[63] GOB, L/PJ/6/2021, BRGF, Extract from the Proceedings of the Burma Legislative Council (BLC) Relating to the Burma Criminal Law Amendment Bill 1931, at a meeting held on 14 February 1931, pp. 139–62.

[64] *Ibid.*

Indian subcontinent could explain the terrorist tendencies of the Bengali community.

> The Hindus believe, Sir, that the Brahmins proceed from the mouth of Brahma and therefore they are the most intellectual people because they are the teachers of the people. They are known as Brahmins, but the Kshatriyas and the fighting classes proceed from the arms and chest of Brahma. Now if you take the map of India, you will see that Bengal is the head of India, that the North-West Province of Punjab, where the fighting races come from, are the arms and chest of India. The Bengalis are efficient people and very highly intellectual. They are a mild mannered people and well disposed as a rule, but out of all the different districts in Bengal, there is one that lies right to the east nearest to the hills where the wild tribes go in for head hunting and that is Chittagong, and it is in the district of Chittagong that the Bengal Revolutionary Association had its birth and the majority of the members of the Association come from Chittagong.[65]

In objection to these and other curious statements made by Acting Governor Joseph Maung Gyi, several members of the legislature questioned whether an emergency situation actually existed by disputing the interpretation of events that led to the Ordinance's promulgation. Although scholars suggest that urban elites were unimpressed and embarrassed by the rebellion, significant questions were raised by opposition members as to how the rebellion was being portrayed and responded to by local government. Local members of the Burma Legislative Council were deeply engaged in considering the powers delineated by counter-insurgency legislation.[66] One member, U Ni complained:

> The Government is pursuing a chimera when, among its objects and reasons, it tries to draw a connection between the Tharrawaddy rebellion, the U Soe Thein GCBA, and the Bengal Revolutionaries. Ever since the rebellion started Government issued communiques from time to time. From the beginning no mention was made that this rebellion was the result of revolutionary activities. The first information was that it was due to economic depression. Later on it was changed into the statement that a pretender was aspiring to the throne of Burma. Subsequently, when Government thought fit to introduce this bill, they ingeniously tried to connect two outrages that occurred in Burma with the rebellion.[67]

Along the same lines, Mr Rafi from Moulmein found it hard to believe that any of the rebels in Tharrawaddy 'had even heard of Bengal and know

[65] *Ibid.* Tharrawaddy region was also deemed a haven for robbers, dacoits and pretender kings. The criminalisation of geography is a common trait in counter-insurgency documents.
[66] *Ibid.* [67] *Ibid.*

anything about it'.[68] This statement was followed by another observation by Mr E. P. Pillay, who, in commenting on the government's position that it had the Bengali organisation under observance since 1922, stated:

> There had been a careful watch, and yet they were not in a position to discover the connection of these revolutionaries with the rebellion long before this! It is only to-day they open their mouths and say, 'Oh, these revolutionaries are connected with the rebellion!' Could it, by any stretch of the imagination, be said that persons unacquainted with the language, custom, and manners of the people of this country would have gone and influenced the villagers who are now taking part in this rebellion? . . . It strikes me that the Bengal revolutionaries were thrown into the scale in order to hoodwink the Viceroy into granting permission to introduce this Bill.[69]

After continued heated debates over particulars in the bill, the bill was narrowly defeated in a vote of 46–39.[70] Despite this defeat in the legislature, Governor Charles Innes invoked his powers of certification to override the Council's decision, which to all intents and purposes signalled the transformation of the Ordinance into a longer-lasting Bill. Although the Criminal Law Ordinance was not officially directed toward the rebellion, it gave special powers to enact other legislation that was specifically aimed at dealing with the uprising. One such example was the Burma Emergency Powers Ordinance which was later secured in order to confer powers to local government to suppress and prevent rebellion in Burma.[71] Not only would this third Ordinance extend the powers of the British counter-insurgency plan, but it would define more directly those people against whom these provisions would be used. One noticeable feature was that the government sought to apply specific powers throughout the whole of Burma (rather than in limited 'affected areas'), in order to curb the movement of political monks who were associated with tattooing and the recruitment of rebels.[72] Though these specific measures were regarded by London as of 'doubtful legality' and despite instructions that no further proposals should make reference to tattooing or supernatural charm use, later tribunal records would demonstrate that arrests,

[68] *Ibid.* [69] *Ibid.* [70] *Ibid.*

[71] GOB, L/PJ/6/2021, BRGF, Burma Emergency Ordinance, 1 June 1931; GOB, L/PJ/6/2021, BRGF, Governor's Statement, Enclosure no. 3, 1 August 1931.

[72] GOB, L/PJ/6/2020, BRGF, Government of India, Home Department, to S/S India, Telegram, repeating telegram from GOB, 11 June 1931; L/PJ/6/2021, BRGF, Government of India, Home Department, to S/S India, Telegram, Part I, repeating telegrams from and to GOB, 9 June 1930.

detainment and association with the rebellion were in fact based on the arrest of these 'agents' of Burmese rebellion culture.[73] In essence, the new Ordinance extended counter-insurgency attention from Tharrawaddy and neighbouring districts to include the entire province while simultaneously narrowing the ethnographic profiles associated with rebellion. At a stroke, measures against wandering monks and royal pretenders were combined to form an image of the rebellion that labelled monks as recruiters, village associations as terrorist cells and the resurrection of the Burmese monarchy as the ideological platform upon which peasants were motivated to participate. Just as official reports began to conceptualise the rebellion as a single, coherent expression of Burmese resistance, so too did counter-insurgency legislation reflect and enable this change in perspective.

In the end, the Emergency Powers Ordinance came to embody the combined intents of the Rebellion Trials and Criminal Law Ordinances. While the latter two were secured through a narrative depicting the Bengal Revolutionary Party involvement in the uprising, the full weight of emergency power was directed against Burmese rebels who were responding to a variety of local concerns and interests. Once these legal powers were established, traces of the Bengali role in the rebellion begin to fade out in official accounts as administrators returned their focus to a local explanation. What matters here is that three narratives were produced simultaneously by colonial scholar-officials in an attempt to explain the rebellion: the royal model, the Bengali terrorist conspiracy and the image of the modern, politicised monk. Of these three narratives, two would be conflated to form the picture of Saya San that we accept today. The exclusion of the Bengali connection in practically every account of the Saya San rebellion and the conflation of the royal/monk model reflects the manner in which the narrative involving the alleged role of kingship was prioritised and normalised in official documentation in order to render the rebellion as traditional, while providing the means of regulating political expression that in fact departed from pre-colonial forms of protest. As U Oktama would eventually fade from view, Saya San would be depicted not only as a quack doctor who saw himself as the restorer of the Burmese monarchy, but also as a political operative exploiting GCBA-connected village associations as the infrastructure for the rebellion network. Counter-insurgency legislation both produced and

[73] GOB, L/PJ/6/2021, BRGF, Government of India, Home Department, to S/S India, Secret Telegram, Part III, 23 May 1931; GOB, L/PJ/6/2021, BRGF, Government of India, Home Department, to S/S India, Telegram, Part II, repeating telegrams from and to GOB, 9 January 1931.

reduced narratives of Burmese resistance while creating the epistemological context for their articulation and authorisation in the special rebellion tribunals.

In pursuit of expansive legal and municipal powers, emergency policy enabled and was enabled by ethnographic constructions of Burmese culture. By identifying, textualising and codifying cultural practices that were quite common throughout rural society, colonial officials produced legislation that defined the contours of Burmese social culture through the language and priorities of counter-insurgency policy. The resulting discourse reified differences among Burmese in what Vasuki Nesiah identifies as the 'normalising' feature of emergency, suggesting entrenched divisions between urban and rural communities and between politically capable Indian politicians and incapable Burmese activists, and more generic differences between colonised and coloniser.[74] Legislation, like official reports, represented both a stage in the formation of the official narrative of Saya San and an institutional expression of what rebellion meant to colonial officials in a particular context. It marked a moment, referred to in Anil Kalhan's chapter, where the colonial executive attempted not only to maintain central control over state matters, but also to preserve its autonomy from both the military (who actively sought a formal declaration of martial law) and the judicial sector.[75] Yet it also signalled a particular stage in the codification of what constituted a Burmese 'rebellion'. Ideas of 'normality' did not – in British eyes – involve or include space for tattooing, wandering monks or kingship in the realm of the political. Emergency legislation was as much a textual expression of and debate over these cultural perspectives as those found in official reports and other documentation. For counter-insurgency officials, rebellion was about migrant communities (Bengalis) and transnational activists (U Oktama) as much as it was about a hopeless Burmese nostalgia for its vanquished monarchy (royal model).

Although the British pacification of the Burmese Kingdom (1886–1890) provided profiles of criminals and rebels that would endure in colonial documentation, it was specifically the use of emergency legislation that projected many of these generic traits into the particular events of 1930–1. The Rebellion Trials Ordinance and the Burma Criminal Law Amendment Ordinance codified many of these traits of crisis by making them a part of the legal discourse on rebellion matters. As objects of debate in correspondences, reports and legislative proceedings, elements of Burmese

[74] Nesiah, Chapter 5, p. 123. [75] Kalhan, Chapter 4.

culture were embedded in the administrative context of rebellion, reshaping their meaning and significance to observers. Most importantly, the records that would evolve out of this discourse would establish the interpretive framework in which future nationalists, scholars and governments would engage them.

VII. Contemporary currents and colonial antecedents

In the context of colonial Burma, emergency was more than a series of counter-insurgency policies that were enacted by authorities to deal with the threat of rebellion. It was more than a legal tussle between the principles of civilian rule (which was somewhat curbed, even with some liberal institutions in place) and those of military rule, more than a negotiation between opposition members in the Burmese legislative council, New Delhi and London. Emergency was also a discourse, a set of operational terms and perspectives through which the Burmese past, its culture and its communities were identified and categorised. As Vasuki Nesiah observes in the context of colonial and postcolonial Sri Lanka, emergencies produced similar discourses and epistemologies about the 'riot' and 'hooliganism', creating perceptions about the ability of certain communities to participate in political channels that are approved by the state. Emergency legislation in colonial Burma was intimately involved in prescribing the procedures, settings and paradigms that were directly connected to forming not only the evidential record of the rebellion, but the shape of the official narrative itself. Special powers in colonial Burma were not, following comments by Johan Geertsema, secured in a context of 'lawlessness', but were firmly embedded in the colonial state's discursive structures.[76] Law's ability to write history and its role in the registering of that past can be charted through this epistemology of emergency in colonial Burma.

Understanding contemporary Myanmar and its challenges through emergency can be useful as well. Clearly, the postcolonial predicament that is similarly discussed in this volume by Nesiah, Thiruvengadam and Kalhan is directly connected to two aspects of emergency's predicament: the legal continuities that connect the colonial and postcolonial state (despite attempts by the latter to distinguish itself) and the frequent application of emergencies as 'normal' (rather than 'exceptional') raise issues

[76] J. Geertsema, 'Exceptions, Bare Life, and Colonialism', in V. V. Ramraj (ed.), *Emergency and the Limits of Legality* (Cambridge: Cambridge University Press, 2008).

with how scholars define the parameters of normality in Myanmar. The notion of emergency is embedded in the way the military has viewed its role in governance since 1962, when it decided to formally take over from a civilian administration that had endured the beginnings of a multifaceted civil war, communist insurgencies, KMT invasion, separatist movements and urban violence since independence from the British in 1948.[77] Under General Ne Win (who came to power in 1962), the government regarded itself continually under threat from foreign and internal parties, much as British colonial authorities had articulated in reports that anticipated periodic 'disturbances' and rebellions by pretender-kings were of constant concern. This perspective of being continually under siege is something that Mary Callahan has identified as being central to the way in which the military has conceptualised itself in relation to Burmese society.[78] Just as the emergency of the Saya San rebellion produced particular expectations of Burmese peasants and limited their capacity to articulate reform in terms other than the traditional, so too has this notion of emergency characterised, to some extent, the Myanmar government's assessment of its own people as not being ready to embrace alternative forms of government until very recently. Separatist movements, ethnic tensions, political opposition movements and internal competition have fallen under this notion of continual threat and potential crisis, making stability and security key principles that have guided the direction of government policy. Overstated or not, this view has been articulated in an interesting way as a struggle against enemies within and without; it is apparent in recent movies (about the annexation of the Kingdom), museums, textbooks and monuments. Ironically, in its attempt to establish this cultural continuity, much of the state's emergency discourse appropriates both the form and perspective of colonial counter-insurgency policies and practices. While legal concepts of special powers were adopted from the British in the 1947 Constitution, emergency has also been very much a part of state discourse, inherited from colonial antecedents and the circumstances following independence in 1948.

As Myanmar prepares for its transition to what it sees as democracy, it is important to remember that it might not be seen exclusively as a 'return' to democracy (as is often reported in the media), a working assumption we tend to apply in studying emergency powers. Many within the current

[77] Myanmar Historical Commission, *Myanmar Politics 1958–1962*, 2 vols. (Yangon: University Press, 2006/7).

[78] M. P. Callahan, *Making Enemies: War and State Building in Burma* (Ithaca: Cornell University Press, 2003).

government and a few scholars abroad regard the era following independence (1948–62) not in terms of representative government but in terms of 'emergency' as well – a period that almost saw the disintegration of the Union. Factionalism within the educated elite, the Karen rebellion, communist insurgencies and the various divisions within the former Burmese Defence Army (formed during the Second World War) contributed to the sense of chaos and instability that characterised Burma and many new nations in the region. An assessment of emergency law, regimes and powers in the context of Asia might do well to consider colonialism and its forms as a complementary framework from which to start. The encounter with colonialism has been shown to have lasting legacies in contemporary Asian societies, providing an attractive field through which legal histories and epistemologies can be explored from a variety of interdisciplinary perspectives.[79]

[79] N. B. Dirks, *Castes of Mind: Colonialism and the Making of Modern India* (Princeton: Princeton University Press, 2001).

8

Emergency and Islamic law in Aceh

MICHELLE ANN MILLER AND R. MICHAEL FEENER

I. Introduction

Indonesia's province of Aceh on the northwestern tip of the island of Sumatra has been the site of catastrophic natural disaster, as well as the scene of one of Asia's most enduring and bloody armed separatist conflicts. Until August 2005, when an internationally mediated peace process in Helsinki led to resolution of the Aceh conflict, the Indonesian government exercised powers of emergency (*darurat*)[1] in various forms against the armed separatist Free Aceh Movement (Gerakan Acheh Merdeka, or GAM).[2] These emergency powers included both constitutional and extra-legal measures, and their exercise coincided with measures facilitating the state implementation of Islamic law in Aceh in complex and mutually reinforcing ways. After Indonesia initiated its

Research for this chapter was undertaken partially with the support of the Singapore Ministry of Education's Academic Research Fund (MOE AcRF no. R-110-000-029-750). We would like to thank Dan Birchok, Clark Lombardi and the participants in the Emergency Powers in Asia Symposium for their helpful comments on earlier drafts of this chapter.

1 This Indonesian term is derived from the Arabic *darura*, a technical term in Islamic jurisprudence (*fiqh*) that deals with the justification of sometimes necessary departures from established rules in order to protect, in times of imminent threat, the most fundamental aims of the Shari'a: life, property, progeny, reason, and religion itself. Despite this linguistic overlap in the terminologies of traditional jurisprudence and modern states of exception, we have not yet found any significant invocations of *darura* in its *fiqh* sense connecting the simultaneous calls for a declaration of a state of emergency and the formal implementation of Islamic law in Aceh that are discussed in this chapter.

2 The British spelling of 'Acheh' was generally preferred by GAM, reflecting the rebels' rejection of the modern Indonesian spelling. Despite his outspoken opposition to most other things Dutch, GAM's founding leader, Hasan di Tiro, also used the old Dutch spelling of 'Atjeh' to establish the Atjeh Institute in America and GAM's Ministry of Information of the State of Atjeh Sumatra (*Kementerian Penerangan Negara Atjeh Sumatra*). See, for example, H. di Tiro, *The Political Future of the Malay Archipelago* (New York: Atjeh Institute in America, 1965).

Reformasi decentralisation process in 1999, the country's political and military establishment called for the concurrent implementation of emergency rule and Islamic law (Shari'a) in the almost entirely Muslim province.[3]

While this particular combination of initiatives to increase the extent of state control may seem surprising to some, it actually has considerable precedent in a number of other countries in which the Islamisation of laws has been promoted within contexts of the exercise of emergency powers since the 1970s. Examples of this type of 'coincidence' are numerous and diverse. For instance, under the broader rubric of the exercise of extraordinary powers Anwar Sadat promulgated the 1979 Egyptian Constitution declaring Islamic jurisprudence as *the* principal source of legislation,[4] while in Pakistan Zia ul-Haq campaigned to make the country an 'Islamic state'.[5] In Sudan, too, Muhammad Ja'far al-Numayri initiated programmes for the implementation of Shari'a law codes and an Islamising unification of the previously separate civil and religious courts contemporaneously with various attempts at reasserting control over an emerging civil war in that country.[6] In Aceh the appeals to both emergency powers and Islamic law were not merely simultaneous, but actually formed two prongs of a strategy to strengthen Indonesian state control against the threat of Acehnese separatism.

This chapter considers how invocations of emergency and appeals to Shari'a have sought both to contain the armed struggle for Acehnese independence and to legitimate Indonesian state authority in its exercise of emergency powers in the province. Through a narrative of events in Aceh since 1989, it explores the evolving relationships between different forms of emergency rule and Shari'a, with a focus on the means by which they together served both to empower and to constrain Indonesian state authority in Aceh during and after the period of armed conflict.

3 Some 98 per cent of Acehnese are Muslims, compared with the Indonesian national average of 88 per cent.

4 For more on these developments, see C. B. Lombardi, *State Law as Islamic Law in Modern Egypt: The Incorporation of the* Shari'a *into Egyptian Constitutional Law* (Leiden: E. J. Brill, 2006), pp. 123ff.

5 Various aspects of these developments are discussed in C. Kennedy, *Islamization of Laws and Economy: Case Studies on Pakistan* (Islamabad: Institute of Policy Studies, 1996).

6 These developments are treated in detail in A. Layish and G. R. Warburg, *The Reinstatement of Islamic Law in Sudan Under Numayri: An Evaluation of a Legal Experiment in the Light of Its Historical Context, Methodology, and Repercussions* (Leiden: E. J. Brill, 2002).

II. Indonesia's emergency powers

In its exercise of coercion to contain the spectre of armed separatism in Aceh, the Indonesian state has used emergency powers in both formal and informal ways. There are three formal states of emergency recognised under Indonesian law: civil emergency, military emergency and a state of war. These three distinct conditions are regulated by Law No. 23/1959 on a 'state of danger' (*keadaan bahaya*), which was introduced after a period of frequent legislative and constitutional change in Indonesia.[7] In the 1950s and early 1960s, the young Indonesian Republic was threatened by the Darul Islam rebellions, which began in West Java and spread to Central Java, South Sulawesi, Kalimantan and Aceh with very loosely integrated agendas for the formation of an Islamic state (Negara Islam Indonesia, or NII).[8] Indonesian authorities responded to this emergency by developing a legal framework that built upon the Dutch colonial era 'state of war' law, the Regeling op Staat van Oorlog en van Beleg.[9]

Following a rash of subsequent emergency laws that were introduced between 1950 and 1957, Law No. 23/1959 was passed in an effort to remove inconsistencies that had arisen in relation to the emergency powers outlined in Indonesia's 1945 Constitution. As Nadirsyah Hosen explains in his contribution to this volume, although numerous laws, regulations and presidential decrees on state security have been introduced since, Law No. 23/1959 has remained the primary source of legislation in dealing with threats to Indonesian national security.[10] This law empowers the President as Supreme Commander of the Armed Forces to declare or abolish a state of emergency. It also outlines three conditions under which a state of emergency may be declared: rebellion, rioting or a natural disaster that threatens national security and the protection of public order where there is reasonable concern that the state's normal apparatus cannot cope with the situation. In addition to its formal emergency powers, Indonesia has often conducted military operations in Aceh without declaring a formal

[7] A brief overview of Indonesian constitutional developments in comparative perspective can be found in Kevin Tan's chapter, 'From Myanmar to Manila: A Brief Study of Emergency Powers in Southeast Asia' (Chapter 6), this volume.

[8] S. H. Hardi, *Daerah Istimewa Aceh: Latar Belakang Politik dan Masa Depannya* (Jakarta: PT Cita Panca Serangkai, 1993), p. 132. For more on the background of the Darul Islam movement in Acehnese history, see C. van Dijk, *Rebellion under the Banner of Islam: The Darul Islam in Indonesia* (The Hague: Martinus Nijhoff, 1981), pp. 269–339.

[9] B. Widjajanto and D. Kammen, 'The Structure of Military Abuse', *Inside Indonesia*, no. 62 (April–June 2000), http://insideindonesia.org/content/view/557/29/.

[10] N. Hosen, 'Emergency Powers and the Rule of Law in Indonesia' (Chapter 10), this volume.

state of emergency there. For example, after the formation of GAM on 4 December 1976, which marked the start of the contemporary conflict in Aceh, President Suharto's New Order regime did not invoke Indonesia's emergency legislation or the 1945 Constitution to provide a legal basis for its military operations in Aceh.

The legality or otherwise of Indonesia's ongoing counter-insurgency campaign in Aceh was not called into question until 1998 – after the collapse of Suharto's New Order government. From 1989 to 1998, the New Order's intolerance of separatist movements was demonstrated by its establishment of a 'Red Net Operation Implementation Command' (Komando Pelaksana Operasi Jaring Merah) in Aceh, which effectively transformed the province into a 'Military Operations Area' (Daerah Operasi Militer, or DOM) for a decade.[11] In 1998, when Suharto's appointed successor, B. J. Habibie, 'lifted DOM' and withdrew thousands of 'non-organic'[12] troops from Aceh, there arose considerable disagreement about whether or not DOM had any legal status in the first place. The general belief both in Aceh and amongst a wide cross-section of the broader Indonesian population was that DOM had indeed formally existed and that Aceh had been under a state of military emergency, or martial law. But in fact DOM did not have any legal 'emergency' status as the Red Net operations and command structure provided the *de facto* basis for the counter-insurgency operations against GAM.

Questions about the legality of DOM were manipulated by sections of the Indonesian military in an attempt to disavow responsibility for the murder, rape, torture and a litany of other crimes committed against Aceh's civilian population by Indonesian security forces personnel during the decade of military operations. Indonesia's military leadership claimed that DOM had never existed because there was no legal doctrine by that name, which was technically correct but also misleading. In November 1999, when several senior generals were summoned before Indonesia's national parliament (Dewan Perwakilan Rakyat, or DPR) to explain their role and interventions in human rights abuses in Aceh during DOM, all

[11] M. A. Miller, 'From Reform to Repression: The Post-New Order's Shifting Security Policies in Aceh', (2004) 38 *Review of Indonesian and Malaysian Affairs* 134.

[12] 'Non-organic' refers to troops deployed to a province on a short-term basis for specific combat exercises and counter-insurgency operations. 'Organic' denotes troops recruited within their own province, which are permanently attached to the local territorial command structure. In provinces like Aceh, however, the deep mistrust between the civilian population and the Indonesian military made it difficult to recruit ethnic Acehnese into organic battalions, so troops organic to other territorial commands were deployed to Aceh to reinforce counter-insurgency operations against GAM.

denied its existence and argued that the Indonesian government had only 'lifted' DOM because most Acehnese and sections of the wider Indonesian population believed DOM had existed.[13] For practical purposes, however, Aceh was a military operations area and issues of the legal status of DOM were beside the point. Soldiers could not be blamed for DOM as such, but they could be prosecuted for atrocities committed against the civilian population. That there was no legal doctrine called DOM should have afforded security forces personnel less, not more, state protection for their abuse of Indonesia's coercive powers.[14] However, this fact was generally overlooked by Indonesia's military and political establishment.

During the 'DOM period', the New Order regime had also sought to legitimise its authority in Aceh by co-opting Acehnese Islamic leaders (*ulama*) into the Indonesian military's campaign against GAM. Acehnese *ulama*, like religious leaders in the rest of the country, had become weakened by the New Order's secularising and centralising policies and those who had survived did so by becoming embedded in institutional niches within the authoritarian regime itself.[15] In Aceh, the *ulama* were broadly split into two camps: the traditionalist rural-based *ulama* were primarily based in independent Islamic boarding schools (*dayah*), whereas the urban-based, mostly reformist *ulama* broadly coalesced under the umbrella of the state-sanctioned Indonesian Ulama Council (Majelis Ulama Indonesia, or MUI).[16] This latter group (often referred to within Aceh as 'modern' *ulama*) tended to support the Indonesian military's campaign against GAM, and many of them became active in this by holding mass prayer rallies and making door-to-door visits distributing anti-GAM propaganda.[17] However, this should not be taken to imply that there was any simple distinction between 'modern' and 'traditional' (*dayah*) *ulama* with regard to their respective relationships with the Indonesian government and armed forces in Aceh. In fact a number of leading *ulama* from *dayah* circles also lent their support to the government – for example, by holding religious ceremonies at Indonesian National Day (17 August)

[13] 'Try Sutrisno Bertanggung Jawab', *Harian Suara Merdeka*, 30 November 1999.

[14] M. A. Miller, *Rebellion and Reform in Indonesia: Jakarta's Security and Autonomy Policies in Aceh* (New York: Routledge, 2009), p. 20.

[15] E. E. Morris, 'Islam and Politics in Aceh: A Study of Center–Periphery Relations in Indonesia', unpublished PhD thesis, Cornell University (1983), pp. 270–6.

[16] For documents on the history of the MUI in Aceh during this period, see B. Ismail, *Amal Bakti Empat Windu: Majelis Ulama Indonesia Propinsi Daerah Istimewa Aceh* (Banda Aceh: MPU, 2002).

[17] T. Kell, *The Roots of Acehnese Rebellion, 1989–1992* (Ithaca: SEAP, Cornell University, 1995), pp. 77–82.

and Military Foundation Day (5 October) observances.[18] The Indonesian government and armed forces thus came to view the *ulama* as a potential bulwark against Acehnese separatist sentiment and activity, a local strategy that appears analogous to the ways in which Suharto himself began to court Islamic political groups and organisations to attract support for his weakening presidency during his final decade in power.[19]

Following Suharto's resignation in May 1998, Aceh experienced less than six months of relative quietude before the Indonesian military forced a return to counter-insurgency operations. The army had been institutionally weakened by internal divisions and was widely discredited after the New Order's collapse as its primary instrument of authoritarian repression. Yet sections of Indonesia's military establishment attempted to use the separatist conflicts in Aceh, East Timor and Irian Jaya (now Papua) to justify their gradual re-entry into national politics. By mid-1999, several senior generals who were frustrated with Habibie's uncertain experiment with democracy and the opportunities it created for GAM's expansion called on the President to impose martial law in Aceh. To his credit, Habibie refused their request on the basis of Aceh's negative experience during the DOM period and the inevitable human rights violations and internal displacement of civilians that undertaking such a policy would have entailed.

Instead, Habibie and Indonesia's military leadership agreed upon a decision to grant Aceh limited 'special autonomy' (*otonomi khusus*), including the right to implement aspects of Islamic law. Indonesia's democratisation process included some new initiatives to deal with the country's territorial disputes, and there was general consensus among Indonesia's political and military establishment that decentralisation, or regional autonomy, was the best way to prevent national disintegration and to accommodate some of Indonesia's increasingly self-assertive provinces within the unitary state. However, Habibie's remarkable decision to settle the national identity problem in East Timor by granting that province a referendum on independence was widely seen in Indonesia as unacceptable and contributed to his defeat in the 1999 presidential election.

[18] Some prominent *ulama dayah* also served in more formal positions within the Indonesian state structure, including as representatives in both the Acehnese regional and Indonesian national legislative assemblies (DRPD and MPR respectively).

[19] R. W. Hefner, 'Islam, State and Civil Society: ICMI and the Struggle for the Indonesian Middle Class', (1993) 56 (October) *Indonesia* 1; A. Bahar *et al.*, *ICMI Kekuasaan dan Demokrasi* (Yogyakarta: Pena Cendekia Indonesia, 1995); A. Schwarz, *A Nation in Waiting: Indonesia's Search for Stability*, 2nd edn (St Leonards, NSW: Allen & Unwin, 1999), pp. 182–4.

For Indonesian nationalists, any debate about national identity had to be constructed within, and seek to strengthen the integrity and cohesion of the unitary state – not to weaken or destroy it.[20]

Though sections of Indonesia's military leadership were unhappy that their demand to declare a state of emergency in Aceh was not met, the armed forces faction in the national parliament enthusiastically supported the introduction in September 1999 of legislation that granted Aceh limited special autonomy and the right to implement aspects of Islamic law.[21] Law No. 44/1999, which formally recognised the 'Special Status of the Province of Aceh Special Region' in the fields of religion, education and customary law (*adat*), was passed three weeks after the East Timorese voted in an internationally monitored referendum to separate from Indonesia, at a time when concerns about national disintegration peaked in Jakarta. The Indonesian government no longer saw an entirely non-military solution to the Aceh conflict as a realistic option, but was prepared to offer the Acehnese some concessions in a limited effort to persuade them that it was worth remaining part of Indonesia.[22]

The decision to allow Aceh to start implementing Shari'a was based to a considerable extent upon the then dominant assumption among Indonesia's ruling elite that support for GAM would wane if Acehnese *ulama* were returned to their pre-New Order position of socio-political influence. Related to this assumption was the belief that Aceh's contemporary conflict had stemmed from Jakarta's failure to honour the terms of the Darul Islam settlement in Aceh. The involvement by an earlier generation of Acehnese rebels in the Darul Islam rebellion had gradually subsided after 1959 when President Sukarno conferred, in principle, 'special autonomy' status to Aceh and later, in 1962, issued a decree granting the province the right to start implementing Islamic law within its borders.[23]

However, while Acehnese rebels from the Darul Islam era would have welcomed national legislation on Shari'a, by September 1999 Aceh – and Acehnese demands on the Indonesian government – had changed substantially. Many Acehnese now saw Jakarta's offer of limited special autonomy and the formal implementation of Islamic law as too little too late and were

[20] Miller, *Rebellion and Reform*, p. 20.

[21] H. M. Kaoy Syah and L. Hakiem, *Keistimewaan Aceh Dalam Lintasan Sejarah. Proses Pembentukan UU No. 44/1999* (Jakarta: Pengurus Besar Al Jam'iyatul Washliyah, 2000), p. 165.

[22] 'Aceh Sudah Bisa Terapkan Otonomi', *Kompas*, 30 August 1999; '20 Masyarakat Aceh "Adili" Menteri', *Serambi Indonesia*, 29 August 1999.

[23] Morris, 'Islam and Politics', pp. 232–3; N. Sjamsuddin, *The Republican Revolt: A Study of the Acehnese Rebellion* (Singapore: Institute of Southeast Asian Studies, 1985), p. 310.

more receptive to the agendas of GAM, student groups and NGOs than to those of Indonesian government officials and *ulama*. The precariousness of Indonesian state authority in Aceh was shown on 8–9 November 1999 at a mass rally in the provincial capital of Banda Aceh, when some 500,000 of Aceh's 4.2 million people gathered at the Baiturrahman Mosque to demand an East Timor-style referendum on Aceh's political status. There was also some public opposition to Jakarta's offer of Shari'a implementation. GAM and Aceh's university student-led referendum movement, SIRA (Sentral Informasi Referendum Aceh), which quickly filled the post-Suharto political vacuum in Indonesian state authority, saw the imposition of Islamic law as a 'political trick' by the Indonesian government to justify the military's 'slaughter' of the Acehnese people by portraying Islam in Aceh as being of 'a fundamentalist type'.[24] Reflecting Acehnese popular opinion, GAM and SIRA argued that as the Acehnese could already practise Shari'a under the 1945 Constitution they did not need a 'concocted' government version like that which had been imposed in Aceh during Dutch colonial times.[25]

Although virtually all GAM rebels and SIRA activists were Muslims, their political demands were explicitly nationalist in nature. GAM based its claims to territorial sovereignty on the construct of a distinctive Acehnese ethnic, linguistic, cultural, historical and geographically specific identity, rather than upon a religiously oriented political ideology. Aceh's independence movement was certainly far broader than GAM, encompassing as it did civil society groups and organisations covering the entire political spectrum. Yet public opinion was overwhelmingly in favour of GAM's nationalist imperative and there was a strong lack of grassroots support for what was at that time widely seen as Jakarta's 'unwanted gift' of Islamic law. According to GAM, the *real* reason why Jakarta was imposing Shari'a in Aceh was to attract international support for its plans to intensify the counter-insurgency campaign against them by portraying the Acehnese as 'fundamentalist' and 'fanatical' Muslims, or as some expressed it, 'to make us look like Afghanistan'.[26]

GAM's claim, however, was only partly true given that many political leaders in Jakarta had already acknowledged that centre–periphery imbalances and human rights violations were at the heart of Acehnese grievances. For instance, when Habibie's elected successor President

[24] 'SIRA Tolak Gus Dur ke Aceh', *Serambi Indonesia*, 13 December 2000.
[25] 'Aceh Separatists Snub Offer of Islamic Law', *Indonesian Observer*, 15 December 2000.
[26] 'Interview: Islamic Law to Soothe Aceh', *Reuters*, 11 December 2000.

Abdurrahman Wahid visited Aceh in January 2001, he apologised for his inability to provide redress for these problems, stating that 'if I were not a Muslim I would probably have killed myself'.[27] However, some military and political hawks in Jakarta *did* believe that the counter-insurgency operations against GAM would gain legitimacy in the eyes of the international community if the rebels were portrayed as Islamic extremists or terrorists. For the Indonesian military, the conferral of international legitimacy to the counter-insurgency campaign in Aceh stood to strengthen their aim to win national political support for imposing martial law there, which promised to seal the military's control over the province and provide a legal framework to protect the activities of soldiers stationed there.

International pressure and developments also helped to shape Jakarta's security policy discussions on Aceh in the post-Suharto era. After East Timor's 1999 referendum ballot, the USA in particular opposed the army's calls for emergency rule in Aceh, having severed all military ties with Indonesia because of atrocities committed by Indonesian security forces against the East Timorese. Following the September 2001 terrorist attacks on the USA, however, Washington revisited its military relations with the world's most populous Muslim nation and started offering funding for Indonesian military and police training programmes in exchange for security sector reforms.[28] This emphasis on reforming Indonesia's security sector was tied to concerns in the United States that its improved bilateral military relations with Indonesia would suffer reversals if the armed forces resorted to excessive acts of internal repression. Another factor in Washington's decision to revive military ties with Jakarta was that the USA, along with Japan, Australia and other countries, held a stake in Aceh's rich oil and gas industries and wanted to avoid major disruptions to the production rate of multinational companies such as ExxonMobil Oil Indonesia.

Although Jakarta continued to 'postpone' declaring a formal state of emergency in Aceh after the 11 September 2001 terrorist attacks on the USA, it was around this time that Indonesian military and political hardliners began to position GAM within the US global 'War on Terror'. In her post-9/11 speech in Washington, for instance, Megawati Sukarnoputri, who replaced Abdurrahman Wahid as president in July 2001 after his impeachment by the national parliament, attempted to win US support for her government's hardening approach against GAM by describing the 'terrorist acts' committed by the rebels against the Indonesian

[27] 'Give Peace a Chance', *Asiaweek*, 12 January 2001.
[28] 'Bantuan Militer AS: Untuk Apa?', *Kompas*, 15 August 2002.

state.[29] Then, in October 2001, when the administration of George W. Bush responded to the terror attacks on US soil by invading Afghanistan, governments around the world increasingly began to look toward 'military solutions' to finish off their various separatist movements. Megawati's then Coordinating Minister for Political Affairs and Security, Susilo Bambang Yudhoyono, explained that 'Any separatist movement must be crushed, and we have the international support to maintain our territorial integrity.'[30] This was a position, however, that he would later abandon after he himself became president of Indonesia in 2004.

Beyond its claims to international legitimacy for the intensifying counter-insurgency campaign against GAM, by 2001 the Indonesian government was still in the process of trying to win national legitimacy through the introduction of reforms aimed at proving its democratic credentials. Declaring a state of emergency in Aceh without first pursuing ameliorative policies to persuade the Acehnese to remain part of Indonesia threatened to invite criticism from the international community and domestic reform-minded civil society organisations alike. It was largely for these reasons that the Megawati administration postponed declaring a state of military emergency in Aceh until May 2003, despite growing scepticism that democratic resolution of Indonesia's internal conflicts was possible.

To balance the competing interests of Indonesia's security forces and those of the international community and reform-minded local political actors, the Megawati administration decided to pursue a combined persuasive-repressive approach to Acehnese demands rather than to immediately impose emergency rule. This involved intensive counter-insurgency operations aimed at pressuring GAM into agreeing to participate in a limited peace process that would culminate in the rebels' acceptance of Jakarta's offer of special autonomy as a final solution to the Aceh conflict. Variations of this dual-track Aceh approach had already been in place under the two previous post-Suharto administrations. Under Habibie, this approach took the form, on the one hand, of police and military operations against GAM, and, on the other, of conciliatory gestures such as launching human rights investigations into Aceh, granting amnesty to Acehnese political prisoners and offering Aceh limited

[29] H. E. Megawati Sukarnoputri, President of the Republic of Indonesia, 'Address at the USINDO Gala Dinner in Washington DC' (19 September 2001), www.indonesiamedia.com/2001/october/english-1001-megaspeech.htm

[30] '"Crushing" GAM: A Military Mission', *Indonesian Observer*, 8 February 2002.

special autonomy and the implementation of Shari'a pursuant to Law No. 44/1999.

During his erratic and unpredictable presidency, Abdurrahman Wahid had initially followed in Habibie's footsteps by ordering human rights investigations and withdrawing all non-organic troops from Aceh, although he redeployed them less than two months after coming to power under military pressure and thereafter generally relied more heavily on coercion to compel Acehnese compliance with Indonesian authority. However, Wahid did go further than his predecessor in his search for a negotiated settlement by initiating a series of internationally facilitated and mediated peace talks with GAM, even though this peace process was limited to achieving a ceasefire and the distribution of humanitarian aid and did not address any of the substantive issues dividing the two sides. During his final days in power, the national parliament also introduced more comprehensive special autonomy legislation for Aceh after recognising that Law No. 44/1999 was too limited to deal with Aceh's specific set of grievances. Law No. 18/2001, which was passed on 19 July 2001, formally changed Aceh's name to Nanggroe Aceh Darussalam (NAD; lit. 'State of Aceh, Abode of Peace') and conferred broader powers of self-governance to the province in the fields of religion (Shari'a), governance, economics, security and defence.

This so-called 'NAD law' became the 'main pillar' of Megawati's persuasive strategy for resolving the Aceh conflict,[31] while the repressive component comprised intensifying military operations aimed at crushing GAM. In practice, however, Megawati gave Indonesia's security forces a free rein in Aceh and eventually succumbed to their demands to declare a formal state of military emergency there in May 2003. During Megawati's presidency, important revisions to Aceh's revenue-sharing arrangements with Jakarta were mismanaged and a key concession granting Aceh direct democratic local elections was never implemented.[32] Substantive efforts to implement the NAD law were in fact largely restricted to the sphere of Shari'a implementation.

There were several reasons for this growing emphasis on military operations and Islamic law in Jakarta's handling of the Aceh conflict.

[31] Speech by Megawati Sukarnoputri, President of the Republic of Indonesia, delivered at the Annual Session of the People's Consultative Assembly, Jakarta (1 August 2002), http://kepustakaan-presiden.pnri.go.id/articles/index/.

[32] M. A. Miller, 'What's Special About Special Autonomy in Aceh?', in A. Reid (ed.), *Verandah of Violence: The Historical Background of the Aceh Problem* (Singapore: Singapore University Press, 2006), pp. 292–314.

First, in contrast to Habibie and Wahid, who had maintained uneasy relations with Indonesia's military establishment, Megawati was far more amenable to a military response to threats to Indonesia's territorial integrity and national cohesion.[33] By granting the military generous political concessions over the Aceh issue and other key policy areas, Megawati also hoped to ward off potential challenges to her leadership.[34] While the military's increased involvement in government decision-making threatened to reverse many of the gains that had been made during the early years of Indonesia's post-Suharto democratisation process, it also promised to provide a degree of national stability after Wahid's chaotic leadership, when separatist activity in the country's disaffected regions had sharply escalated. In Aceh, however, where 'stability' had long been associated with state repression, Jakarta's hard-line security approach represented a return to DOM in everything but name.

Also, unlike Habibie and Wahid who believed that granting Aceh special autonomy would help to end the conflict, Megawati was basically opposed to decentralisation and her personal reservations about granting 'too much' power to outlying regions were well known. In her former capacity as Wahid's vice-president (and reflecting, perhaps, her background as the daughter of Indonesia's founding father, Sukarno), Megawati had condemned the introduction of limited autonomy laws for all of Indonesia's sub-provincial administrations as being 'on a different path, or even against the basic principles adopted by the Constitution'.[35] Megawati, as well as many ministers in her cabinet, believed that granting broad autonomy to regions like Aceh heightened the risk of national fragmentation and disintegration. Little wonder, then, that her administration relied far more heavily on military force in dealing with the Aceh problem than on remedial policies. Although Megawati had no choice other than to ratify the NAD law, which was passed by the DPR just days before her presidential appointment, she warned the Acehnese that if they abused special autonomy then her government would 'initiate stern law enforcement measures in the province'.[36]

[33] For more on Megawati's engagement with the Indonesian military, see, for example, M. Mietzner, *The Politics of Military Reform in Post-Suharto Indonesia: Elite Conflict, Nationalism and Institutional Resilience* (Washington, D.C.: East–West Center, 2006), pp. 34–5.

[34] *Ibid.*, p. 34.

[35] 'Indonesian Regional Autonomy Architect Warns of "Recentralization"', *Associated Federated Press*, 23 May 2001.

[36] 'Mega Tells Aceh to Focus on Autonomy', *Jakarta Post*, 29 August 2001.

Given the Megawati administration's suspicions about the NAD law, few efforts were made to disseminate public information about the specific terms of this special autonomy legislation in Aceh. Of all the provisions of the NAD law, the only one that received any real attention was the implementation of Islamic law. This dominant emphasis on Shari'a was strongly supported by Aceh's then newly re-formed Consultative Council of Ulama (Majelis Permusyawaratan Ulama, MPU – developed out of the existing MUI) and the provincial government's Shari'a Agency (Dinas Syariat Islam), which were established in July and August 2001 respectively.[37] Both of these institutions worked diligently to promote their Islamic agenda by distributing pamphlets about Islamic law, by convening public forums and by launching Shari'a 'socialisation' programmes in schools throughout the province.[38] The central government, it seemed, was content to allow these Acehnese institutions to assume responsibility for distributing public information about the provisions of the NAD law, if only to effectively reduce it to little more than a reconstituted version of Law No. 44/1999.

As an ameliorative policy, the NAD law generally failed to win Acehnese hearts and minds back into the Indonesian national fold. GAM demonstrated its rejection of both special autonomy and its accompanying provisions for the implementation of Shari'a by stepping up its attacks on Indonesian state institutions and facilities.[39] SIRA, too, saw the NAD law as an unacceptable substitute for a referendum on Acehnese self-determination. For many ordinary Acehnese, whose daily experience of Indonesian state authority was of violence, special autonomy did not promise to bring any palpable improvements to their daily lives, just as the new Shari'a legal regime appeared to offer no immediate redress for their substantive grievances about past and ongoing human rights abuses.

As the violence spiralled out of control, the political leadership in Jakarta became increasingly receptive to the military's calls to impose emergency rule in Aceh. Initially Indonesia's political and military leadership were divided over the competing merits of imposing civil or military emergency rule in the province. For the military, the 'worst possible scenario would be

[37] For an official statement on the mandate and legal status of the Dinas Syariat Islam, see Al Yasa' Abubakar, *Syariat Islam di Provinsi Nanggroe Aceh Darussalam: Parjadigma, Kebijakan dan Kegiatan* (Banda Aceh: Dinas Syariat Islam, 2005), pp. 149–52.

[38] 'DPRD Aceh Sambut Pembentukan Dinas Syariat Islam', *Analisa* (28 August 2001); 'Sosialisasi Syariat Islam bagi Guru SD', *Serambi Indonesia*, 8 October 2002; 'Walikota Buka Forum Diskusi Syariat Islam', *Serambi Indonesia*, 15 October 2002.

[39] 'A Rejection of NAD Law', *Kompas*, 27 August 2001.

a civilian emergency status in Aceh and not a military emergency' because Aceh's civilian political leadership had lost their governing presence to GAM in many parts of the province and had failed to restore Acehnese faith in Indonesian rule.[40] However, while Aceh's provincial authorities were deeply unpopular and were widely seen as corrupt, they were not the primary perpetrators of the violence. The Indonesian military's main motivation for seeking to impose martial law in Aceh was to establish a legal framework to protect its counter-insurgency operations against GAM and to formalise its authority over the province. By contrast, sections of Indonesia's political leadership and Aceh's provincial government wanted a state of civil emergency and expressed concerns that martial law would further undermine the authority and legitimacy of Aceh's civilian leadership. After a limited peace process between GAM and the Indonesian government began to unravel in early 2003, however, Megawati Sukarnoputri eventually acquiesced to the military's growing calls to annihilate the rebels by pronouncing martial law in Aceh via Presidential Instruction No. 18/2003.

III. Emergency rule and Shari'a: empowering or constraining state authority?

Jakarta's efforts to contain the separatist insurgency in Aceh by imposing emergency rule and by offering Shari'a to the Acehnese can be seen as having both strengthened and constrained Indonesian authority in different ways. During the year of martial law (May 2003–May 2004), Indonesia's security forces successfully weakened GAM's military capabilities and regained control over Aceh's urban centres, forcing the rebels to scale back their activities to the sub-district level.[41] The armed forces also put an end to public displays of anti-Indonesian sentiment and often orchestrated televised mass rallies of crowds of Acehnese singing nationalist songs and waving little Indonesian flags. However, while emergency rule had by all accounts dealt a bitter blow to GAM and allowed the Indonesian state forcefully to reassert its authority in Aceh, it ultimately failed to achieve its objective of crushing the rebels. This became apparent three days before the December 2004 Indian Ocean tsunami, when Aceh's then regional commander, Maj. Gen. Endang Suwarya, announced that 2,500 GAM

[40] Home Affairs Minister Lt-Gen. (ret.) Hari Sabarno, in 'Govt Moves Towards Imposing Civil Emergency in Aceh', *Jakarta Post*, 9 July 2002.

[41] International Crisis Group, *Aceh: A New Chance for Peace* (Jakarta and Brussels: International Crisis Group, 2005), p. 4.

combatants with 844 guns remained at large in Aceh,[42] indicating that the military saw its mission there as being far from over. The inability of Indonesia's security forces to break the rebel movement militarily was also shown at the signing of a peace agreement in Helsinki on 15 August 2005 by Indonesian government representatives and GAM, when the rebels pledged to demobilise their 3,000 active troops.

To a great extent, Indonesia's exercise of its formal emergency powers in Aceh weakened the state from within as security forces personnel often acted in ways that ran counter to state goals and objectives. In conflict with the Indonesian state's goal of ending Aceh's separatist insurgency through its imposition of martial law, sections of Indonesia's armed forces had vested economic and political interests in perpetuating the conflict. With the Indonesian state only providing one-third of the national defence budget, the armed forces remained heavily reliant on alternative funding sources, which Aceh's war economy and rich natural resources provided in abundance. Soldiers and police officers were involved in every sector of the local economy, such as providing private security services to multinational companies, participating in Aceh's illegal logging and marijuana industries, extortion, commercial agriculture, the export of native fauna such as Sumatran tigers and exotic birds, and selling arms to GAM (including the direct sale of weapons from the Indonesian military's PT Pindad arms factory in Bandung).[43] These business interests operated outside state control and encouraged security forces personnel to subvert or ignore central government policy directives that endangered benefits derived from the pre-existing order. In this context, the resolution of the Aceh conflict threatened to bring an end to these opportunities for personal and institutional enrichment.

Politically, too, the Indonesian military benefited from the perpetuation of the Aceh conflict. Under weak successive post-New Order administrations, the Indonesian military was able to claw back some of its former political influence by portraying itself as the primary defender of national unity and cohesion. The seemingly intractable conflict in Aceh thus created new opportunities for the Indonesian military to become re-embedded in the state's nascent democratic institutions and prevent weak civilian

[42] 'Pangdam: Kekuatan GAM Tersisa 2,500 Orang', 23 December 2004, www.dephan.go.id.

[43] See, for example, 'Disinyalir Barter dengan Ganja, Senjata Ilegal TNI Mengalir ke GAM', *Indomedia.com*, 4 March 2000; 'Peluru M-16 dan Granat dari Depok untuk GAM', *Kompas*, 7 April 2001; 'Aceh dalam Genggaman GAM dan TNI', *Pikiran Rakyat*, 16 December 2002; 'Menghentikan GAM dengan Senjata', *Kompas*, 4 May 2003; Fahmi A. P. Pane, 'Kesalahan Pencegahan Teror Bom', *Republika*, 11 August 2003.

authorities from internalising critical aspects of democratic procedure. However, as the administration of Susilo Bambang Yudhoyono showed after the 2004 tsunami, by honouring the terms of the Helsinki peace agreement with GAM it effectively de-legitimised the TNI's claim that its suppression of separatist threats justified its role in Indonesian political life.

Throughout Aceh's contemporary conflict, military operations had consistently been the primary cause of GAM's regeneration because of the atrocities committed by Indonesian security forces against the civilian population. The Indonesian military, on the other hand, interpreted and justified its use of statist violence as a necessary mechanism for defending Indonesia's territorial sovereignty and national cohesion. Normative legal constraints to minimise the abuse of the state's coercive powers were rarely enforced, with the great majority of human rights violations cases never going to trial. Even without a formal declaration of emergency, Indonesia's judiciary implicitly legitimised the use of excessive state (and extra-state) violence by granting impunity to human rights violators while depriving their civilian victims of legal recourse to justice.[44] As Arun Thiruvengadam demonstrates in his contribution to this volume, Indonesia's judiciary was not unique in this sense, and conformed to a similar pattern amongst judiciaries worldwide of failing to protect and defend individual rights during periods of emergency.[45] Past counter-insurgency operations in Aceh had shown, however, that the violent methods by which Indonesia's security forces defended Indonesia's sovereignty over the territory of Aceh only hardened Acehnese attitudes against Indonesian rule.

Within the context of emergency rule, the Indonesian state's authority and legitimacy in Aceh were also strengthened and constrained in diverse and complex ways by the formal implementation of Islamic law in the province. Jakarta did achieve one of its limited objectives during the period of emergency: that of securing the co-operation of a significant

[44] See, for example, Human Rights Watch, *Indonesia: Accountability for Human Rights Violations in Aceh*, vol. 14, no. 1(C), March 2002; Amnesty International, *Briefing on the Deteriorating Human Rights Situation in Aceh for Participants in the ASEAN Regional Forum*, July 2001; Tapol, *A Reign of Terror: Human Rights Violations in Aceh, 1998–2000*, Executive Summary, March 2000.

[45] A. K. Thiruvengadam 'Asian Judiciaries and Emergency Powers: Reasons for Optimism?' (Chapter 17), this volume. However, Thiruvengadam then goes on to develop a more optimistic normative argument about the potential ability of the courts to check the abuse of emergency powers by the state in the foreseeable future, given some significant contextual changes allowing courts in the region to engage more robustly with existing constitutional provisions.

portion of Aceh's Islamic leadership. Following the introduction of Law No. 44/1999, a number of *ulama* (particularly – but by no means exclusively – those affiliated with the MUI) welcomed Jakarta's offer of Shari'a, but at the same time others publicly announced that they were ready to 'face the consequences' if their demand to hold an internationally monitored referendum on Acehnese independence was not met.[46] Eventually, however, Aceh's Islamic leaders became increasingly united in their common goal to expand their own political influence through the state implementation of Islamic law. This became even more apparent after the July 2001 formation of a mixed modernist/traditionalist MPU.

While the MPU did provide new means for establishing links between Acehnese religious leaders and Indonesian political and military authorities, the Indonesian state's Shari'a project in Aceh still failed to achieve its ultimate goals of undermining local support for GAM and reducing anti-Indonesian sentiment. In large part, this was because of the escalating violence on the ground and the ongoing depredations by Indonesian security forces against Acehnese civilians. That the political ascendancy of the MPU did not translate into a reduction in local support for GAM was also due to the MPU's perceived close working relationship with Aceh's widely discredited provincial administration. Indeed, the biggest objection to Shari'a in Aceh was not to Islamic law itself, but rather to the provincial government's handling of Shari'a, which GAM, SIRA and many Acehnese NGOs argued had reduced Islamic law to a tool in the hands of the Indonesian political elite. This common perception was reinforced by incidents such as the payment by Aceh's then governor, Abdullah Puteh, of Rp.7, 500 (US$0.75) each to some 20,000 people to march as 'Shari'a supporters' in the 2002 Islamic New Year (1 Muharram 1423H.) parade.[47] Among the civilian population, there was also general resentment that the provincial administration's emphasis was on what some criticised as 'symbolic' religious issues rather than on more 'substantive' matters such as corruption and human rights. There were also frequently voiced objections by various NGOs in Aceh over the unequal treatment of women, the poor and other vulnerable groups who were targeted and prosecuted most vigorously for infractions of the new Shari'a legislation.[48]

46 Tgk. Syamaun Risyad (HUDA Representative), in 'Referendum Sudah Final', *Serambi Indonesia*, 18 November 1999; see also 'Ulama Dan Tokoh Masyarakat Aceh: Alhamdulillah, Gus Dur Restui Referendum', *Waspada*, 10 November 1999.

47 'Gubernur Deklarasikan Hidup Tanpa', *Serambi Indonesia*, 16 March 2002.

48 See, for example, 'Syari'ah in Aceh Silencing Women's Voices', *Jakarta Post*, 8 April 2002; 'Pakai Jilbab Karena Takut pada Manusia: Syariat Islam untuk Aceh Cek Kosong', Radio

One important area in which Indonesian state authority was particularly compromised by the introduction of Shari'a related to provincial security. Within the context of Aceh's parlous security environment, the initially limited application of Shari'a could even be said to have added to the chaos and confusion on the ground, as the government's early efforts to implement aspects of Islamic law were accompanied by an increase in extra-state violence by moral vigilantes. After the introduction of Law No. 44/1999, there was a sharp rise in 'headscarf raids' (*razia jilbab*) and other forms of extra-judicial violence against those accused of moral misconduct by various Islamist groups. Unmarried couples caught in public displays of affection, transvestites and sex workers were publicly humiliated by gangs of Muslim youth and paraded around the streets of Banda Aceh.[49] Non-Muslims, and especially non-Muslim Batak women traders from North Sumatra, were also subjected to growing acts of violence.[50] This growth of moral vigilantism by non-state actors in turn constrained Indonesian state authority in Aceh by further compromising its monopoly over the legitimate exercise of physical force.

The introduction of Islamic law in Aceh also attracted Islamist groups from other parts of Indonesia who saw the implementation of Shari'a there as a model for the rest of the country. In particular, Islamic militias who were said to be recruited, armed and trained by the TNI flocked to Aceh after the imposition of martial law. These Muslim militias conceptualised *jihad* (holy war) in Indonesian nationalist terms and saw the purpose of *jihad* as being to eliminate 'infidel' separatists who threatened Indonesia's territorial integrity and national cohesion. According to GAM, however, such Islamist militias were 'terrorists' who came to Aceh to incite 'racial and religious sentiment' amongst the local population and to detract outside attention away from their nationalist cause.[51]

Although the Indonesian government's Shari'a project did not at first meet with an enthusiastic response from many Acehnese, in the long run it did facilitate the re-establishment and maintenance of bureaucratic control over much of the province through the creation and expansion of new governmental departments. Since 2001, a number of new offices

Nikoya 106.15FM (transcript), Banda Aceh, 30 September 1999; Tapol, *Defending Women's Rights in Aceh*, April 2000; '"Eagerly Awaited" Implementation of Islamic Law in Aceh', *Islamonline*, 5 January 2002.

49 E. Aspinall, 'Whither Aceh?' *Inside Indonesia*, April–June 2000, 7.

50 S. Tiwon, 'From East Timor to Aceh: The Disintegration of Indonesia?', (2000) 32.1–2 *Bulletin of Concerned Asian Scholars* 101.

51 T. Kamaruzzaman, in Amy Chew, 'Aceh Links to al Qaeda Dismissed', *CNN World News*, 14 July 2002.

have been created to oversee the implementation of Islamic law, including a system of Islamic religious courts with expanded jurisdiction (known as Mahkamah Syariah), the provincial government's Islamic Law Agency (Dinas Syariat Islam) and the Wilayatul Hisbah (WH), a body of officers who police public morality with a mandate only to 'admonish and advise'.[52] Despite the persistence of problematic issues such as staffing and budget shortfalls, these various new governmental institutions have grown in size and have come to exert influence over many aspects of life in contemporary Aceh. The move for instituting Islamic law within the context of emergency rule has thus helped to establish mechanisms for state control that have outlasted the immediate crisis and appear to be creating a new order of regulation for post-conflict Aceh.

IV. From emergency rule to Islamic law

Emergency rule in Aceh officially ended on 15 August 2005 when the signing of a peace agreement in Helsinki by the Indonesian government and GAM ushered in a new era of peace. The signing came after several months of heated negotiations that were mediated and facilitated by the former Finnish president Martti Ahtisaari's Crisis Management Initiative NGO. The talks had commenced shortly after the December 2004 tsunami, which created a window of opportunity (as well as strong international pressure) for both sides to reassess their own positions and to work toward a negotiated settlement. As part of the Helsinki agreement, Jakarta agreed to withdraw all non-organic military and police troops from Aceh, while 14,700 organic soldiers and 9,100 local police officers were to remain. GAM agreed to demobilise all of its 3,000 fighters and to hand over 840 weapons. This process, which was monitored by a European Union-led Aceh Monitoring Mission (AMM), took place from September to December 2005 and went remarkably smoothly. By the year's end, all Indonesian non-organic troops had been redeployed from Aceh and GAM had demobilised its fighters and decommissioned its weapons.

The Helsinki peace process highlighted the limits of Indonesia's military emergency powers in Aceh in at least two ways. First, it showed that in order for conflict resolution to occur, the armed forces had to become subordinate to civilian authorities and respect the rule of law. As in

[52] Qanun 11 (2002), VI.14.1–5. Initially affiliated with and housed in the same building as the Dinas Syariat Islam, the WH was moved in early 2008 to the offices of the civilian police (*pamong praja*) in Banda Aceh.

Northern Ireland, where 'a retreat from legality appeared to send a message from the state to affected communities that the "gloves are off"',[53] the indiscriminate use of force in Aceh by Indonesian security personnel sent a powerful message to Acehnese separatists that extra-state violence was an appropriate response to statist repression. Under weak civilian administrations, sections of Indonesia's security forces fuelled a growing acceptance of anti-state violence among Aceh's civilian population through their sustained lack of commitment to legality and their active perpetuation of the conflict for political and financial gain. Under the presidency of Susilo Bambang Yudhoyono, however, who was himself a retired general, the non-organic troop withdrawal was made possible by the combination of Indonesia's strong civilian leadership and pressure from the international community to reach a negotiated settlement in exchange for ongoing post-tsunami reconstruction funds and humanitarian assistance.

Second, the Helsinki peace process pointed to the ineffectiveness of Indonesia's exercise of military emergency powers as a response to the country's internal conflicts. Contrary to the common perception that the counter-insurgency campaign made GAM more amenable to reaching a negotiated settlement with Jakarta after the tsunami,[54] attempts by previous Indonesian governments to engage GAM in dialogue had consistently shown that the rebels had never agreed to negotiate with Jakarta solely on the basis of the strength of their military capabilities. GAM's participation in peace talks had always been contingent on the involvement of an international mediating body, in part because of their basic distrust that Jakarta would honour any peace agreement, and in part because the rebels had sought international recognition and support for their separatist cause. Military operations (which were as closely linked to the root causes of Aceh's contemporary conflict as they were to its continuation) had only ever forced GAM to retreat temporarily and the rebels' numbers had always multiplied during periods of relative quietude.

In the context of Aceh's post-conflict, post-tsunami landscape, the expanding application of Shari'a both empowered and constrained Indonesian state authority in the province. With the end of emergency rule, increasing numbers of Acehnese came to look positively at this

[53] C. Campbell, 'Law, Terror and Social Movements: The Repression–Mobilisation Nexus', in V. V. Ramraj (ed.), *Emergencies and the Limits of Legality* (Cambridge: Cambridge University Press, 2008), pp. 172–98, at p. 184.

[54] See, for example, K. Schulze, *Mission Not so Impossible: The Aceh Monitoring Mission and Lessons Learned for the EU* (Singapore: Rajaratnam School of International Studies, 2007).

development as an expression of Aceh's 'special' status and distinctive regional identity. In this way, it appears that the agenda for Shari'a implementation in Aceh during the period of emergency rule laid the foundations for the establishment of greater Indonesian government control and stability, at least for the immediate post-conflict period.

After the tsunami, Aceh's religious bureaucracy became more assertive in expanding its own authority. In particular, the Islamic Law Agency (Dinas Syariat Islam) and the Wilayatul Hisbah (WH), which shared headquarters in Banda Aceh, became increasingly zealous in their efforts to further expand and monitor the implementation of Islamic law. When the WH was first established in 2004 under emergency rule, it only operated in and around Banda Aceh. By late 2006, however, the so-called 'moral police' had established a province-wide presence and were far more vigilant in defending public morality. In the first half of 2007 alone, the WH handled 397 Shari'a violation cases, compared with 376 cases for the entire year of 2006.[55]

Some aspects of these expansionary tendencies, however, served to weaken the popular legitimacy of Aceh's religious administration. The WH, in particular, was criticised for its perceived 'arrogance and thuggery' in its dealings with the civilian population as it became more assertive.[56] Although its authority was limited to conducting identity checks and it was legally required to obtain police assistance before conducting investigations and making arrests, there were numerous reports of its involvement in more invasive activities. While the WH empowered the state in the sense that it increased Indonesia's authoritative presence in Aceh, the anti-vice squad's existence and expansion was contingent on the presence of social maladies. As such, its involvement in the aggressive policing of public morality could not be divorced from its expansionary tendencies and desire to attract more state power and funding.[57]

The legitimacy of Aceh's religious bureaucracy was also undermined by its interpretation and implementation of Islamic law. Just as Shari'a had been widely seen as targeting the most marginalised elements of Acehnese society during the conflict, there was a lingering perception in its aftermath that Islamic law mainly targeted women and the poor. With the exception

[55] 'WH Tangani 770 Kasus', *Serambi Indonesia*, 24 August 2007.

[56] 'Acehnese Accuse Religious Police of "Arrogance" and Thuggery', *Jakarta Post*, 23 February 2006.

[57] International Crisis Group (ICG), *Islamic Law and Criminal Justice in Aceh*, Asia Report No. 117 (Jakarta and Brussels: International Crisis Group, 2006), p. 11.

of a very few high-profile cases,[58] the vast majority of those arrested for violations of Islamic laws on gambling, alcohol consumption and *khalwat* (close proximity between unrelated men and women) were from the lower classes of Acehnese society. Nevertheless, while many people viewed the implementation of Islamic law as discriminatory and unfair, corporal punishment was highly popular. Public canings generally attracted large audiences and were sometimes televised for mass consumption in other parts of Indonesia and in neighbouring Malaysia.[59] In his defence of Aceh's Islamic penalty system, however, one 'lashing executioner' argued that 'The law is equal for everybody. It's just that the people who have been caught are poor people.'[60]

Though few, if any, Acehnese Muslims would criticise Islamic law itself, certain groups and individuals did, as noted above, express concerns about its interpretation and application by the governmental bodies charged with its administration. Although many former GAM rebels remained basically opposed to what they saw as the imposition of Islamic law by outside forces, they were mindful of the political sensitivity of the Shari'a issue and became increasingly circumspect in their criticism of Shari'a implementation during their 2006 election campaigns. Still, there remained a distinct gap between in-principle support for Shari'a and specific points of criticism of its practical application by the government, which served to de-legitimise the government's interpretation of Islamic law among some sections of the local population even as aspects of it were implemented. For example, there have been critiques that although the expanding application of Islamic law in the post-conflict period could have potentially assisted the Acehnese in coming to terms with their legacy of violence and social trauma, it has instead tended to reinforce unequal power hierarchies rather than promote the formation of a more egalitarian society. Particularly problematic have been reports of moral vigilantism (said by some to be encouraged by sections of Aceh's religious leadership) by state and non-state actors alike, leaving little possibility for the public openly to criticise abuses of the state's coercive powers and religious authority.[61] Nevertheless, some Acehnese social critics and activists have

[58] The best known of these is that of Zainal Abidin bin T.M. Ali, a member of the local parliament (DPRD) from the Parṭain Bulan Bintang (*Putusan* (Decision) No. 04/JN/2006/MSy.Lsm). The decision was appealed through review in the provincial capital to the Indonesian Supreme Court, which eventually upheld it (Mahkamah Agung *Putusan* No. 02K/AG/JN/2007).

[59] Personal observation, Michelle Ann Miller, Kuala Lumpur, July–August 2006.

[60] 'Aceh Enforces Shari'a Law with Lash of Cane', *Financial Times*, 6 October 2006.

[61] 'Public Canings to Start in Aceh for Gamblers', *Jakarta Post*, 23 June 2005.

repeatedly called into question why it is that the new Shari'a system seems to place much greater emphasis on prosecuting cases pertaining to moral misconduct (for example, alcohol consumption and extra-marital sexual relations) than on issues such as human rights violations and corruption cases.[62]

V. Conclusion

In considering the correlation between the Indonesian state's exercise of its emergency military powers and its programme for the implementation of Shari'a in Aceh, we have described some of the ways in which the simultaneous calls for emergency powers and Islamic law have served to both empower and constrain Indonesian state authority in Aceh. The formal imposition of military and civil emergency rule in Aceh forcefully reasserted Indonesian control over the territory of Aceh, while counter-productively alienating the Acehnese people from Indonesian rule and radicalising a victimised community in support of violent anti-state action.[63] As Indonesia's security forces abused the state's coercive powers by committing human rights violations against the civilian population with impunity, Jakarta's efforts to persuade the Acehnese to remain part of Indonesia through its different offers of 'special autonomy' and the implementation of Islamic law initially met with significant scepticism from various sectors of Acehnese Muslim society.

Since the end of emergency rule, however, state programmes for the implementation of Islamic law have come to play a more important role in asserting Indonesian governmental authority in Aceh. There has thus been a considerable shift over time in the relative importance of the two prongs of Jakarta's repressive/persuasive strategy in Aceh. When Indonesia asserted its coercive emergency powers during the period of armed conflict, the power and appeal of Shari'a implementation was somewhat limited by both institutional constraints and popular sentiment. Following the signing of the Helsinki agreement, however, the Indonesian military presence has receded while simultaneously the scope and strength of state Islamic institutions has grown markedly to establish a province-wide presence. That is, while during emergency rule the Islamisation of laws was relatively unsuccessful compared to the success of

[62] Aguswandi, 'Why Islamic Conservatism is Up in Aceh?' *Jakarta Post*, 26 January 2006.

[63] In this respect, there are important parallels between Aceh and Northern Ireland. See, for example, Campbell, 'Law, Terror and Social Movements'.

military measures against Acehnese separatism, in the post-conflict period of demilitarisation the Shari'a system has served to strengthen state control in the province. In this sense, the exercise of Indonesia's emergency powers can be understood to have prepared the ground not for the restoration of a previously existing state of normalcy, but rather for the establishment of a new legal order.[64] Over the course of these developments, the new Shari'a system appears to be offering – in the eyes of many Acehnese – an alternative legal order for post-conflict Aceh as a special autonomous region within Indonesia. Nevertheless, considerable obstacles remain in the way of ensuring that this new form of rule *by* law can also guarantee the establishment of a meaningful rule *of* law in this long-troubled region.[65]

[64] The importance of this distinction for understanding the relationship between the exercise of emergency powers and the rule of law is discussed in V.V. Ramraj, 'The Emergency Powers Paradox' (Chapter 2), this volume.

[65] Drawing on the work of Lon Fuller, Rueban Balasubramanian has argued for the importance of considerations of legal subjects as rational self-directing agents bearing moral interests – and not just the introduction of formal regulatory mechanisms upon the exercise of state power – in establishing a meaningful rule of law. See R. R. Balasubramanian, 'Indefinite Detention: Rule by Law or Rule of Law?' in Ramraj (ed.), *Emergencies*, pp. 129–35.

9

UNaccountable? The United Nations, emergency powers and the rule of law in Asia

SIMON CHESTERMAN

> Above all we must remember that the ways of Orientals are not our ways, nor their thoughts our thoughts. Often when we think them backward and stupid, they think us meddlesome and absurd. The loom of time moves slowly with them, and they care not for high pressure and the roaring of the wheels. Our system may be good for us; but it is neither equally, nor altogether good for them. Satan found it better to reign in hell than to serve in heaven; and the normal Asiatic would sooner be misgoverned by Asiatics than well governed by Europeans.
>
> Lord Curzon, 1889[1]

In 1952 a committee of the American Society of International Law considered whether the laws of war should apply to United Nations enforcement actions. After struggling with the question, they noted that the UN held a 'a superior legal and moral position'[2] to the states which are parties to the relevant conventions and concluded that the Organisation should 'select such of the laws of war as may seem to fit its purposes'.[3] This conferred extraordinary latitude upon the United Nations, which at the time consisted of only sixty countries. Since that time the membership of the UN has more than tripled and the Organisation itself has

This chapter draws upon a few passages first published in *You, The People: The United Nations, Transitional Administration, and State-Building* (Oxford: Oxford University Press, 2004). I am deeply indebted to Mark Fenwick, Victor V. Ramraj, Barnett Rubin and Arun Thiruvengadam for comments on earlier drafts.

1 G. N. Curzon, *Persia and the Persian Question* ([1892] London: Frank Cass, 1966), vol. II, p. 630.

2 Committee on the Study of the Legal Problems of the United Nations (C. Eagleton, Chairman), 'Should the Laws of War Apply to United Nations Enforcement Action?' (1952) 46 *American Society of International Law Proceedings* 217.

3 *Ibid.*, at 220.

affirmed – though only in 1999 – that international humanitarian law does indeed apply to peacekeeping and other operations.[4]

For a body ostensibly so committed to the rule of law in theory,[5] the question of whether the rule of law applies to the United Nations itself in practice remains oddly unclear. A historical reason for this was the uncertain legal personality of this club of states when it was created, which had to be inferred by the International Court of Justice four years later.[6] With respect to specific bodies of law, an ongoing problem is that the United Nations is not itself a party to, among other things, the human rights treaties negotiated under its auspices.

This chapter will not consider the *personal* responsibility of UN officials, who generally enjoy personal or functional immunity from legal process in the territories where they work.[7] Rather the focus is on the quasi-constitutional question of the liability of the Organisation itself. As the United Nations has assumed more state-like functions – in particular through the coercive activities of its Security Council – the question of what limits there are on the powers thus exercised has become more pressing. Though there are significant problems in applying concepts such as the rule of law uncritically onto the international level,[8] here the focus will be the manner in which the UN Security Council has *used* the rule of law as a tool, particularly in situations of actual or potential conflict, and the extent to which the rule of law has *constrained* the exercise of power by the Council or its delegate.

The Council's powers thus invoked derive from Chapter VII of the UN Charter, which is the sole exception to the saving clause that renders

[4] Secretary-General's bulletin: Observance by United Nations Forces of International Humanitarian Law, UN Doc. ST/SGB/1999/13 (6 August 1999), www.un.org/Docs/journal/asp/ws.asp?m=ST/SGB/1999/13.

[5] See, for example, 2005 World Summit Outcome Document, UN Doc. A/RES/60/1 (16 September 2005), www.un.org/summit2005, para. 134(a) (member states unanimously reaffirmed their commitment to 'an international order based on the rule of law and international law, which is essential for peaceful coexistence and cooperation among States').

[6] *Reparation for Injuries Suffered in the Service of the United Nations (Advisory Opinion)* (1949) ICJ Rep. 174.

[7] For discussion of this topic, see Convention on the Privileges and Immunities of the United Nations, 13 February 1946, 1 UNTS 15, www1.umn.edu/humanrts/instree/p&i-convention.htm; F. Rawski, 'To Waive or not to Waive: Immunity and Accountability in UN Peacekeeping Operations', (2002) 18 *Connecticut Journal of International Law* 103; A Comprehensive Strategy to Eliminate Future Sexual Exploitation and Abuse in United Nations Peacekeeping Operations (report of Prince Zeid to the Secretary-General), UN Doc. A/59/710 (24 March 2005), www.un.org/apps/docs/ws.asp?m=A/59/710.

[8] See, for example, S. Chesterman, 'An International Rule of Law?' (2008) 56 *American Journal of Comparative Law* 331.

the domestic jurisdiction of member-states otherwise inviolable;[9] these powers may be invoked when the Council determines that there has been a 'threat to the peace, breach of the peace, or act of aggression'.[10] Such a framework clearly resonates with a doctrine of emergency powers.[11] What is interesting, for the purposes of this volume, is that whereas states of emergency are traditionally invoked in order to justify a departure from or stretching of the rule of law,[12] here the existence of an emergency is a prerequisite to invoking the rule of law at all. At the same time, however, those promoting the rule of law themselves generally lie beyond the reach of the jurisdiction in question – both during times of emergency *and* in times of quiet.

This chapter will examine these two questions – the use of the rule of law at the international level as a tool, and its application to those who wield it – with a particular emphasis on UN operations in Asia, notably East Timor (Timor-Leste) and Afghanistan. Part I will examine the ways in which the rule of law has been used to stabilise conflict zones, focusing on the activities of the UN Security Council from the mid-1990s onward and in particular on East Timor. Part II will consider the extent to which the rule of law has constrained the decisions and actions of the Council, focusing on accountability issues and the apparent compromise of these principles in Afghanistan. A concluding section will consider what light (if any) these operations shed on larger questions raised by the book, such as whether there are discernibly 'Western' or 'Asian' approaches to the role law plays in times of crisis.[13]

Of particular interest is the extent to which the United Nations can be said to reflect Western values, as is frequently alleged. A tentative conclusion is that there may be some rhetorical merit to this claim: Western states do largely set the agenda for the human rights framework that is commonly used to judge state actions. Nevertheless, the United Nations

[9] UN Charter, Article 2(7): 'Nothing contained in the present Charter shall authorise the United Nations to intervene in matters which are essentially within the domestic jurisdiction of any state or shall require the Members to submit such matters to settlement under the present Charter; but this principle shall not prejudice the application of enforcement measures under Chapter VII'.

[10] UN Charter, Article 39.

[11] J. Schott, 'Chapter VII as Exception: Security Council Action and the Regulative Ideal of Emergency' (2007) 6 *Northwestern University Journal of International Human Rights* 24.

[12] See V. V. Ramraj, 'The Emergency Powers Paradox' (Chapter 2), this volume.

[13] On the transplanting of rule-of-law discourse from Western to non-Western states, see A. H. Y. Chen, 'Emergency Powers, Constitutionalism and Legal Transplants: The East Asian Experience' (Chapter 3), this volume.

and the international system wield executive authority so infrequently and inconstantly that broad conclusions are not yet possible. More interesting, for the purposes of this book, is the manner in which internationally administered 'emergency' powers demonstrate the willingness of even established democracies to invoke the rule of law instrumentally, as a tool to provide stability – and thus implicitly to compromise rule of law principles in the name of security. This may be a case of what Victor Ramraj calls in his chapter the 'emergency powers paradox'.[14]

At the same time, it is hoped that this chapter also sheds some light on the underlying question of whether it even makes sense to speak of 'emergency' powers before the rule of law has been established in a meaningful sense. Other chapters in this volume point to two types of problem that have historically confronted Asian states: the routine invocation of extra-constitutional measures without reference to formal emergency powers provisions in a basic law (as discussed in Maitrii Aung-Thwin's chapter on Myanmar and Andrew Harding's chapter on Thailand)[15] and the availability to some regimes of extraordinary executive powers that remove the need to assert emergency powers in the first place (as discussed in Kevin Y. L. Tan's chapter with respect to Singapore and Malaysia).[16] Both types of problem have arisen in Security Council authorised administration of territory, leading to predictable problems when power is transferred from international to 'Asiatic' and other hands.

I. Invoking the rule of law as a response to emergency

The rule of law has long been invoked in human rights treaties as the foundation of a legitimate state[17] and in development policies as the basis

[14] Ramraj, Chapter 2.

[15] M. Aung-Thwin, 'Discourses of Emergency in Colonial and Postcolonial Burma' (Chapter 7) and A. Harding, 'Emergency Powers with a Moustache: Special Powers, Military Rule and Evolving Constitutionalism in Thailand' (Chapter 11), this volume.

[16] K. Y. L. Tan, 'From Myanmar to Manila: A Brief Study of Emergency Powers in Southeast Asia' (Chapter 6), this volume.

[17] The preamble to the 1948 Universal Declaration of Human Rights states that 'it is essential, if man is not to be compelled to have recourse, as a last resort, to rebellion against tyranny and oppression, that human rights should be protected by the rule of law'. Universal Declaration of Human Rights, GA Res. 217A(III) (1948), UN Doc. A/810 (1948), preamble. On the relationship between human rights and the rule of law, see R. Peerenboom, 'Human Rights and Rule of Law: What's the Relationship?' (2005) 36 *Georgetown International Law Review* 809.

for a sustainable economy.[18] Frequently this invocation has been of greater rhetorical than political significance, in the same way that a great many states invoke the rule of law in theory with little effort to implement it in practice.[19] More recently, however, the rule of law has also been used at the international level by the UN Security Council as a means of conflict resolution. This section considers the manner in which Council has used the rule of law as a response to 'emergencies' before considering how this played out in East Timor. Following Dyzenhaus,[20] an examination of the relationship between the rule of law and emergencies may be best pursued through consideration of practical examples. Two elements are of special interest: what the United Nations did while exercising a degree of control over the territory, but also what influence this had (if any) on subsequent governance practices.

A. *The Security Council's uses of the rule of law*

Apart from a preambular reference in relation to the deterioration of law and order in the Congo in 1961,[21] the Council first used the words 'rule of law' in the operative paragraph of Resolution 1040 (1996), where it expressed its support for the Secretary-General's efforts to promote 'national reconciliation, democracy, security and the rule of law in

[18] For an early link between the rule of law, the free market and economic prosperity, see A. Smith, *An Inquiry into the Nature and Causes of the Wealth of Nations* ([1776] Chicago: University of Chicago Press, 1976). In the 1960s, the US Agency for International Development, the Ford Foundation, and other private American donors began an ambitious programme to reform the laws and judicial institutions of countries in Africa, Asia and Latin America. The 'law and development' movement, steeped in dependency theory, generated hundreds of reports and articles – yet, a decade later, leading academic participants and a former official at the Ford Foundation declared it a failure. D. M. Trubek and M. Galanter, 'Scholars in Self-Estrangement: Some Reflections on the Crisis in Law and Development' (1974) 4 *Wisconsin Law Review* 1062; J. H. Merryman, 'Comparative Law and Social Change: On the Origins, Style, Decline and Revival of the Law and Development Movement' (1977) 25 *American Journal of Comparative Law* 457; J. Gardner, *Legal Imperialism: American Lawyers and Foreign Aid in Latin America* (Madison: University of Wisconsin Press, 1980).

[19] See, for example, J. deLisle, 'States of Exception in an Exceptional State: Emergency Powers Law in China' (Chapter 13) and Harding, Chapter 11, this volume.

[20] D. Dyzenhaus, 'The State of Emergency in Legal Theory', in V. V. Ramraj, M. Hor and K. Roach (eds.), *Global Anti-Terrorism Law and Policy* (Cambridge: Cambridge University Press, 2005).

[21] SC Res. 161B (21 February 1961), preamble ('*Noting with deep regret and concern* the systematic violations of human rights and fundamental freedoms and the general absence of the rule of law in the Congo'; the relevant French text was 'l'absence générale de légalité au Congo').

Burundi'.[22] (It is noteworthy that the French text rendered rule of law as 'le rétablissement de l'ordre'.)[23] Many peace operations have subsequently had important rule-of-law components, such as those in Guatemala (1997),[24] Liberia (2003–),[25] Côte d'Ivoire (2004–),[26] Haiti (2004–)[27] and the Democratic Republic of the Congo (2007–).[28] The mandates for such missions tend to be broad, calling for the 're-establishment' or 'restoration and maintenance' of the rule of law, without formally articulating what this might entail. In practice, the dominant activities have tended to be training of personnel, assisting institution-building, advising on law reform issues and monitoring, with the emphasis on criminal law processes.[29] Less attention has been paid, for example, to land law.[30]

[22] SC Res. 1040 (29 January 1996), para. 2.

[23] 'The reestablishment of order'. *Ibid.* (French text available at http://documents.un.org).

[24] UN Verification Mission in Guatemala (MINUGUA).

[25] UN Mission in Liberia (UNMIL).

[26] SC Res. 1528 (27 February 2004), para. 6(q) (authorising the UN Operation in Côte d'Ivoire (UNOCI) to 'assist the Government of National Reconciliation in conjunction with ECOWAS and other international organisations in re-establishing the authority of the judiciary and the rule of law throughout Côte d'Ivoire').

[27] SC Res. 1542 (30 April 2004), para. 7(I)(d) (authorising the UN Stabilisation Mission in Haiti (MINUSTAH) 'to assist with the restoration and maintenance of the rule of law, public safety and public order in Haiti through the provision inter alia of operational support to the Haitian National Police and the Haitian Coast Guard, as well as with their institutional strengthening, including the re-establishment of the corrections system').

[28] SC Res. 1756 (15 May 2007), para. 3, deciding that the UN Organisation Mission in the Democratic Republic of the Congo (MONUC)

> will also have the mandate, in close cooperation with the Congolese authorities, the United Nations country team and donors, to support the strengthening of democratic institutions and the rule of law in the Democratic Republic of the Congo and, to that end, to: . . . (c) Assist in the promotion and protection of human rights, with particular attention to women, children and vulnerable persons, investigate human rights violations with a view to putting an end to impunity, assist in the development and implementation of a transitional justice strategy, and cooperate in national and international efforts to bring to justice perpetrators of grave violations of human rights and international humanitarian law; . . . (e) Assist in the establishment of a secure and peaceful environment for the holding of free and transparent elections; (f) Contribute to the promotion of good governance and respect for the principle of accountability.

The UN Observer Mission in El Salvador (ONUSAL, 1991–5) had a rule-of-law component within its human rights division.

[29] V. O'Connor, 'Rule of Law and Human Rights Protections through Criminal Law Reform: Model Codes for Post-Conflict Criminal Justice' (2006) 13 *International Peacekeeping* 517.

[30] D. Fitzpatrick, 'Land Policy in Post-Conflict Circumstances: Some Lessons from East Timor' (Evaluation and Policy Analysis Unit, United Nations High Commissioner for Refugees, Working Paper No. 58, Geneva, February 2002), www.unhcr.org/publ/RESEARCH/3c8399e14.pdf.

In addition to supporting domestic rule-of-law institutions, the Council has created international criminal tribunals to replace domestic processes for trials arising from the former Yugoslavia (1991–)[31] and Rwanda (1994).[32] These tribunals were explicitly created as part of an effort to bring peace to war-torn territories, though they have been criticised for spending significant resources in order to prosecute few individuals, with little lasting impact on the judicial institutions of the territory concerned. Hybrid tribunals, such as the Special Court for Sierra Leone[33] and the Extraordinary Chambers in the Courts of Cambodia,[34] were intended to blend international supervision with development of national capacity but have had limited success.

In two situations, Kosovo (1999–2008)[35] and East Timor (1999–2002),[36] the United Nations assumed direct responsibility for the administration of justice, including control of police and prison services. (Similar powers were exercised in Bosnia and Herzegovina through the Office of the High Representative from 1996.) Resolution 1272 (1999), for example, determined that the situation in East Timor constituted a threat to peace and security and invoked the Security Council's Chapter VII powers.[37] It established the UN Transitional Administration in East Timor (UNTAET) and endowed it with 'overall responsibility for the administration of East Timor', granting the new body power 'to exercise all legislative and executive authority, including the administration of justice'.[38] UNTAET was further authorised 'to take all necessary measures to fulfil its mandate'.[39] These potentially dictatorial powers were tempered by the political understanding that the Timorese people had voted overwhelmingly for independence and that this transition should be overseen by the United Nations.[40] East Timor duly became independent two-and-a-half years later.

The frequency with which the rule of law is now invoked through the United Nations as a means of preventing or responding to crisis has led to a proliferation of institutions, notably including a new Rule of Law

[31] SC Res. 827 (25 May 1993).
[32] SC Res. 955 (8 November 1994).
[33] Agreement between the United Nations and the Government of Sierra Leone on the Establishment of a Special Court for Sierra Leone, done at Freetown, 16 January 2002.
[34] Agreement between the United Nations and the Royal Government of Cambodia Concerning the Prosecution under Cambodian Law of Crimes Committed During the Period of Democratic Kampuchea, done at Phnom Penh, 6 June 2003, www.eccc.gov.kh.
[35] UN Interim Administration Mission in Kosovo (UNMIK).
[36] UN Transitional Administration in East Timor (UNTAET).
[37] SC Res. 1272 (25 October 1999), preamble.
[38] *Ibid.*, para. 1. [39] *Ibid.*, para. 4. [40] *Ibid.*, preamble.

Coordination and Resource Group and a Rule of Law Unit.[41] The roles attributed to the rule of law as a response to crisis have also been reflected in the burgeoning literature on the subject.[42]

That literature rarely considers the irony that lawless means are being used to promote law (though that irony tends not to be lost on the locals[43]). Analogies are sometimes made to the laws of military occupation and colonialism, in particular the civilising mission incorporated more openly in texts such as the League of Nations Covenant, which explicitly provided that 'the tutelage of [peoples not yet able to stand by themselves] should be entrusted to advanced nations who by reason of their resources, their experience or their geographical position can best undertake this responsibility, and who are willing to accept it'.[44] This language of a 'sacred trust' survived into the present UN Charter.[45]

A more interesting analogy for present purposes is that which one might draw between the UN Security Council and the Roman law concept of *iustitium*. As Agamben has argued, this state of exception represents not the fullness of powers, but 'an emptiness and standstill of the law'.[46] In times of crisis, the Security Council does not invoke emergency powers in the sense of enhanced centralised authority – rather, the crisis (a threat to international peace and security) justifies a temporary suspension of the law (the non-intervention principle enshrined in

[41] UN Doc. A/61/636-S/2006/980 (2006).

[42] See generally, T. Carothers, 'The Rule of Law Revival' (1998) 77 *Foreign Affairs* 95; R. Caplan, *International Governance of War-Torn Territories: Rule and Reconstruction* (Oxford: Oxford University Press, 2005); J. Stromseth, D. Wippman and R. Brooks, *Can Might Make Rights? Building the Rule of Law after Military Interventions* (New York: Cambridge University Press, 2006); D. Zaum, *The Sovereignty Paradox: The Norms and Politics of International Statebuilding* (Oxford: Oxford University Press, 2007).

[43] See, for example, Jose 'Kay Rala Xanana' Gusmão, 'New Year's Message: The Right to Live in Peace and Harmony' (Dili, East Timor, 31 December 2000), www.cpa.org.au/garchve3/1031xan.html:

> We are witnessing another phenomenon in East Timor; that of an obsessive acculturation to standards that hundreds of international experts try to convey to the East Timorese, who are hungry for values: democracy (many of those who teach us never practised it in their own countries because they became UN staff members); human rights (many of those who remind us of them forget the situation in their own countries); gender (many of the women who attend the workshops know that in their countries this issue is no example for others).

[44] Covenant of the League of Nations, Article 22.

[45] See, for example, UN Charter, Article 73.

[46] G. Agamben, *State of Exception* (Chicago: University of Chicago Press, 2005), p. 48; S. Humphreys, 'Legalizing Lawlessness: On Giorgio Agamben's *State of Exception*' (2006) 17 *European Journal of International Law* 677 at 681–2.

Article 2(7) of the UN Charter) for a specific purpose (restoration of peace and security).[47]

Formally, states have agreed to this arrangement through their membership of the United Nations, even though such powers go somewhat beyond what was originally contemplated when the Charter was drafted. Through the 1990s that expansion could be tracked by the language used to justify each step as 'unique' (Somalia in 1992),[48] 'unique and exceptional' (Haiti in 1993)[49] and again 'unique' (Rwanda in 1994).[50] Predictably, these powers have become most controversial when they slipped from the exceptional into the normal, as the Council's powers arguably have in the over-use of targeted financial sanctions and legislative resolutions. In the former case, sanctions in principle operate, *inter alia*, to prevent the financing of terrorist acts: as asset freezes stretch into more than a decade these preventive acts based on secret intelligence look more like a form of punitive confiscation based on no evidence.[51] In the latter case, the ability of the Council to respond swiftly and robustly to international threats has crept toward using those powers to issue norms of general application without operating through the normal – and cumbersome – processes of international law.[52]

Though the United Nations is highly unusual in the coercive powers granted to its security organ, regional organisations of more recent vintage have been granted explicit powers to be critical of, among other things, non-constitutional changes of government. The OSCE, in its previous incarnation as the CSCE, adopted the Copenhagen Document in 1990, in which member-states recognised their responsibility to defend and protect 'the democratic order freely established through the will of the people against the activities of persons, groups or organisations that engage in or refuse to renounce terrorism or violence aimed at the overthrow of that order or of that of another participating state'.[53] The European Union has even more intrusive powers with respect to its members. In 1992 the

[47] Cf. N. Bhuta, 'The Antinomies of Transformative Occupation' (2005) 16 *European Journal of International Law* 721.

[48] SC Res. 794 (3 December 1992).

[49] SC Res. 841 (16 June 1993).

[50] SC Res. 929 (22 June 1994).

[51] See notes 94–100 below and accompanying text.

[52] S. A. Talmon, 'The Security Council as World Legislature' (2005) 99 *American Journal of International Law* 175. See also S. Chesterman, 'The UN Security Council and the Rule of Law', UN Doc. A/63/69-S/2008/270 (2008), http://documents.un.org.

[53] Conference on Security and Co-operation in Europe, Document of the Copenhagen Meeting of the Conference on the Human Dimension (Copenhagen Document) (29 June 1990). See also M. Halberstam, 'The Copenhagen Document: Intervention in Support of Democracy' (1993) 34 *Harvard International Law Journal* 163.

Organisation of American States (OAS) amended its Charter to permit suspension of a member whose democratic government has been overthrown by force.[54] Going one step further, the African Union (AU) in 2000 adopted a Constitutive Act that recognised 'the right of the Union to intervene in a Member State pursuant to a decision of the Assembly in respect of grave circumstances, namely: war crimes, genocide and crimes against humanity'.[55] Most recently, the United Nations at the 2005 World Summit endorsed the 'responsibility to protect', and member-states declared their preparedness

> to take collective action, in a timely and decisive manner, through the Security Council, in accordance with the Charter, including Chapter VII, on a case-by-case basis and in cooperation with relevant regional organisations as appropriate, should peaceful means be inadequate and national authorities are manifestly failing to protect their populations from genocide, war crimes, ethnic cleansing and crimes against humanity.[56]

These developments may be contrasted with the more traditional conception of sovereignty that tends to be embraced in Asian institutions, such as they are. Asia lacks comparable bodies to the EU/OSCE, the OAS or the AU. Those bodies that do exist either have no provision at all for scrutiny of members, such as the Shanghai Cooperation Organisation, or extremely weak mechanisms such as the embryonic human rights body within ASEAN.[57] This is not to say that such questions of institutional design are explicable by Asian cultural or political differences, but it does suggest that – at least in this respect – Asia provides a useful counterpoint to the general trend toward greater delegation of powers to international organisations.

B. *Applying the rule of law in East Timor*

Leaving aside the question of what international organisations have been empowered to do in theory, what happens in practice when forces are

[54] OAS Charter (1948), Article 9, as amended by the Protocol of Washington, adopted on 14 December 1992 by the Sixteenth Special Session of the General Assembly of the OAS (amendment entered into force 1997). Suspension is not automatic, however, and must be approved by a two-thirds majority of the OAS member-states.

[55] Constitutive Act of the African Union, done at Lomé, Togo, 11 July 2000 (in force 26 May 2001), www.africa-union.org, Article 4(h).

[56] 2005 World Summit Outcome Document, para. 139.

[57] Charter of the Association of Southeast Asian Nations (ASEAN Charter), done at Singapore, 20 November 2007, in force 15 December 2008, at www.aseansec.org/AC.htm, Article 14.

deployed on the ground? This chapter will not rehearse the pre-1999 history of East Timor.[58] When the Australia-led INTERFET force landed – formally authorised by both a Security Council resolution[59] and Indonesian consent[60] – they swiftly drew up a Detainee Ordinance that provided for temporary detention of persons suspected of or on trial for committing a serious offence, voluntary detainees, and persons detained as 'a security risk'. 'Serious offence' was defined by reference to certain chapters of the Indonesian Penal Code.[61] Plans had been made to transfer persons so detained to Indonesian civilian authorities, but the collapse of those structures soon led to the creation of a Detainee Management Unit (DMU) to review detention cases, comparable to a bail hearing, except in its use of written submissions. Between 21 October 1999 and 12 January 2000 the DMU reviewed sixty cases, after which all detainees were handed over to civilian authorities under the auspices of UNTAET.[62]

Following the transfer of power to the civilian UNTAET operation, an early order of business was to determine what law applied. In Kosovo, the controversial mission authorised just months earlier, choice of law had been politically fraught. At Russian insistence, and consistent with the terms of Resolution 1244 (1999), the first UNMIK regulation established that the law in force prior to 24 March 1999 (the day on which NATO's air campaign commenced) would apply, provided that this law was consistent with internationally recognised human rights standards and Security Council Resolution 1244.[63] The largely Albanian judiciary that was put in place by UNMIK rejected this, however, with some judges reportedly stating that they would not apply 'Serbian' law in Kosovo. Though they accepted some Federal laws, such as the Federal code of criminal procedure, the judges insisted on applying the Kosovo Criminal Code and other provincial laws that had been in effect in March 1989, asserting

[58] See generally, J. Ramos-Horta, *Funu: The Unfinished Saga of East Timor* (Lawrenceville, N.J.: Red Sea Press, 1987); D. Kingsbury (ed.), *Guns and Ballot Boxes: East Timor's Vote for Independence* (Clayton, Australia: Monash Asia Institute, 2000); I. Martin, *Self-Determination in East Timor: The United Nations, the Ballot, and International Intervention*, International Peace Academy Occasional Paper Series (Boulder, Colo.: Lynne Rienner, 2001).

[59] SC Res. 1264 (15 September 1999).

[60] Statement of the President of Indonesia, 12 September 1999, cited in SC Res. 1264 (1999), preamble. From a legal perspective this consent would appear to be redundant.

[61] INTERFET Detainee Ordinance, 21 October 1999. See B. M. Oswald, 'Model Codes for Criminal Justice and Peace Operations: Some Legal Issues' (2004) 9 *Journal of Conflict and Security Law* 269.

[62] M. J. Kelly *et al.*, 'Legal Aspects of Australia's Involvement in the International Force for East Timor' (2001) 83 *International Review of the Red Cross* 101.

[63] UNMIK Regulation 1999/1 (25 July 1999), ss. 2, 3.

that these had been illegally revoked by Belgrade. The judges nevertheless 'borrowed' from the 1999 law to deal with cases involving crimes not covered in the 1989 Code, such as drug-trafficking and war crimes. In addition to lowering hopes that Serb judges would return to office, this dispute further undermined local respect for UNMIK – especially when, in December 1999, it finally reversed its earlier decision and passed a regulation declaring that the laws in effect on 22 March 1989 would be the applicable law in Kosovo.[64]

In East Timor, by contrast, choice of law was uncontroversial. UNTAET Regulation 1999/1 defined the applicable law as 'the laws applied in East Timor prior to 25 October 1999'.[65] This language (referring to 'the laws applied', rather than 'the applicable laws') was chosen in order to avoid the retroactive legitimation of the Indonesian occupation.[66] These laws were not translated from Indonesian to English, however, greatly complicating the efforts of international judges to inform themselves of the laws governing the territory. Institutions were sometimes developed idiosyncratically: East Timor found itself, for example, with German-style investigative judges – an outcome not unconnected with the fact that UNTAET's legal advisor at the time happened to be German.[67]

Though East Timor had fewer security and political problems than Kosovo, lack of local capacity presented immense challenges. Under Indonesian rule, no Timorese lawyers had been appointed as judges or prosecutors. A Transitional Judicial Service Commission was established, comprising three Timorese and two international experts,[68] but the absence of a communications network meant that the search for qualified lawyers had to be conducted through leaflet drops by INTERFET planes. Within two months, sixty qualified Timorese with law degrees had applied for positions and the first eight judges and two prosecutors were sworn in on 7 January 2000.[69]

The decision to rely on inexperienced local jurists came from a mix of politics and pragmatism. Politically, the appointment of the first Timorese legal officers was of enormous symbolic importance. At the same time,

64 UNMIK Regulation 1999/24 (12 December 1999), s. 1.1.

65 UNTAET Regulation 1999/1 (27 November 1999), s. 3.1

66 H. Strohmeyer, 'Building a New Judiciary for East Timor: Challenges of a Fledgling Nation' (2000) 11 *Criminal Law Forum* 267 at n. 18.

67 H. Strohmeyer, 'Collapse and Reconstruction of a Judicial System: The United Nations Missions in Kosovo and East Timor' (2001) 95 *American Journal of International Law* 46; Zaum, *Sovereignty Paradox*, p. 232.

68 UNTAET Regulation 1999/3 (3 December 1999), s. 2.

69 Strohmeyer, 'Collapse and Reconstruction', at 53–4.

the emergency detentions during the Australian-led INTERFET operation required the early appointment of judges who understood the local civil law system and who would not require the same amount of translation services demanded by international judges. In addition, appointment of international judges would necessarily be an unsustainable temporary measure that would cause further dislocation when funds began to diminish.

In the end, UNTAET was more aggressive in Timorising the management of judicial systems than the institutions working in political and civil affairs.[70] The trade-off, of course, was in formal qualifications and practical experience. Some of the appointees had worked in law firms and legal aid organisations in Indonesia; others as paralegals with Timorese human rights organisations and resistance groups.[71] None had ever served as a judge or prosecutor. Timorisation thus referred more to the identity of a particular official, rather than the establishment of support structures to ensure that individuals could fulfil their responsibilities. UNTAET developed a three-tier training approach, comprising a one-week 'quick impact' course prior to appointment, ongoing training and a mentoring scheme. However, limited resources and difficulties in recruiting experienced mentors with a background in civil law posed serious obstacles to the training programme, which UNTAET officials later acknowledged was grossly insufficient.

Quite apart from the limited legal training that was possible during the period of UNTAET administration (which was shorter than even a three-year law degree), a greater source of potential instability was the political situation upon independence. It is arguable that continuing the international administration or a large foreign military presence would ultimately have encouraged free-riding on the part of the government, and that limited peacekeeping resources needed to be deployed elsewhere. Nevertheless, the international presence can certainly take some responsibility for laying the foundations for disorder by leaving in place a government where the first president (Xanana Gusmão) enjoyed massive popular support (including that of the military) without meaningful constitutional power, while the prime minister (Mari Alkatiri) had constitutional authority but little personal public support.[72] This contributed to outbursts of violence in December 2002, June 2006 and February 2008.

[70] See, for example, J. C. Beauvais, 'Benevolent Despotism: A Critique of UN State-Building in East Timor' (2001) 33 *New York University Journal of International Law and Politics* 1149.

[71] Strohmeyer, 'Collapse and Reconstruction', at 54.

[72] See further, Chesterman, *You, the People*, p. 233.

Given the subsequent instability in East Timor, what lessons if any were drawn from the period of international administration? East Timor's emergency powers in the Constitution adopted upon independence in May 2002 are, unusually, gathered under an Agambenesque sub-heading:

> Section 25 (State of exception)
>
> 1 Suspension of the exercise of fundamental rights, freedoms and guarantees shall only take place if a state of siege or a state of emergency has been declared as provided for by the Constitution.
> 2 A state of siege or a state of emergency shall only be declared in case of effective or impending aggression by a foreign force, of serious disturbance or threat of serious disturbance to the democratic constitutional order, or of public disaster.
> 3 A declaration of a state of siege or a state of emergency shall be substantiated, specifying rights, freedoms and guarantees the exercise of which is to be suspended.
> 4 A suspension shall not last for more than thirty days, without prejudice of possible justified renewal, when strictly necessary, for equal periods of time.
> 5 In no case shall a declaration of a state of siege affect the right to life, physical integrity, citizenship, non-retroactivity of the criminal law, defence in a criminal case and freedom of conscience and religion, the right not to be subjected to torture, slavery or servitude, the right not to be subjected to cruel, inhuman or degrading treatment or punishment, and the guarantee of non-discrimination.
> 6 Authorities shall restore constitutional normality as soon as possible.[73]

Subsequent provisions set out the means by which such a declaration is to be made. The power to do so is granted exclusively to the President, but this is to follow 'authorisation of the National Parliament, after consultation with the Council of State, the Government and the Supreme Council of Defence and Security'.[74] When Parliament is not in session, the power of authorisation falls to the Standing Committee.[75] The government, for its part, has the power to propose such a declaration to the President.[76]

[73] Constitution of the Democratic Republic of Timor-Leste (East Timor) (2002), www.constitution.org/cons/east˙timor/constitution-eng.htm, s. 25.

[74] *Ibid.*, s. 85(g). The National Parliament's power to 'authorize and confirm the declaration' is provided in s. 95(3)(j).

[75] *Ibid.*, s. 102(3)(g). [76] *Ibid.*, s. 115(2)(c).

The Timorese Constitution draws in part on the Constitution of Portugal.[77] In particular, the threshold for the declaration of a state of emergency is very similar, with the Portuguese Constitution (under the more prosaic heading 'Suspension of the Exercise of Rights') allowing for such a declaration in cases of 'actual or imminent aggression by foreign forces, a serious threat to or disturbance of constitutional democratic order, or public disaster'.[78] This is a significantly broader set of circumstances than that recognised in the International Covenant on Civil and Political Rights, to which East Timor acceded, which limits derogations to 'a public emergency which threatens the life of the nation'.[79] Indeed, East Timor goes beyond the Portuguese baseline of either '*serious threat to* or disturbance of constitutional democratic order' by allowing for a state of emergency to be declared if there is a 'serious disturbance or *threat of serious disturbance to* the democratic constitutional order'.[80]

Nevertheless there would appear to be little question that the higher threshold had been reached on the two occasions when a state of emergency was declared. The first followed a dispute between the military and the Fretilin-dominated leadership, with 600 soldiers deserting and an escalation of violence through March and April 2006 that saw about forty deaths, including nine unarmed police killed by soldiers. President Gusmão declared a state of emergency on 31 May 2006 – in part to reassert control over the armed forces, but also in order to force the resignation of Prime Minister Alkatiri. Alkatiri ultimately resigned on 26 June 2006.[81]

A state of emergency was declared for a second time following assassination attempts on the President and Prime Minister on 11 February 2008, apparently led by Alfredo Reinado – a rebel soldier who had deserted in the May 2006 unrest. Reinado had been detained by Portuguese and Australian troops but escaped a month later. As President Jose Ramos-Horta had been shot, the Speaker of the National Parliament took on the function of Acting President.[82] On behalf of the government, Xanana

[77] For a critique of the failure to engage with legal pluralism in East Timor, see L. Grenfell, 'Legal Pluralism and the Rule of Law in Timor Leste' (2006) 19 *Leiden Journal of International Law* 305.

[78] Constitution of the Portuguese Republic (seventh revision) (2005), art. 19.

[79] International Covenant on Civil and Political Rights (ICCPR), 16 December 1966, 999 UNTS 171 (in force 23 March 1976), Article 4. Cf. 'Freedom of Expression and the Media in Timor-Leste' (Article 19 and Internews: London and Dili, 2005), pp. 39–40, www.Article19.org.

[80] Constitution of East Timor, s. 25(2).

[81] T. Hyland, 'Charges over Timor Violence', *Sunday Age* (Melbourne), 8 October 2006; G. Lloyd, 'Trio Holds Key to Resolving Conflict', *Courier Mail* (Australia), 3 June 2006.

[82] Constitution of East Timor, s. 84.

Gusmão, now Prime Minister, requested an initial state of emergency of forty-eight hours in order to suspend the right to free movement, impose a dusk-to-dawn curfew and prohibit any assembly or demonstration.[83] This was subsequently extended by ten days in order to cover Reinado's funeral,[84] and then by a further thirty days.[85]

It is far too early to draw any meaningful conclusions about how emergency powers will be invoked in East Timor in the future. It is not clear that it is possible to distinguish an 'Asian' or non-Western position, however. Relations with Indonesia remain somewhat tense and the Constitution and the ruling elite look more to Portugal for guidance.[86] ASEAN has been reluctant to consider East Timor as a potential member. Australia's ongoing military support will be essential for stability; the United Nations presence, extended until February 2009, has provided additional oversight. East Timor thus has little Asian identification and enjoys far closer formal and substantive relations with Western states and the United Nations, even if those relations resemble the colonial ties of earlier times. It demonstrates, if anything, the extent to which even this newest of states found itself swiftly drawn to a familiar discourse on, and practice of, the rule of law.

II. Compromising the rule of law because of emergency

Whereas the previous section looked at efforts by the United Nations to promote the rule-of-law, invoking exceptional powers to do so, this section will consider the application of rule-of-law principles to the United Nations itself, before examining the manner in which it was prepared to compromise them in the hope of achieving a more modest form of organised political life in Afghanistan.

A. *Does the rule of law apply to the United Nations?*

The United Nations is not a party to the human rights treaties negotiated under its auspices or monitored through its agencies. In part this reflects

[83] Jose 'Kay Rala Xanana' Gusmão, 'Message to the Nation by the Prime Minister' (Dili, East Timor, 11 February 2008).

[84] ABC (Australia) News Radio, 'State of Emergency Extended in East Timor' (14 February 2008).

[85] 'President Improves', *The Australian*, 22 February 2008. The state of emergency was ultimately lifted in all but one district on 22 April 2008. M. Metherell, 'E. Timor Told to Follow the Rules', *Sydney Morning Herald*, 23 April 2008.

[86] Cf. N. Hosen, 'Emergency Powers and the Rule of Law in Indonesia' (Chapter 10), this volume.

the traditional view that only states properly enter into such treaties, a view also supported by the understanding that it is primarily states that violate or protect human rights. As the United Nations has assumed state-like functions, however – including administrations that ran entire territories – the question of whether the United Nations is required to abide by basic human rights standards has become more pressing. Arguments that the United Nations should be bound sometimes proceed on the basis that such a conclusion is self-evident from the purposes and principles of the UN Charter. A second approach asserts that the United Nations has sufficient legal personality to be bound by customary international law. A third approach focuses on the activities of the United Nations and the state-like functions that it is now exercising. In a series of cases arising from the use of targeted financial sanctions, the European Court of First Instance has held that Security Council decisions, by virtue of the UN Charter's primacy clause in Article 103, are constrained only by norms of *jus cogens*.[87] This is one of only a few cases in which a tribunal has reviewed, even indirectly, the validity of Council action.[88]

Apart from the general 'state of exception' that might be used to characterise the Security Council's use of Chapter VII powers[89] – most obviously to authorise the use of military force to restore peace and security – two sets of activities undertaken with the authority of the Council warrant closer analysis for their proximity to national debates about states of emergency and thus the subject of this book: detention without trial in a period of relative calm, and confiscation of assets without judicial review.

1. Kosovo – executive detentions

Kosovo, like East Timor, was an unusual situation in which the United Nations exercised *de facto* day-to-day governance over a territory and population – at the time technically part of what remained of the Federal Republic of Yugoslavia (later renamed Serbia and Montenegro, and after further secession simply 'Serbia'), but always destined for a political future separate from that of Belgrade. As indicated earlier, however, UNMIK's

[87] See n. 96 below.

[88] See also *Legal Consequences for States of the Continued Presence of South Africa in Namibia (South-West Africa) Notwithstanding Security Council Resolution 276 (1970) (Advisory Opinion)* (1971) ICJ Rep. 16, para. 118 (referring to 'a situation which the Court has found to have been *validly* declared illegal' by the Security Council (emphasis added)); *Prosecutor* v. *Tadic (Appeal on Jurisdiction)* (ICTY Appeals Chamber, 2 October 1995) Case No. IT-94-1-AR72, available at www.un.org/icty, paras. 28–30 ('neither the text nor the spirit of the Charter conceives of the Security Council as *legibus solutus* [unbound by law]').

[89] See n. 11 above.

faith in the judiciary and its own credibility as a lawmaker were shaky. One consequence of this was recourse to executive detentions.

On 28 May 2000, Afram Zeqiri, a Kosovar Albanian and former Kosovo Liberation Army (KLA) fighter, was arrested on suspicion of murdering three Serbs, including the shooting of a four-year-old boy. An Albanian prosecutor ordered him released for lack of evidence, raising suspicions of judicial bias. The decision was upheld by an international judge, but the Special Representative of the Secretary-General, Bernard Kouchner (later Foreign Minister of France), nevertheless ordered that Zeqiri continue to be detained under an 'executive hold', claiming that the authority to issue such orders derived from 'security reasons' and Security Council Resolution 1244 (1999). Similar orders were made by Kouchner's successor, Hans Haekkerup. In February 2001, a bus carrying Serbs from Nis into Kosovo was bombed, killing eleven. British KFOR troops arrested four ethnic Albanians in mid-March on suspicion of being involved, but on 27 March a panel of international judges ordered that three of them be released (the fourth escaped). The following day, Haekkerup issued an executive order extending their detention for thirty days, later extended by six more such orders.[90]

Following criticism by the OSCE Ombudsperson,[91] as well as international human rights organisations such as Human Rights Watch and Amnesty International, a Detention Review Commission of international experts was established by UNMIK in August 2001 to make final decisions on the legality of administrative detentions. The Commission approved extension of the detentions of the alleged Nis bombers until 19 December 2001 – a few weeks after Kosovo's first provincial elections – ruling that 'there are reasonable grounds to suspect that each of the detained persons has committed a criminal act'. At the end of that period, the three-month mandate of the Commission had not been renewed; in its absence, the Kosovo Supreme Court ordered the release of the three detainees. The last person held under an Executive Order, Afrim Zeqiri, was released by a judge on bail in early February 2002 after approximately twenty months in detention.

Two years into the mission, UNMIK officials argued that Kosovo still ranked as an 'internationally-recognised emergency'. And, in such circumstances, 'international human rights standards accept the need for special

[90] Chesterman, *You, the People*, pp. 167–8.

[91] Ombudsperson Institution in Kosovo, Special Report No. 3: 'On the Conformity of Deprivations of Liberty under "Executive Orders" with Recognised International Standards' (29 June 2001), www.ombudspersonkosovo.org.

measures that, in the wider interests of security, and under prescribed legal conditions, allow authorities to respond to the findings of intelligence that are not able to be presented to the court system'.[92] Human rights law does indeed provide for derogation from particular norms including the right to a fair trial, although this is generally limited to a time of 'war or other public emergency threatening the life of the nation' and there must be some form of official notification of this situation.[93] No such notification was offered in Kosovo – largely because of political reservations against admitting that Kosovo even two years after UNMIK arrived remained a 'public emergency'. Rather, the view was taken that a Chapter VII resolution adopted by the Security Council somehow absolved a UN operation from certain human rights obligations – an odd conclusion to a war that was justified precisely on the grounds of its support for human rights.

2. Targeted financial sanctions

A second instance of quasi-emergency powers being invoked through the United Nations is the use of targeted financial sanctions. Security Council Resolution 1267 (1999) established a committee (the '1267 Committee') to oversee implementation of a sanctions regime that initially targeted Afghanistan's Taliban government but was later expanded to apply to Osama bin Laden and 'individuals and entities associated with him as designated by the Committee, including those in the Al-Qaida organisation'.[94] In January 2002, following the 11 September 2001 attacks on the United States and the successful military operation in Afghanistan, the regime was further expanded with the removal of a geographic connection to Afghanistan and any time-limit on its application.[95]

The targeted sanctions in question entailed the worldwide freezing of an individual's assets. The process for identifying those individuals whose assets should be frozen, however, was somewhat opaque. Only in January 2004, with the passage of Resolution 1526, were member-states proposing individuals to be listed called upon to provide information demonstrating an association with al Qaeda. The same resolution '*encourage[d]*' member-states to inform such individuals that their assets were being frozen. In

[92] 'UNMIK Refutes Allegations of Judicial Bias and Lack of Strategy', *UNMIK News* (Pristina), 25 June 2001.

[93] See European Convention for the Protection of Human Rights and Fundamental Freedoms, done at Rome, 4 November 1950, 213 UNTS 222 (in force 3 September 1953), Article 15; ICCPR, Article 4.

[94] SC Res. 1333 (19 December 2000), para. 8(c).

[95] SC Res. 1390 (16 January 2002), para. 3.

July 2005 – almost six years after the listing regime was first established – Resolution 1617 required that when states proposed additional names for the consolidated list they should henceforth provide to the Committee a 'statement of case describing the basis of the proposal'. This did not affect the more than four hundred individuals and entities that had been listed without such a formal statement of case. The resolution also '*request[ed]* relevant States to inform, to the extent possible, and in writing where possible, individuals and entities included in the Consolidated List of the measures imposed on them, the Committee's guidelines, and, in particular, the listing and delisting procedures'. Meanwhile, the sanctions regime had been challenged in European courts on the basis that assets were being frozen without adequate legal protections.

The European Court of First Instance held that the ability to review decisions ultimately made by the Security Council was severely limited. Nevertheless,

> the Court is empowered to check, indirectly, the lawfulness of the resolutions of the Security Council in question with regard to *jus cogens*, understood as a body of higher rules of public international law binding on all subjects of international law, including the bodies of the United Nations, and from which no derogation is possible.[96]

The Court found that this very high threshold had not been reached in the cases before it. In January 2008 the Advocate-General of the European Court of Justice argued that measures adopted by the Council applied within the European Community only to the extent that this was compatible with Community law: 'There is no reason, therefore, for the Court to depart, in the present case, from its usual interpretation of the fundamental rights that have been invoked by the appellant.'[97] As for what

[96] *Ahmed Ali Yusuf and Al Barakaat International Foundation* v. *Council of the European Union and Commission of the European Communities* (Case T-306/01) (Court of First Instance of the European Communities, 21 September 2005), http://curia.eu.int/, para. 277. See also *Yassin Abdullah Kadi* v. *Council of the European Union and Commission of the European Communities* (Case T-315/01) (Court of First Instance of the European Communities, 21 September 2005), http://curia.eu.int/; *Faraj Hassan* v. *Council of the European Union and Commission of the European Communities* (Case T-49/04) (Court of First Instance of the European Communities, 12 July 2006), http://curia.eu.int/; *Chafiq ayadi* v. *Council of the European Union* (Case T-253/02) (Court of First Instance of the European Communities, 12 July 2006), http://curia.eu.int/.

[97] *Opinion of Advocate General Poiares Maduro Regarding the Case of Yassin Abdullah Kadi* v. *Council of the European Union and Commission of the European Communities* (Case C-402/05 P) (European Court of Justice, 16 January 2008), http://curia.eu.int, para. 46.

this might mean for states bound by Article 103 of the UN Charter,[98] the Advocate General merely noted its understanding that such a ruling might 'inconvenience the Community and its Member States in their dealings on the international stage'.[99]

In September 2008 the European Court of Justice ultimately held that, while it did not purport to challenge the primacy of the Council's resolutions as a matter of international law – contradicting the Court of First Instance on this point – it found that it could nevertheless review the lawfulness of the Community act intended to give effect to those resolutions.[100] The European regulation in question violated fundamental rights (effective judicial protection and respect for property) and was therefore struck down. Nevertheless, as annulment with immediate effect 'would be capable of seriously and irreversibly prejudicing the effectiveness' of the measures imposed by the Council, the effects of the regulation would be maintained for three months.

3. Compromising the rule of law in Afghanistan

The rule of law was compromised in a quite different manner in Afghanistan, which faced challenges distinct from East Timor and represented an entirely different context. A 'light footprint' approach was advocated by the United Nations as a means of promoting local ownership – though it was also only practical given the size and population of the country, and only politically viable given the undisputed sovereignty of the Afghan government under Hamid Karzai. This substantially limited the role that the international presence played, though key areas were still potentially 'externalised'.

Justice in Afghanistan under the Taliban had been notoriously capricious and brutal; their overthrow was brutal in its own way. In addition to allegations that anti-Taliban forces summarily executed prisoners of war during the fighting, there were several reports that Rashid Dostum's troops killed hundreds of Taliban detainees while transporting them in sealed freight containers. There was little willingness to investigate

98 UN Charter, art. 103: 'In the event of a conflict between the obligations of the Members of the United Nations under the present Charter and their obligations under any other international agreement, their obligations under the present Charter shall prevail'.

99 *Maduro Opinion*, para. 39.

100 *Ahmed Ali Yusuf and Al Barakaat International Foundation* v. *Council of the European Union and Commission of the European Communities* (Cases C-402/05 P and C-415/05), (European Court of Justice, 3 September 2008), available at http://curia.eu.int/, paras. 286–8.

these and other allegations against members of Hamid Karzai's new government.[101]

The Bonn Agreement provided that the Interim and later Transitional Authority should, 'with the assistance of the United Nations, establish an independent Human Rights Commission, whose responsibilities will include human rights monitoring, investigation of violations of human rights, and development of domestic human rights institutions'. At the same time, the United Nations was separately granted 'the right to investigate human rights violations and, where necessary, recommend corrective action', as well as developing and implementing a human rights education programme.[102] In keeping with the 'light footprint' philosophy, senior UN staff were circumspect about taking the lead in human rights.

Also under the Bonn Agreement, the Interim Authority was to establish, 'with the assistance of the United Nations, a Judicial Commission to rebuild the domestic justice system in accordance with Islamic principles, international standards, the rule of law and Afghan legal traditions'.[103] A document from the Office of the Special Representative emphasised the need for a careful, strategic approach:

> all agree that global experience in justice reform and development has shown that non-strategic, piecemeal and 'interventionist' approaches can have dire consequences for the effective development of [the justice] sector. A strategic, comprehensive, Afghan led, integrated programme of justice sector reform and development can only begin with a comprehensive sectoral review and assessment of domestic needs, priorities, initiatives and capacities for reconstruction and development of this crucial sector. To date, none has been undertaken.[104]

Given the experiences of Kosovo and East Timor, these assumptions are highly debatable. UNMIK in particular found that failure to engage *immediately* with rule-of-law questions can lead to missed opportunities for the maximum impact of international engagement. It is true that a strategic, comprehensive approach is desirable – but not if it means indefinite delays

[101] Human Rights Watch, *World Report 2003* (New York: Human Rights Watch, 2003), p. 198. The detention of Taliban and alleged al Qaeda forces on US military bases raised serious questions of international humanitarian law.

[102] Agreement on Provisional Arrangements in Afghanistan Pending the Re-establishment of Permanent Government Institutions (Bonn Agreement), done at Bonn, 5 December 2001, UN Doc. S/2001/1154, Article III.C(6), Annex II, para. 6.

[103] *Ibid.*, Article II(2).

[104] Office of the SRSG for Afghanistan, 'Proposal for a Multi-Agency Review of Justice Sector Development in Afghanistan' (UNAMA-OSRSG, Kabul, May 2002), p. 2.

until the security environment allows for a thorough review. If necessary, skeletal legal reforms might be made on an emergency basis until a more strategic approach can be formulated.[105]

In Afghanistan, UNAMA's mandate was interpreted as requiring the United Nations to facilitate rather than lead. In areas such as the choice of laws, the structure of the legal system and the appointment of judges, this was entirely appropriate. Such arguments were less persuasive in relation to basic questions of rebuilding courthouses, procuring legal texts and office equipment and the training of judges. Instead, it appeared that rule of law was simply not a priority. In the forty-eight-page National Development Framework drafted by the Afghan Assistance Coordination Authority (AACA) in April 2002, the justice system warranted only a single substantive sentence.[106] Italy agreed to serve as 'lead donor' on the justice sector at the Tokyo pledging conference in January 2002 – essentially because the other 'lead donor' portfolios had already been taken – and there was little evidence of activity in this area. The Afghan Interim Authority did appoint some new judges, including a number of women, but those courts that functioned at all continued to do so erratically. This was not helped by Karzai's appointment of a septuagenarian Chief Justice who had never studied secular law.[107]

Of still greater concern than the relative inattention to establishing the rule of law – admittedly difficult in a country that had known little peace in a generation – was the preparedness of both international and national actors to look the other way as war criminals moved into political office and narco-trafficking was used to supplement ministerial appropriations.[108]

The formal laws on declarations of a state of emergency in the Constitution ultimately adopted in 2004 are not especially controversial; if anything the relevant chapter is restrictive, setting up a potentially tense relationship between the President and the National Assembly which must 'consent' to a state of emergency longer than two months, but the 'endorsement' of which is also required for a shorter period.

[105] See, for example, 'A Review of Peace Operations: A Case for Change' (King's College London, March 2003), p. 263.

[106] 'National Development Framework' (draft for consultation) (Afghan Assistance Coordination Authority, Kabul, April 2002), p. 47: 'The judicial system will be revived through a sub-program that provides training, makes laws and precedents available, and rehabilitates the physical infrastructure of the judicial sector'.

[107] H. Gardish, 'Chief Justice under Scrutiny', IWPR Afghan Recovery Report, no. 54 (1 April 2003).

[108] Cf. F. Ahmed, 'Afghanistan's Reconstruction Five Years Later: Narratives of Progress, Marginalised Realities, and the Politics of Law in a Transitional Islamic Republic' (2007) 10 *Gonzaga Journal of International Law* 269.

Chapter Nine: State of Emergency

Article 143. If because of war, threat of war, serious rebellion, natural disasters or similar conditions, protection of independence and national life become impossible through the channels specified in this Constitution, the state of emergency shall be proclaimed by the President, throughout the country or part thereof, with endorsement of the National Assembly.[109] If the state of emergency continues for more than two months, the consent of the National Assembly shall be required for its extension.

Article 144. During the state of emergency, the President can, in consultation with the presidents of the National Assembly as well as the Chief Justice of the Supreme Court, transfer some powers of the National Assembly to the government.

Article 145. During the state of emergency, the President can, after approval by the presidents of the National Assembly as well as the Chief Justice of the Supreme Court, suspend the enforcement of the following provisions or place restrictions on them:

1. Clause Two of Article Twenty-Seven [no detention without due process];
2. Article Thirty-Six [right to free assembly];
3. Clause Two of Article Thirty-Seven [privacy of personal correspondence];
4. Clause Two of Article Thirty-Eight [restrictions on power to search personal residences].

Article 146. The Constitution shall not be amended during the state of emergency.

Article 147. If the presidential term or the legislative term of the National Assembly expires during the state of emergency, the new general elections shall be postponed, and the presidential as well as parliamentary terms shall extend up to four months. If the state of emergency continues for more than four months, the President shall call the Loya Jirga. Within two months after the termination of the state of emergency, elections shall be held.

Article 148. At the termination of the state of emergency, measures adopted under Article One Hundred Forty-Four and One Hundred Forty-Five of this Constitution shall be void immediately.[110]

These provisions broadly correspond to the relevant provisions of the 1964 Constitution, with the role of the King being taken by the President

[109] Article 64(8) provides that the President has the power to proclaim *and terminate* a state of emergency 'with the endorsement of the National Assembly'.

[110] Constitution of Afghanistan (2004), www.mfa.gov.af/Documents/The%20Constitution.pdf.

and slightly greater power being granted to the National Assembly than was enjoyed by the Loya Jirga (Great Council).[111]

The threshold established by the Constitution is significantly higher than that in East Timor and more closely follows the model of the ICCPR – though not its limitation of any derogation 'to the extent strictly required by the exigencies of the situation'.[112] Significantly greater checks do exist on the potential exercise of powers, including enumeration of those rights from which derogation is possible (rather than saving of specific rights) and oversight of such derogation by both the legislature and the Chief Justice.

As with East Timor, however, it is difficult to generalise from the case of Afghanistan to a larger non-Western or Asian context. Afghanistan's regional identification is weak, though unlike East Timor it successfully resisted colonisation and thus lacked an externally derived legal system that could be reintroduced. In any case, the resurgence of the Taliban and the limited ability of the central government to exercise power in much of the country continue to pose grave threats to the life of the nation. It is not clear that a declaration of a state of emergency – as opposed to enhanced international military support – would alter this.[113]

In fact, despite its troubled recent history Afghanistan has never invoked its state of emergency provisions. Some Afghan scholars and watchers wryly speculate that the government might instead one day declare a state of 'normality'.[114]

III. Conclusion: the 'ways of Orientals'?

This brief survey of the ways in which the United Nations has supported and compromised the rule of law in Asian contexts may, in the end, offer more heat than light on the themes uniting this book.

On the relationship between formal and informal institutions, recurrent tensions in UN peace operations have been between form and substance and between short-term stability and longer-term sustainability. In East Timor the government inherited a country that was both the newest and

[111] The 1964 Constitution is available at www.afghan-web.com/history/const/const1964.html. See Title Nine: State of Emergency.

[112] ICCPR, Article 4(1).

[113] Contrast the experiences of Pakistan and Thailand, discussed respectively in A. Kalhan 'Constitution and "Extraconstitution": Colonial Emergency Regimes in Postcolonial India and Pakistan' (Chapter 4) and Harding, Chapter 11, this volume.

[114] Cf. Aung-Thwin, Chapter 7.

the poorest in the region, with a constitutional structure that set in place an inevitable clash of personalities. Remarkably, the consequences of that clash were managed within the four corners of the Constitution, though this depended heavily on the ongoing support of the United Nations and military contributions from Australia and other states. In Afghanistan the rule of law was seen by some UN officials as a luxury for a state that could hope for, at best, a kind of organised anarchy even in good times. This essentially acknowledged through default the ongoing importance of informal institutions at the local level, even as such local commanders (*sc.* warlords) were formally denounced as undermining the hopes of stability. In both cases area specialists have been critical of foreign receptiveness to existing local institutions, though it is not clear that either suggests broad lessons for a coherent non-Western narrative.

On the relationship between emergency powers and the rule of law, one interesting dimension of the examples considered here is the manner in which the invocation of extraordinary powers at the international level is grounded on a claim to establish or support the rule of law. As indicated earlier, these powers are properly understood as 'exceptions' both in the formal sense that the Security Council only enjoys *any* power to intrude upon the domestic jurisdiction in a time of crisis, and also in the practical sense that the powers are invoked infrequently. As that frequency has increased and they have been applied to general rather than particular problems (to 'terrorism' rather than to Libyan support for terrorism, for example), so has the controversy about the limits to be applied to them. At the national level, where these extraordinary powers have been used to impose order it would be too much to imply a kind of original sin to the institutions thus created. Nevertheless, the contradictions between what international administrators say and what they do have complicated administration of territory while under international control and left an uncertain legacy for those who inherit it.

On the larger question of Asian versus Western discourses on emergency powers, it is hard to draw general conclusions. East Timor does not identify strongly as Asian in a constitutional sense: its colonial and post-conflict baggage, ongoing ties to Portugal and Australia, and continuing UN presence bind it to a global (and perhaps Western) discourse.[115] Certainly the two occasions on which states of emergency were declared more closely approximate the Western constitutionalist approach to dealing with crises

[115] This colonial experience contrasts markedly with, among others, the account of Pakistan and India: Kalhan, Chapter 4.

than, say, similar experiences in recent Indonesian history. Afghanistan for its part suffers from such weakness of central institutions that it is barely a meaningful state – in the sense of an organised polity with institutions that can offer some basic public goods and claim a monopoly over the legitimate use of violence. As with East Timor, much of the discourse on emergencies is offered in language intelligible to the Western ear, though this may bear little relation to the conflict as it plays out on the ground.

This disconnect between rhetoric and reality is perhaps the most interesting and troubling aspect of the cases considered here. Upon his return from an 1889 trip to Persia, Lord Curzon noted thoughtfully the different perspectives on governance held by Europeans and 'Orientals', who might legitimately regard their own systems of government as more appropriate than those of Europeans, and in any case would generally prefer to misgovern themselves than be well governed by foreigners.[116] Such observations were insightful but uncharacteristic. As Viceroy of India a decade later, Curzon did not appoint a single Indian to his advisory council; when asked why, he replied, absurdly, that in the entire country there was not an Indian fit for the post.[117] If there is, indeed, an 'Asian' approach to the development of constitutional structures emerging from conflict, it is that those structures inevitably reflect the varied colonial heritage of the region, are cast with an eye to international legitimacy, but stand or fall on the basis of local politics.

[116] Curzon, *Persia*, vol. II, p. 630.
[117] D. Gilmour, *Curzon* (London: J. Murray, 1994), p. 168.

PART III

Emergencies, executive power and constitutional order

10

Emergency powers and the rule of law in Indonesia

NADIRSYAH HOSEN

I. Introduction

While Indonesia has had experience in dealing with the use of emergency powers for more than fifty years, it has had to face severe problems that have challenged its goals of national resilience, development and, more importantly, the absence of the rule of law. The focus of my chapter is the tensions inherent between emergency powers and the rule of law in Indonesia, particularly in the post-Suharto era.

From 1998 Indonesian politics has progressed to a fully functional democratic system: all political parties can easily participate in general elections for the Parliament and for the office of the President. There is no restriction placed on establishing new political parties. Contrary to previous years, the military, at least ostensibly, is not involved in the political realm. The 2004 General Election in Indonesia was illustrative. The Indonesian people exercised their constitutional rights to rotate elites, to select leaders and to express grievances and desires, in free and fair elections.

Despite Indonesians' willingness to embrace the processes of democracy, as the biggest Muslim country in the world Indonesia has also faced the problems of terrorism, such as in the Bali bomb blasts of 12 October 2002, the attack on the JW Marriott hotel in Jakarta in 2003, and the further one against the Australian embassy in 2004.[1] Indonesians were shocked when they found that foreign tourists had become the targets of terrorism. At the time there was general incredulity that the people

I am grateful to Victor V. Ramraj, Simon Chesterman and Arun K. Thiruvengadam for their insightful comments on an earlier draft.

[1] S. Sherlock, 'The Bali Bombing: What it Means for Indonesia', (2002–3) 4 *Current Issue Brief*, www.aph.gov.au/Library/Pubs/cib/2002–03/03cib04.pdf; D. M. Jones and M. L. Smith, 'The Changing Security Agenda in Southeast Asia: Globalization, New Terror, and the Delusions of Regionalism' (2001) 24 *Studies in Conflict and Terrorism* 271.

involved were Indonesian and that an attack such as the Bali bombings could ever have occurred.

There are two main questions in this chapter: can Indonesia's advances in, and aspirations toward, a thicker conception of the rule of law survive the international and domestic pressure to facilitate the use of emergency powers by the executive? And how does Indonesia's experience assist in understanding the paradox of emergency powers?

To answer these questions, I first provide a brief overview of emergency powers in Indonesian history. Second, I demonstrate how the Indonesian government has to consider and calculate international and national pressures to uphold the rule of law, which has been extended beyond civil and political rights to social and economic entitlements, while at the same time using emergency powers in dealing with national threats. Finally, I assess whether the anti-terrorism and emergency powers regime is compatible with the 'thick' concept of the rule of law.

I argue that one root of the concerns in this chapter can be traced to the phenomenon of legal transplant, both in legal reform, which had been driven mainly by the IMF, and in establishing anti-terrorism law, which had been pushed by the United States (and also Australia). Drawing on Indonesian experience in the post-Suharto era, this chapter suggests that the counter-terrorism agenda has influenced negatively the efforts to uphold the rule of law, good governance and constitutionalism. What we see is a pragmatic and politically oriented rule of law. Unfortunately, there can be no shortcuts in establishing a meaningful rule-of-law state.

II. Emergency power in Indonesia: an overview

Indonesia has had experience in dealing with the use of emergency powers for more than fifty years. The first president of Indonesia, Sukarno, declared a state of emergency on 14 March 1957 (known as 'UU SOB', *De Regeling op de Staat van Oorlog en Beled*).[2] This declaration was based on Article 12 of the 1945 Constitution, which says that the President may declare a State of Emergency in accordence with statutory law. As Indonesia did not have such a law, Sukarno's government applied the law on states of emergency inherited from the Dutch.[3]

[2] B. Susanti, 'National Security, Terrorism, and Human Rights in Indonesia', paper presented at International Workshop on National Security and Constitutional Rights in the Asia-Pacific Region, The Australian National University, Canberra, 8–9 October 2002.

[3] A brief history of Indonesia in the colonial period can be read in K. Y. L. Tan, 'From Myanmar to Manila: A Brief Study of Emergency Powers in Southeast Asia' (Chapter 6), this volume.

Sukarno, backed up by the military leaders, dissolved the Konstituante (a parliament established by the 1955 election) through his Presidential Decree of 5 July 1959, arguing that it could not make any progress in creating a new constitution. The Decree abrogated the 1950 Constitution and enforced the 1945 Constitution. In an analysis of these events, Adnan Buyung Nasution suggests that Sukarno and the military leaders played a 'game', by providing evidence that the Konstituante had nearly finished its task at the point when Sukarno's decision dissolved it.[4] The demise of the Konstituante led Indonesia back to the 1945 Constitution, which still remains in force.

Sukarno and General A. H. Nasution also drafted a law on states of emergency which then became Law No. 23/Prp/1959. Under this law, the Sukarno government allowed the military to take over all Dutch-owned companies operating in Indonesia, which was perhaps the beginning of the military-business era. Several political parties were banned by Sukarno under this emergency law.[5] Furthermore, at least thirty-three newspapers and magazines were also banned.[6]

Following the alleged attempted Communist coup of 1965, General Suharto received emergency power from Sukarno, on 11 March 1966, to restore order. Suharto then arrested cabinet ministers and members of the Communist Party, and established an emergency body, the Provisional MPR, provided for in the 1945 Constitution, to strip Sukarno of his powers and transfer them to himself. Despite the absence of the rule of law at all other levels of the legal system, even the most authoritarian leaders in Indonesia's modern history have wrapped themselves in the legitimacy of the Constitution, and have been very careful to be seen as abiding by its tenets. Following continental European norms, legal formalism is very important in Indonesian legal and political practice. Former-President Suharto built on this aspect of Indonesian political culture and practice by carefully ensuring that all of his actions could be considered, at least formally, legal. For instance, unlike Sukarno, who was proclaimed as President for life, Suharto held general elections every fifth year until 1998 in which the Peoples' Consultative Assembly (MPR)

[4] More information can be found in A. B. Nasution, *The Aspiration for Constitutional Government in Indonesia: A Socio-legal Study of the Indonesian Konstituante 1956–1959* (Jakarta: Pustaka Sinar Harapan, 1992).

[5] Susanti, 'National Security, Terrorism, and Human Rights in Indonesia'.

[6] See K. Sen and D. T. Hill, *Media, Culture and Politics in Indonesia* (Melbourne: Oxford University Press, 2000) and A. Romano, *Politics and the Press in Indonesia: Understanding an Evolving Political Culture* (London: RoutledgeCurzon, 2003).

unanimously re-elected Suharto to the presidency.[7] Although the outcome might be similar, the method of election was different.

During his presidency, Suharto employed extensively the 1963 Anti-subversion Law, which had been issued by the previous president, Sukarno, originally as a Presidential Decree in the context of the period of confrontation with Malaysia. This Decree was eventually ratified, and formally incorporated into law in 1969, by the Suharto regime. The Anti-subversion Law is considered as the harshest of the repressive legislation available in the history of Indonesia to silence a government's alleged opponents. This law contained provisions for the death penalty, for arrest and imprisonment for peaceful expression of opinion, detention for up to one year without charge or trial, the imprisonment of witnesses, an absence of the obligation to inform detainees of the charges against them, the denial of legal representation, prohibition of family visits to prisoners, denial of defence lawyers' access to court documents, and the widespread use of torture.[8]

President Suharto and the military held the 1945 Constitution essentially sacred, not least because it granted broad powers and tremendous flexibility to the President and created a weak legislature and judiciary, thereby facilitating the authoritarian project of the military and President. Proposals to amend the Constitution were considered tantamount to treason and all political and social organisations were required to include loyalty to the Constitution in their charters.[9]

Following the economic crisis which hit Indonesia in mid-1997, mass demonstrations and student demands for reform, along with international pressures, were critical in the fall, after thirty-two years, of the Suharto government. Before he stepped down, however, Suharto issued a Presidential Decree which empowered General Wiranto to employ emergency measures. However, Wiranto hesitated to follow the order, since he was aware that by following the order, he would be declaring martial law, and clashes between the security forces and the people would take place. The

[7] The MPR under the Suharto regime had 1,000 members, which consisted of the 500 members of Parliament and another 500 representatives of different functional groups and of Indonesia's 27 provinces. The appointment of these 500 delegates, together with that of the 100 appointed members of the military faction of Parliament, was in the hands of the President. In practice, Suharto controlled the appointment of 60 per cent of the delegates in the assembly which elected him. But Suharto managed to get 100 per cent support.

[8] See Amnesty International, 'Indonesia: The Anti-subversion Law: A Briefing', London (1 February 1997); ASA 21/003/1997; see G. Simons, *Indonesia: The Long Oppression* (London: Macmillan, 2000).

[9] See H. Thoolen (ed.), *Indonesia and the Rule of Law: Twenty Years of 'New Order' Government* (London: Frances Pinter, 1987).

situation would become worse. Therefore he decided not to implement the Decree.[10]

Habibie, as Vice-President, replaced Suharto. While his government revoked the Anti-subversion Law, the most controversial issue of Habibie's tenure as President was the status of East Timor. On 26 January 1999, Habibie raised the option of giving the province independence if it refused a special autonomy package. Thus he laid the seeds for the horrific events which broke out there following the 30 August referendum. In his mind, the offer of independence was the most sensible solution to a two-decade-old problem. The territory was both a drain on scarce resources and a foreign-policy millstone.

However, unlike Suharto, who had been a five-star general, Habibie, a civilian president, could not control the military effectively. He then declared martial law in East Timor in an effort to restore peace. Militias in the former Portuguese colony had been on the rampage for three days. The declaration of martial law meant the military had the power to arrest anyone suspected of causing a disturbance.[11] However, the declaration of martial law failed. This rule by martial law was then abolished by Habibie, through Presidential Decree No. 112 of 1999 and subsequently Habibie accepted the presence of an international peacekeeping force in East Timor.

General Wiranto proposed to Habibie the draft law concerning state security (Undang-Undang tentang Keselamatan dan Keamanan Negara). Afterward, on 6 September 1999, the Parliament changed the title of the law to 'A Law Concerning Emergency Situations' (Undang-Undang tentang Keadaan Bahaya).[12] However, the passage of the law ignited the most violent turmoil. Students objected to both the content of the law, which they said would grant sweeping new powers to the military to impose martial law, and the way it was approved, in a hastily arranged vote on the next-to-last day of the parliamentary session. Four people were killed and more than one hundred were injured, leading Habibie to refuse to sign the bill, despite the fact that Parliament had already passed it. To date, the national security law currently operating in Indonesia is the old 1959 law, which was created under Sukarno. Any attempt to issue a law such as the above-mentioned Emergency Situation law would be considered against

[10] A. F. Azhari *et. al.*, *Dari Catatan Wiranto Jenderal Purnawirawan Bersaksi di Tengah Badai* (Jakarta: IDe Indonesia, 2003), p. 35.

[11] More information can be found in J. Purnawanty, 'Various Perspectives in Understanding the East Timor Crisis' (2000) 14 *Temple International and Comparative Law Journal* 73.

[12] 'Jakarta Delays Security Bill as Riots Rage', *New York Times*, 25 September 1999.

the spirit of reform. However, as will be shown below, the Constitution still provides another legal tool to deal with emergency situations.

At the end of his presidency, Habibie's accountability speech before the MPR was narrowly rejected. The rejection leads to the assumption that the MPR took the view that Habibie was not capable of carrying on his reform agendas. Subsequently, Abdurrahman Wahid was elected as the fourth president of Indonesia. Wahid refused to give way to the military, who wanted to impose martial law in Aceh. However, the military was not the only institution that was unhappy with Wahid's policy. Wahid was unpopular among members of parliament and political parties. The conflict between the Parliament and the President led the Parliament to initiate impeachment proceedings against Wahid.[13] He insisted that the legislature did not have the constitutional right to remove the President and threatened to declare a state of emergency. On 22 July 2001 he declared such a 'state of emergency', thereby dissolving the Parliament. However, unlike under Sukarno's Presidential Decree in 1959, the security forces refused to implement Wahid's orders, and the Parliament convened an emergency session on 23 July, at which it overwhelmingly voted to end President's Wahid's mandate and to install Vice-President Megawati Sukarnoputri as President. On advice from one of her senior ministers (Susilo Bambang Yudhoyono, who is the current President), President Megawati declared martial law in Aceh on 19 May 2003. This martial law was extended in November 2003.[14]

Previously, under the emergency power stipulated in Article 22 of the 1945 Constitution, President Megawati had issued Government Regulations in Lieu of Law (*Peraturan Pemerintah sebagai Pengganti Undang-undang* (Perpu), which have authority equivalent to a statute, to deal with the 2002 terrorist attack in Bali. The use of the Perpu has demonstrated that Megawati's government treated the Bali bombing as an emergency situation. However, President Megawati also issued a Perpu (No. 1/2004)

[13] President Wahid was then alleged to have misappropriated a US$ 2 million gift from the Sultan of Brunei. The money was given by the Sultan Hasanal Bolkiah for humanitarian aid in Aceh, but the gift was handled informally, with no record kept of its disbursement. It was claimed that the money was a 'personal gift' from the Sultan to the President for the people of Aceh. The Attorney-General's office found, in early June 2001, that legally there was no evidence to support claims that the President had been involved in any wrongdoing in relation to this matter. However, politically, this case became one of the reasons why the MPR moved to impeach the President, on 23 July 2001, leading to the replacement of President Wahid by his vice-president, Megawati Sukarnoputri.

[14] See M. A. Miller and R. M. Feener, 'Emergency and Islamic Law in Aceh' (Chapter 8), this volume.

on 11 March 2004, amending Forestry Law No. 41/1999 to allow the thirteen companies that had been given permits before 1999 to continue their mining operations in protected forests.[15] This controversial use[16] of the Perpu suggests that her government took the view that the absence of new investment over a long period would constitute a threat to the nation.

President Yudhoyono continues to invoke the Perpu to deal with ostensible emergencies. For instance, he issued Perpu No. 2/2007 on the Management of Legal Issues and Implementation of Rehabilitation and Reconstruction of the Regions and Communities of the Nanggroe Aceh Darussalam (NAD) Province and Nias following the tsunami which hit Aceh and Nias in December 2004. He is also planning to issue an emergency government regulation to justify the formation of the West Papua province, which has been a source of tension between Jakarta and Papua for the last five years. Such a Perpu would provide the legal basis for the West Papua province and resolve all problems related to the establishment of the new province, which was declared illegal by the Constitutional Court in 2003.[17]

I have briefly examined above the use of emergency powers and, to some extent, the impact of such laws on the application of the rule of law, in post-independence Indonesia. The next section will focus on efforts within Indonesia to move from a formalistic version of the rule of law, as has been demonstrated by previous governments to ensure that all of their actions could be considered legal and constitutional, to a more substantive version of the rule of law, and the difficulties these efforts have encountered.

III. Rule of law in Indonesia

From 1945 to 1998, the concept of the rule of law was subordinated to the romantic vision of Sukarno's notion of unfinished revolution; and to the goals of economic development, stability, security and order under

[15] 'Law No: 1/2004 Causes Loss of Rp70 Trillion to the State.' *Indonesian Investment Highlights* 172 (April 2004), 5(1).

[16] As will be discussed in more detail below (pp. 290–1), these companies were alleged by NGOs to have had dismal records in environmental management in Indonesia, as could be seen from the disposal of their industrial waste into the environment: D. Bachriadi, 'The Forestry Law Has Not Stopped Mining in Indonesia's State Forests', *Inside Indonesia*, October–December 2004, www.insideindonesia.org/edit80/p4–5dianto.html.

[17] 'New Law to End Papua Legal Dispute', *Jakarta Post*, 5 March 2008.

the Suharto government.[18] However, since 1998, Indonesia has amended its Constitution four times. There existed a school of thought that the Amendments would convert Indonesia into a *negara hukum* (literally, a nation of law), which is based on the rule of law, not the law of the ruler. But, is it true that Indonesia now is a *negara hukum*?

A. Negara hukum *in Indonesia*

The term *negara hukum*, or *rechtsstaat*, is used in Indonesia as a practical equivalent of the Western notion of the rule of law. According to Lindsey, the rule of law 'is a highly charged notion that has played a central role in Indonesian political and legal thinking'.[19] However, as Lindsey has correctly pointed out, 'the use of common law traditions of "the rule of law" to understand *negara hukum* is problematic' since no consensus has been reached on the exact meaning of *negara hukum*.[20] The literal meaning of *rechtsstaat* was stipulated in the Elucidation of the 1945 Constitution. However the Elucidation did not explain the notion of *rechtsstaat*. It said only that 'Indonesia is a state based on law (*rechtsstaat*), not merely based on power (*machtsstaat*).' In other words, the spirit of the 1945 Constitution is that Indonesia is based on right rather than might. The constitutional amendments in 1999–2002, however, abolished the Elucidation, and did not make any attempt to define the concept of *negara hukum*.

The debate over the meaning of *negara hukum* in Indonesian legal history is reflected in the writings of (to name but a few):[21] Sunaryati Hartono, who interpreted *negara hukum* in the light of the rule of law;[22] Oemar Seno Adji, who opined that *negara hukum* has its own Indonesian characteristics, based on the family principle;[23] Padmo Wahyono, who

[18] T. M. Lubis, 'The *Rechtsstaat* and Human Rights', in T. Lindsey (ed.), *Indonesia: Law and Society* (Sydney: Federation Press, 1999), p. 172.

[19] T. Lindsey, 'From Rule of Law to Law of the Rulers – to Reformation?', in Lindsey (ed.), *Indonesia: Law and Society*, p. 13.

[20] T. Lindsey, 'Indonesia: Devaluing Asian Values, Rewriting Rule of Law', in R. Peerenboom (ed.), *Asian Discourses of Rule of Law: Theories and Implementation of Rule of Law in Twelve Asian Countries, France, and the U.S.* (London: RoutledgeCurzon, 2004), p. 299.

[21] Other views can be read in H. Feith and L. Castles (eds.), *Indonesian Political Thinking (1945–1965)* (Ithaca: Cornell University Press, 1970) and D. S. Lev, *Legal Evolution and Political Authority in Indonesia: Selected Essays* (Boston: Kluwer Law International, 2000).

[22] S. Hartono, *Apakah Rule of Law Itu?* (Bandung: Alumni, 1982), chap. 5.

[23] O. S. Adji, *Peradilan Bebas negara hukum* (Jakarta: Erlangga, 1980), pp. 24–58; and O. S. Adji, 'An Indonesian Perspective on the American Constitutional Influence', in L.W. Beer (ed.), *Constitutionalism in Asia: Asian Views of the American Influence* (Berkeley: University of California Press, 1979), pp. 102–10. His view is supported by T. Azhary, *negara hukum* (Jakarta: Bulan Bintang, 1992), p. 99.

related the concept of *negara hukum* to the political philosophy of organic statism (integralism or *integralistik*);[24] Ismail Suny, who adhered to the literal meaning of *negara hukum* as *rechtsstaat*;[25] and Hartono Mardjono, who took the view that the elements of *negara hukum* are the supremacy of the law, equality before the law and the due process of law.[26] This debate reflects a similar controversy in German legal theory over the concept of *rechtsstaat* in the early nineteenth century. Some have tried to distinguish the rule of law from *rechtsstaat* by stressing that the former is a theoretical ideal while the latter is concerned with actual obedience to the law.[27] However, the concept of *rechtsstaat* has evolved over time in Europe to incorporate democracy and fundamental human rights.

Recent debates in Asia juxtapose competing 'thin' and 'thick' versions of the rule of law. The 'thin' version focuses on the formal or procedural aspects 'that any legal system allegedly must possess to function effectively as a system of laws, regardless of whether the legal system is part of a democratic or a non-democratic society, capitalist, liberal or theocratic'.[28] The civil law *rechtsstaat* is often described, by Peerenboom[29] and Lindsey[30] for example, as a 'thin' version of the rule of law. A more apt label for this version might be 'rule *by* law', for it entails no connotation of legal limitations. The idea of rule *by* law is that law is a means by which the state operates in the conduct of its affairs; 'that whatever a government does, it should do through laws'.[31] Another theoretical version of the rule of law is the 'thick' (substantive) concept.[32] It consists of the basic elements of the formal rule of law, and then goes further by adding content requirements in various combinations of 'particular economic arrangements . . . forms

[24] P. Wahyono, *Guru Pinandita: Sumbangsih untuk Prof. Djokosoetono, SH* (Jakarta: Lembaga Penerbit Fakultas Ekonomi Universitas Indonesia, 1984).

[25] I. Suny, *Mekanisme Demokrasi Pancasila* (Jakarta: Aksara Baru, 1978), pp. 10–12.

[26] H. Mardjono, *negara hukum yang Demokratis* (Jakarta: Yayasan Koridor Pengabdian, 2001), p. 139.

[27] See R. Grote, 'Rule of Law, Rechtsstaat and Etat de Droit', in C. Starck (ed.), *Constitutionalism, Universalism and Democracy – A Comparative Analysis* (Baden-Baden: Nomos Verlagsgesellschaft, 1999), p. 270; R. Peerenboom, 'Varieties of Rule of Law' in Peerenboom (ed.), *Asian Discourses*, p. 2.

[28] Peerenboom, 'Varieties of Rule of Law', p. 2.

[29] *Ibid., passim.*

[30] T. Lindsey, 'Legal Infrastructure and Governance Reform in Post-Crisis Asia: The Case of Indonesia' (2004) 18 *Asian Pacific Economic Literature* 1 at 17.

[31] N.B. Reynolds, 'Grounding the Rule of Law' (1989) 2 *Ratio Juris* 1 at 3.

[32] Whilst Peerenboom has classified the rule of law into the 'thick' and the 'thin', Paul Craig has used the terms 'formal' and 'substantive'. See P. Craig, 'Formal and Substantive Conceptions of the Rule of Law' (1997) *Public Law* 467.

of government . . . or conceptions of human rights'.[33] That is what makes this conception of the rule of law 'thicker' than the formal version.

Although the concepts of *negara hukum*, *rechtsstaat*, and the rule of law have different meanings,[34] I take the position that they share the common view that the government and the State apparatus should be subject to the law, that areas of discretionary power should be defined and limited, and that citizens should be able to turn to the courts to defend themselves against the State and its officials.[35] The rule of law entails equal protection of the human rights of individuals and groups, as well as equal punishment under the law. It protects citizens against arbitrary state action. It ensures that all citizens are treated equally and are subject to the law rather than to the whims of the powerful. The law should also afford vulnerable groups protection against exploitation and abuse. In this context, it is important to highlight that the rule of law should be recognised as an essential element of constitutional government in general, and of representative democracy in particular.[36]

B. Implementing the rule of law: economic and political pressures

Debates over the meaning of *negara hukum* and the rule of law will continue, but all Indonesian jurists agree that Indonesia needs law reform as a basis for becoming a *negara hukum*.[37] However, history has shown that such an ideal is not easy to achieve. Both the Sukarno (1945–66) and the Suharto (1966–98) governments used the notion of *negara hukum* in their rhetoric. Neither government created appropriate institutions and frameworks, nor did they establish basic infrastructure. Legal frameworks are necessary for creating a predictable and secure living and working environment for ordinary citizens, and for entrepreneurs and investors. Those legal frameworks have long been absent in Indonesia.

[33] Peerenboom, 'Varieties of Rule of Law', p. 4.

[34] See Lindsey, 'From Rule of Law to Law of the Rulers – to Reformation?', p. 13; See also G. Dietze, *Two Concepts of the Rule of Law* (Indianapolis: Liberty Fund, 1973).

[35] Stern distinguishes the following elements of the *rechtsstaat* principles: the constitutional state, liberty and equality, the separation and control of government authority, legality, judicial protection, a system of reparation and the prohibition of the excessive use of government authority. See F. Venter, *Constitutional Comparison: Japan, Germany, Canada and South Africa as Constitutional States* (Cape Town: Juta & Co., 2000), p. 49.

[36] J. N. Shklar, 'Political Theory and the Rule of Law', in A. C. Hutchinson and P. Monahan (eds.), *The Rule of Law: Ideal or Ideology* (Vancouver: Carswell, 1987), p. 14.

[37] In the remainder of this chapter, I use both terms (*negara hukum* and the rule of law) interchangeably.

In the Suharto era, Indonesia was a complex web of corrupt deals and political pay-offs. Suharto's New Order government focused mainly on economic development, in order to provide steadily improving standards of living for Indonesians. However, the economic performance was built on debt. It was not from a convergence of expectations based on commonly understood and enforced legal rules, but from a system of hierarchical relationships: unlimited state power, control and authority, in which orders flowed down from the 'top' with little input from the 'bottom'. This is one explanation as to why Indonesia, under Suharto, was quite successful in economic development terms, even though there was little regard for the state of its laws and legal system.[38] Both political and legal systems were engineered to support the development strategy of the nation, but this also explains why Indonesia was so fragile when it was hit by the economic and political crises. Unlike other Asian countries, and without the support of the rule of law, Indonesia faced chaos and riots.

What went wrong with Indonesia's choice of development rather than the rule of law? It was an economic crisis, not an economic achievement, which launched Indonesia into its transition. In other words, the Suharto legacy suggests that legal flaws were an important element of the economic and political crisis which hit Indonesia during 1997–8, and therefore legal reform is considered essential for a stable future.

The transition which took place immediately after the resignation of Suharto begins with the assumption that law reform is an inherently *political* process, i.e. one that is explicitly rooted in the give-and-take of mundane conflicts over the distribution of power. Apart from an economic crisis, it was politics which opened the window for the law reform movement to develop. Law reform is not only political, but also a struggle between the status quo and change for the better. As Gary Goodpaster observes, '[s]imply put, Indonesia will find that it cannot manage and function effectively in the global economy, nor continue strong economic growth, without the rule of law and widespread rule-based behaviour'.[39] A lesson to be learned from the Suharto era, then, is that the centralisation of power in the hands of Suharto damaged the idea of the rule of law. Suharto's intervention in the military, the courts, political parties and

[38] M. McGillivray and O. Morrisey, 'Economic and Financial Meltdown in Indonesia: Prospects for Sustained and Equitable Economic and Social Recovery', in A. Budiman, B. Hatley and D. Kingsbury (eds.), *Reformasi: Crisis and Change in Indonesia* (Clayton: Monash Asia Institute, 1999).

[39] G. Goodpaster, 'The Rule of Law, Economic Development and Indonesia', in Lindsey (ed.), *Indonesia: Law and Society*, p. 24.

Parliament was against the concept of the rule of law. Suharto's power was reflected in the corrupt behaviour of many military officers, much of government apparatus and judges. There was neither transparency nor a system of checks and balances.

After Suharto's resignation, Indonesia had to deal with economic, political and legal crises. Accordingly, during the economic, political and legal crisis, Indonesia adopted the neo-liberal adjustment policies imposed by the International Monetary Fund. Despite the fact that not all aspects of the reform agenda pursued in the post-Suharto era were driven by the IMF, it was clear that this drive led the Indonesian government to revisit the connection between the rule of law and economic development. It is in this context that the idea of a 'thick' version of the rule of law was proposed. For instance, during the Habibie period (May 1998 to October 1999), the Indonesian government was required to sign no less than sixteen Letters of Intent to the International Monetary Fund, indicating its agreement to act in accordance with several reform programmes.[40] Some of the agreements required the cancellation of huge industrial projects and trading cartels at the heart of the Suharto regime. Moreover, the two crucial IMF demands were those relating to the recapitalisation of Indonesia's banks and the decentralisation of administrative authority (*otonomi daerah).* In these areas, the IFIs (international financial institutions) played a very active role in 'helping' the Indonesian government to draft the required bills.

The basic assumption of the 'thick' version of the rule of law can be traced back to the new law and development movement, now frequently couched in terms of the rule of law and good governance. In the 1990s, the World Bank and the International Monetary Fund required loan and aid recipients in the developing world to adopt Western-style commercial law as a *condition* of receiving help.[41] This emphasis on Western-style

[40] See the official documents of Indonesia and the IMF at www.imf.org/external/country/idn/index.htm?pn=9.

[41] In October 1999, Kaufmann, Kraay and Zoido-Lobatón provided 'new empirical evidence of a strong causal relationship from better governance to better development outcomes such as higher per capita incomes, lower infant mortality, and higher literacy'. They claim that their analysis is based on more than 300 governance indicators compiled from a combination of sources. See D. Kaufmann, A. Kraay and P. Zoido-Lobatón, 'Governance Matters', World Bank Policy Research Working Paper 2196, October 1999, http://siteresources.worldbank.org/INTWBIGOVANTCOR/Resources/govmatrs.pdf. The data and methodology used to construct the indicators are described in 'Governance Matters III: Governance Indicators for 1996–2002', World Bank Policy Research Working Paper 3106, 25 July 2003, www.worldbank.org/wbi/governance/govdata2002/.

commercial law contains assumptions about the importance of establishing the rule of law in developing countries, in the light of the pressures exerted by global economic and capital markets.

In this sense, one of the criticisms which have been advanced relates to the use of legal transplants.[42] The IFIs often suggest importing foreign legislative schemes or institutional models to developing countries. Critics assert that one of the most significant reasons for the failure of IFI programmes is the naive belief that the Western legal system, particularly the American model, can easily be transplanted to recipient countries.[43] Gunther Teubner has examined the difficulty of legal transplants, preferring to describe a foreign legal element as an 'irritant' rather than a transplant. According to Teubner, the transfer of a legal concept from one system to another will have unpredictable effects, because structural coupling will change.

> When a foreign rule is imposed on a domestic culture ... it is not transplanted into another organism, rather it works as a fundamental irritation which triggers a whole series of new and unexpected events ... 'Legal irritations' cannot be domesticated; they are not transformed from something alien into something familiar, not adapted to a new cultural context, rather they will unleash an evolutionary dynamic in which the external rule's meaning will be reconstructed and the internal context will undergo fundamental change.[44]

There is little agreement among scholars on transplant feasibility and the conditions for successful transplants, or even how to define 'success'.[45] Those who oppose legal transplants generally point out that it is a form of colonial imposition and, as such, contrary to the principles of democratic governance. It interferes substantially with the sovereignty of the

[42] Some problems of legal transplants in the context of East Asian states can be seen in A. H. Y. Chen, 'Emergency Powers, Constitutionalism and Legal Transplants: The East Asian Experience' (Chapter 3), this volume.

[43] See J. R. Thome, 'Comment on McAuslan's "Law, Governance and the Development of the Market: Practical Problems and Possible Solutions"', in J. Faundez, *Good Governance and Law: Legal and Institutional Reform in Developing Countries* (New York: St Martin's Press, 1997).

[44] G. Teubner, 'Legal Irritants: Good Faith in British Law or How Unifying Law Ends Up in New Divergences' (1998) 61 *Modern Law Review* 12.

[45] See A. Watson, *Legal Transplants* (Edinburgh: Scottish Academic Press, 1974); O. Kahn-Freund, 'On Use and Misuse of Comparative Law' (1974) 37 *Modern Law Review* 1; W. Ewald, 'Comparative Jurisprudence (II): The Logic of Legal Transplants' (1995) 43 *American Journal of Comparative Law* 489.

recipient country and clashes with the concept of local ownership of the reform process, as the process does not originate in a home-grown product, but is externally imposed. From this perspective, the rule of law promoted by IFIs is seen as a form of economic, legal, cultural and political hegemony.[46]

Another significant criticism is that the donor community is imposing neo-liberal models of governance on the developing world. Ohnesorge labels the model as 'the neoliberal rule of law of the 1990s'.[47] It is often seen as synonymous with the phrase 'Washington Consensus', coined by Williamson in 1990,[48] which focuses on privatisation, deregulation, trade liberation, and so on. The phrase 'Washington Consensus' has become a lightning rod for dissatisfaction among anti-globalisation protesters, developing-country politicians and officials, trade negotiators, and numerous others.

The critics also claim that most of the reforms that President Habibie made as the successor of Suharto were driven not by government commitment to change, but rather by the pressure of the IMF or 'IMF conditionalities'.[49] It appears that President Habibie's interest in legal reform was geared primarily toward meeting the minimum requirements for the continuation of international financial assistance, including a US$ 43 billion IMF financial assistance package, tied to an economic reform programme. The World Bank, and over thirty countries comprising the Consultative Group on Indonesia, pledged another $7.9 billion in aid to Indonesia. For instance, the Habibie government received technical assistance from donors in preparing for the June 1999 general election and in the voting process concerning the East Timorese conflict.[50]

[46] See B. M. Hager, 'The Rule of Law: Defining It and Defending It in the Asian Context', in *The Rule of Law: Perspectives from Pacific Rim* (Mansfield Centre for Pacific Affairs, 2000), www.mcpa.org/programs/program˙pdfs/03chap1.pdf. It should be noted, however, that Hager's article defends the notion of rule of law.

[47] J. K. M. Ohnesorge, 'The Rule of Law, Economic Development, and the Developmental States of Northeast Asia', in C. Antons (ed.), *Law and Development in East and Southeast Asia* (London: RoutledgeCurzon, 2003), pp. 91–127.

[48] See J. Williamson, 'What Should the World Bank Think about the Washington Consensus?' (2000) 15 *World Bank Research Observer* 251.

[49] See T. Lindsey, 'Introduction', in D. Duncan and T. Lindsey (eds.), *Indonesia after Suharto: Reformasi and Reaction*, International Colloquium Proceedings (Victoria, BC: Centre for Asia-Pacific Initiatives, 1999), p. 1.

[50] See A. M. Clear, 'Democracy and Donors in Indonesia', unpublished PhD thesis, Columbia University (2002).

C. *Toward rule of law in Indonesia*

Despite the criticisms above, it is worth noting that, after assuming office, President Habibie began the release of political prisoners.[51] In total, during its sixteen months in office, President Habibie's government released 213 political prisoners.[52] In order to deal with the protection of human rights, President Habibie issued Presidential Decree No. 129 of 1998, on the National Human Rights Plan. The Decree states that Indonesia, as a member of the international community, holds in high esteem the Universal Declaration of Human Rights and the 1993 Vienna Human Rights Declaration and Programme of Action. On 23 September 1999, a month before the presidential election, President Habibie signed Law No. 39 of 1999 on Human Rights. This law implemented MPR Decree XVII on Human Rights, which had been adopted by the MPR at its session in November 1998. Law No. 39 of 1999 sets out a long list of internationally recognised human rights which Indonesia is obliged to protect.

Significant reforms were also undertaken in the area of press freedom. Habibie signed Law No. 40 of 1999 on the Press. This law is broadly acceptable to the media in Indonesia and forms the basis for meaningful legal protection for the Press for the first time in Indonesia's history. The stampede into publishing began as soon as Suharto stepped down. In the year following his resignation, the government granted 718 new press licences, quite a leap from the 289 issued in the fifty-three years since the country's independence. The proof is on the streets, as broadsheet newspapers compete for public attention with saucy entertainment magazines, racy tabloids and a host of full-colour magazines.

In addition, in April 1999, the Anti-subversion Law, which had carried a maximum penalty of death and made it a crime to engage in acts which could distort, undermine or cause deviation from the state ideology, or the broad outlines of state policy, or which could disseminate feelings of hostility, or arouse hostility, or cause disturbances or anxiety amongst the population, was repealed by the Parliament.[53] The excessive vagueness of this law made it possible to prosecute

[51] See Presidential Decree Nos. 80, 81, 82, 105, 123, 124 and 125 of 1998.

[52] US Department of State, 'Indonesia Country Report on Human Rights Practices for 1998', 26 February 1999, www.state.gov/www/global/human_rights/1998_hrp_report/indonesi.html.

[53] See Asian Human Rights Commission, 'Indonesia: Plea to Repeal Anti-subversion Law', www.hrsolidarity.net/mainfile.php/1998vol08no06/1486/.

persons merely for peaceful expression of views contrary to those of the government.[54]

Another significant step in Indonesian law reform is the reform of the 1945 Constitution. When Suharto was in power, he did not permit any attempt to propose amendments to the 1945 Constitution since this Constitution gave him greater authority than the legislative and judicial bodies. However, since the end of his presidency in 1998, Indonesia has amended the Constitution four times (1999–2002).[55] This achievement is notable for a number of reasons. First, it has broken 'the sacred statement' of former President Suharto that people must not change their Constitution. Second, constitutional reform is a critical aspect of Indonesia's transition, for the original form of the 1945 Constitution was an inadequate foundation for democracy. Third, the amendments have altered the basis of the political structure. For instance, the First Amendment limits presidential tenure to two terms.[56] There is a new Chapter comprising ten Articles regarding human rights.[57] The structure and the power of three bodies (executive, legislative and judiciary) are reformed.[58] In fact, thirty-one articles (84 per cent) have been amended or modified and only six articles (16 per cent) have not been changed.

Despite some significant achievements, noted above, all the governments in the post-Suharto era have been unable to punish perpetrators of human rights abuses involving top military officers, and to bring Suharto to justice, as demanded by the reform movement. The changing of the Press paradigm has not led to professionalism in the Press. Corruption is still a common practice. What we see today is the product of the overcrowded

[54] Indonesia's National Human Rights Commission (Komnas HAM) commented on the anti-subversion law, 'The Anti-subversion Law can be used to punish people whose ideas are different from those of the government. It allows prosecutors and judges to act as if they can read the accused's mind.' See *Jakarta Post*, 9 April 1996.

[55] See N. Hosen, *Shari'a and Constitutional Reform in Indonesia* (Singapore: ISEAS, 2007); G. F. Bell, 'Obstacles to Reform: The 1945 Constitution' (2001) 3(6) *Van Zorge Report on Indonesia – Commentary and Analysis on Indonesian Politics and Economics*, 7. See also T. M. Lubis, 'Constitutional Reforms', in Hadi Susatro (*et al.*), *Governance in Indonesia: Challenges Facing the Megawati Presidency* (Singapore: ISEAS, 2003); T. Lindsey, 'Indonesian Constitutional Reform: Muddling Towards Democracy' (2002) 6 *Singapore Journal of International and Comparative Law* 244; B. A. King, 'Empowering the Presidency: Interests and Perceptions in Indonesia's Constitutional Reforms, 1999–2002', unpublished PhD thesis, Ohio State University (2004).

[56] See Article 7 of the First Amendment of the 1945 Constitution: 'The President and the Vice-President hold their office term for five years, and afterwards, can be re-elected for the same position, for only one office term.'

[57] See Chapter XA, Articles 28A–28J of the Second Amendment of the 1945 Constitution.

[58] See the Third and Fourth Amendments of the 1945 Constitution.

reform agenda, hurried through in a very short time. For instance, the draft bill on the Press was discussed for only thirteen working days. On the other hand, every time Indonesia has a new government and Parliament as a result of a general election, it always proposes and then issues a new electoral law.[59] This shows not only that Indonesia is still in the process of finding the right direction, but also that Indonesian elites are in a battle to gain benefit from the new electoral laws. These problems have occurred mainly because of huge problems left by the Suharto government, and the fact that all parties, such as students, new political parties and non-governmental organisations (NGOs), including the IMF, World Bank and other international donors, required the government to reform the economic, political and legal systems *simultaneously.*

Suharto made himself the fulcrum between civilians and soldiers, Christians and Muslims, indigenous Indonesians and ethnic Chinese. He was the only effective institution for thirty-two years. When he fell from power, the balance was shattered. Its components, including the reform group, were left to battle each other. This means that the 1998 reform movement did not sweep aside the political forces nurtured by the New Order government. In such circumstances, through the networks, power, money and political machinery they had developed in the past, they could take advantage of the opening-up of political space. This partly explains why the Golkar party and the military still play a significant role in the post-Suharto era.[60] In Lindsey's words, 'the compromises inherent in the political process . . . are often the only way effective reform can be achieved from a *realpolitik* perspective'.[61]

So far I have examined the shifting focus of the discourse on the rule of law in Indonesia. Under Suharto the focus was on economic development with little attention to the rule of law, whereas in the post-Suharto era the focus was more on a 'thick' version of the rule of law (formal rule of law plus human rights protection and economic development). I have also mentioned several problems faced by the reform movement: corruption, human rights protection, lack of effective institutions, political battles between old and new forces, and so on. It is time to move to the period after the 2002 Bali bombing, wherein Indonesia faces a dilemma between maintaining the rule of law and maintaining its national security. One thing never changes: Indonesia is under pressure from the political and

[59] Electoral laws in the post-Suharto era: Law No. 10 of 2008, Law No. 12 of 2003 and Law No. 3 of 1999.

[60] Tan, Chapter 6.

[61] Lindsey, 'Legal Infrastructure and Governance Reform', at 36.

economic power of foreign governments. Ignoring such pressure would be impossible, given the importance of Indonesia's strategic location, its size and also the significant fact that it is the world's most populous Muslim country, which is still in search of a path to constitutionalism.

IV. Post 9/11 and Indonesia's dilemma

Post-9/11 concerns over terrorism have brought attention to the rule of law as a means to hold terrorists accountable and to legitimise their capture and punishment, often through the promulgation of national defence and anti-terrorist laws. The question then is the extent to which the 'thick' rule of law in Indonesia has to support this 'war on terror'? First, before assessing whether the anti-terrorism and emergency powers regime is compatible with a 'thick' concept of the rule of law, I need to examine the international and domestic pressure to facilitate the use of emergency powers. Second, I answer the main question posed in this chapter by specifically focusing on the use of the Perpu as a legal instrument to deal with emergency situations. As has been shown earlier, the Indonesian government has used this instrument extensively. In the context of constitutionalism and the rule of law, I argue that the use of the Perpu is problematic. Finally, I examine several cases in order to illustrate my point that the anti-terrorism and emergency powers regime has in fact undermined Indonesia's attempt to uphold the rule of law in the post-Suharto era. More importantly, Indonesia *would step* back from a 'thick' version of the rule of law discussed above to what I call a 'stick' version of the rule of law – a combination of formal and substantive elements of the rule of law, and when necessary the use of the stick – any means at all to protect national security.

A. *Under pressure*

While Indonesia is clearly in need of US and Australian assistance in terms of military and economic support, Western governments also need Indonesia's full support in the 'war on terror'. The potential and centrality of Indonesia has long been noted: 'the outcome of how Indonesia deals with the future will almost certainly have a ripple effect in other, smaller countries in the region facing similar economic and political situations'.[62] Given its size and importance, including its strategic location, Indonesia is critical to stability in Southeast Asia.

[62] D. M. Snow, *Cases in International Relations: Portraits of the Future* (New York: Longman, 2003), p. 157.

While Singapore and Malaysia still use their Internal Security Acts (ISA) to deal with terrorists, prior to the Bali bombing in 2002, Indonesia no longer had an Anti-subversion Law. Reinstating draconian laws like the Anti-subversion Law would not be an option since the Indonesian people would reject it, whereas using the ordinary penal code would not impress the US and Australian governments, who had constantly been asking Indonesia to issue an anti-terrorism law, even before the Bali bombing occurred. The Bush administration's framing of Southeast Asia as the second front in the 'war on terror'[63] led the Asian region to revisit the discourse on the rule of law – this time in the context of emergency powers. It seems that after 9/11 the focus has no longer been on either the 'thin' or the 'thick' concept of the rule of law, but rather on the limits of legality, particularly as the concept of 'emergency' is becoming very powerful.

The Asian financial crisis of 1997–8 and the increase in terrorism across the region are separated, but highly connected, in explaining the designation of Southeast Asia as the second front. With the Taliban in Afghanistan having apparently been routed, Southeast Asia – home to radical Islamist groups such as the Jemaah Islamiah (JI), Abu Sayyaf and the Kumpulan Mujahideen Malaysia (KMM) – was starting to seem like the new home base for the terrorist movement that had brought down the World Trade Center. Across Southeast Asia there are thousands of remote islands and expanses of jungle ideal for extremist groups to hide and train.[64] Co-operation among Singapore, Malaysia, the Philippines and the United States has led to the arrests of dozens of suspected JI members, including several top leaders. In August 2002, the United States and all ten members of ASEAN signed an agreement to co-operate in counter-terrorism activities.[65] It seems that the intent of these agreements was to block terrorist financing, enhance intelligence exchange and improve border controls.[66] Another sign of increased attention given to terrorism occurred in July 2003, when the Southeast Asia Regional Centre for Counter-Terrorism opened in Kuala Lumpur. The centre houses researchers and hosts training sessions for regional officials.

[63] A. Acharya and A. Acharya, 'The Myth of the Second Front: Localizing the "War on Terror" in Southeast Asia' (2007) 30 *The Washington Quarterly* 75.

[64] C. S. Bond, 'Indonesia and the Changing Front in the War on Terrorism', Heritage Foundation, www.heritage.org/Research/AsiaandthePacific/hl875.cfm

[65] B. Pereira, 'ASEAN Countries Benefit from Anti-Terror Pact', *Strait Times*, 3 August 2002; see also Declaration on Terrorism by the 8th ASEAN Summit, www.aseansec.org/13154.htm.

[66] K. W. Chin, 'Southeast Asia in 2002: From Bali to Iraq – Co-operating for Security', in D. Singh and Chin Kin Wah (eds.), *Southeast Asian Affairs 2003* (Singapore: ISEAS, 2003), pp. 3–23.

However, it is important to note that the 1997 economic crisis in Southeast Asia generated grievances among groups that development has left behind. In both Indonesia and Malaysia, which have Muslim majorities, as well as in Singapore, the southern Philippines and southern Thailand where there are sizeable Muslim minorities, these grievances have combined to produce Islamist movements.[67] Although poverty alone cannot explain the existence of transnational terrorist networks such as the JI, poverty and inequality have contributed to popular discontent and thus encouraged support for such groups as Laskar Jihad and Abu Sayyaf. Long-standing economic grievances have also created support for secessionist groups in southern Thailand, Indonesia and the Philippines. At their January 2007 summit, ASEAN leaders reiterated their concern over 'the grave danger posed by terrorism to innocent lives, infrastructure and the environment, regional and international peace and stability, as well as to economic development.'[68]

In the context of Indonesia, the wider pattern of human insecurity derives not just from high-profile acts of horror such as the Bali bombing.[69] Day-to-day economic insecurity, communal violence, sporadic riots and violence, unresolved conflict in Papua, plus unfinished democratic and decentralisation transitions, are in fact greater dangers to national and regional development. The combination of economic crises from 1997, governmental transition reform since 1998 and the 'war on terror' from 2001 generated a renewed sense of crisis through 2002–3 which has begun to wane only slowly through 2003–9. However, in the wider context, this challenge remains. With some 50 million Indonesians living in dire poverty, the potential for growing radicalism and terrorism is very real in Indonesia. From this perspective, it can be stated safely that terrorist groups have used Indonesia's fragile political and economic transition to attack the Indonesian government and 'Western' interests.

The Megawati government was aware of the delicate balance between its position in the international community and domestic reactions to it. When Megawati announced support for the US 'war on terror', the United States pledged financial aid in return for that support. However, this was met with scepticism in Indonesia in radical Islamic circles and the

[67] A. Collins, *Security and Southeast Asia: Domestic, Regional and Global Issues* (Singapore: ISEAS, 2003).

[68] 'ASEAN Convention on Counter Terrorism', 31 January 2007, www.aseansec.org/19250.htm.

[69] A. Azra, 'Contemporary Islamic Militant Movements: Challenges to Democracy in Indonesia', paper presented at the International Conference on *The Future of Islam, Democracy, and Authoritarianism in the Muslim World*, International Centre for Islam and Pluralism, Jakarta, 6–7 December 2004.

public was angered, resulting in mass demonstrations against the USA in several cities. As the protests intensified, Megawati bowed to pressure and revised her position to issue criticisms of the US-led military campaign in Afghanistan.[70]

B. *Emergency response*

Without it being known by the Indonesian public, the Indonesian government drafted the Anti-terrorism Law in April 2002 in response to the events of 11 September 2001. However, the Bali bombing on 12 October 2002 forced President Megawati, six days after the attack, to issue Perpu No. 1/2002 and Perpu No. 2/2002. This was because of US allegations that Indonesia was one of the most important headquarters of terrorist organisations, especially that of Jemaah Islamiah, an affiliate of al Qaeda. The Australian government was also not happy with the Bali bombing, with the killing of 202 people and injury to a further 209, most of whom were Australian. Both US and Australian governments asked the Megawati government to take the problems of terrorism seriously, and to provide the necessary legal framework to deal with the attack. It was clear then that the Indonesian government treated the attack as an emergency matter and therefore took over the debate within Parliament on the Anti-terrorism Bill.

According to the Constitution, a Perpu must obtain the approval of Parliament during its next session. The Indonesian parliament approved the two Perpu on terrorism. Perpu No. 1 was adopted by the DPR through Law No. 15 of 2003 on 4 April 2003, whereas Perpu No. 2 of 2002 was adopted in the form of Law No. 16 of 2003. Perpu No. 2 of 2002 (or Law No. 16 of 2003) merely states that Perpu No. 1 of 2002 can be used retrospectively with respect to the Bali bombings. The two anti-terrorism laws were used as the basis for the arrest, prosecution and conviction of twenty-five of the now infamous Bali bombers. Given that the laws were enacted only after the bombings had occurred, the suspects were tried and punished for a crime which, according to law, was not strictly a crime at the time it was committed.[71]

Masykur Kadir was found guilty under Article 13(a) of Law No. 15 of 2003 of assisting the Bali bombers. Lawyers for Kadir claimed that he had

[70] See R. Sukma, 'Indonesia and 9–11: Reactions and Implications', in Han Sung-Joo (ed.), *Coping With 9–11: Asian Perspectives on Global and Regional Order* (Tokyo: JCIE, 2003).

[71] See H. Juwana, 'Indonesia's Anti-Terrorism Law', in V. V. Ramraj, M. Hor and K. Roach (eds.), *Global Anti-Terrorism Law and Policy* (Cambridge: Cambridge University Press, 2005), pp. 295–306 at p. 304.

been investigated, charged, prosecuted and convicted under an unconstitutional law (Law No. 16 of 2003). They argued that Article 28I(1) of the Indonesian Constitution provides citizens with a right not to be prosecuted under retrospective laws. The Constitutional Court agreed, exercising its powers of constitutional review to declare Law No. 16 of 2003 to be invalid.[72] The decision of the Indonesian court was reached by a majority of five justices to four. The decision demonstrates the potential dilemma faced by the court. On the one hand, the majority displayed their commitment to upholding the Constitution,[73] but on the other they were criticised for providing an unjust outcome, particularly for victims of the bombings and their families, both Indonesian and Australian.

The dilemma continues: should all the convicted Bali bombers use the Constitutional Court's decision and the constitutional invalidity of the law as a basis for an appeal? Butt and Hansell report:

> Apparently fearing that the convictions would be lost, Justice Minister Yusril Ihza Mahendra and Constitutional Court Chief Justice Professor Dr Jimly Asshiddiqie announced their own interpretation of the decision to the press. They claimed that the bombers would remain in jail because the Constitutional Court's decision itself could not operate retrospectively. In other words, the decision, whilst binding, only prevents future investigations, prosecutions and convictions being carried out retrospectively. It would not, therefore, impact upon convictions that have already been obtained. This statement, particularly from Asshiddiqie, constitutes an inappropriate politicisation of the court. That Asshiddiqie's statement and that of the Justice Minister were announced at around the same time, and conveyed the same view, gives the impression that Asshiddiqie may have collaborated with the government, even though he might not actually have done so.[74]

Specifically, the dilemma is this. Do we want to keep the terrorists in jail, although they were convicted under an unconstitutional anti-terrorism

[72] S. Butt and D. Hansell, 'The Masykur Abdul Kadir Case: Indonesian Constitutional Court Decision No 013' (2004) 6 *Australian Journal of Asian Law* 176.

[73] Under international law an exception is sometimes allowed to permit trial or punishment for any act (or omission) which, at the time it was committed, was criminal according to the general principles of law recognised by civilised countries. This expression is drawn directly from the statute of the International Court of Justice. However, the Indonesian Constitution states in Article 28I: 'The rights to life, freedom from torture, freedom of thought and conscience, freedom of religion, freedom from enslavement, recognition as a person before the law, and the right not to be tried under a law with retrospective effect are all human rights that cannot be limited under any circumstances.'

[74] Butt and Hansell, 'The Masykur Abdul Kadir Case', at 181.

law, which is basically against the principles of human rights and the rule of law; or to let them go free, which puts the country at higher risk from the bombers themselves, and also from the criticism of foreign countries, including the USA and Australia, which certainly will not be happy to see the convicted terrorists walk free? As has been stated above, Justice Minister Mahendra and Constitutional Court Chief Justice Asshiddiqie take the view that the court's decisions affect only the application of the law in the future, and therefore Masykur Kadir and other convicted bombers should remain in jail. This is a clear example of Indonesian potentially moving toward a 'stick' version of the rule of law, when the court bows to international pressure and pressure from the government.

Apart from the matter of retrospectivity, the use of the Perpu itself as a legal instrument to deal with emergency power remains questionable. Under Indonesia's Constitution the President is given emergency powers to issue a Perpu in situations where the government must take swift and decisive action to guarantee security. Before a Perpu is formalised, the President is required to outline the threat to security which has prompted its introduction. It is still open to interpretation in what types of emergency situation the state must be deemed to be for a President to have the right to issue a Perpu.

I have mentioned earlier that the Megawati government also issued a Perpu (No. 1/2004) on 11 March 2004, which amends the Forestry Law. The Parliament then approved this Perpu. NGOs unhappy with this decision requested the Constitutional Court to review the validity of that Perpu. One of their arguments was that the government did not explain the emergency situation which led to the President issuing this Perpu. Moreover, Article 22 of the Constitution, which has been used frequently to issue Perpus in emergency cases, must be related to Article 12 ('The President may declare a state of emergency') and Law No. 23 of 1959 on National Security. In Perpu No. 1 of 2004, President Megawati did not refer to them. The question of whether such a condition existed in relation to mining in protected areas consumed hours of hearings and pages of the court's decision. To the great concern of civil society, the Constitutional Court found that whether there is a pressing crisis is not measured objectively by reference to whether there exists a national emergency which cannot be dealt with by Parliament. Instead it is a subjective measurement at the discretion of the President. The court cited as precedents previous Perpus, most of which date from the time of Suharto's New Order regime. The court did not even refer to the Perpu on terrorism to illustrate its point.

There were allegations that the government's hand was forced primarily by pressure from the Australian government, which held twelve closed-door meetings with high-ranking officials before the regulation was issued. Australian Embassy spokesperson Elizabeth O'Neill told the *Jakarta Post* that several meetings between Australian and Indonesian representatives had indeed taken place, but dismissed the allegation that they were not transparent.[75] She said Australia had been concerned for some time about the impact of the 1999 Forestry Law on Australian mining firms operating in Indonesia, as many of them had signed contracts with the government prior to 1999 to develop mineral resources and had already made significant investments.[76] This suggests that the neo-liberal approach to the rule of law remains influential in Indonesia.

Meanwhile, NGOs alleged that several legislators took bribes prior to the start of the House plenary session to vote on the Perpu, when several State Secretariat officials had been seen lobbying the legislators. The judges considered evidence (including testimony from a member of parliament) that parliamentarians received bribes of US$5,000 to $15,000 in order to ratify the Perpu but concluded that the Constitutional Court was unable to consider the bribery issue until it was proven in a criminal court. Once again, this illustrates the difficulties in Indonesia of prosecuting cases involving allegations of corruption, which is inconsistent with the idea of both 'thin' and 'thick' rule of law.

According to NGOs, the thirteen companies had demonstrated very bad performance in environmental management in Indonesia, as could be seen from the disposal of their industrial waste into the environment. The NGOs were upset that the government ignored these violations.[77] The Director-General of Geological and Mineral Resources, Simon Sembiring, also told the *Jakarta Post* that the regulation was expected to spur new investment of about US$17 billion for the next three years.[78] The Constitutional Court responded to the issue by stating:

> Although this Court shares the opinion of all the experts brought by the appellants regarding the danger and negative impacts of open-pit mining in protected forests, nevertheless this Court also understands the reasoning for the need for a transitional regulation which continues the rights or legal status gained by mining companies before the advent of the Forestry Law (1999).[79]

75 'NGOs Up Pressure on Forest Mining', *Jakarta Post*, 17 July 2004. 76 *Ibid.*

77 Bachriardi, 'The Forestry Law Has Not Stopped Mining in Indonesia's State Forests'.

78 'NGOs Up Pressure on Forest Mining'.

79 See Constitutional Court Decision No. 008/PUU-III/2005 [2005] IDCC 16 (19 July 2005), www.asianlii.org/id/cases/IDCC/2005/16.html

The court took the view that the subjective discretion of the President to measure the threat to national security becomes objective once it is ratified by Parliament. It seems that this decision allows the government to maintain the legal fiction of an emergency in order to justify its policy. Even the judges themselves seemed uncomfortable with this unclear definition of 'emergency' in the Constitution, ambiguously recommending that, in future, the President must consider more objective conditions before issuing a further Perpu.[80] In other words, the Constitutional Court failed to outline the criteria for the government in issuing a Perpu to deal with an emergency situation.

V. Conclusion

I have examined how Indonesia has attempted to revisit the discourse on the rule of law and emergency powers. Arguably, Indonesia has moved from the 'thin' to the 'thick' concept of the rule of law since 1998. However, the 2002 Bali bombings have tested whether Indonesia's counter-terrorism agenda will have a negative impact on the efforts aimed at upholding the rule of law. The rule-of-law tensions and ambiguities (retrospective law, etc.) discussed in this chapter arguably support what Victor Ramraj calls the 'emergency powers paradox'.[81] Ramraj explains, with reference to examples in Southeast Asia, that countries in democratic transition may in some circumstances be justified in using emergency powers in their initial phase as this may help in establishing legality in the long run for legal, political and economic reforms to take hold. Indonesia's experience in maintaining a balance between upholding the rule of law and using emergency powers to deal with terrorist attacks is illustrative in understanding such a paradox.

In the context of Indonesia, I suggest, first of all, that we might question the unclear definition of 'emergency' in the Constitution and how the Constitutional Court is ready to accept any conditions or criteria provided by the government as long as the Parliament accepts it. As has been demonstrated, the subjective criteria might operate practically at two levels: political and/or financial emergencies. Theoretically, the two levels can be traced back to the phenomenon of 'legal transplant' and to the neo-liberal agenda. I should clarify that I use the paradox of emergency powers above as an explanation rather than as a justification.

In Indonesia, the paradox therefore begins with the vagueness of emergency powers stipulated in the Constitution and its failure to set out the

[80] *Ibid.* [81] V. V. Ramraj, 'The Emergency Powers Paradox' (Chapter 2), this volume.

criteria or the time-frame within which the powers may be exercised. This failure, in turn, facilitates the justification and use of these powers. The only limitation is Parliament's ability to approve or disapprove the Perpu. However, this is exactly the second concern of this paradox: the unstable nature of political alignments, the weakness of party structures, economic crisis, along with international pressures, all contribute to a pragmatic and politically oriented rule of law. For instance, the basis of discretion in establishing Perpu may be questioned if it is seen as derogating from the tenets of the rule of law. This has resulted in more emphasis being placed on empowering the state, rather than limiting its powers. It seems the finality of discretionary power would rest with the primary decision-maker.

Third, Indonesia's experience of the inability of Parliament and the courts to limit emergency powers is dissonant to the Gross–Dyzenhaus debate.[82] Dyzenhaus retains some faith in the ability of the courts (or specialised administrative tribunals under judicial supervision) to uphold the rule of law in emergency situations, while, for Gross, the solution lies outside the courts (it should involve a political check on abuses of power). The debate assumes either Parliament or the courts can provide adequate checks and balances – a function that has not been fully exercised by either institution in Indonesia because of its choice of pragmatic rule of law in some cases.

Fourth, while I share the concerns expressed by Anil Kalhan and Vasuki Nesiah on the risks of using emergency powers and the premises of liberal constitutionalism, respectively,[83] I take the view that Indonesia's experience shows how constitutionalism and the rule of law do matter in a normative sense. Given the vagueness of emergency powers and the Perpu stipulated in the Constitution and the very fact that the national security law currently operating in Indonesia is the old 1959 law, I suggest that constitutional reform in this sense remains unfinished. The 2002 Bali bombings and other terrorist attacks should not interrupt this process.

A hard lesson to be learned from Indonesia is that gradualism and long-term planning are critical to the agenda of a reformist government. Understanding the paradox above, together with the challenges from international and domestic pressures, would assist us to acknowledge that there

[82] See the debate in V. V. Ramraj (ed.), *Emergencies and the Limits of Legality* (Cambridge: Cambridge University Press, 2008).

[83] See, in this volume, A. Kalhan, 'Constitution and "Extraconstitution": Colonial Emergency Powers in Postcolonial India and Pakistan' (Chapter 4) and V. Nesiah, 'The Princely Impostor: Stories of Law and Pathology in the Exercise of Emergency Powers' (Chapter 5).

can be no shortcuts in establishing a meaningful 'rule-of-law' state. If Indonesia does not succeed in limiting the use of emergency powers and upholding the rule of law, what we will see is not 'thin' or 'thick' but the 'stick' version of the rule of law, in which the government will not only use any means to protect national security, but also set its own criteria for dealing with emergency situations. The struggle for *negara hukum* is still a long way from success in Indonesia.

11

Emergency powers with a moustache: special powers, military rule and evolving constitutionalism in Thailand

ANDREW HARDING

I. Introduction

On 16 July 2005 the Thai-language newspaper *Thai Post* in Bangkok published as its front-page article comment on the Decree on Public Administration in Emergency Situation 2005, which had been passed by the executive the day before, under the headline 'Decree with a Moustache'.[1] The article likened the powers assumed by the executive under the decree to those of the Nazi Gestapo in Hitler's Germany. The decree, a response to the continuing separatist insurgency in the Malay/Muslim southern provinces of Thailand, and ostensibly intended to consolidate several existing applicable laws, empowered the Prime Minister to order wire taps, censor the press, restrict freedom of assembly and movement, confiscate and destroy property and preventively detain suspects in undesignated places without criminal charge; it also transferred all governmental authority in an area subject to an emergency declaration into the Prime Minister's own hands. These powers were expressed to be exercisable with no, or minimal, judicial oversight or access to justice and with immunity from legal consequences. The decree sparked extensive public debate about the role of emergency powers and the legitimate powers of the executive and the military. This debate continued in 2006–7 during which period a military coup (19 September 2006) overthrew the Constitution and the government and the interim legislature passed the Internal Security Act 2007. The debate revealed great concern, both in Thailand and internationally, over numerous aspects of these exceptional laws and military actions.

[1] *Thai Post*, Bangkok, 16 July 2005, p.1 (in Thai). This decree ceased to be effective on 19 July 2008.

Thailand has been grappling in recent decades with two related problems. First, and especially since 2003, with the central dilemma presented by emergency powers, namely how to deal with exceptionally dangerous and destabilising circumstances, such as the insurgency and violence in Thailand's southern provinces of Yala, Narathiwat and Pattani, without giving up on the project, begun in earnest in 1991, of building constitutionalism and the rule of law: to put it in a more general way, the issue is how can we draw limits to powers which are of necessity illimitable or at least exceptionally broad?[2] Yet it will be seen here that the context in which this dilemma presents itself in Thailand is somewhat different from other states in the era of international terrorism and the post-9/11 world, both in Asia and in the West, and this leads us to the second problem. As Kevin Tan, adverting to Thailand's chequered political history since 1932, observes, 'Thailand deals with exceptional political situations through *coups d'état* rather than through the invoking of emergency powers.'[3] While justifications based on emergency and national security considerations are very frequently resorted to by military leaders mounting *coups d'état* in Thailand, emergency powers in the strict sense, contiguous as they are in some respects with the device of the military coup, have generally been invoked for reasons connected with law and order or insurgency, as was the case with the decree of 2005. The most recent military coup, that of 19 September 2006, was essentially one designed to oust from government Prime Minister Thaksin Shinawatra and his Thai Rak Thai Party, who had become unpopular (at least in Bangkok if not elsewhere in Thailand) as a result of abuses of power and corruption; nonetheless, the generals had to include in the justification of their actions a reference to a very imminent threat to law and order resulting from the protests against Thaksin and the acute polarisation of Thai society. It is still nonetheless increasingly true, as Tan indicates in his conclusion, in Thailand as elsewhere, that 'the key lies not in the inherited tradition or system, but in how the state and its governing elite view their own survival'.[4] This notion can be seen clearly in the Thai case, as will be seen in this chapter, as it can in the case of, for

[2] For discussion of this issue in a Southeast Asian context, see the chapters in this volume by Victor V. Ramraj and Kevin Y. L. Tan: respectively, 'The Emergency Powers Paradox' (Chapter 2) and 'From Myanmar to Manila: A Brief Study of Emergency Powers in Southeast Asia' (Chapter 6).

[3] Tan, Chapter 6, p. 185. See Tan's chapter, further, for a historical overview of Thai constitutional history in comparative perspective.

[4] *Ibid.*, p. 184. See, for example, H. P. Lee's chapter where he refers to 'the key impetus [in invoking emergency powers being] the desire of the ruling government to cling to power at any cost', H. P. Lee, 'Constitutionalised Emergency Powers: A Plague on Asian Constitutionalism?' (Chapter 14), this volume, p. 409; A. H. Y. Chen, 'Emergency Powers,

example, the Philippines and Pakistan. What Pangalangan refers to[5] as 'the bizarre "disconnect" between legality and normativity' and the 'manipulation of constitutional text'[6] are phenomena very clearly evidenced in the Thai case. Even more apposite here is the example of Pakistan, discussed by Anil Kalhan, who examines the use of exceptional powers (to use a comprehensive term) as a 'pattern' technique of government.[7] Here the issue is not simply state survival but a more ambitious agenda of using these powers as a means of reconfiguring the political order on a basis intended to be permanent and according to the preferences or interests of the ruling faction. Comparison with Pakistan reveals, however, an interesting difference in approach.

The central dilemma of emergency powers, as I have described it, is presented in Thailand not just in the context of emergency powers, martial law and standing internal security powers, as will be explored in some detail in this chapter, but in relation to constitutional development more generally. As Victor V. Ramraj argues,[8] there is a distinction to be drawn between the use of emergency powers to preserve legality and their use to establish legality. In Thailand, while it might be hasty to present all uses of emergency powers in a similar light, the use of extraconstitutional measures, principally the military coup, as a means of establishing legality, can be easily recognised; the problem here (Ramraj's emergency powers paradox) is that the very attempt to establish legality by what are strictly illegal means itself tends to undermine attempts to establish the rule of law as a binding principle.

In this respect Anil Kalhan's chapter on Pakistan resonates very appositely in the Thai context, because on seventeen occasions in the last seventy-six years, since the end of the absolute monarchy of Siam in 1932, a military coup has brought existing constitutional arrangements to an end and inaugurated the emplacement of further constitutional arrangements. Much the same has occurred in Pakistan, in relation to which Kalhan postulates an 'extraconstitution' whose purpose is to reconfigure the constitution according to the political agenda of the leader in actual power, and whose legal-analytical description could be either

Constitutionalism and Legal Transplants: The East Asian Experience' (Chapter 3), this volume, p. 64.

5 R. Pangalangan, 'Political Emergencies in the Philippines: Changing Labels and the Unchanging Need for Legitimacy' (Chapter 15), this volume, p. 434.

6 Compare Lee's reference in Chapter 14 (p. 410) to '[seeking] to give a veneer of constitutional respectability to . . . unscrupulous actions'.

7 A. Kalhan, 'Constitution and "Extraconstitution": Colonial Emergency Regimes in Postcolonial India and Pakistan' (Chapter 4), this volume, p. 100.

8 Ramraj, Chapter 2, p. 22.

unconstitutional or authorised by emergency powers. One important difference is that the *coup d'état* in Thailand normally displaces the existing government (as in Thailand, 2006) rather than attempting to reconstitute the state around the existing leadership (as in Pakistan, 2007). In the Thai case, the revocation of the Constitution is generally thought to be necessary in order to provide legal immunity for the coup-promoters, usually enshrined in an interim constitution. Additionally, in Thailand, where the sole politically acceptable definition and description of the state is 'the democratic regime with the King as head of state' the monarchy carries considerable constitutional weight, and it is crucial for any *coup d'état* to have royal approval. Since constitutional powers historically derive from the monarchy, royal approval has the function of legitimating any constitutionally relevant act such as the adoption of a new constitution or installation of a new government; and occasionally royal prompting is required before the legal machinery grinds into motion, as happened when the Constitutional Court invalidated Thaksin's snap election of April 2006 in the midst of constitutional crisis.

The *coups d'état* have usually cited national security, often along with other aspects of public interest, such as government corruption or constitutional breakdown, as the justification for intervention in the political system, and without exception the leaders of such military coups have acted under subsequently granted legal immunity for their actions; indeed when the issue of legality of a coup first arose in the courts it was decided in effect (again reflecting the Pakistan courts' view based on the doctrine of necessity) that a successful coup begets its own legality.[9] In the most recent instance in 2006, the military junta was able to enjoy complete immunity in respect of all of its actions.[10] The 2006 coup was peaceful, but the same principle applies even where those concerned have been

[9] 'The high court held that it was immaterial how a government came into being and that the only real test of its legitimacy was whether in fact it could rule': W. Blanchard *et al.*, *Thailand: its People, its Society, its Culture* (New Heaven: HRAF Press, 1958), p. 202, referring to a decision relating to the 1947 coup. The reasoning is also familiar in common law jurisdictions; cf. T. Mahmud, 'Jurisprudence of Successful Treason: Coup d'Etat and Common Law' (1994) 27 *Cornell International Law Journal* 49.

[10] The Constitution of the Kingdom of Thailand (Interim) 2006 stated at s. 37:

> All acts performed on account of the Acts of the seizure and control of State governing power on 19 September 2006 of the Chairperson of the Council for Democratic Reform, including all acts of persons incidental to such performance or of persons entrusted by the Chairperson or [*sic* – of] the Council for Democratic Reform or of persons ordered by persons entrusted by the Chairperson or [*sic* – of] the Council for Democratic Reform whereby such acts have been done for the benefit of the above mentioned performance, irrespective of their legislative, executive or judicial force as well as punishments and other official administrative acts and irrespective of whether

guilty of gross human rights abuses.[11] Thus the military coup has become virtually a constitutional remedy legitimised by frequent usage. Interestingly enough, in the present situation (that is, during the last few months of 2008) in Bangkok where widespread protest against the government has been thought by many to presage another coup,[12] demonstrations have been mounted against a coup, *in advance* of it taking place, which phenomenon seems to indicate a counter-discourse in which the *coup d'état* is seen as no longer having such legitimacy. Support for the coup of 2006, which was apparently supported by 80 per cent of Bangkok residents, evaporated quickly after the military and its 'technocrat' government displayed self-serving authoritarianism combined with a lack of economic competence.

The frequently occurring situation where military power has not been held accountable under the rule of law has encouraged the adoption of similar approaches in contexts other than the military coup. For example, during 2003–5 it was government policy to pursue a 'war on drugs', conducted against 'dark forces' which were undermining Thai society. It is estimated that up to 2,500 people, alleged drug-traffickers, died in this episode, effectively executed without any resort to judicial procedure;[13] nobody has been punished for any actions relating to this matter. And although eighty-seven people died, mainly of suffocation as they were

> those acts have been done as a principal, abettor, agent provocateur or commission agent and whether those acts have been done on, before or after the aforesaid date, if those acts are offences under the laws, the persons who commit those acts shall be entirely discharged from such offences and liabilities (official certified translation, available at www.senate.go.th/pdf/const.pdf).

See, further, Constitution of the Kingdom of Thailand 2007, s. 309, which validates this immunity provision.

[11] A. J. Harding, 'Thailand's Reforms: Human Rights and the National Commission' (2006) 1 *Journal of Comparative Law* 88.

[12] As this chapter was being finalised in December 2008, a prolonged and tense political situation appeared to be reaching boiling point as anti-government protesters occupied the two main airports in Bangkok and the compounds of the Prime Minister's office and Parliament, and an emergency limited to the area of the main airport had been declared. As is often the case in Thailand, yet another military coup was being forecast. Given the history of the 2006 coup, which became rapidly unpopular, the military has indicated its extreme unwillingness to intervene, but intervention of some kind seems highly likely as the government is in effect prevented from dealing with the global economic crisis or indeed carrying on anything resembling normal government. The protesters, without apparent irony, are known as the 'People's Alliance for Democracy'. An earlier declaration of an emergency in Bangkok was simply ignored by the police and the military.

[13] See http://in.reuters.com/article/worldNews/idINIndia-31814820080207. Worryingly this article reports an intended revival of the 'war on drugs' by the present PPP government.

stacked on top of each other in police trucks, in the Tak Bai incident in the south in 2003, nobody has been punished or even called to account with consequences for their actions, even though the National Human Rights Commission reported extensively, and adversely, on this incident. Despite evidence of wrongdoing by the local police in the south, and possibly even higher up in the government, the disappearance of Muslim human rights lawyer Somchai Neelaphaijit in 2003, also remains unexplained. Concerning the Krue Se Mosque incident in 2004 the Asian Committee on Human Rights had this to say:[14]

> In one of the bloodiest actions by the security forces, 107 persons, mostly teenagers were killed and 17 others were arrested on 28 April 2004. The killed youth, mostly armed with machetes and only a few carrying assault rifles, allegedly battled policemen and soldiers in Pattani, Yala and Songkhla. More than 30 were killed inside the historic Krue Se Mosque alone on the outskirts of Pattani in Narathiwat province. The probe panel into the Krue Se mosque headed by Suchinda Yongsunthron, a former constitution[al court] judge found that the security forces did not use peaceful means to end the standoff and described the killings as an over reaction by the security forces. The inquiry commission observed that the circumstances at the mosque were not so overwhelming that troops had to resort to 'excessive force.' The panel also found that the bodies of the slain militants were not examined in accordance with judicial procedures.

Again there was no accountability. The Internal Security Act 2007, discussed further below, also creates extensive immunities and places national security powers, not in the realm of temporary emergency powers, but on a permanent footing. For this reason it would be artificial to discuss only 'emergency powers' strictly defined; the seepage of emergency or special powers into the regular legal system, and the cynical use or abuse of such powers as a 'technique of government' is clearly a problem of twenty-first-century jurisprudence; and if recent protests in Thailand, Pakistan and Malaysia are indicative, it is also an endemic political problem in Asia.[15] It seems clear that, despite many advances in recent years in Thai constitutionalism and governance, the exercise of special powers by the police and the army remain beyond the scope of such positive

[14] See www.achrweb.org/reports/Thailand/Thailand0105.pdf.

[15] Even so, as Lombardi and Aung-Thwin indicate in their chapters, the colonial discourse of emergency evidences the same phenomenon at an earlier period, and even though Siam was not a colony, its tendency to copy the techniques of colonial powers is well documented. See C. B. Lombardi, 'Islamism as a Response to Emergency Rule in Pakistan: The Surprising Proposal of Justice A. R. Cornelius' (Chapter 16), and M. Aung-Thwin, 'Discourses of Emergency in Colonial and Postcolonial Burmese History' (Chapter 7).

developments, maintaining a regime of exception which now exists apparently as a permanent feature of Thai jurisprudence and legal culture, and which contradicts and undermines sterling efforts in some sectors to entrench the rule of law and good governance.[16]

This chapter examines the nature of, and critiques the exercise of, emergency and analogous powers in contemporary Thai constitutionalism. It looks at the constitutional basis and origins of these powers and the opportunities for achieving accountability for their exercise. The conclusion is depressing. The rule of law operates only as a competing, not as a fundamental, value in the Thai context, and in emergency and security contexts competes with a striking lack of compulsion. The repeated exercise of exceptional and even unconstitutional (but still, by one means or another, legitimated) power by the military has undermined attempts over the last sixteen years to establish the rule of law on a permanent constitutional basis. Clearly if the constitution itself can be overthrown with immunity simply by a decision of the military then relatively less important laws can easily be either manipulated or ignored.

II. Emergency powers: the constitutional provisions

In examining any aspect of Thai constitutionalism, it is important to keep in mind that, despite the rapid turnover of constitutions in Thailand, many provisions of these constitutions remain hardly altered. Indeed, emergency powers offer a clear example of this. The last three constitutions (other than the Interim Constitution of 2006), that is, those of 1991, 1997 and 2007, have contained virtually identical provisions with regard to emergency powers.[17] Even the first 'permanent' (that is to say, other than interim) Constitution of Siam of December 1932 contained emergency powers quite similar to those in recent constitutions.[18] We can therefore

[16] See, further, A. J. Harding, 'May There Be Virtue: "New Asian Constitutionalism" in Thailand' (2001) 3 *Australian Journal of Asian Law* 24; A. J. Harding, 'A Turbulent Innovation: The Constitutional Court of Thailand, 1998–2006', paper presented at the conference on *New Courts in the Asia-Pacific Region*, University of Victoria, July 2007; P. Leyland, '*Droit Administratif* Thai Style: A Comparative Analysis of the Administrative Courts in Thailand' (2006) 8 *Australian Journal of Asian Law* 121; P. Leyland, 'Thailand's Constitutional Watchdogs: Dobermans, Bloodhounds or Lapdogs?' (2007) 2 *Journal of Comparative Law* 151.

[17] 1991: ss. 175–7; 1997: ss. 218–20; 2007: ss. 184–6. Even the Interim Constitution 2006, s. 15, contains rather similar provisions.

[18] The precise provenance and reasoning behind the inclusion of emergency powers in the first Constitution is not clear, but it may be that the factor mentioned in note 15 above, the tendency to copy the techniques of powers perceived to be stronger and better equipped legally, may be relevant.

take the current statement of these powers under the 2007 Constitution, approved by referendum in August 2007, not simply as the current law on this subject, but as typical of emergency powers in recent times and indeed throughout Thai constitutional history since 1932. Having said this, it is worth keeping in mind the very practical point recently made by Thai historian Thanet Aphornsuvan that 'Thai constitutions served as histories of political development and conflict, and in terms of law, they were the sum total, not the source, of the lesser and organic laws that existed prior to the promulgation of these constitutions'.[19] Constitutions in Thailand should therefore be seen in terms of their legitimating function and as a statement of the present state of constitutionalism rather than as an embodiment of the unchanging Kelsenian *grundnorm*.

This can be clearly seen in the following discussion of the present constitutional arrangements relating to emergency powers. Under the relevant provisions of the 2007 Constitution, ss. 184–8, an emergency decree may be issued by the King acting on the advice of the Cabinet where the latter is of the opinion that it is necessary for the purpose of maintaining national or public safety or national economic security, or averting public calamity. The decree must be submitted to the National Assembly without delay, and the approval of both houses is required for the decree to take effect. One fifth of the members of either house can have the constitutionality of the decree referred to the Constitutional Court within three days. An emergency decree may also be passed if it is necessary to have a law on taxes, duties or currency, which, in the interests of state, requires an urgent and confidential consideration. The King also has a prerogative power, without legislature approval, to declare martial law, and the military can declare martial law for a given locality where it is necessary to do so. Some observations are made in this section concerning the emergency powers provisions.

A. *Scope of the powers*

'Maintaining national or public safety or national economic security, or averting public calamity' spells out, as is typical of emergency powers, a broad range of possible circumstances which would justify an emergency decree. If one takes s. 186 along with ss. 184–5, clearly the power to pass emergency decrees based purely on economic contingency is very broad, but also contains an unusual degree of specificity. It is not clear precisely what genealogy led to the framing of emergency powers in this manner.

[19] *Bangkok Post*, 3 August 2007, p. 5.

However, their breadth may be seen from the very first decision by the Constitutional Court on its inauguration under the 1997 Constitution in 1998,[20] ruling on the constitutionality of four emergency decrees issued by the government in response to the economic crisis of 1997–8. The government had issued the decrees in May 1998, thereby expanding the role of the Financial Restructuring Authority of Thailand and the Assets Management Corporation, settling the debts of the Financial Institutions Development Fund through the issue of 500 billion baht in bonds and authorising the Ministry of Finance to seek 200 billion baht in overseas loans. On the last day of parliamentary debate on these decrees, when it was clear they would be passed and in order to postpone a vote, a minor political party invoked s. 219 of the 1997 Constitution (equivalent to s. 185 of the 2007 Constitution) to question their constitutionality. It was argued that, since there was no 'emergency nor necessary urgency' as required by s. 218(2) (precisely equivalent to s. 184 of the 2007 Constitution), the government could not make any emergency decrees. Section 218(1) allowed emergency decrees to be passed on the basis of 'national economic security', and the court ruled that it was obvious that the nation was in an economic crisis, and that the decrees were in fact designed to deal with national economic security.[21] As in other jurisdictions, and increasingly in the practice of constitutional law internationally, national security is defined not just in terms of war, rebellion, insurgency, organised violence, natural disaster, etc. but also in terms of economic security.[22] In a long series of cases during 1998–2002 the court took a

[20] Case 1/1998 (23 May).

[21] A similar suit by the same party, impeaching Prime Minister Chuan Leekpai for signing Letters of Intent with the International Monetary Fund to secure an emergency loan without parliamentary approval under s. 224 of the Constitution, was also rejected on the grounds that the Letters of Intent were not in the nature of treaties which the government was obliged to bring before Parliament for approval, nor were they contractual agreements, as they lacked any enforcement provisions. As McDorman says in connection with decisions under the 1991 Constitution, it is at least positive that the Constitutional Court (or Constitutional Tribunal under the 1991 Constitution) appears willing to look at the actual situation in which the decree is made, rather than simply say that the court has no power to review the exercise of discretion by the executive, which is the sole judge of necessity for the decree: see T. L. McDorman, 'The 1991 Constitution of Thailand' (1993) 3 *Pacific Rim Law and Policy Journal* 257.

[22] In some jurisdictions, for example, the law permits preventive detention (under emergency or national security powers) for a wide range of economically sensitive actions, e.g. smuggling, in addition to unlawful actions having purely social effects, such as drug-trafficking, or even actions which involve organised or violent crime.

similar approach to challenges to emergency decrees based on the response to the 1997 economic crisis.[23]

B. Scrutiny

Given the drastic consequences of the collapse of currency values in 1997 and the need for a speedy response, it is difficult to argue that national security was not in some sense at issue or that the response of the Constitutional Court in refusing to hold these decrees unconstitutional was incorrect. It would seem that, if anywhere, Parliament is the place where the exercise of such powers should be accounted for, since Parliament rather than the Constitutional Court is better able to assess all substantive aspects of the need for emergency powers to be assumed. The emergency powers provisions do, of course, recognise the pre-eminent role of Parliament; indeed the Decree of 2005, which purported to make emergency provision for the making of emergency declarations (that is, abstractly and in general) without any parliamentary scrutiny was surely unconstitutional in that it attempted to replace and bypass constitutional provisions with an executive decree proclaiming an emergency; presumably only a constitutional amendment could achieve that result.[24]

23 These challenges have been based on various grounds, as though some vested interests were attempting to find different ways of unpicking the lock which the decrees had created. See, for example, Cases 23 and 24/2002, where it was held that an emergency decree was not operated discriminatorily as it applied to all financial institutions; Case 4/2003 dealt with a challenge based on the separation of judicial powers. See also Cases 11/1999, 9 and 10/2001, 9 and 19–34/2002, 8, 14, 22 and 30/2002.

24 The relevant provision, s. 5, is as follows:

> [If in] the event of the occurrence of emergency situation, the Prime Minister deems it appropriate to mobilise administrative officials or police officers, civil officials or military officers to jointly prevent, remedy, suppress, contain the emergency situation, provide rehabilitation or assistance to the people, the Prime Minister upon the approval of the Council of Ministers is empowered to declare a state of emergency be it applicable to the whole Kingdom or in some area or locality as necessary under the circumstances. In the case where the approval of the Council of Ministers cannot be obtained in a timely manner, the Prime Minister may declare the emergency situation and subsequently shall seek the approval of the Council of Ministers within three days. If approval of the Council of Ministers is not sought within the time prescribed, or the Council of Ministers refuses approval, such Declaration of a state of emergency shall cease to be in force. The Declaration of a state of emergency under paragraph one above shall be in force for the duration prescribed by the Prime Minister but shall not exceed three months from the date of declaration. In the case where it is necessary to extend such period, the Prime Minister upon the approval of the Council of Ministers shall have the power to declare the extension of duration of enforcement provided that each extension shall not exceed three months.

Notwithstanding extensive debate concerning emergency powers under the Thaksin Shinawatra government of 2001–6 and a generally enhanced role for the Constitutional Court under the 2007 Constitution, the actual constitutional position has changed only very marginally since 1991, in that the Constitutional Court has powers to control emergency decrees, although it is unlikely to exercise those powers in any significant way. Perhaps the most positive development is the fact that, despite government control over the media, public concern about emergency powers has found a voice, and that voice may be heard in Parliament.

It is clear from the 2007 emergency powers provisions that it is for Parliament to consider the validation of emergency decrees, although the Constitutional Court also has a limited role to play. It is right that, whatever the circumstances in which the powers are invoked, the matter should be required to be placed before Parliament at the earliest available opportunity and this is the thrust of the provisions. It is also right that if there is a constitutional challenge it should be made and determined promptly. In this respect the 2007 Constitution makes a slight improvement on the 1991 and 1997 versions by prescribing three days for the forwarding of any petition to the Constitutional Court. This does not of course say anything about the standards to be applied by the court in such cases. The only ground for interference is that 'the Emergency Decree is not in accordance with [s. 184 (1) or (2)]'; given the broad nature of those provisions it is clearly very difficult for the court to invalidate an emergency decree or even to limit the operation of any of its provisions. Conceivably the court has power only to check whether the stated purpose of a decree is consistent with s. 184. Indeed, given that Parliament cannot debate the decree until the court has given its verdict, a petition before the court might in practice actually delay the operation of parliamentary scrutiny. However, it should be noted that the court considers only whether the decree falls within the constitutional powers of the executive, whereas Parliament considers the substantive issue of whether the decree should be validated irrespective of whether there is legal power to make it – a much broader basis of scrutiny. Having noted this, it should also be pointed out that where the Constitutional Court has explained its reasons for not interfering with an emergency decree, it has simply said that the factual basis existed or that it was obvious to the public (for example, during the 1997–8 economic crisis) that such a factual basis existed. This would mean that the court does not consider the extent of executive discretion but simply whether the executive's judgement was substantively correct; this test could actually ensure that emergency decrees could not be used fraudulently or as an obvious over-reaction.

One other improvement on the 1997 version of emergency powers is that where the Constitutional Court rules an emergency decree unconstitutional this does not now have to be achieved by a two-thirds majority of the court. It is indeed very hard to see why a decree considered unconstitutional by, say, five members of a nine-member court, but considered constitutionally valid by four, should be deemed to be valid.

C. *Relationship to fundamental rights*

A further issue which is not made clear by the emergency powers provisions themselves is to what extent they allow overriding of other constitutional provisions in an emergency. They do not, for example, say that the fundamental rights provisions are suspended during an emergency, or restricted to a stated extent. Thus while there is in general no overriding of constitutional provisions by an emergency decree, law or regulation, emergency decrees are themselves laws, and the terms of particular constitutional provisions allow a restriction 'as provided by law' or 'by virtue of the law'. A pertinent example of this can be found in s. 32, of the 2007 Constitution, which grants a right to enjoy the right and liberty of life and person and prohibits torture, brutal acts or punishment by cruel or inhumane means, other than punishment under judgments of the courts or by virtue of the law. It further provides that arrest and detention of persons shall not be made except by order or warrant issued by the courts or where there is a ground as provided by law; and that search or acts affecting the right to liberty of life or person shall not be made except by virtue of the law. The combined effect of such provisions is that a law (including an emergency decree) may restrict a fundamental right, but such restriction is only allowed (i) by a specific law; (ii) only to the extent of necessity; and (iii) provided it does not affect the substance of the right. In general this constitutional dispensation delivers to the executive potentially enormous powers with some restrictions but little in the way of accountability; however, unlike the position in some constitutions, there is at least an obligation to bring the decree before Parliament at an early opportunity.

D. *Martial law*

Section 188 of the 2007 Constitution creates another executive power, quite distinct from emergency powers but again usual in the context of Thai constitutional history, to proclaim martial law, and this can even be done by the military itself in a particular locality as an emergency measure. It is difficult to see why this provision exists, given that in principle anything that could be done under a martial law decree could also be done under an emergency decree, yet a martial law decree does not require parliamentary scrutiny – or even in some cases scrutiny by any non-military arm of the executive. There is however a Martial Law Act which prescribes on a permanent footing the conditions for martial law rule. Martial law applied initially to the whole of Thailand and later to much of the country following the coup of September 2006, and was only partially rescinded, that is, restricted to parts of thirty-one, mainly border, provinces, shortly before the elections of December 2007, before being completely rescinded except for parts of the three disturbed southern provinces in April 2008. The permanent nature of exceptional powers is further reinforced by the Internal Security Act 2007, discussed below.

III. The Internal Security Act 2007

In this section, it is proposed to examine in some detail the Internal Security Act (ISA), which was passed in 2007 during the period in office of the military-appointed government of Surayud Chulanond (2006–8). This law represents current jurisprudence regarding national security, and, as we see with other countries under discussion in this volume, tends to obliterate the distinction between emergency powers and national security powers. The worrying aspect of the ISA is the extent to which it gives powers directly to the military and that these powers are conferred, not temporarily as an exception, but on a permanent footing. It remains a matter of speculation whether this relates to the precise situation in which the ISA was enacted – by an interim National Assembly appointed by the military-installed government under the Interim Constitution 2006, after the 2007 Constitution became effective but before the National Assembly elected under the 2007 Constitution was in session.[25] In January 2008 a new People Power Party government was appointed having a political colour close to the Thai Rak Thai Party which had been ousted from government by the military coup of 2006. A question mark against the ISA even before one looks at its provisions is why such a far-reaching measure was enacted, as a result of an initiative by a temporary government, by a temporary, appointed legislature under an interim constitution.

[25] For further discussion, see V. Muntarbhorn, 'A Very Dangerous Precedent: Ten Reasons against Thailand's Proposed New Law on National Security', *Bangkok Post*, 5 November 2007, p. 6.

Democratic normality is contradicted not only by the ISA's provisions but even by the circumstances of its enactment.

The ISA sets up an Internal Security Operations Board (ISOB) which formulates national security policy. This is implemented by an Internal Security Operations Command (ISOC), which has power to give directions even to civilian public servants. In this capacity the ISA imposes restrictions, potentially imposed simply by executive decision, on liberty of the person (2007 Constitution, s. 32), liberty of dwelling (s. 33), liberty of travel and residence (s. 34), liberty of communication (s. 36), freedom from forced labour (s. 38), property rights (s. 41) and freedom of assembly (s. 63).[26]

The preamble to the ISA cites security problems 'at present' threatening the independence and integrity of the realm, and justifies the creation of a principal agency for national security 'to resolve the threats promptly and completely'. The necessity of such a law is attributed to a need to guard against threats which may arise in times of normalcy, and to lay down measures to be used at times when a security threat has arisen in any area to regulate the use of power according to the level of seriousness of the situation, so that it may be resolved efficiently and with unity. The ISOC would have responsibility to integrate and co-ordinate actions between government offices and promote public participation in preserving security.

Leaving aside the curious ambiguity of the preamble regarding the particular situation of its enactment as against the general nature of the need for such legislation in 'normal' times, the inspiration for the ISA seems to lie in approaches which were taken during the 1970s and 1980s to deal with the threat of communist terrorism. The essence of this approach, which drew on the experience of British Malaya in dealing with a similar type of threat during the 1950s, was to deal with terrorism as a community issue and separate the terrorists from communities which were sources of sustenance, information, recruitment and logistical support.

One of the most significant provisions of the ISA is s. 4 under which the Prime Minister has responsibility for the execution of the Act. In the draft ISA the Royal Army Commander was responsible, which would have created an intolerable situation of giving vast and permanent powers to the Army Commander, and seriously disturb the already problematical constitutional relationship between the civil and military powers.[27] In

[26] See above for the relationship between fundamental rights provisions and legislation.

[27] It was a purpose of the 1997 Constitution to confine the military to the barracks. As we have seen, in this respect it was unsuccessful.

effect the draft law had the potential to create an entirely separate and parallel, military, government. Under s. 5 the ISOC is to operate from within the Prime Minister's Office, the Prime Minister being the Director of Internal Security and the Army Commander being Deputy Director. The Cabinet determines the organisation of the ISOC, so that the Prime Minister possesses his powers under the ISA as head of the government subject to normal principles of cabinet government. However, the Prime Minister also has power under s. 5 to delegate his powers in writing to the Army Commander; for the same reason as with the draft law, this presents an alarming prospect. The ISOC has responsibility for maintaining internal security, defined in s. 2 as 'operations to control, resolve, and restore any situation which is or may be a threat in order to restore normalcy for the sake of peace and order of the people, and the security of the nation, including prevention against such a situation'. The relationship of the ISA to emergency powers as such is clarified by s. 14, which states:

> Should any matter arise which affects internal security but which does not yet require the declaration of a state of emergency under the Act on Government Administration in a State of Emergency, and this matter has a tendency to persist for a long time, and falls under the power and responsibility for solving problems of several government agencies, the Cabinet shall pass a resolution for ISOC to take responsibility for prevention, suppression, and eradication or mitigation of this matter which affects internal security, within an assigned area, and shall make a general announcement of this fact. In the event that the matter in paragraph 1 subsides or can be overcome within the powers of the government agencies which have normal responsibility, the Prime Minister shall declare that the powers of ISOC as assigned under paragraph 1 are revoked.

The ISOC is also overseen by the ISOB, comprising senior members of government, civil service and military (s. 9), and lies at the head of a potentially vast administrative network comprising Regional and Provincial ISOCs each advised by an advisory board comprising people trusted in all parts of the region or province in question (ss. 10–13), as well as 'special operations centres' (s. 16). Section 5 specifically gives the ISOC Director power to 'undertake juristic acts, prosecute or defend lawsuits and perform any actions in connection with lawsuits which are related to the duty of the ISOC, acting in the name of the Prime Minister's Office'. The implications of this provision are potentially alarming in taking control over prosecutions and security-related lawsuits away from the prosecution authorities and the Attorney-General, who are accountable, and giving them to the military, who are not.[28]

The powers and duties of the ISOC are set out in ss. 6 and 15, and include the expected powers of monitoring, investigating, evaluating, reporting and making proposals on internal security matters as well as directing and co-ordinating action, and (remarkably) overseeing government agencies if assigned this task by the Cabinet. Even more remarkably, in language redolent of the period of right-wing dictatorship in the 1940s and 1950s, ISOC has the power and duty to 'encourage people to be aware of their duty in upholding nation, religion, and king; to build love and unity among people in the nation; as well as to promote popular participation in preventing and overcoming various problems which affect internal security and the peace and order of society'. More generally the ISOC has powers to prevent, suppress, eradicate or mitigate a matter assigned under s. 14; to draw up a plan of execution for approval by the ISOB; to oversee and expedite implementation of the plan; and, astonishingly, 'to order that any government official whose behaviour is a threat to internal security or an obstruction to the maintenance of internal security, be excluded from a designated area', which event requires the government agency in question to relieve the official of his duties.

In pursuance of matters falling under s. 14 the Director has powers under s. 17 to require government officials to perform or withhold performance of any action; to prohibit entry or exit at a locality, building or

[28] See also s. 18 which makes the Director or official designated by him an investigating officer for the purposes of the Code of Procedure for Criminal Investigation; and s. 19 which provides:

> Within the area assigned for ISOC operations under a Cabinet resolution in Section 14, if an investigating officer believes that any accused person has committed an offence which affects internal security as designated by Cabinet by mistake or out of ignorance, and that granting the suspect the opportunity to reform will be of benefit to the maintenance of internal security, the investigating officer shall submit records about that accused along with his opinion to the Director. If the Director concurs with the opinion of the investigating officer, the Director shall send the aforesaid accused to undergo training at a designated place for a period not exceeding 6 months and under any other conditions so designated in place of court proceedings, according to principles, methods, and conditions determined by the Cabinet. The procedure under paragraph 2 may be carried out only when the accused agrees to undergo training and abide by the aforesaid conditions. When the accused has undergone training and fulfilled all the conditions, the investigating officer shall submit the matter to the public prosecutor to order the withdrawal of the case under his responsibility, and when the public prosecutor has ordered the withdrawal of the case against the accused, nobody shall bring charges against the accused for the same offence.

designated area; to prohibit exit from dwelling places within a designated time; to prohibit meetings or gatherings in public places when it appears that those meetings or gatherings will create inconvenience for the people using that public place, and may give rise to public disorder; to prohibit the carrying of weapons outside dwelling places; to prohibit the use of communication routes or vehicles or to impose conditions on the use of communication routes or vehicles; to order persons to perform or not perform any action in connection with electronic equipment in order to guard against danger to life, limb or property of the people. Violation of a regulation under s. 17 involves a penalty of imprisonment for up to one year.

Section 22, similar to the 2005 Decree, exempts any regulations, notifications, orders and actions under the ISA from the law on administrative procedures and the law on the establishment of the Administrative Court and procedure for administrative cases. Furthermore, s. 23 creates legal immunity for any official acting in execution of his duty under the ISA in respect of 'civil, criminal, or disciplinary liability if that official is acting under orders of a superior officer and has reasonable cause to believe that the order falls within the law and the action is appropriate to the cause, but with no abrogation of the rights of any person who suffers loss to petition for compensation from government according to the law on liability of officials for wrongful acts'.

These provisions are worrying in several respects. The vagueness of many of the provisions granting powers to the ISOC, and the lack of recourse to the courts or even to normal procedures of criminal justice creates the potential for widespread abuse of power and human rights violations without any recourse. The ISA places exceptional powers on a permanent footing, a phenomenon which seems to have become a regular feature of national security law during the international war on terror since 2001. It gives extraordinary powers to military as opposed to civilian personnel, thereby exacerbating the main problem that Thailand has been trying to deal with since 1992, namely defining a limited and appropriate role for the military.

Still, things could be worse. The military could have attempted to hold onto power in 2008 citing issues of national security. The ISA was amended in the course of its passage through the Cabinet and the legislature to reassert control over the ISOC by elected, civilian officials. While the ISA gives extensive powers to the military, and that is a major concern, at least the prospect of exclusively military powers was avoided. The ISA could also have contained even more draconian provisions with regard to freedom of expression, assembly and association, privacy and personal liberty. It does not, surprisingly, contain any provision for preventive detention, which forms part of the ordinary law of many Asian states.

But these are small compensations. The ISA moves Thailand, a country that has been making much progress in other areas of constitutional experimentation, further than before down the path of making the rule of law an exception, clothing the executive and the military with legal immunity, and arming it to the teeth with a veritable panoply of security laws comprising not just the ISA, but also the emergency powers in the Constitution, the Emergency Decree of 2005, which is still in force, the Martial Law Act, and many 'emergency' provisions of the Criminal Code. The government has indicated that it will implement the ISA 2007 in disturbed areas to combat drug-trafficking, in place of martial law.[29]

IV. Conclusion

Emergency powers in general present considerable difficulties for constitutionalists. It appears that every society recognises that there is a need for special executive powers of (at least) a temporary nature that go beyond what is permissible in normal times, and that these may be justified by a particular situation of danger presented by war, rebellion, insurgency or natural disaster, and perhaps other situations. We have seen that in Thailand a constitutional culture which validates what is otherwise an act of treason – overthrowing the elected government and legislature and the Constitution itself – inevitably also tends to entrench and 'normalise' what are in essence to be regarded as exceptional powers and provide for substantial areas of legal immunity quite apart from political or constitutional crisis situations. But additionally it can be seen that the 'deed'[30] whereby law and order are established and the Constitution settled (by no means an unknown facet of emergency powers even in Western jurisprudence) has proved extraordinarily elusive. It is as though when, in 1932, King Prajadhipok (Rama VII) reached an accommodation with the coup leaders and added the word 'interim' to the draft Constitution they presented for his signature, he condemned Thailand to a permanently interim constitution, which would only ever reflect rather than provide the basis of the current state of legality.

[29] 'End of Martial Law', *Bangkok Post*, 17 April 2008.

[30] Ramraj refers in Chapter 2, p. 43, to Bernard Williams, *In the Beginning was the Deed* (Princeton: Princeton University Press, 2005).

Such a situation is not entirely surprising and is in conformity with some other Asian states, but we should not be led into thinking that Thai legal culture in general regards the rule of law as trivial. The rule of law may be described here as a competing principle, and if we were to compare the field of emergency and national security powers with other fields relevant to the rule of law, a task which forms no part of this chapter but is undertaken elsewhere, we would see a much more nuanced picture in which elements of the rule of law have been successfully established, such as a system of judicial review of administrative actions in the administrative courts and the scrutiny of human rights issues by the National Human Rights Commission. Nor is a critical discourse around emergency powers, human rights abuses, military immunities and corruption absent; indeed a protest movement presently (in early December 2008) cripples government's ability to run the country and the Prime Minister is forced to carry out his functions from temporary accommodation, his office having been occupied by protesters. Ever since the horrors of the 1973 and 1976 military crackdowns, and the 1992 Black May incident, there has been an important strand of political opinion supporting democratic development, good governance and human rights. This political trend of popular protest, although in general aligned with the coup of 2006, which was ostensibly itself carried out in the interests of furthering constitutional reform, is probably the best hope for a long-term improvement in the control of emergency powers. As Ramraj has shown, it is plausible to see the establishment and maintenance of legality as an essentially ongoing political act, a project of the legal complex.[31] Constitutionalism in Thailand is therefore indeed a project rather than a fact, and presents paradoxes which are actually symptomatic of democratic transition. The project has achieved only very patchy success, and it may be some time before it truly engages with the major concerns of this chapter.

As we have seen in Thailand there is little in this context of emergency powers, positive or negative, that can be attributed to Thai legal culture (except perhaps the culture of military immunity, but even that is hardly found only in Thailand). Nonetheless, as Ramraj argues,[32] close attention is needed to the social and historical context of the legal and constitutional order, particularly in societies where constitutional norms are not firmly entrenched. This applies forcefully in Thailand, where the rule of law is difficult to establish firmly when any government or constitution can be overthrown with relative ease. The law imposes virtually no restraint on

[31] Ramraj, Chapter 2, p. 40. [32] Note 2 above.

executive powers in emergency and security contexts, and only public and international opinion act as anything near to a check at the present time. It is the expectation of many that the small but significant advances of the post-1992 period can be transformed over time from elements of political protest into living law.

Establishing a theory of emergency powers that deals with such situations is highly problematical. While it might be tempting to look to less formal mechanisms such as 'people power' or mass demonstrations, such as those in Bangkok during 2006, or even to entirely new forms of accountability, for example in the legislature, it seems that the only real constraint is a sense of legal restraint and moderation amongst those in power, and a politics that favours those values. Even so, there is clearly much that courts can do in terms of preserving as much legality as is possible. If the rule of law fails to hold the line against increasingly elaborated and *permanent* 'emergency' or 'national security' powers, then to be governed by tyrants with moustaches will undoubtedly prove to be our destiny.

12

Emergency powers and the limits of constitutionalism in Japan

MARK FENWICK

I. Introduction

If emergency powers are conceptualised as involving the partial suspension of the rule of law for reasons of necessity (political or otherwise), and the principal justification for such action is the long-term preservation of the legal order and various basic liberties underlying that order, then the so-called Northeast Asian developmental state, of which Japan is a prominent example, poses something of a conundrum. After all, a recurring feature of developmental state discourse has been the contention that the law has, at least historically speaking, played a limited role in regulating political and social life, and that the rule *of* law has not yet fully emerged.[1] It has often been suggested that the primary function of law within such states has been to bolster the position of the executive and to insulate, often 'extra-legal', administrative action from judicial scrutiny. This has been achieved by curtailing judicial independence and the scope of human rights, and has resulted in a greatly diminished zone of legality compared to other jurisdictions with comparable levels of economic development.

In the absence of a strong rule of law and human rights tradition one might conclude that the crucial elements that allow us to distinguish, in an analytically precise way, between a 'normal' and an 'emergency' situation are absent. This, in turn, casts some doubt on the necessity of constitutional or legislative provision for emergency powers or a 'state'

[1] For the classic statement on the Japanese developmental state, see C. Johnson, *MITI and the Japanese Miracle: The Growth of Industrial Policy, 1925–1975* (Palo Alto: Stanford University Press, 1981); and C. Johnson, *Who Governs Japan? The Rise of the Developmental State* (New York: Norton, 1994), chap. 6.

of emergency. In the absence of substantive legal constraints on executive action, why legislate for their suspension?[2]

At the very least, these preliminary concerns highlight the need to exercise some caution when transplanting to a Northeast Asian context arguments advanced in the contemporary English language debate on responding to emergency situations. After all, these arguments have been made against the backdrop of functioning, albeit imperfect, legal orders in which rule-of-law values and human rights are, relatively speaking, well entrenched.

One might then explore the possibility that a different dynamic is at work in a Northeast Asian context and that the distinction between the 'normal' and 'emergency' situation has a different basis and requires a different analytical framework. This line of inquiry raises a number of further questions: what does constrain the exercise of executive power under 'normal' circumstances if not the law, and are such constraints effective? What is being suspended in the emergency situation if not the rule of law? Finally, what is being preserved if not the long-term future of a legal order and the protection of certain basic liberties underlying that order?

This chapter will attempt to tackle in a tentative way some of these issues through a discussion of post-1945 Japan.[3] Perhaps unsurprisingly given its post-conflict and post-authoritarian origins, the Japanese Constitution contains no provisions pertaining to emergency powers. It is a classic 'business-as-usual' constitution with no mechanism for derogating from constitutional norms.[4] Article 11 states that the people 'shall not be prevented from enjoying any of the fundamental human rights' and that such rights are 'eternal and inviolate'. Article 97 affirms that 'the fundamental human rights guaranteed to the people of Japan' shall remain 'for all time inviolate'. Finally, Article 98 declares the Constitution to be the 'supreme law' and that any law, ordinance or government act that contravenes the

[2] A similar, albeit more stark version of this question or 'paradox' can be found in J. deLisle's account of emergency powers in China; see 'States of Exception in an Exceptional State: Emergency Powers Law in China' (Chapter 13), this volume.

[3] The discussion in this chapter is restricted to Japan and no conclusions about other developmental states in Asia or elsewhere will be offered. On this issue, see A. H. Y. Chen, 'Emergency Powers, Constitutionalism and Legal Transplants: The East Asian Experience' (Chapter 3), this volume; and deLisle, Chapter 13.

[4] Although the Japanese Constitution – unlike the German Basic Law (Article 79(3)) – does not have a provision explicitly prohibiting amendments of a certain kind, most Japanese constitutional law scholars think the effect of Articles 11 and 97 is to render respect for human rights unchangeable even by amendment.

Constitution shall be invalid. In fact, the only reference to an emergency of any kind is a provision, Article 54(2), empowering the Cabinet to convene a special session of the upper house of the national parliament 'in time of national emergency'. A reading of the plain text of the Constitution suggests that *all* government action, including that responding to a factual emergency, must comply with the Constitution.

Although several special laws contain provisions for emergency situations, they did not, until 2003, authorise a systematic derogation from constitutional norms. The Police Law, for example, authorises the Prime Minister to declare a 'national emergency' but the only significant legal consequence in such a case is that the national government temporarily assumes direct control over the prefectural (i.e. regional) police.[5] Although post-1945 Japanese law has made some provision for emergencies, until 2003 it had not made any legal provision for the widespread or systematic suspension of the constitutional order.

However, beginning in June 2003, a package of legislative measures were enacted (the so-called *Yūjihō*, i.e. 'Emergency' or 'Contingency Legislation'), which for the first time, empowered the executive in the event of an 'armed attack from overseas' to derogate from constitutionally guaranteed rights 'as necessary' and to deploy the Self-Defence Forces inside Japan. As such, the new legislative framework represents an important break in the post-war regulation of emergency situations.

At first glance, it might be tempting to interpret these events as a familiar tale of a liberal-democratic state retreating in the face of the post-9/11 'new normal' and, as such, evidence supporting those who argue that 'business-as-usual' constitutional arrangements are prone to naivety and hypocrisy in the face of perceived crises of a certain kind.[6] However, this chapter will set out to problematise this view. Rather than focusing exclusively on recent legislative developments, it proceeds from the assumption that in order to understand the contemporary Japanese situation *vis-à-vis* emergency powers a more expansive approach is required, one that situates recent events in the broader context of post-1945 debates on the rule of law and constitutionalism. The chapter, therefore, begins by characterising in

[5] See Police Law (*Keisatsu Hō*) No. 162 of 8 June 1954. Chapter 6 (Articles 71–5) deals with 'national emergencies'. National emergencies include such events as a foreign invasion, a large-scale natural disaster or a major internal disturbance. It is also worth noting that the Prime Minister can only implement these measures upon a 'recommendation' from the civilian-controlled National Public Safety Commission.

[6] See, in particular, O. Gross 'Chaos and Rules: Should Responses to Violent Crises Always be Constitutional?' (2003) 112 *Yale Law Journal* 1011.

rather general terms three well-documented features of post-war Japanese governance, namely the prevalence of 'extra-legal' executive action; judicial review as a facilitator of executive action; and the constraining effects of the political culture. In a preliminary way, these general features of the developmental state will be connected to the problem of responding to emergencies. Taken together, this part of the chapter argues that in a post-war Japanese context, the law has often failed to function as a powerful normative constraint on executive action, and that the rule *of* law has exhibited certain structural weaknesses. As a consequence, it is hard to distinguish between the *normal* (understood as the rule of law) and *exception* (understood as entailing, at least in part, the suspension of the rule of law) in Japan. As such, there has been a significant gap between the constitutional text and the realities of post-1945 Japanese governance.

The second part of the chapter will examine one major reason for the weakness of the rule of law, namely the *origins* of the Constitution. In particular, it will be suggested that a key legacy of the vexed origins of the Constitution is that it has inhabited and continues to inhabit a conceptual 'grey zone' in which it is something more than political fact but something less than full public law. The lack of normative force surrounding the Constitution explains, to a large degree, why the constraints on executive power in a post-war Japanese context have not been legal, or at least not to any significant degree, and provides a potent symbol of the complexities and ambiguities of the rule of law in contemporary Japan.

The final part of the chapter will then consider the recent enactment of emergency laws. It will be argued that carving a space for the exception within the legal order has not been primarily driven by the desire for rule of law legitimation. Instead, it is best interpreted as a symptom of the failures of constitutionalism, but also – more interestingly – as a challenge to the authority of the Constitution. Legislating the exception is a strategic move in an ongoing project on the part of conservative factions within the ruling elite to reinvigorate a process of constitutional reform designed to return Japan to the status of a 'normal country' *(futsu no kuni)*.

II. The developmental state, the rule of law and emergencies

A. *The prevalence of 'extra-legal' administrative guidance*

Administrative guidance (*gyōsei shidō*) refers to informal actions taken by administrative agencies without legally binding force that are intended to influence the actions of other private parties in order to realise some administrative aim.[7] Simple examples might be an official request to limit voluntarily the number of goods to be exported to a particular country or a request to a private party to comply with an extra-legal policy standard. The essence of administrative guidance is that the action undertaken by the public official is intended to persuade private entities into *voluntarily* co-operating with some purpose that the guiding agency deems desirable, despite the non-existence of any authoritative legislative or even administrative enactment on the question.

In Japan and abroad many commentators have suggested that 'extra-legal' administrative guidance of this kind is either unique to Japan (which it is not) or widely prevalent in post-war Japan (which it would appear to be). Administrative guidance has been praised as a flexible, responsive form of policy-making that was a key strategy in Japan's post-war industrial policy and a crucial factor in the remarkable post-war economic recovery. Alternatively, it has been condemned as an abuse of executive power that has undermined the separation of powers by empowering an unaccountable and secretive bureaucracy. Explanations why private parties comply with such administrative requests range from rational-choice theories (focusing on the negative effects of non-compliance) to the cultural (focusing on Confucian respect for authority).

The general attitude of the courts, at least when dealing with cases of administrative guidance involving *central* government, has been either to uphold the legality of the guidance or to avoid directly ruling on the issue. As such, courts have taken the 'voluntary' nature of compliance with such guidance at face value and as reason for precluding the need for legal grounds for administrative action. In the leading decision, the Supreme Court held that an administrative agency's prima-facie illegal delay in issuing a licence (in this case planning permission) would be justified if it was connected to efforts to resolve a conflict between private parties (in this case local residents who opposed the plan and the construction company).[8] A social obligation to comply with a government request to resolve a private conflict was thus given legal effect since the agency's intervention was aimed at prompting a negotiated resolution to a socially disruptive dispute. Interestingly, a substantial judicial opinion on the legality of administrative guidance as an instrument of national economic

[7] For the English language literature, see, in general, Michael Young, 'Judicial Review of Administrative Guidance', (1984) 84 *Columbia Law Review* 923, and Mark Ramseyer, 'Rethinking Administrative Guidance', in Masahiko Aoki (ed.), *Finance, Development and Competition Law* (Oxford: Oxford University Press, 2000).

[8] *Nakatani* v. *Tokyo Metropolitan Government*, 39 *Minshu* 989 (Supreme Court, 1985).

regulation has yet to be delivered in spite of the fact that such guidance is said to be very common.

Acting 'outside' of the law has thus been a routine feature of executive action in Japan. In the context of a discussion of emergency powers, however, the most interesting form of administrative guidance involves government agencies acting extra-legally to ameliorate an emergency situation. Given that such guidance has been prevalent under normal conditions, it is hardly surprising to discover that it has also been deployed as an instrument of crisis management.

Although there are a number of examples of central government utilising administrative guidance to this end from throughout the post-war period, the best-documented concerns the Ministry of International Trade and Industry's (MITI) guidance to the major oil companies in the middle of the 'oil shock' in December 1973.[9] At that time, in response to serious difficulties in the oil market and the possibility of social disorder, all the major Japanese oil companies agreed to harmonise their pricing and co-ordinate production levels. Such action was in clear violation of various criminal law provisions of the Antimonopoly Law. However, it was done at the express request of officials from MITI who were concerned about the disruptive effects of a sudden decline in oil supply and a resulting sharp rise in prices of important oil-dependent products, such as gasoline and kerosene. Crucially, MITI had no legal authority in issuing these instructions. In fact, MITI's request exceeded the powers conferred on the Ministry by emergency legislation enacted weeks earlier in response to the crisis. The oil companies were, therefore, from a legal point of view, free to ignore MITI's guidance, without fear of any formal reprisals.

Complicating the issue in this case, was the fact that the competition law regulator, the Fair Trade Commission (FTC), did not share MITI's view that a prolonged policy of price fixing was appropriate or necessary, and a criminal prosecution was initiated against several executives of oil companies that had participated in these illegal cartels. The case went to the Supreme Court, and one of the key issues was whether the defendants by complying with a clear direction from MITI had a justification for their actions that precluded a criminal conviction (the so-called 'illegality preclusion defence').[10]

In its ruling, the Supreme Court held that the cartel agreement among the oil companies was in violation of the criminal law provisions of the

[9] A compilation of materials on the 'oil shock' can be found in C. Milhaupt *et al.* (eds.), *Japanese Law in Context* (Cambridge, Mass.: Harvard University Press, 2003), chap. 11.

[10] *Japan* v. *Idemitsu et al.* 38 *Keishu* 1287 (Supreme Court, 1984).

competition law. However, the court held that if it had been entered into with the purpose of complying with 'legally appropriate' administrative guidance then the illegality of any such action would be precluded. The court ruled that administrative guidance would be 'legally appropriate' when (i) its purpose was 'to deal with an emergency situation and was necessary to avert social disorder'; (ii) the existing legal framework was 'inadequate' to deal with the emergency; and (iii) the guidance took an 'appropriate form' given the circumstances.[11] In applying this standard, the court deferred to MITI's evaluation of the situation and found that all three conditions were met. The court noted the rapidly changing circumstances and the necessity of price controls. However, illegality preclusion did not help the defendants in this particular case, as it was found that they did not simply follow MITI's instructions, but had taken additional actions not part of the original guidance. The effect of the judgment was to absolve MITI of any responsibility for their extra-legal but 'legally appropriate' action, but punish the oil companies for exploiting the situation to their own advantage.

The stance of the Supreme Court in *Idemitsu* has some superficial similarities with the kind of extra-legal approach to emergencies advocated by scholars such as Oren Gross.[12] On one interpretation, the *Idemitsu* standard informs public officials that they can act extra-legally when 'they believe such action is necessary for protecting the nation and the public in the face of calamity' and it adopts a mechanism for considering *ex-post* (in this case, judicial) ratification of such unlawful acts.[13] However, in contrast to Gross's model, the Japanese approach does not seem to require officials to openly and publicly acknowledge their actions nor does it seem to envisage popular deliberation of any kind. Moreover, the fact that the court formalises this doctrine into an, albeit vague, legal standard would appear to differ from the kind of *ad hoc*, particularistic process envisaged by Gross.

There is one further difference from Gross's model. Although the court seems to concede that such action is not *legally* authorised in the sense that it derives from the constitution, or any other law, it suggests that the act derives its normative force from *necessity*, conceived of in terms of protecting the national interest and social order broadly defined. However, in the court's formulation, necessity seems to function as something akin to a *source* of law, i.e. it is not that 'necessity has no law' but rather that necessity provides the administrative act with a certain

[11] *Ibid.* at 1295. [12] See Gross, 'Chaos and Rules'. [13] *Ibid.* at 1023.

legal quality – what the court calls 'legal appropriateness' – and this enables it to be incorporated into the legal order. From this perspective, the normal operation of a particular law (in this case, the Antimonopoly Law) is suspended whilst the law – understood in the broader sense of the legal order – remains in force. Of course, this approach is hard to reconcile with the doctrine of the supremacy of the constitution. Moreover, since it represents an attempt to incorporate the extra-legal into the legal order it is more akin to what Gross characterises as judicial 'accommodation'.

In summary, the distinctive feature of administrative guidance in Japan is not that it occurs, but the degree to which it occurs, and – more significantly – the fact that the courts have consistently allowed government agencies, particularly central government ministries, to engage in informal policy-making of this kind. Policy choices have thus been made without any prior legislative balancing of interests (or, as in the oil case, in spite of them) and courts defer to these political judgements of the executive, even when the requested actions are prima facie illegal. Extra-legal executive action has thus been a normalised means of governance and has been retroactively approved by courts. Given the fact that administrative guidance has been sanctioned during ordinary times, it comes as little surprise that an emergency situation is one of the principal grounds justifying such action.

B. *Judicial review as facilitator of executive action*

Article 81 of the Constitution states that the Supreme Court has the 'power to determine the constitutionality of any law, order, regulation or official act'. The prevailing view is that this article permits judicial review of statutes, orders and official acts, although only in the case of a concrete dispute. That is to say, there is no abstract judicial review of the kind found in Germany, for example. However, in exercising its powers of judicial review the Supreme Court has, according to most commentators, been extremely cautious, particularly in cases involving the executive.[14] Examples of this conservatism abound, from the recent decisions upholding the constitutionality of Prime Minister Koizumi's visits to Yasukuni Shrine, in spite of an apparently clear constitutional rule on the separation of state and religion, through to the very small

[14] For the most comprehensive English language review, see M. Ramseyer and E. Rasmusen, *Measuring Judicial Independence: The Political Economy of Judging in Japan* (Chicago: University of Chicago Press, 2003).

number of cases in which legislation (which in a Japanese context is executive-driven) has been declared unconstitutional (less than ten cases in over sixty years). Moreover, in the context of criminal procedure, the extensive constitutional protection afforded to defendants and suspects in criminal investigations has been neutralised by the judiciary on the grounds of the public interest in crime control.[15] And, as we saw in the previous section, the courts have been unwilling to challenge the administrative guidance of central government.

Of particular importance in the context of a discussion of judicial review and emergency powers has been the Supreme Court's development of an expansive conception of the political question doctrine, notably as a strategy for avoiding decisions on the constitutionality of the Self-Defence Forces (SDF) and other politically sensitive issues. In the so-called *Nike II* case the plaintiffs challenged the government's decision to construct an anti-aircraft base in a forest near the town of Nike.[16] One claim by the plaintiffs was that the existence of the military base violated Article 9 of the Constitution. As is well known, Article 9 – the so-called pacifism clause – 'renunciates' war and prohibits 'the maintenance of any war potential'. However, successive Japanese governments have argued that Article 9 was never intended to infringe upon Japan's inherent right to self-defence in international law and that retaining the minimum military potential necessary to defend Japan from attack is constitutional (hence the SDF).[17] However, in the post-war period a number of legal challenges have been made against the government position; not surprisingly, as this is one of the most controversial issues in Japanese politics. On appeal of *Nike II* to the Supreme Court, the court rejected the plaintiff's claim on the grounds that the question of the constitutionality of the SDF was non-justiciable and in the course of the judgment expanded upon the political question doctrine.

As presented by the court, the power of judicial review contained in Article 81 is subject to the requirement that it does not infringe on the

[15] See D. Johnson, *The Japanese Way of Justice: Prosecuting Crime in Japan* (Oxford: Oxford University Press, 2001).

[16] *The Ministry of Agriculture, Forestry and Fisheries v. Ito* et al. 27 *Gyosai Reishu* 8 (1974). An edited translation of *Nike II* can be found in L. Beer and Hiroshi Ito (eds.), *The Constitutional Case Law of Japan, 1970 through 1990* (Seattle: University of Washington Press, 1996) pp. 83–7.

[17] On the recent history of Article 9 debates, particularly in the context of the post-9/11 'war on terror', see M. Fenwick, 'Japan's Response to 9/11', in V. V. Ramraj, M. Hor and K. Roach (eds.), *Global Anti-Terrorism Law and Policy* (Cambridge: Cambridge University Press, 2005), pp. 327–50.

basic principle of the separation of powers underlying the Constitution. However, the separation of powers has not been understood by the court in *formalistic* terms (i.e. the legislature makes law, the executive implements law and the judiciary interprets the law) nor in *instrumental* terms (i.e. the view that the separation of powers is a *means* of upholding certain basic values of the rule of law or legality that underscore the legal order). Instead, the separation of powers has been understood by the Supreme Court as the responsibility of the judicial branch to defer to the 'specialized and technical judgment' of the executive in 'politically sensitive' cases.[18]

More specifically, the test developed in *Nike II* states that in cases where (i) 'the meaning of a legal rule is not clearly obvious' (i.e. there is room to 'establish logically contradictory interpretations') and (ii) the issue concerns political matters, then the court should refrain from deciding the case in order to avoid the 'social and political confusion' that might ensue from a judicial decision.[19] 'Politically sensitive' cases are defined in rather vague terms, as those matters 'concerning essential state affairs', including issues that 'directly affect the preservation of the nation'.[20] In *Nike II*, the court held that Article 9 fell squarely within this class of cases and declined to address the issue of the constitutionality of the SDF.

A comparison with the US Supreme Court's approach to this issue is instructive. In the landmark ruling of *Baker* v. *Carr*, the court identified six situations where it would be appropriate for the Supreme Court to refrain from a ruling on the grounds that it is a political question:

> [A] textually demonstrable constitutional commitment of the issue to a coordinate political department; or a lack of judicially discoverable and manageable standards for resolving it; or the impossibility of deciding without an initial policy determination of a kind clearly for non-judicial discretion; or the impossibility of a court's undertaking independent resolution without expressing lack of the respect due coordinate branches of government; or an unusual need for unquestioning adherence to a political decision already made; or the potentiality of embarrassment from multifarious pronouncements by various departments on one question.[21]

However, most contemporary US constitutional law scholars agree that the only real components of the political question doctrine are the first two, namely a textually demonstrable transfer of authority to a political

[18] *Nike II*, at 116. [19] *Ibid.* at 117. [20] *Ibid.*
[21] *Baker* v. *Carr*, 369 US 186, 217 (1962).

branch or the lack of judicially manageable standards.[22] This contraction in the scope of the doctrine is usually explained by the emergence and acceptance over the last thirty years within US political and legal culture of a strong form of judicial supremacy.

In a Japanese context, however, a similar contraction in the scope of the doctrine has not occurred. Take the Article 9 jurisprudence as an example.[23] Article 9 does not express a *clear* transfer of authority to the political branch nor does it obviously involve a lack of judicially manageable standards. As such, according to the modern US standard, Article 9 would appear to be justiciable. In contrast, the Japanese court seems to rely on variations of the other four factors listed in *Baker* v. *Carr*, notably a lack-of-respect rationale (framed in terms of deference) and a potentiality-of-embarrassment (resulting in uncertainty and disorder) rationale. However, the Japanese court's principal argument for the non-justiciability of Article 9 cases – namely the politically sensitive subject matter – is not obviously covered by any of the *Baker* v. *Carr* components.

Moreover, the Japanese Supreme Court's hollowing out of the separation of powers doctrine suggests that a comparable doctrine of judicial supremacy has not yet emerged. Various explanations have been advanced for this, namely the fact that Japan has a parliamentary rather than a presidential system, and the fact that the executive and legislature are controlled by a single political party.[24] However, even within parliamentary systems, particularly so within those with written constitutions, the courts are duty-bound to uphold the law. In a Japanese context, it is hard to avoid the conclusion that the Supreme Court has used the political question doctrine in an expansive way in order to avoid a political backlash whilst giving a veneer of legality to a judicially sanctioned suspension of certain controversial constitutional norms.

[22] See M. Tushnet, 'Law and Prudence in the Law of Justiciability: The Transformation and Disappearance of the Political Question Doctrine' (2002) 80 *North Carolina Law Review* 1203.

[23] Constitution (1947), Article 9: 'Aspiring sincerely to an international peace based on justice and order, the Japanese people forever renounce war as a sovereign right of the nation and the threat or use of force as a mean of settling international disputes. (2) In order to accomplish the aim of the preceding paragraph, land, sea, and air forces, as well as other war potential, will never be maintained. The right of belligerency of the state will not be recognized.'

[24] See S. Calabrasi, 'The Virtues of Presidential Government' (2001) 18 *Constitutional Commentary* 51, and Ramseyer and Rasmusen, *Measuring Judicial Independence*.

C. *The constraining effects of factionalism and consensus politics*

It would be a mistake, however, to conclude from the absence of effective *legal* constraints on executive power that successive post-war Japanese governments have been especially powerful or that political power has been concentrated in either the hands of a few individuals within the higher echelons of the bureaucracy or the dominant Liberal Democratic Party (LDP). Instead, various embedded norms and practices within the political culture – in particular factionalism and the demands of consensus politics – have acted as a strong and effective check on executive action. Although the task of mapping this political constitution is principally one for political scientists and historians, it is worth highlighting a number of important points.

Most commentators on Japanese politics seem to agree that it has been the elite bureaucracy (i.e. high-ranking officials within the national-level ministries) who have been the crucial actors in post-1945 Japanese decision-making, drafting all legislation, controlling the national budget and inspiring all of the major policy initiatives.[25] Even those revisionists who have sought to emphasise the role of pressure groups, politicians or business leaders have done so by focusing on the ability of these other actors to exert influence over the bureaucrats.[26]

Although a full review of this debate is not necessary, it is worth noting that accounts of elite bureaucrats emphasise factionalism and territorial consciousness (*nawabari ishiki*) as key features of the bureaucratic culture. A characteristic feature of decision-making in Japan, therefore, has been the prevalence of internal bureaucratic disputes, factional in-fighting and conflict between officials from different ministries.[27] Intense rivalry among officials has prevented any one group from achieving general dominance over Japanese policy-making. Similarly, in spite of the fact that Japan has been governed for most of the post-war period by a single party (the LDP) or a coalition led by the LDP, Japanese politics is also highly factional with party loyalty coming

[25] K. van Wolferen, *The Enigma of Japanese Power: People of Politics in a Stateless Nation* (London: Vintage, 1990), chap. 5.

[26] M. Muramatsu and E. Krauss, 'Bureaucrats and Politicians in Policy-Making: The Case of Japan' (1984) 78 *American Political Science Review* 126.

[27] Johnson, *Who Governs Japan?*, chap. 6. In 2001 an attempt was made to reorganise the bureaucracies and introduce greater political control. By most accounts, however, these measures were only partially successful. See A. G. Mulgan, *Japan's Failed Revolution: Koizumi and the Politics of Reform* (London: Asia Pacific Press, 2002).

second to loyalty to the clique (*habatsu*) to which a particular politician belongs.[28]

The effects of this institutionalised factionalism are compounded by a second feature of Japanese political culture, namely a requirement of consensus in policy-making and executive action. Although the issue of consensus politics is debated among scholars, it is clear that an aversion to winner-takes-all models of decision-making as well as to formal, public procedures for resolving disagreements remain a feature of the political culture. Consequently, territorial jealousies among ministries and agencies, which frequently turn into well-publicised policy 'wars' have, on many occasions, obstructed the formulation of policy. The requirement of consensus amongst all stakeholders on any particular issue has meant that *controversial* policy choices will almost certainly result in an intractable impasse and a veto from a ministry or political faction opposed to the proposal. This is even more the case given the absence of any independent means or criteria for breaking the deadlock caused by an unco-operative ministry that opposes a particular policy. The lack of mechanisms for negotiated consensus thus results in weak formal legal regimes that facilitate and, on occasion, require administrative guidance in order to function.

For example, the populist Junichiro Koizumi, Prime Minister from April 2001 to September 2006, found his neo-liberal economic reform programme frustrated by obstacles of this kind. The ministerial bureaucrats consistently blocked initiatives coming from the PM's office. Another source of obstruction was members of parliament who are organised into 'tribes' (*zoku*) and control specific areas of policy. Such 'tribes' worked closely with the bureaucrats to block or at least delay changes to the status quo, notably the 'privatisation' of the Post Office. Finally, the complex committee system of the LDP would often reject or dilute Koizumi's reform proposals, in spite of the fact he was party president throughout his tenure as PM.[29]

Of course, as Koizumi found, the more controversial the policy issue the more likely deadlock is to ensue. For example, the conflict mentioned above between MITI and the FTC over the content of the emergency legislation responding to the 1973 'oil shock' is a good example of such a dispute. It was precisely because the FTC was unwilling to concede the necessity of legalising cartels that MITI felt compelled to act extra-legally

[28] See J. A. A. Stockwin, *Governing Japan: Divided Politics in a Resurgent Economy* (Oxford: Blackwell, 2008).

[29] See Mulgan, *Japan's Failed Revolution.*

in order to avert catastrophe. More generally, the desire on the part of certain conservative elements within the LDP to amend the Constitution or to enact legislation that would empower the SDF's public order role was, for similar reasons, frustrated for most of the post-war period. The institutional culture has acted as a powerful check on executive power. But the price of this inability to act has been weak formal regimes that create an incentive to engage in the kind of extra-legal activities outlined in section II.A above.

A number of commentators, notably Mark Tushnet, have recently drawn attention to the way that *political* constraints can promote rule-of-law values extra-legally as it were, and that one need not be committed to 'the exclusivity of law as a system of normative regulation of state power'.[30] Tushnet describes how a 'moralised politics', in which political leaders appeal for popular support on the basis of moral claims, might function as a powerful normative constraint, particularly in an emergency situation.

A necessary, if not sufficient, pre-condition for the successful operation of this kind of 'normatively infused politics', however, would seem to be that public officials and politicians are closely attuned to public opinion. In a Japanese context, this structural feature is lacking, or at least counter-pressures may be of greater significance. Although in recent years a more populist style of politics has emerged, for most of the post-war period public opinion did not act as a particularly important constraint on any of the key actors in the policy-making process on account of the sequestration of the political and bureaucratic elite. In contrast to the United States, for example, where the presidential appointment of many leading civil service positions results in greater diversity in the background of civil servants, and frequent moves between civil service and employment in other sectors such as academia, law firms and private business, the Japanese system is based on a career bureaucracy that ties decision-makers closely into the state apparatus while keeping them at arm's length from the populace. The same point also applies to the judicial and legislative branches as well. In the judicial branch, American judges and prosecutors are elected officials in many jurisdictions while their Japanese counterparts are life-tenured civil servants. The difference holds further for the legislative branch, where American legislators are only loosely tied to their parties. Political parties

[30] See, for example, M. Tushnet, 'The Political Constitution of Emergency Powers', in V. V. Ramraj (ed.), *Emergencies and the Limits of Legality* (Cambridge: Cambridge University Press, 2008), pp. 145–55.

may endorse candidates, but candidates have to win primaries, that is to say, they are nominated directly by the constituents. Japanese politicians, in contrast, are nominated by highly organised and bureaucratised national parties that exert greater control over their activities. In particular, LDP candidates/politicians are bound to the faction or political clique that promotes their candidacy. As a consequence of these structural differences, the attention of American politicians and officials, as compared to their Japanese counterparts, is much more attuned to public opinion polls and other measures of their constituents' opinions and anxieties.

III. The limits of constitutionalism

In the Introduction it was suggested that on a plain reading of the text Japan has a 'business-as-usual' constitution in the sense that it makes no explicit provision for either the suspension of, or derogation from, constitutional norms. The language of the Constitution, therefore, seems to assume that *all* government action, including that carried out in response to an emergency situation must comply with rights guaranteed in ordinary times and be in accordance with the principles of legality. On paper, Japan has a model liberal constitution.

The previous section, however, sought to complicate this picture, by identifying three aspects of governance in post-war Japan and showing how they relate to the problem of responding to emergencies. It was revealed that, in practice, the ideals of the Constitution were not always attained, and that political constraints were more important. In this section, this line of argument will be developed by suggesting that the rule-of-law weaknesses identified above are intimately connected with the limits of post-war Japanese constitutionalism. A full account of these limits is beyond the scope of this chapter, but in this section one crucial explanatory factor, namely the origins of the post-war Constitution will be considered.[31] The ongoing controversy surrounding this issue highlights an important point, namely the relationship between the origins of a constitutional order, the legitimacy of that order and the willingness of a state to maintain a commitment to that order during times of crisis. Moreover, as we shall see in the final section of this chapter, the controversy surrounding the origins of the Constitution is important for an understanding of the recent enactment of emergency legislation.

[31] A full account of this issue would also need to consider, in particular, the circumstances and legacy of the reception of Western law in the late nineteenth century.

The problem of the legitimacy of the Japanese Constitution is well known. Stated simply, the status of the Constitution remains, to this day, one of the most divisive issues in Japanese politics and society.[32] Given the high procedural requirements for constitutional amendment (two-thirds majority in both chambers of Parliament and majority support in a national referendum), this controversy explains, in large part, why no amendment of the Constitution has been attempted, much less achieved. Much of this controversy is connected to the origins of the Constitution.[33] This debate largely focuses on whether the Japanese Constitution was imposed (*oshitsuke*) by the United States occupying forces or whether it reflected the genuine post-war aspirations of the Japanese people.

Generalising somewhat, there are two standard responses to the question of whether the Constitution was imposed. On the one hand, there are the conservatives and nationalists who regard the Constitution as a simple case of victor's justice, lacking legitimacy of any kind. In particular, they object to Article 9 (the renunciation of war/demilitarisation clause), the downgrading of the status of the Emperor and the imbalance between citizen rights, of which there are many, and duties, of which there are very few (most significantly, the duty to pay tax). Moreover, the lack of any obligation on individuals to be 'loyal' to the state is regarded as a serious weakness that has resulted in various social problems, such as crime and the breakdown of traditional notions of filial duty.

Conservatives point to the fact that the Constitution was drafted without serious Japanese input.[34] It is certainly clear that the original draft of the Constitution was written in English at the GHQ of US forces in Tokyo over the course of 4–10 February 1946. This occurred after the commander of the US occupation, General Douglas MacArthur, became frustrated at the slow pace and lack of imagination in the proposals coming from the Japanese side and ordered his staff to draft a text.

[32] See N. Field, *In the Realm of the Dying Emperor: Japan at Century's End* (London: Vintage, 1991).

[33] Classic accounts include R. E. Ward, 'The Origins of the Present Japanese Constitution' (1956) 50 *American Political Science Review* 980; C. Whitney, *MacArthur: His Rendezvous with History* (New York: Norton, 1956); and J. Maki, 'The Documents of Japan's Commission on the Constitution' (1965) 24 *Journal of Asian Studies* 475. For contemporary accounts, see S. Koseki, *The Birth of Japan's Post-War Constitution* (New York: Westview, 1997); and J. Dower, *Embracing Defeat: Japan in the Aftermath of World War II* (London: Penguin, 1999).

[34] See generally, S. Yoshida, *The Yoshida Memoirs* (New York: Houghton Mifflin, 1962). (Yoshida was Prime Minister at that time.)

Of the twenty-four individuals involved in this drafting process ('GHQ's Constitutional Convention'), none was Japanese and sixteen were officers in the US military, although none had a professional military background. Four had previously worked as lawyers, with the others coming from a variety of professions. Only three of the participants had any real experience or knowledge of Japan, and only one, a civilian, Beate Sirota (a twenty-two-year-old Austrian woman who had been to high school in Tokyo before the war), was fluent in Japanese.

More controversial is the 13 February meeting at which the English draft was presented unannounced to select members of the Japanese Cabinet. The exact events of that meeting are hotly contested. In his account, Joji Matsumoto – the government minister and Tokyo University law professor whose modest proposals for constitutional reform were rejected by MacArthur after they were leaked to the *Mainichi Shinbun* – suggests that threats to the personal safety of the Emperor were used in order to coerce the Cabinet into accepting the draft.

The alternative view of whether the Constitution was imposed is associated with more social democratic strands of Japanese political thinking and emphasises the emergence of a popular democratic reform movement in the period between the Japanese surrender in August 1945 and the promulgation of the Constitution in November 1946, in order to support the contention that the Constitution does indeed reflect Japanese values and aspirations, irrespective of the precise circumstances that surrounded its drafting. The argument made is that the democratic and pacifist values contained in the Constitution emerged out of Japan's painful experience of authoritarian rule and military defeat. The apparent reservations of the post-surrender government are dismissed on the grounds that they were the remnants of a discredited authoritarian regime. Proponents of this view are inclined to oppose any kind of constitutional reform on the grounds that it might instigate a descent into authoritarianism or militarism.

This view is given strong support by John Dower in his Pulitzer Prize winning account of post-war Japan.[35] Dower concedes that the Constitution was imposed on the Japanese *government* but that it did embody the wishes of the long-suffering Japanese *people*, i.e. the conservatives are wrong to insist the Constitution was imposed on *Japan*, and the distinction between people and government is vital. In making this argument, Dower places a great deal of emphasis on several factors. First, he describes

[35] See Dower, *Embracing Defeat*.

popular – largely liberal-democratic and leftist – initiatives for a new national charter that emerged particularly in the wake of the publication of the discredited Matsumoto Committee's reform proposals.[36] Second, Dower stresses the role of Beate Sirota.[37] The reason Dower emphasises her role is rather obvious: as the only person capable of reading these popular reform proposals in Japanese (none of which were translated) she is presented by Dower as a conduit for the aspirations of the Japanese people in the drafting process. Finally, Dower shows how in the process of translating the English draft the Japanese exerted influence over the content of the final version.

The scope of this part of the discussion is relatively well known, in large part as a result of the recent historical research conducted by scholars like Dower and Koseki. The issue is complicated, however, by a second problem with the Constitution. This relates to a much less well documented aspect of the Constitution that both sides in this debate – albeit for different reasons – often seek to obscure, namely the precise role of the Emperor in its promulgation.

A notable feature of the post-war Constitution is that it was formally enacted as an *amendment* to the Meiji Constitution of 1889. This was because the US government, and MacArthur in particular, believed that the Japanese people would be more willing to accept a new national charter if it was presented to them by the Emperor. Once it was decided to utilise residual loyalty to the Emperor as a means for facilitating a transition to democracy, it made sense to introduce the new Constitution as an amendment. However, this decision had important procedural implications. Under the terms of the Meiji Constitution any amendment had to be initiated by an Imperial order and ultimately depended on Imperial approval.[38] An Imperial Rescript, therefore, authorised what in substance was the complete dismantling of the Meiji Constitution, but was formally speaking, a series of amendments to it.[39]

[36] *Ibid.* pp. 351–5.

[37] *Ibid.* pp. 365–7. Dower suggests that it was Sirota's influence that resulted in many of the Constitution's more progressive provisions, notably gender equality.

[38] Imperial Constitution of Japan (1889), Article 73.

[39] Constitution (1947), Imperial Rescript: '*I* rejoice that foundation for the construction of a new Japan has been laid according to the will of the Japanese people, and *hereby sanction and promulgate the amendments of the Imperial Japanese Constitution . . . made in accordance with Article 73 of the said Constitution.* Signed, Hirohito, Seal of the Emperor, Twenty Sixth year of Showa, November 3 1946' (emphasis added).

It is interesting to note that this Rescript is often omitted from both English and Japanese versions of the Constitution.[40] Reprints of the Constitution usually begin with the Preamble.[41] The reason for the omission of the Rescript is perhaps rather obvious. Its very existence exposes something of a contradiction at the core of the post-war Japanese Constitution, namely *who* is the precise source of its legitimacy: the People (the 'We' of the Preamble) or the Emperor (the 'I' of the Rescript)? Was the Constitution a parting gift from a divine Emperor or a genuine expression of the democratic will of the People?

The existence of this doubt as to the precise identity of the constituting power of the new constitutional order poses a problem for both sides in the political debate on the legitimacy of the Constitution. Those on the right (who disapprove of the Constitution or, at least, favour its revision) are forced to concede that the Emperor approved of the changes, whilst those on the left (who wish to defend the values of democracy and pacifism enshrined in the Constitution) are forced to confront the troubling fact that the new Constitution ultimately depended on the authority of an Emperor whom they blame for plunging Japan into a destructive period of authoritarian rule.

The ambiguity surrounding the identity of the constituting power of the new Constitution was a consequence of an intentional decision on the part of the US occupying forces. A recurring challenge of constitutionalism in the context of a transition to democracy is that a new constitution narrates a new collective identity that promotes identification with the new order and provides it with legitimacy.[42] The difficulty with this project is that if the addressees of the new constitution are to identify with the new order, then it must, at least in part, contain values and aspirations that exist in some form within that society. In the absence of such values, the temptation for any new liberal order, therefore, is to retain cultural myths or images from the old regime as a way of facilitating this process of transition. The danger of such a strategy, however, is that residual tensions will remain. The 'solution' in post-war Japan to this dilemma of

[40] The date of promulgation, 3 November 1946, was also one of some significance, as it would have been Emperor Meiji's ninety-fourth birthday. This is something that would not have been lost on Japanese people at that time.

[41] Constitution (1947), Preamble: '*We, the Japanese people . . . do proclaim that sovereign power resides with the people and do firmly establish this Constitution.* Government is a sacred trust of the people, the authority for which is derived from the people . . .' (emphasis added).

[42] On this issue, in general, see R. Teitel, *Transitional Justice* (Oxford: Oxford University Press, 2002).

transitional constitutionalism was to appeal to the pre-existing identity of 'Subjects of the Emperor' as a way of providing some moral authority to the new democratic order. However, by retaining the Emperor and then relying on his authority to introduce the Constitution, the legitimacy of the new order was undermined. As a consequence of this strategy, questions of responsibility for wartime atrocities, both international and domestic, were never satisfactorily resolved.

Ideally, any new constitutional framework must mediate the transition from authoritarianism and provide the basis for a new, more democratic, social order. But – as the Japanese experience shows – if that process of constitution-building is perceived as flawed the legacy of that illegitimate foundation will continue to haunt the legal and political culture for many years. This is particularly so during times of perceived crisis when a commitment to the values of that constitutional order are most likely to be tested, and when any failing in the legitimacy of a particular norm or the constitutional order, as such, can provide a convenient pretext for negating its intended effect.

IV. Carving a space for the exception and constitutional politics

The above discussion suggested that post 9/11 emergency legislation in Japan is not to be read as a familiar tale of a liberal-democratic state retreating from rule-of-law values in the face of the 'new normal'. This type of narrative presupposes a well-entrenched constitutional order and sections II and III of this chapter have sought to cast some doubt on this presupposition by examining the realities of post-war Japanese governance and the controversial status of the Constitution. However, if this argument is correct, it points to something of a conundrum: given the weak constitutional/legal constraints on executive action, why has it been necessary to legislate for their suspension? What have been the regime's objectives in pushing for legislation of this kind?

It is important to emphasise that the focus of the recent debate in Japan has been on legislating for *war* contingencies, and the key issues have thus been in delineating the domestic role of the SDF, the powers that would accrue to the Prime Minister and the rights and duties of citizens in the event of an armed attack on Japan. Japanese interest in war contingency legislation dates back to 1963 when the SDF secretly initiated an internal study of how to deal with a crisis on the Korean Peninsula. Two years later, revelations about the study touched off a heated debate in the Diet, with opposition parties criticising the SDF for preparing for war. In 1977, the then Prime Minister Fukuda formally established a study group within the Defence Agency to examine the issue. Although efforts were periodically made to introduce some form of war contingency legislation, they all failed. The last of these failures occurred in 2002 when three Bills failed because of parliamentary and media-driven opposition amid concerns about human rights protection. However, in June 2003, slightly amended versions of the Bills were enacted. A further package of legislation was introduced in 2004, and various amendments were made in each of the subsequent three legislative sessions. Significantly, these reforms authorised the suspension of constitutional norms by the executive and the domestic deployment of the SDF in the event of an 'armed attack' on Japan. A preliminary question that, therefore, needs to be addressed is why, after more than four decades of controversy and thwarted efforts, such legislation finally succeeded.

A number of factors accounted for the earlier difficulties in enacting such laws. First, for much of the post-1945 period the major opposition parties were the Social Democratic Party and the Communist Party. Both were strongly opposed to any such legislation on the grounds that it entailed acknowledging the legality of the SDF. As such, the whole issue of war contingency laws became entwined with the divisive question of whether the SDF was constitutional or not. Second, the powerful economic ministries (of Finance, as well as MITI) were fearful of the concentration of power that would accrue to both the Prime Minister and SDF if emergency powers were permitted, and therefore acted to veto such measures. A final consideration was the attitude of successive US administrations. Stated bluntly, for most of the post-war period there was no pressure from the USA on Japan to adopt a more 'active' security policy. At that time, the United States was comfortable with Japan's so-called 'check book' approach to diplomacy and international affairs. Consequently, the role of the SDF was strictly limited to self-defence (understood in terms of defending Japanese territory) and any attempt to empower the SDF by giving them a public order role during a state of emergency, for example, was deemed too controversial.

Significantly, all of the above factors changed over the course of the 1990s. First, there was a reconfiguration of the domestic political landscape in which the traditional leftist opposition parties declined in popularity and a new main opposition party – the Democratic Party – emerged.[43]

[43] See I. Neary, *The State and Politics in Japan* (Cambridge: Polity, 2005) for a history of post-war party politics.

Crucially, the Democratic Party was a breakaway of certain LDP factions, i.e. it was not ideologically united in its opposition to the SDF in the way that traditional leftist parties were and hence was much less opposed to acknowledging the existence of, or empowering, the SDF. As such, it supported the government by voting for the proposed legislation. In addition, there was also a generational shift in the LDP as older politicians, who, having experienced the war, took a principled stance on Article 9 and preferred a limited role for the SDF, stepped down to be replaced by a younger generation of more hawkish conservatives.

Second, there was the various internal administrative reforms introduced in 2001 that were designed to strengthen the power of politicians *vis-à-vis* the bureaucracy, and in particular to empower the Prime Minister's Office.[44] These structural reforms coincided with the election of Junichiro Koizumi as PM in 2001. With his populist, non-conformist style and reform agenda he was able to concentrate political power in a way that few post-war Japanese prime ministers had been able to achieve. On domestic policy, as mentioned above, his economic agenda was often frustrated as it placed him in conflict with his own party. However, at least on security policy Koizumi's nationalistic stance (evidenced by his continued visits to the Yasukuni Shrine and seeming disregard for relations with Asian neighbours, notably China and North Korea) and strong support for the United States' foreign policy post-9/11 (evidenced by the enactment of the Anti-Terrorism Special Measures Law in 2001 and SDF participation in military operations in Afghanistan and Iraq) earned him the strong support of certain more nationalistic factions of the LDP. Koizumi's strong personal commitment to *Yūjihō* was thus a key factor in its success. Specifically, it meant that the institutional constraints discussed in section II. C above could be overcome by an appeal to popular support for such measures.

Third, there has been a significant shift in the attitude of the United States toward Japanese security policy.[45] Post-1990 (i.e. after the first Iraq war), Japan was heavily criticised for its refusal to contribute military support for the operation to liberate Kuwait, in spite of the fact that Japan was a major importer of oil. Although Japan made a major financial contribution, the US government's criticism of Japan's limited role in

[44] See Mulgan, *Japan's Failed Revolution*.

[45] For recent studies, see H. Dobson, *Japan and UN Peacekeeping: New Pressures, New Responses* (London: Routledge, 2003); M. Green, *Japan's Reluctant Realism* (London: Palgrave Macmillan, 2003); and C. Hughes, *Japan's Re-emergence as a 'Normal' Military Power* (London: Routledge, 2005).

international affairs and its encouragement to play a more active security role contributed to a gradual expansion of the SDF's role post-1990. In 1992, the PKO Law permitted Japanese troops to participate in UN-sponsored peacekeeping operations. The events of 11 September 2001 led to further US pressure. Subsequent legislation permitted the deployment of the SDF in Afghanistan, Iraq and, most controversially, in support of the US 'war on terror'.[46]

Finally, US rhetoric over the 'Axis of Evil' and the 'new normal' – the notion that the current security threat is of indefinite duration and is intimately linked to the activities of certain 'rogue' states – allowed the Japanese government to connect the question of the necessity of emergency legislation with concerns over North Korean militarism.[47] There is no doubt that the success of enacting legislation empowering the SDF in international affairs, as well as the post-9/11 geopolitical climate, greatly encouraged the government to push through emergency legislation and created a political climate in which the whole issue of emergency legislation was less controversial than it was at any other time post-1945.

Although *Yūjihō* has involved the enactment of a number of new laws, as well as amendments to existing laws, perhaps the most significant of these laws are the Law Concerning Measures to Ensure National Independence in a Situation of Armed Attack, Law No. 79 of June 2003 (hereinafter SAAL) and the Law Concerning Measures to Ensure the Protection of the People in a Situation of Armed Attack, Law No. 112 of June 2004 (hereinafter PPSAAL). SAAL is significant because it establishes the general framework and basic principles for dealing with armed attacks, whereas PPSAAL provides much of the detail.

SAAL identifies the triggering conditions that authorise the Prime Minister to declare an 'armed attack situation'. Article 2 enumerates three situations, namely an actual 'armed attack' (Article 2(1)), the 'clear and imminent danger of such an attack' (Article 2(2)) or a 'tense situation' where an armed attack is 'forecast' (Article 2(3)). The law does not provide any real guidance as to what constitutes an 'armed attack', other than it must come from 'outside the country' (Article 2(1)). Although there is no general triggering condition – such as 'urgent necessity' – as is often found

[46] See Fenwick, 'Japan's Response to 9/11', for further discussion.

[47] Interest in the fate of Japanese citizens kidnapped by the North Korean regime in the 1970s and 1980s, as well as the launching of missiles over the Sea of Japan and the intrusions of 'spy ships' has undoubtedly played an important role in creating a mood of fear that has made it easier to generate public support for war contingency legislation.

in emergency powers laws, academic critics of the legislation were quick to remark on the vagueness of the wording of Article 2. In particular, it was pointed out that any 'armed attack' on SDF forces deployed overseas or even the 'anticipation' of such an attack would provide grounds to trigger an emergency situation *inside* Japan. Given the broad range of deployments in which the SDF is currently engaged, there is a genuine concern that the triggering conditions can be met at any time the SDF is engaged in operations. Such concerns may be rather far-fetched. However, fears about the vagueness of the triggering conditions were given real credence when Prime Minister Koizumi explicitly stated that 'war is not the only emergency', suggesting that terrorism and 'mysterious intruders' from overseas might be encompassed within the SAAL standard.[48] Although this kind of vagueness in legislative drafting is not unusual in a Japanese context, the particularly sensitive nature of the subject-matter in this instance, as well as the comments at the time of its enactment, have given rise to concerns about the scope of the legislation and the potential for abuse.

In the event of an 'armed attack situation' being declared, a broad range of powers would accrue to the Prime Minister. In particular, the PM can assume control over a number of 'public organs' including the Bank of Japan, NHK, public utility companies, as well as local government institutions. Moreover, Article 10 authorises the PM to convene a 'Special Security Council' consisting of 'experts in military affairs' as well as high-level bureaucrats to 'assist' the Cabinet in governing Japan in such a situation. At the time SAAL was enacted, a number of amendments were also made to the SDF Law to permit the domestic deployment of SDF in a public order role, as well as the military expropriation of land and other property and conscription of certain categories of workers (including doctors and engineers).

Of particular importance are SAAL, Article 3 and PPSAAL, Article 5, as both provisions relate to the protection of constitutional rights in an emergency situation. The provisions are very similar in content. PPSAAL, Article 5(1), in rather general language, affirms the importance of respecting the freedoms guaranteed by the Constitution. However, it is in Article 5(2) that one finds the punch line: constitutional rights and freedoms may be limited 'as necessary in order to protect the people'.

Article 5(2) does, however, impose three restrictions on such derogations: the curtailing of rights must be (i) the 'minimum necessary'; (ii) done 'according to fair and proper procedures'; and (iii) cannot

[48] *Asahi Shimbun*, 18 June 2003.

infringe upon certain rights, i.e. rights protecting equality before the law (Constitution, Article 14), freedom of expression (Constitution, Article 21) and freedom of conscience (Constitution, Article 19). These three constitutional rights cannot be curtailed but, by implication, all others can. It goes without saying that many rights are therefore subject to derogation on the grounds of necessity in the event of a prime ministerial declaration that an 'armed attack situation' has arisen. The law thus confers broad discretion on the executive, i.e. the PM, the Cabinet and the Special Security Council. The danger of this approach is that it is insufficiently attentive to the fact that some power cannot be controlled once authorised, or at least needs strong incentives within the political system to ensure that abuse does not occur. Whether the kind of political constraints described in section II. C are sufficient to this task is an open question.

A further distinctive feature of both SAAL and PPSAAL is the degree to which they are infused with the language of obligation, at least when compared to the Constitution. For example, SAAL, Articles 4–8 impose general obligation on local communities, local government and individuals to 'co-operate' with government. Chapter 10 of the PPSAAL provides for criminal sanctions in the event of non-compliance. As has already been noted, one of the objections of conservatives to the current Constitution is the imbalance between rights and duties. For example, the Preamble has long been the focus of LDP criticism of the Constitution and the insertion of a 'love-of-the-nation' clause a key element of their constitutional reform agenda. It is perhaps unsurprising, therefore, that the emergency laws emphasise the duty to obey the government.

Given the broad range of powers accruing to the executive, the system of checks and balances appears weak. SAAL, Article 9(4) requires legislative approval prior to the declaration of an armed attack situation. However, SAAL, Article 9(4)(2) says that this can be retroactive if circumstances prevent legislative deliberations. Furthermore, the parliamentary decision to approve the declaration is a one-off. There is no 'sunset clause', for example, that either time-limits or requires a renewal of a state of emergency. In the context of the 'new normal', when the threat is perceived to be of indefinite duration, the possibility of a semi-permanent state of exception is raised. Finally, since there is no abstract judicial review in Japan, challenging the constitutionality of the law, in the absence of an actual state of emergency, would seem to be difficult. And even in the event that the law were to be utilised it is hard to imagine that the Supreme Court would find against the executive in such a case, given its conception of the separation of powers and the political question doctrine, as well as its long history of deference to the executive.

A striking feature of the recent Japanese legislation is that although it provides a clear *legal* basis for curtailing constitutional rights and the creation of a new normative order, it has not involved a constitutional amendment of any kind. For the time being, the Japanese Constitution contains no provision for emergency powers. Constitutional norms can thus be suspended without any *constitutional* authorisation. Given the supremacy of the Constitution within the Japanese legal order, this seems to result in something of a contradiction. On the one hand, the Constitution states that the 'fundamental human rights guaranteed to the people of Japan' are 'inviolate' and that the Constitution is the 'supreme law'. On the other, a special law (i.e. a law that has to be in conformity with the Constitution to be valid) makes express provision for derogation from constitutional norms. A crucial feature in liberal accounts of the state of exception, namely that a constitution must suspend its own operation in order to justify the government acting outside of the law, is thus lacking in the Japanese context.

If the objective of the *Yūjihō* project were liberal rule-of-law legitimation (i.e. increasing legal and institutional control over public decisions and strengthening the principle of legality) it would seem hard to avoid the conclusion that the whole enterprise has been self-defeating. Surely, the recent legislation has merely served to further undermine the authority of the Constitution by effectively ignoring two fundamental principles of the legal order. The commitment to pacifism has been undermined by the acknowledgment of a conflict situation and respect for human rights has been undermined by the possibility of derogation from fundamental rights without constitutional authority.

However, it would be wrong to conclude that advocates of *Yūjihō* are unaware of these contradictions. Quite the contrary. Most Japanese liberals are convinced that the long-term agenda of those supporting *Yūjihō* is to expose the inadequacies of the Constitution and move closer toward constitutional reform. Public pronouncements by politicians from both major political parties stressed that without legislative provision for a war-like situation the lives of Japanese citizens would be in grave danger. This fuelled public anxieties that a 'business-as-usual' constitution is inadequate to the realities of the post-9/11 world. Similarly, by emphasising that what is at stake in wartime contingency legislation is the survival of the nation, a powerful appeal was made to everyday conceptions of nationality and political community that transcend the contemporary commitment to constitutionalism.

As mentioned above, conservatives – notably the ruling LDP – have long felt that the Constitution is lacking in legitimacy and in need of urgent reform. Although this process has a long and tortuous history it took on greater impetus with the publication in December 2005 of the LDP's long-awaited proposals for a revised constitution, as well as the enactment in May 2007 of a law regulating the national referendum that is required as part of the amendment process.[49] Revising Article 9 to acknowledge formally the existence of the SDF and to allow it greater operational freedom is obviously a key plank in the LDP's proposals. For conservatives, the ambiguous status of the SDF is a potent symptom of Japan's post-war 'abnormality'. As such, amending Article 9 is part of the constitutional reform process whereby Japan can once again become a 'normal country'. The war contingencies legislation is inextricably linked to that project.

Although there is no doubt that public debate on the status and content of the Japanese Constitution is vital, there does seem to be an inherent danger in approaching the issue of constitutional reform through the route of the status of the SDF, war contingencies and emergency powers legislation. This is particularly so in the context of the 'new normal' where these issues can be sensationalised in a way that monopolises the agenda and excludes other important questions from public discussion. As illustrated in the first part of this chapter, the law has not always functioned as an effective normative constraint on executive action. At the very least, this suggests that there are a number of rule-of-law concerns that also need to be addressed as part of the constitutional reform process. However, focusing the reform debate around issues that are inherently concerned with empowering the executive and imposing new duties on the people, as is currently the case, seems unlikely to result in these rule-of-law concerns receiving adequate attention. It should be emphasised, of course, that there are forces in Japanese society advocating such issues. The danger, however, is that these voices will be drowned out. And until these other issues are confronted, the ideals of liberalism that David Dyzenhaus identifies in his recent work on emergency powers – namely 'banishing

[49] The LDP draft can be found at www.jimin.jp. The proposals do not contain any general 'state of emergency' provision although revised Article 9(2)(3) does provide for the domestic deployment of the SDF in response to an emergency situation. It is debatable whether this provides sufficient constitutional authority for the SAAL in its current form.

the exception'[50] and 'affirming the normative desirability of the idea that the authority of the state is prior to law'[51] – may well remain frustratingly elusive in a Japanese context.

[50] D. Dyzenhaus, 'The State of Emergency in Legal Theory', in Ramraj *et al.* (eds.), *Global Anti-Terrorism Law and Policy*, pp. 65–89 at p. 73.

[51] D. Dyzenhaus, 'The Compulsion of Legality', in Ramraj (ed.), *Emergencies and the Limits of Legality*, pp. 33–59 at p. 58.

13

States of exception in an exceptional state: emergency powers law in China

JACQUES DELISLE

I. The puzzle of emergency powers law in a 'Chinese-style' regime

Laws governing emergency powers are a puzzle in China and similar systems. Despite changes since the Reform Era began in the late 1970s, China remains an authoritarian regime without a robust rule of law, strong constitutional restraints on state power and reliable legal protections for citizens' rights. Laws authorising or defining extraordinary authority are not the significant and controversial matters that they often are elsewhere, especially in liberal constitutional democracies.

A regime of China's type (at least in pure form) operates in a permanent, but almost never declared, state of emergency. Laws conferring special powers seem superfluous. China does not have the aspirationally or episodically liberal, democratic, rule-of-law constitutional order that Albert Chen, Raul Pangalangan, H. P. Lee, Andrew Harding[1] and other contributors to this volume describe as partly explaining frequent or lasting – if legally hard to justify – states of emergency in many Asian states. Even this dilute form of what David Dyzenhaus calls a 'compulsion of legality' would seem to have little purchase for PRC rulers.[2]

Conversely, a regime of China's type cannot easily bind itself to the mast. Laws articulating preconditions for extraordinary powers or restricting their scope seem meaningless. In China's constitution and politics, courts do not play the vigorous role in policing such legal commitments

[1] See, in this volume, A. H. Y. Chen, 'Emergency Powers, Constitutionalism and Legal Transplants: The East Asian Experience' (Chapter 3), R. Pangalangan, 'Political Emergencies in the Philippines: Changing Labels and the Unchanging Need for Legitimacy' (Chapter 15), H. P. Lee, 'Constitutionalised Emergency Powers: A Plague on Asian Constitutionalism?' (Chapter 14), A. Harding 'Emergency Powers with a Moustache: Special Powers, Military Rule and Evolving Constitutionalism in Thailand' (Chapter 11).

[2] D. Dyzenhaus, 'The Compulsion of Legality', in V. V. Ramraj (ed.), *Emergencies and the Limits of Legality* (Cambridge: Cambridge University Press, 2008), pp. 33–59.

that judiciaries are – or were – expected to perform in Western constitutional democracies, or the modestly constraining role that Arun K. Thiruvengadam envisions emerging in some Asian states in his chapter.[3] As Mark Fenwick argues for Japan in his chapter,[4] regimes lacking longstanding, secure commitments to the rule of law or law's central place in governance – a description applicable to China – find it hard not to blur distinctions between 'normal' and 'exceptional' conditions.

Nonetheless, China has adopted, and employed, laws addressing emergency powers. These include a 1982 constitutional provision on martial law (or states of siege), a 1996 Law on Martial Law,[5] a 2004 constitutional amendment on states of emergency, and a 2007 Emergency ('Sudden Incidents') Response Law.[6] Formal resort to such law has been rare and broader invocations of its norms opaque, but its development has been closely entwined with challenges the leadership has defined as profound.

China's rulers invoked the constitution's martial law provision in 1989 to address the Tiananmen Democracy Movement,[7] which they depicted as the gravest challenge to the regime since the Cultural Revolution, and unrest in Tibet, which was among the most serious eruptions of ethnoreligious discontent since the PRC's founding. The constitutional amendment and legislation on emergencies reflected lessons from the SARS crisis of 2003, in which a disease brought social panic and threatened serious economic harm.[8] Beijing issued the first major provincial implementing

[3] A. K. Thiruvengadam, 'Asian Judiciaries and Emergency Powers: Reasons for Optimism?' (Chapter 17), this volume.

[4] H. Fenwick 'Emergency Powers and the Limits of Constitutionalism in Japan' (Chapter 12), this volume.

[5] The Chinese term is *jieyan*, rendered in English as 'martial law' or 'state of siege'.

[6] The English term 'emergency' covers two Chinese terms. The constitutional provision, and a contemplated 'State of Emergency Law', address 'states of emergency [*jinji zhuangtai*]' while the statute is the 'Emergency [*tufa shijian*, or "sudden incidents"] Response Law'.

[7] The Tiananmen Democracy Movement began in April 1989, when students at Beijing universities mobilised after former Chinese Communist Party General Secretary Hu Yaobang died. He was widely regarded as a liberal reformer who had been ousted partly for being too soft on previous student protests. Initially focused on student concerns, the movement grew into mass action by tens of thousands of students, workers and other urban residents who occupied Tiananmen Square in Beijing (and other cities), pressing for wide-ranging democratic and liberal political reforms. The movement ended with a crackdown by People's Liberation Army troops on 4 June 1989.

[8] SARS (severe acute respiratory syndrome) appears to have originated in China in late 2002. By the end of the outbreak several months later, the pneumonia-like illness had affected more than 8,000 people, nearly two-thirds in China, and killed around 800, nearly half in China. World Health Organisation, *Summary of Probable SARS Cases* (2004), www.who.int/csr/sars/country/table2004_04_21/en/index.html. Analysts predicted that a moderately prolonged outbreak (lasting only nine months) could shave 2 per cent

regulations under the Emergency Response Law in anticipation of the 2008 Olympics (at which China's leaders would not countenance disorder) and against the backdrop of an earthquake in Sichuan and disturbances in Tibet (which were the worst natural disaster since 1976 and the most unsettling mass opposition since 1989).[9]

Why would China's rulers adopt and employ emergency powers laws? A simple, but incomplete, answer is that such laws appear nearly costless. In a residually Leninist order, altering the law remains relatively easy. Because laws do not strongly constrain the state, they present little evident risk to the regime and its prerogatives. Because legal protection of rights is already weak, mandates for exceptional power threaten only limited damage to such law and modest additional danger for possible victims of state action.

Another partial answer is that China no longer may be the type of regime for which emergency powers laws are unnecessary and empty. Three decades after the Cultural Revolution, China scores respectably in 'rule-of-law' measures, ranking at the forty-fifth percentile globally and above median for lower-middle-income countries.[10]

Neither a 'cheap talk' nor a 'developmental' account, however, resolves the paradox of China's emergency powers law. The former cannot account for the regime's sustained effort to develop legal frameworks for emergency powers, the authorities' reluctance to invoke those powers or critics' and reformers' ardent attempts to shape those laws and their interpretation. It overlooks the prospect that Chinese emergency powers law could have state-limiting and rights-protecting features analogous to those asserted by some analysts for liberal constitutional democracies. The latter explanation slights the problem that efforts to 'legalise' emergency powers may be futile or undermine rule of – or by – law in China as in more robustly law-governed systems. It invites unduly benign inferences that China's emergency powers law reflects – or will help achieve – a level of

off China's GDP growth while an epidemic would have had far worse consequences. E. X. Fang, 'SARS: Economic Impacts and Implications', Economics and Research Department Policy Brief Asian Development Bank, Manila, 2003, www.adb.org/Documents/EDRC/Policy_Briefs/PB015.pdf.

9 Beijing Municipality, Measures for Implementing the Emergency Response Law of the PRC (2008); 'Beijing Publishes Implementation Measures of Emergency Response Law', *Xinhua*, 22 June 2008; 'Emergency Response Law to be Implemented', *Xinhua*, 23 June 2008.

10 World Bank, *World Bank Governance Indicators, 1996–2008* (Washington: World Bank, 2008); J. deLisle, 'Traps, Gaps and Law: Prospects and Challenges for China's Reforms', in R. Peerenboom (ed.), *Is China Trapped in Transition? Implications for Future Reforms* (Oxford: Oxford Foundation for Law, Justice and Society, 2007), chap. 6, pp. 2–3.

legality higher than China has or soon will have, or than its rulers will accept.

If one assumes Reform Era PRC leaders seek capacity and discretion to address challenges while limiting costs to other important goals, four features of Chinese emergency powers law and practice help explain their appeal to China's rulers and illuminate their character. First, putting emergency powers in legal form has been consistent with sustaining China's wider Reform Era 'legal development' project. Second, Chinese emergency powers law reflects a power-creating – and often power-centralising – concept of law. Third, emergency powers laws are defined and defended as means to ends that China's leaders deem essential. Fourth, putting emergency powers in legal form allows the regime to draw upon law's emergent legitimacy in China to support extraordinary authority.

Chinese emergency powers law thus serves regime agendas and threatens law's stature and citizens' rights. It is, however, also an imprecise tool and potentially a double-edged sword. It can help limit state power and implement relatively liberal promises that laws – and policies – make to Chinese citizens. This chapter examines how Chinese emergency powers law and practice reflect the four identified features. It then assesses the prospects that China's emergency powers law may limit the state's power and discretion to depart from ordinary law and derogate from citizens' legal rights. A concluding section addresses, in comparative and theoretical perspective, implications of China's approach to emergency powers for the emergence of legality.

II. Limiting damage to the '(socialist) rule of law' project

Emergency powers can undermine law in any system, but they pose special threats in China, where norms of legality are only starting to emerge and legal protection for citizens' rights is merely nascent. The regime's approach to 'legalising' emergency powers can limit damage to a 'rule-of-law' or 'rule-by-law' project that China's Reform Era leaders have long pursued. PRC emergency powers law holds an appeal analogous to one cited – and disputed – in more strongly rule-of-law systems: such law may be less costly to legality than other means of addressing perceived or purported crises. Putting rules for emergencies in legal form offers a backhanded compliment to law, pays some deference to norms of legality and reaffirms commitments to using law to structure state behaviour. Putting rules for emergency in legal form, and adhering to those laws, can limit emergencies' damage to the broader legal order by defining clearer zones of exception to ordinary legal rules.[11]

Chinese emergency powers law here faces an illiberal variation on a dilemma that Chen, Harding and Ramraj identify in their chapters on emergent or aspiring constitutional, rule-of-law regimes in Asia: how to allow authorities to invoke emergency powers, which is sometimes necessary to establish conditions for *creating* legality, without having such powers sweep so broadly (or so undermine confidence in the regime's commitment to law) that they destroy the possibility of achieving legality.[12] China also presents a less-than-rule-of-law variant on the conundrum that Ramraj, Chen and others suggest is less common in Asia but that is central to discussions of emergency powers in constitutional democracies: how to accommodate the state's use of emergency powers, which is sometimes needed to *preserve* the legal order, without accepting unconstrained, unreviewable state power that can be fatal to rule of, or by, law.

The 'turn to law' has been a valuable, if incipient and vulnerable, element in the Reform Era strategy for ruling China. The post-Mao leadership has relied on law to bolster its ability to govern, by enhancing state capacity and by supporting economic transformations that generate legitimacy and material resources for the regime. The founding document of the Reform Era in 1978 emphasised creation, implementation and enforcement of laws. The Deng Xiaoping years brought a renaissance of 'socialist legality' far surpassing its mid-1950s antecedent. Ideological commitments of the Jiang Zemin period included 'ruling the country by law' and creating a 'socialist rule-of-law state' – notions that attained constitutional status in 1999. Under Hu Jintao, this agenda evolved, with new prominence for the constitution and law, especially at the Seventeenth Party Congress in 2007.[13]

[11] For this type of argument about liberal, democratic rule-of-law regimes, see K. Roach, 'Ordinary Laws for Emergencies and Democratic Derogations from Rights', in Ramraj (ed.), *Emergencies*, pp. 229–57. For a view that such laws would permit positivistically valid emergency powers that 'seep' corrosively into the legal order, see O. Gross, 'Chaos and Rules: Should Responses to Violent Crises Always Be Constitutional?' (2003) 112 *Yale Law Journal* 1011.

[12] V. V. Ramraj, 'The Emergency Powers Paradox' (Chapter 2); Chen, Chapter 3; Harding, Chapter 11, all this volume.

[13] See generally, S. Lubman, *Bird in a Cage: China's Post-Mao Legal Reforms* (Stanford: Stanford University Press, 2000); R. Peerenboom, *China's Long March toward the Rule of Law* (Cambridge: Cambridge University Press, 2000); J. deLisle, 'Legalization without Democratization in China under Hu Jintao', in Cheng Li (ed.) *China's Changing Political Landscape* (Washington: Brookings, 2008), pp. 185–211.

Although not seeking – much less achieving – full-fledged rule of law, the programme behind such rhetoric brought much lawmaking, investment in legal personnel and institutions and efforts to raise popular legal awareness. Key policies increasingly were put in legal form. They promised citizens greater predictability, stability and transparency in the rules governing their lives. Although imperfectly implemented, laws became much more elaborate and liberal. Economic contract law moved toward market-conforming norms of party autonomy. Criminal law moved toward less politicized and more positivist definitions of sanctionable behaviour and promises of due-process-like rights. Administrative law created rights to challenge improper government acts and abuses of citizens' rights.

With 'law' and 'rule by law' occupying elevated positions among means for ruling China, the calculus of preserving or augmenting party-state power that inevitably informs decisions about how to address real or concocted crises has had to weigh damage to the broader, regime-valued 'law project'. Harm to legality must figure in assessments of when to declare, and how to manage, emergencies that purportedly warrant measures displacing ordinary law. Chinese authorities thus have significant self-interest in creating conditions that are conducive to a 'compulsion of legality with Chinese characteristics'.[14]

A. *Establishing legal frameworks for emergency powers*

The development of Reform Era PRC emergency powers law includes much that appears consistent with realising the dubious – but potentially important – legality-protecting benefits of laws to address exceptional powers. Against the backdrop of Cultural Revolution chaos and Mao's resort to the military to restore order, the 1982 constitutional provision on martial law, although skeletal, signalled increased legalisation of means for controlling disorder. It restored and refined an article from the 1954 Constitution that had been dropped in the radical charter adopted near the end of the Cultural Revolution decade and omitted from the 1978 version. In 1989, China's rulers (many of whom had been victims of the

[14] Dyzenhaus characterises the compulsion of legality as the perceived imperative among regimes to establish a legal framework for state action such that public officials' acts are legally constituted ('The Compulsion of Legality'). The phrase 'Chinese characteristics' has been appended to borrowed concepts in Reform Era China to indicate a distinctive approach that diverges from the original meaning. The most famous example is 'socialism with Chinese characteristics', describing the adoption of market-based capitalist elements in post-Mao economic policies.

Cultural Revolution) meticulously invoked this provision as a legal basis for extraordinary measures to suppress the 'turmoil' of the Tiananmen Democracy Movement and unrest in Tibet. Orthodox sources and more liberal commentators explained that this lawful use of martial law differed from military government immediately after 1949, when civilian authority had yet to be established, and military intervention in politics during the Cultural Revolution, when the government had become paralysed. It also contrasted with the late-Mao-era use of martial means, then without constitutional foundation, to terminate the 1976 demonstrations at Tiananmen Square which were the most obvious progenitor of the 1989 movement.[15]

Official accounts stressed that martial law conformed to constitutional requirements. They defended the State Council's declaration of martial law for Beijing as consistent with the provision mandating action by the National People's Congress (NPC) Standing Committee to impose martial law throughout a provincial-level entity such as Beijing, but permitting proclamation by the State Council for subprovincial areas. Official and orthodox sources explained that martial law reached only Beijing's urban districts, excluding rural regions that are legally part of the capital.[16] (Serious politics may have lain behind this point of procedural law. Key NPC Standing Committee members were widely viewed as less willing to use force against the demonstrators than were Premier and State Council

[15] Yao Jianguo, 'A Few Words About Martial Law', *Beijing Review*, 18–24 September 1989, p. 7; Mo Jihong, 'Perfect Emergency Response Legislation: Protecting Citizens' Constitutional and Legal Rights' (2004) 6 *China Judicature [Zhongguo Sifa]*, sect. 2.1, www.iolaw.org.cn/showArticle.asp?id=1670. Accounts of martial law and the regime's reaction to the Tiananmen Movement, include S. Ogden, K. Hartford, L. Sullivan and D. Zweig (eds.), *China's Search for Democracy* (Armonk, N.Y.: M. E. Sharpe, 1992); M. Oksenberg, L. R. Sullivan and M. Lambert (eds.), *Beijing Spring, 1989* (Armonk, N.Y.: M. E. Sharpe, 1990); Zhang Liang, P. Link and A. J. Nathan, *The Tiananmen Papers* (New York: Public Affairs, 2001). The 1976 Tiananmen Demonstrations began as mourning for Premier Zhou Enlai – popular for his perceived efforts to rein in Mao's excesses – and quickly became a mass expression of opposition to the Gang of Four – radicals led by Mao's wife, Jiang Qing, who sought to continue Cultural Revolution policies and reverse incipient more moderate approaches associated with Zhou and a resurgent Deng Xiaoping.

[16] Constitution of the PRC (1982), Articles 67, 89; 'An Important Indicator of Stability in China', *Renmin Ribao [People's Daily]*, 11 January 1990; 'Yuan Mu on Revolt and Martial Law', *Xinhua*, 16 August 1989; State Council of the PRC, Order on Enforcing Martial Law in Parts of Beijing Municipality, 20 May 1989; 'Li Peng Stresses Law and Order', *Beijing Review*, 12–25 June 1989, p. 8; C. W.-H. Lo, *China's Legal Awakening* (Hong Kong: Hong Kong University Press, 1995), pp. 193–294; Mo, 'Perfect Emergency Response Legislation', sec. 2.1.

Chairman Li Peng and other senior leaders.)[17] For Tibet, official sources noted that the State Council's martial law declaration covered only Lhasa, not the rest of the provincial-level Autonomous Region. They cited the constitutional provision on martial law and another on the state's obligation to maintain order and suppress counter-revolution.[18]

Decrees suspending rights and granting the military and other state actors special powers were explicitly issued pursuant to the State Council's martial law declaration and by authorities thereby created or empowered.[19] One Beijing notice emphasised that martial law authorities were enforcing their own initial martial law orders, including those banning demonstrations.[20] Directives in Beijing noted constitutional and other legal foundations for the People's Liberation Army's (PLA) actions quelling the 'rebellion' and the PLA's role of 'martial law enforcement'. Official media claimed the troops came to enforce martial law, not to suppress the students.[21] Leaders and spokesmen expounded on the illegality of activities by the targets of martial law: unauthorised demonstrations and organisations, defiance of martial law decrees, assaults on police officers, party and state institutions, social order and the rights of other citizens (which violated the Criminal Law), and disregard for the Four Basic Principles (which insist on socialism and Communist Party leadership, which the constitution and criminal law oblige all PRC citizens to uphold, and which reportedly drove Deng Xiaoping's assessment that the movement was illegal).[22] In Tibet, Party Secretary Hu Jintao and martial law orders

[17] See Zhang, Link and Nathan, *Tiananmen Papers*, pp. 223–77; D. Southerland, 'Military Group Opposes Martial Law in China', *Washington Post*, 23 May 1989; Ogden *et al.*, *China's Search*, pp. 292, 306, 321.

[18] 'News Agency Cites Deng Xiaoping on Legality of Martial Law', *Zhongguo Xinwen She*, 7 March 1989; State Council of the PRC, Order on Imposing Martial Law in Lhasa City, Tibet Autonomous Region; Mo, 'Perfect Emergency Response Legislation', sect. 2.1.

[19] For example, Beijing Municipal People's Government and Martial Law Military Command, Order No. 16; 'Interview with Public Security Spokesman on Martial Law', *Xinhua*, 22 May 1989; Tibet Autonomous Region People's Government Martial Law Orders Nos. 1–4, March 1989.

[20] Martial Law Military Command, 'Urgent Notice', 3 June 1989; BBC Summary of World Broadcasts, 5 June 1989.

[21] Beijing Municipal Government and Headquarters of PLA Martial Law Units, Circular (Various Defensive Measures), 3 June 1989; BBC Summary of World Broadcasts, 5 June 1989; State Council of the PRC, 'Letter of Comfort' to Martial Law Troops, 25 May 1989; 'Martial Law Enforcement Spokesman on People's "Misunderstanding" of Martial Law', *Xinhua*, 23 May 1989; Shi Wei, 'Why Impose Martial Law in Beijing?', *Beijing Review*, 26 June–2 July 1989, pp. 24–5.

[22] This critique began before martial law, with the 26 April 1989 *People's Daily* editorial condemning the movement as lawless 'turmoil'. See also Criminal Law of the PRC (1980),

similarly warned of sanctions for protesters who violated state laws and martial law orders.[23]

After the crackdown, attention to positivist legality continued. The NPC Standing Committee expressed approval of prior martial law actions, and the NPC passed new legislation governing demonstrations.[24] Later, the Law on Martial Law went beyond the constitutional text, which had provided awkwardly thin legal support in 1989. The statute stated that it was rooted in the constitutional provision. It articulated substantive conditions and specific procedures for declaring martial law and the powers and departures from ordinary law that followed therefrom (and provided for lesser, provisional uses of similar powers by local authorities). The statute also set forth limits to derogations. Official and mainstream Chinese commentators cited the legislation's vital contribution in providing a clearer positive law basis, and articulating conditions and procedures, for martial law.[25] Responding to the SARS crisis, authorities again relied on legal forms to confer – or discerned in existing law – extraordinary powers. Moves included republication and amendment of a law on control of epidemic diseases, a formal determination that SARS came within that law's ambit, State Council emergency regulations on responding to public health emergencies (which supplemented the infectious disease law, criminal law and other statutes), a judicial-prosecutorial joint interpretation asserting, clarifying and expanding criminal sanctions, a joint notice from the party's Central Committee and key ministries, new

Article 10; Chen Xitong, 'Report on Checking the Turmoil and Quelling the Counterrevolutionary Rebellion', *Beijing Review*, 17–23 July 1989 (Deng's views); Lo, *China's Legal Awakening*, pp. 281–93; Shi, 'Why Impose Martial Law?'; Propaganda Department, Beijing Municipal Party Committee, 'Recognize the Essence of Turmoil and the Necessity of Martial Law', *People's Daily*, 3 June 1989.

23 'Martial Law Protects Best Interests of Tibet', *Xinhua*, 17 March 1989 (quoting Hu Jintao); People's Government of the Tibet Autonomous Region, Martial Law Orders Nos. 1–3; 'Tibet Regional Government Issues Orders to Enforce Martial Law', *Xinhua*, 7 March 1989; D. Southerland, '300 Tibetans Said Arrested After Rioting', *Washington Post*, 31 March 1989.

24 'NPC Meeting Focuses on Rebellion', *Beijing Review*, 17–23 July 1989, pp. 4–5; Law of the PRC on Assemblies, Processions and Demonstrations (1989).

25 Law of the PRC on Martial Law (1996), Articles 1–3, 7–8, 12–29, 31; Li Yuede and Zhang Yu, 'Several Questions on Legislation for the Emergency Response Law' (2007) 4 *Administrative Law Review [Xingzheng Faxue Yanjiu]* 70; Wang Yongqing, 'State of Emergency Legal Institutions', *People's Daily [Renmin Ribao]*, 28 February 2005; Xie Huimin, 'On Adjusting the Scope of Coverage and Limits to Decision-Making Authority in the Law on Martial Law,' *Journal of the Jilin Public Security Academy [Jilin Gongan Gaodeng Zhuanke Xuexiao Xuebao]* (1999), No. 1; Mo, 'Perfect Emergency Response Legislation', sect. 2.1. Li, Zhang and Wang are State Council Legislative Affairs Office researchers and deputy director.

ministerial and local rules on SARS-related issues, and repeated references to powers conferred in pre-existing public health, transportation and other laws.[26] Such measures asserted or assumed proper positivist pedigrees for sanctions that included capital punishment for knowingly spreading the disease, multiyear incarceration for negligently spreading the illness or breaking quarantine, and lesser sanctions for violating orders implementing reporting requirements and quarantines. Officials and commentators explained that these were important measures for coping with the crisis that must, and did, find foundation in existing laws or satisfy requirements of higher laws.[27]

Defences of measures adopted during SARS, and arguments for the constitutional amendment to authorise exceptional powers in future emergencies, employed another argument asserting consistency with existing laws and the broader legal order: such law protected the legal rights of other citizens. Official sources claimed harsh sanctions were needed against rumour-spreaders during SARS to protect potential victims from blackmail and extortion. An advocate for a constitutional 'state of emergency' provision explained that special powers permitted by the new Article were necessary to protect the rights of the majority.[28]

[26] Law of the PRC on the Prevention and Treatment of Infectious Diseases (1989); 'China to Amend Anti-Epidemic Law to Eliminate Legal Loopholes in SARS Fight', *Xinhua*, 16 June 2003; State Council of the PRC, Regulations on Dealing with Public Health Emergencies, 9 May 2003; 'Chinese Premier Urges Overcoming SARS at Forum on "Contingency Regulations"', *Xinhua*, 15 May 2003; 'Chinese Official Answers Questions on Regulations for Health Contingencies', *Xinhua*, 12 May 2003; Supreme People's Court and Supreme People's Procuracy, Interpretation of Applicable Provisions of Criminal Law with Respect to Deliberately Endangering Public Safety and Other Crimes, 9 May 2003; PRC Ministry of Health, 'Atypical Pneumonia Control Management Measures', 12 May 2003; Zou Keyuan, 'SARS and the Rule of Law in China', in J. Wong and Y. Zheng (eds.), *The SARS Epidemic: Challenges to China's Crisis Management* (Singapore: World Scientific Press, 2004), pp. 99–113; 'China Threatens SARS Death Penalty', BBC News, 15 May 2003; C. Liu, *Chinese Law on SARS* (Buffalo, N.Y.: William S. Hein, 2004), pp. 39–50.

[27] Yin Yao, 'We Should Prevent and Fight Atypical Pneumonia Virus According to Law', *Xinhua*, 10 May 2003; 'China Amends Anti-Epidemic Law after SARS Outbreak', *Xinhua*, 17 June 2003; 'New SARS Regulations to Improve China's Emergency Response Mechanism', *Xinhua*, 17 May 2003; Zou, 'SARS and the Rule of Law', p. 103. Some outside commentaries were sceptical: Ding Wang, 'The Phenomenon of Legal Double Talk Aggravates Spread of the Epidemic', *Hsin Pao* (Hong Kong), 7 May 2003; Wang, 'State of Emergency', sect. 3.1.

[28] 'Public Security Organs in Various Localities Uncover Some 150 Cases of Using Atypical Pneumonia to Disrupt Public Order', *Xinhua*, 29 April 2003; 'Uphold "Taking the Person as the Base", Respect and Ensure Human Rights – An Interview with Famous Constitutional Law Scholar and People's University Professor Xu Chongde' ('Interview with Xu Chongde'), www.humanrights-china.org/china/magazine/200402/p29–30.htm.

Arguably legal but disconcertingly *ad hoc* steps taken mid-crisis were followed by systematic moves to address future emergencies and to close identified – and criticised – gaps in pre-SARS emergency laws. The troubled response to SARS, including lapses into improvised and politicised 'campaign' and 'people's war' rhetoric and methods and strained efforts to assert legal bases, pressed Chinese officials and commentators to pursue a firmer legal footing for emergency powers and to make their use more transparent.[29] The constitutional Article on 'states of emergency' offered clearer underpinnings for exceptional powers in situations (such as public health crises and natural disasters) not addressed by the superseded martial law clause.[30] One orthodox legal expert asserted that the amendment showed the party's commitment to rule in strict accordance with constitutional requirements. Another noted that it created constitutional regulation of the types of restriction imposed on some citizens' legal rights during the SARS epidemic. Other commentators, both official and more liberal, stressed the new provision's bringing greater comprehensiveness and coherence to fragmented laws on emergency powers and creating a basis for further legislation.[31]

The amendment spawned a protracted process of drafting legislation. Orthodox commentaries stressed the importance of putting the constitutionally embedded policies into concrete legal form. An extensive debate addressed whether to adopt a comprehensive State of Emergency Law or to focus first on a more modest Emergency Response Law. The latter approach prevailed, purportedly because it promised to make better use of limited legislative resources, and provide more quickly a framework for relatively modest departures from the ordinary legal order in many situations that demanded exceptional measures but did not pose

[29] J. Lawson and Feng Xu, 'SARS in Canada and China' (2007) 20 *Governance* 209; Lai Hongyi, 'Local Management of SARS in China', in Wong and Zheng (eds.), *The SARS Epidemic*, pp. 94–5; J. deLisle, 'SARS, Greater China, and the Pathologies of Globalization and Transition' (2003) *Orbis* 595; Mo Jihong (ed.), *SARS Period Exceptional Rule of Law ['Feidian Shiqi de Feichang Fazhi']* (Beijing: Law Press 2003), pp. 24–7; Chen Ziwei, 'Interpretation of the Emergency Response Law: Greatest Limitations Protecting Democracy and Freedom', *Outlook Weekly [Liaowang Xinwen Zhoukan]*, 17 April 2006 (interviewing scholar and participant in law-drafting Yu An).

[30] Meng Na, 'China's First Emergency Law in Pipeline', *Xinhua*, 6 January 2004; 'Interview with Xu Chongde'.

[31] Sun Yanxin and Li Xuanliang, 'Legal Experts Praise Constitutional Amendment on State of Emergency', *Xinhua*, 8 March 2004; 'Interview with Xu Chongde'; Li and Zhang, 'Several Questions', at 70–2; Mo, 'Perfect Emergency Response Legislation,' sect. 2.2–2.4; Wang, 'State of Emergency', sect. 1.2.

the rare, severe threats requiring martial law.[32] Facing their colleagues' concerns that the narrower law might leave unacceptable legal lacunae, defenders of the Emergency Response Law argued that the constitutional provision and the Law on Martial Law provided adequate foundations for handling major crises left uncovered by the draft emergency response legislation.[33]

The 2007 Emergency Response Law did, for aspects of the 2004 constitutional amendment, what the Law on Martial Law had done for the 1982 constitutional provision. It specified conditions triggering exceptional powers, and colour-coded levels of emergency and accompanying powers. It directed government units to formulate and implement emergency response plans and directives. It provided extensive procedures, prohibitions and sanctions and tied some to existing criminal and administrative laws.[34] Proponents and drafters argued that the legislation would integrate provisions relevant to emergencies that were scattered across many laws and were unclear.[35]

Authorities pointed to such laws in explaining uses of exceptional powers, *absent* formal legal states of emergency. The State Council cited the Emergency Response Law as the basis for regulations governing reconstruction for earthquake-stricken Sichuan in 2008. Orthodox and mainstream commentators variously argued that the earthquake itself or existing laws were adequate grounds for emergency measures.[36] Accounts of the PLA's role in responding to the earthquake referred to the statutes' institutional and procedural frameworks.[37] After severe snowstorms in

[32] Li Fei (ed.), *Explanations of the PRC Emergency Response Law [Zhonghua Renmin Gongheguo Tufa Shijian Yingdui de Shiyi]* (Beijing: Law Press, 2007), pp. 2–3, 160–1; Chen, 'Interpretation' (Yu An); Qin Ping, 'Economic Emergencies Also Should be Brought under Legal System', *Legal System Daily [Fazhi Ribao]*, 26 June 2008 (Yu An); Li and Zhang, 'Several Questions', at 70; 'Emergency Response Law's Breakthrough in Managing Five Major Difficulties', http://npc.people.com.cn/GB/6465064.html.

[33] Li (ed.), *Explanations*, pp. 137–9; Li and Zhang, 'Several Questions', at 70; Wang, 'State of Emergency', sect. 1.2; Qin Ping, 'Yu An: Can the Earthquake Speed the Birth of China's State of Emergency Law?', *Legal System Daily* [*Fazhi Ribao*], 27 May 2008.

[34] Emergency Response Law of the PRC (2007), Articles 3, 7–26, 42–53, 63–9.

[35] For example, Mo, 'Perfect Emergency Response Legislation'; Chen, 'Interpretation' (Yu An's description of the law as a 'dragon's head law' that leads other, lesser laws).

[36] State Council, Regulations on Wenchuan Earthquake Post-Disaster Recovery and Reconstruction (2008), Article 1; '"Ten Firsts" that Follow China's Massive Quake', *Xinhua*, 12 June 2008; Various Legal Questions in Contending with the Earthquake and Recovery Work', 30 June 2008, www.civillaw.com.cn/Article/default.asp?id=39647; Qin, 'Yu An: Can Earthquake Speed?'

[37] 'Ten Firsts'; 'An Earthquake of Magnitude 7.8 Occurred in Sichuan's Wenchuan County', *Xinhua*, 13 May 2008.

January 2008, officials explained that the 'constitution and laws' directed the PLA to undertake relief efforts through exceptional measures, displacing ordinary legal rights.[38]

The 2008 crises brought calls for improved laws. Widely publicised comments from drafters of the Emergency Response Law identified local authorities' failure to follow or implement the law, and the law's failure to provide clearer procedures and substantive authority, as being responsible for problems in handling the snowstorms and earthquake.[39] Those experiences prompted the head of the NPC to call for research on revising the law. Official and orthodox commentaries endorsed a more complete legal framework, including laws on disaster aid, recovery and reconstruction, and a State of Emergency Law. A contributor to the initial law proposed more elaborate delineation of local officials' legal powers and responsibilities at each phase in a crisis, and new legislation covering previously unaddressed calamities.[40]

As such developments also illustrate, Reform Era Chinese emergency powers law includes another aspect that may limit harm to broader legal development – one familiar from other legal systems. Using law to define the scope and terms of crisis-driven departures from the ordinary legal order can do more than assign law another function. It also places grounds for derogation from ordinary (if weakly implemented) laws on a footing formally no higher than that of those laws themselves.

B. 'Incidents' and exceptional powers without 'emergencies'

China's emergency powers law, practice and discourse caution that according law a central role might be cold comfort for broader legal development agendas. Official reports claim approximately 80,000 'incidents' of unrest annually. Although the definition is murky, incidents are thought to be protests that might, and often do, draw uses of state force. Discussions of the draft Emergency Response Law cited high numbers of potentially covered events. Some suggested there were millions annually.[41] Legal definitions of circumstances warranting declarations of

[38] 'Chinese Army Mobilizes 306,000 Troops to Combat Snow Disasters', *Xinhua*, 2 February 2008.

[39] Qin, 'Economic Emergencies'; Qin Xudong, 'Quake Propels the Improvement of Emergency Laws', *Finance [Caijing]*, 29 May 2008; 'Various Legal Questions'.

[40] Qin, 'Economic Emergencies'; Chen, 'Interpretation' (Yu An).

[41] Irene Wang, 'Incidents of Social Unrest Hit 87,000', *South China Morning Post*, 20 January 2006; 'Teleconference Highlights Implementing Law on Emergency Response', *Xinhua*, 14 November 2007; Chen, 'Interpretation'.

martial law or emergency are sufficiently vague – and Chinese interpretive norms and implementing institutions sufficiently tractable – that legally declared exceptional states too easily could swallow the rule of ordinary law, making a textually defensible but substantively problematic state of emergency commonplace.[42] Reports, especially in international media, refer to declarations of martial law or emergencies by local authorities to address unrest and natural disasters.[43] Chinese sources recount exceptional measures, especially after the 2008 earthquake and snowstorms, in terms that imply or assert use of the Emergency Response Law.[44]

There has, however, been no widespread invocation of martial law or states of emergency. Media accounts often use such terms colloquially for unusual measures that may have bases in other laws or have no legal basis. Some may refer to local officials using the authority which emergency powers laws grant for limited, interim measures. Some appear to involve elements in the Emergency Response Law that apply in the absence of a fully fledged emergency. The Emergency Response Law has been especially conducive to confusion, incompletely addressing constitutional states of emergency, spawning debates about the source and scope of authority to declare emergencies under circumstances not covered by the statute and offering sprawling and general local powers and obligations that await interpretive regulations from above or the formulation of mandated plans from below. Chinese official and conservative to mainstream commentators have argued that most incidents can be handled by ordinary legal means and that emergency powers – and especially martial law – should be deployed in rare, extreme circumstances and forgone in some cases where they are legally warranted. Otherwise, the rule of law would be put needlessly at risk. Authorities eschewed states of emergency in cases in when they seemed plausibly lawful, such as the 2008 earthquake and Tibetan unrest (with fear of international embarrassment at the Beijing Olympics perhaps

[42] Vasuki Nesiah documents a process similar to this in her chapter, 'The Princely Impostor: Stories of Law and Pathology in the Exercise of Emergency Powers' (Chapter 5), this volume. The same pattern characterises aspects of the Philippines experience as analysed by Pangalangan, Chapter 15.

[43] See J. Kahn, 'Martial Law Declared as Nearly 150 Die in Clashes in Central China', *New York Times*, 1 November 2004; Shi Ting, 'No End in Sight for Martial Law in Henan Riot Villages', *South China Morning Post*, 4 November 2004; Li Xi, 'Martial Law Imposed in China's Rioted City Yongzhou', *Epoch Times*, 4 March 2007.

[44] 'Ten Firsts', but cf. 'Various Legal Questions' and Qin, 'Quake Propels Improvement'.

prompting authorities to dub *de facto* martial law in Tibet as the lesser 'special measures').[45]

Such murkiness and inconsistency are troubling for the project of building or preserving broader legality. The pattern might show the regime's ultimate aversion to legal regulation of emergency powers. Nonetheless (and partly because Chinese emergency powers law includes much that serves regime interests), another interpretation is also plausible: rarely using full formal emergency powers, and undertaking shaky or strained assertions of other legal authority for uses of exceptional powers, may reflect a regime grappling with the difficult task of creating a legal structure that authorises exceptional powers while avoiding too-frequent formal invocations of exceptional powers that would imperil the wider legal order that the regime rationally values.

It is, at least, hard to reach confident and strongly negative conclusions from the Reform Era Chinese pattern. Ideally the state might assert exceptional prerogatives rarely and only after formal declarations of emergency, but evidence from other Asian cases suggests much peril for legality, or rule of law, or rule by law, in many 'second best' options, such as near-constant formal emergencies (as in Sri Lanka) or refusal to invoke emergency powers law despite recurrent resort to exceptional authority (as in Arroyo's Philippines).[46]

III. Creating state power through law

Although putting authority for emergency powers in legal form can limit harm to the broader legal order, such laws most fundamentally authorise extraordinary power. They reflect a view of law as a means to enhance state capacity. As chapters by Anil Kalhan, H. P. Lee, Andrew Harding and others in this collection show, this phenomenon is pronounced in many Asian states, where it is sometimes a legacy of illiberal colonial rule or a priority for vulnerable regimes. In China too, a power-creating concept of law is prominent. In such contexts, a dilemma familiar in more liberal

[45] Wang, 'State of Emergency', sect. 1.1, 3.2; Xie, 'Adjusting the Scope', at 41; Zhu Hengshun, 'Martial Law in the Legal System of Exception: Proposal for Amending China's Law on Martial Law', (2004) 20 *Journal of Qingdao University of Science and Technology (Social Sciences Edition) [Qingdao Keji Daxue Xuebao (Shehui Kexue Ban)]* 89; Chen, 'Interpretation'; 'Trashing the Beijing Road – A Week in Tibet', *Economist*, 22 March 2008; J. Yardley, 'China Lets Olympic Torch Spend Two Hours in Lhasa', *International Herald Tribune*, 23 June 2008; Mai Wei, '"State of Emergency Law": Initial Framing', Caijing [*Finance*], 22 February 2004.

[46] See Pangalangan, Chapter 15, and Nesiah, Chapter 5.

systems eases: if building state power is emergency powers law's primary function, such law poses prudential problems, not dilemmas of principle.

The idea of power-creating law pervades reforms that began in 1978 with rebuilding state capacity after the depredations of the Cultural Revolution. The Leninist notion of the state and law as disciplined 'organisational weapons' runs through Reform Era legal discourse.[47] The seven major laws that began a torrent of lawmaking in 1979 mostly constituted and empowered state organs.[48] Later, the agenda became more complex, but a steady flow has continued of organic laws for state institutions, regulatory statutes addressing key organs' powers, and other laws to build such bodies' capacity and legitimacy.

Legal and institutional reforms during the 1990s and 2000s aimed to reclaim central authority that had leached to recalcitrant local organs. This concern animated reforms ranging from tax law (which recentralised revenue collection and rate-setting), to attempts to redress local protectionism (which flouted national laws and undermined the administration of justice), to WTO entry (which Premier Zhu Rongji sought partly to recentralise authority through treaty-based requirements for national legal uniformity), to rural fiscal rules (which dropped central levies, outlawed irregular local exactions and warned officials to pay compensation when taking land for development).

A. *Authorising and defining emergency powers*

Power-creating notions run through Chinese emergency powers law. The constitutional provisions assert or enhance authority, with the 1982 version permitting martial law and the 2004 amendment seeking to remedy its predecessor's inadequacies in handling SARS and other crises.[49] On some accounts, delay in deploying the PLA in Beijing in 1989 reflected senior leaders' expectation that merely invoking constitutional authority to declare martial law would disperse the protesters.[50] The 2004 state of emergency amendment, like the Emergency Response Law, was described

[47] P. B. Potter, *From Leninist Discipline to Socialist Legalism* (Stanford: Stanford University Press, 2003); P. Selznick, *The Organizational Weapon* (New York: Free Press, 1960).

[48] Peng Zhen, 'Explanation of the Seven Laws', *Beijing Review*, 13–19 July 1979, p. 8.

[49] PRC Constitution (1982, 2004), Articles 67, 80, 89; Wen-chieh Wang and Min-Chiuan Wang, 'The 2004 Amendment to China's Constitutional Law' (30 June 2005) 6(2) *Perspectives*, sect. II.5; 'Official Explains Draft Amendment to China's Constitution', *Xinhua*, 9 March 2004, sect. 2.10; Li and Zhang, 'Several Questions', 70.

[50] J. Hoagland, 'Martial Law Backfires in Beijing, but Many Chinese Demonstrators Fear a Phase-Two Crackdown', *Washington Post*, 24 May 1989.

as enhancing the state's ability to control crises, ensuring that 'all possible government and social resources' could be mobilised, assuring that nothing impeded the state's access to necessary powers and closing the legal authority gap that had contributed to haphazard, ineffective responses to SARS.[51] The Law on Martial Law and the Emergency Response Law authorised seizing social resources. The Law on Martial Law focused on authority to use force, to displace ordinary laws and institutions, and to limit citizens' rights.[52] The Emergency Response Law addressed less dire situations, specifying legal bases and authorisations for derogations and powers under different 'levels' and types of crisis. Mainstream commentators emphasised the statute's state-capacity-enhancing aspects. A scholar-drafter opined that a state of emergency (beyond the statute) rightly would entail major departures from ordinary policymaking and constitutional rules. One State Council source praised it for supporting a more proactive government.[53] The laws authorised interim or limited exceptional powers for local authorities confronted with sudden, serious incidents.[54] The Emergency Response Law's directive to state organs to formulate emergency response plans and its integration of scattered emergency-response-related laws were supposed to make state responses to the most likely emergencies more effective.[55] Concerns that they might help enhance the state's repressive capacity appear to have dissuaded usually forthcoming foreign advisors from acceding to requests for assistance with constitutional amendment-implementing legislation from PRC drafters – whose reviews of foreign emergency powers law often adopted expansive, statist readings.[56]

The earthquake, snowstorms and Tibetan unrest in 2008 brought criticisms of the Emergency Response Law for leaving local authorities to use improvised, legally questionable measures that lacked the timeliness and efficiency achievable under a lawfully declared state of emergency. Such

51 Chen, 'Interpretation'; Sun and Li, 'Legal Experts Praise'; Meng Na, 'Constitutional Amendment Paves Way for Drafting Emergency Law', *Xinhua*, 6 January 2004; Li (ed.), *Explanations*, pp. 1–3, 160–2; Mo, 'Perfect Emergency Response Legislation', sect. 2.3; Mo (ed.), *SARS Period*, pp. 2–4; Wang, 'State of Emergency', sect. 3; L. A. Jacobs, 'Rights and Quarantine during the SARS Global Health Crisis' (2007) 41 *Law and Society Review* 525; Lai, 'Local Management', pp. 77–8.

52 Law on Martial Law, Articles 13–28; Zhu, 'Martial Law', at 89–90.

53 Emergency Response Law, Articles 11–14, 42–62; Li and Zhang, 'Several Questions', at 74; 'Emergency Response Law's Breakthrough'; Chen, 'Interpretation'; Qin, 'Yu An: Can Earthquake Speed?'

54 Law on Martial Law, Article 31; Emergency Response Law, Articles 7–10, 16, 42–53, 69.

55 Emergency Response Law, Articles 3–4, 7–9, 17–20, 23–6, 42–5, 63–9.

56 Author's interviews, 2008; Li and Zhang, 'Several Questions', at 70–1; Wang, 'State of Emergency', sect. 2.

difficulties prompted reconsideration of the choice to adopt an Emergency Response Law, rather than a State of Emergency Law, because the former was expected to provide effective means to deal with the most immediate likely problems. Advocates of a State of Emergency Law, to implement more fully the constitutional provision, argued that it would unite emergency law, including martial law, under a single framework, clarify roles of officials and institutions in emergencies and improve state responses.[57]

Concrete emergency response measures also reflect a power-creating dimension of emergency powers law. The pattern – in martial law for Beijing and Tibet, the SARS crisis and the troubles of 2008 – of claiming that special powers and measures were authorised by existing law was not merely a matter of preserving the broader legal order from the corrosive effect of legally undefended or indefensible departures from ordinary law. It also asserted that valid, often higher-level, positivist legal sources conferred any extraordinary powers state agents wielded and attendant limitations on citizens' rights. Substantively, these sources of legal authority purported to enhance powers of state agents in crisis situations. Nearly twenty martial law orders in Beijing and a handful in Lhasa imposed derogations from ordinary legal rights and rules and pledged zealous efforts and severe methods to enforce long-standing laws and new martial law prohibitions. One Beijing directive explained that still 'stronger measures' were necessary and appropriate responses to 'lawless acts' violating martial law orders.[58] An order in Tibet asserted the PLA's authority to take 'necessary and strong measures' to enforce martial law orders.[59]

SARS brought a similar dynamic. Government sources and official media invoked existing laws, new State Council regulations and Supreme People's Court and Procuracy 'interpretations' not just to parry concerns that exceptional measures were at odds with the prior legal order, but also as power-conferring mandates for state authorities to impose extraordinary information control, quarantines, detentions and stiff penalties, including capital punishment – all methods employed during SARS.[60] Mid-outbreak regulations and institutional changes were touted as increasing state capacity to handle the crisis and reflecting

[57] Qin, 'Economic Emergencies' (quoting Yu An); Qin, 'Quake Propels Improvement'; 'Various Legal Questions'; Mo, 'Perfect Emergency Response Legislation'; Qin, 'Yu An: Can Earthquake Speed?' (expectation that earthquake would hasten state of emergency legislation).

[58] Circular (Various Defensive Measures).

[59] Tibet Autonomous Region People's Government, Martial Law Order No. 2, 7 March 1989.

[60] Liu, *Chinese Law*, pp. 26, 39–42, 64–5; 'Basic Knowledge for the Study and Implementation of the "Infectious Disease Prevention and Treatment Law" and the Prevention and Treatment of Atypical Pneumonia in Accordance with the Law', *Xinhua*, 27 April 2003; Tian Yu,

lessons learned early in the crisis about the need for stronger emergency response powers.[61] Although the Sichuan earthquake prompted no full, declared state of emergency, official accounts loosely invoked the Emergency Response Law, portraying its infrastructure as contributing to the state's successful response and implying that the law supported unprecedented PLA-led response efforts.[62]

In Beijing and Lhasa, martial law orders had another power-expanding feature: they ordered or implored citizens to help enforce martial law, exposing and detaining those who caused unrest or committed other offences.[63] The Law on Martial Law imposed duties to obey martial law decrees and 'actively assist' martial law authorities.[64] The Emergency Response Law obliged economic entities and individuals to co-operate with authorities in planning for and responding to emergencies.[65] Accounts of the response to the Sichuan earthquake pointed to the Emergency Response Law framework and praised resulting success in mobilising non-state resources.[66]

B. *Strengthening state institutions and central control*

Power-creating aspects of emergency powers law also targeted perceived deficiencies in governmental institutions that emerged in responses to crises. Amid the Tiananmen protests in 1989, Deng and senior leaders chose martial law reportedly after concluding that municipal authorities

'Chinese Officials Explain Judicial Interpretation of SARS-Related Crime', *Xinhua*, 16 May 2003; Li Shufeng and Tian Yu, 'During the Period When China is Preventing and Fighting the Atypical Pneumonia Epidemic, Those Who Gather Together to Attack Others, Smash and Plunder Property or Cause Injuries, Disabilities or Death to Others Shall be Severely Punished', *Xinhua*, 15 May 2003; Mo (ed.), *SARS Period*, pp. 3–4, 25–7.

61 Wu Jing and Huang Fuhui, 'New SARS Regulations Improve China's Emergency Response Mechanism', *Xinhua*, 17 May 2003; N. C. Wiest, 'Powerful Disaster Agency is Unveiled', *South China Morning Post*, 13 May 2003; Liu, *Chinese Law*, pp. 50–4; Mo (ed.), *SARS Period*, pp. 25–7.

62 'Ten Firsts'; 'Earthquake of Magnitude 7.8'; Lu Chuanzhong, 'Disaster Response, Disaster Release Faster than Ever', *Xinhua*, 15 May 2008.

63 Beijing Municipal People's Government and Martial Law Military Command, Order No. 16; Tibet Autonomous Region People's Government, Martial Law Orders Nos. 2, 5; Lhasa City People's Government and Martial Law Headquarters, 'Message to Lhasa Residents', BBC Summary of World Broadcasts, 8 March 1990.

64 Law on Martial Law, Article 6; Zhu, 'Martial Law'.

65 Emergency Response Law, Articles 6, 11, 23–6, 34, 39, 66–8; Li and Zhang, 'Several Questions', at 74; Chen, 'Interpretation'.

66 'Ten Firsts'; 'Earthquake of Magnitude 7.8'.

and reformers and moderates among the top elite had allowed the capital to lapse into chaos and become unwilling or unable to restore order and protect the regime's authority.[67] Official media defences of martial law argued that the demonstrators had been 'making use of some failings in the work of the party and government' to stir up turmoil and that rebellious citizens had sought to oust and replace the government and legislature.[68] Worries about organisational discipline also surfaced in martial law authorities' directive to government personnel to remain at their posts and perform their duties.[69]

In the SARS crisis, central authorities became alarmed at – and took urgent regulatory measures to address – undisciplined behaviour by local officials, who covered up the disease's outbreak, erected unauthorised roadblocks to exclude sources of contagion, allowed protests impeding the establishment of SARS treatment facilities, alienated local citizens and otherwise responded too passively or too harshly to the feared epidemic – often in violation of applicable law.[70] Critiques stressed inadequate transparency in local officials' reporting and management and resulting damage to the regime's ability to handle the crisis.[71] Perceived shortcomings also afflicted the central bureaucracy, with the Ministry of Health seen as a major source of the state's poor response.[72]

[67] 'Beijing Mayor Defends Martial Law', *Japan Economic Newswire*, 10 October 1989; see also Zhang, Link and Nathan, *Tiananmen Papers*, pp. 175–223; Lo, *China's Legal Awakening*; Ogden *et al.*, *China's Search*, pp. 235–53.

[68] Shi, 'Why Impose Martial Law?'

[69] Beijing Municipal People's Government and Headquarters of PLA Martial Law Units, 'Notice', 22 May 1989, BBC Summary of World Broadcasts, 23 May 1989.

[70] deLisle, 'SARS, Greater China', at 598–604; Zheng Yongnian and Lye Liang Fook, 'SARS and China's Political System', in Wong and Zheng (eds.), *The SARS Crisis*, pp. 52–6; Lawson and Xu, 'SARS in Canada and China', at 210–25; Zhong Kaibin, 'Crisis Management in China', (2007) *China Security* 92; Nan Chen, 'Key Words to Preventing "Atypical Pneumonia" in Rural Areas – Law Abiding and Science', *Xinhua*, 12 May 2003; 'A High Price for Progress: Five Years Since a Deadly Virus Hit', *South China Morning Post*, 26 February 2008; 'New SARS Regulations Improve China's Emergency Response', *Xinhua*, 17 May 2003; 'Chinese Official Answers Questions on Regulations for Health Emergencies', *Xinhua*, 13 May 2003; S. V. Lawrence, 'The Plague Reaches Much Deeper', *Far Eastern Economic Review*, 1 May 2003, pp. 26–8; 'Slack Officials Face Crackdown in SARS Crisis', *People's Daily*, 8 May 2003; Liu, *Chinese Law*, pp. 21–32, 45, 105–6.

[71] Lai, 'Local Management', pp. 78–83; Liu, *Chinese Law*, pp. 14, 28–32; J. Kahn, 'Seven at Chinese Paper Held After Article on New SARS Case', *New York Times*, 7 January 2004.

[72] Lawson and Xu, 'SARS in Canada and China', at 210–12; Zhong, 'Crisis Management', at 92–5; Zheng and Lye, 'SARS and China's Political System', pp. 57–8; Liu, *Chinese Law*, pp. 56–8.

The constitutional provision on martial law addressed concerns of state weakness due to fragmentation and unaccountability. It mandated determinations at the highest levels before extraordinary measures could be undertaken. In 1989, martial law came through top-level declarations and was implemented through decrees that were reviewed by central leaders, and issued by bodies captained by a top leader (Premier Li Peng in Beijing) or someone with ambitions and potential to become one (Hu Jintao in Tibet). The Law on Martial Law mandated central authorisation, control and monitoring of martial law powers and activities. It called for martial law measures to be implemented under a 'unified plan', required the Central Military Commission to designate an institution to command PLA units enforcing martial law and subjected local authorities' use of temporary special measures to State Council review.[73]

Initial unco-ordinated responses to SARS were followed by reassertions of central authority. Many measures superseded or constrained local and ministry discretion, including the State Council regulations on public health emergencies and the Supreme People's Court and Supreme People's Procuracy interpretation on applying criminal laws. Mid-crisis directives and commentaries emphasised restoring central leadership, ensuring reliable reporting to the centre and effective implementation at the grassroots and holding local officials accountable to higher authorities. Additional reforms sought to centralise control and co-ordinate emergency responses across geographic and functional bureaucratic divides.[74]

The Emergency Response Law responded to perceived problems in handling SARS and addressed fragmented authority and excessive autonomy.[75] It mandated 'uniform leadership' and 'integrated co-ordination', and higher-level monitoring and direction of lower-level

[73] Law on Martial Law, Articles 3, 5, 10, 31; Zhu, 'Martial Law', at 91 (legislation reflected lessons from the Tiananmen incident); Xie, 'Adjusting the Scope', at 41.

[74] 'New SARS Regulations Improve China's Emergency Response Mechanism'; 'Chinese Premier Urges Overcoming SARS'; 'Chinese Official Answers Questions on Regulations'; 'China's New Health Regulation Spurs Emergency', *Xinhua*, 19 May 2003; E. Eckholm, 'China Gets Strict Rules on Disease Reporting', *International Herald Tribune*, 14 May 2003; Jacobs, 'Rights and Quarantine', at 525–9; Zou, 'SARS and the Rule of Law', pp. 104–7; Zheng and Lye, 'SARS and China's Political System', pp. 65–6; Liu, *Chinese Law*, pp. 58–65, 100–6; 'China Improving Legal System to Cope with Public Health Emergencies', *Xinhua*, 13 May 2003.

[75] Chen, 'Interpretation' (quoting Yu An); 'China Builds Emergency Response System', *People's Daily*, 3 February 2005; 'Premier Wen Calls for Stepping Up Emergency Management', *Xinhua*, 24 July 2005; 'Emergency Law Mooted to Tackle Crises', *Xinhuanet*, 4 February 2004, http://news.Xinhuanet.com/english/2004–02/04/content˙1332952.htm; Cheng Zhiliang, 'China Gets Rewarded in Combating Major Disasters', *Xinhua*, 6 March 2008.

responses. Capacity enhancement, centralisation and clear allocation of roles among functional and regional state organs, reinforced by punishments for officials who failed to report or otherwise handle emergencies properly, were central themes of discussions of the Emergency Response Law.[76] Commentaries stressed reporting and transparency, essential elements for monitoring and control. Some worried that a draft provision harshly punishing false reports might encourage local cover-ups or re-muzzle the media. These concerns may have generated revisions in the draft law and an emphasis on transparency in accounts of Beijing's municipal implementing regulations.[77]

Familiar concerns resurfaced in crises after the law's adoption, including severe snowstorms, Tibetan unrest and the Sichuan earthquake in 2008. Although state responses won praise in official media and sometimes from foreign observers, Chinese critics pointed to local authorities' inadequate reporting of emerging problems, their slow, timid or uncoordinated reactions, and their failure to accomplish all that they might have to ameliorate crises or their consequences. Analysts blamed these problems on local officials' failure to respect or employ the law, and problems with the law itself. The latter included insufficiently clear and graduated powers and responsibilities for local officials, and inadequate mechanisms for co-ordinating and reviewing local responses and checking local authorities' *ad hoc* methods. Such assessments brought calls for new legal measures to augment central management and oversight, limit local discretion, and thereby enhance overall state power.[78]

[76] Emergency Response Law, Articles 4–7, 16; 'China's Assembly Begins Hearing Draft Emergency Law', *Xinhua*, 4 July 2006; 'China to Improve Emergency Response System', UPI, 10 March 2004; Li, *Explanations*, pp. 160–1; Wang, 'State of Emergency', sect. 1.1; Li and Zhang, 'Several Questions', at 74.

[77] 'High Price for Progress'; 'Chinese Lawmakers Demand Severe Penalties for False Accident Information', *Xinhua*, 26 June 2007; 'Emergency Response Law "Will Ensure Accurate Info"', *China Daily*, 4 July 2006; 'China Improving Legal System to Cope'; 'China's Assembly Begins Hearing'; 'China Adopts Emergency Response Law', *Xinhua*, 30 August 2007; Emergency Response Law, Articles 54, 65; 'Making the News Media into Responsible Media', *Xinhua*, 12 July 2006; 'Emergency Response Law to be Implemented' (Beijing regulations).

[78] 'Earthquake of Magnitude 7.8'; 'Various Legal Questions'; P. Goodspeed, 'China Sees Seismic Shift in Censorship', *National Journal*, 16 May 2008; '43 Punished for Quake Relief Frauds', *China Daily*, 24 June 2008; J. Yardley, 'As Tibet Erupted, China Wavered', *New York Times*, 24 March 2008; J. Ma, 'Slow Response to Crisis Shows Deficiencies in Relief Efforts', *South China Morning Post*, 4 February 2008; Qin, 'Quake Propels Improvement' (quoting Mo Jihong); Mo, 'Perfect Emergency Response Legislation'; Qin, 'Economic Emergencies' (quoting Yu An); 'Wuhan to Enforce Governmental Reporting of Emergent Events', *Xinhua*, 19 November 2008.

IV. Pursuing substantive priorities

Emergency powers law in Reform Era China has been framed in terms of defeating threats to goals that are vital to the regime's success or survival – a pattern familiar from assertions of exceptional powers, and laws conferring them, in many systems. Eschewing other, lesser justifications can limit damage to the broader legal order, and invoking such priorities in relevant laws can enhance state power. But the more salient point here is simpler and blunter: for the regime, significant costs to legality are worth bearing if emergency powers law helps preserve or advance essential aims and interests. This calculus is hard for those in power to resist; Simon Chesterman's chapter in this collection argues that even the United Nations – merely an interim wielder of sovereign authority and presumably more attentive to human rights and rule of law than is a typical Asian authoritarian regime – is not immune.[79] As assessments of China's fragile near-neighbour regimes by Kevin Tan, Maitrii Aung-Thwin, Raul Pangalangan and others in this volume indicate,[80] authorities can mitigate costs to legality and legitimacy where they persuade relevant constituencies that emergency powers are essential to preserving vital and valid goals or that existing law authorises exceptional measures in pursuit of those ends.

Throughout the PRC period, the regime's claim to legitimacy has been cast more in substantive terms (achieving policy ends, whether revolution, development, or advancement of the interests of 'the people', 'the nation' or particular 'classes') than procedural ones (holding power through a legitimate process, representing properly expressed preferences of constituencies or adopting and enforcing rules that meet positivist requirements). During the Reform Era, the commitment to law has been instrumental (on some views, devastatingly so for the rule of law), based on expectations that law can advance substantive reform agendas.[81] While such

[79] S. Chesterman, 'UNaccountable? The United Nations, Emergency Powers and the Rule of Law in Asia' (Chapter 9), this volume.

[80] Respectively, K. Y. L. Tan, 'From Myanmar to Manila: A Brief Study of Emergency Powers in Southeast Asia' (Chapter 6); M. Aung-Thwin, 'Discourses of Emergency in Colonial and Postcolonial Burma' (Chapter 7); and Pangalangan, Chapter 15.

[81] J. deLisle, 'Chasing the God of Wealth while Evading the Goddess of Democracy', in S. Ramaswamy and J. W. Cason (eds.), *Development and Democracy: New Perspectives on an Old Debate* (Hanover, N.H.: University Press of New England, 2003), pp. 252–93; Lubman, *Bird in a Cage*. See T. Nardin, 'Emergency Logic: Prudence, Morality and the Rule of Law', in Ramraj (ed.), *Emergencies*, pp. 97–117 (arguing that such an instrumentalist approach to emergency powers law is irreconcilable with the rule of law).

phenomena exist in many – probably all – systems, they have been especially prominent in China.

Economic development has been the defining goal for Reform Era leaders. This has been evident from the Four Modernisations[82] that began the post-Mao era through the 'socialist market economy' that was later enshrined in the Constitution, from Deng Xiaoping's early assertion that 'to get rich is glorious' to the Jiang–Hu era pursuit of a 'relatively well off' society and embrace – including in a constitutional amendment – of capitalist entrepreneurs as among the groups that the party and state represent. Three decades averaging nearly 10 per cent annual growth – and relatively scant attention until near the end of that period to growth's social, human and environmental costs – underscore the seriousness and effectiveness of this project.

Social and political stability has been another core pursuit, in its own right and as a precondition to economic development. In mainstream comparative definitions of the rule of – or even by – law, maintaining the state's monopoly of coercion, preventing anarchy and providing citizens the predictability and stability needed to order their other affairs are minimal components.[83] In Reform Era China, such aims animate key laws such as constitutional articles obliging and empowering the state to provide national security and domestic order, as well as economic progress. It also surfaces in the principal ideological slogans of the Hu Jintao era: building a 'harmonious society' and achieving 'scientific' or 'human' development. Stability and order have been still more compelling because of the turmoil of the Cultural Revolution and other campaigns, chronic disorder that preceded the PRC's founding, and, on some accounts, a cultural 'fear of chaos'.

A. *Preserving social and political order*

Preserving order and preconditions for economic success have loomed large in explanations of Reform Era uses of emergency powers and legal

[82] The 'Four Modernisations' comprise agriculture, industry, science and technology, and national defence. Originating with Zhou Enlai in the final Mao years, the phrase became shorthand for the emphasis on economic development that has dominated the post-Mao era.

[83] See J. Stromseth, D. Wippman and R. Brooks, *Can Might Make Rights? Building the Rule of Law after Military Interventions* (New York: Cambridge University Press, 2006), pp. 78–9; R. Fallon, 'The Rule of Law as a Concept in International Discourse' (1997) 97 *Columbia Law Review* 1 at 7–9.

frameworks for them. Defences of martial law in 1989 emphasised protecting state and society from dangers posed by groups allegedly acting to overthrow the regime, seeking to oust top leaders and usurp government powers and attacking party and state offices.[84] Official and orthodox sources asserted that no government would, or should, fail to use necessary means to stop such seditious behaviour.[85]

Martial law orders, regime spokespeople and ostensibly man-in-the-street interviews explained that authorised military force and other exceptional measures were necessary – and successful – means to end the 'turmoil' in Beijing, restore order, maintain the state's ability to function and protect ordinary citizens.[86] From this perspective, huge numbers of people at Tiananmen Square (some of them armed) who defied orders to disperse, city residents who assaulted or obstructed troops, and citizens who disregarded martial law restrictions were proper targets of exceptional measures that the state was legally empowered and obliged to employ. For China's rulers, these extraordinary means seemed still more clearly warranted because the Democracy Movement's disorder and challenge to authority were reminiscent of the Cultural Revolution.[87]

In Tibet, official sources and martial law decrees explained that the authorities had responded to 'riots' and fulfilled constitutional duties to maintain public order and security. These sources emphasised that martial law and the PLA successfully re-established stability and defeated efforts to undermine the unity and security of the state.[88] A smaller-scale use of

[84] For example, Shi, 'Why Impose Martial Law?'; Martial Law Military Command, 'Urgent Notice'; Yao, 'A Few Words'; 'An Important Measure to Safeguard the Stability of the Capital and the Whole Nation', *Liberation Army Daily [Jiefangjun Bao]*, 21 May 1989.

[85] 'Yuan Mu on Revolt and Martial Law'.

[86] Shi, 'Why Impose Martial Law?'; Circular (Various Defensive Measures); 'Urgent Notice'; 'An Important Measure to Safeguard the Stability of the Capital'; Beijing Municipal Government and Headquarters of PLA Martial Law Units, 'Notice on Restoring Order in the Capital as Soon as Possible', 21 May 1989; 'Residents Support Reasons for and Lifting of Martial Law', *Xinhua*, 26 January 1990; 'An Indicator of Stability, A Correct Policy Decision', *Liberation Army Daily*, 11 January 1990; 'Premier Li Peng Announces Lifting of Martial Law in Peking', BBC Summary of World Broadcasts, 12 January 1990; 'Important Indicator of Stability'.

[87] 'An Important Measure to Safeguard the Stability of the Capital'; 'Martial Law Command Launches Publicity Blitz in China', *Japan Economic Newswire*, 22 May 1989; Zhang, Link and Nathan, *Tiananmen Papers*, pp. 277–96, 318–65.

[88] 'Martial Law Declared in Lhasa', BBC Summary of World Broadcasts, 9 March 1989 (text of declaration); 'News Agency Cites Deng Xiaoping on Legality of Martial Law'; 'Chinese Official Says Martial Law Quelling Violence in Tibet', UPI, 9 March 1990 (Hu Jintao); 'Li Peng Signs Order Lifting Martial Law in Lhasa', *Xinhua*, 1 May 1990; 'Consolidate Stability, Unity and Build and Develop Tibet', *Xinhua*, 1 May 1990.

martial-law-like powers in Henan in 2004 resonated with these themes. Exceptional measures were adopted to handle ethnic conflict that erupted in an already restive county after a Hui Muslim taxi driver killed a Han Chinese girl.[89] Events in Tibet in 2008 reprised patterns of two decades earlier. Although no emergency was formally declared, the party secretary – who had previously held the equivalent post and borne similar duties of controlling ethnic unrest in the largely Muslim Xinjiang Autonomous Region – resorted to martial-law-like methods to quash an uprising. Local authorities won praise for making sure that the 'incident' had 'subsided' when the Olympic torch's pass through the region demonstrated the 'firm basis' of Tibet's 'social stability'.[90]

Official and quasi-official sources emphasised the threat of social chaos from reactions to SARS. The risk that travel by the infected would spread the disease underpinned public welfare justifications for extraordinary measures to limit citizens' mobility and impose quarantines. The spectre of panic triggered by false reports or cover-ups of outbreaks – and attempted blackmail and extortion – provided a rationale for hurriedly adopted measures authorising harsh sanctions for anyone who spread rumours and officials who failed to report cases accurately.[91] Advocates of the post-SARS constitutional amendment argued that clearer authorisation for 'states of emergency' imposing restrictions on citizens' liberties were necessary, internationally common means to serve the state's need for order and the 'fundamental goal' of protecting the rights of the majority.[92]

Commentaries on emergency powers legislation, and the laws themselves, rooted exceptional powers in the imperative to maintain stability. The Law on Martial Law provided that martial law would be imposed under conditions of 'turmoil, riot or disturbance' where 'emergency measures' were necessary to 'preserve social order and protect people's lives and property'. It mandated strengthened security for state and military institutions and infrastructure and permitted requisitioning of necessary assets.[93] One NPC Standing Committee member described the statute's purpose as

[89] Kahn, 'Martial Law Declared'; Ting, 'No End in Sight'.

[90] 'Trashing the Beijing Road'; M. Magnier, 'Expect a Crackdown, Experts Say', *Los Angeles Times*, 25 March 2008; 'China Resumes Foreign Tourism to Tibet after March Riots', *Deutsche Presse-Agentur*, 24 June 2008.

[91] 'Public Security Organs in Various Localities Uncover Some 150 Cases of Using Atypical Pneumonia to Disrupt Public Order', *Xinhua*, 29 April 2003; deLisle, 'SARS, Greater China', at 594–604; Liu, *Chinese Law*, pp. 83–4, 104–5.

[92] 'Interview with Xu Chongde'; Wang, 'State of Emergency', sect. 2, 3.2; Mo, 'Perfect Emergency Response Legislation', sect. 2–3.

[93] Law on Martial Law, Articles 2, 5, 17–18.

providing means to deal with 'riots stirred up by hostile forces attempting to endanger the country's current political power'. Commentators pointed to martial law legislation's roots in Deng Xiaoping's Tiananmen-era call to protect stability.[94] The Emergency Response Law, and explanations from participants in its drafting, focused on natural or man-made threats that imperilled social or political order. The law provided mandates for commandeering resources and strengthening security around key institutions to maintain order during emergencies. Drafters described the law as helping the state pursue its principal task – preserving the lives and security of the people – amid threats or crises.[95] In the first major disaster following the law's adoption, authorities emphasized preserving social stability alongside providing relief to Sichuan earthquake victims. Observers argued that effective response to the crisis was important to assure stability.[96] Such concerns quickly overrode initial moves toward openness and accountability as local authorities pressured or bribed discontented victims into silence.[97]

Rationales for emergency powers also invoked the spectre of disorder stoked by external enemies. Defences of martial law in Beijing in 1989 asserted that the demonstrators conspired with foreign elements. Official justifications of crackdowns on Tibetan unrest in 1989 and 2008 linked targets of exceptional measures to 'outside forces', including 'separatist' Tibetans in exile, and denounced the 2008 uprising as timed to embarrass China as it hosted the Olympics.[98] (Unlike the Indonesian regime in Aceh, as described by Michelle Miller and R. Michael Feener in their chapter,[99] the Chinese regime has not had to be accommodating; it benefits from politically weak secessionists, ineffective international pressure and strong support among majority Han Chinese for keeping Tibet a 'part of China'.)

[94] 'National People's Congress Legislators on Draft Law Covering Martial Law', *Xinhua*, 29 February 1996; Xie, 'Adjusting the Scope', at 41.

[95] Emergency Response Law, Articles 1, 3, 49–52; Mo, 'Perfect Emergency Response Legislation'; Qin, 'Economic Emergencies'; Wang, 'State of Emergency', sect. 3.2; Chen, 'Interpretation' (Yu An).

[96] E. Cody, 'Crises Cloud China's Olympic Mood as Quake Tests Party's Mantle', *Washington Post*, 17 May 2008; 'Ten Firsts'; 'Various Legal Questions'.

[97] E. Wong, 'China Pushes Hush Money on Grieving Parents', *New York Times*, 24 July 2008.

[98] Shi, 'Why Impose Martial Law?'; Southerland, '300 Tibetans'; 'Political Commissar of Tibet Military District Zhang Shaosong on Lhasa Riots and Martial Law', *Zhongguo Xinwen She*, 30 March 1989; 'Martial Law Aims to Safeguard National Unity', *Xinhua*, 8 March 1989; J. Yardley, 'After Fury in Tibet, Firm Hand Trembles', *New York Times*, 18 March 2008.

[99] M. A. Miller and R. M. Feener, 'Emergency and Islamic Law in Aceh' (Chapter 8), this volume.

Explanations of the Olympics-linked Beijing implementing regulations for the Emergency Response Law and arguments for additional emergency powers laws asserted their contributions to thwarting international terrorism.[100]

B. *Sustaining economic growth*

Maintaining economic growth has been another key justification for exceptional powers. Disrupting transportation, industry and commerce were prominent among evils attributed to Tiananmen protesters and reasons given for martial law. State media reports, comments from senior officials and Premier Li Peng's order lifting martial law cited the 'turmoil's' damage to production, foreign investment and hard-won gains from economic policies of reform and opening to the outside world. They praised martial law's contribution to redressing those harms.[101] Outside assessments saw securing World Bank loans, avoiding human-rights-based trade sanctions and reassuring foreign investors as impetuses to lifting martial law.[102]

Official sources stressed unrest-caused damage to Tibet's economy in 1989 and the regime's commitment to lifting Tibet out of poverty. Foreign commentators attributed the end of martial law to worries about reduced tourism and costs to China's trade from other states' opposition to repression in Tibet.[103] The 2008 Tibetan uprising brought similar assessments, with concerns about harms to Han Chinese businesses in Tibetan regions, and Beijing Olympics-driven tourism seen as reasons for martial-law-like measures (as well as reluctance formally to declare martial law).[104]

The resort to special measures amid SARS reflected economic costs from fear and disorder, with production in urban centres threatened by

[100] Qin, 'Quake Propels Improvement'; 'Emergency Response Law to be Implemented'.

[101] Shi, 'Why Impose Martial Law'; Yao, 'A Few Words'; 'Peking Residents Support Reasons'; 'Vice Mayor Says Martial Law "Protecting Foreign Economic and Trade Activities"', *Zhongguo Xinwen She*, 6 November 1989; 'Premier Li Peng Announces Lifting of Martial Law'.

[102] R. Pear, 'US Easing Curbs as China Declares Martial Law Over', *New York Times*, 11 January 1990; D. Southerland, 'Premier Ends Martial Law in Beijing', *Washington Post*, 11 January 1990.

[103] 'Consolidate Stability, Unity and Build and Develop Tibet', *Xinhua*, 1 May 1990; 'Hu Jintao Says Martial Law Does Not Change Policy on Tibet', *Xinhua*, 22 March 1989; Y. Sharma, 'Tibet: Beijing Lifts Martial Law for Economic Reasons', Inter Press Service, 2 May 1990.

[104] 'Trashing the Beijing Road'.

migrant workers fleeing affected cities to return to inland areas, foreigners decamping to safer locations, urban Chinese staying home from work and local authorities restricting entry of people and goods.[105] Rationales for the Emergency Response Law's extraordinary powers included minimising the economic consequences of natural disasters, public health crises and social disorder. Participants in the drafting and other commentators emphasised protection of citizens' property and public property among the law's key goals. One senior official asserted that the law partly embodied the 'Three Represents' policy, under which PRC authorities committed to supporting the interests of China's emergent business class.[106] A prominent expert involved in drafting the law later argued for revisions adding economic crises to the list of covered emergencies, new legislation implementing special measures permitted by the WTO to manage economic crises, and other moves strengthening emergency laws in recognition of the economic costs of natural disasters such as the 2008 earthquake and snowstorms.[107] The most formal emergency lawmaking in response to the earthquake – State Council regulations issued under the Emergency Response Law – focused on economic reconstruction.

V. Drawing on law's legitimacy

Using law to authorise and define emergency powers allows the regime to tap the legitimacy that law holds in society. Law's legitimacy is more than something to be protected from unnecessary harm in the regime's quest for emergency powers, or expected to help legality endure despite derogations during crises. It is also a resource that can make it easier and less costly for the regime to claim and use exceptional powers. Drawing on law's legitimacy also supplements invocations of substantive policy imperatives and partly explains emergency powers law's ability to enhance state power. Moreover, phenomena that Pangalangan observes in Marcos's Philippines[108] and that Colm Campbell suggests can be discerned in

[105] deLisle, 'SARS, Greater China', at 588, 594–5; Zheng and Lye, 'SARS and China's Political System', pp. 51–66; Lai, 'Local Management', pp. 82–91; 'Public Security Organs Uncover 150 Cases'. Ironically, fears that reports of SARS would trigger an economy-harming panic contributed to the initial cover-up and, in turn, poor state response; Chen, 'Interpretation'; Wang, 'State of Emergency', sect. 3.2.

[106] Emergency Response Law, Articles 1, 51, 58–62; National Comprehensive Contingency Plan for Emergencies, sect. 1.5, BBC Summary of World Broadcasts, 29 January 2006; 'China Adopts Emergency Response Law'.

[107] Qin, 'Economic Emergencies' (quoting Yu An).

[108] Pangalangan, Chapter 15.

Northern Ireland[109] may have loose Chinese analogies: ideological commitment to (or acceptance of) the rule of law among constituencies that are generally sceptical of extraordinary state powers (and that may be targets of those powers) means the regime can defang critics and opponents if it can credibly claim legal legitimacy for exceptional measures.

Such potential for using law's legitimacy has become more significant than might be supposed in China. Even though law's foothold is insecure, especially when measured against the USA, Europe and much of East Asia, China has moved far from Mao Era baselines. The regime's insistence on ruling through law and law's central place in the regime's creed reflect substantial – and partly successful – investments of political capital in building law during the Reform Era. Embodying major policies in laws, casting such 'legalisation' as a marker of those policies' durability, and devoting resources to constructing legal institutions, crafting laws, training lawyers and increasing public legal knowledge have broadened arenas in which legal arguments carry weight, and constituencies that believe law should matter and usually benefit when it does.[110]

'Rights consciousness' has risen among ordinary Chinese. Despite a flawed judicial system, millions each year file civil claims and many tens of thousands sue the state, with significant prospects for success. Investigative reporters, 'rights protection' lawyers and officials in state offices that receive 'letters and visits' and other entreaties routinely encounter citizens who assert, seek help in asserting, and are outraged at violations of their legal rights. Such legal rights were central to two politically charged and mediagenic incidents of the early Hu years: Sun Zhigang (a recent college graduate, who was mistaken for an illegal migrant and beaten to death in custody, and whose death led to calls on the NPC to declare unconstitutional the regulations under which Sun was detained and to action by the State Council to replace the challenged regulations) and the owners of the Chongqing Nailhouse (who resisted local government efforts to remove them to make way for a development project, insisted on the illegality of the expropriation process, and extracted greater compensation on the eve of a new Property Law's entry into force).[111]

109 C. Campbell, 'Law, Terror and Social Movements: The Repression–Mobilisation Nexus', in Ramraj (ed.), *Emergencies*, pp. 172–98.

110 deLisle, 'Chasing the God of Wealth'; deLisle, 'Legalization without Democratization'.

111 K. J. Hand, 'Using Law for a Righteous Purpose: The Sun Zhigang Incident' (2006) 45 *Columbia Journal of Transnational Law* 114; H. W. French, 'In China, Fight over Development Creates a Stir', *New York Times*, 26 March 2007.

Many mass 'incidents' invoke legal rights. The Tiananmen Movement in 1989 provided dramatic early examples, with protesters denouncing unprosecuted corruption among officials and calling on the regime to respect constitutional rights to freedom of speech and organisation. Examples from the 2000s include peasants who asserted land rights in resisting a power plant in southeastern China, and middle-class residents who mixed legal rights and political action in opposing a maglev railway in their Shanghai neighbourhood.[112] Further contributing to law's rising legitimacy under Hu has been the rise of those specialising in law or advocating legality as advisors to top leaders and as public intellectuals, and the rise of a group of next-generation leaders who have, formally at least, educations partly in law.

Elements that draw on law's growing legitimacy permeate Reform Era approaches to emergency powers law. The PRC Constitution is a complicated and ambivalent instrument. It is variously empty rhetoric, an aspirational programme, a set of weakly and unevenly implemented rules and a mechanism for entrenching principles to which the regime is most committed. Still, official insistence that the Constitution is China's highest law, leadership assertions that it should be taken more seriously and law reformers' appreciation that constitutionalism and constitutional provisions might advance liberal legalist agendas have given constitutional law special stature. By including martial law and states of emergency in the Constitution and suggesting that they belong in the informal, functional category of serious, imbedded commitments, China's rulers have exploited constitutional law's distinctive, if limited, legitimacy to enhance the stature of emergency powers law, and the propriety of the limits on rights it imposes. Commentaries on emergency powers law pointedly assert the special force crisis conditions give the hoary PRC constitutional norm that citizens' legal rights are correlative with public duties and must not be exercised to injure others' rights.[113]

Proponents of emergency powers legislation have invoked other supra-statutory law to legitimate its content and enhance its standing.

[112] Lo, *China's Legal Awakening*, pp. 280–9; Ogden *et al.*, *China's Search*, pp. 47–50, 55–8, 113–15, 174–6, 217–18; J. Kahn, 'Military Officer Tied to Killings is Held by China', *New York Times*, 12 December 2005; M. Fan, 'Shanghai's Middle Class Launches Quiet, Meticulous Revolt', *Washington Post*, 26 January 2008; E. Pils, 'Land Disputes, Rights Assertion and Social Unrest in China' (2005) 19 *Columbia Journal of Asian Law* 235.

[113] deLisle, 'Legalization without Democratization'; J. A. Cohen, 'China's Changing Constitution' (1978) 76 *China Quarterly* 794; PRC Constitution, Article 51; Mo (ed.), *SARS Period*, p. 27.

Drafters of China's emergency response legislation sought advice – and, some recipients of their requests worried, implicit endorsement – from those who shape, implement and study US and other foreign systems' emergency powers law. PRC scholars and commentators, both quasi-official and somewhat more eclectic, defended emergency powers laws' restrictions on civil liberties as consistent with what all other legal systems do. A more liberal advocate of adding economic crises to emergency response legislation opined that such a law was authorised by, and could implement, the WTO agreement. Another argued that a State of Emergency Law should be conceptualised as implementing international human rights law, especially UN treaties.[114]

Efforts in legislative texts, executive regulations and directives, official explanations, orthodox accounts and expert commentaries to ground emergency powers laws and exercises of emergency powers in constitutional law – and constitutionally grounded laws – make sense if authorities and advocates think these might reduce resistance to assertions of extraordinary powers. To be sure, references to constitutional and other legal authority in the texts and discussions of the Law on Martial Law, the Emergency Response Law, martial law decrees, and regulations rooted in the Emergency Response Law are boilerplate. But such ubiquitous citation increases the likelihood – or reflects the hope – that such laws and actions will enjoy whatever legitimacy proper, lawful status can confer.

Some assertions of underlying legal authority have been so striking in their circumstances that they imply recognition of law's legitimating prowess. Despite tumult in the capital's streets and breakdown of norms of partially office- and rule-based authority and semi-collective rule among the top elite in 1989, senior leaders and official sources punctiliously defended martial law as being imposed according to legal and constitutional requirements.[115] In a volatile Tibet, official accounts similarly insisted relentlessly on the legal propriety of martial law. Faced with another crisis of order and public confidence amid SARS, central authorities proffered elaborate glosses on existing laws, or adopted new laws,

[114] Li, *Explanations*, pp. 159–160 (research on foreign law); author's interviews; Xie, 'Adjusting the Scope', p. 41; Wang, 'State of Emergency', sect. 2; 'Interview with Xu Chongde'; Qin, 'Economic Emergencies' (WTO); Mo, 'Perfect Emergency Response Legislation', sect. 1 (human rights); Jiang Bixin, 'Emergency Situations and Administrative Rule of Law' (2004) 2 *Legal Research [Faxue Yanjiu]* sections 3, 4.7.

[115] 'Li Peng Stresses Law and Order'; Lo, *China's Legal Awakening*, pp. 281–294; Gerrit W. Gong, 'Tiananmen: Causes and Consequences' (Winter 1990) 13:1 *Washington Quarterly* 79.

to bolster assertions that the restrictions citizens endured were lawful. One prominent analyst argued that shortcomings in the response to SARS reflected local governments' and citizens' insufficient understanding of existing laws and the extensive duties they imposed.[116]

Even when such arguments strained credulity or threatened to backfire (inviting charges that authorities manipulated or disregarded law) and even in the absence of declared emergencies, official and sympathetic sources sought to ground exceptional powers in legitimating sources of emergency-powers-related law.[117] Examples include the adoption of arguably retroactive prohibitions and sanctions amid SARS, vague claims that the constitution or laws authorised exceptional PLA roles and powers during the snow disasters, and accounts of emergency measures responding to the Sichuan earthquake that asserted or implied bases in the Emergency Response Law.[118]

Conversely, official and mainstream assessments saw questionable positive law authorisation as undermining the legitimacy of uses of exceptional powers. Adopting legislation or State Council regulations, rather than relying on discretion or policy, was seen as enhancing the stature of crisis-response measures. In the handling of SARS, the absence of a complete, coherent legal framework drew blame for delegitimating mid-crisis measures and the regime more generally. In the run-up to the Emergency Response Law (which reflected lessons from SARS), one prominent reformist legal scholar said the law would help assure that the country was thereafter 'ruled by law even under emergency circumstances'.[119] Charges that the Emergency Response Law might leave a gap in the legal foundation for emergencies left the legislation's drafters and supporters arguing defensively that the Constitution and the Law on Martial Law were sufficiently comprehensive.[120]

The crises of 2008 prompted law reform agendas that reflected perceptions of, and efforts to tap, law's capacity to legitimate. This is a plausible,

[116] See Part II above, on 'Limiting damage to the "(socialist) rule of law" project'; Mo (ed.), *SARS Period*, p. 27.

[117] Resort to strained legal arguments, and reluctance to declare formal emergencies, parallel the Philippines under Arroyo. See Pangalangan, Chapter 15.

[118] deLisle, 'SARS, Greater China', at 598–600; 'Chinese Army Mobilizes'; 'Ten Firsts'.

[119] Na, 'China's First Emergency Law'; 'Chinese Premier Urges Overcoming SARS'; Mo (ed.), *SARS Period*, pp. 3, 25; Li and Zhang, 'Several Questions', at 69–70; 'Constitutional Amendment Paves Way'; 'Experts: Law Must Specify Rights', *China Daily*, 31 March 2004 (quoting Yu An); see also the discussion of SARS in the section on 'Creating State Power through Law'.

[120] 'Emergency Response Law's Breakthrough'; Mo, 'Perfect Emergency Response Legislation' sect. 2; Li , *Explanations*; Qin, 'Yu An: Can Earthquake Speed?'

if incomplete, reading of calls from the head of the NPC and mainstream sources to revise the Emergency Response Law and pass legislation, including a State of Emergency Law, to address flaws in the legal structure that severe snows, a massive earthquake and Tibetan unrest had revealed as problems for the legitimacy – and legitimating efficacy – of state crisis management. Perhaps most tellingly, liberal legal experts supported such moves even characterizing a state of emergency as a potential 'mini-constitution' for emergency situations.[121] While their arguments reflected hope that such laws would better protect citizens' rights, the logic of their positions was that such laws – even if illiberal – would legitimate exceptional state powers properly claimed under their auspices.

VI. Constraining the state?

Emergency powers law in China includes much that enhances state power and discretion and threatens citizens' legal rights and law's broader roles. Still, Chinese emergency powers law has potential to constrain the state in ways akin to those asserted in defence of analogous law in more rule-of-law-based systems. In China as elsewhere, emergency powers law defines procedural requirements and substantive preconditions for exceptional powers, acknowledges law's role in regulating state action even in crises, exposes assertions of emergency powers to distinctively legal scrutiny and shapes and reflects political expectations about the use of extraordinary state authority. These features – which potentially range across the legal, institutional and normative types of checks that Vasuki Nesiah critically assesses in her chapter[122] and that loom large in the broader theoretical discourse on emergency powers – can limit the frequency and severity of departures from ordinary legal rights and the erosion of legality.

In China, such factors may be particularly significant. Although still comparatively low levels of solicitude for citizens' legal rights and legal checks on the state mean that laws authorising their suspension are especially worrisome, those same traits can make emergency powers laws a more unmixed (if still limited) good. Although Chinese authorities retain much capacity to circumvent them, such laws do purport to impose limits, and – given the regime's broader interest in a functioning legal system

[121] Qin, 'Economic Emergencies'; Qin, 'Quake Propels Improvement'; 'Various Legal Questions'; Mo, 'Perfect Emergency Response Legislation'; Mai, 'State, of Emergency'.

[122] Nesiah, Chapter 5.

and the legitimacy that law can confer – they may help forge restraints on derogations where few otherwise would exist.

A. *Power-creating law as state-limiting law*

Even primarily state-strengthening elements in PRC emergency powers law and practice can constrain the state. Many of the most seriously meant provisions assert, or reassert, central authority over uses of exceptional authority 'on the ground', where such power ultimately is exercised, often in disregard of laws as well as central leadership preferences. In Reform Era China, complaints about the abuse of citizens' rights frequently focus on local officials who disobey law, disregard policy and use harsh, unauthorised methods. Top leaders publicly regard this as a significant threat to their regime's legitimacy.[123]

Legal measures to address such ills by overseeing, directing or eliminating lower authorities' discretion can impose meaningful limits on state power. Imposing top-down discipline and reining in wayward officials imply restraining state power as a whole, including acts that overstep legal restrictions. Especially in the abuse-prone and transgression-inviting contexts of declared emergencies, purported crises, tens of thousands of local 'incidents' and numerous natural disasters, binding the state's hands to follow more faithfully the dictates of the state's head can limit the degree to which citizens encounter iron fists, battering ordinary law and rights.

Some Reform Era developments in emergency powers law and practice fit this scenario. Although martial law in 1989 might appear to be a pure instance of using emergency powers law to remove restraints on the power wielded under the direct control of top leaders, the reality was more complex. Plans to use military force to quash the Tiananmen Movement briefly raised the prospect that radical enhancement of central state power could backfire as rumours spread of divisions – and potential clashes – within the military.[124] Here, the backstory to Reform Era laws may matter. Among the most scarring aspects of the Cultural Revolution was internecine violence that reached near-combat levels in 1967,

[123] See K. J. O'Brien and Linjiang Li, 'Suing the Local State: Administrative Litigation in Rural China', in N. J. Diamant, S. B. Lubman and K. J. O'Brien (eds.), *Engaging the Law in China* (Stanford: Stanford University Press, 2005); Hand, 'Using Law for a Righteous Purpose'; Pils, 'Land Disputes;' M. Pei, *China's Trapped Transition* (Cambridge, Mass.: Harvard University Press, 2006).

[124] P. Ellingsen, 'Army Orders Soldiers to Enforce Martial Law', *Sydney Morning Herald*, 26 May 1989; Southerland, 'Military Group Opposes'; Gong, 'Tiananmen', at 87–9.

when military units appeared poised to fight one another and the army intervened to restore order and suppress armed civilian factions (some of which had seized power in beleaguered government institutions).

For post-Mao leaders and many of their subjects, recurrence of such loss of central control over means of coercion was to be resolutely avoided. Coups – or near coups – are major crises for any legal order, including laws governing emergency powers. One of the more disturbing apparent lessons from 1989 was that avoiding military rule or armed conflict may have depended on the personal authority with the PLA that Deng Xiaoping, Yang Shangkun and other elders held and that Jiang, Hu and other successors could not replicate.[125]

The Law on Martial Law stressed central authorisation and close oversight of resorts to martial law and threatened sanctions for state agents who acted beyond the powers conferred upon them by the statute and subordinate decrees.[126] The regime eschewed full emergency powers and relied initially and primarily on non-PLA resources to suppress the Tibetan uprising in 2008 and stressed the PLA's peaceful relief role after the Sichuan earthquake.[127] Such laws, wariness about using the military and determination to maintain central civilian control over military units responding to crises can reduce the likelihood, and likely severity, of derogation from ordinary laws in a crisis.

SARS brought new alarm about – and central reactions to – lower-level authorities' lawlessness and unaccountability to higher levels. Although the response contained significant illiberal and rights-restricting elements (including measures limiting individual mobility and mandating sanctions for spreading unauthorised but accurate information), much of the response and subsequent reforms targeted acts by local officials who overreached in stripping citizens of their limited freedoms to report outbreaks of the disease or to travel.[128]

[125] Chien-wen Kou, 'Why the Military Obeys the Party's Orders to Repress Popular Uprisings' (2000) 46:6 *Issues and Studies* 27; Gong, 'Tiananmen'; Zhang, Link and Nathan, *Tiananmen Papers*, pp. 273–317.

[126] Law on Martial Law, Articles 3, 7, 9–10, 30–1; Xie, 'Adjusting the Scope', at 42–4; Zhu, 'Martial Law', at 92–3.

[127] J. Yardley, 'As Chaos Erupted in Tibet, the Police Fled', *International Herald Tribune*, 25 March 2008; R. Spencer, 'China Unleashed Guns and Tear Gas as Tibet Protests Turn Violent', *Daily Telegraph*, 15 March 2008; 'Earthquake of Magnitude 7.8'.

[128] Wang Xiangwei, 'China Uses Criminal Penalties in Virus Battle', *South China Morning Post*, 25 April 2003; 'Chinese Official: Draft Law Will Not Affect Objective Reporting on Disasters', *Xinhua*, 6 July 2006; 'Emergency Law Mooted'; 'New SARS Regulations Improve China's Emergency Response'; deLisle, 'SARS, Greater China', at 598–604; Zheng and Lye.

Following SARS and the Law on Martial Law, the Emergency Response Law reflected similar concerns. It threatened sanctions for local officials who disregarded the law's requirements. It adopted means – including requiring emergency response plans – to assert central control, co-ordination and review of local authorities' assertions of extraordinary powers, including powers to limit citizens' rights.[129] Crises following adoption of the Emergency Response Law, but not bringing its full implementation or declarations of states of emergency, reprised these themes. Amid earthquake recovery efforts, top leaders pledged that incompetent or corrupt officials would be held accountable for transgressions that included violations of legal obligations to citizens.[130] In assessing responses to the 2008 earthquake and weather disasters, experts who played key roles in crafting emergency powers laws credited the 'people's spirit' not (failed) laws, and cited local authorities' unaccountable actions and *ad hoc* measures that illegally overrode citizens' rights as evidence of the need for better legislation and more effective implementation.[131]

More broadly and diffusely, elements in Chinese emergency powers law that authorise departures from ordinary legal rights and state-restraining legal rules create space for arguments that other derogations are, at least, suspect. Notwithstanding a legal tradition of relatively open-ended state powers, liberal participants in emergency response law debates sometimes argued for implied denial of formally ungranted powers. Such analyses supported calls for more finely differentiated and fully defined types of emergency and accompanying powers.[132] Especially among official and orthodox circles, such power-limiting dimensions of power-granting

'SARS and China's Political System', pp. 52–6; Liu, *Chinese Law*, pp. 45, 100–6; Lawson and Xu, 'SARS in Canada and China', at 210–20; Zhong, 'Crisis Management', at 92–101. Travel increased the risk of contagion but local authorities' moves to bar 'outsiders' flouted central authority, poorly fitted disease-containment goals and threatened economic harms.

[129] Emergency Response Law, Articles 63, 66–8; 'Chinese Official: Draft Law Will Not Affect'; Jiang, 'Emergency Situations', sect. 4.5, 4.8; Li and Zhang, 'Several Questions', at 73–4; Wang, 'State of Emergency', sect. 2.2, 3.1.

[130] Wang Aihua and Yu Zheng, 'Interpreting the Sichuan Earthquake', *Xinhua*, 11 June 2008; '43 Punished'; R. Callick, 'Beijing Muzzles Quake Families', *Australian*, 23 June 2008.

[131] Mo, 'Perfect Emergency Response Legislation'; Qin, 'Economic Emergencies'; Qin, 'Quake Propels Improvement' (quoting Yu An); Mai, 'State of Emergency'.

[132] Qin, 'Economic Emergencies'; Chen, 'Interpretation'; Jiang, 'Emergency Situations', sect. 2–3. On implications of different levels or types of emergency derogation from ordinary laws, see Lee, Chapter 14; M. Hor, 'Law and Terror: Singapore Stories and Malaysian Dilemmas', in V. V. Ramraj, M. Hor and K. Roach (eds.), *Global Anti-Terrorism Law and Policy* (Cambridge: Cambridge University Press, 2005), pp. 273–94.

emergency law may have most traction where they most strongly tie emergency powers to protecting substantive aims and values.

B. *Substantive justifications as narrowing constructions*

The regime's reliance on a few substantive justifications for exceptional measures can help constrain state power. When the regime has used formal legal means to articulate conditions and justifications for declaring emergencies or martial law, it has interpreted and potentially narrowed capacious authority for extraordinary powers.[133] The Law on Martial Law and the Emergency Response Law did this for the terse and vague 1982 and 2004 constitutional provisions. The 2004 amendment itself was undertaken to articulate – and thus potentially constrict – conditions that warrant emergency powers (including those short of martial law).[134]

The Law on Martial Law provided that martial law would be imposed only under conditions of turmoil, riot or disturbance in which nothing less would do to protect order, lives and property.[135] Some NPC lawmakers endorsed restrictive understandings of the legislation, arguing that the law must 'make clear' the 'detailed' conditions triggering martial law, and that those excluded 'demonstrations arising from economic disputes' or 'minor unrest confined to a small area'. Martial law should be introduced only with 'great caution' to serve those ends, only under the law's procedures and only until 'social order' returned.[136]

A decade later, the Emergency Response Law mandated that emergency measures be commensurate in 'nature, extent and scope' with the hazards to life, property, security and order that constituted the emergency and cease when emergency conditions were eliminated or controlled.[137] A broad spectrum of legal experts, including some who helped frame emergency powers legislation, argued that conditions warranting martial law and states of emergency had been defined, and should be construed, narrowly, and that such conditions would not often arise. They opined that

[133] Some analyses from liberal-democratic constitutional contexts conclude that detailed provisions defining the scope and terms of emergency powers can constrain the state. See Campbell, 'Law, Terror and Social Movements', and Roach, 'Ordinary Laws'.

[134] Wang and Wang, '2004 Amendment', sect. 2.5; 'Official Explains Draft Amendment'.

[135] Law on Martial Law, Articles 2, 12.

[136] 'National People's Congress Legislators on Draft Law Covering Martial Law', *Xinhua*, 1 March 1996; 'Further Details of Draft Martial Law', *Zhongguo Xinwen She*, 21 December 1995; A. Cheung and C. Yeung, 'Martial Law Boost for PLA', *South China Morning Post*, 21 December 1995; 'China Mulls Law Covering Martial Law', *Xinhua*, 20 December 1995.

[137] Emergency Response Law, Articles 1, 11, 58.

a good, mature system of emergency law was one that was effective and available but rarely used. Some asserted that only war or severe domestic disorder warranted martial law; lesser threats such as most public health crises, most natural disasters and merely localised unrest merited lesser responses, whether under the colour-coded categories of the Emergency Response Law or under other, ordinary laws. Such commentaries insisted on proportionality between the severity of the challenge and the extent of departure from the ordinary legal order.[138] Where state-limiting interpretations have been embodied in such formal legal terms or highly publicised and officially condoned glosses, their too easy abandonment would invite doubt about the regime's commitment to the broader project of ruling by law and imperil the benefits it provides in terms of legitimacy, prosperity and order.

The political contexts of the principal emergency powers statutes and the 2004 constitutional amendment indicate potentially state-constraining effects of tying legitimacy of exceptional authority to particular or narrow substantive justifications. Absence of clear substantive criteria for imposing martial law in 1989 or adopting SARS-related measures in 2003 gave critics room to challenge, and elements within the party-state apparatus reason to question, the propriety of using extraordinary means to address challenges that arguably did not severely threaten political stability or obviously require radical departures from the ordinary legal order.[139] Perceptions that the regime overreached – or lacked viable standards for defining overreaching – and thereby sacrificed legitimacy in 1989, amid SARS and again in 2008 appear to have helped advance more formally state-restraining constitutional and legislative changes.

[138] Zhu, 'Martial Law', at 90; 'Constitutional Amendment Paves Way' (Li Shuguang on content and rarity of conditions for martial law); Xie, 'Adjusting the Scope', at 42 (similar); Mo, 'Perfect Emergency Response Legislation', sect. 2.4 (types and levels of crisis and proportional response); Chen, 'Interpretation' (Yu An making similar point); Wang, 'State of Emergency', sect. 1.1, 3.2; 'Interview with Xu Chongde'.

[139] Southerland, 'Military Group Opposes' (senior military leaders and NPC chief doubted martial law was warranted and opposed using military); A. Mitchell, J. Mulvaney and J. Sommer, 'Troops Blocked in Beijing; Martial Law Declared in City', *Newsday*, 20 May 1989 (official newspaper commentary and ordinary citizens see no martial-law-warranting violence among protesters); D. Holley, 'China Orders Martial Law, Deploys Troops in Tibet', *Los Angeles Times*, 6 March 1989; Southerland, '300 Tibetans' (lack of violence before resort to military force); Zou, 'SARS and the Rule of Law', pp. 104–7 (belated turn to legal measures and extensive criticism of excessive harshness indicate rule-of-law deficiencies); He Baogang, 'SARS and Freedom of the Press: Has the Chinese Government Learnt a Lesson?', in Wong and Zheng (eds.), *The SARS Epidemic*, pp. 186–95 (problematic restrictions on information flows).

Proponents of relatively limited scope for emergency powers have adumbrated or embraced this analysis. On these views, the response to SARS showed the need for a stronger legal 'mechanism' to address emergencies and a sharper legal 'definition' of substantive conditions triggering emergency powers. For other legal commentators, the 'illegal' resort to emergency powers in response to the crises of 2008 taught a similar lesson. More broadly, some presented as models for Chinese reform the emergency powers laws of foreign 'rule-of-law' states, which they portrayed as imposing strict limits and conditions.[140]

By relying heavily on particular – and dire – justifications for martial law in 1989 and special anti-SARS measures, China's rulers undertook one of the more binding steps available to them to define emergencies warranting extraordinary measures. In China's undemocratic politics, and despite China's ostensibly civilian legal culture, a common-law-like mechanism of precedent can be relatively powerful among the comparatively modest means for limiting state discretion. It can make it harder to expand the universe of 'exceptional states' to include lesser threats to core values or serious perils to previously peripheral goals. Fortuity may enhance the constraining effect here: in the few cases where Reform Era Chinese authorities clearly and formally have asserted emergency powers, they faced apparently serious threats that they portrayed in near-apocalyptic terms. For future invocations of emergency powers, it may matter that Tiananmen, SARS and purportedly violent secessionist movements provide poor foundations for declaring states of exception when more mundane challenges arise. It may matter that China's rulers have forgone claims of martial-law-justifying emergencies in the face of other threats, including unrest that swept cities beyond Beijing and Lhasa in 1989, resistance by Falun Gong (which authorities described as a major threat) in the late 1990s, tumult in Tibet in 2008 (which echoed 1989) or the earthquake in Sichuan the same year. Such uses and non-uses may have helped set a high bar for invoking legal emergency powers (although this may come at the price of more frequent use of exceptional powers without legal authorisation and the undermining of modest constraints such authorisation might impose).

[140] 'Emergency Law Mooted' (SARS showed 'our society lacks the experience and mechanism to deal with emergencies' and requires new law); 'Constitutional Amendment: A Look through Expert Eyes', http://chinaorg.cn, 13 March 2004, available at www.10thnpc.org.cn/english/features/90166.htm (Hu Jinguang saying constitutional amendment on states of emergency would provide 'clear-cut definition' for suspension of rights that was lacking in SARS context); Qin, 'Quake Propels Improvement' (2008 crises); Jiang, 'Regulation of Law Concerning Administrative Rights under a State of Emergency' (foreign models).

Broader features of Chinese politics increase the difficulty of abandoning such potentially state-limiting legal commitments and informal precedents. Against the Mao-era backdrop of wild ideological swings and the recasting of orthodox positions as heretical and even criminal, Reform Era China's leaders pledged, and significantly bound themselves, to provide increased stability, predictability and non-retroactivity in policies and the laws embodying them.

Modest political liberalisation, increased transparency, weakened ideology and emergent critical media – along with the official turn to law – have lessened the Reform Era Chinese regime's capacity to define politically salient facts and control their interpretation. The absence of democratic accountability and the party-state's monopoly of organised political power do not give leaders unbounded discretion to define an emergency that legitimates a special response, especially a fully lawful one.[141] Although China's resiliently authoritarian and residually ideological system still accords rulers much latitude in defining when severe challenges to order, security and prosperity exist, Reform Era changes assure that not all circumstances present plausible (much less convincing) cases for exceptional powers in the eyes of a changed and broadened universe of relevant political actors and constituencies.

C. Rights-protecting law, law's legitimacy and critiquing the state

State-constraining and rights-protecting provisions in Chinese emergency powers law have made facially promising commitments that much official and orthodox discourse pledged the state would respect. The regime's moves to tap law's emergent legitimacy to support emergency powers further open the door to legal analysis and critique. State actors who invoke laws authorising martial law or states of emergency – or deploy exceptional authority formally regulated by law – are more likely to face, or even undertake, serious assessments of their fidelity to such law's letter and spirit.

In 1989, participants in the Tiananmen Movement and sympathisers argued that the martial law proclamation was invalid because it effectively covered all of Beijing and therefore should have been issued by the NPC Standing Committee, not the State Council. In critics' eyes, China's rulers

[141] See A. J. Nathan, 'Resilient Authoritarianism' (January 2003) 14:1 *Journal of Democracy* 6; R. Baum, *Burying Mao: Chinese Politics in the Age of Deng Xiaoping* (Princeton: Princeton University Press, 1994); deLisle, 'Legalization without Democratization'.

probably violated the letter and definitely violated the spirit of the Constitution. At worst, martial law reflected unconstitutional usurpation of the NPC Standing Committee's role by senior leaders, or even a coup by a few leaders in collaboration with parts of the PLA.[142] Tiananmen activists called on the NPC to meet, and NPC members sought to gather enough signatures from their ranks to force a special session. Their aim was to have the NPC exercise its constitutional authority to remove the Premier or declare unconstitutional – or override – the martial law proclamation, as well as protect constitutional rights of speech and organisation from restrictions improperly imposed by government authorities.[143] Critics later denounced trials of Tiananmen dissidents for failing, without legally adequate cause, to respect open trial requirements and other criminal procedure laws.[144]

Prominent assessments of the handling of SARS criticised failures to use the existing infectious disease statute to frame the state's response. On these views, the handling of SARS suggested a troubling and incorrect view that extraordinary conditions justified 'breaking' the ordinary constitutional and legal rules and demonstrated the need for clear and strict constitutional and statutory rules to ensure that responses to emergencies stayed within the rule of law (albeit of an 'exceptional' type). This exceptional rule of law required state actors to regard proper legal authorisation as an indispensable condition for exercising emergency powers and to obey legal procedures and time limits.[145]

The Law on Martial Law added clearer commitments and standards for measuring state behaviour. This is one dimension of provisions that reiterated and added detail to constitutional procedures for imposing martial law, restated and elaborated allocations of institutional roles and articulated narrow and extreme circumstances warranting martial law and abrogation of citizens' legal rights. The statute declared citizens' 'legitimate rights' would be protected, requisitioned property would be returned and

[142] Lo, *China's Legal Awakening*, p. 293; J. A. Cohen, 'Tiananmen and the Rule of Law', in G. Hicks (ed.), *The Broken Mirror: China After Tiananmen* (London: Longman, 1991); Ogden *et al.*, *China's Search*, pp. 246–51; see also Zhang, Link and Nathan, *Tiananmen Papers*, pp. 175–365.

[143] 'Protest Staged in Peking on 25th May', *Zhongguo Tongxun She*, 25 May 1989, BBC Summary of World Broadcasts, 31 May 1989; S. Handelman, 'Chinese Students Demand Lifting of Martial Law', *Toronto Star*, 23 May 1989; Southerland, 'Military Group Opposes'; Lo, *China's Legal Awakening*, pp. 290–1; Ogden *et al.*, *China's Search*, pp. 217–18, 246–51.

[144] Lo, *China's Legal Awakening*, pp. 304–15.

[145] Mo (ed.), *SARS Period*, pp. 5–6, 25–31, 101–3; Mo, 'Perfect Emergency Response Legislation', sect. 1.3; Liu, *Chinese Law*, pp. 26–32.

compensation provided, detentions would be registered and reasons given, and arrests would require prosecutorial approval. It pledged that martial law enforcement personnel would obey relevant laws and be 'responsible under law' for violations.[146] NPC Standing Committee members and State Council officials elaborated on such restrictions and stressed that the law mandated 'restraint' in using martial law powers, restricted martial law to situations where its triggering conditions were clearly met and embodied the principle that the use of force be 'as prudent as possible'. As some critics saw it, legal regulation of martial law needed to go further still to keep state power within proper and constitutional limits under conditions conducive to excess.[147]

The Emergency Response Law and the underlying constitutional amendment on states of emergency continued these patterns. Going beyond martial law predecessors, they framed specific substantive and procedural standards for multitiered emergency powers and restrictions on citizens' legal rights. These offered a clearer law-based foundation for evaluating whether authorities declared the proper level of emergency by proper means, whether they stayed within the bounds of accompanying special powers and whether they ceased using special powers when crisis conditions ceased.[148]

In official media, the law received praise for unifying scattered and patchy rules for crises, articulating broad principles governing emergencies and undercutting the legitimacy of once-prevalent *ad hoc* and mobilisational approaches. Senior State Council officials explained that the law aimed to restrict administrative power to what is necessary and appropriate in the authorities' judgement under conditions when the government could most easily abuse power and violate rights and when protection of such rights was especially important.[149] Unofficial commentators echoed these themes and argued that enhanced restrictions on – and stricter requirements of legal bases for – state authority in emergencies had become necessary as China had reformed and developed and as citizens' 'awareness of autonomy' had grown.[150]

[146] Law on Martial Law, Articles 2–3, 7, 17, 27, 29–30.
[147] 'National People's Congress Legislators on Draft Law'; Wang, 'State of Emergency', sect. 2.1, 3.2; Zhu, 'Martial Law', at 92–3.
[148] Emergency Response Law, Articles 1–11, 42–52.
[149] See, for example, 'Emergency Law Mooted'; Meng, 'China's First Emergency Law'; 'China's Assembly Begins Hearing Draft Emergency Law'; 'Emergency Response Law's Breakthrough'; Wang, 'State of Emergency'; Li and Zhang, 'Several Questions', at 73.
[150] Mo (ed.), *SARS Period*, pp. 101–3; 'Constitutional Amendment Paves Way'.

Provisions in the law limiting suspensions of citizens' rights received extensive favourable discussion.[151] Relatively orthodox legal analysts discerned in the 'state of emergency' constitutional amendment a commitment to protecting 'the basic rights of the masses' – a feature that would extend to legislation.[152] Leading legal scholars called for China to emulate 'modern rule-of-law states' in which the special emergency powers remain limited by law – and legislative intent – and may not infringe 'basic' civil rights and freedoms.[153] Some argued that when an emergency powers statute grants the state power to abrogate specified rights, it also draws 'a line' concerning 'individual rights that the state could not surpass', offers a 'clear-cut definition' of which rights can be suspended and should minimize derogations from rights of criminal defendants, civil litigants and even plaintiffs in administrative litigation suits.[154] Prominent academic commentators and participants in drafting the Emergency Response Law asserted that the goals of the statute and proper state of emergency law included minimising the impact on civil rights and citizens' freedom and protecting citizens' legal, constitutional and international human rights – including those embodied in the International Covenant on Civil and Political Rights and especially those rights which the Covenant declared non-derogable.[155] Such comments gained force from the regime's earlier acceptance of the long-rejected principle of universal human rights and from growing constituencies for human rights and kindred norms among Chinese liberal law reformers.[156]

151 'Emergency Law Mooted'; 'China Mulls Emergency Management Law'; Qin, 'Quake Propels Improvement' (original law has 'no flaws'); cf. 'Experts: Law Must Specify Rights'.

152 Sun and Li, 'Chinese Legal Experts Praise' (Hu Jinguang); 'Interview with Xu Chongde'.

153 Jiang Mingan, 'Regulation of Law Concerning Administrative Rights under a State of Emergency', *Chinese Constitution [Zhongguo Xianfa]* (2002), http://big5.chinalawinfo.com/article.chinalawinfo.com/article/user/article_display.asp?ArticleID=26215; cf. Jiang, 'Emergency Situations' (foreign, rule-of-law country practices as lessons for China); 'Interview with Xu Chongde' (conservative assessment that all countries suspend citizens' legal rights when necessary in emergencies).

154 'Emergency Law Mooted' (quoting Jiang Mingan); 'Constitutional Amendment: A Look through Expert Eyes' (quoting Hu Jinguang); Sun and Li, 'Legal Experts Praise'; Mai, 'State of Emergency'.

155 Jiang, 'Regulation of Law'; Mo, 'Perfect Emergency Response Legislation', sect. 1.3–1.4, 2.4; Mo (ed.), *SARS Period*, p. 25; Chen, 'Interpretation'; Wang, 'State of Emergency', introduction and sect. 3.3; Jiang, 'Emergency Situations', sect. 4.7.

156 A. H. Y. Chen, 'Conclusion: Comparative Reflections on Human Rights in Asia', in R. Peerenboom, C. J. Petersen and A. H. Y. Chen (eds.), *Human Rights in Asia* (New York: Routledge, 2006), pp. 487, 502–5; R. Peerenboom, 'Competing Conceptions of the Rule of Law in China', in R. Peerenboom (ed.), *Asian Discourses on the Rule of Law* (New York: Routledge, 2004), pp. 113–45.

Perhaps equally telling were critiques of provisions that were not included – or claimed not to be included – in emergency powers legislation. With Hong Kong's reversion to China nearing, some in the colony worried that the Law on Martial Law would extend to the future Special Administrative Region. This elicited reassurance – albeit of questionable legal accuracy and against the problematic backdrop of PRC officials' insistence on the central Chinese government's ultimate legal authority to impose martial law in Chinese territory – from prominent members of relevant NPC bodies that the Basic Law for the Hong Kong Special Administrative Region governed and precluded application of the Law on Martial Law.[157]

Diverse Chinese critics contended that a provision in the draft Emergency Response Law punishing 'irregular' or 'unauthorised' reporting (even if accurate) on 'sudden events' and media violations of relevant 'regulations' (which might include administrative rules) was too open to interpretation and abuse by local authorities, and insufficiently rights-protecting.[158] The article faced especially sharp attacks as a departure from the regime's post-SARS commitment to greater openness (especially about crises) and as an infringement of a 'right to know' that some liberal intellectuals saw emerging from the SARS debacle and that seemed to gain ground in party orthodoxy at the Seventeenth Party Congress. After an initial defence from official sources, key offending elements were dropped.[159]

[157] C. Law and R. L. Wan, 'Martial Law May be Used in HK', *South China Morning Post*, 24 December 1995; Cheung and Yeung, 'Martial Law Boost'; 'Martial Law in Hong Kong', *South China Morning Post*, 22 December 1995; Mo, 'Perfect Emergency Response Legislation', sect. 2.2 (Hong Kong Basic Law provision as part of PRC state of emergency law); Y. Ghai, *Hong Kong's New Constitutional Order*, 2nd edn) (Hong Kong: Hong Kong University Press, 1999), pp. 447–8.

[158] 'Draft Emergency Law Bans False Information on Accidents', *Xinhua*, 24 June 2007; 'Emergency Law Mooted'; 'Scholar Calls for Caution on Making Press-Related Law', *Ta Kung Pao* (Hong Kong), 27 July 2006; J. Ma, 'Disquiet Among Journalists over Chinese Draft Media Law', *South China Morning Post*, 6 July 2006; M.-A. Toy, 'China Law Aims to "Shut Up" Media', *The Age* (Melbourne), 5 July 2006; http://danwei.org/media_regulation/draft_bill_breaking_news'stori.php (postings from Mind Meters Blog); J. Kahn, 'China Weighs Fines for Reports on "Sudden Events"', *New York Times*, 26 June 2006.

[159] Meng, 'China's First Emergency Law'; Sun and Li, 'Legal Experts Praise'; 'Emergency Response Law "Will Ensure Accurate Info"'; Mei Tzu, 'Legislate to Safeguard the Public's Right to Know', *Ta Kung Pao* (Hong Kong), 27 June 2003; He, 'SARS and Freedom of the Press'; Liu, *Chinese Law*, p. 14 (Guangzhou newspaper deputy director's argument for media transparency to promote accountability); Meng Na and Lu Chuanzhong, 'Government Transparency in Quake Relief Not "Forced Reaction" for Hosting Olympics', *Xinhua*, 26 May 2008; Goodspeed, 'China Sees Seismic Shift'.

Also significant were criticisms of state responses to crises that followed the Emergency Response Law's adoption. Prominent legal scholars – some of whom participated in the law's drafting – and other commentators offered a sweeping indictment. Local authorities failed to report emergent threats in accordance with the law and resorted to concocted measures rather than those provided under the law.[160] Such behaviour permitted or invited more severe infringements of legal rights than the laws authorised. Not invoking and following the Emergency Response Law to address the Sichuan earthquake reduced vital trust in the government's actions.[161] Some of the faults lay in the law's excessively thin content, which left local officials to resort to 'necessary but illegal' measures that lacked the legitimacy (and limits) they might have had under a proper legal mandate. Such problems showed that the Emergency Response Law needed revision to create a 'stricter emergency rights system' so that emergency powers would be 'effectively supervised through the rule of law'.[162]

The regime's enduring dilemma concerning emergency powers provides another indication of emergency powers law's potential to constrain the state. We have seen Chinese leaders' reluctance to invoke fully and formally martial law and other emergency powers and a long march toward more comprehensive legislation to regulate emergency powers. We also have seen the expansion of exceptional legal states from martial law to a wider variety of emergencies and lesser crises, legislative authorisation of temporary exceptional measures by local authorities and departures from background legal rights and rules for different levels of emergency, and vague official assertions of legal support for informal exceptional measures. The tension here suggests the regime may be navigating between two potentially damaging law-based lines of criticism that the regime's self-interested commitment to legal development and the regime-valued rise of law's legitimacy have made tenable and effective: lawyerly arguments against small departures from fairly clear and elaborate laws, and a broader attack on using extraordinary powers too much and too often outside the law.

Finally, some of emergency powers law's most significant prospects for limiting the state may lie beyond emergencies, real or concocted. Once

[160] Qin, 'Economic Emergencies' (quoting Yu An); Qin, 'Quake Propels Improvement' (quoting Mo Jihong); Ma, 'Slow Response'.

[161] Li Datong, 'China's Soft Power Failure', *Open Democracy*, 20 May 2008, http://en.chinaelections.org/newsinfo.asp?newsid=1574.

[162] Qin, 'Quake Propels Improvement'; 'Various Legal Questions'.

laws and power-holders articulate substantive conditions for emergencies and processes for arrogating exceptional power, disregard of ordinary legal limits likely becomes more illegitimate in other contexts, including where legal means to special powers are formally available but unused. To the seemingly considerable extent that the leadership seeks to preserve a broader project of legality and law's legitimacy, this line of argument has promise. As relatively liberal participants in recent Chinese emergency powers law debates have asserted, legal rules for emergencies can support a 'division of spheres' or 'acoustical separation' or 'cordon sanitaire' between exceptional conditions when ordinary law is suspended and non-emergency circumstances when it is not. This, in turn, can support rule-of-law agendas by reducing the likelihood that 'lawlessness under pressure' will 'spill over' to undermine confidence in the regime's commitment to law in service of economic development, political stability or other goals.

VII. Conclusion: emergency powers and emerging legality

Rights-protecting and state-restraining provisions in emergency powers law, and favourable official or orthodox glosses and pledges concerning them, are not self-enforcing. Where well-crafted legal restraints threaten to bind, China's rulers may evade them, asserting that non-emergency laws authorise the powers the state seeks or that exceptional conditions demand extraordinary measures despite the possible absence of a proper legal mandate. Worse yet, Oren Gross[163] and H. P. Lee[164] may be right in warning that trying to keep emergency powers within the framework of law may undermine legal restraints, in the end augmenting the state's power and reducing the reviewability of its actions. In Dyzenhaus's terms, a little legality may be worse than none.[165] Relatively liberal, and fairly influential, Chinese legal experts' arguments are not certain to prevail despite their resonance with international norms that PRC authorities increasingly accept in principle. Regime interests and agendas that parallel such arguments do not reliably trump other party-state priorities.

Liberal, pro-legality agendas in China can overreach and provoke pushback, especially where backed by foreign pressure or closely associated

[163] Gross, 'Chaos and Rules'. [164] Lee, Chapter 14.

[165] D. Dyzenhaus, 'State of Exception', in M. Troper (ed.), *Traité International de Droit Constitutionnel* (Paris: Presse Universitaire de France, 2009).

with foreign sources.[166] Clark Lombardi's[167] and Simon Chesterman's[168] chapters illustrate such perils in other Asian states. As Nadirsiyah Hosen's account of Indonesia in this volume and the contemporary discourse over emergency powers in the West illustrate, emergency powers-limiting pro-rule-of-law influences from abroad have been undercut by post-9/11 anti-terrorism agendas.[169] Similar problems are potentially serious in the PRC, where rulers are perennially wary of outsiders' drives to change China, increasingly confident in a Chinese alternative model of law, politics and development and zealously opportunistic in invoking China's modest terrorism worries and 'war on terror'-driven shifts in US and other Western laws and practices.[170] More fundamentally, China's emergency powers law is the product of a capable and durable authoritarian regime that has had much scope and motivation to craft law that confers much power and discretion in responding to real, perceived or concocted emergencies (and governing under more ordinary conditions).

Nonetheless, state-restraining elements in Chinese emergency powers law and developments surrounding it show at least potential for meaningful impact. On its own or under pressure at home or abroad, the Chinese regime may steer between the Scylla of asserting legal bases for emergency powers and other exceptional measures so frequently that it destroys the force of ordinary law, and the Charybdis of resorting to extraordinary authority without purported or plausible legal foundations so often that it renders emergency powers law and other legal restraints impotent. Relatively liberal, pro-legality Chinese critics and participants in shaping those laws may prove right in siding implicitly with Bruce Ackerman[171] and, in this volume, Chen[172]: there may be promise in a neo-Roman (or

[166] Jiang, 'Emergency Situations' (foreign emergency powers laws as models for China); deLisle, 'Legalization without Democratization', pp. 187–8, 201–3; J. deLisle, 'Lex Americana?: United States Legal Assistance, American Legal Models, and Legal Change in the Post-Communist World and Beyond' (1999) 20 *University of Pennsylvania Journal of International Economic Law* 179.

[167] C. B. Lombardi, 'Islamism as a Response to Emergency Rule in Pakistan: The Surprising Proposal of Justice A. R. Cornelius' (Chapter 16), this volume.

[168] Chesterman, Chapter 9.

[169] N. Hosen, 'Emergency Powers and the Rule of Law in Indonesia' (Chapter 10), this volume.

[170] R. Peerenboom, 'Varieties of Rule of Law', in Peerenboom (ed.), *Asian Discourses*, pp. 13–21; J. deLisle, 'Development without Democratization: China, Law and the East Asian Model', in J. V. Ciprut (ed.), *Democratizations: Comparisons, Confrontations and Contrasts* (Cambridge, Mass.: MIT Press, 2008).

[171] B. Ackerman, *Before the Next Attack: Preserving Civil Liberties in an Age of Terrorism* (New Haven: Yale University Press, 2006); 'The Emergency Constitution', (2004) 113 *Yale Law Journal* 1029.

[172] Chen, Chapter 3.

French Republican) approach that seeks to realise some of the potential of emergency powers law to constrain the state by building down from a thin veneer of legality, and exploiting the regime's apparent susceptibility to the remarkably widespread compulsion to argue that its uses of exceptional powers are lawful. Herein also may lie the shoots of a Chinese version of Mark Tushnet's 'moralised politics', capable of generating extra-legal limits (rooted partly in ideologies of legality) on emergency powers.[173] Such politics might constrain regime behaviour that otherwise might be as unchecked as in the world analysed by Carl Schmitt and arguably until recently inhabited by China's rulers, wherein the sovereign has uncontrollable discretion to determine states of exception.

Emergency powers law is a puzzling, but not inexplicable, phenomenon in a system with China's characteristics. Although they might seem to have little reason to do so, China's leaders have turned to law to address emergency powers for reasons that are specific to Reform Era China but also are intelligible in terms familiar from experiences and ideals of liberal, democratic, constitutional, law-governed regimes. In China, as in other Asian states and the West, the turn to law to address emergency powers can devastate legal rights and law's roles but also could impose meaningful constraints on the state. How much either potential is realised in China depends on still-evolving choices by the ruling elite, efforts of those who seek to enhance law's roles, the extent to which norms of legality take hold and the relative prevalence of conditions that present compelling or plausible cases for using exceptional powers in what remains an exceptional state.

[173] M. Tushnet, 'The Political Constitution of Emergency Powers: Some Conceptual Issues', in Ramraj (ed.), *Emergencies*, pp. 145–55; C. Schmitt, *Political Theology: Four Chapters on the Theory of Sovereignty* (Cambridge, Mass.: MIT Press, 1988).

PART IV

The role of the courts

14

Constitutionalised emergency powers: a plague on Asian constitutionalism?

H. P. LEE

I. Introduction

A conspicuous distinction between Asian constitutional frameworks and those of many constitutional liberal democracies – particularly those in the Anglo-American tradition, such as the United States, the United Kingdom, Canada, New Zealand and Australia – is the omission of a constitutionalised and elaborate framework of emergency powers from the national constitutions of these liberal-democratic countries. Does the existence of such a framework in many Asian constitutions uphold or undermine the rule of law? To what extent can the courts protect the rule of law in the face of a deployment of sweeping powers following a declaration or proclamation of emergency? Can specific constitutional norms be crystallised by the courts so that the constitutionality of emergency powers might continue to be tested in the courts? The theme running through this chapter is that in times of crisis (real or imaginary) the invocation of sweeping powers embodied in a constitution poses a more serious threat to constitutionalism than when such powers are in ordinary statutory form. The next part of the chapter (Part II) examines the experience of constitutionalised emergency powers in Asia, explaining how those powers operate and the problems arising from their use. The following part (Part III) defends the use of ordinary emergency powers in light of this experience.

II. The dilemmas of constitutionalised emergency powers

In many Asian countries, the framers of the constitution were motivated by the best of intentions when they advocated the embodiment of emergency powers as a set of constitutional powers. In many of these countries, the maintenance of national stability in terms of national peace and security could not be regarded as a given. Many of them, emerging from the shadow of colonial rule, were (and many still are) grappling with inter-ethnic rivalry and violence, religious warfare or terrorist insurgency. In consequence, the decolonisation process 'has resulted in a structural legacy that treats as normal, the exceptional situation of emergencies'.[1] This section will show how constitutionalised emergency powers have been abused in Asia and how they have eroded constitutionalism, both through their invocation in questionable contexts and by way of constitutional amendments that have removed many of the procedural safeguards that were intended to keep the powers in check.

A. *Constitutionalised emergency powers: general features*

The constitutionalised emergency powers of many constitutions of the post-World War II independent polities have a number of common features. First of all, there is provision for a 'proclamation of emergency' to be made generally by the Head of State on the advice of his/her ministers. The formal statement tends to recite the conditions articulated in the constitution as the basis for the proclamation. In the case of the Malaysian Constitution, the Yang di-Pertuan Agong (or 'King') is empowered by Article 150(1) to issue a Proclamation of Emergency if he is 'satisfied that a grave emergency exists whereby the security, or economic life, or public order in the Federation or any part thereof is threatened'. While a Proclamation of Emergency is in force, the executive authority of the Malaysian Federation shall, 'notwithstanding anything in this Constitution', extend to any matters within the legislative authority of a State and to the giving of directions to the Government of a State or to any officer or authority thereof. Subject to some specified limitations, the Malaysian Parliament is also empowered, 'notwithstanding anything in this Constitution', to make laws with respect to any matter, 'if it appears to Parliament that the law is required by reason of the emergency'. Entrenched emergency powers can be found in the constitutions of countries such as East Timor, Fiji, India, the Philippines, Singapore, Sri Lanka and Thailand.

B. *Abuse of emergency powers*

The record in many developing countries of the invocation of emergency powers is a dismal one. In the case of Malaysia, the Malaysian Constitution

[1] K. Y. L. Tan, 'From Myanmar to Manila: A Brief Study of Emergency Powers in Southeast Asia' (Chapter 6), this volume, p. 151.

since the attainment of independence in 1957 has been weathering a 'storm of exigencies'.[2] A state of emergency was declared by the King on 3 September 1964 following the launching of a 'confrontation' by Indonesia during the Sukarno era. A constitutional imbroglio between the State government of Sarawak and the Federal Government resulted in the invocation of Article 150 on 14 September 1966.[3] The outbreak of racial riots in Kuala Lumpur in the midst of a general election led to a national state of emergency on 15 May 1969.[4] Another tussle between State and Federal governments, this time involving the State of Kelantan, resulted in a proclamation of emergency on 8 November 1977, with the main aim of extending Federal executive authority to Kelantan.[5]

In the case of the 1966 proclamation of emergency targeting the State of Sarawak, the purpose of ousting a State Chief Minister who had fallen out of favour with the Federal Government was achieved. In the case of the 1977 proclamation of emergency to counter a perceived threat to 'the security and economic life' of the State of Kelantan, the Federal Government was able to prevent the ousting of a State Chief Minister against whom a motion of 'no confidence' had been passed by the Legislative Assembly of Kelantan. In both instances, there were serious doubts whether in fact there was 'a real emergency or an emergency of convenience'.[6]

In India, a blatant abuse of the emergency powers in the Indian Constitution arose when Prime Minister Indira Gandhi was found guilty of electoral violations which would have led to her being barred from holding office for six years. Imtiaz Omar explained:

> Faced with the threat of losing power to the Opposition, Prime Minister Gandhi, apparently without consulting the Cabinet, asked the President to

[2] See H. P. Lee, 'Emergency Powers in Malaysia', in F. A. Trindade and H. P. Lee (eds.), *The Constitution of Malaysia: Further Perspectives and Developments* (Singapore: Oxford University Press, 1986), p. 136.

[3] H. P. Lee, 'The Ningkan Saga: A Chief Minister in the Eye of a Storm', in A. Harding and H. P. Lee (eds.), *Constitutional Landmarks in Malaysia* (Petaling Jaya: LexisNexis, 2007), pp. 77–87.

[4] C. Das, 'The May 13th Riots and Emergency Rule', in Harding and Lee (eds.), *Constitutional Landmarks*, pp. 103–13.

[5] K. A. bin Mokhtar, 'The Emergency Powers (Kelantan) Act 1977', in Harding and Lee (eds.), *Constitutional Landmarks*, pp. 135–43.

[6] D. Asri, Malaysian Parliamentary Debate (Dewan Rakyat) 8 November 1977, para. 4132 and 4143, as cited in bin Mokhtar, 'The Emergency Powers (Kelantan) Act', p. 141. See also C. Das, *Governments and Crisis Powers: A Study of the Use of Emergency Powers Under the Malaysian Constitution and Parts of the Commonwealth* (Kuala Lumpur: Malaysian Current Law Journal, 1996), p. 178.

> proclaim an Emergency on the ground that the security of India was threatened by internal disturbances. The Proclamation of Emergency, which was issued on June 26, 1975, inaugurated an era of draconian measures, designed to suppress political dissent and purportedly implemented to bring about fundamental social and political reforms.[7]

Analysing the state of constitutionalism particularly in the context of the African continent, B. O. Nwabueze in 1973 described emergent nations as 'having to live under an almost continual state of emergency'.[8] In a study of fifteen countries in 1983, the International Commission of Jurists referred to the 'disturbing tendency' for a state of emergency in many countries 'to become perpetual or to effect far-reaching authoritarian changes in the ordinary legal norms'.[9] The record of many instances of the abuse of entrenched emergency powers raises the issue of whether constitutionalism in many of these countries has been undermined by the entrenchment of these powers.

C. *Entrenched emergency powers and constitutionalism*

Constitutionalised emergency powers are often contemplated by the constitutional founders to be used on a temporary basis. In Malaysia, the Proclamation of Emergency made to counter the outbreak of racial riots in Kuala Lumpur was effected in 1969 but today still continues to provide the underpinning of draconian emergency laws. As Cyrus Das explains:

> The resort to crisis powers and a continuous state of emergency has a direct bearing on the question of constitutionalism. More importantly, the legal domain created by a state of emergency generally enhances executive power and provides for executive law-making under the rubric of emergency legislation. This has resulted in two parallel legal regimes subsisting in Malaysia; one, the parliamentary system with a Cabinet which is answerable to an elected Parliament, and the other, the emergency regime where the Government may at its option invoke its emergency powers and undertake action without first reference to Parliament.[10]

[7] I. Omar, *Emergency Powers and the Courts in India and Pakistan* (The Hague: Kluwer Law International, 2002), p. 32.

[8] B. O. Nwabueze, *Constitutionalism in the Emergent States* (London: C. Hurst & Co., 1973), p. 173.

[9] International Commission of Jurists, *States of Emergency: Their Impact on Human Rights* (Geneva: International Commission of Jurists, 1983), p. 415.

[10] Das, *Governments and Crisis Powers*, p. i.

When one walks the streets of Kuala Lumpur or any major city in Malaysia today, one does not sense a serious threat to the security or economic life of the Federation. How is it possible to maintain the validity of the Proclamation of Emergency when the very factual substratum nourishing it no longer exists? This poses a fundamental issue of the justiciability of a Proclamation of Emergency. On this issue, the judicial approach provides little comfort to those who look to the judiciary to maintain the rule of law. When confronted with this issue, a majority of the Federal Court of Malaysia in *Stephen Kalong Ningkan* v. *The Government of Malaysia*[11] were simply prepared to recognise the King as 'the sole judge'[12] (per Lord President Barakbah and Azmi CJ). However, a significant dissenting view on this issue was expressed by Ong Hock Thye FJ:

> The inbuilt safeguards against indiscriminate or frivolous recourse to emergency legislation contained in article 150, specifically provide that the emergency must be 'whereby the security or economic life of the Federation or of any part thereof is threatened'. If those words of limitation are not meaningless verbiage, they must be taken to mean exactly what they say, no more and no less, for article 150 does not confer on the Cabinet an untrammelled discretion to cause an emergency to be declared at their mere whim and fancy.[13]

Ong Hock Thye FJ was critical of the other judges for holding the view 'that the Cabinet have *carte blanche* to do as they please'. He also described this as 'a strange role' for the judiciary who are supposed to be 'bulwarks of individual liberty and the Rule of Law and guardians of the Constitution'.[14]

Constitutionalism was not enhanced by the guarded non-committal approach of the Privy Council. Lord MacDermott, delivering the advice of the Privy Council, held that whether 'a Proclamation under statutory powers by the Supreme Head of the Federation can be challenged before the courts on some or any grounds is a constitutional question of far reaching importance which, on the present state of the authorities, remains unsettled and debatable'.[15] The stark political reality regarding the invocation of constitutionalised emergency powers is that the making of a proclamation of emergency is, in truth, an act pursuant to the wishes of the government of the day, with the Head of State being regarded as an automaton. So in *Teh Cheng Poh* v. *Public Prosecutor*, the Privy Council observed that the King's functions 'are those of a constitutional monarch

[11] [1968] 1 MLJ 119.
[12] *Ibid.*, at 122 (per Barakbah LP) and 124 (per Azmi CJ (Malaya)).
[13] *Ibid.*, at 128. [14] *Ibid.* [15] [1968] 2 MLJ 238 at 242.

and except on certain matters that do not concern the instant appeal, he does not exercise any of his functions under the Constitution on his own initiative but is required by Article 40(1) to act in accordance with the advice of the Cabinet'.[16] The Privy Council explained that when the Malaysian Constitution or a Federal law specifies that powers conferred upon the King are to be exercisable if he is of opinion or is satisfied that a particular state of affairs exists or that particular action is necessary, the reference to his opinion or satisfaction is in reality a reference to the collective opinion or satisfaction of the members of the Cabinet, or the opinion or satisfaction of a particular Minister to whom the Cabinet have delegated their authority to give advice upon the matter in question.[17]

Furthermore, proceeding on the assumption that the state of emergency was a justiciable issue, the Privy Council found that the 'heavy' onus of proof of an absence of an emergency situation had not been discharged. It is not difficult to note that by arriving at the conclusion in that way it had adroitly avoided the justiciability issue. Even Ong Hock Thye FJ, who was highly critical of his judicial brethren, concluded that he was unable to say, with any degree of confidence, 'that the Cabinet advice to His Majesty was not prompted by *bona fide* considerations of security'.[18] Another perspective on the Proclamation of Emergency in the *Ningkan* case is that the state of emergency was simply a convenient mode of overcoming the constitutional and political impasse stemming from the frustrated attempt by the Federal Government to remove a recalcitrant State Chief Minister.[19] When the President of India, on the advice of the Prime Minister, Indira Gandhi, proclaimed a state of emergency in 1975, it was motivated by the Prime Minister's desperate desire to save her political career.[20]

The constitutionalisation of emergency powers has become too tempting for political leaders who seek to entrench themselves in power or to destroy political opponents who threaten their grip on the reins of government. Unscrupulous resort to constitutionalised emergency powers is facilitated by the courts adopting a 'judicial deference' approach, an approach encapsulated in the following description by Professor Zellick: '[T]he courts . . . run from questions of national security as a fox does

[16] [1979] 1 MLJ 50 at 52. [17] *Ibid.* [18] [1968] 1 MLJ 119 at 128.

[19] Lee, 'The Ningkan Saga', pp. 77–87; S. M. Thio, 'Dismissal of Chief Ministers' (1966) 8 *Malaya Law Review* 283.

[20] H. M. Seervai, *Constitutional Law of India*, 2nd edn (Bombay: N. M. Tripathi Pty. Ltd. 1979), vol. III.

from hounds.'[21] The Privy Council gave its endorsement to such a passive approach in the 1916 case of *Zamora*: 'Those who are responsible for the national security must be the sole judges of what the national security requires. It would be obviously undesirable that such matters should be made the subject of evidence in a court of law or otherwise discussed in public.'[22] The courts are placed in an invidious position. A deferential approach to the interpretation of entrenched emergency powers provides a cloak of legitimacy for what essentially are acts that erode constitutionalism.

D. Constitutionalised emergency powers and constitutional amendments

In his analysis of the operation of emergency powers in Hong Kong, Taiwan, South Korea and mainland China in this volume, Albert Chen observes:

> Thus constitutional emergency provisions, when transplanted to countries that aspire toward liberal constitutional democracy and express such aspirations in the text of their constitutions, can be a two-edged sword. On the one hand, they may be easily abused by power-holders for the purpose of legitimising their authoritarian rule. On the other hand, insofar as they presuppose the distinction between normalcy and states of exception, those who struggle for democracy can use the discourse of normalcy and emergency to challenge the justifications for emergency and demand the return of normalcy.[23]

However, Chen's remarks fail to take into account the situation of a government which is determined to preclude such a discourse from even occurring.

The constitutionalisation of emergency powers enables the executive arm of government, through its control of Parliament, to amend the constitution to further enlarge these powers. When the constitutional framers drafted the constitution they had also ensured some safeguards to prevent an abuse of the emergency powers. Thus, a Proclamation of Emergency was to be made only in exceptional circumstances. Before 1963, the Malaysian Constitution, in Article 150(1), required that the King must be satisfied 'that a grave emergency exists whereby the security

[21] G. Zellick, 'Government Beyond Law' [1985] *Public Law* 283 at 308.

[22] [1916] 2 AC 77 at 107 (per Lord Parker of Waddington).

[23] A. H. Y. Chen, 'Emergency Powers, Constitutionalism and Legal Transplants: The East Asian Experience' (Chapter 3), this volume, p. 86.

or economic life of the Federation or any part thereof is threatened whether by war or external aggression or internal disturbances' as a pre-condition to issuing a Proclamation of Emergency. The qualifying words, 'whether by war or external aggression or internal disturbances' were deleted by a constitutional amendment in 1963. A constitutional amendment in 1981 introduced a new element of 'public order' alongside 'security' and 'economic life' in Article 150(1).

Another safeguard embodied in the original Constitution provided that a Proclamation of Emergency should cease to have force at the expiration of two months from the date on which it was issued, and similarly, any ordinance promulgated by the King automatically lapsed, and ceased to have effect, at the expiration of fifteen days from the date on which both Houses of Parliament were first sitting. This safeguard ensures a greater oversight role by Parliament. The government, in the face of such a safeguard, would be required to seek the approval of Parliament if it desired to prolong a Proclamation or an ordinance. Such a safeguard was diluted by a constitutional amendment in 1960 which provided for a Proclamation of Emergency or an ordinance to continue in force until such time as resolutions are passed by both Houses of Parliament to nullify it.

The most audacious constitutional amendment, which struck at the very heart of constitutionalism, is the insertion in 1981 of a new clause (8) into Article 150. This new clause provides that, notwithstanding anything in the Malaysian Constitution, the satisfaction of the King 'shall be final and conclusive' and 'shall not be challenged or called in question in any court on any grounds'. The Constitution was also amended to excise the power of a court to determine the validity of a Proclamation of Emergency or an ordinance. Article 150(8) now provides that 'no court shall have jurisdiction to entertain or determine any application, question or proceeding, in whatever form, on any ground', regarding the validity of a Proclamation of Emergency or its continued operation, or any ordinance promulgated under Article 150 or its continuation in force. If such a provision is an ordinary statutory provision and not a constitutionalised one, the court would be able to query its validity. However, by securing this excision of the courts' jurisdiction through a constitutional amendment, it is unlikely that the Malaysian courts would invalidate it.[24]

The constitutional amendment excising the courts' jurisdiction to determine the validity of a Proclamation of Emergency or an ordinance makes a mockery of the rule of law. If a point is reached when it is clear

[24] For a discussion of this amendment, see Lee, 'Emergency Powers', pp. 148–51.

to everyone that the facts invoked to justify a Proclamation of Emergency have ceased to exist, this amendment compels the courts to maintain a fiction. If the amendment procedures have been followed to effect the amendment, how can the courts invalidate it? Andrew Harding has argued for the adoption by the Malaysian courts of the 'basic structure' doctrine enunciated by the Indian Supreme Court.[25] Under this doctrine, there can be implied limits to the power of Parliament to amend the Constitution. On an earlier occasion I have argued that clause (8) has undermined the basic structure of the Constitution, as all questions concerning emergency powers are left to the absolute discretion of the government of the day, resulting in the eclipse of constitutional government.[26]

III. Emergency powers as non-entrenched powers

In view of the perils associated with entrenched emergency powers, a better option would be to use ordinary legislation to deal with an emergency. In 1996 the Fiji Constitution Review Commission submitted its report *Towards A United Future* to the President of Fiji. The Commission noted that the 1970 Fiji Constitution did not give the Governor-General any express power to declare a state of emergency and that the 1990 Constitution was designed 'to fill the perceived gap'.[27] Section 163 of the 1990 Constitution empowered the President of Fiji to issue a Proclamation of Emergency, if 'satisfied that a grave emergency exists whereby the security or economic life of Fiji is threatened'. The Commission recommended the repeal of section 163.[28] It also recommended that the Fiji Parliament should be encouraged to enact 'sector' emergency legislation, enabling the emergency powers granted to the executive to be specially tailored to the particular type of emergency.[29] Similar arguments have been made by contemporary scholars. For example, Kent Roach has argued that it may

[25] A. Harding, 'The Death of a Doctrine? *Phang Chin Hock* v. *Public Prosecutor*' (1979) 21 *Malaya Law Review* 365.

[26] Lee, 'Emergency Powers', p. 151.

[27] *The Fiji Islands: Towards a United Future* (Suva: Government Printer, 1996) (Report of the Fiji Constitution Review Commission 1996, Parliamentary Paper No. 34 of 1996), p. 635, para. 19.6.

[28] *Ibid.*, p. 640 (recommendation 667).

[29] Similarly, in its 1991 *Final Report on Emergencies*, the New Zealand Law Commission recommended a 'sectoral' approach to the passage of legislation conferring powers to respond to emergencies. See New Zealand Law Commission, *Final Report on Emergencies*, Report No. 22, p. 88, para. 4.11. In Canada, a legal framework relating to public welfare emergencies, public order emergencies, international emergencies and war emergencies, is set out in the Emergencies Act which received the Royal Assent in 1988.

be better to 'look to the ordinary law as a starting point' for dealing with modern emergencies.[30] This part of the chapter sets out the case for emergency powers and shows how these powers remain within the purview of the courts, before considering and refuting recent attempts to defend the constitutionalisation of emergency powers.

A. *The case for ordinary emergency powers*

Embodying emergency powers in an ordinary Act of Parliament, rather than constitutionalising them, is more in accord with constitutionalism. When dealing with an ordinary statute, the courts have more room to manoeuvre in terms of judicial review. The exercise of a statutorily invested power to proclaim a state of emergency will be treated like the exercise of a statutory discretionary power. Courts can draw on grounds such as reasonableness and improper purpose to impugn an abuse of a discretionary power. The guarded non-committal approach of the Privy Council in the *Ningkan* case on the issue of justiciability of a Proclamation of Emergency is unconvincing. That the discretion to proclaim a state of emergency pursuant to a statutory (not constitutional) power is invested in a supreme head does not insulate the exercise of that power from judicial scrutiny.

One example of the courts jettisoning a Crown immunity doctrine is found in the decision of the High Court of Australia in *Re Toohey*[31] and signifies a fundamental shift in the High Court's perception of its role in judicial review. Gibbs CJ, Stephen, Mason, Aickin and Wilson JJ held that the court could inquire whether a power granted to the Crown by statute had been exercised by the Crown for a purpose which the statute did not authorise. Mason J regarded a Crown immunity doctrine as being 'out of harmony with the current approach of the courts to the review of statutory discretions'.[32] Aickin J pointed out that if a minister's exercise of a statutory power could be reviewed by a court, it would seem 'anomalous and irrational to say that it is impossible to examine a decision made by more than one Minister to advise the Governor-General to do an act which in constitutional reality he is obliged to do once advised so to do'.[33]

The Australian High Court has also shown that where special powers are invoked pursuant to an ordinary Act of Parliament, it enables the court to

[30] K. Roach, 'Ordinary Law for Emergency Powers and Democratic Derogations from Rights', in V. V. Ramraj (ed.), *Emergencies and the Limits of Legality* (Cambridge: Cambridge University Press, 2008), pp. 229–57.

[31] *Re Toohey (Aboriginal Land Commissioner); Ex parte Northern Land Council* [1981] 56 ALJR 164. See H. P. Lee, *Emergency Powers* (Sydney: Law Book Co., 1984), pp. 274–7.

[32] *Re Toohey*, at 184. [33] *Ibid.*, at 201.

consider the constitutionality of the Act. In *Australian Communist Party* v. *Commonwealth*[34] the High Court was thus able to invalidate the legislation which sought to dissolve the Australian Communist Party by determining that the 'defence power' in the Australian Constitution did not provide the constitutional anchorage for the legislation. The court invoked 'a stream cannot rise higher than its source'[35] doctrine to deny the legislation its constitutional validity. Of this decision, Professor George Winterton has this to say:

> For unelected judges to invalidate legislation enacted unanimously, and for which the Government had a clear electoral 'mandate', would itself demonstrate judicial independence of a high order. To do so at a time of national hysteria against an 'enemy', the subject of the legislation, whose supposed overseas allies were fighting and killing Australian troops, is surely a remarkable, virtually unique, achievement.[36]

The Australian approach demonstrates how, when faced with ordinary emergency powers, the courts can continue to serve as a check on those powers.

B. Ordinary emergency powers and proportionality

One important advantage of ordinary emergency legislation is that it is subject to review for proportionality. The need for normal constitutional principles to yield to the invocation of emergency powers is recognised by a number of international instruments. Article 4(1) of the International Covenant on Civil and Political Rights 1966 provides:

> In times of public emergency which threatens the life of the nation and the existence of which is officially proclaimed, the State Parties to the present Covenant may take measures derogating from their obligations under the present Covenant to the extent strictly required by the exigencies of the situation, provided that such measures are not inconsistent with their other obligations under international law and do not involve discrimination solely on the ground of race, colour, sex, language, religion or social origin.

Article 15 of the European Convention on Human Rights permits a member-state to take measures derogating from the obligations under the Convention 'in times of war or other public emergency threatening the life of the nation'. The Convention does not permit derogation, even

[34] (1951) 83 CLR 1. [35] *Ibid.*, at 258 (per Fullagar J).
[36] G. Winterton, 'The Communist Party Case', in H. P. Lee and G. Winterton, *Australian Constitutional Landmarks* (Cambridge: Cambridge University Press, 2003), pp. 131–2.

in times of emergency, from guarantees against torture or inhuman or degrading treatment or punishment, the guarantee that no one shall be held in slavery or servitude and the guarantee against retrospective legislation in the criminal law.

However, under both of these instruments, any derogation from rights is subject to various limitations.[37] The exigency must be of such a degree as to threaten 'the life of the nation' and the derogation must be to 'the extent strictly required by the exigencies of the situation'. These limitations enable the courts to apply a test of 'proportionality' to determine the validity of emergency measures invoked to cope with a crisis. This test, which quite often is described as not using a steam hammer to crack a nut,[38] enables the courts to compel a reasonable relationship between the means and the end they seek to achieve. This proportionality test is not always applicable, however, if the means (i.e., the emergency powers) are constitutionally entrenched and are empowered to override constitutional safeguards.

The limited grounds for review in these circumstances can be seen from the experience of Singapore and Malaysia with their preventive detention laws.[39] For a long time, the courts in both Malaysia and Singapore persisted with the application of a 'subjective test' when the power to order the preventive detention of a person is invoked. The Malaysian Internal Security Act (ISA) provides for the detention power to be exercised '[i]f the Minister is satisfied' and in the case of the Singapore ISA, '[i]f the President is satisfied'. According to the subjective test, the only issue for the courts to consider in cases of detention under the ISA was whether the executive was in fact satisfied (subjectively) that the detainee posed a threat to national security; they did not have to ask whether reasonable (objective) grounds existed to justify that belief. The problem with the subjective test, however, was 'that it allowed the government to claim rule-of-law legitimacy for its actions despite the fact that under that test, governments could effectively exercise a wholly arbitrary power'.[40] The majority decision of the House of Lords in the wartime case *Liversidge* v. *Anderson*,[41] which affirmed the subjective test, has continued to echo loudly in Singapore

[37] See also Roach, 'Ordinary Law'.

[38] See M. Aronson, B. Dyer and M. Groves, *Judicial Review of Administrative Action*, 3rd edn (Pyrmont: Lawbook Co., 2004), p. 345; *R* v. *Goldstein* [1983] 1 WLR 151, at 155B (per Lord Diplock).

[39] See R. R. Balasubramaniam, 'Indefinite Detention: Rule by Law or Rule of Law?', in Ramraj (ed.), *Emergencies*, pp. 118–41.

[40] *Ibid.*, p. 124. [41] [1942] AC 206.

and Malaysia, even though a broad consensus had emerged elsewhere in the Commonwealth that Lord Atkin's dissent represented the better legal position.[42]

In 1989, the subjective test of *Liversidge* was jettisoned in Singapore by a bold decision of the Singapore Court of Appeal in *Chng Suan Tze* v. *Minister of Home Affairs, Singapore*.[43] The government's response was swift. On 25 January 1989, within weeks of the decision, Parliament amended both the Constitution and the ISA to restore the subjective test.[44] Given the entrenched status of this special power of preventive detention, the constitutional amendment in Singapore has virtually ousted any significant role of the courts in judicial oversight of the use of such a power. A new Article 149(3) in the Singapore Constitution provides:

> If in respect of any proceedings whether instituted before or after [27 January 1989], any question arises in any court as to the validity of any decision made or act done in pursuance of any power conferred upon the President or the Minister by any law referred to in this Article, such question shall be determined in accordance with the provisions of any law as may be enacted by Parliament for this purpose; and nothing in Article 93 shall invalidate any law enacted pursuant to this clause.

The aim of this provision was to bring the scope of judicial review in national security cases under the ambit of the Internal Security Act. And thus, in a parallel move, a new provision, s. 8B(1), was added to the ISA which provided that the law governing judicial review of executive detention 'shall be the same as was applicable and declared in Singapore on 13th July 1971', the date on which the subjective test was affirmed by the Singapore High Court in *Lee Mau Seng* v. *Minister for Home Affairs,*

[42] In his celebrated dissent in which he defended the objective test, Lord Atkin declared:

> I view with apprehension the attitude of judges who on a mere question of construction when face to face with claims involving the liberty of the subject show themselves more executive minded than the executive . . . In this country, amid the clash of arms, the laws are not silent. They may be changed, but they speak the same language in war as in peace. It has always been one of the pillars of freedom, one of the principles of liberty for which on recent authority we are now fighting, that the judges are no respecters of persons and stand between the subject and any attempted encroachments on his liberty by the executive, alert to see that any coercive action is justified in law. In this case I have listened to arguments which might have been addressed acceptably to the Court of King's Bench in the time of Charles I (*Ibid.*, at 244).

[43] [1989] 1 MLJ 69.

[44] K. Y. L. Tan, 'Recent Developments in the Law and Practice of Preventive Detention', in Wu Min Aun (ed.), *Public Law in Contemporary Malaysia* (Petaling Jaya: Longman, 1999), p. 306.

Singapore.[45] The complete freezing of the law was reinforced by the further declaration that 'no part of the law before, on or after that date of any country in the Commonwealth relating to judicial review shall apply'.

Following the amendments in Singapore, the Malaysian Parliament amended its Internal Security Act in June 1989. Kevin Tan points out that the Malaysian amendment of the ISA was 'far more comprehensive'. A new s. 8B(1) which was inserted into the ISA reads:

> There shall be no judicial review in any court of, and no court shall have or exercise any jurisdiction in respect of any act done or decision made by the Yang di-Pertuan Agong or the Minister in the exercise of their discretionary power in accordance with this Act, save in regard to any question on compliance with any procedural requirement in this Act governing such act or decision.

As Tan observes, while the Singapore amendments sought to freeze the scope of judicial review of executive decision as at the date of the *Lee Mau Seng* decision, the Malaysian approach was to 'oust judicial review completely'.[46] But, argues Tan, both approaches give rise to distinct problems:

> Let us first take the Singapore position. Requiring judges to interpret a law by legislatively binding them to a single High Court decision made at a certain point in time would, it is argued, be a usurpation of the judicial power conferred on the courts by Article 93 of the Constitution. It is tantamount to directing the court to decide cases in a certain way. Unfortunately, the legality of the legislative intervention was affirmed in *Teo Soh Lung* v. *The Minister for Home Affairs & Ors* [1989] 2 MLJ 449 first in the High Court and then subsequently in the Court of Appeal. The Malaysian approach is problematic in the sense that like most other ouster clauses, the new section 8B(1) can be overcome on grounds of *ultra vires*. Neither approach makes legal sense, and it is hoped that the courts will one day strike down these legislative interventions as unconstitutional and void.[47]

[45] [1971] 2 MLJ 137. [46] Tan, 'Recent Developments', p. 307.

[47] *Ibid*. It is instructive to note that in a recent case, *Raja Petra bin Raja Kamarudin* v. *Menteri Hal Ehwal Dalam Negeri* (7 November 2008), file no. MTJ1: 44-217-2008 (Malaysia H. C.), Datuk Syed Ahmad Helmy bin Syed Ahmad J rejected the challenge to the constitutional validity of s. 8B(1) but overcame the ouster clause in the section by finding that the Minister had acted *ultra vires* the object of the ISA. The words 'in accordance with the Act' in s. 8B(1), if they were not to amount to 'excess verbiage', meant that the Minister's decision was not completely unfettered. As the judge found an absence of correspondence between the grounds stipulated in the detention order and those specified in the ISA he acceded to the application for habeas corpus and ordered the release of the detainee.

A challenge to the constitutionality of Article 149(3) of the Singapore Constitution is unlikely to succeed if the basis of the challenge is that it amounts to a usurpation of judicial power. This is because Article 149(3) was inserted through a constitutional amendment process and has become constitutionalised. The only glimmer of hope is if the Singapore Supreme Court is prepared to entertain the application of the Indian 'basic structure' doctrine.[48] The usurpation of judicial power may, arguably, be more convincingly raised against the *statutory* amendment to the ISA (i.e. s. 8B(1)). However, this argument is ostensibly undermined because Article 93, which vests the judicial power in the courts, is declared by Article 149(3) as not having any effect of invalidating any law enacted pursuant to Article 149(3).

Similarly, in Malaysia, the argument based on the usurpation of judicial power must take into account that a constitutional amendment in 1988 to Article 121 of the Malaysian Constitution deleted the expression 'the judicial power of the Federation'. The amended Article 121 now simply states that 'the High Courts and inferior courts shall have such jurisdiction and powers as may be conferred by or under federal law'. Sultan Azlan Shah once remarked that as a result of this amendment, 'it would appear that the judicial power is no longer vested in the courts'.[49]

C. Ordinary emergency powers: objections and refutations

Some contemporary theorists still insist that constitutionalised emergency powers are preferable to ordinary emergency legislation. For instance, John Ferejohn and Pasquale Pasquino have argued that constitutionalised emergency powers, in the form of a modern version of the Roman model of dictatorship, would help to insulate the ordinary legal system from the extraordinary measures required in an emergency.[50] Specifically, they claim that such a model, given its 'conservative' aim to restore the constitutional status quo ante, would 'not impose any permanent change on the

[48] In *Kesavananda Bharati* v. *State of Kerala* AIR 1973 SC 1461, the Supreme Court of India held that the amending power does not extend to abrogating or destroying the 'basic' or 'essential' features of the Indian Constitution. See also *Minerva Mills Ltd* v. *Union of India* [1981] 1 SCR 206. For a discussion of *Kesavananda*, see D. G. Morgan, 'The Indian "Essential Features" Case' (1981) 30 *International and Comparative Law Quarterly* 307.

[49] S. A. Shah, 'The Role of Constitutional Rulers and the Judiciary Revisited', in V. Sinnadurai (ed.), *Constitutional Monarchy, Rule of Law and Good Governance* (Kuala Lumpur: Professional Law Books, 2004), p. 403.

[50] J. Ferejohn and P. Pasquino, 'The Law of the Exception: A Typology of Emergency Powers' (2004) 2 *International Journal of Constitutional Law* 210 at 234.

legal ordering'.[51] Second, they stress the importance of fixing the limits of emergency powers *in advance* of the emergency.[52] Finally, they argue that by entrenching emergency powers, the regulation of those powers is 'fixed constitutionally and operates before or after the exercise of emergency power itself'.[53] As the preceding discussion suggests, however, these arguments are unconvincing.

As far as the first argument is concerned, the experience of emergency powers in the jurisdictions discussed earlier show that entrenching emergency powers in the constitution does not insulate the ordinary legal system from emergency measures. Indeed, as the Malaysian experience shows, there is a real danger of those powers becoming normalised. The proclamations of emergency effected to counter armed aggression by Indonesia in 1964, resolve a political and constitutional impasse in the Malaysian state of Sarawak in 1966 and deal with the outbreak of racial riots on 13 May 1969 have never been expressly revoked.[54] The proclamations of 1964 and 1966, according to Andrew Harding, could be considered to have lapsed by effluxion of time or been implicitly superseded by the 1969 emergency proclamation. Draconian emergency laws enacted pursuant to the 1969 proclamation still remain in force to this day, leading him to observe that 'what has become normal is the existence of emergency laws in parallel with the operation of the ordinary constitutional and legal systems'.[55] Second, the ease with which constitutionalised emergency powers are amended (in Malaysia and Singapore, for example) suggests that despite appearances, these powers are not genuinely fixed in advance. Moreover, when the courts try to step in to check those powers, the government has responded quickly, reversing the impact of the judicial intervention.[56] In *Teh Cheng Poh* v. *Public Prosecutor*,[57] the appellant was convicted and sentenced to death under special emergency regulations made pursuant to an ordinance made by the King. The Privy Council declared his trial a nullity as the King's ordinance-making power was curtailed once Parliament had sat. The appellant's trial and many other trials were retrospectively validated through legislation enacted by

[51] *Ibid.*, at 235. [52] *Ibid.* [53] *Ibid.*

[54] A. Harding, *Law, Government and the Constitution in Malaysia* (Kuala Lumpur: Malaysian Law Journal Sdn Bnd, 1996), pp. 160–1.

[55] *Ibid*, p. 159.

[56] See M. Hor, 'Singapore Stories and Malaysian Dilemmas', in V. V. Ramraj, M. Hor and K. Roach (eds.), *Global Anti-Terrorism Law and Policy* (Cambridge: Cambridge University Press, 2005), pp. 273–94.

[57] [1979] 1 MLJ 50. For a commentary on this case, see V. V. Ramraj, 'The *Teh Cheng Poh* Case', in Harding and Lee (eds.), *Constitutional Landmarks*, pp. 145–55.

the Malaysian Parliament. The legislation also revived the operation of the special emergency regulations.[58] For similar reasons, the claim that under a constitutional framework, the regulation of emergency powers operates 'before or after' the exercise of those powers is questionable. The examples discussed in this chapter demonstrate, as in Indira Gandhi's case, that at the height of an emergency, politics becomes more important than law in determining the course that emergency powers will take.

When constitutionalised emergency powers are invoked, courts have been very reluctant to provide vigorous and effective oversight of the exercise of these powers. It is important to provide the civil authorities with ample powers to cope with an emergency situation. 'Stand-by' emergency powers embodied in ordinary legislation ensure that their exercise is subject to judicial review. By defining the different categories of emergencies, e.g. natural disasters, public disorders, terrorist attacks, war, etc., and statutorily prescribing the nature of the powers appropriate for handling these emergencies and the safeguards that can be made applicable, ordinary emergency powers legislation does not pose a threat to the rule of law.

IV. Conclusion

The International Commission of Jurists has recognised that '[r]eal emergencies do occur, and many governments resort to emergency powers in good faith'.[59] By the same token, Victor V. Ramraj argues, in his contribution to this volume, that 'emergency powers pose a threat not to an established legal order with a deep tradition of constitutionalism, but to a nascent and fragile legal order struggling to establish its rule-of-law credentials'.[60] It should, however, also be acknowledged that a number of occasions on which emergency powers were invoked in less established legal orders were, in truth, pseudo-emergencies. In most of these occasions, the key impetus was the desire of the ruling government to cling to power at any cost. In 1973, S. A. de Smith observed that the 'nationalists who took over political power found too many seductive temptations to cling to office regardless of constitutional restraints or respect for minority

[58] H. P. Lee, *Constitutional Conflicts in Contemporary Malaysia* (Kuala Lumpur: Oxford University Press, 1995), pp. 103–5.

[59] International Commission of Jurists, *States of Emergency*, p. 432.

[60] V. V. Ramraj, 'The Emergency Powers Paradox' (Chapter 2), this volume, p. 28.

interests'.[61] This is a familiar refrain in modern times. Thus, Anil Kalhan describes the 2007 invocation of emergency powers by then President Musharraf of Pakistan as 'a pretextual attempt . . . to maintain power, not a means to combat terrorism'.[62]

An irony which can be observed is that many political leaders who have undermined constitutionalism through a *mala fide* invocation of emergency powers have also sought to give a veneer of constitutional respectability to their unscrupulous actions. Many of them would prefer not to be shunned as pariahs in the international community. The constitutionalisation of emergency powers enabled them to claim constitutional legitimacy when they imposed emergency rule, through, to adopt a phrase of Raul Pangalangan, a 'manipulation of constitutional text'.[63] That claim has less credibility when they act under ordinary statutory powers. Furthermore, an invocation of statutory emergency powers lends itself to a stronger case for judicial review.

Several scholars, including some of the contributors to this volume, have noted a role for the courts in holding the executive in check. The 'importance of upholding legality in times of crisis has been eloquently defended by judges around the globe, sometimes in lone dissent, at other times in unanimous resistance to a determined executive'.[64] But as Arun Thiruvengadam observes in this volume, 'a set of supportive factors is needed to facilitate judicial review of emergency powers', including 'a political climate where judges can feel confident that their actions will find favour'.[65] Yet waiting for a change of political climate before a court would 'act more robustly in times of emergency' is akin to asking judges to display courage when such a display is not necessary. In truth, the judicial role in countries without an entrenched 'culture of accountability' is severely constrained when an unscrupulous executive resorts to constitutionalised emergency powers, especially as limitations on such powers can

[61] Foreword to B. O. Nwabueze, *Constitutionalism in the Emergent States*, p. ix.

[62] A. Kalhan, 'Constitution and "Extraconstitution": Colonial Emergency Regimes in Postcolonial India and Pakistan', Chapter 4, this volume, p. 89.

[63] R. Pangalangan, 'Political Emergencies in the Philippines: Changing Labels and the Unchanging Need for Legitimacy', Chapter 15, this volume, p. 435.

[64] V. V. Ramraj, 'No Doctrine More Pernicious? Emergencies and the Limits of Legality', in Ramraj (ed.), *Emergencies*, pp. 3–29 at p. 5.

[65] A. K. Thiruvengadam, 'Asian Judiciaries and Emergency Powers: Reasons for Optimism?', Chapter 17, this volume, p. 493.

be undermined by constitutional amendments. When emergency powers, whether in a constitutionalised or statutory form, are invoked, the state of constitutionalism will ultimately depend on the *bona fides* and integrity of those pulling the levers of power. However, if the emergency powers are not constitutionalised, at least the constitution cannot be used as a cloak to provide a veneer of constitutional legitimacy for abuses of powers.

15

Political emergencies in the Philippines: changing labels and the unchanging need for legitimacy

RAUL C. PANGALANGAN

I. Introduction

It was former President Ferdinand Marcos who boldly declared that his emergency measures aimed to reform society. He claimed that he wanted not just to quell a rebellion but to remedy the social inequalities that fuelled it. He still invoked every positivist cover for his dictatorship, constitutional text as well as manipulated referenda masquerading as the people's voice, but he did not shirk from fundamentally reconceiving the notion of emergency, shifting from a preservative 'national security' purpose to a transformative and 'revolutionary' rationale. The post-Marcos Constitution of 1987 rejected Marcos's ideological challenge by reiterating the tried and tested liberal formula, reinstating the national security rationale as the sole basis for emergency rule and instituting procedural checks-and-balances that cabined the national security powers. The 1987 Constitution was designed deliberately to forestall a return to a Marcos-style dictatorship, and allowed emergency powers only under several layers of institutional safeguards.

Yet the real irony is that whatever was left of those powers was not invoked during the truest emergency in recent history, the January 2001 uprising that actually toppled a sitting President, Joseph Estrada. Worse, his successor, Gloria Macapagal-Arroyo, has since faced several actual threats and has thrice declared one or another sort of emergency triggered by the endless corruption scandals that elsewhere – as with Thaksin in Bangkok – would have sufficed to topple a leader who – in contrast to Thaksin – did not enjoy a popular mandate. Incumbent President Gloria Macapagal-Arroyo has invoked the extraordinary 'commander-in-chief' powers thrice, each time deliberately avoiding the exact language under the Constitution to disable precisely those safeguards.

The Arroyo government's dismal record in restraining the excesses of state power – whether in transgressing the civil liberties of its citizens or in stopping the use of public power for private enrichment – shows that the legalistic constraints preferred by the drafters of the 1987 Constitution have not constrained presidential abuse and may have, in fact, abetted it. Arroyo has surmounted every intra-constitutional challenge, namely, impeachment (blocked by her minions in Congress), anti-corruption investigations (quashed by her handpicked Ombudsman), and Senate inquiries in aid of legislation (stonewalled by executive privilege). By manipulating the law and the levers of political patronage, she has undermined the very constitution by which she reigns.

The final irony is that Arroyo, having thus pushed the text of the law to the limit, each time calls on the nation 'to defend the rule of law' whenever threatened by restless soldiers. By purporting to deal with uprisings without invoking her emergency powers, she uses the letter of the law to defeat its spirit; reinforces the literal notion and weakens the substantive notion of the rule of law; and strains the legitimacy of a constitutionalism that asserts itself only selectively to favour Arroyo and her allies and punish her enemies.

This chapter will demonstrate what we might call in the vernacular the 'schizoid' attitude that swings from excessive textualism to open-ended ideological and consequentialist argument, and asks how Filipinos, as a political community, can reconcile this overweening obsession for legal formalism while in the end recognising the enduring primacy of substantive claims. The Philippine experience should have confirmed – repeatedly – the limits of formal legality, yet Filipinos persist in the folly of excessive legalism. The chapter therefore uses the debate on states of emergency to situate the different theories of law that, either wittingly or more probably unwittingly, Filipinos have imbibed: the bizarre alchemy of a highly formalist rule-of-law tradition, the judicial flamboyance so uncharacteristic of a historically civil law jurisdiction, and the instrumentalism and social engineering in which both the legal realists (of the 1950s and 1960s) and the Left-inspired (of the 1970s and early 1980s) have found a common path.

II. Historical and doctrinal context

This chapter consists of two parts. Considering that it deals with the formalistic treatment of doctrine and the deft manipulation of discourse, the chapter, in the first part, deals with the intricacies of constitutional text, before proceeding, in the second part, to asking how Philippine discourse on emergency powers has taken on the extreme literalism which it exhibits today. The first part provides the concrete historical and doctrinal material in order to avert the peril, in the second part, of theorising in a vacuum.

A. *Survey of the constitutional history*

Philippine constitutional history begins with a brief experiment under the Malolos Constitution promulgated by the triumphant revolutionaries who had waged a war of independence against Spanish colonialism.[1] It established a parliamentary government and contained an entire section entitled 'The Filipinos and their National and Individual Rights', recognising the typical list of rights protected in a liberal democracy.[2] However, the Spanish-American War soon brought Admiral George Dewey to Manila Bay. The United States took over the city of Manila; before long, the Philippine–American War broke out, and the Philippines became a US colony.[3]

Accordingly, in strict doctrinal terms, the current constitutional order in the Philippines is not traced to the aborted Malolos charter, but to the various 'organic acts' by which the United States exercised governmental power over the islands, all of which contained guarantees for fundamental liberties.[4] That process culminated with the 1935 Constitution, a virtual clone of the US Constitution and its Bill of Rights. The Philippines

[1] C. Majul, *The Political and Constitutional Ideas of the Philippine Revolution* (Quezon City: University of the Philippines Press, 1967), pp. 178–82; O. D. Corpuz, *Saga and Triumph: The Filipino Revolution Against Spain* (Quezon City: University of the Philippines Press and Cavite Historical Society, 2002), pp. 201–31, 273–97.

[2] S. Guevara (ed.), *The Laws of the First Philippine Republic (The Laws of Malolos, 1898–1899)* (Manila: National Historical Institute, 1994), pp. 104–19. See also T. Agoncillo, *Malolos: The Crisis of the Republic* (Quezon City: University of the Philippines Press, 1997), pp. 305–35.

[3] Treaty of Peace between Spain and the United States (1898).

[4] V. V. Mendoza, *From McKinley's Instructions to the New Constitution: Documents on the Philippine Constitutional System* (Quezon City: Central Lawbook Publishing Co., 1978). The very first organic act was President William McKinley's Instructions to the Second Philippine Commission (7 April 1900), which transferred legislative powers from the military commanders to a civilian commission appointed by the US President and chaired by William Howard Taft, a Federal judge who would later serve as US President. The second was the Philippine Bill (1 July 1902), which transferred the administration of the Islands from the US President to the US Congress, and vested legislative power in an elected assembly. The third was the Philippine Autonomy Act (Jones Law) (29 August 1916), which established a tripartite separation of powers and completed the 'Filipinisation' of the legislature with the election of a Senate to take the place of the Philippine Commission. See also W. C. Forbes, *The Philippine Islands* (Cambridge, Mass.: Harvard University Press, 1945).

became independent after World War II, and from 1946 until 1972, when Marcos began his one-man rule, the nation was governed under the 1935 Constitution. The 1935 Constitution created a government of separated powers, with a bicameral Congress, a nationally elected President and an independent judiciary. It contained a Bill of Rights that guaranteed civil and political rights. Significantly for our purposes, it gave the President emergency powers – to suspend the writ of habeas corpus and to proclaim martial law – to respond to threats to national security.[5]

In September 1972, Ferdinand Marcos, the sixth President of the Republic and two years away from the end of his second and last allowable term in office, proclaimed martial law and shut down the Congress. He invoked the threat of a Maoist rebellion waged by a peasant army, led by urban intellectuals, and supported by foreign communist states.[6] By January 1973 a new constitution was adopted, whose Transitory Provisions granted him extraordinary powers.[7] In successive referenda in which a cowed populace voted under duress, the Filipino people supposedly agreed not to convene the parliamentary assembly provided under the 1973 Constitution, to vest legislative power in Marcos, and for him 'to continue the reforms he ha[d] instituted'.[8] Marcos was ousted in 1986 by a civilian-led, military-backed uprising that installed Corazon Aquino as president. A new constitution[9] was adopted, containing elaborate checks against a repeat of the Marcos dictatorship. The President was granted his commander-in-chief powers to protect the state from national security threats. At the same time, the Constitution subjected those powers to automatic review by the Congress, judicial review by the Supreme Court, and substantive constraints against military jurisdiction over civilians and assured access to civilian courts.

President Joseph Estrada was ousted in 2001 after a civilian uprising, protesting the suppression of evidence during his impeachment trial for corruption.[10] Even on the verge of being overthrown, Estrada did not invoke any of the emergency measures provided in the 1987

[5] See also K. Y. L. Tan, 'From Myanmar to Manila: A Brief Study of Emergency Powers in Southeast Asia' (Chapter 6), this volume, pp. 152–3.

[6] Proclamation No. 1081 (21 September 1972), *Proclaiming a State of Martial Law in the Philippines.*

[7] Proclamation No. 1102 (17 January 1973), *Announcing the Ratification by the Filipino People of the Constitution.*

[8] Jau-Yuan Hwan (ed.), *Direct Democracy in Asia: A Reference Guide to the Legislations and Practices* (Taipei: Taiwan Foundation for Democracy, 2006), pp. 171–4.

[9] Hereinafter, the '1987 Constitution'.

[10] See A. Doronila, *The Fall of Joseph Estrada* (Manila: Inquirer Books, 2002).

Constitution. In contrast, his successor, Gloria Macapagal-Arroyo, has thrice been threatened with civilian protests and has just as often proclaimed some form of emergency. Ominously, each time, she has deliberately avoided using the exact language of the Constitution in order not to trigger off the built-in safeguards, and she has not been fundamentally repudiated either by the Supreme Court, the Congress or the people. This chapter analyses the impact of this extreme formalism on Philippine constitutionalism, and the changing meaning of the rule of law as a constraint on emergency powers.

B. *Institutionalised emergency under Marcos*

There was one historical moment when the Philippines confronted the societal – and not just military – origins of emergency rule. In doing so, it saw national security not solely as the clash of arms that triggers off the commander-in-chief clause but more broadly in terms of the political unrest fuelled by social inequality and absolute levels of poverty. The hero of that moment is, strangely but not surprisingly, Ferdinand E. Marcos, the last president under the 1935 Constitution through which the country regained its independence from American colonial rule, and who used the commander-in-chief clause to establish 'constitutional authoritarianism'. The nature of his emergency powers, however, evolved in the following decade. He seized power using the classic national security purposes of the commander-in-chief clause; he remained in power by virtue of the 'transitory provisions' of a new constitution, riding on the crest of bogus referenda where the people supposedly asked him to remain in power; and he institutionalised that power via a 'new Republic' that fully constitutionalised his dictatorship.

Marcos suspended the writ of habeas corpus on 21 August 1971 and declared martial law on 21 September 1972, citing a communist plot to overthrow the government by force.

> [O]n the basis of carefully evaluated and verified information, it is definitely established that [there is] an armed insurrection and rebellion against the Government of the Republic of the Philippines in order to forcibly seize political and state power in this country, overthrow the duly constituted government, and supplant our existing political, social, economic and legal order with an entirely new one . . . based on the Marxist-Leninist-Maoist teachings and beliefs.[11]

[11] Proclamation No. 1081.

He soon inaugurated what would be called the 1973 Constitution after it was approved by a bogus plebiscite[12] and after the Supreme Court, invoking the political question doctrine, declined to reject the results.[13] From September 1972 to January 1973, Marcos justified his emergency rule solely in terms of the commander-in-chief clause and invoked mainly the national security rationale for emergency powers.

That suddenly changed with the approval of a new constitution on 15 January 1973. From then on, Marcos aggrandised executive and legislative powers unto himself under the Transitory Provisions of the new constitution. The transition clauses allowed the incumbent president to exercise his powers under the presidential system of the 1935 charter and the powers of the Prime Minister under the parliamentary system of the 1973 charter.[14] Having accomplished the shift from 'emergency' to 'transition', he next engineered the shift from 'military' to 'social reform'. His term of office as President would have come to an end in 1973, so in July of that year, he called for a referendum which asked: 'Do you want President Marcos to continue after 1973 and *finish the reforms he has initiated under martial law*?' (emphasis added). Ninety per cent of the voters gave a resounding yes. Suddenly 'martial law', a pre-eminently national security power, was uttered in the same breath as 'reforms' and the building of a 'New Society'.

Marcos consolidated this justificatory rhetoric by releasing books in his name. Soon after he suspended the writ of habeas corpus in 1971, he published the book *Today's Revolution Democracy*,[15] setting forth what he would call a 'blueprint' for his reform projects. He later published the book *Notes on the New Society of the Philippines*,[16] wherein he fused the national security, the transition and the reformist justifications for his regime:

> The Proclamation [of martial law] was immediately necessitated by a clear and present danger [posed by communist rebels]. Beyond this, however, was the imperious demand for revolutionary change. And this meant . . . a much more enormous responsibility than restoring public order . . . That enormous responsibility . . . was laying the foundations for an entirely new society. The transformation, no less, of Philippine society . . .

[12] Proclamation No. 1102.

[13] *Javellana* v. *Executive Secretary*, GR No. L-36142, 31 March 1973, 50 SCRA 30.

[14] Note that Marcos held the Prime Minister's office, though he refused to convene the new Parliament called for in the new charter. The people supposedly suspended the convening of the Parliament, according to the 1973 plebiscite.

[15] F. Marcos, *Today's Revolution: Democracy* (Philippine Government, 1971).

[16] F. Marcos, *Notes on the New Society of the Philippines* (Philippine Government, 1973).

> [M]artial law is a temporary constitutional expedient of safeguarding the republic; at most, it is a necessary transition . . . between the old and the new society . . . Thus martial law in the Philippines takes on a unique character: from the untenable strategy of protecting or restoring the status quo to a militant, constitutional and legal strategy for creating and building, from the ashes of the old, a new society.[17]

Finally in the 1977 reissue of the two works, Marcos affirms his 'revolutionary' use of the martial law powers:

> Martial law was never conceived nor has it ever been utilized to attain revolutionary or radical reforms. On the contrary, it was the ultimate weapon for stability – in short, the final power to freeze the status quo. Injustices there may be in the status quo; it was not for martial law to redress them . . . For the Philippines, history dictated this persuasion. The [martial law clause] was lifted verbatim from [the American-period] organic laws . . . They were meant to consolidate the power of the American Governor-General over a colony . . . The legalist and historian were outraged that martial law, the weapon *against* Revolution, should now be converted in a weapon for reform![18]

The 'institutionalization of the Revolution'[19] was solidified with the 1976 Amendments, which further entrenched the concentration of legislative and executive powers in one man:

> The incumbent President *shall continue to exercise* legislative powers until *martial law* shall have been lifted.[20]
>
> Whenever in the *judgment of the President/Prime Minister*, there exists a grave emergency or a threat or imminence thereof, or whenever the interim Batasang Pambansa or the regular National Assembly fails or is unable to act adequately on *any* matter for *any* reason that *in his judgment* requires immediate action, he may, in order to meet the exigency, issue the necessary decrees, orders or letters of instruction, which shall form part of the law of the land.[21]

Note how the language of national security blended seamlessly into the language of boundless discretion. The text of the 1976 Amendments segues from 'martial law', 'grave emergency', 'threat or imminence thereof' into unalloyed discretion ('any matter', 'for any reason', 'in his judgment').

Finally, through all these developments, Marcos made a show of his scrupulous respect for the rule of law: 'It will be noted I had submitted

[17] *Ibid.*, pp. vi–vii.

[18] F. Marcos, *The Democratic Revolution in the Philippines* (Manila: Philippine Government 1977) p. 11 (emphasis in the original).

[19] *Ibid.*, Constitution, p. 239.

[20] 1973 Constitution, Amendment V (emphasis added).

[21] 1973 Constitution, Amendment VI (emphases added).

myself to the jurisdiction of the Supreme Court in all cases questioning my authority.'[22]

> Certainly no dictator would submit himself to the judgment of a higher body like the Supreme Court on the question of the constitutionality or validity of his actions.
>
> At the same time, I wanted to emphasize that the revolution which I was leading was a constitutional revolution. It was constitutional because it did not depart from the strictures and limitations of the old and new Constitutions.[23]

However, as subsequent cases now document, Marcos used those powers to suppress dissent through torture, disappearance and summary executions.[24]

Indeed, the Supreme Court held unanimously that the martial law declaration was constitutional because there was an escalating rebellion.[25] The transitional government ended officially only in 1981, after Marcos had consolidated control and formed a 'new' republic. The 1981 Amendments provided for direct election of the President, who presided over a parliament led by a Prime Minister. He retained his immense powers until he was ousted during the uprising of February 1986 under Corazon Aquino.

C. The post-Marcos Constitution: institutional checks on emergency powers

The nightmare under Marcos was seared into the nation's memory by the time the drafters of the 1987 Constitution convened. Their antidote to dictatorship was a constitution that combined grand statements with detailed and technical constraints on executive power. The normative statement is made in the Declaration of Principles and State Policies: 'The Philippines is a democratic and republican State. Sovereignty resides in the people and all government authority emanates from them.'[26] Yet this declaration stands in tension with another normative statement, which was intended to preclude a Marcosian reliance on the military but has actually been invoked to justify military intervention during the 2001 uprising that ousted President Joseph Estrada:[27] 'Civilian authority is, at

[22] Marcos, *Democratic Revolution*, p. 215. [23] *Ibid.*, p. 214.

[24] *Trajano* v. *Marcos (In re Estate of Ferdinand E. Marcos, Human Rights Litigation)*, 978 F.2d 493, 499 (9th Cir. 1992), and *Hilao* v. *Estate of Marcos (In re Estate of Ferdinand Marcos, Human Rights Litigation)*, 25 F.3d 1467, 1473 (9th Cir. 1994).

[25] *Aquino* v. *Ponce Enrile* (GR No. L-35546, 17 September 1974 59 SCRA 183).

[26] 1987 Constitution, Article II(1). [27] Doronila, *Fall of Joseph Estrada.*

all times, supreme over the military. The Armed Forces of the Philippines is *the protector of the people and the State.*'[28] Leaving aside this tension at the level of constitutional principle between the sovereignty of the people and the 'protective' role of the military, there are three specific emergency powers clauses that warrant our attention: the commander-in-chief clause, the war powers clause and the economic emergencies clause.

1. The commander-in-chief clause

The 1987 Constitution recognises several kinds of emergency. The first and most traditional is what I call the national security emergency under the extended commander-in-chief clause, all six paragraphs of it. The clause lists three such powers: the power to call out the armed forces (hereinafter, the calling-out power);[29] the power to suspend the writ of habeas corpus;[30] and the power to proclaim martial law.[31] The drafters codified many *substantive* constraints: martial law does not suspend the Constitution, supplant the courts or allow military jurisdiction over civilians;[32] the writ can be suspended only for rebellion-related offences[33] and there is a three-day detention limit for warrantless arrests.[34] In addition to these, the next set of constraints is *institutional*, through the Congress: it may revoke[35] or extend[36] the emergency, with fixed twenty-four-hour[37] and forty-eight-hour[38] deadlines to act. The last set of constraints is still institutional, but is specifically *judicial* in character: (i) the Supreme Court may determine the 'sufficiency of the factual basis of the proclamation . . . or

[28] 1987 Constitution, Article II(3) (emphasis added).

[29] The following conditions must concur: 'whenever it becomes necessary' and in order to 'prevent or suppress lawless violence, invasion or rebellion'.

[30] The following condition must hold: 'in case of invasion or rebellion, when the public safety requires it, he may, for a period not exceeding sixty days . . . '.

[31] The same conditions apply as for the suspension of the writ of habeas corpus (1987 Constitution, Arttícle VII(18)(1).

[32] *Ibid.*, Article VII(18)(4) (martial law 'does not suspend the operation of the Constitution, nor supplant the functioning of the civil courts or legislative assemblies, nor authorize the conferment of jurisdiction on military courts and agencies over civilians where civil courts are able to function, nor automatically suspend the privilege of the writ of habeas corpus').

[33] *Ibid.*, Article VII(18)(5) (only those 'persons judicially charged for rebellion or offenses inherent in, or directly connected with, invasion').

[34] *Ibid.*, Article VII(18)(6) (person thus arrested or detained shall be released unless he is judicially charged within three days).

[35] *Ibid.*, Article VII(18)(1).

[36] *Ibid.* ('if the invasion or rebellion shall persist and the public safety requires it').

[37] *Ibid.*, Article VII(18)(2) (within twenty-four hours from the suspension or proclamation, the Congress must convene if it is not in session, and without need of a call).

[38] *Ibid.*, Article VII(18)(1) (within forty-eight hours, the President must report the suspension of the writ or proclamation of martial law.)

the suspension . . . or the extension thereof'; (ii) the Constitution vests standing in any citizen to challenge emergency powers, in effect creating a legislated standing to sue (thus setting aside the traditional requirement of a Hohfeldian plaintiff); and (iii) the Court must decide the challenge within thirty days.[39] Note that judicial review of national security decisions may be traced to a pre-martial law Supreme Court ruling that libertarians of that period saw initially as the triumph of judicial power, but which revisionist jurists[40] and commentators[41] have exposed as the first legal step taken by Marcos in preparation for his *coup de grâce* on the Philippine democracy.

In *Lansang* v. *Garcia*,[42] the Supreme Court reviewed the suspension of the writ of habeas corpus by Marcos, following a grenade-thrower's attack at an opposition election rally, which Marcos blamed on the communists (as indeed would be confirmed two decades later[43]). The erstwhile controlling doctrine decreed judicial deference to the President on national security through the political question doctrine. *Lansang* however asserted the court's power to review not the correctness but the validity of the President's call, and since the challenge was cast procedurally as a certiorari petition, would rule solely on whether or not the call was 'arbitrary', that is to say, bereft of any factual basis. In hindsight, since the facts are available mainly from military intelligence, the *Lansang* court merely set itself up inevitably to ratify the challenged act. Thus, as revealed in the subsequently published Marcos diaries, when he learned of the court's unanimous ruling in *Lansang*, he wrote in his diary, 'I am ecstatic!'[44]

Signficantly, when Marcos proclaimed martial law one year later, he actually invoked *Lansang*'s judicial confirmation of the existence of the threat to national security.[45] In a way, this is parallel to the leading US authority on judicial review, *Marbury* v. *Madison*,[46] wherein Chief Justice

[39] *Ibid.*, Article VII(18)(3).

[40] P. Fernandez, *From Javellana to Sanidad: An Odyssey in Constitutional Experimentation*, in J. L. Cabildo (ed.), *1976 Amendments and the New Constitution* (Quezon City: University of the Philippines, Law Center, 1978), pp. 38–54.

[41] W. C. Rempel, *Delusions of a Dictator: The Mind of Marcos as Revealed in His Secret Diaries*, (Boston: Little, Brown and Company, 1993), p. 117.

[42] GR No. 33964, 11 December, 1971, 42 SCRA 448.

[43] J. R. Salonga, *Journey of Struggle and Hope: The Memoir of Jovito R. Salonga* (Quezon City: University of the Philippines Centre for Leadership, Citizenship and Democracy, 2001), pp. 177–81. This is the autobiography of Salonga, former Senate President, who was among the most seriously injured in the grenade blast. He survived and today remains the senior statesman in Philippine politics. He records personal findings based on the testimony of former rebels. See chapter XII, 'Responsibility for the Plaza Miranda Bombing'.

[44] Rempel, *Delusions of a Dictator*, p. 133.

[45] Proclamation No. 1081.

[46] 5 US (1 Cranch) 137, 176 (1803).

John Marshall aggrandised judicial power as a principle while strategically deferring to the executive in practice. The difference is that in the case of the United States, the judiciary eventually seized upon that power to challenge the political branches of government, while in the Philippines, it merely allowed the court to serve as the loyal justifier of the dictatorship.

2. War powers clause

The second kind of emergency is the extraordinary condition of 'war or other national emergency'. The ultimate power 'to declare the existence of a state of war' was reposed in Congress alone,[47] though the Congress was authorised to give additional powers to the President under the following conditions: (i) in 'times of war or other national emergency'; (ii) where authorised by law; (iii) 'for a limited period and subject to such restrictions as [Congress] may prescribe'; and (iv) limited to the 'powers necessary and proper to carry out a declared national policy'.[48] The war powers clause of the 1987 Constitution was invoked only once, when the Congress granted emergency powers to President Corazon Aquino after the 1989 coup attempt.[49]

3. Economic emergencies clause

Finally, the 1987 Constitution recognised economic emergencies in its clauses on the National Economy and Patrimony.

> In times of national emergency, when the public interest so requires, the State may, during the emergency and under reasonable terms prescribed by it, temporarily take over or direct the operation of any privately-owned public utility or business affected with public interest.[50]

The clause, 'the State may' could have meant either the President or the Congress. Until recently, this ambiguous drafting had led to the view that the President may act alone without need of congressional authority.[51] Thus emboldened, President Arroyo sought to do so in 2003, but was rebuffed in *David* v. *Arroyo*.[52] The court ruled that those powers can be

[47] 1987 Constitution, Article VI(23)(1). [48] *Ibid.*, Article VI(23)(2).

[49] Republic Act 6826 ('An Act to Declare, in View of the Existence of a National Emergency, a National Policy in Connection therewith and to Authorize the President of the Republic of the Philippines for a Limited Period and Subject to Restrictions, to Exercise Powers Necessary and Proper to Carry Out the Declared National Policy and for Other Purposes').

[50] 1987 Constitution, Article XII(17).

[51] See, for example, J. Bernas, SJ, 'The Takeover Provision', *Philippines Daily Inquirer*, 8 May 2006, http://archive.inquirer.net/view.php?db=0&story_id=75022.

[52] GR No. 171396, 3 May 2006, 489 SCRA 160.

exercised only by Congress, and that Arroyo exceeded her powers when she threatened to seize unco-operative broadcast networks on her own.

D. *Arroyo's 'rule-of-law' brinkmanship: formalism pushed to the hilt*

President Corazon Aquino faced down seven coup attempts during her presidency but finally declared a 'state of national emergency'[53] only for the last, almost fatal coup attempt of 1989.[54] Even then, before the month ended, the Congress affirmed her emergency powers,[55] but invoked the war powers[56] rather than the commander-in-chief clause, and confined its exercise mainly to stop destabilising economic saboteurs.[57] On the other hand, President Joseph Estrada invoked his 'calling out' powers at the height of terrorist attacks from an Islamic secessionist group, and sent the marines into Metropolitan Manila – including its shopping malls, veritably the centre of public activity. *Integrated Bar of the Philippines* v. *Executive Secretary Zamora*[58] upheld his decision, citing his 'widest leeway and broadest discretion' while avoiding the constitutional constraints inherent in the suspension of the writ or the declaration of martial law. The intent was to give the President the 'full discretion . . . to determine the factual basis' on whether it has become 'necessary' to call out the armed forces. These are 'graduated power[s]' on national security, of which the calling out power 'is considered as the lesser and more benign power' compared to the martial law and suspension of the writ powers, 'both of which involve the curtailment and suppression of certain basic civil rights and individual freedoms, and thus necessita[e] affirmation by Congress and, in appropriate cases, review by this Court'.[59]

But most significantly, when President Estrada faced the most serious threat to his presidency, the January 2001 uprising that actually brought his downfall, he did not invoke his emergency powers. In other words, to his credit, Joseph Estrada, faced with people's wrath over the suppression of evidence in the impeachment charges against him, backed down and

[53] Proclamation No. 503 (6 December 1989).

[54] See the *Final Report of the Fact-Finding Commission, pursuant to R. A. No. 6832* (October 1990), the Davide Commission, which was the investigative panel convened by President Aquino after the December 1989 coup attempt.

[55] Republic Act 6826. [56] 1987 Constitution, Article VI (23)(2).

[57] The law cited, *inter alia*, 'hoarding, profiteering, injurious speculations, manipulation of prices, product deceptions, and cartels, . . . , or other pernicious practices affecting the supply, distribution and movement of food, clothing, medicine and medical supplies'.

[58] GR No. 141284, 15 August 2000, 338 SCRA 81. [59] *Ibid.*, at 110.

vacated the seat of power.[60] As his successor, Arroyo assumed power under a cloud of 'constitutional ambiguity',[61] through a popular uprising that 'had sufficiently, though barely, pushed People Power within the pale of constitutional legitimacy'.[62] She has since faced the same wrath but has survived, deftly manipulating the Constitution's procedural safeguards to betray the Constitution's most deeply held values.

1. Arroyo: textual compliance, normative evasion

Incumbent President Arroyo has thrice invoked her military powers, and has shown a tendency for excessive textualism coupled with substantive evasions. The first time was in May 2001, when she declared a 'state of rebellion' after an 'angry and violent mob . . . attempt[ed] to break into Malacañang with the avowed purpose of overthrowing the duly constituted Government and forcibly seiz[ing] power'.[63] Loyalists of ousted President Estrada, mainly unorganised and uneducated, trooped to the presidential palace to protest when their leader was arrested on plunder charges. Arroyo ordered the military immediately to 'suppress and quell the rebellion with due regard to constitutional rights'.[64] These actions were impugned before the Supreme Court, but the 'state of rebellion' was soon lifted[65] and the court dismissed the petitions for being moot and academic.[66]

A dissenting opinion stated, however, that the 'state of rebellion' can be used to 'skirt the constitutional safeguards' for civil liberties and thus 'partakes the nature of martial law without declaring it as such'. It was effectively a 'subterfuge' to avoid procedural safeguards:

> It is a truism that *a law or rule may itself be fair or innocuous on its face, yet, if it is applied and administered by public authority with an evil eye so as to practically make it unjust and oppressive, it is within the prohibition of the Constitution.* In an ironic sense, a 'state of rebellion' declared as a subterfuge

60 Doronila, *Fall of Joseph Estrada*, p. 5. 61 *Ibid.*, pp. 6–11.

62 R. Pangalangan, 'The Impact of People Power on Our Legal System', in *The Supreme Court Centenary Lecture Series* (Manila: Supreme Court Centenary Celebration Committee, 2001), pp. 389–96. The author has written elsewhere on the rule-of-law implications of the 2001 uprising that ousted President Estrada and installed President Arroyo. See R. Pangalangan, 'The Philippine "People Power" Constitution, Rule of Law, and the Limits of Liberal Constitutionalism', in R. Peerenboom, (ed.), *Asian Discourses of Rule of Law* (New York: RoutledgeCurzon, 2004), pp. 371–84; and R. Pangalangan, 'Anointing Power with Piety', in R. Pangalangan (ed.), *Law and the Newly Restored Democracies: The Philippines Experience in Restoring Political Participation and Accountability* (Tokyo: Institute of Developing Economies, IDE-JETRO, 2002).

63 Presidential Proclamation No. 38 (1 May 2001).

64 General Order No. 1 (1 May 2001). 65 Presidential Proclamation No. 39 (7 May 2001).

66 *Lacson* v. *Perez*, GR No. 147780, 10 May 2001, 357 SCRA 757.

> to effect warrantless arrest and detention for an unbailable offense places a heavier burden on the people's civil liberties than the suspension of the privilege of the writ of habeas corpus and the declaration of martial law because in the latter case, *built-in safeguards are automatically set in motion.*[67]

Another dissenting opinion noted Arroyo's 'deviation from the concise and plain' language of the Constitution and her failure to follow the proper procedure:

> To accept the theory that the President could disregard the applicable statutes . . . on the mere declaration of a 'state of rebellion' is *in effect to place the Philippines under martial law without a declaration of the executive to that effect and without observing the proper procedure.* This should not be countenanced. In a society which adheres to the rule of law, resort to extra-constitutional measures is unnecessary where the law has provided everything for any emergency or contingency. *For even if it may be proven beneficial for a time, the precedent it sets is pernicious as the law may, in a little while, be disregarded again on the same pretext but for evil purposes.*[68]

Significantly, the dissenting justice derided the President's timing in lifting the declaration by invoking the well-settled principle that the courts could decide an otherwise moot question if the alleged unconstitutional acts were 'capable of repetition, yet evading review'.[69]

The prophecy of repetition came to pass when the President declared a 'state of rebellion'[70] for a second time on in July 2003, after the Oakwood Mutiny, when military officers protesting corruption in government took over a posh apartment complex (called the Oakwood Towers, hence the label) in the heart of the financial district.[71] Once again, the President

[67] *Ibid.*, at 774 (Kapunan J, dissenting) (emphasis added).

[68] *Ibid.*, at 790 (Sandoval-Gutierrez J, dissenting) (emphasis added). [69] *Ibid.*

[70] Presidential Proclamation No. 427 (27 July 2003). It read in part: 'Certain elements of the [military] seized a building in Makati City, put bombs in the area, publicly declared withdrawal of support for, and took arms against the duly constituted Government, and continue to rise publicly and show open hostility, for the purpose of removing allegiance to the Government . . . and depriving the President of the Republic of the Philippines, wholly or partially, of her powers and prerogatives which constitute the crime of rebellion.' Through General Order No. 4 (27 July 2003), she once again directed the armed forces and police 'to immediately carry out the necessary and appropriate actions and measures to suppress and quell the rebellion with due regard to constitutional rights'.

[71] See the *Report of the Fact Finding Commission, pursuant to Administrative Order No. 78 of the President of the Republic of the Philippines* (30 July 2003), issued by the Feliciano Commission, the investigative panel convened by President Arroyo after the Oakwood Mutiny.

tried to pre-empt the court's review by lifting the declaration.[72] This time, the court asserted the 'capable of repetition, yet evading review' standard and remained seized of jurisdiction. In its decision in *Sanlakas* v. *Executive Secretary*,[73] the court held that the declaration of a 'state of rebellion' was an 'utter superfluity' which was 'devoid of any legal significance' and is 'deemed not written'.[74] The dissenting opinion called it a 'constitutional shortcut', noting that nowhere does the Constitution grant 'the executive the power to declare a "state of rebellion," much more, to exercise on the basis of such declaration the prerogatives which a president may validly do under a state of martial law'.[75] When the President resorts to a subterfuge, she exercises a power 'not subject to clear legal restraints'.[76] The other danger therefore is that this 'unorthodox measure [is] unbounded and not canalized by the language of the Constitution'.[77]

> *The purpose of the Constitution is not only to grant power, but to keep it from getting out of hand.* The policy should be – where the Constitution has laid down specific procedures on how the President should deal with a crisis, it is imperative that he must follow those procedures in meeting the crisis. These procedures serve as limitations to what would otherwise be an unbounded exercise of power . . .
>
> If President Arroyo's only purpose was merely to exercise her 'calling out power,' then she could have simply ordered the AFP to prevent or suppress what she perceived as an invasion or rebellion . . . . *However, adopting an unorthodox measure unbounded and not canalized by the language of the Constitution is dangerous.* It leaves the people at her mercy and that of the military.[78]

The third state of emergency was declared during the coup attempt of February 2006,[79] the culmination of popular protests after Arroyo was caught on tape conspiring with an election official to cheat in the 2004 presidential elections. She was able to defeat an impeachment attempt by resorting to technicalities and her control over Congress, the impeaching body.[80] Arroyo invoked the commander-in-chief powers and the economic emergency clause. True to form, Arroyo lifted 'national emergency' just before the cases were scheduled for argument before the Supreme

[72] Presidential Proclamation No. 435 (11 August 2003).
[73] GR No. 159085, 3 February 2004 421 SCRA 657.
[74] *Ibid.* at 677 . [75] *Ibid.* at 692 (Sandoval-Gutierrez J dissenting).
[76] *Ibid.* at 694. [77] *Ibid.* at 693. [78] *Ibid.* (emphasis added).
[79] Presidential Proclamation No. 1017 (24 February 2006).
[80] M. de Jesus, 'The Death of Public Accountability: An Analysis of Presidential Impeachment Proceedings', unpublished LLB thesis, University of the Philippines (2007).

Court.[81] In *David* v. *Arroyo*,[82] the court struck down the violations of the freedom of speech and freedom of assembly, and the warrantless arrests carried out under the emergency declaration, but characterised the declaration itself as within the valid exercise of the 'calling out' powers of the President.

Arroyo has also attempted to arrogate emergency powers unto herself by purporting merely to exercise the generic powers of the state to punish common crimes. In *Bayan* v. *Executive Secretary Ermita*,[83] the Supreme Court struck down the Calibrated Pre-emptive Response (CPR) policy by which the President authorised the violent dispersals of protesters in public rallies. The Public Assembly Law mandated a policy of 'maximum tolerance', defined as 'the highest degree of restraint that the military, police or other peace keeping authorities shall observe during a public assembly or in dispersal of the same'.[84] However, the President's chief cabinet officer, the Executive Secretary, had announced in a press conference that the new policy would be the infamous CPR. The irony, therefore, was that what the court struck down was an unconstitutional press release, but one that nonetheless caused actual injury to protesters and real violations of the Bill of Rights.

The government has twice attempted to cite ostensibly non-political grounds to silence unsympathetic media. The National Telecommunications Commission, citing violations of the anti-wiretapping law, threatened to cancel the franchise of broadcast networks if they played the famed 'Garci tapes'. On these tapes a woman's voice – recognisably the President's – spoke to an election commissioner, plotting to cheat, intimidate witnesses and kidnap the family of an unco-operative election officer. Challenged in *Chavez* v. *Secretary of Justice*,[85] the court threw out the government's excuse that the warning was a mere press statement.

> [I]t is not decisive that the press statements . . . were not reduced in or followed up with formal orders or circulars. It is sufficient that the press statements were made by respondents while in the exercise of their official functions . . . The concept of an 'act' does not limit itself to acts already converted to a formal order . . . *Otherwise, the non-formalization of an act . . . will result in the easy circumvention of the prohibition on prior restraint.*[86]

[81] Presidential Proclamation No. 1021 (3 March 2006).
[82] GR No. 171396, 3 May 2006 489 SCRA 160.
[83] GR No. 169659, 14 February 2006, 488 SCRA 226.
[84] Batas Pambansa Blg. 880, s. 3(c) (Public Assembly Law of 1985).
[85] GR No. 168338, 15 February 2008. [86] *Ibid.*

The police likewise proposed to issue guidelines, under pain of franchise cancellation, to these networks under the emergency declaration of 2006.[87]

As if this were not enough, the same Secretary of Justice once more issued a 'media advisory' threatening action against overzealous journalists for 'criminal liabilities under the law, if [their personnel] will disobey lawful orders . . . during emergencies which may lead to collateral damage to properties and civilian casualties'.[88] In suppressing the latest attempt to oust Arroyo in November 2007 with the takeover of the Manila Peninsula Hotel by the same officers who were linked to the 2003 Oakwood Mutiny, and annoyed by the media coverage that stymied the anti-coup operations despite repeated appeals and requests for them to leave, two busloads of journalists were handcuffed with plastic tie wraps and herded into the military camps. The official rationale was, first, to evacuate the civilians for their safety and, second, to stop the rebels from escaping by pretending to be reporters. Accordingly, in official accounts, the newsmen were not arrested but merely 'processed' to establish their identity.

In *Tordesillas* v. *Secretary of Interior*,[89] the journalists sued for damages for the violation of the constitutional freedom of the press during the Peninsula stand-off. The trial judge dismissed their claim without hearing the merits of the case, saying that they had disobeyed a generic penal law on 'disobedience to a person in authority':

> The right of the plaintiffs as members of the press as guaranteed under the Constitution was not violated and trampled upon by the respective acts of the defendants. [The order to vacate the premises was] lawful and appeared to have been disobeyed by . . . the plaintiffs, when they intentionally refused to leave the hotel premises for which an appropriate criminal charge [for 'resistance and disobedience to a person in authority' under] the Revised Penal Code, which is applicable to all, including the media personalities, could have been initiated against them.[90]

The government had equivocated on whether the journalists were evacuated, processed or arrested and on whether there was a request, appeal, or order for them to vacate.[91]

[87] *David* v. *Arroyo*.

[88] Media Advisory, addressed to the chief executive officers (CEOs) of media networks and press organisations (11 January 2008) (see 'Int'l group slams [Department of Justice] threat', *Philippine Daily Inquirer*, http://newsinfo.inquirer.net/inquirerheadlines/nation/view_article.php?article_id=112166.

[89] Order (20 June 2008), Regional Trial Court, Branch 56, Makati City, Civil Case No. 08–086.

[90] *Ibid.*

[91] In *Senate* v. *Executive Secretary Ermita*, GR No. 169777, 20 April 2006, 448 SCRA, the Supreme Court partially struck down President Arroyo's claim of executive privilege in

As regards the right to free assembly, the government has perfected the art of the pre-emptive strike. Each time there is a big anti-Arroyo protest, the government confines the attendance of provincial protesters by blocking their buses and 'jeepneys' on the national highways leading to Manila. Sometimes they invoke national security, and conduct a vehicle-by-vehicle, passenger-by-passenger search that delays the protesters and prevents them from reaching time-bound protests. Sometimes the police invoke the Public Assembly Law literally; student protesters from the University of the Philippines were barred as they marched to a protest in Manila. The reason? Their rally permit was for Manila, not for Quezon City where the school is located. In other words, since the Supreme Court has struck down the Calibrated Pre-emptive Response policy, the President's men simply engage in tried and tested 'parsing', reading the law so literally as to defeat its animating purposes.

2. Dismal human rights record

The Arroyo government has been similarly disingenuous in justifying impunity in the face of the alarming rise in heinous human rights violations. The United Nations Special Rapporteur on extrajudicial, summary or arbitrary executions has confirmed in a 2007 report the extrajudicial executions of left-wing activists (at least 96 deaths confirmed, and dossiers regarding 271 other such murders filed) and the killings of journalists (2 to 3 per year in 1986–2002, and 7–10 in 2003–6).[92] Yet, the report lamented, the military has been in a 'state of almost total denial'.

> [M]any of the accountability mechanisms which are invoked as checks on governmental abuses have been rendered ineffectual . . . *On paper, they*

issuing a gag order on government officials called to testify in congressional investigations: Executive Order 464 (25 September 2005). Despite this, in *Gudani* v. *Senga*, GR No. 170165, 15 August 2006, 498 SCRA 671, the court upheld the ban on the testimony of two generals summoned to testify on election cheating. The court invoked not the privilege of the president as Chief Executive, but as commander-in-chief whose orders to her generals must prevail. More recently, the Supreme Court upheld the refusal of a cabinet official to answer questions on President Arroyo's involvement in a $132 million bribe offer over a telecommunications deal. This time, the court relied solely on executive privilege: *Neri* v. *Senate*, GR No. 180643, 25 March 2008.

92 Statement by Professor P. Alston, Special Rapporteur on extrajudicial, summary or arbitrary executions, Human Rights Council, UNGA A/HRC/4/20/Add.3* (22 March 2007). See also statement by E. G. John, Deputy Assistant Secretary for East Asian and Pacific Affairs, before the Senate Committee on Foreign Relations, Subcommittee on East Asian and Pacific Affairs (14 March 2007); and Amnesty International, Testimony before the Committee on Foreign Relations, Subcommittee on East Asian and Pacific Affairs (14 March 2007).

> *remain strong. In practice, they are of all too little use, and often this is the result of official design.* [F]or present purposes it is sufficient to focus upon some key examples of institutional passivity.[93]

The UN Special Rapporteur gave examples of responses from the passive government agencies. First, the Senate Committee on Justice and Human Rights, which 'insisted that there was no role for Congress because no new legislation was required, given that murder was already a punishable offence' and denied 'any proactive oversight role [by the Senate] regarding the executive's execution of the law'.[94] Second, the Secretary of Justice 'saw [his] role as a passive one' because prosecutors must show 'total impartiality'. 'If a file presented to them was insufficient, their role was simply to return it and hope that the police would do better next time. It was not for them to observe or respond to clearly shoddy dossiers designed to ensure that the police could be said to have done their job while at the same time no prosecution would follow.'[95] And finally, the Ombudsman's record was appalling: forty-four complaints of extrajudicial killings by state agents between 2002 and 2006, and 'the Ombudsman's office concluded that it was unable to act on even a single case'.[96] Under Marcos, it took the draconian measure of martial law to create a human rights nightmare. Under Arroyo, even worse human rights violations are committed and remain unpunished simply through 'a passivity, bordering on an abdication of responsibility by government'.[97]

III. A nation of juridical 'schizoids': pre-emption, subterfuge and 'doing without naming'

At different points in Philippine constitutional history, the discourse on states of emergency has segued from the formalist to the legal realist, from the legalistic to the instrumentalist. Marcos, the legalist and revolutionary has given way to Arroyo, who through the use of pre-emption, subterfuge and 'doing without naming' has subverted the Constitution through artifice.

Marcos marshalled the strengths of both the 'legalist' and the 'revolutionary'. He took pride that he exercised emergency powers under a

[93] *Preliminary Note on the Visit of the Special Rapporteur on Extrajudicial, Summary or Arbitrary Executions, Philip Alston, to the Philippines* (12–21 February 2007), UNGA A/HRC/4/20/Add.3* (22 March 2007), at 4, para. 10 (emphasis added).

[94] *Ibid.* at 5, para. 11.

[95] *Ibid.* at 5, para. 12.

[96] *Ibid.* at 5, para. 13.

[97] *Ibid.* at 5, para. 10.

'constitutional authoritarianism', which governed by law and was ratified each step of the way either by the sovereign will (through periodic referenda) or by the Supreme Court. He portrayed himself as the dictator who humbled himself before the majesty of the Supreme Court and was vindicated. But by that account, he was also the revolutionary who transformed martial law 'from the untenable strategy of protecting or restoring the status quo, to a militant, constitutional and legal strategy for creating . . . from the ashes of the old, a new society'.[98] He imputed that conservatism to law's colonial baggage in Philippine history, and impugned as elitists those who would insist that martial law should be confined to restoring order rather than restructuring society. After he was ousted, the new democracy reinstated a liberal constitution that limited emergency powers to national security and grave 'economic emergencies', and effectively barred Marcos's transformative rationale as bogus (because he failed to deliver) and illegitimate (because it can be used as an excuse to 'trade-off' civil liberties for economic and social reforms).[99]

Arroyo, on the other hand, has persisted in trying to evade constitutional checks in several ways. The first is by pre-emption, that is to say, by mooting the case and forestalling judicial review through the expedient of lifting the emergency before the case is decided. This worked during the first emergency but failed the second and third times. The second is through 'subterfuge', in the words of the court itself. Arroyo 'deviat[es] from the concise and plain' text of the Constitution, avoids the Constitution's 'graduated' levels of powers and checks, and simply calls her emergency powers by another name. The Constitution sets out the gradations: 'calling out', suspending the writ and proclaiming martial law. Arroyo instead used the terms 'state of rebellion' (in 2001 and 2003) and 'state of national emergency' (in 2006). And why persist in what the court validated at best as a suspect legal superfluity? Because to use the exact text of the Constitution would have triggered the institutional safeguards. Change the labels, escape the checks. The third is by what I call 'doing without naming'. Arroyo sought to achieve her political aims without resorting to legal measures, or by simply applying the generic, non-emergency-related provisions of the criminal code.

Arroyo's logic is uncanny twice over. First, she could have wondered: 'If I don't issue any law, what is there for the court to strike down?' The

[98] Marcos, *New Society*.

[99] *See Simon* v. *Commission on Human Rights*, GR No. 100150, 5 January 1994, 229 SCRA 117.

Constitution speaks of the freedom of assembly and the statute ensures a Maximum Tolerance Policy for protesters, but the Presidential Spokesman declares a Calibrated Pre-emptive Response by press release. The Constitution speaks of freedom of the press, but the Justice Secretary issues a media advisory prohibiting the playing of incriminating tapes of a presidential conversation. Both times, the Supreme Court strikes it down. 'The [mere] non-formalization of an act... will result in the easy circumvention of the [rule] on prior restraint.'[100] ... Second, she could also ask: 'If I simply rely on existing non-emergency laws, why would a court strike down the stock provisions of the penal law?' Arroyo needed no state secrets law to suppress the playing of incriminating tapes and block a cabinet officer's testimony on gargantuan bribe-money changing hands; all she invoked was a generic claim of 'executive privilege'. She invoked good old-fashioned rules on insubordination to bar two generals who were about to testify on election cheating without asking for her permission. Two busloads of journalists were herded into the military camps, but they were being 'processed' to ascertain their media credentials. Protesters may have the right to public assembly, but their buses can be stopped at every checkpoint along the way, whether to verify that a bus is following its authorised route, or to check each passenger for weapons and bombs. By parsing the law, who needs emergency powers? Finally, gross human rights violations – the extrajudicial execution of left-wing activists and of journalists – have been committed and remain unpunished, and impunity reigns not through blatant means but through 'passivity, bordering on the abdication of responsibility' by state agencies.

The Philippine experiment shows how formal constraints on power have failed: by pre-emption of institutions; by subterfuge to cheat the spirit by manipulating the text; and by 'doing without naming' and thus remaining below the radar of the courts. Finally, human rights violations remain unpunished by default because accountability mechanisms are lackadaisical, strong on paper but useless in fact, 'often [by] official design'. The overall effect, however, is to not 'surface' the sense of being in an emergency, to make extraordinary measures – intimidation, killings and all – look ordinary, commonplace and invisible. While, in China, the challenge was how to construe emergency powers in a one-party state where the starting point is roughly liberalism's idea of a permanent emergency,[101] in the Philippines, the challenge is how to recognise the

[100] See text at note 86.

[101] See J. deLisle, 'States of Exception in an Exceptional State: Emergency Powers Law in China' (Chapter 13), this volume.

emergency in the first place. It is as if the response is: 'Duh, emergency? What emergency?' Indeed the best proof is that each time Arroyo lifted yet another state of rebellion, nobody really cared whether the lifting was bogus or genuine – the way it was an issue when Marcos 'lifted' martial law in 1981. The reason is that it does not really matter whether the emergency was declared or not.

Indeed we may carry the contrast to the perennial national security laws in Malaysia, Singapore, Indonesia under Suharto's New Order,[102] or even the Philippines under Marcos, where the emergency was justified on the basis of an ever-present communist threat to an entire society, and emergency powers were a form of communal action against the enemy. Arroyo has structured the discourse such that the notion of an emergency is relevant only to the troublemakers, because the rest of society, apolitical and self-absorbed, is made to think simply that they inhabit a different place. She has de-ideologised the 'enemy' by making it generic. Stated otherwise, Arroyo has called liberalism's bluff and pushed its fictions to the outer edge of credulity. She is merely the duly elected chief executive, carrying out a mandate to enforce the laws of the land, against all foes of whatever ideology.

IV. Conclusion

In the Philippine constitutional narrative, the preferred concept of emergency powers is one that is grounded on threats to national security, to the exclusion of the deeper structural causes that foster political restiveness. Emergency powers are contained in the commander-in-chief clause that empowers the state to deal with rebellion, and are by necessity blind to the larger reasons that drive people to rebel. Thus construed, emergency powers are likewise more easily subjected to constitutional constraints. The irony is that the most candid challenge to that account was offered by Marcos, namely, that the truest and most persistent cause of political unrest is social inequality, and that government needed to short-circuit the separation of powers and sacrifice the Bill of Rights in order to address those problems. That was fundamentally incompatible with the constitutional design, because to so conceive extraordinary powers was likewise to

102 See Tan, Chapter 6; H. P. Lee, 'Constitutionalised Emergency Powers: A Plague on Asian Constitutionalism?' (Chapter 14); and N. Hosen, 'Emergency Powers and the Rule of Law in Indonesia' (Chapter 10), all in this volume.

institutionalise the emergency and, as the Marcos years sadly confirmed, allow a long-term dictatorship.

When the Marcos experiment failed, the constitutional response of the democratic movement that overthrew Marcos was twofold. The first response was formal, restoring the national security approach to emergency powers and hemming it in with layer upon layer of checks and balances. The second was normative, codifying in the Constitution several grand affirmations of democracy, civilian supremacy and respect for human rights. Those responses worked with both Corazon Aquino and Joseph Estrada. They both faced severe threats to their presidencies. Aquino faced down several coup attempts without resorting to unilateral assumption of emergency powers. Estrada faced one civilian uprising, did not invoke emergency powers, but eventually relinquished the presidency.

Those same constraints have failed with incumbent President Gloria Macapagal-Arroyo, who has complied with the literal text of the Constitution while betraying its foundational norms. The Arroyo presidency represents an unprecedented positivistic turn in Philippine rule-of-law debates. The last such brazen manipulation of the constitutional text was by Marcos, but even he took care to appeal to substantive norms that bore a legitimating power distinct from the Constitution. Arroyo is different. She has violated civil liberties, but when faced with coup attempts, instantly takes refuge in the same Constitution she has violated. The legalistic turn shows the bizarre 'disconnect' between legality and normativity, when text trumps norms. The post-Marcos Constitution began as a grand statement against dictatorship and is now transformed into a mere backdrop for evasion and abdication.

What Arroyo has achieved is to expose the folly of the anti-Marcos movement in seeing legal constraints as the chief deterrent to dictatorship. The anti-Marcos movement was an ideological hotchpotch that unified under Corazon Aquino's presidency a whole spectrum from the Communist Party to the traditional politicians of the pre-martial law political order. The movement's lowest common denominator was its opposition to Marcos and his one-man rule, and its ideological expression was the rule of law, or to be more precise, governance through the mechanical working of institutions oblivious to ideology. Arroyo has seized upon that reluctance, that aversion to open ideological contestation. By foisting the supremacy of the Constitution as text, she claims to exemplify the highest form of constitutionalism, the trump card that prevails without having to appeal to external and substantive norms of justice, accountability and respect for human dignity. The crisis of Philippine constitutionalism today lies in its inability to explain why Arroyo's manipulation of constitutional text is itself unconstitutional and why compelling institutions to work – and devising extra-constitutional measures to make them work – is a duty that we must read into the Constitution.

16

Islamism as a response to emergency rule in Pakistan: the surprising proposal of Justice A. R. Cornelius

CLARK B. LOMBARDI

I. Introduction

Few countries can claim as rich and varied an experience of extraordinary rule as Pakistan. Pakistan has been governed under either emergency rule or martial law for the greater part of its history. Pakistani lawyers and intellectuals have given a great deal of thought to the problems posed by these kinds of extraordinary rule and their effect on the rule of law. In this Chapter, I will discuss how one famous and thoughtful liberal judge in Pakistan responded to the repeated imposition of emergency rule, martial law and guided democracy during his years on the bench. I will describe how he came up with a most surprising proposal for strengthening the rule of law so that extraordinary rule was either unnecessary or, when imposed, restrained. The judge in question is A. R. Cornelius, a famous Christian justice of the Pakistani Supreme Court – renowned for his repeated defence of the position that judges must play an active role in defending fundamental rights against executive overreach. His proposal was to Islamise the Pakistani legal system.

Cornelius has long stood as a hero to liberals in Pakistan and abroad for his courageous defence of fundamental rights during periods of extraordinary rule.[1] He is particularly admired for dissents he wrote during

[1] For laudatory academic analyses of Cornelius's career and commitment to the judicial protection of individual rights, see, for example, R. Braibanti, 'An Analysis of the Thought of Cornelius', in R. Braibanti, *Chief Justice Cornelius of Pakistan: An Analysis with Letters and Speeches* (Karachi: Oxford University Press, 1999), pp. 1–66; S. M. Haider, 'Preface', in A. R. Cornelius, *Law and Judiciary in Pakistan*, ed. S. M. Haider (Lahore: Lahore Law Times Publications, 1981), pp. 1–45; P. Newberg, *Judging the State: Courts and Constitutional Politics in Pakistan* (Cambridge: Cambridge University Press, 1995), pp. 48–9, 61, 76–7. For a sense of his status among Pakistani liberals today, see N. Iqbal, 'Disqualification Clause Doesn't Hit

Pakistan's first state of emergency and first martial law. In these dissents, Cornelius decried his colleagues' unwillingness to challenge executive assertions of power. Deeply frustrated by the judiciary's inability (or unwillingness) to assert the power to protect fundamental rights in Pakistan, he came up with a remarkable proposal. To strengthen the rule of law in Pakistan and ensure the ability of the judiciary to protect fundamental rights, this Christian liberal proposed the systematic Islamisation of the Pakistani legal system – albeit Islamisation of a certain kind.

I do not here have space to do justice to the story of Justice Cornelius or to the complexity of his thought. In the following pages, I can simply introduce Justice Cornelius and make clear that he is a most unlikely champion of Islamisation. Having established this, I will describe how I believe he arrived at his surprising Islamist position. Cornelius's move toward Islamism allows us to reflect upon several themes being explored in this book, and it helps us to evaluate some of the arguments made by contributors to this volume.

Victor V. Ramraj has presciently pointed out in this book that emergency laws or military rule in states where rule-of-law values are more established function differently from emergency laws or military rule in states where the basic constitutional infrastructure and culture of accountability are weak.[2] Where the former seeks to preserve or restore an existing state of legality, the latter is imposed with the goal of establishing legality. Normatively, he suggests that we should refrain from criticising in emerging constitutional states forms of emergency rule in the same way that we would criticise them in established constitutional states. The challenge for academics and policy-makers is, he suggests, to identify the characteristics of a positive, constructive form of emergency for emerging constitutional systems in Asian jurisdictions. A number of contributors to this volume have responded to the points made in Ramraj's piece. I would suggest that in a number of dissents and speeches, Cornelius anticipated some of Ramraj's points, and he weighed in on some of the questions that Ramraj asks.

Musharraf', *Dawn* (Karachi), 28 September 2007, www.dawn.com/2007/09/28/top1.htm. This is an article in one of Pakistan's leading papers describing the arguments on 28 September 2007 before the Supreme Court of Pakistan during the so-called 'Lawyers' Revolt'. The article reports that the president of the Supreme Court Bar Association is said to have described Justice Cornelius in oral arguments as 'one of the most outstanding, dynamic and independent judges in the history of Pakistan' and urged the justices to make the choice to protect the principle of democracy, which he characterised as a choice to follow Justice Cornelius.

[2] V. V. Ramraj, 'The Emergency Powers Paradox' (Chapter 2), this volume.

For example, in an important series of dissents in the late 1950s, Cornelius argued that emergency and military rule in Pakistan was essentially different from the types of extraordinary rule that British and American courts had previously dealt with – precisely because it was invoked not to save an existing state of legality to which the people had consented but rather to impose a new state of legality. Like Ramraj and some contributors to this volume, Cornelius also recognised that there was a paradox built into the idea of constructive emergency. The executive claims to embrace authoritarian rule only because it wants to establish a new constitutional system where, for the first time, the executive will be effectively constrained. Finally, Cornelius recognised that, as Ramraj suggests and some other contributors to this volume vigorously argue, the emergency powers paradox is not just a curiosity. Rather, it points to practical problems that would have to be addressed by any constitutionalists who think about co-operating with rulers in countries like Pakistan who claim to have established emergency rule only as a step toward building, for the first time, a robust constitutionalist tradition. Cornelius asked how one could tell whether a declaration of emergency had been taken in good faith as a step to constitutionalism – and thus whether this declaration was legitimate and judicially cognisable by courts. And how can judges or the polity help ensure that a legitimate, constructive state of emergency will, in fact, give way to rule of law?

In answering his own questions, Cornelius argued that extraordinary rule could only help establish a culture of legality if that extraordinary rule was exercised in a manner that respects the basic constitutional expectations of the people. In countries without strong democratic mechanisms, he suggested that these popular expectations were best recognised by judges. Thus, to his mind, judges should accept emergency or military rule only if that rule respected judicially articulated constraints on the power of the ruler. Cornelius argued in vain. When his judicial colleagues refused to assert any power to impose liberal restraints on emergency and military governments, Cornelius was forced to develop his arguments in dissent. When the now unconstrained military government promulgated by presidential decree its new Constitution, Cornelius realised that this government had refused voluntarily to accept the restraints that he believed should have been judicially imposed.

Cornelius's theory of constitutionalism and his frustration at the behaviour of both judges and military rulers in Pakistan ultimately drove him toward Islamism. First, he came to believe that the settled constitutional expectations of the people included an expectation not only that the state would respect the fundamental rights of the citizenry but also that the state would always act in a manner that was consistent with God's law – the *shari'a*. Thus, if judges asserted the inherent right to impose liberal restraints on the executive because they represented the aspirations of the people, those same judges should, as a logical matter, support Islamisation too. Second, Cornelius came to believe that, as a practical matter, judges could not restrain an unwilling military ruler unless their orders were understood to speak for both the common-law constitutionalist tradition *and* for the Islamic heritage that the people wanted the state to honour. For it was only in such a situation that judicial orders might create both a desire to obey on the part of rulers and political pressure for obedience from the masses.

II. A. R. Cornelius

Alvin Robert Cornelius was born in 1903 to an established family of Indian Christian background.[3] Cornelius's grandfather converted to Christianity in the early nineteenth century. Cornelius's father was an accomplished professor of mathematics. Raised a Protestant, Cornelius converted to Catholicism after marrying an Indian Catholic, and he remained a practising Catholic his whole life. Excelling at school in India and later at Selwyn College, Cambridge, Cornelius earned a commission in the powerful and prestigious Indian Civil Service (ICS), an appointment that placed him automatically at 'the pinnacle of [Indian] society and the political order'. The ICS was a small cadre of highly competent British officials and elite native Indians who served as equals and provided the Raj with an administrative and judicial elite which oversaw the day-to-day operation of the empire. Cornelius opted to serve in the ICS's judicial branch, the organisation from which the Raj's elite judges mostly came.

Serving for much of his career in Lahore, he made a choice at the time of partition that was unusual for an ICS member – and particularly for a Christian one. He chose to remain in Lahore, a city that was to become part of Pakistan, and to serve the new Pakistani state as a judge.[4] Cornelius's choice to serve the Pakistani state did not reflect any attraction to the

[3] The biographical information in this section is drawn from Braibanti, 'An Analysis of the Thought of Cornelius', pp. 21–31, and from Haider, 'Preface', pp. 1–7.

[4] At partition, India and Pakistan each needed the services of experienced bureaucrats. Members of the ICS were given the option of serving either Pakistan or India. Braibanti, who was a leading expert on the Indian Civil Service and the Civil Service of Pakistan, notes that the majority of ICS officers chose to serve India. More striking, only two Indian

romantic idea of Pakistan as a land where Muslims could achieve some authentic identity. Indeed, he would later tell his friend Ralph Braibanti that he initially found the discussions about Pakistani identity and the role of Islam in the Pakistani state to be 'repellent'. He chose Pakistan, he said, because Lahore was familiar, and many of the regions that would make up Pakistan were, he believed, unusually well run. As a judge and member of the ICS, he apparently respected good management.[5]

Having made the choice to stay in Pakistan, Cornelius served from the start among its judicial elite. At the time of partition, Cornelius was serving on the Lahore High Court, which had jurisdiction over the Punjab, West Pakistan's most populous and wealthy province. In 1951, he was appointed to Pakistan's Federal Court, soon to be renamed the Supreme Court.

Almost immediately after Cornelius's arrival on the Supreme Court, Pakistani politics began to unravel. The drafting of a controversial Constitution was followed by the dismissal of the Constituent Assembly and the Governor-General's assertion of emergency power to rule alone over Pakistan. This in turn led to the restoration of civilian rule, the drafting of a new Constitution, the abrogation of that Constitution by martial law and then thirteen years of martial law and guided democracy. During the tumultuous years in which he served on Pakistan's highest court, Cornelius sought consistently to convince his colleagues that judicial power could and should be invoked to protect the individual rights that had traditionally been enjoyed by British subjects. In a series of frustrating cases, however, he failed to sway a majority to his views and was forced to issue bitter dissents.

In his dissents and later in important speeches, Cornelius reflected deeply about extraordinary rule in a postcolonial state and the effect emergency rule had on the rule of law in the country. He thought too about the proper judicial response to extraordinary rule. As his thinking evolved, Cornelius, who had once found public discussions of Islam's role in the state to be 'repellent', came to argue in the 1960s that a liberal constitutional tradition of restrained government could not emerge in Pakistan unless it was embedded in a legal system that was not merely liberal but was accepted by the majority of Pakistanis as being consistent with Islamic law. He urged legal professionals to call for (and take part in) a systematic programme to explore Pakistani law and amend it as necessary

Christian members of the ICS chose to serve Pakistan. See Braibanti, 'An Analysis of the Thought of Cornelius', pp. 4, 24.

5 Letter from A. R. Cornelius to R. Braibanti, 14 November 1977, reprinted in Braibanti, *Chief Justice Cornelius*, p. 193.

to ensure that it was consistent with Islamic law. In a later section of this chapter, I will discuss some ambiguities in Cornelius's understanding of Islam and in his understanding of the role it might play in the strengthening of liberal constitutionalism in Pakistan. Before doing so, it will be useful to explore the frustrations he felt as he tried to impose from the bench a form of liberal constitutionalism that was justified in purely secular terms.

III. Litigation during the first emergency

To understand Cornelius's intellectual evolution and, in particular, his turn to Islamisation as a guarantor of constrained government, we must consider the events to which he was responding – political dysfunction in a newly independent postcolonial state, which led to military rule and, most important, a decision by his colleagues on the Supreme Court to hold that as a result of an extraconstitutional martial-law order, Pakistan's judges had lost all power to review or correct violations of individual rights.

Pakistan gained independence in 1947. It was granted independence very suddenly, however, and the grant of independence was followed by traumatic violence and dislocation. As a result, Pakistan failed to prepare for independence and after independence it needed to draft a constitution. As a stopgap measure, Pakistan took the statutes defining the government of British India, and, with minor modifications, used them as the interim constitutional documents for Pakistan. The Pakistani legislature was assigned the task of drafting a new constitution but it found itself unable to complete the task for many years.

The constitution-making process started well enough. In 1949, the legislature, in its capacity as constitutional assembly, enacted an 'Objectives Resolution' that announced broad principles.[6] These supposedly represented the core expectations of the Pakistani people for their government and should animate the new Constitution. The principles included popular sovereignty along with 'democracy, freedom, equality, tolerance and social justice, as enunciated by Islam'. The resolution also provided a place for Islamic law, by announcing that Muslims had the right to be governed

[6] The Objectives Resolution was adopted by the Constituent Assembly on 12 March 1949. For a brief history and reprint of the resolution, see Justice (Rtd) F. Karim, *Judicial Review of Public Actions* (Karachi: Universal Law Publishing, 2006), vol. I, pp. 30–3. For a history of the resolution and its eventual incorporation into the Pakistan Constitution, see M. Lau, 'Article 2a, the Objectives Resolution and the Islamisation of Pakistani Laws', in H. G. Ebert and T. Hanstein (eds.), *Beitraege zum Islamischen Recht*, vol. III (Frankfurt and New York: Peter Lang, 2003), pp. 173–204.

by 'the teachings of Islam as set out in the Qur'an and Sunna'. Finally it called for religious freedom for minorities, federalism, respect for independence of the judiciary and respect for fundamental rights – which were undefined but presumably were understood in light of the common-law constitutional tradition.

Having reached easy agreement on those fundamental principles, however, the legislators failed for many years to agree on the details of the new constitution. In 1954, when the legislators finally *did* come to agreement, they found that the chief executive of the state did not like what they had come up with. Upset about the terms of a draft constitution that was about to be ratified by the Constituent Assembly, the Governor-General dismissed the legislature and declared a state of emergency under which, he claimed, he could legislate. The Supreme Court, with Justice Cornelius on the bench, heard two cases that grew out of this action. In *Tamizuddin Khan*,[7] the ousted prime minister of Pakistan argued that the dissolution of the Constituent Assembly in 1954 violated the fundamental rights of the assembly members and the people they represented.

There is no space in this article to discuss the background to this case, nor, unfortunately, to analyse the extraordinarily complex opinions that were produced. We can only note that in these opinions, the majority and Cornelius in dissent each proceeded as if the powers of the Pakistani government were defined entirely by (i) statutory documents left over from the British Raj and (ii) the unwritten limits on executive and legislative power that had been elaborated over the years by common-law courts in the United States and United Kingdom, each elaborating what they took to be the common-law constitutionalist tradition. The two sides, however, understood the inherited legal texts very differently. The majority of justices, led by Chief Justice Munir, argued in a formalistic mode that the Supreme Court of Pakistan had not been vested by statute or custom with the power to compel the executive to respect fundamental rights. Justice Cornelius, in dissent, argued that the constitutional documents Pakistan had inherited from the British should be interpreted differently. Citing British treatises and Thomas Cooley's nineteenth-century treatise on American constitutional law, Cornelius argued that the majority's conclusions were untenable. He asserted that the Governor-General had no right to prevent the legislature from meeting in its capacity as a constitutional convention to enact a constitution.[8]

[7] *Federation of Pakistan* v. *Maulvi Tamizuddin Khan*, PLD 1955 Federal Court 240.

[8] See *Tamizuddin Khan*, at 363, 365, 395 and 399 (Cornelius J, dissenting); for an analysis of the case, see Newberg, *Judging the State*, pp. 48–9.

Shortly after this decision, a second case challenged the right of the Governor-General to declare an 'emergency' and his right during any emergency to assume legislative powers. In *Special Reference #1 of 1955*[9], Chief Justice Munir and a majority of justices concluded that a state of emergency had been properly declared and that the Governor-General had all the powers he claimed. Again, Munir's argument rested entirely on traditional common-law analysis of statutes and precedents.[10] Citing multiple common-law cases and numerous English treatises on constitutional law and legal maxims, Munir asserted that the Roman maxim *salus populi supreme lex* was good law in Pakistan's common-law-based legal system, and that this maxim justified all the Governor-General's actions.[11] In a dismissive, sometimes sarcastic dissent, Cornelius argued that the majority violated both the letter and spirit of the Pakistan Constitution and, more broadly, of common-law constitutional traditions. To his mind, if one interpreted the constitutional documents in force using traditional common-law tools of construction and if one filled in gaps with rules established in other common-law jurisdictions, the Governor-General did *not* have absolute discretion to declare an emergency or to determine what response was appropriate. Thus, a court would have to find that the Governor-General's assumption of legislative power was inappropriate.[12]

[9] *Reference by His Excellency, the Governor-General*, PLD 1955 Federal Court 435 (subsequently referred to as 'Governor-General's Reference').

[10] For a slightly different account of the case from the one I give below, see Newberg, *Judging the State*, pp. 51–60.

[11] See particularly, *Governor-General's Reference*, at 478–80 (Munir CJ). See also Munir's comment at 485: 'an act which would otherwise be illegal becomes legal if it is done bona fide under the stress of necessity, the necessity being referable to an intention to preserve the constitution, the State or the Society and to prevent it from dissolution, and [this] affirms Chitty's statement that necessity knows no law and the maxim cited by Bracton that necessity makes lawful which otherwise is not lawful'.

[12] Ultimately, Cornelius concluded the Governor-General cannot on the grounds of necessity engage in any act that a court does not agree is necessary. He pointedly noted a leading treatise on executive power and the way in which it treats the argument that a Governor-General can do anything that he reasonably and in good faith believes to be necessary to meet an emergency. Cornelius argues: 'This is doubtless unsound doctrine . . . Every member of the executive may violate in case of emergency ordinary laws, but the Governor, like every other officer, runs the risk of finding that a Court of law may conclude that the emergency was not such as to justify his action despite its good faith and reasonableness' (*Governor-General's Reference*, at 497 (Cornelius J, dissenting)). Later, in a delightfully sarcastic passage, Cornelius argues that, in looking to history, it would seem that the decision to exercise accepted emergency powers is extremely counterproductive. There is thus no good policy reason to grant an executive any more of these self-destructive powers. Indeed, he asks whether the Governor-General really

These two cases provide no hint that Cornelius in the mid-1950s believed the propriety of government action should ever be measured against Islamic norms. They do reveal, however, clear frustration on his part about the weakness of 'law' in Pakistan and about the absence, even among judges, of a commitment to upholding the rule of law in Pakistan.

In 1958, a new crisis would force the justices again to decide whether they should assert the constitutional power to restrain an executive which was claiming expansive powers during a period of extraordinary rule. The crisis was brought on by the imposition of martial law. The Supreme Court, led by Chief Justice Munir, issued two opinions abjuring any right or responsibility to review military actions or to protect the individual rights that had been mentioned in the Objectives Resolution and were protected under the abrogated 1956 Constitution. In two famous dissents, Cornelius developed ideas that would evolve over time and would eventually lead him into the paradoxical position of being a liberal Christian Islamist.

IV. Opinions written after the first imposition of martial law

After the Supreme Court opinions in *Tamizuddin Khan* and the *Governor-General's Reference*, the Governor-General had established dominance over the legislature. By 1956, the Governor-General of Pakistan had convinced the legislature to produce a new draft constitution and then to enact it. This Constitution established a parliamentary form of government in which most power was held by the prime minister. It also identified certain 'fundamental rights' and gave the courts the power to enforce them against the government.

The new constitutional regime did not work smoothly. After two years of fractious politics, the President, military and bureaucracy lost patience with the new constitutional order that they had helped to create. In 1958, the civilian President of Pakistan declared martial law and voided the Constitution. Soon thereafter, the President resigned his post as chief martial law administrator (CMLA), and Army Chief of Staff Ayub Khan

would want to exercise such powers for himself: 'For they [precedents in which the British Crown asserted emergency powers] can bring but cold comfort to any protagonist of the autocratic principle against the now universal rule that will of the people is sovereign. In the case of North America, the territory was lost eventually to the British Crown through the maintenance of just such reactionary opinions, as those which Senior Counsel for the Federation of Pakistan has been pleased to advance for acceptance by the Court'. *Governor-General's Reference*, at 515–16 (Cornelius J, dissenting).

assumed the role. The Martial Law Authorities argued that politicians had systematically failed to serve the interest of the people. They pledged that they would sideline the politicians who had failed the nation. Thus, they promised, democracy would be restored, but it would be democracy in a form that placed limits on corrupt or demagogic popular politicians and thereby (at least according to the military) increased the real enjoyment of democracy.

So as to avoid a total legal vacuum in the country, the Martial Law Authorities issued the cryptic 'Order (Proclamation) No. 1 of 1958', which was known as the 'Laws (Continuance in Force) Order'. This Order was a short and nebulous document identifying which of the previous government's laws would apply while the military government established itself. In explaining which laws would apply, it incorporated by reference many, but not all, of the existing laws. Its ambiguities made it something of a Rorschach test for Pakistanis – testing their understanding of the fundamental nature and sources of law in Pakistan.[13]

The Order provided that the Constitution, which had established judicial protection of fundamental rights, would no longer be valid. It proceeded enigmatically to say (in arguably mandatory terms) that state 'shall be governed as nearly as may be in accordance with the late Constitution'. In a similar mixed message, the Order provided that the courts of Pakistan would continue to operate under the new regime and would have the power to identify and issue interpretations of the rules that applied in the new order,[14] but they had no power to compel 'the Chief Administrator of Martial Law or the Deputy Chief Administrator of Martial Law or any person exercising powers or jurisdiction under the authority of either' to respect their interpretation.[15]

Shortly after the issuance of the Laws (Continuance in Force) Order, cases came before the Supreme Court asking it to restrain the government from violating the fundamental rights that had been guaranteed by the (supposedly abrogated) 1956 Constitution and that might or might not

[13] The Rorschach inkblot test is one in which a patient is given a series of inkblots and asked to describe them to a psychiatrist. Its advocates believe that the answers reveal important aspects of the patient's personality. For a history of the evolution of the test, see H. F. Ellenberger, 'The Life and Work of Hermann Rorschach (1884–1922)' (1954) 18 *Bulletin of the Menninger Clinic* 173.

[14] '[A]ll courts in existence immediately before the Proclamation shall continue in being and, subject further to the provisions of this Order, in their powers and jurisdictions.'

[15] Instead of compulsive writ power against the executive, the courts maintained only the right to issue a non-binding advisory opinion.

have been protected under the Order. These cases raised questions both about the validity of the Order and about its construction.

In *State* v. *Dosso and Another*, the Supreme Court considered whether a military government could by fiat abrogate a duly enacted constitution and, if so, whether the court could read into the Laws (Continuance in Force) Order (which claimed to abrogate the 1956 Constitution) any power for judges to provide legal protection for the fundamental rights that had been guaranteed by that abrogated constitution. Speaking for the majority, Justice Munir said yes to the first question and no to the second.[16]

Concurring in result, Cornelius accepted Munir's claim that courts had no choice but to accept the military's claim that the Laws (Continuance in Force) Order superseded the Constitution. He also accepted that the Order could not be read, as a general matter, to preserve fundamental rights.[17] Nevertheless, uncomfortable with this conclusion, he produced a highly technical argument for why in two of the criminal cases the court could interpret the Order as empowering the courts to issue a writ compelling the government to respect fundamental rights.[18] The opinion was

[16] See *Dosso*, PLD 1958 (SC) 533 at 541. In his opinion, Munir notoriously (mis)cited Hans Kelsen for a proposition that was really closer to that of Carl Schmitt. Justice Munir argued that whenever a military ruler declared a change in the legal order and proved able, through threat or force, to suppress all effective opposition to the change, then a legal 'revolution' had occurred. In such a state, the only law was the ruler's command. If the ruler said that a constitution that had protected fundamental rights was void and if he did not issue any new law explicitly re-establishing those rights, then there were no fundamental rights. This was the position that Munir saw in Pakistan in 1958. Thus, he concluded, 'the so-called fundamental rights which were described in Part II of the late Constitution are therefore no longer a part of the national legal order' and cannot be protected by courts.

[17] See *Dosso*, at 553 (Cornelius J, concurring).

[18] The argument begins with an extremely abstract discussion. Cornelius focuses, *inter alia*, on how one should interpret retrospective laws and on what a law might mean when it says that a writ guaranteeing rights would 'abate' (see 558–60). He argues that one could plausibly read the statute to provide limited protections for fundamental rights. And, he went on, judges were obliged to read it in this manner because it protected what he understood to be human rights that governments were morally obliged to protect. Admitting, implicitly, that his argument was strained, he stated that he was driven to adopt it, in part, by his belief that a statute must be interpreted whenever reasonably possible to protect 'essential human rights which inherently belong to every citizen of a country governed in a civilized mode':

> One final reason for my being in a state of doubt [that the appeals could not continue] may be added in brief... It may further be said with reference to a number of Fundamental Rights enumerated in Part II of the Constitution of 1956 that they do not derive their entire validity from the fact of having been formulated in words and enacted in that Constitution. A number of these rights are essential human rights

a concurrence rather than a dissent because he admitted that the petitioners' claims, though they could be heard, would fail on the merits. The fact that he chose to issue it reflected his deep concern about the implications of the majority opinion. The concurrence also contained an enigmatic statement upon which Cornelius would soon have cause to elaborate: 'essential human rights do not derive their entire validity from the fact of having been formulated in words and enacted in that Constitution'.[19]

The elaboration of that sentence began one year later when Cornelius dissented from the majority opinion in the case of *Province of East Pakistan* v. *Mehdi Ali Khan*.[20] The facts in *Mehdi Ali Khan* were similar to those in *Dosso*, and a majority of Supreme Court justices used the case to reaffirm the positions that they had adopted in *Dosso*. Cornelius dissented at great length. Feeling that his *Dosso* opinion did not go far enough in defending fundamental rights, he used *Mehdi Ali Khan* as an opportunity to rethink the question of whether (and why) courts might have the power to restrain Pakistan's martial authorities by issuing orders protecting fundamental rights. Cornelius began by arguing briefly that the case at bar was distinguishable from *Dosso*.[21] He then turned to an argument that – based on the space he allotted to it – he felt more important. Cornelius argued that *Dosso* should be overruled. In the process, he articulated a thoughtful argument for why, during the period of martial law, Pakistani courts should assert their continuing power to protect certain fundamental rights. These were the fundamental rights that had been protected in the 1956 Constitution and that the Laws (Continuance in Force) Order

> which inherently belong to every citizen of a country governed in a civilized mode, and speaking with great respect, it seems to me that the view pressed before us by the learned Attorney General involves a danger of denial of these elementary rights, at a time when they were expressly assured by writing in the fundamental law of the country, merely because that writing is no longer in force.
>
> *Dosso*, at 560–1 (Cornelius J, concurring).

19 *Dosso*, at 561 (Cornelius J, concurring).

20 *Province of East Pakistan* v. *Mehdi Ali Khan*, 1959 PLD (SC) 387.

21 Cornelius argued that the case *could* plausibly be distinguished and thus it *should* be distinguished because in all cases of doubt judges should interpret statutes and precedent in a rights-protective manner.

> I am conscious that it is possible to criticise the view I have taken as savouring of technicality. I propose to answer that the rule laid down in the *Dosso* case is equally of a technical character and as it operates to deprive subjects of a right to protect interests by certain well-recognised modes in law, I conceive that to defeat such a rule by the aid even of purely technical submissions involves no contravention of law
>
> *Mehdi Ali Khan*, at 436.

had explicitly said were constitutionally protected – even though they were not to be interpreted and enforced by judges.

Cornelius's argument was, I suggest, one whose implications may not have been immediately clear to its author. It anticipates Ramraj's argument in this volume that emergency rule in countries with weak traditions of constitutionalism is essentially different from emergency rule in countries with strong traditions.[22] Where the latter seeks to preserve or restore a state of legality that is broadly understood and accepted but which is under temporary threat, the former is imposed with the goal of establishing a new culture of legality. Nevertheless, Cornelius took this insight in a direction that Ramraj might find surprising. He argued that a government that invokes emergency powers in order to establish a previously non-existent culture of legality, should sometimes be considered *more* constrained than a government in a nation with a strong history of legality that invokes emergency powers in order to preserve the existing culture of legality. The argument deserves a close look.

Cornelius argued in his *Mehdi Ali Khan* opinion that all the justices writing in the *Dosso* case (including himself) had misconstrued the 1958 coup and the documents produced by the military government. They had all failed to recognise that under common-law precedents martial law can apparently be of two types, unconstrained or constrained, and that the current martial law was of the latter, constrained type. His argument went, roughly, as follows: The 'ordinary' type of martial law is the type that occurs in a society with an established and popular constitutional system when a military ruler asserts extraordinary power to respond to a military emergency or civil unrest, with the goal of suppressing the violence and restoring the traditional constitutional order.[23] The common-law precedents tend to deal with military rule of this sort, and they suggest that, during such a period of martial law, the military ruler is largely unconstrained and permitted to do whatever he believes necessary to respond to the emergency. However, this latitude has only been granted in circumstances where courts expect the protections provided by the old Constitution to come back into force.[24]

[22] Ramraj, Chapter 2.

[23] See *Mehdi Ali Khan*, at 439 (Cornelius J. dissenting) ('[T]he Martial Law under which the country was placed by the Presidential Proclamation in 1958 is different in essential respects from the ordinary conception of Martial Law').

[24] Although he is not explicit, Cornelius's lifelong commitment to judicial power probably led him to the view that judges are empowered to determine when the emergency is such that constitutional constraints come back into force.

Cornelius suggested that Pakistan was *not* in this type of martial law. Pakistan had not been invaded, nor did it face an internal rebellion and, in any case, the martial law was not designed to restore the old order. The new type of martial law imposed by the army was analogous to the martial law that applies when one country occupies another and tries to establish in the conquered territory a new rule of law. In this different type of martial law, the government may have different and, ironically, more constrained powers.

Cornelius's dissent is dense and multilayered and must be read against his conviction that legitimate government rests on the consent of the governed. According to Cornelius, judicial precedents and history each suggest that people are willing temporarily to give up many rights in order to defeat a challenge to a legitimate constitutional order (to which they have consented) so long as they understand that this constitutional order will be restored. However, there is no comparable tradition suggesting consent to the theory that a military government that has quashed opposition should be, during the period that it is establishing a new constitutional order, 'purely arbitrary as to power or unrestricted as to method'. Admittedly, a government that has extraconstitutionally removed a previous government and purports to establish a new government is not bound by the rules of the government that it has conquered and displaced. Nevertheless, like all governments, it is bound to respect the people's settled expectations of good governance and their core understandings of 'justice'.[25]

Cornelius argued that the Constitution of Pakistan was the Order insofar as it was not inconsistent with the core values of the Pakistani people and their expectations regarding legitimate government. 'Like any form of rule over human beings, it [military rule of the sort operative in Pakistan] is obliged by the circumstances to adapt itself to the circumstances in order to attain its ends, and one such circumstance of the utmost importance is the settled habits and sentiments of the people'.[26] In the context of the case before him, Cornelius meant that the Pakistani people

[25] See *Mehdi Ali Khan*, at 439 (Cornelius J, dissenting) where drawing (without citation) upon an old muse, Thomas Cooley, Cornelius defined the constitution of a country as 'that body of rules and maxims in accordance with which the powers of Sovereignty are habitually exercised'. (The phrase appears in T. M. Cooley, *A Treatise on the Constitutional Limitations Which Rest upon the Legislative Power of the States*, 5th edn (Boston: Little, Brown & Co., 1883), p. 3. Cornelius seems to have agreed with Cooley that these rules and maxims might be written or unwritten. If a written 'Constitution' was inconsistent with them, that document could not claim truly to be the Constitution of the country.

[26] *Mehdi Ali Khan*, at 439.

expected their government invariably to respect at least some of the fundamental rights that had been elaborated over the years by common-law courts.

More interesting still, Cornelius argued that, when judges interpreted martial law pronouncements, they should presume that the military government wanted to be restrained whenever it was violating the settled expectations of the polity. In other words, in the absence of explicit instructions to the contrary, judges should assume that a conquering government wants its judges to help the government avoid acting in a way that undermines its legitimacy. With this presumption in place, Cornelius argued that judges should interpret the Order itself to permit judicial protection of some rights. By adopting this presumption, Cornelius was able to avoid asking trickier questions: in cases where a conquering government unmistakably rejects the judiciary's power to limit its action, should a court assert an inherent power to void a military government action that the court believes deviates unacceptably from the core values of the people? If so, how would the courts be able to ensure that the government respected their rulings?

Cornelius's avoidance of those questions was typically shrewd. Cornelius no less than Chief Justice Munir recognised that in Pakistan in 1959, it would be quixotic to claim that the courts had the power to issue orders against an unwilling executive. Cornelius instead flattered the military government, suggesting that in its cryptic Order it had wisely permitted judges to protect some fundamental rights. He hoped that the government would agree with him and that as it planned the new constitutional order, the military government would recognise that the legitimacy of any Pakistani government depended in part upon its willingness to accept judicial constraints, including an obligation to respect fundamental rights as articulated by judges.

As I will discuss, Cornelius was ultimately disappointed in this hope that the military would agree that it was limited in the way he proposed. Thus, in subsequent years, he would have to begin thinking about the things that judges and lawyers could do to create external pressures on a military government. His goal would be to create pressures that would lead to a situation where the military found itself psychologically or politically compelled to respect judicial orders that protected fundamental rights. Among the steps that he thought would be helpful was the beginning of a systematic programme led by legal professionals to harmonise the Pakistani legal system with Islamic law.

V. Dialogue with the executive

As already suggested, Cornelius's dissent in *Mehdi Ali Khan* was probably not directed primarily at his colleagues on the bench, but rather at the military government. As a dissenter, Cornelius's opinion did not define the law for Pakistan. Rather, it described what the law should be. The most important audience for Cornelius's opinion was, thus, the military regime itself. Cornelius was telling that government that, even if judges refused to assert themselves, the military government would never enjoy legitimacy until it bound itself to respect judicial rulings enforcing human rights. Cornelius knew that the military authorities were planning to draft a new constitution. Implicitly in *Mehdi Ali Khan* and later explicitly in advice provided to the Constitutional Drafting Commission, Cornelius called for the military to refuse the Supreme Court's offer of unrestrained legislative and executive discretion. The military government should draft a constitution confirming in writing, that, as Cornelius had suggested, it was bound by supra-legislative norms embedded in the expectations of the people.

In 1960, Chief Justice Munir reached retirement age and Cornelius ascended by dint of seniority to the position of Chief Justice. In that capacity, he was expected to advise the committee drafting the new Constitution. In written comments presented to the Chief Martial Law Administrator, Army Chief of Staff Ayub Khan, Cornelius stated explicitly that *Dosso* and *Mehdi Ali Khan* were wrongly decided and that in its new Constitution, the government should explicitly recognise that the government was, as Cornelius's dissent had argued, bound to respect any fundamental rights to which Pakistanis fundamentally believed they were entitled.[27] Nevertheless, Cornelius did not seem very optimistic that the military would voluntarily relinquish power or would subject itself to judicial oversight in areas involving fundamental rights. Thus he began to think both about why the military might be reluctant to accept checks on its power and about why the public did not demand that it did so. In 1960, Cornelius gave a speech at the Political Science Association at Edwardes College in Peshawar.[28] In his speech, Cornelius explicitly fretted about the tendency of post-conflict and postcolonial governments to abuse

[27] A. R. Cornelius, 'Some Constitutional Proposals for Pakistan', proposals presented in writing to the Military President of Pakistan, Field Marshal Ayub Khan, reprinted in Cornelius, *Law and Judiciary*, pp. 184ff.

[28] A. R. Cornelius, 'Speech at Edwardes College, Peshawar, 1960', reprinted in Cornelius, *Law and Judiciary*, pp. 47ff.

their power asserting emergency powers and then refusing to relinquish them.[29] Implicitly suggesting that the Pakistani government was just such a government, he went on to analyse the problem, the conditions that made it possible and its possible solution.

Cornelius argued that 'today we automatically think in terms of the laws being derived from the consent of the governed and we lay the foundations of our liberty upon that proposition'.[30] But in an unrepresentative or dysfunctional political system 'one who is of perverse and antisocial mind and tyrannical in his outlook can utilise the political processes and by achieving power can pervert the laws and press them ruthlessly to his advantage . . . I think you would agree that if that be the condition then the law affords no guarantee of liberty . . . '.[31] A solution could theoretically lie with the judiciary. In some common-law jurisdictions, judges had demonstrated that they could preserve liberty by defending the rights that the people expect to be honoured but which the people have not been able to enact – through democratic political means – into positive law. In an interesting section, Cornelius speculated about the mechanics by which some courts had been able to impose their will on a reluctant executive.

He suggested that courts could only hope to bind a powerful executive if they spoke with moral force and in a fashion that clearly resonated with the people such that powerful rulers would feel both psychological and mass political pressure to comply.[32] Judges who had spoken with such power had often spoken in a religious idiom – tying their legal rulings to a religious faith that compelled the obedience of most citizens.

As an Anglophile speaking in an elite British-founded, English-language educational institution, Cornelius, predictably, tried to demonstrate the mechanics of judicial empowerment by pointing to the constitutional history of Britain. He claimed that in Britain's early development, its judges had not felt obliged to apply a statute that was contrary to English customary law 'illuminated and inspired by the dictates of their religion'.[33] Even

[29] *Ibid.*, pp. 50–1:

> Experience during the last two World Wars clearly proves that once possessed of emergency powers, Governments are most reluctant to part with them. What then is the ray of hope in this climate of deterioriation and despair? . . . The world in its darkest corners is now gravitating towards universal suffrage and if the peoples are not to be subjected to further extremes of tyranny in the form of laws, it is necessary that each individual should be educated into a proper understanding of and belief in himself as the possessor, by right of birth, of basic human rights . . . And then, of course, there are the courts.

[30] *Ibid.*, p. 49. [31] *Ibid.*, p. 50. [32] *Ibid.*, pp. 51ff. [33] *Ibid.*, p. 51.

when they submitted to the supremacy of positive law, judges continued to defend the ethical values of the people by systematically interpreting statutes so far as possible to comport with the principle of equity and the overarching notion that the law must be 'made for the people and not the people to be subjected to the laws'.[34] Courts in Britain had been able to continue defending fundamental individual rights because they were able convincingly to argue that aggressive interpretations were necessitated by the principles of the Christian religion. Cornelius did not, in this speech, call judges to start phrasing their rights-protecting opinions in an Islamic vein. But he seemed to suggest that it might be an effective mode of protecting rights.

One year later, in a speech given in Karachi to celebrate the anniversary of the promulgation of the Universal Declaration of Human Rights, Cornelius suggested that the British experience merely exemplified a broader principle. Human rights were more likely to be respected if their champions could articulate the demand for 'rights' in language that resonated with the great masses of people – people who often equated proper behaviour with religiously ethical behaviour and, thus, equated proper governance with governance that respected religious commands:

> Organized and established [sic] religion, such as we are familiar with, still remains the most powerful safeguard against man's inhumanity to man . . . I submit that this Universal Declaration of Human Rights is founded too exclusively on the concept of the secular state . . . I suggest that the safer sanction is that of the religious conscience and that the future calls for a great deal of consideration whether this Declaration would not be more effective over large parts of the Earth's surface if it gave a real place to religion in its formulation.[35]

Perhaps inevitably, in the following year, Cornelius came out dramatically in favour of the systematic Islamisation of the Pakistani legal system. He argued that in a state such as Pakistan, Islamisation would be necessary to ensure the rule of law, including respect for the fundamental rights to which Cornelius himself was committed.

VI. The explicit turn to Islamism

In 1962, the military government in Pakistan promulgated a new constitution. That Constitution disappointed many in Pakistan, including the

[34] *Ibid.*, p. 52.

[35] A. R. Cornelius, Unpublished speech on the thirteenth anniversary of the Universal Declaration of Human Rights (1961), quoted in A. R. Cornelius, 'Islamic Concept of Human Rights', speech (8 November 1977), reprinted in Cornelius, *Law and Judiciary*, pp. 344–5.

new Chief Justice Cornelius. It made reference to fundamental rights, but refused to make them binding on the executive. It also outraged Islamists by setting up advisory committees to look into the possibility of Islamising the law, but failing constitutionally to recognise a role for Islamic law in the state.

As Chief Justice, Cornelius quickly made a number of important speeches arguing that the constitutional system enshrined in the new Constitution was fatally flawed because it failed accurately to reflect the settled expectations of the people – something that his *Mehdi Ali Khan* dissent had suggested was the 'real' constitution of Pakistan. The gist of the speeches was this: whether or not Pakistan's written constitution formally required the government to respect fundamental rights (as understood by the judiciary) or Islamic norms, the military, bureaucracy and judiciary needed to recognise that the majority of Pakistanis would consider Pakistani law illegitimate if they deemed it inconsistent with their core expectations. These core expectations included expectations that their fundamental individual rights would be respected and that their government would respect Islamic norms. And, if Pakistani law was deemed illegitimate, the judges who spoke in the name of the law would lose their power to control either the government or the governed.

There is one thing that should be noted about Cornelius's demand that all legal claims in Pakistan be rooted, ultimately, in a respect for the sanctity of Islamic law. Cornelius was heavily influenced by the family of movements that are known as liberal Islam.[36] Thus, he admitted that a few rules, such as the rules of criminal procedure, might require some change. Nevertheless, he seemed to have thought that much of the inherited legal system could be preserved. This may have been rooted in his growing familiarity with the experience of Middle Eastern nations that were then purporting to 'Islamise' their laws according to liberal visions of Islamic law – including the many countries that were Islamising their laws according to the theories of Egypt's `Abd al-Razzaq al-Sanhuri.[37] There is no room here to discuss the phenomenon of liberal Islam and of

[36] For brief overviews and bibliographies of modernist Islamic movements, including the movements together subsumed under the title 'liberal Islam', one can look at the introductions to Charles Kurzman's sourcebooks on modernist and liberal Islam as well as the contributions therein. See C. Kurzman, 'The Modernist Islamic Movement', in C. Kurzman (ed.), *Modernist Islam 1840–1940* (New York: Oxford University Press, 2002) and C. Kurzman, 'Liberal Islam and its Islamic Context', in C. Kurzman (ed.), *Liberal Islam* (New York: Oxford University Press, 1998).

[37] For a discussion of Sanhuri's theories and their influence in the Middle East, see generally, E. Hill, *Sanhuri and Islamic Law: The Place and Significance of Islamic Law in the Work of Abd*

governmental programmes to Islamise law according to a liberal Islamic vision. Nor is there room to ask whether it was naive for Cornelius to believe that Pakistan could effectively implement a programme of 'liberal Islam'-isation. For the purposes of this chapter, it is simply important to recognise that based on the evidence before him, Cornelius, like many Muslims of his era, believed that Islamisation might require some significant changes to the Pakistani legal system – but not too many. Most important, Islamisation would not require the abandonment of the principle that governments must respect the fundamental civil and political rights historically protected at common law.[38] Indeed, Islamisation might be the only thing that could create the conditions in which judges could compel government to respect these rights. Thus, when he demanded that Pakistani law be harmonised with Islamic values, Cornelius believed that he would be 'resanctifying' a liberal constitutionalist vision of the law – a vision that he believed had come to be viewed with suspicion by Pakistanis as an imported British vision of law that did not provide robust protections for their rights.

This belief is evident in one of the most interesting of Cornelius's speeches and surely the gutsiest. This was a 1962 speech delivered to the military command itself at its headquarters in Rawalpindi. In this speech, Cornelius urged the military to commit itself to respecting the fundamental wishes of the people – wishes that included not just judicial protection of fundamental rights but also a demand that all Pakistani law be demonstrably consistent with Islamic law. That this speech represented a milestone in the evolution of his thought can be seen by the fact that in later speeches Cornelius referred to it and quoted from it.[39]

Al-Razzaq Ahmad Al-Sanhuri, Egyptian Jurist and Scholar, 1895–1971 (Cairo: American University Press, 1987). See also A. al-Shalakany, 'Between Identity and Redistribution: Sanhuri, Geneaology and the Will to Islamize' (2001) 8 *Islamic Law and Society* 201, and C. B. Lombardi, *State Law as Islamic Law in Modern Egypt* (Leiden: Brill, 2007). For evidence of Cornelius's interest in Middle Eastern codification projects in which Sanhuri was often involved (and in which his thinking was always influential), see, for example, A. R. Cornelius, 'Integration of Nation through Law', speech (23 December 1962), reprinted in Cornelius, *Law and Judiciary*, pp. 51–2.

[38] See A. R. Cornelius, 'Function of Law as a Link Between Nations' speech (4 June 1964), reprinted in Cornelius, *Law and Judiciary*, pp. 147–51; A. R. Cornelius, 'Leadership Needs to Promote the Ethos of Constitution', speech (13 February 1965), reprinted in Cornelius, *Law and Judiciary*, p. 215; A. R. Cornelius, 'Reorganization of Judicial System' (no date listed), reprinted in Cornelius, *Law and Judiciary*, p. 313.

[39] See, for example, A. R. Cornelius, 'Crime and Punishment of Crime', speech (27 August 1965), reprinted in Cornelius, *Law and Judiciary*, p. 80.

Cornelius began by challenging the military's government's implicit claim that its new Constitution respected a basic 'law' that would be obeyed and, as the root of all other laws, would bring stability to Pakistan. Asking the assembled officers to reflect on their own attitudes toward 'law', he pointed out that the mere fact that an act is declared 'legal' does not mean that it is considered to be legitimate or that it will command obedience.

> The mere fact that cases are decided does not necessarily mean that the system followed is fully adapted to the understanding and sentiment of the people. We all know of civil cases where after getting a decision from the final Court, the parties have to go home and make a compromise so as to produce a practical result more in consonance with what they know to be the natural justice of the matter . . . [40]

For this reason, Cornelius went on, a successful government will never rest simply upon a 'thin' notion of legality, and successful rulers are never lulled into believing that people will respect and obey their government simply because the government abides by laws that may be formally legitimate but are perceived to be unjust.[41]

> [I]ndependence . . . cannot be sustained by a mere paper constitution. The machinery of popular representation, the technique of law-making, all the familiar activities of politicals have come to be understood as mere motions in a foreign mode. The more vigorously they are pursued, the nearer the infant State is brought to the point of dissolution.[42]

In short, he suggested, the state cannot be stable and cannot survive in the long term without recognising a judicially administered, 'thick' form of legality – that demanded respect not only for the positive law of the state, but also for supra-legislative principles that grew from the people's understanding of justice.

Cornelius suggested it would be wise for the architects of the new constitutional order to heed carefully Simone Weil's argument that after a constitutional breakdown, the new constitutional order has no inherited legitimacy. A government must build a new constitutional order that is popularly supported and compels obedience from the government simply because it reflects the people's deepest moral convictions and their

[40] A. R. Cornelius, 'Speech at Army Command, Rawalpindi, 1962', reprinted in Cornelius, *Law and Judiciary*, p. 208

[41] The 'thin' and 'thick' versions correspond to what Ramraj in his contribution to this volume calls 'formal' and 'substantive' conceptions of the rule of law. Ramraj, Chapter 2, pp. 47–8.

[42] Cornelius, 'Speech at Army Command', p. 218

understanding of 'the eternal source of all legality'.[43] Building upon this, he insisted that it was a matter of 'political therapeutics'[44] in Pakistan that courts be empowered to create and apply law in a manner that is consistent with both fundamental rights and Islamic law – two bodies that he saw as at their deepest level consistent.

> The most important of these powers [necessary to create a viable government in Pakistan] in my opinion, is the judicial power... It is only necessary to redivise for them the basic principles and procedures of the laws they administer [in Islamic terms]. This is a matter of fundamental importance.[45]

In a second speech that year, Cornelius took his message to the lawyers who were struggling to define their place in a military-dominated, quasi-democracy. He had already told the military that they would have to respect both fundamental individual rights and Islamic law. This raised the question of who should interpret Islamic law and oversee the harmonisation of Pakistani law (including any judicially elaborated doctrine of fundamental rights) with Islamic law. In a speech delivered to the All-Pakistan Lawyers Convention, he repeated that anyone who has an interest in guaranteeing obedience to the law must ensure that the law is framed in Islamic terms. The people only respect laws that they believe to be consistent with their understanding of the religion that was the ultimate source of all legality. 'There is', he said,

> great weight in the popular demand to bring all laws in conformity with the dictates of religion... [F]rom whatever angle it is represented it represents the feeling of a people who are seeking to shape their lives according to Quran and Sunnah. We cannot take refuge behind the argument that the people are already equipped with a thorough complex of laws under which they have lived successfully for many decades.[46]

[43] *Ibid.*, pp. 219–20:

> The point is put very clearly by a notable French woman writer, Simone Weil, in a book entitled *The Need for Roots*, written during the years 1940–45 when France lay under German occupation... This is what she has to say: 'Seeing that we have in fact recently experienced a break in historical continuity, constitutional legality can no longer be regarded as having an historical basis; it must be made to derive from the eternal source of all legality. The men who offer their service to the country to govern it will have to publicly recognise certain obligations corresponding to essential aspirations of the people eternally inscribed in the depths of popular feeling; the people must have confidence in the work and in the capacity of these men, and be provided with means of expressing the fact; they must also be made to feel that, in accepting these men, they give an undertaking to obey them.

[44] *Ibid.*, p. 219 [45] *Ibid.*, p. 220.

[46] Cornelius, 'Integration of Nation through Law', p. 58.

Cornelius pointed out that the Pakistani government could bring compulsive force to bear and thus could for a time apply some thin form of the rule of law.[47] But, he argued 'these things are clearly not enough'.[48] The colonial powers had also upheld the thin rule of law, and as his listeners well knew, their rule was considered illegitimate and they were ultimately driven out. The strength of a nation and the stability of its legal order rests, he suggested, on its people's consent to their government and thus cannot be assured unless the people understand and accept the 'source of the laws under which they and the administration live and work'.[49]

In a provocative comment, Cornelius claimed that this caused him, as a judge, to 'suffer' whenever he was asked to apply the death penalty in some cases of honour killings. This was not because, to his mind, the act of murdering one's daughter was ever morally excusable. Implying that his own views on the matter were beside the point, he simply argued that the state should not ask its judges to punish people for things that 'are esteemed among the highest in their community'. For in doing so, judicial acts would simply create disrespect for the state and, ultimately, disorder. '[T]his type of capital punishment is being administered for over a century. It has not resulted in the diminution of the sentiments with which the code of honour is maintained. On the contrary, it is the deterrent effect of the death sentence which has been dulled.'[50]

According to Cornelius, if lawyers and judges understood this fact, they would see that their highest duty was to help the government to legitimise itself by systematically engaging in a course of study, legal drafting and judicial opinion-writing that would result in a body of constitutional law and a corpus of subsidiary positive laws that spoke in Islamic language and did not contradict the Islamic principles 'esteemed among the highest' by Pakistanis.[51] If legal professionals succeeded in this task, Pakistanis would be more likely to respect the law and demand that the government respect it as well. If the constitutional principles enunciated by judges were understood to be Islamic, the military rulers, themselves Muslim and also sensitive to the possibility of popular revolt, would feel both morally and politically compelled to obey the law.[52] Cornelius thus concluded that lawyers can (and must) help the government 'shape the laws in such a way that they become [seen as] instruments for the manifestation and fulfillment of the will of the Almighty, through the lives of the people and the organization of their State. If that ideal is achieved, the [state's] laws

[47] *Ibid.*, p. 57. [48] *Ibid.*, p. 58 [49] *Ibid.* [50] *Ibid.*, pp. 59ff.
[51] *Ibid.*, pp. 60–2. [52] *Ibid.* (note particularly the passages at p. 60).

would have a natural force to project and sustain them in the same way as [moral] principles are maintained and universally accepted.'[53]

VII. The further evolution of Cornelius's thought

After 1962, Cornelius's commitment to Islamisation became ever more pronounced. Cornelius continued to link this commitment to his desire for a legal system in which the government could be expected to respect judicial orders protecting fundamental rights. Indeed, his speeches started to suggest repeatedly that Islam and liberalism could not be separated. Islam, properly interpreted, was fundamentally liberal. And, given popular support among Pakistanis for Islamisation, there could be no liberal rule of law in Pakistan unless it could realistically be characterised as a liberal 'Islamic' rule of law.

By 1965, the government had amended the Constitution to make fundamental rights justiciable. Cornelius welcomed the move, but, having lived through the imposition of both emergency rule and martial law, he was clearly concerned that respect for fundamental rights would cease whenever the military found respect to be inconvenient. That year, in a speech to the Pakistan Institute of International Affairs, he returned to a theme he had articulated four years earlier in his speech at Edwardes College. He argued that the common-law principles of restrained government and individual rights had been respected in the early years and thus had become part of the fabric of English society. Why? At least in part, he said, this was because judges had drawn them from religious principles that were widely respected by both thc government and the governed.[54]

In another speech the following year, Cornelius argued that in Pakistan, judges would not be able to ensure respect for fundamental rights listed in the Constitution unless they could plausibly argue that fundamental rights were connected to religious values shared by both the governors and the governed.

> The Constitution lays down in the Fundamental Rights, the path which leadership is to follow, the over-riding principles that are to govern thought and behavior and policy. It is a misfortune that these are expressed in terms derived from other Constitutions which have been in existence for

[53] *Ibid.*, p. 62.

[54] Cornelius, 'Function of Law as a Link Between Nations', pp. 141ff. (see particularly, pp. 147–8).

> perhaps half a century. It may be convenient for judicial interpretation that the expression should be in the English language, but from the point of view of making these amendments a matter of conscience, would there not be in Pakistan enormous advantage to be gained from setting them out in a Scriptural language, that is in the Arabic language? I conceive that each Fundamental Right can be shown to derive from the dictates contained in the Holy Scriptures of Islam. If expressed in Arabic, in suitable terms, would they not be invested with overtones of undeniable obligation? Would not their assimilation into the public conscience be vastly enhanced thereby? [55]

Consistently from the mid-1960s until his death, he built upon the themes that germinated during his dissents under martial law and blossomed in the early years of Ayub Khan's military regime. He reiterated in speeches the following themes: (i) only if they enforce a law that is recognised as fundamentally moral as well as formally 'legal' will judges be able to command the obedience of all people in Pakistan – both citizens and rulers; (ii) if properly trained, Islamic legal professionals will be able to demonstrate to the satisfaction of the Pakistani people that Islamic law is consistent, in most respects, with common-law rules, and indeed it requires governments to respect most of the fundamental rights that common-law courts have recognised and protected; (iii) Islamists and liberals should recognise that they share a common cause in the defence of fundamental rights, and the government should recognise that it will fail to command obedience unless it establishes a rule of law that respects these values, which are shared by both Islamists and liberals. To give just one example, in 1969, Cornelius was asked to teach the officers in training for the Civil Service of Pakistan (the elite bureaucratic apparatus that was the successor to the ICS). He reflected upon the principles of political science that had been taught to him when he was about to enter the civil service. He explained that one who wanted to apply those principles in Pakistan would be led to a 'liberal Islam'-ism:

> Reverting now to the proposition that an integrated idea of Right or Law pervading the entire community is essential for the healthy operation of a democratic society which observes the Rule of Law, there is no escape from the conclusion that the Ethical System of Islam must provide the medium through which the body of laws and institutions together with the moral conscience of the citizens is to function.[56]

[55] Cornelius, 'Leadership Needs to Promote the Ethos of the Constitution', p. 215.

[56] A. R. Cornelius, 'Judicial System of Pakistan', speech (12 May 1965), reprinted in Cornelius, *Law and Judiciary*, pp. 274–5.

VIII. Criticism of Cornelius and the declining awareness of his Islamist tendencies

When Cornelius first championed the cause of Islamisation in Pakistan, he shocked colleagues both in Pakistan and abroad. He immediately attracted criticism from former friends in the ICS and the high judiciary – bastions of Anglophilia and ideological commitment to secular government.[57] One such observer reflected the feelings of many when he suggested in print that Cornelius's Islamism could only be due to some schizophrenia or some neurotic insecurity about his status as a Christian in a majority Muslim country.[58]

Why might this be? Cornelius's contemporaries in the postcolonial Pakistani elite tended to have little, if any, systematic education in Islam. The only thing that they knew with confidence about Islam was that it appealed to the less educated members of the Pakistani polity and that they often followed demagogues who had a profoundly anti-liberal vision of the state. As a result, they disagreed with Cornelius's conclusion that for legal liberals the promise of Islamisation outweighed its dangers. Little in the subsequent history of Pakistan caused them to change their mind.[59]

In the 1970s and 1980s, a new Pakistani dictator, General Zia al-Haq reached out to illiberal Islamist elements in Pakistan. He imposed a series of statutes that imposed 'Islamic' laws. These laws reflected a very narrow and illiberal interpretation of Islam – one diametrically opposed to the version that Cornelius believed could support a liberal state. Al-Haq also enacted institutional reforms that empowered conservative Islamic thinkers. While one can to this day find liberal Islamic thinkers in Pakistan, including some active in politics and the judiciary, Islamism has come to be associated in the minds of many liberals primarily with anti-liberal movements. And

[57] One eminent liberal and fellow member of the ICS, Justice M. R. Kayani, of the Lahore High Court, publicly ridiculed Cornelius's theory that the rule of law would be strengthened by trying systematically to demonstrate congruence between liberal legal principles and Islamic legal principles. See Braibanti, *Chief Justice Cornelius*, p. 47.

[58] See the acid comments of I. A. Khan, SQA, reprinted in Braibanti, *Chief Justice Cornelius*, pp. 46–7. Similar comments were made to me in 2008 during interviews with secularist lawyers and intellectuals of Cornelius's generation.

[59] In the 1970s and 1980s, a few judges took up Cornelius's challenge and justified controversial liberal experiments by arguing that they were mandated by Islamic law. See generally, M. Lau, *The Role of Islam in the Pakistani Legal System* (London: Martinus Nijhoff, 2007). Nevertheless, for many liberals, Islamism in Pakistan came increasingly to be associated with anti-liberal Islamist thinkers and with an illiberal programme of statutory 'Islamisation' in the 1970s by the military dictator, Zia al-Haq.

Islamisation was thought to be very dangerous to fundamental rights – particularly those of minorities and women.

Not surprisingly, many liberal constitutionalist thinkers who are aware of Cornelius's liberal Islamist writings seem to think that his ideas have been discredited. And many seem to fear that if they drew attention to Cornelius's Islamist writings, those writings might be wilfully misinterpreted and used to legitimise Islamist programmes that Cornelius would have found repugnant.[60] Ironically, powerful Islamists in Pakistan also have little incentive to draw attention to the role that a Christian played in Islamising Pakistan – particularly as he called for Pakistan to study and integrate a form of Islam that is far more tolerant and liberal than the brand that they practise. They too fail to talk about Chief Justice Cornelius as an important supporter of Islamism.

As a result, it seems that many younger Pakistani legal and political figures have no idea that Cornelius, whom they knew as a liberal lion of Pakistan's Supreme Court, had systematically advocated a form of Islamisation in Pakistan's legal system. During interviews I conducted in the spring of 2008, more than one well-informed young lawyer seemed truly shocked to hear that Pakistan's only Catholic Chief Justice, the liberal lion of the Pakistani Supreme Court in the 1950s and 1960s, had thought a programme of Islamisation was essential if liberal principles were ever to take root in Pakistan and were to provide a source of protection from authoritarian overreach.

IX. Conclusion

While one can understand the conspiracy of silence in Pakistan about A. R. Cornelius's turn to Islamism, it seems a shame that Cornelius's writings are not better known. In this volume, several contributors have noted the profound questions that emergency rule and martial law have posed for modern Asian nations that have not yet established a strong tradition of legality – particularly newly independent nations that emerged from colonial rule with a limited tradition of constitutionalism and the rule of law. Contributors to this volume have raised questions about how one should conceptualise emergency rule in such countries and how these countries might best manage them in order to (i) permit emergency

[60] This is based on interviews conducted in Lahore and Islamabad in April 2008 and May 2008. As should be clear from the text, the discussants wished to remain anonymous insofar as they talked about the subject of Cornelius and Islamism.

rule to play whatever productive roles it can, in fact, play, but also (ii) ensure that emergency rule gives way to a state of legality in which the executive whose power was aggrandised during a period of emergency rule again comes under effective restraint from other branches and/or democratic processes. It seems to me that Cornelius's thought implicitly represents his own answers to these questions.

Cornelius clearly felt strongly the weight of what Ramraj calls the 'emergency powers paradox'. He accepted that the political system in Pakistan had been dysfunctional in the years prior to the repeated declarations of emergency and martial law. Although the imposition of martial law was probably not his preferred method of dealing with political dysfunction, he seems to have accepted that the imposition of martial law might help provide the stable type of situation in which a postcolonial state could establish a new culture of legality. Nevertheless, he found that the terms under which military rule operated were more authoritarian than they needed to be, and they suggested a lack of commitment to principles of governmental restraint. Furthermore, he thought it depressing that his colleagues on the Supreme Court would be unable to find any theoretical justification for the assertion of judicial power during the period of martial law that followed the 1958 coup or (for this is probably what they were really driving at) for them to assert that the judiciary had enough respect among the military rulers or the populace to ensure that orders against the executive would be obeyed. He thus seems to have seen it as his mission to identify a theoretical justification for judicial power to restrain martial law authorities and also to come up with a plan to ensure that judicial orders were viewed with respect.

In thinking about the restraints that should apply to an executive who had established emergency rule ostensibly to facilitate the establishment for the first time of a new constitutional order and in thinking too about the factors that would facilitate the emergence of judicial power in the emerging Pakistani constitutional order, the thoughtful, Catholic Justice Cornelius came to a surprising conclusion. A liberal constitutional order was unlikely to take root in Pakistan without Islamisation mediated by liberal lawyers and judges. This type of Islamisation could legitimise the legal system and empower the judges who administered that legal system.

In responding to Ramraj's essay in this volume, Arun Thiruvengadam has suggested in his own contribution to this volume that 'judges can be important allies for those who seek to mitigate the excesses of Asia's many repressive emergency laws. However . . . [they] can only do so against the backdrop of supportive factors such as a political climate where judges can feel confident that their actions will find favour.'[61] Cornelius's embrace of Islamisation reflects, I suggest, agreement with Thiruvengadam's basic point. Cornelius would have added, however, that the 'supportive factors' that judges need will inevitably reflect the cultural assumptions of the citizenry. Thus, factors that might weaken liberal judges in one culture, might empower them in another. Bringing this closer to home, he would argue that Pakistani judges could never enjoy a supportive 'political' environment and could never effectively serve as a constraint on executive power unless the following conditions were met: judges would have to be understood to be the representatives of a legal system in which the laws conform to the religious sensibilities of the people; and the legal system needed to be explicitly Islamised, so that when judges issued orders against the executive, these were understood by the masses and, indeed, by the executive, as orders that resonated with the moral weight of the nation's official religion. As Cornelius put it in a 1965 letter to Ralph Braibanti, Islamisation need to be part of the 'resanctification' of the Pakistani state and, by extension, of its judges' constitutional role as checks on executive power.[62]

Cornelius admitted that Islamisation might require judges to apply some laws that they personally found distasteful, such as the mitigation of punishments in honour killings. However, Cornelius thought these instances rare. Looking to the experience of other Muslim states at that time – particularly the Arab states then being influenced by the work of al-Sanhuri – Cornelius believed that legal professionals who were expert in both Islamic and Western law would be able to convince most Muslims that Islam, properly understood, demanded respect for almost all the human rights that liberals hold dear. Some then said, and some today might still say, that Cornelius's views on the consistency of Islam and human rights were naïve and that they were, ultimately, the weak point in his thought. To his credit, Cornelius always admitted that his were rebuttable presumptions.

For the purpose of this chapter, we do not need to determine finally whether Cornelius's position was correct or incorrect. Here it is useful simply to note that Cornelius anticipated some of the conclusions of contributors to this volume. These contributors have identified in the legal history of other Asian nations a tendency by executives to invoke

61 A. K. Thiruvengadam, 'Asian Judiciaries and Emergency Powers: Reasons for Optimism?' (Chapter 17), this volume.

62 Letter from A. R. Cornelius to R. Braibanti, 3 July 1965, reprinted in Braibanti, *Chief Justice Cornelius*, pp. 183–4.

extraordinary emergency powers or powers of martial law ostensibly in the service of building a previously non-existent culture of legality. They have commented that the idea of autocracy as a necessary step toward legality is paradoxical and that, in practice, autocracy has rarely given way to a genuine culture of constitutionalism, separation of powers and respect for fundamental rights. For legality fully to replace autocratic emergency rule, it seems, extra-legal factors must help to push an autocrat to accept restraints and must establish the power of the legal institutions that will be entrusted with the job of applying these restraints. Cornelius agreed with all these points. He believed with ever more conviction that an environment must be built up in which the executive respects the moral values that inform the law and in which the people refuse to accept the legitimacy of someone who defies the law as enunciated by judges. Looking at the history of the common law and at the recent trends in his country, Cornelius thought that the most efficient way to build up this kind of culture would be to connect the legal system with the predominant religion in the country. Whether he was right or wrong, he is not alone. That a liberal, British-educated, cricket-loving, Catholic living in a Muslim country should come to embrace Islamism as the only hope for the establishment of the rule of law in his land is both a fascinating phenomenon and an illuminating one. It may help us understand the remarkably broad appeal that Islamist parties seem to have in many contemporary Muslim nations with weak cultures of legality.

17

Asian judiciaries and emergency powers: reasons for optimism?

ARUN K. THIRUVENGADAM

I. Introduction

This chapter addresses the issue of the institutional checks on the invocation and use of emergency powers, by focusing on the role of judiciaries. Historically, judiciaries across the world have performed poorly when it comes to safeguarding the rights of individuals in times of emergency. This has led, over time, to the axiom that in times of emergency, judges cannot – and should not – reasonably be expected to act as the guardians of the constitution.[1] Throughout this chapter, I will refer to this as the 'conventional view' of the role of courts during times of emergency.

The conventional view has witnessed a shift in the post-9/11 era. In recent years, courts in a number of jurisdictions have resorted to a variety of innovative strategies that are designed to curb executive power against the backdrop of the ongoing 'war on terror'. At the time of writing, such decisions which have thwarted the traditional deference accorded to executive governments by courts have almost invariably emanated from jurisdictions within 'the West'. My primary purpose in this chapter is to analyse whether a similar shift is likely to be occasioned by judiciaries in Asia.

I thank Albert Chen, Simon Chesterman, Andrew Harding, Anil Kalhan, H. P. Lee, Vasuki Nesiah and Kevin Tan for their questions and/or comments that helped me revise the preliminary draft presented at the symposium. Michael Ewing-Chow and V. Venkatesan challenged some of my claims, forcing me to be clearer about their scope. Special thanks go to Victor V. Ramraj for his substantive and stylistic suggestions that have greatly improved both the content and central argument of this chapter. The usual caveat applies.

[1] See generally, G. Alexander, 'The Illusory Protection of Human Rights by National Courts During Periods of Emergency' (1984) 5 *Human Rights Law Journal* 1; O. Gross and F. Ní Aoláin, 'From Discretion to Scrutiny: Revisiting the Application of the Margin of Appreciation Doctrine in the Context of Article 15 of the European Convention on Human Rights' (2001) 23 *Human Rights Quarterly* 625.

Asia has been described as the 'home of illiberal democracy' and an area which is 'perhaps the most difficult regional context for establishing the rule of law'.[2] It is also the region where some leaders sought to oppose what they perceived as 'Western imperialism' in spreading ideas of universalism, by arguing that Asian political traditions (especially the Confucian legacy) are fundamentally incompatible with, and offer an alternative to, Western-style liberal democracy. Ironically, many of the countries which espoused these 'Asian values' possessed legal systems that were still recognisably foreign in origin, being the remnants of the colonial legal system that was in place for centuries prior to independence. This is particularly evident in the arena of laws regulating terrorism and threats to national security. Asia as a whole has been wracked by the effects of terrorism (domestic, regional and global) for decades prior to 9/11, and governments across Asia have developed complex anti-terrorism regimes, many originating in (or inspired by) colonial laws that were put in place by Western powers. Equally, people who have opposed the adoption of such oppressive laws (be they lawmakers, lawyers for people charged under such laws, or public intellectuals) have often relied upon normative arguments drawn from liberal constitutional discourse. The issue of emergency powers is therefore a rich site to test claims about the applicability of liberal constitutional discourse to countries in Asia.

Legal scholars focusing on Asia in the 1980s would have found few judicial institutions outside South Asia that were willing to exercise strong forms of judicial review. That general trend has changed over the last two decades. During the 1990s, many Asian judiciaries have begun acting in unprecedented ways. In India, a phase of judicial activism that began in the mid to late 1970s expanded impressively in the 1990s, encompassing a vast range of issues that has led commentators to describe the Indian Supreme Court as the 'most powerful court in the world'. Courts elsewhere in South Asia (particularly in Bangladesh and Pakistan) also sought to emulate the Indian Supreme Court's methods, especially in public interest litigation relating to the environment. Across the continent, courts in Taiwan, South Korea and Mongolia have developed a body of cases in the 1990s that does not fit into the old characterisation of quiescent Asian judiciaries. Courts in other Asian jurisdictions such as Hong Kong, Malaysia and Indonesia have decided cases (even if only occasionally) that should give pause to anyone who thinks Asian judiciaries are timid institutions.

[2] T. Ginsburg, *Judicial Review in New Democracies* (Cambridge: Cambridge University Press, 2003), p. 11; D. Bell, D. Brown, K. Jayasuriya and D. M. Jones (eds.), *Towards Illiberal Democracy in Pacific Asia* (New York: St Martin's Press, 1995), p. 10.

Despite all this, the fact remains that courts in Asia have generally been more reluctant to interfere when the executive and legislative branches have asserted national security concerns. My focus in this chapter is on this narrow range of cases, and I seek to analyse the path that is likely to be pursued by courts in Asian jurisdictions in future cases. The question whether judiciaries in Asian nations will adopt a more aggressive stance toward judicial review of emergency powers needs to be viewed from multiple perspectives, taking serious account of sociological, cultural and political studies of Asian societies.

Let me first clarify the scope of this chapter. Other chapters in this volume focus on situations where formal or informal emergencies are declared and implemented. I take a broader view of emergency powers, focusing also on ordinary times when extraordinary measures such as preventive detention are used. My central argument in this chapter is that there are good reasons to expect that Asian judiciaries will indeed exercise robust judicial review in cases involving national security or emergency powers more generally. My argument has two components.[3] The first is in part an empirical argument, based on changing socio-political circumstances. Here, I show that the political circumstances that are now in play in many Asian countries favour the exercise of robust forms of judicial review over cases involving national security in ways that were not possible in earlier times. The second component of my argument is a limited normative one. The robust exercise of constitutional review over cases involving emergency powers or national security is justified because the constitutional regimes in many Asian countries actually expect and provide the basis for such robust review. The order in which I argue these components is deliberate. The normative reasons for exercising constitutional review over cases involving emergency powers have always existed in Asia; a facilitative environment and support structures did not. My claim is that the change in those circumstances in recent years provides hope that a more robust review will indeed be possible in future years.

The argument is developed in five parts. Following this introduction, Part II focuses on judiciaries in Western liberal democracies. This part considers whether the conventional view is valid in contemporary times. The focus here is on recent post-9/11 cases that are said to herald a new trend in the judicial treatment of cases involving emergency powers and national security. Part III examines whether the conventional view is valid in Asian jurisdictions, and focuses on the post-independence experience

[3] I thank Victor Ramraj for helping me identify the different strands of my argument.

of India with emergency laws. In Part IV, I draw attention to the fact that despite a timorous record in cases on emergency powers, more recently, many Asian judiciaries have exercised more robust forms of review over several areas in which they previously would have meekly deferred to the other branches. In Part V, I argue that the Supreme Court of India's interpretive strategies in recent cases could form the basis for a more rigorous review of laws regulating emergency powers in future. In Part VI, I deal with the normative basis for such a robust form of constitutional review.

II. The shift in the conventional view: judicial checks on emergency powers post-9/11

In an influential study of the US Supreme Court in wartime, Clinton Rossiter concludes that 'the courts of the United States, from the highest to the lowest, can do nothing to restrain and next to nothing to mitigate an arbitrary presidential military program suspending the liberties of some part of the civilian population'.[4] Other scholars have echoed his views doubting the capacity of judiciaries to prevent executive excess in times of emergency.[5] There is clearly a long line of court decisions from across the common-law world that can be cited in support of the conventional view.[6] In this section, I examine recent cases from a number of Western liberal

[4] C. Rossiter, *The Supreme Court and the Commander-in-Chief*, expanded edn (Ithaca: Cornell University Press, 1976), p. 52.

[5] O. Gross, 'Chaos and Rules: Should Responses to Violent Crises Always Be Constitutional?' (2003) 112 *Yale Law Journal* 1011 at 1034. See also L. Epstein *et al.*, 'The Supreme Court During Crisis: How War Affects Only Non-War Cases' (2005) 80 *New York University Law Review* 1 (providing empirical, quantitative evidence that the US Supreme Court has historically been less protective of individual rights in times of crisis); Alexander, 'The Illusory Protection of Human Rights'.

[6] Prominent cases in the USA, the UK and Canada include the following: in the US Supreme Court: *Schenk* v. *United States* 249 US 47 (1919) (upholding a law which, during World War I, authorised the criminalisation of speech despite strong textual foundations for the right to speech, and the existence of a body of case law that could have been used to support the striking down of such a law), *Korematsu* v. *United States* 323 US 214 (1944) (upholding detentions of Japanese-Americans within concentration camps during World War II based purely on race) and *Dennis* v. *United States* 341 US 494 (1951) (upholding convictions based on guilt by association citing concerns about the Cold War); in the UK House of Lords, *R* v. *Halliday, ex parte Zadig* [1917] AC 260 (validating Regulation 14B of the Defence of the Realm Act 1914–15 which was employed to intern 30,000 'enemy aliens' and 160 British citizens on the ground that the general words of the parent statute were sufficient to provide implied authorisation) and *Liversidge* v. *Anderson* [1942] AC 206 (refusing to review, and thereby validating, regulation 18B of the Defence (General) Regulations, under the authority of which, 28,000 enemy aliens and 2,000 British citizens were detained); and the decisions of the Supreme Court of Canada in *In Re Gray* (1918) 57

democracies that have led some scholars to assert that the conventional view (even if correct in describing what happened in the pre-9/11 era), does not hold true in the first decade of the twenty-first century. I rely on the analysis of Eyal Benvenisti who has, in recent work, focused on the manner in which courts around the world have begun to exercise more robust forms of judicial review over cases involving the use of emergency powers in the post-9/11 world.[7]

As has now been well documented, legislatures in the USA, UK, Canada, Israel and New Zealand, as well as a number of European and Asian countries, rushed to update their existing anti-terrorism laws, or enact new ones, in the wake of 9/11.[8] By 2009, courts in a number of these jurisdictions have built up a corpus of jurisprudence around such laws. As mentioned earlier, the first few cases decided in the post-9/11 era adhered to the expectations of the conventional view, with courts deferring to executive and legislative branches on most issues.[9] However, more recently, the old trend has witnessed a dramatic shift, or 'transformation' to use Benvenisti's preferred term. The decisions which, in Benvenisti's analysis, signal this shift are the House of Lords' decision in the *Belmarsh detainees* case (2004);[10] the US Supreme Court's decisions in *Rasul* (2004), *Hamdi* (2004) and *Hamdan* (2006);[11] the Israeli High Court of Justice's ruling in the *Sourik* case (2004);[12] the German Constitutional Court's decisions in

SCR 150 (upholding the War Measures Act which was enacted in World War I to authorise internment, and under which law, more than 80,000 Canadians were classified as 'enemy aliens' because they had family ties to the countries with which Canada was at war) and in *Reference as to the Validity of Orders in Council of the 15th Day of December 1945 in Relation to Persons of the Japanese Race* [1946] SCR 248 (20 February 1946) (upholding the orders of the Canadian government passed during World War II that seized the property of 22,000 Japanese-Canadians and deported them to Japan).

[7] E. Benvenisti, 'United We Stand: National Courts Reviewing Counterterrorism Measures', in A. Bianchi and A. Keller (eds.), *Counterterrorism: Democracy's Challenge* (Oxford: Hart Publishing, 2008), pp. 251–76.

[8] See generally, V. V. Ramraj, M. Hor and K. Roach (eds.), *Global Anti-Terrorism Law and Policy* (Cambridge: Cambridge University Press, 2005).

[9] Here I cite one example each from the US, UK and Canada: *N. Jersey Media Group Inc.* v. *Ashcroft*, 308 F 3d 198 (3d Cir. 2002), cert. denied, 123 S Ct 2215 (2003); *Secretary of State for the Home Department* v. *Rehman* [2001] 3 WLR 877; and *Suresh* v. *Canada (Minister of Citizenship and Immigration)* (2002) 1 SCR 3, 2002 SCC 1.

[10] *A (FC) and Others (FC) (Appellants)* v. *Secretary of State for the Home Department* (Respondent) [2004] UKHL 56 (2004).

[11] *Rasul* v. *Bush*, 542 US 466 (2004); *Hamdi* v. *Rumsfeld*, 542 US 507 (2004); *Hamdan* v. *Rumsfeld*, 126 S Ct 2749 (2006). To this list, we may now add *Boumediene* v. *Bush*, 128 S Ct 2229 (2008).

[12] HCJ 2056/04 *Beit Sourik Village Council* v. *Government of Israel* (2004) (English trans. available at http://elyon1.court.gov.il/files_eng/04/560/020/a28/04020560.a28.pdf).

the *European Arrest Warrant* case (2005) and the *Air Transport Security Act* case (2006);[13] the decision of the Indian Supreme Court in the PUCL case (2004);[14] and the decision of the Supreme Court of Canada in the *Charkaoui* case (2007).[15]

Benvenisti argues that in these and other cases, courts around the globe have used five distinct strategies to try and respond to the challenges raised in the post-9/11 emergency powers scenario. He argues that these five responses can be depicted as five steps up the ladder of judicial review. Depending on the level of political resistance, Benvenisti argues that courts can be expected to climb 'up or down the ladder, summoning the political branches to enter into a dialogue and thereby also seeking to share with them responsibility for the outcome'.[16] Benvenisti describes the first three strategies as involving referrals to the executive and legislative branches, whereas the third and fourth strategies involve the exercise of weak and robust forms of constitutional review. I now provide a brief overview of these strategies. Later in the chapter, I address the issue of whether similar strategies can be adopted by Asian judiciaries.

The first of these strategies is referring the issue or case back to the executive for reconsideration. Benvenisti contends that though this may seem like a very timid response (and is certainly the least controversial), it can often have an impact. He argues that the Canadian Supreme Court's decision in *Suresh* (2002)[17] is one such example. A second step would be to refer the matter to the legislature, seeking a clarification on the scope of authorisation granted to the executive in the particular instance. Benvenisti argues that this is a shrewd strategy because it shows that courts are sensitive to the claim that they lack democratic legitimacy, and by involving the legislature and giving it an opportunity to intervene, courts can position themselves as guardians of the democratic process. Benvenisti describes the majority decision in *Belmarsh* as following this precise logic.

The third strategy consists of referring the case or law in question to the legislature, requiring it to depart from international treaty obligations

[13] Judgment of 18 July 2005, 2 BvR 2236/04, available at www.bverfg.de/entscheidungen/rs20050718_2bvr223604en_html.

[14] (2004) 9 SCC 580. I discuss this case in greater detail in Part V of this chapter.

[15] *Charkaoui v. Canada (Citizenship and Immigration)*, 2007 SCC 9.

[16] Benvenisti, 'United We Stand', p. 257.

[17] Above, note 9. Note, however, that other scholars consider *Suresh* to be a regressive decision, more in line with the 'conventional view'. Benvenisti's analysis can be considered a more optimistic reading of the decision, without necessarily contesting that description; in his scheme, it can at best represent the first level in the five steps he outlines.

and imposing significant limits on the legislature's discretion. The fourth and fifth steps directly involve the exercise of constitutional review. In Benvenisti's analysis, the fourth step consists of sending the law back to the legislature, with the court requiring a re-enactment of the law so as to remove the specified unconstitutionality. This was what happened in the *European Arrest Warrant* case (2005), where the German Constitutional Court referred the European Arrest Warrant Act back to the German legislature so that the restriction on the fundamental right to freedom from extradition could be made to comply with the requirement of proportionality.

The fifth and most radical step is where the court strikes down an emergency statute as clearly unconstitutional. Once again, Benvenisti cites the example of a decision of the German Constitutional Court for this strategy. In what has been described as a remarkable decision,[18] the *Air Transport Security Act* case (2006), the German Constitutional Court struck down a provision in an anti-terrorism statute which empowered the Minister of Defence to order that a passenger aircraft be shot down, if it could be assumed that the aircraft would be used against the life of others and if the downing of the plane would be the only means of preventing the present danger.

Benvenisti's analysis helps us understand the different strategies that courts in some prominent jurisdictions have deployed to exercise judicial review over emergency powers in the post-9/11 era. As stated before, one of the principal questions in this chapter is whether such strategies might be emulated by judiciaries in Asia – a question I address in section V. First, however, some background context on judiciaries in Asia is necessary.

III. Post-independence India and emergency laws

There is considerable evidence supporting the conventional view of judiciaries in times of crisis in Asia. Asian judiciaries have historically been reluctant to exercise strong judicial review even in routine cases, making their entry into the highly charged arena of emergency powers that much more unlikely. Other contributors have shown how judiciaries in various

[18] O. Lepsius, 'Human Dignity and the Downing of an Aircraft: The German Federal Constitutional Court Strikes down a Prominent Anti-terrorism Provision in the New Air-Transport Security Act' (1 September 2006) 7 *German Law Journal* no. 9, www.germanlawjournal.com/article.php?id=756; see also R. Young, 'Germany: Shooting Down an Airplane and Analyzing Computer Data' (2008) 6 *International Journal of Constitutional Law* 331.

Asian jurisdictions have either avoided or failed in their attempts to exercise judicial review in cases on emergency powers. H. P. Lee provides a vivid account of how courts were thwarted in Malaysia and Singapore.[19] Mark Fenwick, Clark Lombardi and Raul Pangalangan demonstrate similar failures of courts in Japan, Pakistan and the Philippines.[20] In this part, I discuss how courts in India have historically reacted to cases where they were required to exercise judicial review over emergency powers. The Indian case study, I argue, provides important lessons on emergency powers in Asia more generally.[21] Some have argued that India is an exceptional case within Asia because of its relatively strong tradition of constitutional democracy since its independence in 1947. While this is true to some extent, I endeavour to show that in regard to emergency powers, India's experience has been much closer to other Asian jurisdictions.

Like many other Asian countries, India has a complex web of laws and regulations on anti-terrorism and emergency issues dating back to colonial times.[22] During the period of direct colonial rule (1813–1947), the British passed several laws that enabled the colonial authorities to exercise various forms of emergency powers, some as early as the 1860s.[23] One of the most draconian of these laws was the Rowlatt Act of 1919 which allowed for arrests without warrants, imposition of restrictions on the freedom of movement and residence of persons suspected of involvement with the freedom movement, and trials by special tribunals with summary

[19] H. P. Lee, 'Constitutionalised Emergency Powers: A Plague on Asian Constitutionalism?' (Chapter 14), this volume.

[20] See, respectively, M. Fenwick, 'Emergency Powers and the Limits of Constitutionalism in Japan' (Chapter 12), C. Lombardi, 'Islamism as a Response to Emergency Rule in Pakistan: The Surprising Proposal of Justice A. R. Cornelius' (Chapter 16), and R. Pangalangan, 'Political Emergencies in the Philippines: Changing Labels and the Unchanging Need for Legitimacy' (Chapter 15), all in this volume.

[21] There is, by now, an extensive literature on the Indian experience of emergency laws. For the analysis that follows, I draw upon the following: V. Iyer, *States of Emergency: The Indian Experience* (New Delhi: Butterworths, 2000); D. P. Jinks, 'The Anatomy of an Institutionalised Emergency: Preventive Detention and Personal Liberty in India' (2001) 22 *Michigan Journal of International Law* 311; G. Subramanium, 'Emergency Provisions under the Indian Constitution', in B. N. Kirpal *et al.* (eds.), *Supreme But Not Infallible* (New Delhi: Oxford University Press: 2000); V. Vijayakumar, 'Legal and Institutional Responses to Terrorism in India', in Ramraj *et al.* (eds.), *Global Anti-terrorism Law and Policy*; A. Kalhan, Gerald Conroy, Mamata Kaushal, Sam Scott Miller and Jed S. Rakoff, 'Colonial Continuities: Human Rights, Terrorism, and Security Laws in India', (2006) 20 *Columbia Journal of Asian Law* 93 (referred to in the text as Kalhan *et al.*).

[22] See generally, N. Hussain, *The Jurisprudence of Emergency* (Ann Arbor: University of Michigan Press, 2003).

[23] Iyer, *States of Emergency*, pp. 67–75.

procedures that did not provide for appeal. Later, the Government of India Acts of 1919 and 1935 enabled the representative of the British colonial authority in India, the Governor-General, to issue a proclamation of emergency 'in cases of emergency... for the peace and good government of British India'.[24]

A number of these emergency powers were used quite liberally in the last phase of British colonial rule, resulting in grave violations of the civil liberties of many Indians. Unsurprisingly, therefore, such laws became a focal issue for the leaders of the freedom movement, several of whom were preventively detained for long periods of time under these draconian laws. Leaders such as Gandhi, Nehru and others often cited these laws as proof of the brutality and exploitative nature of the colonial regime, necessitating the immediate withdrawal of colonial rule. It is quite ironic, therefore, to find that many of these repressive colonial laws were continued under the post-independence constitutional regime. The Constitution of India (1950) is generally viewed as having heralded an era of liberal constitutionalism in India. Yet one of the enduring paradoxes of this liberal constitutional order is that it also sustains a regime of emergency laws amounting to a near-permanent state of emergency, where thousands of people are routinely and regularly detained preventively and several hundred others are denied basic civil liberties. Thus, even as the Indian Constitution specifically guarantees fundamental rights (including civil, political, as well as social rights) to its citizens, justifications for preventive detention and other emergency laws are also woven into the very text of these fundamental rights.[25]

As Kalhan *et al.* have explained, India's various emergency laws can be grouped in three broad categories: (i) constitutional provisions and statutes authorising the declaration of formal states of emergency and the use of special powers during those declared periods, (ii) constitutional provisions and statutes authorising preventive detention during non-emergency periods, and (iii) substantive criminal laws which define terrorism and other security-related offences and establish special rules to adjudicate these offences during non-emergency periods.[26] Emergency

[24] The satisfaction of the Governor-General as to the existence of an emergency was judicially interpreted to be absolute, as was his opinion as to whether any ordinance promulgated was necessary for peace and good government of the country. *Ibid.* pp. 70–1.

[25] Thus, the text of Article 22 provides the justification and circumstances under which preventive detention can be used.

[26] Kalhan *et al.*, 'Colonial Continuities', at 125.

laws under each of these three categories have been employed by successive governments in India since 1947, and reports from human rights and civil society organisations have revealed that, collectively, these have led to the trampling of the civil liberties of several hundred thousand people. More importantly for our purposes, judicial challenges to each of these laws have been unsuccessful, giving, at least at first blush, credence to the validity of the conventional view. In what follows, I will provide a brief overview of the working history of these emergency laws.

The Constitution of India, following the model of the Government of India Act of 1935 outlined earlier, allows the President to declare a formal state of emergency in specified situations.[27] Under the original provisions, upon declaration of such a formal state of emergency, several rights, including the right to approach courts for enforcement of fundamental rights, were automatically suspended. Between 1950 and 1975, this formal state of emergency was invoked twice (in 1962 and 1971 during periods of war with China and Pakistan), resulting in long periods of emergency rule where the civil liberties of citizens were adversely affected. As Venkat Iyer has demonstrated, judicial challenges to aspects of these proclamations of emergency and the laws that were passed under their aegis, proved to be unsuccessful.[28] A third invocation of the formal state of emergency occurred in 1975; it lasted for two years, and was the most controversial use of such powers. Later, in Part VI, I examine the decision of the Supreme Court in the infamous case of *ADM Jabalpur* v. *Shivkant Shukla* (1976)[29] where it rubber-stamped the government's strained interpretation of its expansive powers during a time of emergency. Since 1975, in part because of the increased attention that such a declaration necessarily entails, no government has resorted to this means of exercising emergency powers. Significantly, the pressure to avoid using them appears to have come not from the judiciary, but from civil society. Governments have instead adopted a different strategy, using specialised criminal anti-terrorism laws.

Although the use of the first category of emergency powers identified by Kalhan *et al.* has become less prevalent, the deployment of laws from the second and third categories has been a regular part of the political and historical landscape of post-independence India. India's Constitution explicitly authorises the use of preventive detention in a variety of contexts during ordinary, non-emergency periods. Such laws have been in force

[27] For the logic behind such provisions, see A. Kalhan, 'Constitution and "Extraconstitution": Colonial Emergency Regimes in Postcolonial India and Pakistan' (Chapter 4), this volume, and Lee, Chapter 14, which focus on analogous provisions in other Asian jurisdictions.

[28] Iyer, *States of Emergency*, pp. 117–21, 142–7.

[29] AIR 1976 SC 1207.

almost continuously since the adoption of the Constitution. The first such law, the Preventive Detention Act of 1950, was enacted as early as February 1950 and remained in force until December 1969. It was succeeded by the Maintenance of Internal Security Ordinance in 1971 (which became a law soon afterwards), which lasted until 1978. The National Security Act 1980 continues to be in force today. While there has almost always been an overarching central statute for preventive detention in force, it has invariably been supplemented by a host of state laws which authorise preventive detention. Once again, foundational challenges to these preventive detention laws, although frequently raised, have been unsuccessful in the courts.

Since the 1980s, having learnt the lesson of avoiding the fallout of formal declarations of emergency, the Indian Parliament has enacted specialised anti-terrorism laws (which fall under the third category mentioned above), starting with the Terrorist and Disruptive Activities Act (TADA) which was in force between 1985 and 1995. Similarly, in the aftermath of 9/11, Parliament enacted the Prevention of Terrorism Act (POTA) 2002, which was in force until 2004, when it was repealed following public outrage at its reported misuse. However, since prior laws relating to terrorism are still in force, even after the repeal of POTA, there are valid concerns about the way in which the Indian state is able to misuse anti-terrorism laws.[30]

Judicial challenges to both TADA and POTA were unsuccessful, and the Supreme Court in fact upheld the constitutional validity of these draconian laws.[31] The fact that they were ultimately repealed speaks more to the strength of the forces of democracy and civil society in India, than to the courage of its judges. In defence of the judiciary, it must be stated that the case for strong judicial review over such emergency laws is considerably weakened by the fact that the text of the Constitution itself authorises the invocation and exercise of such extensive powers. Judges have repeatedly explained that their own liberal instincts had to be reined in because of the explicit commands of the Constitution. Some judges have noted that their options will remain limited until the text of the Constitution and existing laws are changed to reflect a greater respect for individual liberty, even in times of national and security crises. The better question to ask, then, is why the framers of India's Constitution, as well as those responsible for enacting such emergency laws since independence, felt compelled to make provision for such strong and vigorous emergency powers.

[30] Kalhan *et al.*, 'Colonial Continuities', at 105–7.

[31] Both these decisions are analysed in detail in Part V of this chapter.

In his contribution to this volume, Victor V. Ramraj forcefully argues that in order to theorise about emergency powers meaningfully, one needs to distinguish between older constitutional regimes (where rule-of-law values are more established) and newer states (where the basic constitutional infrastructure and culture of accountability are weak or absent). Ramraj goes on to emphasise the importance of 'the emergency powers paradox': this is the logic that 'in states that are struggling to establish legality in the face of a violent political crisis, emergency powers may be seen by the government as necessary to establish the conditions of relative stability in which a legal infrastructure and culture of accountability can take hold'.[32] As Ramraj insightfully recognises, the paradox lies in the fact that 'the invocation of these powers throws into question the government's commitment to legality . . . in the first place'.[33] Looking into the debates among the framers of the Indian Constitution, and the subsequent debates in the Indian Parliament when various emergency laws were introduced, one is struck by the fact that both the advocates and opponents of the laws facilitating the use of emergency powers were deeply conscious of the paradox identified by Ramraj. While this tension is revealed in debates among the framers about other aspects of emergency powers,[34] it is also reflected in debates on preventive detention laws, the subject of my immediate concern.

As several commentators have noted, the drafting of the Constitution of India occurred at a tumultuous time. Outside the meeting hall of the Constituent Assembly, the impending partition of India and the creation of the new republic of Pakistan was causing huge stresses; many of the erstwhile rulers of princely states were refusing to join the newly emerging federal state and were on the brink of armed revolt; communist groups in the southern state of Andhra Pradesh were resorting to armed insurrection; and the papers were reporting the disturbing news in neighbouring Burma where large-scale political violence including the assassination of prominent leaders was occurring.[35]

These events had a clear and discernible impact on the provisions which were ultimately included in the Constitution, especially those relating to

32 V. V. Ramraj, 'The Emergency Powers Paradox' (Chapter 2), this volume, p. 22.

33 *Ibid.*

34 In his detailed analysis, Venkat Iyer refers to debates among the framers of India's Constitution on the provisions relating to the formal declaration of emergencies where several members expressed disquiet over the wide discretionary powers conferred upon the President in relation to the circumstances under which they could be declared, and the exclusion of judicial review. Iyer, *States of Emergency*, pp. 83–91.

35 *Ibid.*, pp. 76–77.

emergency powers. They caused leaders such as Prime Minister Nehru, the Chairman of the Drafting Committee, Dr B. R. Ambedkar, and the noted constitutional lawyer, Alladi Krishnaswami Iyer, who otherwise had impressive liberal constitutional credentials, to argue that the Indian state should be equipped through the use of emergency powers to respond to these dire challenges. A. K. Iyer termed such laws 'a necessary evil' and articulated his concern as follows:

> It is agreed on all hands that the security of the state is as important as the liberty of the individual . . . Even the most enthusiastic advocate of liberty says there are people in this land at the present day who are determined to undermine the Constitution and the State, and if we are to flourish, and if liberty of person and property is to be secured, unless that particular evil is removed or the State is invested with sufficient power to guard against that evil there will be no guarantee even for that individual liberty of which we are all desirous.[36]

The provisions in the Constitution authorising preventive detention were vehemently opposed by a small minority of members of the Constituent Assembly. One member described such a provision as being 'obnoxious to the whole idea of democracy'.[37] Another member, Mahavir Tyagi, maintained that the provision should be withdrawn in its entirety. In an impassioned appeal to his fellow members, Tyagi argued that incorporating such a provision would undercut their purpose in drafting a people's charter in a fundamental way:

> Now we are making a Constitution guaranteeing these inherent rights. What relevance is there for a detention clause in the Constitution which is meant to guarantee fundamental rights to the citizens? I am afraid the introduction here of a clause of this kind changes the chapter of fundamental rights into a penal code worse than the Defence of India Rules of the old government. I have suffered under the Defence of India Rules long detentions. . . . How I wish Dr. Ambedkar was with me in jail after being arrested and hand-cuffed for a whole night? I wish he had had my experience. If he had been hand-cuffed along with me, he would have experienced the misery. I fear, Sir, the provisions now proposed by him would recoil on himself. Sir, as soon as another political party comes to power, he along with his colleagues will become the victims of the provisions now being made by him.[38]

[36] Speech made on 15 September 1949, Constituent Assembly Debates, vol. IX, 1536.

[37] Speech of Ms Purnima Banerjee, 15 September 1949, Constituent Assembly Debates, vol. IX, 1511.

[38] Speech made on 16 September 1949, Constituent Assembly Debates, vol. IX, 1547.

Several other members asserted that incorporating such authorising provisions that amount to 'blank cheques' in the Constitution would make it impossible for them to be removed in future, when conditions improved, as no government would voluntarily give up such powers. They therefore advised against constitutionalising powers of preventive detention, leaving such matters to be justified in parliamentary laws that could be adjusted to the demands of changing circumstances.

The advocates of strong emergency powers sought to allay such fears by incorporating procedural safeguards against abuse. They asserted that these, coupled with their faith that future governments would make sagacious and selective use of such powers, would act as restraining factors. Though the advocates of emergency powers won in the Constituent Assembly, history has proved that the fears expressed by the opponents of such laws were well founded. Emergency laws have been used, as we noted previously, extremely frequently, belying the expectations of the supporters of such powers, and in circumstances beyond those originally envisaged. On several occasions, such laws have been used against political opponents of the government in power, and against dissidents and people on the margins of society.[39] Scholars who have studied India's emergency laws closely have acknowledged that contemporary India continues to face grave threats to its territorial and national solidarity from internal and external sources. Yet, these scholars also note that more often than not, India's repressive emergency laws have been misused, and it is not clear that having them in place has had any appreciable effect in combating forces of terrorism.[40]

This brief overview of debates among the framers of India's Constitution also shows how the paradox Ramraj defines and explains has had considerable historical salience in Asian jurisdictions such as India. This survey highlights the dangers of accepting the persuasive logic of the argument that states should be allowed to exercise strong emergency powers in the formative stages of their evolution. As the Indian case shows, even after a liberal constitutional edifice has arguably been established, the seductive allure of such laws for those who hold power will ensure that they become a permanent part of the constitutional and legal order. More disturbingly, they pose a continuing threat to ways of entrenching liberal constitutionalism more fully within the domestic legal order.

[39] For an extensive cataloguing of the abuses of India's emergency laws, see Kalhan *et al.*, 'Colonial Continuities', at 173–98.

[40] *Ibid.*, at 199–212.

In his contribution to this volume, Albert Chen has argued, based on his analysis of the history of emergency powers in Taiwan and South Korea, that legal orders that enable the exercise and abuse of emergency powers can nevertheless provide avenues for the attainment of liberal democracy over time.[41] Chen further argues that the experiences of these two nations shows that 'the dichotomy between normalcy and exception can make a positive contribution to the project of legality' by serving to 'provoke the people to protest even more, and to demand the lifting of martial law or the state of emergency and the return to the normalcy of civil liberties and political freedoms promised by the Constitution'.[42] While Chen's optimistic analysis is persuasive for those two jurisdictions, the experience of India would suggest a more pessimistic view. As noted earlier, despite relatively strong institutions of democracy (including a judiciary which has often exercised robust powers of review), emergency powers have been invoked almost continuously in the post-independence era in India. And, while there are frequent protests in India, very few uses of emergency powers have resulted in mass protests, often because the problems of such abuse are not always immediately perceived at the level of the masses. Hence, Chen's suggestion that popular protests and people's movements may bring an end to the use of preventive detention and other emergency powers seems unlikely in the Indian context.

My own view is that putting in place a legal framework that allows governments to use emergency powers (including those enabling preventive detention) as frequently as the Indian government has exercised them, carries several risks for *ordinary* constitutional governance and general issues relating to the rule of law beyond issues of emergency powers. Here, I adopt David Dyzenhaus's views where he expresses the following two concerns:

> The first is that judicial lip service to the rule of law in exceptional situations has consequences for the way judges deal with ordinary situations. One finds that judges begin to be content with less substance in the rule of law in situations which are not part of any emergency regime, all the while claiming that the rule of law is well maintained. Second, the law that addresses the emergency situation starts to look less exceptional as judges interpret statutes that deal with ordinary situations in the same fashion. As a package, these concerns seem to show that once the exceptional or emergency situation is normalised . . . *the exception starts to seep into other parts of the law.*[43]

[41] A. H. Chen, 'Emergency Powers, Constitutionalism and Legal Transplants: The East Asian Experience' (Chapter 3), this volume.

[42] *Ibid.*, pp. 87, 86.

[43] D. Dyzenhaus, *The Constitution of Law: Legality in a Time of Emergency* (Cambridge: Cambridge University Press, 2006), p. 27 (emphasis added). I find echoes of this argument

In my view, this statement applies to Indian constitutional jurisprudence as a whole, and to legal actors in the legislative and executive arenas beyond judges, which has led over time to entire areas of constitutional jurisprudence (especially those relating to preventive detention) being quite shaky and vulnerable to the charge that they are not in consonance with the principles enshrined in the Constitution. Indeed, it is the very real danger of such extensive 'seepage' that ultimately weakens the entire community's commitment to ideals of constitutionalism.

Given this depressing scenario, the question is whether anything can be done, short of fundamental changes to the constitutional and legal order that sustains such powerful emergency regimes. In the next part, I argue, somewhat paradoxically (given the record of judges covered so far), that the judiciary may well be one institution that, when bolstered by necessary supportive factors, could provide hope for those who seek progressive change of draconian emergency laws.

IV. Recent trends in judicial review in Asia

The question whether judiciaries in Asia will exercise robust judicial review over emergency powers has to be analysed against traditions of judicial review in Asia more generally.[44] History shows us that courts will not venture into the thorny thickets of emergency powers unless they are assured that their actions will generally be regarded as legitimate and their ultimate judgments will be respected both by the governments in power and by the public at large. My optimistic view of Asian judiciaries is rooted in the fact that there has been an emergence within Asia of strong judicial review in more conventional areas of constitutional law. As mentioned earlier, judiciaries in Asia do not have a long pedigree of activism. Very few countries had experienced strong judiciaries prior to the 1990s. Thanks to colonialism, many nations within Asia have links with common-law traditions, and this initially resulted in a number of judges believing that they too could exercise robust forms of judicial review like their peers in other common-law nations. However, at least for judges in countries such as Pakistan, Bangladesh and Malaysia, this initial optimism

in Vasuki Nesiah's contribution where she similarly questions the distinction between the normal and the exceptional, and also draws attention to the problem of seepage. See V. Nesiah, 'The Princely Impostor: Stories of Law and Pathology in the Exercise of Emergency Powers' (Chapter 5), this volume.

[44] I am grateful to Andrew Harding for impressing upon me the importance of this line of reasoning for developing my overall argument.

was dimmed over time by the realisation that their governments would not countenance the second-guessing of their policies and laws.

In recent work, Andrew Harding has drawn attention to the robust exercise of constitutional review by courts in Thailand, the Philippines and Malaysia, terming this phenomenon, the rise of 'New Asian Constitutionalism'.[45] Here, I will draw upon the work of other scholars who have documented a similar trend in other Asian jurisdictions, before seeking to draw some general conclusions from such trends. To illustrate the themes upon which I seek to focus in this part of the chapter, I rely specifically on developments within India, Taiwan and South Korea. I do not claim that the change over time in these countries of the perception of the legitimate role of judiciaries is representative of Asia as a whole. Rather, my purpose is to analyse the trajectory of events within these nations that led to the acceptance of the legitimacy of ideas of judicial activism.

I start with the case of India. The framers of India's Constitution clearly believed in vesting in the Indian judiciary vast powers of judicial review, and envisaged it as being a strong custodian of constitutional values.[46] However, constant struggles between Parliament and the judiciary in the initial decades after independence led to a series of divisive and destructive conflicts between the two branches, resulting in damage to the perceptions and powers of both institutions. The judiciary in particular suffered great damage to its reputation and its jurisdictional powers especially during the period of internal emergency declared by Prime Minister Indira Gandhi in the period 1975–7. In the aftermath of the emergency, the Indian judiciary, led by a group of public-interest oriented judges of the Supreme Court, heralded a new period of judicial activism, beginning with cases affecting the poor and underprivileged in society. Later, this phenomenon – which is generally referred to as the 'public interest litigation [PIL] movement' – led to massive expansions in the jurisdiction of the courts, which began to encroach upon core governance functions in the 1990s. There is a vast literature documenting the story of the revival of judicial activism in India.[47]

45 A. Harding, 'New Asian Constitutionalism: Myth or Reality' (2006) 14 *International Islamic University Law Journal* 153.

46 See generally, G. Austin, *The Indian Constitution: Cornerstone of a Nation* (Oxford: Oxford University Press, 1966)

47 A recent work which cites much of the earlier work is V. Iyer, 'The Supreme Court of India', in B. Dickson (ed.), *Judicial Activism in Common Law Supreme Courts* (Oxford: Oxford University Press, 2007), pp. 121–68.

For the purposes of this chapter, it is important to emphasise that the rise of the Indian judiciary has much to do with the political fortunes of the other two branches of government in India. It is no coincidence that during the heyday of the Congress party, which enjoyed great popular support because of its influential role as the party that led India to independence, the judiciary enjoyed less power and status, and was more reluctant to intervene in executive and legislative policy-making. The emergence of activism in PIL cases in the 1990s is almost directly attributable to the decline of the Congress as a political party. The arrival of coalition politics in India since the late 1980s has only served to increase the power of the judiciary and the scope of its ambitious forays into policy-making. The fact that India has had a strong civil society, which has bolstered judicial legitimacy, is also crucial. Another contributing factor is the legitimising function played by free and robust media, which in India have done much to improve the public image and prestige of the judiciary. Yet, it is also true, as noted in the previous part, that all this exists alongside the judiciary's dismal record on issues relating to emergency powers. In the next part of this chapter, I try and draw connections between these seemingly irreconcilable aspects of the same judicial record.

I now turn to other Asian jurisdictions that have more recently witnessed activist judiciaries, specifically South Korea and Taiwan.[48] In South Korea, 1987 heralded a 'constitutional moment' as the military prepared to hand over power to civilian authorities after several years of martial law. When constitutional reforms were initiated, it was decided to set up a strong, accessible constitutional court along the German model. After a series of negotiations among the three roughly equal political groupings that drafted the Constitution, the result was a designated court which was accessible to governmental bodies as well as ordinary citizens through the petition process. The Korean Constitutional Court has, from its inception, been a very active court and has not shirked from taking on deeply contentious issues that other courts would have shied away from in order to maintain legitimacy.[49] Thus, the court has carved out new, unenumerated rights, expanded economic and social rights and struck down anti-labour legislation.[50] Most recently, the Korean Constitutional Court

[48] For the analysis in this part, I rely principally on the work of T. Ginsburg, whose recent book analyses the judicialisation of politics in these two jurisdictions: see Ginsburg, *Judicial Review*, pp. 106–57, 206–46.

[49] Dae-Kyu Yoon, 'The Constitutional Court System of Korea: The New Road of Constitutional Adjudication', (2001) 1 *Journal of Korean Law* 1.

[50] Ginsburg, *Judicial Review*, pp. 226–36.

has directly engaged with some of the most controversial issues in Korea. A clear example is its decision overturning the impeachment of President Roh Moo-hyun in May 2004.[51]

The case of Taiwan is quite different from those of India and South Korea, as judicial activism in that nation was not envisaged or conferred by the founders of the nation. The Council of Grand Justices in the Republic of China (COGJ) represents a fascinating judicial institution that served an authoritarian regime for several decades before carefully expanding its own power through a gradual step-by-step process to become an instrument for democracy and human rights. As Ginsburg notes, 'Taiwan is the first historical instance of the entrenchment of modern constitutionalism in a Chinese context, a cultural environment perceived to present severe barriers for the development of independent judicial power.'[52] As Ginsburg demonstrates, the reasons for the rise of the COGJ's power are grounded more in politics than in culture. Once Taiwan embraced democratisation in the mid-1980s, the COGJ gradually began to increase its forays into decisions of the executive and legislative branches. After the arrival of democratisation, the stronghold of the previously dominant party in Taiwan, the Kuomintang (KMT), on political power began to decrease, and this climate provided the COGJ with a favourable environment for activism. Although the COGJ's activism is more restrained than, say, that of its Korean counterpart, there is no doubt that it has emerged as a key institutional player in Taiwanese constitutional politics.[53] Ginsburg cites, for instance, a number of politically important decisions supporting the liberalisation of the political system.[54]

Focusing on these three jurisdictions, I now seek to draw some general lessons from their cumulative experiences about the circumstances that favour the exercise of strong judicial review. As in the case of India, and the post-1987 Korea, a huge impetus for this is the express conferral of powers of judicial review on courts by the framers of constitutional orders. In both countries, courts can rely on strong constitutional provisions and guarantees to justify the legitimacy of their actions. However, as the case of Taiwan indicates, this is not a necessary pre-condition for the exercise

[51] For details, see Youngjae Lee, 'Law, Politics, and Impeachment: The Impeachment of Roh Moo-hyun from a Comparative Constitutional Perspective, (2005) 53 *American Journal of Comparative Law* 403.

[52] Ginsburg, *Judicial Review*, p. 107.

[53] This is a view supported by other scholars of Taiwanese constitutional law, beyond Ginsburg. See, for example, Chen, Chapter 3.

[54] Ginsburg, *Judicial Review*, pp. 106–58.

of judicial review. If political circumstances within a nation change – such as where one-party systems are considerably weakened – a situation may arise where courts become powerful through an incidental process where different political parties see an interest in having a strong, independent institution like the judiciary become the mediator of contentious political disputes. Taiwan is an example of a jurisdiction where despite the lack of a strong constitutional basis for judicial review, courts have, because of favourable political circumstances, been able to exercise robust review.

Ginsburg, focusing on the Korean and Taiwanese examples, terms this the 'insurance model of judicial review'. His starting point is the fact that political parties are self-interested agents. Drawing attention to the question whether a polity has a single, dominant party or has multiple parties with varying degrees of support, Ginsburg argues that 'by serving as an alternative forum in which to challenge governmental action, judicial review provides a form of insurance to prospective electoral losers'.[55] Ginsburg's 'insurance model of judicial review' might help explain recent developments in Malaysia. Following elections held in March 2008, the overwhelming dominance of the governing UMNO regime in the Malaysian parliament has been reduced, resulting in a situation where it now holds a mere simple majority.[56] One of the principal reactions of the leader of the ruling party has been, interestingly, to emphasise the need for a strong and independent judiciary.[57] This is striking because immediately prior to the elections, the ruling party had categorically denied that the judiciary's status required any review. A possible interpretation could be that having come to realise that it may well be in opposition within the foreseeable future, at least some voices in the ruling UMNO party are seeking ways of ensuring that the new ruling party does not victimise them or otherwise run amok. For preventing such a scenario, a strong and independent judiciary suddenly becomes a desirable goal for the weakened ruling party.

[55] *Ibid.*, p. 25. It should be noted, however, that Ginsburg focuses in this book on such calculations at the time of constitutional drafting. I am applying his idea to polities where such conditions emerge later in the evolution of nations, as in India, where the Congress party enjoyed a dominant status for nearly thirty years.

[56] See 'Malaysia's BN Coalition Suffers Worst Electoral Defeat', *Channel News Asia*, 9 March 2008, www.channelnewsasia.com/stories/southeastasia/view/333807/1/.html. (reporting that the ruling BN coalition's strength in the Malaysian Parliament had decreased from 199 to 139 in the 220-member house following the March 2008 elections).

[57] See 'Malaysia Government to Review Judicial Appointments', *ABC Radio Australia*, 18 April 2008, www.radioaustralia.net.au/news/stories/200804/s2220971.htm. (reporting that Prime Minister Badawi has advanced a package of reforms designed 'to strengthen the capacity and credibility of the judiciary').

Similar trends, where judicial review has emerged in polities where it was absent earlier, can be found elsewhere in the world. The foundation of a system of constitutional review in France (which pre-dates the Taiwanese experience) has similarities with it. This is because, as in Taiwan, constitutional review in France was neither envisaged by the Constitution, nor was it endorsed by the legal elite within France in the initial years after the adoption of the existing Constitution. It was only because of changes brought about by the evolving nature of French politics in the mid-1970s that the Constitutional Council began to exercise a strong form of constitutional review.[58] Similarly, a recent work focuses on the reasons behind the emergence of strong judicial review in Egypt in the 1990s, which is all the more striking because it occurred against the backdrop of an authoritarian regime that operated in a one-party state.[59] The larger point of this analysis is that even judiciaries in authoritarian regimes, which have traditionally been considered unworthy of study because of their presumed ineffectiveness, can become activist when provided with supportive circumstances.[60]

My purpose, in this part, has been to draw attention to the fact that courts in Asia have in the recent past begun to exercise strong judicial review more generally, and to examine the causal factors behind this growing trend. In the next part, I revert to the issue of judicial review over emergency powers.

V. Judicial review of emergency powers? Recent cases from India

Having noted that Asian judiciaries are beginning to exercise more robust forms of judicial review in general constitutional cases, I now examine whether they will follow a similar trend in cases involving emergency powers. I continue to use India as a basis for grounding my claims and analysis, although it should also be noted that the Korean Constitutional Court has recently sought to moderate the effect of harsh laws designed to regulate emergency powers by giving them restricted interpretation and application.[61]

[58] See generally, A. S. Sweet, *The Birth of Judicial Politics in France: The Constitutional Council in Comparative Perspective* (New York: Oxford University Press, 1992).

[59] T. Moustafa, *The Struggle for Constitutional Power: Law, Politics and Economic Development in Egypt* (New York: Cambridge University Press, 2007).

[60] It should, however, be noted that while judges in Egypt adopted activist positions with respect to other issues, they steered away from the arena of cases involving national security and emergency powers. As Moustafa explains, the realities of operating in an authoritarian system appear to have dictated this pragmatic stance.

[61] Ginsburg, *Judicial Review*, pp. 236–8.

As courts in Asia continue to exercise strong judicial review on other constitutional issues, they will, inevitably, be confronted with cases which require them to display a similar attitude toward laws involving emergency powers. Over time, to maintain credibility, these courts will have to take steps to correct imbalances in their record, by curbing egregious abuses of emergency powers. At such time, what will become crucial is the question of whether the courts have laid the legal foundations that are necessary for justifying their adventuring into the arena of national security.

Restricting my focus to India for the moment, my claim is that Indian courts have indeed been doing just that in recent cases involving emergency powers. My focus here is on two significant recent decisions. In *Kartar Singh* v. *State of Punjab* (1994),[62] the Supreme Court upheld the validity of the Terrorist and Disruptive Activities (Prevention) Act 1985 (TADA) which was a comprehensive law designed to tackle terrorism in specific parts of India, but had been employed in many states across the nation. The second case is *People's Union for Civil Liberties (PUCL)* v. *Union of India* (2004),[63] where the Supreme Court upheld the successor statute to TADA, POTA.

One reading of these cases is that they are clinching evidence of the correctness of the conventional view of judiciaries in times of crisis, as both resulted in the judicial endorsement of anti-terrorism statutes that were generally regarded as containing provisions that could be easily abused by the executive. Yet, as David Cole reminds us, judicial decisions can often have value in setting the terms for the future development of laws relating to emergency powers.[64] Also, as Benvenisti has argued, courts can place important limits on executive powers even when they refuse to strike down as unconstitutional the emergency laws that have been challenged before them.

In both these cases, the Supreme Court emphasised and asserted its own power to exercise judicial review over the laws in question, despite the subject matter which would in past years have required the exercise of greater (if not absolute) deference. The court, in both cases, made it clear that it would not accept a position where it was required to simply defer to the policy choices of the executive and legislative branches on matters of national security. While this may seem insignificant compared to the fact that both the laws were substantially upheld in the final decision, it gains significance when one considers what may happen in future cases

[62] (1994) 4 SCC 569. [63] (2004) 9 SCC 580.

[64] D. Cole, 'Judging the Next Emergency: Judicial Review and Individual Rights in Times of Crisis' (2003) 101 *Michigan Law Review* 2565 at 2566.

where the court has to strike down parts or the whole of a statute relating to emergency powers.

The Supreme Court flexed its muscles within the space afforded to it in both these cases. In *Kartar Singh*, the court struck down a provision that enabled police to identify a suspect based purely on photographic evidence, doing away with the need for an identification parade. For several other provisions, the court issued 'clarifications' that were designed to avoid some of the harsher consequences of the law by reading down the plain words of the statute. The court also issued guidelines directing the police to construe the provision in a less harsh manner. In *PUCL*, the court did not strike down any part of POTA, but once again issued 'clarifications' and resorted to reading down some provisions in a bid to mitigate their more draconian consequences.

I now compare the strategies used in these two cases with the five-step analysis of Benvenisti that was scrutinised in Part II. The Supreme Court's analysis in both these cases clearly indicates that in an appropriate case, it is ready to exercise full constitutional review and invalidate parliamentary laws that it considers to be beyond the parameters of the Constitution (approximating to steps 4 and 5 in Benvenisti's analysis). The boldness of this move can be appreciated by contrasting the Indian Supreme Court's attitude with those of the Malaysian and Singapore courts, which have been reduced to denying that they can ever exercise judicial review over questions involving preventive detention in the context of national security.[65]

The Indian Supreme Court's overall approach in these two cases offers interesting insights. The court repeatedly emphasises that it has a special role in safeguarding constitutional values, but balances this rhetoric with statements about the need for a co-ordinated response from all three branches to meet the challenges posed by terrorism. This fits well with what Issacharoff and Pildes have described as the 'process-based, institutionally oriented (as opposed to rights oriented) framework for examining the legality of governmental action in extreme security contexts' that the US Supreme Court has adopted over the past century.[66]

[65] For details of the Malaysian and Singapore cases, see M. Hor, 'Law and Terror: Singapore Stories and Malaysian dilemmas', in Ramraj *et al.* (eds.), *Global Anti-Terrorism*, pp. 273–94; and R. Balasubramaniam, 'Indefinite Detention: Rule by Law or Rule of Law?', in V. V. Ramraj (ed.), *Emergencies and the Limits of Legality* (Cambridge: Cambridge University Press, 2008), pp. 118–41.

[66] S. Issacharoff and R. Pildes, 'Emergency Contexts without Emergency Powers: The United States' Constitutional Approach to Rights during Wartime' (2004) 2 *International Journal of Constitutional Law* 296 at 297.

I do not want to exaggerate the extent of what the court actually did in these two cases. Both cases are justifiably excoriated by the human rights community in India for the failure of the court to provide a stronger rebuke to the executive and legislative authorities in light of the documented cases of abuse of these two laws. However, by indicating to the executive and legislature that it will not shirk from exercising constitutional review in cases involving national security or emergency laws, the court is sending out an important signal. In recent years, instances have cropped up in different parts of India that have made clear the tendency of some political parties to use such laws to settle political scores. One effect of the Supreme Court's stance in these cases is to signal that such tendencies may not pass judicial scrutiny. For its part, the judiciary may feel more secure about intervening in such politically charged cases once it knows that it may well find support from the political parties which are at that moment in opposition, and would be critical of such excesses.

There are good reasons, grounded in the political realities of contemporary India, to believe that future circumstances in India will favour a situation where courts can act more robustly in times of emergency. Since the late 1980s, India has experienced the uncertainty of coalition governments, and most observers believe that this may well be a permanent feature of Indian politics in the foreseeable future, given that the two main national parties (the Congress and the BJP, which oppose each other bitterly) together garner less than 50 per cent of the popular vote. Given this, and the fact that India has a long record where abuse of emergency laws consists also of detaining political opponents, it is clear that all political parties have a vested interest in having a judiciary which will check such abuses of emergency laws.

VI. Normative reasons for strong judicial review of emergency powers

I now turn to the normative arguments in favour of judicial review of emergency powers. It might be argued that this should be the starting point of this chapter, not its concluding feature. But the normative arguments favouring strong judicial review of the use of emergency powers have a long pedigree in Asia. They have been articulated and reiterated in case after case by lawyers and dissenting judges in cases dating back to the 1950s in India and Pakistan.[67] Indeed, in the analysis that follows, I rely

[67] See, for instance, the discussion of the arguments advanced by Justice Cornelius in his dissents in the *Dosso* case in C. Lombardi (Chapter 16), this volume, pp. 446–7.

upon such arguments as advanced in an important case decided by the Indian Supreme Court in 1976.

Yet, this issue requires scrutiny because in recent years a number of US scholars have argued that judges should defer to the decisions of elected branches of government in the context of national security and emergency powers, in part because the challenges posed by terrorism today are supposedly even less capable of judicial management.[68] In the words of Judge Richard Posner, 'rooting out an invisible enemy in our midst might be fatally inhibited if we felt constrained to strict observance of civil liberties designed in and for eras in which the only serious internal threat (apart from spies) came from common criminals'.[69] Judge Posner goes on to assert that judges should let the elected branches resolve the often thorny issues that dealing with terrorism involves.[70] Other arguments in support of what I have called the 'conventional view' (advocating judicial deference in cases involving emergency powers) have been catalogued by Aileen Kavanaugh. She identifies three main reasons: first, that when issues of national security are involved, the executive or legislature often claim that some of the information on which their decision was based must be kept secret; second, that judges' awareness of the life-and-death consequences of some decisions made in the national security area will cause them to err on the side of caution; and third, that since many decisions made in the context of emergency powers are anticipatory (based on factual predictions of what people might or might not do), judges have few tools to review such decisions adequately.[71]

Are these arguments persuasive? In recent years, David Dyzenhaus has emerged as the scholar who has provided the most elaborate and sustained arguments against such a position of absolute judicial deference toward executive and legislative decisions in the context of emergency powers.[72]

[68] R. Posner, *Not a Suicide Pact: The Constitution in a Time of National Emergency* (New York: Oxford University Press, 2006); A. Vermuele and E. Posner, *Terror in the Balance: Security, Liberty and the Courts* (New York: Oxford University Press, 2007).

[69] Posner, *Not a Suicide Pact*, p. 6.

[70] To a similar end, Vermuele and (Eric) Posner have recently argued that '[i]n times of emergency, judges should get out of the government's way'. They urge judges to adopt a 'deferential view', recommending that judicial review of government action 'should be relaxed or suspended during an emergency'. Vermuele and Posner, *Terror in the Balance*, pp. 12, 15.

[71] A. Kavanaugh, 'Deference or Defiance? The Limits of the Judicial Role in Constitutional Adjudication', in G. Huscroft (ed.), *Expounding the Constitution: Essays in Constitutional Theory* (Cambridge: Cambridge University Press, 2008), pp. 184–218, at pp. 207–12.

[72] Here, I rely principally upon his recent book, *The Constitution of Law*. Arguably, however, these are concerns that Dyzenhaus has engaged with throughout his academic career,

Dyzenhaus shows that many of these claims are built upon conceptions about the doctrine of separation of powers and the role of judges that are rigid and misguided. Judges should, Dyzenhaus argues, always act to uphold the rule of law. He has a substantive conception of the rule of law, which he defines as consisting of 'fundamental constitutional principles which protect individuals from arbitrary action by the state'.[73] This conception of the rule of law entails linking 'procedural constraints to substantive values' while also requiring 'that all three branches of government regard themselves as participating in a common project of realizing those values'.[74] Judges, argues Dyzenhaus, 'have a constitutional duty to uphold the rule of law even, perhaps especially, in the face of indications from the legislature or the executive that they are trying to withdraw from the rule-of-law project'.[75] And so their role in times of emergency is, in his own words, a 'modest' one; judges should conceive of themselves as 'weathermen', which entails 'having the role of alerting the commonwealth to the storm clouds on the horizon when the rule of law which secures the fabric of civil society is put under strain'.[76]

What would the role of a judge as 'weatherman' involve in practice? An infamous case that had a profound impact on debates about the role of a judge in India provides a useful illustration.[77] The case arose as a result of Indira Gandhi's imposition of a state of emergency in June 1975, which was widely perceived as being legally unsustainable and having been imposed to maintain her political position after an adverse ruling by a High Court judge that would have required her to leave office.[78] Within hours of the official proclamation of the emergency, prominent opposition leaders were arrested across the nation under a pre-existing law authorising preventive detention. The Constitution and existing laws were amended to ensure that (i) the right to move the courts for protection of the fundamental rights to equality, liberty and arbitrary arrest of individual citizens

starting with his doctorate, *Hard Cases in Wicked Legal Systems: South African Law in the Perspective of Legal Philosophy* (Oxford: Clarendon Press, 1991). His previous works on the same theme are referenced in the bibliography attached at the end of *The Constitution of Law*, pp. 235–6.

73 Dyzenhaus, *The Constitution of Law*, p. 2. 74 *Ibid.*, p. 14.

75 *Ibid.*, p. 4. 76 *Ibid.*, p. 12.

77 For a short but gripping account of the case by a respected commentator, see G. Austin, *Working a Democratic Constitution: The Indian Experience* (New Delhi: Oxford University Press, 2000), pp. 334–43. For the perspective of one of the lead lawyers in the case, see S. Bhushan, *Courting Destiny: A Memoir* (New Delhi: Penguin, 2008), pp. 143–5.

78 This invocation of emergency powers by Indira Gandhi, as well as the decision in the *ADM Jabalpur* case, is also covered by Anil Kalhan. See Chapter 4, pp. 111–13.

were suspended, and (ii) the government did not have to disclose the grounds of detention to either those who had been detained or to courts. The political leaders who had been preventively detained challenged their detention, as well as the amendments to the Constitution and pre-existing laws, by filing writs of habeas corpus. Several High Courts across the country granted such writs of habeas corpus, much to the anger of the central government, which appealed to the Supreme Court of India. The Supreme Court's judgment in *ADM Jabalpur* v. *Shivkanth Shukla*[79] is regarded by constitutional scholars in India as the lowest point in its history, where the court completely capitulated to the perceived wishes of the executive, even when the established authorities pointed to a different result. By a 4–1 decision, the Supreme Court held that none of the writs were maintainable. The majority accepted the government's argument that following the proclamation of emergency and the suspension of the right to approach courts for the enforcement of fundamental rights, the executive had overriding power, and the rule of law was suspended. The court also seemed to accept that the rule of law existed only within the four corners of the Constitution, and rights did not pre-exist or exist beyond the text of the Constitution.

In his lone dissent, Justice Khanna relied upon the concept of the rule of law (previously identified as a 'basic feature' of the Indian Constitution) to assert that the basis for the writ of habeas corpus would exist even when rights had been suspended by the proclamation of emergency. He argued that the Constitution was not the sole repository of the rights of citizens, and that well-established principles for challenging the legality of detentions by using writs of habeas corpus would enable the court to examine the grounds of detention. He invoked support from authorities ranging from the Magna Carta to cases from other Commonwealth jurisdictions and established domestic authorities, to argue that there was no contradiction between the power of the executive to detain a person under preventive detention and the power of a court to examine the legality of such detentions.

What makes Justice Khanna's dissent all the more heroic is his knowledge of the personal repercussions that would inevitably follow. When he wrote his dissent, Justice Khanna was next in line to be the Chief Justice of India. He was fully aware of what had transpired three years previously: upon being frustrated by the Supreme Court in a momentous decision in 1973, Indira Gandhi had expressed her wrath by superseding

[79] AIR 1976 SC 1207; MANU/SC/0062/1976.

the two most senior judges of the Supreme Court who ruled against her, and appointing a junior judge who supported her government's stance in several significant cases. Shortly after the judgment in *ADM Jabalpur* was pronounced, Indira Gandhi did in fact supersede Justice Khanna for the post of Chief Justice, appointing in his stead Justice Beg, who had been one of the judges in the majority in the *ADM Jabalpur* case and had adopted the most solicitous attitude among the majority judges toward the government's arguments. This left Justice Khanna no choice but to resign, which is perhaps the result that Gandhi desired. However, in doing so, she created a physical manifestation of all that was wrong with the emergency, and Justice Khanna emerged as one of the rallying points against her regime in the elections that followed and led to the downfall of her government.

In the arguments he deployed, and the courage of conviction he demonstrated, Justice Khanna exemplifies the role of 'judge as weatherman' that Dyzenhaus espouses. This episode is cited by many as being pivotal in turning the attitudes of the general public decisively against Indira Gandhi, yet the personal cost he suffered may well indicate to contemporary judges that it would be prudent to avoid taking on the executive in times of emergency. I realise that requiring contemporary (or future) judges in Asia to feel compelled to emulate Justice Khanna's heroic yet tragic example is unrealistic. An exclusive emphasis on judicial courage seriously underestimates the importance of the deeper structural and institutional reasons that consistently lead judges to define their role in relation to emergency powers cases in specific and limited ways.[80] My argument, instead, has been that a set of supportive factors is needed to facilitate judicial review of emergency powers. Such factors include a shared commitment to the basic values of constitutionalism among important actors within society, members of the general public and significant constituencies such as the practising bar, and other social and legal elites. This list would also include, besides the roles of civil society and a free press that were adverted to earlier, a political climate where judges can feel confident that their actions will find favour, regardless of whether they accord with the view of the holders of power in the executive and legislative arenas. I should clarify that the list of factors catalogued above is only illustrative, not prescriptive. As we have seen, the factors that lead to the emergence of judicial review in individual nations can be very specific to national socio-political

[80] In the US context, Issacharoff and Pildes have argued along similar lines. See, Issacharoff and Pildes, 'Emergency contexts'.

contexts. It may well be that in other contexts, judicial review is strengthened by factors beyond the ones mentioned, which have salience in those jurisdictions.

In my view, judges who do seek to provide effective checks on the misuse of emergency powers will not face difficulty in marshalling the requisite legal and normative arguments. The more difficult issue is whether they will feel confident that the right mix of factors which allow such a message to find favour among the general public, and within crucial segments of those in power, exists within their societies. The purpose of this chapter has been to show that there are reasons to believe that the supportive factors mentioned above have either arisen, or are emerging, in a number of Asian jurisdictions.

VII. Conclusion

I have sought to show that the conventional view – that judges must show near absolute deference to executive and legislative authorities during times of emergency – is beginning to change in the post-9/11 world. I have ventured to suggest that although judiciaries in Asia have yet to do so, they are well positioned to follow this trend. I hope to have also demonstrated that judges and judicial institutions cannot bring about significant change by themselves, especially on sensitive issues involving national security and emergency powers. Judges can be important allies for those who seek to mitigate the excesses of Asia's many repressive emergency laws. However, they can only do so against the backdrop of supportive factors, a number of which I have sought to draw attention to in the body of this chapter. My purpose here is to broaden the focus of constitutional scholars who have a tendency to overemphasise the merits and powers of courts, without paying due regard to the background factors which are crucial for the successful exercise of judicial review over sensitive issues such as national security and emergency powers.

I have argued that in recent years there has been an emergence of strong judicial review in some jurisdictions in Asia, which augurs well for a time when Asian courts will exercise robust judicial review over emergency powers. My hope is that such a situation will come to pass in the foreseeable future, thereby strengthening emerging trends of constitutionalism across Asia.

INDEX